Presidential Elections
1789-1996

Presidential Elections
1789-1996

Congressional Quarterly Inc.
Washington, D.C.

Printed and bound in the United States of America

The paper used in this publication meets the minimum requirements of the American National Standard for Information Science—Permanence of Paper for Printed Library Materials, ANSI Z39.48-1984.

Cover illustration credits (clockwise from top right): Reuters; White House/Bill Fitz-Patrick; Theodore Roosevelt Collection, Harvard College Library; White House/David Valdez; Library of Congress

Library of Congress Cataloging-in-Publication Data

Presidential elections, 1789-1996.
    p.   cm.
    Includes bibliographical references and index.
    ISBN 1-56802-065-1 (alk. paper)
    1. Presidents—United States—Election—History—Statistics. I. Congressional Quarterly, Inc.

JK524.P6783   1997
324.973—dc21   97-19084

Contents

Preface

The election of a president has evolved into the most dramatic political event in the United States. Every four years for more than 200 years, the country has undergone a hectic nominating process based on rhetoric, partisan maneuvering and character analysis as ambitious politicians vie for the nation's, and perhaps the world's, most important job.

Over the years the increase in the number of Americans eligible to participate in the choosing of the president has been one of the most striking measurements of the growth of democracy in the United States. From 1789 to 1996 there have been 53 presidential elections. All of these elections have been decided by the Electoral College, but in the past 44 the electors have been chosen by popular vote. After the 1870 ratification of the 15th Amendment, which prohibited denying the right to vote "on account of race, color, or previous servitude," elections have been open to all races, although it took another 100 years and the 24th Amendment against poll taxes and other voting laws to secure this right for all. The 19th Amendment, ratified in 1920, opened the past 21 presidential elections to women voters. The 26th Amendment has allowed 18-year-olds to vote in the seven elections since 1972.

Despite the continual widening of the base of qualified voters, the last half of the 20th century has witnessed an opposing trend: a decline in electorate turnout. In 1992 more than 100 million Americans went to the polls to cast votes for president, yet that number represented only 71 percent of those registered to vote and only 55 percent of those eligible to vote. For the 1996 presidential contest only 96.2 million turned out to vote. This election was the first time since 1924 that voter turnout in a presidential race dropped below 50 percent. This was surprising in light of passage of the 1993 "motor-voter" law, which made voter registration easier for millions of Americans.

The history of presidential elections has been the subject of countless volumes, monographs and dissertations as well as articles in academic journals. Nevertheless, it is difficult to find a single book that comprehensively and succinctly covers the basic facts and figures on the Electoral College, popular vote returns, presidential primaries, nominations of major and minor party candidates, and biographical data on the candidates.

Presidential Elections 1789-1996 is a unique collection of reference material spanning the time from George Washington's first election as president in 1789 to Democrat Bill Clinton's second election in 1996. It includes popular vote returns for president from 1824 to 1916 obtained from the Inter-University Consortium for Political and Social Research (ICPSR) at the University of Michigan. Congressional Quarterly has updated this material with data on the presidential elections from 1920 to 1996.

The introduction provides a general overview of the changing presidential selection process and looks at the background of those leaders who have run for and have been elected president. A governorship, the vice presidency or a U.S. Senate seat continue to be the most popular backgrounds for candidates who are launching presidential bids.

The first section of the book examines the constitutional origins and historical development of the Electoral College, the uniquely American system of electing presidents. The section details complex and little-known methods used in the various states through 1832 to choose presidential electors, recounts historical anomalies in the functioning of the Electoral College and discusses reasons that a state's electoral votes frequently have been divided among several candidates. It covers the two occasions when a president was elected by the House of Representatives: Thomas Jefferson's close victory over Aaron Burr in 1800 and John Quincy Adams's election from a field of four strong candidates in 1825. It also explains procedures for counting and challenging electoral votes in Congress and describes the famous 1877 Tilden-Hayes contest, which was decided by one electoral vote. This section concludes with a discussion of presidential disability and the ratification of the 25th Amendment to the Constitution.

Electoral maps and tables display all Electoral College results since 1789. Electoral vote totals for vice president from 1804 to 1996 are listed separately.

The expanding role that the popular vote came to play in the election process is examined next. On the first Tuesday after the first Monday in November (a date established in 1845) voters go to the polls to elect the president. Although the voters are actually choosing presidential electors rather than the president, the focus of public attention is the popular vote returns. This section briefly describes voting trends and turnout, the broadening franchise, voting behavior and party affiliation.

Tables provide popular vote returns for the top four candidates for president from 1824 to 1996. These tables are presented in an easily readable format displaying the names and party affiliations of the candidates; state-by-state breakdowns of the total vote and percentage for each candidate; the total vote and winning plurality in each state; and the national totals including national plurality of the leading popular vote candidate. Popular vote returns from 1824 to 1996 for all minor candidates are provided separately.

The next section discusses the origins and development of the presidential primary, which by the 1970s had assumed preeminent importance in the presidential selection process. Overshadowing the caucus method of choosing delegates to a national convention, the primary has become the national stage where the major parties' presidential candidates are chosen. Tables list primary returns for all major candidates from 1912 to 1996.

The final section briefly traces the history of national nominating conventions from their first appearance in 1831 to the most recent gatherings in 1996. Even though they no longer are crucial to the selection of the presidential ticket, conventions have endured because they continue to perform many needed functions — such as bringing the party together on national television to nominate the presidential ticket officially, approve the platform, reconcile any internal party differences and throw a huge political rally. The delegate selection process, credentials disputes, party convention rules, adoption of party platforms and role of the media are discussed here. The section also contains a comprehensive roster of party nominees from 1831 to 1996 that lists minor as well as major party candidates.

The book concludes with a biographical directory of presidential and vice presidential candidates, texts of constitutional provisions and amendments relating to presidential selection, a bibliographical list for further reading and a comprehensive index.

Introduction

The American people and their leaders were ambivalent about the concept of democracy in the early years of the Republic. This ambivalence was evident in the compromise for presidential selection worked out at the Constitutional Convention in 1787 and in the halting steps the nation took toward party competition.

The presidential selection process has changed significantly since George Washington was elected to his first term in 1789. The Electoral College is still the center of the system, but all the related institutions and processes have changed dramatically. In part, this is because the constitutional provisions for presidential selection are so vague.

The major features of the electoral system developed over time, as a process of trial and error. The Constitution contains no provisions for organizing political parties, nominating candidates or campaigning for office. The Framers assumed, incorrectly, that the selection process would be a reasoned one that would transcend partisanship. The original provision for balloting by the Electoral College was flawed and had to be superseded by the 12th Amendment in 1804.

Until the 17th century, elections with opposition were rare. The nation's first legislative body, the Virginia House of Burgesses, usually had uncontested elections until the 1700s. Even when the states' elections involved opponents, there was little active campaigning. Only with the decline of homogenous communities and the end of elite control over politics did contested elections occur. Many elections into the 1790s were uncontested or focused on personalities.

The very concept of the party — the most fundamental way of organizing electoral coalitions — was viewed with distrust by the nation's early leaders. George Washington described the dangers of parties in a letter: "A fire not to be quenched; it demands a uniform vigilance to prevent its bursting into a flame, lest instead of warming it should consume." Only with experience of factional debate in Congress did the idea of parties seem necessary and capable of control. By the third presidential election — when John Adams was elected in 1796 — the idea of party rule was firmly established in new Republic.

From 1796 until 1824, congressional caucuses (when a party had enough representatives to form one) chose almost all the candidates; the electors then chose from the party nominees. Only twice, in 1800 and 1824, as a result of a failure of any candidate to receive a majority of electoral votes, were presidential elections decided by the House of Representatives, and even in those two cases political parties were instrumental in the election. By 1832 all states except Maryland and South Carolina held statewide elections to choose electors pledged to vote for the parties' presidential candidates.

The trend to democratization, as evidenced by the expansion of suffrage and increased importance of the popular vote for president, led to the creation of the national nominating convention. The convention system was initiated by the Anti-Masonic Party in 1831 and adopted by the major parties before the end of the decade.

The birth of the national convention was a milestone in the evolution of the presidential nominating process. In his book, *Politics, Parties, and Pressure Groups* (1964), political scientist V. O. Key Jr., summarized some of the major forces that brought about the rise of the convention system:

> The destruction of the caucus represented more than a mere change in the method of nomination. Its replacement by the convention was regarded as the removal from power of self-appointed oligarchies that had usurped the right to nominate. The new system, the convention, gave, or so it was supposed, the mass of party members an opportunity to participate in nominations. These events occurred as the domestic winds blew in from the growing West, as the suffrage was being broadened, and as the last vestiges of the early aristocratic leadership were disappearing. Sharp alterations in the distribution of power were taking place, and they were paralleled by the shifts in methods of nomination.

The establishment of the national convention solidified the two-party system. Unlike the Founding Fathers, who were suspicious of competitive factions, some political leaders in the late 1820s and 1830s favorably viewed the existence of opposing parties. One of the most prominent of these men, Martin Van Buren, a leading organizer of Democrat Andrew Jackson's 1828 election victory, wrote in 1827: "We must always have party distinctions."

The development of the presidential primary election, in which voters directly elected convention delegates, revolutionized the delegate-selection process. Begun in Florida in 1904, the presidential primary by 1912 was used by 13 states.

In his annual message to Congress the following year, President Woodrow Wilson advocated the establishment of a national primary: "I feel confident that I do not misinterpret the wishes or the expectations of the country at which the voters of the several parties may choose their nominees for the presidency without the intervention of nominating conventions." Wilson went on to suggest the retention of conventions to declare the results of the primaries and formulate the parties' platforms.

Before any action was taken on Wilson's proposal, the progressive spirit that spurred the growth of presidential primaries died out. Not until after World War II, when widespread pressures for change touched both parties, especially the Democratic, was there a rapid growth in presidential primaries.

During the 1970s a dramatic surge occurred in the number of states holding presidential primaries. Twenty-two primaries were held in 1972, 29 in 1976, 35 in 1980, 29 in 1984 and 36 in 1988. (The 1972 to 1988 totals do not include primaries in the District of Columbia and Puerto Rico.) In 1996 41 states and the District of Columbia and Puerto Rico had primaries, but the most important factor was not the number but the timing of primaries. Many states held these elections earlier than ever before in the campaign season.

By the last quarter of the 20th century, presidential primaries became so essential in the selection of the Democratic and Republican national ticket that the nominating conventions were rendered nearly obsolete. Mass politics — mass media presentations of candidates to the public and mass participation of party members in primary elections — had become the most important aspect of choosing presidential candidates.

Roads to the Presidency

Most presidents have come to the White House with long public careers behind them, but there have been notable exceptions. For example, Zachary Taylor's only career was the military; he went straight from the army to the White House. During the 19th century, men changed public jobs frequently as they prepared for the presidency. James Madison, Thomas Jefferson and Andrew Jackson each held nearly a dozen public posts before reaching the White House. During the last half of the twentieth century, however, presidents generally have held fewer public offices. Gerald R. Ford had served 25 years in the U.S. House of Representatives when he was appointed vice president. He became president when Richard Nixon resigned. Ronald Reagan had served only as governor of California for eight years before he won two terms as president in the 1980s.

Bill Clinton's path to the White House followed the most recent trend. Before his first election to the presidency, he had served two years as attorney general of Arkansas and 12 years as governor of Arkansas. However, his predecessor, George Bush, followed the earlier model. Bush was a U.S. representative from Texas, the U.S. ambassador to the United Nations, chief U.S. envoy to the People's Republic of China, director of the Central Intelligence Agency and Reagan's vice president for eight years.

Paths of Glory

As a nation the United States has never made up its mind what background a president ought to have. The earliest tradition concerning the path to the presidency developed around the secretary of state, who was considered the preeminent Cabinet officer and thus the most important man in the executive branch after the president. Jefferson was Washington's first secretary of state. Although he left the Cabinet early in Washington's second term, he went on to become leader of the newly formed Democratic-Republican Party and its candidate for president in 1796, 1800 and 1804. Losing to Adams in 1796, Jefferson came back to win four years later.

In turn, Madison, Jefferson's secretary of state for two terms, won the presidency in 1808. Madison had been a close ally of Jefferson's in the political struggles of the 1790s and served throughout Jefferson's two presidential terms as secretary of state (1801-09). During his first term as president, Madison appointed fellow Virginian James Monroe as his secretary of state. And following in what was rapidly becoming a tradition, Monroe went on to the presidency in 1816, serving two terms (1817-25).

Throughout Monroe's terms, the secretary of state was John Quincy Adams, son of former President John Adams. At the end of Monroe's second term, five major candidates entered the race to succeed him. Three were Cabinet officers, including Adams. None of the candidates managed to acquire a majority in the Electoral College, so the House of Representatives then chose Secretary of State Adams.

Adams was the last secretary of state to go directly from his Cabinet post to the White House. After him, only two secretaries of state made it to the White House at all — Van Buren, who was secretary of state from 1829 to 1831 and president from 1837 to 1841, and James Buchanan, who served as secretary of state under President James K. Polk (1845-49) and as president from 1857 to 1861.

Two other institutions died at approximately the same time as the Cabinet tradition — the Virginia dynasty and "King Caucus," a derogatory term referring to the congressional party caucuses that met throughout the early 1800s to designate presidential nominees.

After the four Virginians who occupied the presidency during the first 36 years of the Republic — Washington, Jefferson, Madison and Monroe — there have been no elected presidents who were born in and made their careers in Virginia. John Tyler was born there but succeeded to the presidency from the vice presidency in 1841 and was not renominated. Three other presidents were born in Virginia but made their careers elsewhere — William Henry Harrison, Taylor and Wilson.

During its heyday, the Washington-centered mentality of King Caucus had virtually guaranteed that Cabinet officers should be among those most often nominated by the party in power. But the caucus came under attack as being undemocratic and unrepresentative and ceased to function as a presidential nominating mechanism after 1824. It was eventually replaced by the national conventions, bodies that are not connected with Congress and that, as of 1996, had never met in the national capital.

Military Men

The next cycle of American politics, from the presidency of Jackson (1829-37) to the Civil War, saw a variety of backgrounds qualify candidates for the presidency. One of the most prevalent was the military. Jackson, who ran in 1824 (unsuccessfully), 1828 and 1832, was a general in the War of 1812, gaining near-heroic stature by his defeat of the British at the Battle of New Orleans in January 1815. Like most military officers who have risen to the presidency, however, Jackson was only a part-time military officer. As a politician, he had served in the U.S. House during Washington's presidency and in the Senate during John Adams' administration, as well as later under Monroe and John Quincy Adams. Only presidents Taylor, Ulysses S. Grant and Dwight Eisenhower were career military officers.

Other candidates during this era who were or had been military officers included Harrison, a Whig candidate in 1836 and 1840; Taylor, the Whig candidate in 1848; Winfield Scott, the 1852 Whig candidate; Franklin Pierce, the Democratic nominee in 1852; and John C. Fremont in 1856, the Republican Party's first presidential candidate. Thus, from 1824 through 1856, all but one presidential election featured a major candidate with a military background.

Like Jackson, Harrison had a mixed military and political career. A member of a distinguished Virginia family, he was the son of a signer of the Declaration of Independence. Harrison served in Congress during the John Adams administration and again under Madison, Monroe and John Quincy Adams. In between, he battled the Indians and the British during the War of 1812.

Taylor and Scott were both career military men who led victorious armies in the Mexican War. Pierce also had a command in the Mexican War, although he had been primarily a politician, with service in both the House and the Senate during the 1830s and 1840s. Fremont was famous as an explorer as well as for a dashing military campaign through California during the Mexican War. Later, he was a U.S. senator from the young state of California (1850-51).

The smoldering political conflicts of the 1840s and 1850s probably contributed to the naming of military officers for the presidency. Generals had usually escaped involvement in national politics and had avoided taking stands on the issues that divided the country — slavery, expansion, the currency and the tariff. In 1840, for example, the Whigs adopted no platform or statement of principle; they simply nominated Harrison and assumed that his personal popularity plus the resentments against Van Buren's administration would suffice for Whig victory. They were right.

Later on, the nature of the Civil War almost automatically led at least one of the parties to choose a military officer as presidential standard-bearer every four years. To have been on the "right" side during the war — fighting to save the Union and destroy slavery — was a major political asset in the North and Middle West, where tens of thousands of war veterans were effectively organized in the Grand Army of the Republic (GAR). The GAR became part of the backbone of the Republican Party during the last third of the 19th century.

Consequently, it became customary for Republicans to have a Civil War officer at the head of their ticket. Except for James G. Blaine in 1884, every Republican presidential nominee from 1868 to 1900 had served as an officer in the Union Army during the Civil War. Blaine, who had spent the war years as a Maine state legislator and a member of the U.S. House, lost the election to Grover Cleveland.

Of all the Republican nominees, however, only Grant, who was elected president in 1868 and 1872, was a professional military man. The others — Rutherford B. Hayes in 1876, James A. Garfield in 1880, Benjamin Harrison in 1888 and 1892 and William McKinley in 1896 and 1900 — were civilians who volunteered for service in the Civil War. Two of them — Hayes and Garfield — were elected to the House while serving in the army. At the time of their presidential nominations. Hayes was governor of Ohio, Garfield was minority leader of the U.S. House and a senator-elect, Harrison was a former senator from Indiana and McKinley was a former governor of Ohio.

The Democrats, who had been split over the war, had few prominent military veterans to choose from. Only twice between 1860 and 1900 did the Democrats pick a Civil War officer as their nominee. In 1864, during the Civil War, the Democrats nominated Gen. George B. McClellan, the Union military commander who had fallen out with President Abraham Lincoln. And in 1880 Gen. Winfield Scott Hancock of Pennsylvania was the Democrats' choice.

The Empire State

Otherwise, Democrats tended to favor governors or former governors of New York. Their 1868 nominee was Horatio Seymour, who had been governor of New York in 1853-55 and again in 1863-65. In 1876 they chose Samuel J. Tilden, New York's reform governor who was battling Tammany Hall. And in 1884 Cleveland, another New York reform governor, captured the Democratic nomination. He went on to become the first Democrat to win the White House in 28 years. Cleveland was again the Democratic nominee in 1888 and 1892.

Besides being the most populous state, New York was a swing state in presidential politics. During the period from Reconstruction through the turn of the century, most Southern states voted Democratic, while the Republicans usually carried Pennsylvania, the Midwest and New England. A New Yorker appeared as the nominee for president or vice president of at least one of the major parties in every election from 1868 through 1892.

This general tradition was maintained through the candidacy of Thomas E. Dewey, Republican governor of New York, in 1948. Only twice between 1868 and 1948 was there no New Yorker on the national ticket of at least one of the major parties — for president or vice president. Once, in 1944, both major party presidential nominees, Democrat Franklin D. Roosevelt and Republican Dewey, were from New York.

From 1952 to 1996, however, no New Yorkers were nominated by a major party for president and only three for vice president. The latter three were Rep. William E. Miller, R, in 1964; Rep. Geraldine A. Ferraro, D, in 1984; and Rep Jack Kemp, R, in 1996. Eisenhower in 1952 and Nixon in 1968 were technically residents of New York, but they were generally identified with other states. President Ford's vice president, Nelson Rockefeller, was a former governor of New York, but he was appointed to the vice presidency. He was not asked to be on the ticket when Ford ran in 1976.

Another major swing state in the years from the Civil War through World War I was Indiana. And, in most elections, a prominent Indianan found his way onto one of the major party's national tickets. In the 13 presidential elections between 1868 and 1916, an Indianan appeared 10 times on at least one of the major parties' national tickets. However, from 1916 to 1992 only two Indianans, Wendell Willkie in 1940 and Dan Quayle in 1988 and 1992, have been major party nominees.

Governors

From 1900 to 1956, Democrats tended to favor governors for the presidential nomination. Democratic governors who received their party's presidential nomination included Wilson of New Jersey in 1912, James M. Cox of Ohio in 1920, Alfred E. Smith of New York in 1928, Franklin D. Roosevelt of New York in 1932 and Adlai E. Stevenson of Illinois in 1952.

During the same period, 1900 to 1956, Republican presidential nominees had a wide variety of backgrounds. There were two Cabinet officers (Secretary of War William Howard Taft in 1908 and Secretary of Commerce Herbert Hoover in 1928), a Supreme Court justice (Charles Evans Hughes in 1916), a U.S. senator (Warren G. Harding in 1920), two governors (Alfred M. Landon of Kansas in 1936 and Dewey of New York in 1944 and 1948), a private lawyer (Willkie in 1940) and a general (Eisenhower in 1952). Calvin Coolidge of Massachusetts, the 1924 nominee, and Theodore Roosevelt of New York, the 1904 nominee, both of whom succeeded to the presidency from the vice presidency, had been governors of their respective states.

Curiously, the two world wars did not produce a plethora of military candidates. The only general besides Eisenhower who made a strong bid for a presidential nomination was Gen. Leonard Wood, who had commands in the Spanish-American War and World War I. Wood led on five ballots at the 1920 Republican National Convention before losing out on the tenth ballot to Harding. Otherwise only a few military men have even been mentioned for the presidency in the 20th century — most notably Gen. Douglas MacArthur in the 1940s and 1950s (he got little support at GOP conventions) and Gen. Colin Powell in the 1990s. Powell the former chairman of the armed forces joint chiefs of staff during the 1991 Persian Gulf War, received a lot of national attention in 1995 before he announced he would not seek the 1996 Republican nomination.

Senators and Former Vice Presidents

A sudden change took place in 1960 with the nomination of John F. Kennedy, a senator, and Nixon, a former senator and sitting vice president. It was only the second time in the 20th century that an incumbent U.S. senator was nominated for the presidency. The first time was in 1920 when the Republicans nominated Harding from Ohio. In the 19th century the phenomenon was also rare, with National-Republican Henry Clay in 1832, Democrat Lewis Cass in 1848 and Democrat Stephen A. Douglas in 1860 the only incumbent senators nominated for president by official party conventions. Republican James A. Garfield was a senator-elect at the time of his election in 1880. Beginning with Kennedy's ascension from the Senate to the White House in 1960, senators dominated presidential campaigns until 1976. During those 16 years every single major party nominee was a senator or former senator.

The nomination of Nixon, like the nomination of Kennedy, was also a sign of things to come. It was the first time since 1860 and only the second time in the history of party nominating conventions that an incumbent vice president was chosen for the presidency. Beginning in 1960 the vice presidency, like the Senate, became a presidential training ground. Vice President Hubert H. Humphrey was chosen by the Democrats for president in 1968. That same year the Republicans renominated Nixon, who went on to win the presidency eight years after being vice president. Vice President Spiro T. Agnew was the leading contender for the 1976 Republican presidential nomination before his resignation in October 1973. In 1984 former vice president Walter F. Mondale, who had served under Jimmy Carter, emerged as the Democratic choice for the presidential nomination. When Bush won the presidency in 1988, after filling the second spot under Reagan for eight years, it marked the first time a sitting vice president had been elected president since Van Buren in 1836.

Even defeated vice presidential nominees have been considered for the nomination — witness Henry Cabot Lodge Jr. of Massachusetts in 1964, Edmund S. Muskie of Maine in 1972, Sargent Shriver of Maryland in 1976 and Bob Dole of Kansas in 1980, 1988 and 1996.

Governors Again

The field of candidates for the 1980 presidential nomination continued a trend that first appeared in the 1976 campaign — the re-emergence of governors as leading contenders in the nomination sweepstakes. While there was no shortage of senators in the 1976 campaign, it was the governors who attracted the most attention. Former California governor Reagan came close to depriving incumbent Ford of the Republican presidential nomination. The Democratic nominee and eventual winner, former Georgia governor Carter, faced a dramatic last-minute challenge from the governor of California at the time, Jerry Brown. Reagan (successfully), Carter and Brown were candidates again in 1980; Reagan was again successful in 1984.

In 1988 and 1992 the field of Democratic presidential candidates contained a near equal mix of governors and senators, but two Democratic governors established momentum early in the primaries. In 1988 Massachusetts governor Michael S. Dukakis won enough delegates by June to take the Democratic nomination, but he lost to Vice President Bush in the November. In 1992 Arkansas governor Clinton secured the nomination by early April and went on to defeat the incumbent Bush.

Looking Outside Government?

In 1996 President Clinton faced no notable challenge from within the Democratic Party in securing his party's renomination. The eventual Republican nominee, Senator Bob Dole of Kansas, had to fend off ten major opponents, that included three senators and two governors. However, Dole's two chief challengers were from outside of government: business executive and millionaire Malcolm S. "Steve" Forbes Jr. and television commentator Pat Buchanan.

Another business executive and billionaire, H. Ross Perot, mounted his second third party run for the presidency in 1996. Perot had won 18.9 percent of the popular vote in 1992, to become the most successful third party candidate since Theodore Roosevelt Bull Moose Party run in 1912. As Reform Party candidate in 1996, he took less than half of that amount. However, the partial successes of these challenges may signal a trend that Americans are willing to look outside of government for future presidential leadership.

Modern Elections

The 1980 primaries concluded in a manner nearly the reverse of 1976, but in both years the incumbent president had to fight for renomination. In 1976 Reagan and President Ford battled on to the Republican convention, while Carter wrapped up the Democratic nomination in the final week of the primary season. Four years later, Reagan became the almost certain nominee early in the primary campaigns, while President Carter continued to face challenges from Sen. Edward M. Kennedy of Massachusetts, up to, and even during, the party's convention.

The Reagan Era

The long 1980 presidential campaign resulted in a landslide victory for Ronald Reagan. Official returns gave the Republican nominee a lead over Carter of 9.7 percentage points. Carrying 44 states, Reagan scored an impressive 489 electoral votes to just 49 for Carter, who carried only six states and the District of Columbia. In rejecting Carter, voters for the second consecutive election turned their backs on an embattled incumbent to elect a challenger promising a fresh approach to government and a dynamic new brand of leadership. But unlike the close contest in 1976 in which Carter narrowly defeated Ford, the results in 1980 were emphatic.

Carter's defeat underscored the Democrats' difficulty in winning presidential elections since the end of World War II. From 1948 to 1980, the Republicans had won five elections to the Democrats' four. But only twice — in 1964 and 1976 — had the Democratic candidate drawn a majority of the popular vote. Carter's share of the vote dropped below that of

1976 in every state by at least 2 percentage points. In nearly half the states it declined by at least 10 percentage points. Reagan easily carried every region of the country, including the keystones of Carter's triumph four years before — the industrial Northeast and the South.

Many Americans did not vote. Only about 54 percent of the nation's voting age population of 160.5 million went to the polls, making 1980 the fifth consecutive election in which turnout had declined.

Running against Mondale in 1984, Reagan was reelected by 59 percent of the popular vote — just shy of President Lyndon B. Johnson's landmark 61 percent in 1964 — and with a record-smashing 525 electoral votes. Reagan won all states but one, a feat performed previously only by Nixon in 1972. Mondale received 13 electoral votes, carrying the District of Columbia and Minnesota. Reagan ran unusually well among young voters (aged 18 to 29), winning more than 55 percent of their ballots. Reagan also decisively reclaimed the conservative white South for the GOP: in fact, he won every Southern state by at least 18 percentage points.

This resounding defeat was another in the Democrats' growing string of presidential election drubbings. At no time during the 20th century had a major party gone through a series of electoral debacles as one-sided as the Democrats had experienced from 1972 to 1984. In 1972 and 1984 the party carried only one state; in 1980 only six states.

Moreover, it has taken unusual circumstances for the Democratic presidential ticket to be competitive. Carter capitalized on public disfavor with the Republicans generated by the Watergate scandal to win in 1976. But even then his victory margin was just 2 percentage points. In 1972, 1980 and 1984, the Democrats lost by margins of 23, 10 and 18 percentage points respectively.

The 1984 election was not a particularly auspicious contest for the Democrats to break the GOP's White House dominance. Reagan enjoyed enormous personal popularity, and the perceived economic upswing served to underscore his themes of peace and prosperity. Adding to the Republican advantage was Mondale's relative unpopularity even within his own party. In the Democratic primaries, more than three voters out of every five cast ballots for a candidate other than Mondale.

The Democrats hoped that the millions of voters who were hurt by Reagan's cutbacks in spending for social programs or who objected to his redirection of the federal government would turn against him at the polls. But their hopes of building a class-oriented, anti-Reagan majority in 1984 evaporated with the economic upswing. Nearly 93 million voters went to the polls, ending the 20-year decline in turnout. Although Mondale's national popular vote total was about 1 million votes higher than Carter's in 1980, Reagan's soared upward by nearly 10 million. Reagan became the first candidate to win more than 50 million votes in a presidential election.

Bush at the Helm

In 1988, the Democrats entered the campaign season with high expectations for winning back the executive branch of the government. There were several reasons for their optimism. First, their candidate, Massachusetts governor Dukakis was not running against Reagan. After two terms, Reagan was passing on his political mantle to his vice president, George Bush. Second, summer polls showed Dukakis with a sizable lead. Third, Bush's choice of Sen. Quayle of Indiana as his running mate was generally unpopular among Republicans.

But Dukakis's early lead evaporated under a withering — and largely unanswered — Republican attack that began at the GOP convention in August. The result was a Bush win that fit neatly into the pattern of recent Republican victories. He swept the South, the Rocky Mountains, much of the Farm Belt and every big state except New York. He won 426 Electoral College votes to 111 for Dukakis and 1 cast for Dukakis's running mate, Sen. Lloyd Bentsen of Texas.

Voter turnout slipped back 3 percent from 1984; a bare majority of the voting age population, 50.1 percent voted. Of the estimated 182.6 million Americans of voting age, only 91.6 million went to the polls in 1988.

Democrats Regain White House

President Bush began the 1992 election cycle looking unbeatable. In March 1991, in the aftermath of the U.S.-led victory over Iraq in the Persian Gulf War, he received a 91 percent approval rating of his performance as president. But as the recession of 1990-91 deepened, Bush seemed increasingly out of touch at home. In addition to his inaction on the economy, the Republican Party's right wing was still angered by his 1990 tax increase, which broke his "no new taxes" pledge. In the 1992 primaries, Bush had to fend off the unusually pointed challenge from conservative columnist Patrick J. Buchanan.

Notwithstanding his poll ratings, President Bush might have been doomed from the start. Historically, "understudy" presidents do not win reelection. Presidents who gain their office by carrying the legacy of their mentors have a hard time developing their own program or strategy. In addition, the tension within their party coalitions burst into the open. John Adams, Madison, Van Buren, Taft, Hoover, as well as Bush, all fit this description.

Bill Clinton, after shaking off questions about his character, locked up the Democratic nomination early in the primaries. By calling himself a "new Democrat," the 46-year-old Arkansas governor hoped to separate himself from rejected candidates such as Carter, Mondale and Dukakis. Clinton promised to move beyond liberal orthodoxy and "reinvent government." His constant campaign slogan was "change." Clinton selected moderate Sen. Al Gore of Tennessee as a running mate.

A bitter anti-incumbent mood dominated the whole campaign. Nationwide reformers promoted the idea of term limits for elected officials as a way of sweeping out career politicians. Texas billionaire Ross Perot, with his folksy anti-government rhetoric about how to "fix" Washington, ran as an independent. Although Perot's erratic on-and-off campaign sank his chances, his relentless attacks on Bush weakened the Republicans in the South and West — the heart of the GOP base since Nixon's 1968 campaign.

Clinton won the White House taking 43 percent of the popular vote and 370 electoral votes, compared with Bush's 38 percent and 168 electoral votes. Perot's 19 percent share of the vote did not win any states. But Clinton's election could be viewed as an aberration. Only the second Democrat elected president since 1968, Clinton won the three-man race. The independent candidacy of Perot might have cost Bush the election, as much by tarnishing his reputation as taking away the votes of the angry middle class.

With the Border states of Arkansas and Tennessee strongly in their camp, the Democrats in 1992 built outward into the old Confederacy (Louisiana, Kentucky, Georgia), north into industrial states (Illinois, Ohio, Michigan) and west and north into farm states (Missouri, Iowa, Wisconsin, Minnesota). Democrats consistently lost those states in presidential elections in the past generation, despite strong support in congressional and statewide races.

The Democrats also built on their core of support in the Northeast (winning all the states from Maine to West Virginia) and capitalized on disgruntlement with Bush in the West (California, Washington, Oregon, Nevada, Montana, Colorado, New Mexico, Hawaii).

The hard anti-incumbent mood of the electorate, stoked by Perot, helped to produce the highest voter turnout since 1960. More than 104,000,000 voters, 55 percent of those eligible, participated in the election. That participation rate was a far cry from rates of earlier periods in U.S. history. But it seemed to stem, momentarily, the apathy and resignation of American politics.

Clinton Again in 1996

In 1994 many voters sent a strong message of disapproval with President Clinton's record by electing a Republican Congress. But the new GOP Congress, led by controversial House Speaker Newt Gingrich of Georgia, incorrectly interpreted the 1994 elections results as a mandate for their conservative ideological agenda. While the Republicans strove hard for conservative — and unpopular — policy change, Clinton adopted more moderate positions and portrayed himself as a check against GOP "extremism." That tack proved successful by the end of 1995. With the president and Republican legislators feuding over spending priorities, Congress failed to pass a budget on time to avoid two temporary government shutdowns. As the budgetary standoff persisted, the GOP Congress began to appear unreasonable in the public's eye, and the president benefited from the comparison.

Clinton entered the 1996 election season with renewed political strength and high approval ratings. In addition to the political miscalculations of the Republican Congress, the president benefited from a strengthening economy, low unemployment, and a falling budget deficit. A third factor also began to weigh in Clinton's favor: he lacked an intra-party challenge for renomination, while the GOP nomination contest was an expensive, highly negative, and divisive process.

From the beginning Senate Majority Leader Bob Dole (Kansas) was the clear front-runner for the Republican Party's nomination. Although there never was any serious doubt that he would be the GOP nominee, for several months Dole had to fight off a large group of presidential aspirants including television commentator Pat Buchanan, former Department of Education secretary and Tennessee governor Lamar Alexander, Texas senator Phil Gramm, California governor Pete Wilson, Pennsylvania senator Arlen Specter, Indiana senator Richard Lugar and multimillionaire publisher Malcolm S. "Steve" Forbes Jr.

After securing the nomination, Dole surprised many with two bold campaign moves. First, he selected former New York representative and secretary of Housing and Urban Development Jack Kemp for vice president. Second, Dole proposed an across-the-board 15 percent income tax cut. This proposal was especially surprising because Dole had cultivated a well-deserved reputation as a "deficit hawk" who opposed supply-side economic theory.

In the meantime Clinton pursued a strategy of one what key aide called "triangulation": that is, separating himself from the unpopular elements of both political parties and moving to the political center. To achieve that end, Clinton supported a number of conservative, but also largely popular, policy initiatives: welfare reform, imposition of a V-chip in televisions, curfews for teenagers, school uniforms and balancing the budget by the year 2002. Clinton also stayed true to his Democratic roots by opposing congressional efforts to reduce Medicare spending and weaken environmental regulation and by proposing tax credits for college education.

Clinton easily won reelection with 49.2 percent of the popular vote and 379 electoral votes to Dole's 40.7 percent and 159 electoral votes. Texas billionaire Perot, running under the Reform Party banner in 1996 had less impact in 1996 than he had as an independent candidate in 1992: Perot polled 8.4 percent of the vote, less than half of his 1992 total, and received no electoral votes. Clinton's victory made him the first Democrat to win reelection since Franklin D. Roosevelt won his second term in 1936. He became the first Democrat to be elected to the presidency along with a Republican-controlled Congress.

Clinton won every state he had captured in 1992, except for Georgia, Montana and Colorado. However, he picked up Florida and Arizona. The regional divisions in the 1996 electoral map confirmed old political trends and revealed new ones. The East solidified as the Democratic stronghold, along with most states in the industrial Midwest and Pacific Coast. The GOP base in the South remained secure, although Clinton became the first Democratic presidential candidate to carry Florida since 1976. The Republicans also retained firm control of the Mountain West and Plains states.

Yet three facts remained discouraging for Clinton. First, for the second straight election he had failed to win a majority of the popular vote. Second, voter turnout was less than 50 percent, the lowest since 1924. Third, Democrats failed to regain control of the Congress, despite the unpopularity of Gingrich and many of his Republican colleagues.

Perhaps what was most remarkable about the 1996 national elections was just how little had actually changed, despite the two major parties having spent about $500 million on campaign activities. Political analysts have aptly referred to the 1996 elections as reaffirming the status-quo, a dramatic difference from both the 1992 and 1994 elections in which voters expressed frustration with the existing political arrangement and sought substantial changes in their government.

The Electoral College

For more than two centuries, Americans have been electing their presidents through the Electoral College. Created by the Framers of the Constitution as a compromise between electing presidents by Congress or by direct popular vote, the system has continued to function even though the United States has undergone radical transformation from an agricultural seaboard nation to a world power.

Under the Electoral College system, each state is entitled to electoral votes equal in number to its congressional delegation — that is, the number of representatives from the state, plus two for the state's two senators. Under the system as it works today, the party that receives a plurality of the popular vote in a state is virtually assured of receiving that state's electoral votes. But in the past there were variations of that procedure including choosing electors by congressional district, statewide votes for each individual elector and selection of electors by state legislatures. There also have been cases of a so-called faithless elector, who cast his or her electoral vote for the candidate of the defeated party. *(Splitting of States' Electoral Votes, box, p. 14)*

Constitutional Background

The method of selecting a president was the subject of long debate at the Constitutional Convention of 1787. Several plans were proposed and rejected before a compromise solution, which was modified only slightly in later years, was adopted (Article II, Section I, Clause 2).

Facing the convention when it convened May 25 was the question of whether the chief executive should be chosen by direct popular election, by the Congress, by state legislatures or by intermediate electors. Direct election was opposed because it was felt generally that the people lacked sufficient knowledge of the character and qualifications of possible candidates to make an intelligent choice. Many delegates also feared that the people of the various states would be unlikely to agree on a single person, usually casting their votes for favorite-son candidates well known to them.

The possibility of giving Congress the power to choose the president also received consideration. This plan was rejected, however, largely because of fear that it would jeopardize the principle of executive independence. Similarly, a plan favored by many delegates, to let state legislatures choose the president, was turned down because the delegates thought the president might feel so indebted to the states as to allow them to encroach on federal authority.

Unable to agree on a plan, the convention Aug. 31 appointed a "Committee of 11" to solve the problem. On Sept. 4 it suggested a compromise under which each state would appoint presidential electors equal to the total number of its representatives and senators. The electors, chosen in a manner set forth by each state legislature, would meet in their own states and each cast votes for two persons. The votes would be counted in Congress, with the candidate receiving a majority elected president and the second-highest candidate becoming vice president.

No distinction was made between ballots for president and vice president. Moreover, the development of national political parties and the nomination of tickets for president and vice president created further confusion in the electoral system. All the electors of one party tended to cast ballots for their two party nominees. But with no distinction between the presidential and vice presidential nominees, the danger arose of a tie vote between the two. That actually happened in 1800, leading to a change in the original electoral system with ratification of the 12th Amendment in 1804.

The committee's compromise plan constituted a great concession to the less populous states, since they were assured of three votes (two for their two senators and at least one for their representative) however small their populations might be. The plan also left important powers with the states by giving complete discretion to state legislatures to determine the method of choosing electors.

Sources

Petersen, Svend. *A Statistical History of the American Presidential Elections.* Westport, Conn.: Greenwood Press, 1981.

Schlesinger, Arthur M., Jr., ed. *History of American Presidential Elections.* 4 vols. New York: McGraw-Hill, 1971.

Stanwood, Edward. *History of the Presidency, 1788-1916.* 2 vols. rev. ed. New York: Kelley, 1921.

U.S. Bureau of the Census. *Historical Statistics of the United States, Colonial Times to 1970.* 2 vols. Washington, D.C.: Government Printing Office, 1975.

U.S. Presidents and Vice Presidents

President and Political Party	Born	Died	Age at Inauguration	Native of	Elected from	Term of Service	Vice President
George Washington (F)	1732	1799	57	Va.	Va.	April 30, 1789-March 4, 1793	John Adams
George Washington (F)			61			March 4, 1793-March 4, 1797	John Adams
John Adams (F)	1735	1826	61	Mass.	Mass.	March 4, 1797-March 4, 1801	Thomas Jefferson
Thomas Jefferson (DR)	1743	1826	57	Va.	Va.	March 4, 1801-March 4, 1805	Aaron Burr
Thomas Jefferson (DR)			61			March 4, 1805-March 4, 1809	George Clinton
James Madison (DR)	1751	1836	57	Va.	Va.	March 4, 1809-March 4, 1813	George Clinton
James Madison (DR)			61			March 4, 1813-March 4, 1817	Elbridge Gerry
James Monroe (DR)	1758	1831	58	Va.	Va.	March 4, 1817-March 4, 1821	Daniel D. Tompkins
James Monroe (DR)			62			March 4, 1821-March 4, 1825	Daniel D. Tompkins
John Q. Adams (DR)	1767	1848	57	Mass.	Mass.	March 4, 1825-March 4, 1829	John C. Calhoun
Andrew Jackson (D)	1767	1845	61	S.C.	Tenn.	March 4, 1829-March 4, 1833	John C. Calhoun
Andrew Jackson (D)			65			March 4, 1833-March 4, 1837	Martin Van Buren
Martin Van Buren (D)	1782	1862	54	N.Y.	N.Y.	March 4, 1837-March 4, 1841	Richard M. Johnson
W. H. Harrison (W)	1773	1841	68	Va.	Ohio	March 4, 1841-April 4, 1841	John Tyler
John Tyler (W)	1790	1862	51	Va.	Va.	April 6, 1841-March 4, 1845	
James K. Polk (D)	1795	1849	49	N.C.	Tenn.	March 4, 1985-March 4, 1849	George M. Dallas
Zachary Taylor (W)	1784	1850	64	Va.	La.	March 4, 1849-July 9, 1850	Millard Fillmore
Millard Fillmore (W)	1800	1874	50	N.Y.	N.Y.	July 10, 1850-March 4, 1853	
Franklin Pierce (D)	1804	1869	48	N.H.	N.H.	March 4, 1853-March 4, 1857	William R. King
James Buchanan (D)	1791	1868	65	Pa.	Pa.	March 4, 1857-March 4, 1861	John C. Breckinridge
Abraham Lincoln (R)	1809	1865	52	Ky.	Ill.	March 4, 1861-March 4, 1865	Hannibal Hamlin
Abraham Lincoln (R)			56			March 4, 1865-April 15, 1865	Andrew Johnson
Andrew Johnson (R)	1808	1875	56	N.C.	Tenn.	April 15, 1865-March 4, 1869	
Ulysses S. Grant (R)	1822	1885	46	Ohio	Ill.	March 4, 1869-March 4, 1873	Schuyler Colfax
Ulysses S. Grant (R)			50			March 4, 1873-March 4, 1877	Henry Wilson
Rutherford B. Hayes (R)	1822	1893	54	Ohio	Ohio	March 4, 1877-March 4, 1881	William A. Wheeler
James A. Garfield (R)	1831	1881	49	Ohio	Ohio	March 4, 1881-Sept. 19, 1881	Chester A. Arthur
Chester A. Arthur (R)	1830	1886	50	Vt.	N.Y.	Sept. 20, 1881-March 4, 1885	
Grover Cleveland (D)	1837	1908	47	N.J.	N.Y.	March 4, 1885-March 4, 1889	Thomas A. Hendricks
Benjamin Harrison (R)	1833	1901	55	Ohio	Ind.	March 4, 1889-March 4, 1893	Levi P. Morton
Grover Cleveland (D)	1837	1908	55	N.J.	N.Y.	March 4, 1893-March 4, 1897	Adlai E. Stevenson
William McKinley (R)	1843	1901	54	Ohio	Ohio	March 4, 1897-March 4, 1901	Garret A. Hobart
William McKinley (R)			58			March 4, 1901-Sept. 14, 1901	Theodore Roosevelt
Theodore Roosevelt (R)	1858	1919	42	N.Y.	N.Y.	Sept. 14, 1901-March 4, 1905	
Theodore Roosevelt (R)			46			March 4, 1905-March 4, 1909	Charles W. Fairbanks
William H. Taft (R)	1857	1930	51	Ohio	Ohio	March 4, 1909-March 4, 1913	James S. Sherman
Woodrow Wilson (D)	1856	1924	56	Va.	N.J.	March 4, 1913-March 4, 1917	Thomas R. Marshall
Woodrow Wilson (D)			60			March 4, 1917-March 4, 1921	Thomas R. Marshall
Warren G. Harding (R)	1865	1923	55	Ohio	Ohio	March 4, 1921-Aug. 2, 1923	Calvin Coolidge
Calvin Coolidge (R)	1872	1933	51	Vt.	Mass.	Aug. 3, 1923-March 4, 1925	
Calvin Coolidge (R)			52			March 4, 1925-March 4, 1929	Charles G. Dawes
Herbert Hoover (R)	1874	1964	54	Iowa	Calif.	March 4, 1929-March 4, 1933	Charles Curtis
Franklin D. Roosevelt (D)	1882	1945	51	N.Y.	N.Y.	March 4, 1933-Jan. 20, 1937	John N. Garner
Franklin D. Roosevelt (D)			55			Jan. 20, 1937-Jan. 20, 1941	John N. Garner
Franklin D. Roosevelt (D)			59			Jan. 20, 1941-Jan. 20, 1945	Henry A. Wallace
Franklin D. Roosevelt (D)			63			Jan. 20, 1945-April 12, 1945	Harry S. Truman
Harry S. Truman (D)	1884	1972	60	Mo.	Mo.	April 12, 1945-Jan. 20, 1949	
Harry S. Truman (D)			64			Jan. 20, 1949-Jan. 20, 1953	Alben W. Barkley
Dwight D. Eisenhower (R)	1890	1969	62	Texas	N.Y.	Jan. 20, 1953-Jan. 20, 1957	Richard Nixon
Dwight D. Eisenhower (R)			66		Pa.	Jan. 20, 1957-Jan. 20, 1961	Richard Nixon
John F. Kennedy (D)	1917	1963	43	Mass.	Mass.	Jan. 20, 1961-Nov. 22, 1963	Lyndon B. Johnson
Lyndon B. Johnson (D)	1908	1973	55	Texas	Texas	Nov. 22, 1963-Jan. 20, 1965	
Lyndon B. Johnson (D)			56			Jan. 20, 1965-Jan. 20, 1969	Hubert H. Humphrey
Richard Nixon (R)	1913	1994	56	Calif.	N.Y.	Jan. 20, 1969-Jan. 20, 1973	Spiro T. Agnew
Richard Nixon (R)			60		Calif.	Jan. 20, 1973-Aug. 9, 1974	Spiro T. Agnew / Gerald R. Ford
Gerald R. Ford (R)	1913		61	Neb.	Mich.	Aug. 9, 1974-Jan. 20, 1977	Nelson A. Rockefeller
Jimmy Carter (D)	1924		52	Ga.	Ga.	Jan. 20, 1977-Jan. 20, 1981	Walter F. Mondale
Ronald Reagan (R)	1911		69	Ill.	Calif.	Jan. 20, 1981-Jan. 20, 1985	George Bush
Ronald Reagan (R)			73			Jan. 20, 1985-Jan. 20, 1989	George Bush
George Bush (R)	1924		64	Mass.	Texas	Jan. 20, 1989-Jan. 20, 1993	Dan Quayle
Bill Clinton (D)	1946		46	Ark.	Ark.	Jan. 20, 1993-Jan. 20, 1997	Albert Gore Jr.
Bill Clinton (D)			50			Jan. 20, 1997-	Albert Gore Jr.

Note: *D—Democrat; DR—Democratic-Republican; F—Federalist; R—Republican; W—Whig.*

The only part of the committee's plan that aroused serious opposition was a provision giving the Senate the right to decide presidential elections in which no candidate received a majority of electoral votes. Some delegates feared that the Senate, which already had been given treaty ratification powers and the responsibility to "advise and consent" on all important executive appointments, might become too powerful. A proposal was made and accepted to let the House of Representatives decide the winner in instances when the electors failed to give a majority of their votes to a single candidate. The interests of the small states were preserved by giving each state's delegation only one vote in the House on roll calls to elect a president.

The system adopted by the Constitutional Convention was a compromise born out of problems involved in diverse state voting requirements, the slavery problem, big-state versus small-state rivalries and the complexities of the balance of power among different branches of the government. Moreover, it was probably as close to a direct popular election as the men who wrote the Constitution thought possible and appropriate at the time.

The term *electoral college* itself does not appear in the Constitution. It was first used unofficially in the early 1800s and became the official designation for the electoral body in 1845.

The 12th Amendment

Only once since ratification of the Constitution has an amendment been adopted that substantially altered the method of electing the president. In the 1800 presidential election, the Democratic-Republican electors inadvertently caused a tie in the Electoral College by casting equal numbers of votes for Thomas Jefferson, whom they wished to be elected president, and Aaron Burr, whom they wished to elect vice president. The election was thrown into the House, and 36 ballots were required before Jefferson was finally elected president. The 12th Amendment, ratified in 1804, sought to prevent a recurrence of this incident by providing that the electors should vote separately for president and vice president. *(Jefferson-Burr Deadlock, p. 11; U.S. Constitution on Presidential Selection, Amendment XII, p. 262)*

Other changes in the system evolved over the years. The authors of the Constitution, for example, had intended that each state should choose its most distinguished citizens as electors and that they would deliberate and vote as individuals in electing the president. But as strong political parties began to appear, the electors came to be chosen merely as representatives of the parties; independent voting by electors disappeared almost entirely.

Methods of Choosing Electors

In the early years of the Republic, states used a variety of methods to select presidential electors. For the first presidential election, in 1789, four states held direct popular elections to choose their electors: Pennsylvania and Maryland (at large) as well as Virginia and Delaware (by district). In five states — Connecticut, Georgia, New Jersey, New York and South Carolina — the state legislatures were to make the choice.

New Hampshire and Massachusetts adopted a combination of the legislative and popular methods. New Hampshire held a statewide popular vote for presidential electors with the stipulation that any elector would have to win a majority of the popular vote to be elected; otherwise,

the legislature would choose. In Massachusetts the arrangement was for the voters in each congressional district to vote for the two persons they wanted to be presidential electors. From the two individuals in each district receiving the highest number of votes, the legislature, by joint ballot of both houses, was to choose one. In addition, the legislature was to choose two electors at large.

Because of a dispute between the two chambers, the New York legislature failed to choose electors. The state Senate insisted on full equality with the Assembly (lower house); that is, the Senate wanted each house to take a separate ballot and to resolve any differences between them by agreement rather than by having one house impose its will on the other. The Assembly, on the other hand, wanted a joint ballot, on which the lower house's larger numbers would prevail, or it was willing to divide the electors with the Senate. The failure to compromise cost the state its vote in the first presidential election.

The 12th and 13th states — North Carolina and Rhode Island — had not ratified the Constitution by the time the electors were chosen, and so they did not participate.

Generally similar arrangements prevailed for the election of 1792. Massachusetts, while continuing to choose electors by district, changed the system somewhat to provide for automatic election of any candidate for elector who received a majority of the popular vote. New Hampshire continued the system of popular election at large, but substituted a popular runoff election in place of legislative choice, if no candidate received a majority of the popular vote.

Besides Massachusetts and New Hampshire, electors were chosen in 1792 by popular vote in Maryland and Pennsylvania (at large) and Virginia and Kentucky (by district). State legislatures chose electors in Connecticut, Delaware, Georgia, New Jersey, New York, North Carolina, Rhode Island, South Carolina and Vermont.

By 1796 several changes had occurred. New Hampshire switched back to legislative choice for those electors who failed to receive a majority of the popular vote. Tennessee entered the Union (1796) with a unique system for choosing presidential electors: the state legislature appointed three persons in each county, who in turn chose the presidential electors. Massachusetts retained the system used in 1792. Other states chose their electors as follows: at-large popular vote: Georgia, Pennsylvania; district popular vote: Kentucky, Maryland, North Carolina, Virginia; state legislature: Connecticut, Delaware, New Jersey, New York, Rhode Island, South Carolina, Vermont.

Political Parties and Electors: 1800

As political parties gained power, manipulation of the system of choosing electors became increasingly widespread. For example, in 1800 Massachusetts switched from popular voting to legislative selection of electors because of recent successes by the Democratic-Republican Party in that state. The Federalists, still in firm control of the legislature, sought to secure the state's entire electoral vote for its presidential candidate, native son John Adams. New Hampshire did likewise.

The Democratic-Republicans were not innocent of this kind of political maneuver. In Virginia, where that party was in control, the legislature changed the system for choosing electors from districts to a statewide at-large ballot. That way, the expected statewide Democratic-Republican majority could overcome Federalist control in some districts and garner a unanimous vote for Jefferson, the Democratic-Republican presidential candidate.

In Pennsylvania the two houses of the state legislature could not agree on legislation providing for popular ballots, the system used in the first three elections, so the legislature itself chose the electors, dividing them between the parties.

In other changes in 1800, Rhode Island switched to popular election and Georgia reverted to legislative elections. The 16 states thus used the following methods of choosing presidential electors in 1800:
- By popular vote: Kentucky, Maryland, North Carolina (by district); Rhode Island, Virginia (at large).
- By the legislature: Connecticut, Delaware, Georgia, Massachusetts, New Hampshire, New Jersey, New York, Pennsylvania, South Carolina, Tennessee (indirectly, as in 1796), Vermont.

Trend to Winner-Take-All System

For the next third of a century, the states moved slowly but inexorably toward a standard system of choosing presidential electors — the statewide, winner-take-all popular ballot. The development of political parties resulted in the adoption of slates of electors pledged to vote for the parties' presidential candidates. Each party organization saw a statewide ballot as being in its best interest, with the hope of sweeping in all its electors and preventing the opposition group from capitalizing on local areas of strength (which could result in winning only part of the electoral vote under the districting system).

From 1804 to 1832 the states used three basic methods of choosing presidential electors — at-large popular vote, district popular vote and election by the state legislature. The following list shows the changing methods of choosing presidential electors for each state from 1804 to 1832:

1804

Popular vote, at large: New Hampshire, New Jersey, Ohio, Pennsylvania, Rhode Island, Virginia.

Popular vote, by district: Kentucky, Maryland, Massachusetts, North Carolina, Tennessee.

State legislature: Connecticut, Delaware, Georgia, New York, South Carolina, Vermont.

1808

Popular vote, at large: New Hampshire, New Jersey, Ohio, Pennsylvania, Rhode Island, Virginia.

Popular vote, by district: Kentucky, Maryland, North Carolina, Tennessee.

State legislature: Connecticut, Delaware, Georgia, Massachusetts, New York, South Carolina, Vermont.

1812

Popular vote, at large: New Hampshire, Ohio, Pennsylvania, Rhode Island, Virginia.

Popular vote, by district: Kentucky, Maryland, Massachusetts, Tennessee.

State legislature: Connecticut, Delaware, Georgia, Louisiana, New Jersey, New York, North Carolina, South Carolina, Vermont.

1816

Popular vote, at large: New Hampshire, New Jersey, North Carolina, Ohio, Pennsylvania, Rhode Island, Virginia.

Popular vote, by district: Kentucky, Maryland, Tennessee.

State legislature: Connecticut, Delaware, Georgia, Indiana, Louisiana, Massachusetts, New York, South Carolina, Vermont.

1820

Popular vote, at large: Connecticut, Mississippi, New Hampshire, New Jersey, North Carolina, Ohio, Pennsylvania, Rhode Island, Virginia.

Popular vote, by district: Illinois, Kentucky, Maine, Maryland, Massachusetts, Tennessee.

State legislature: Alabama, Delaware, Georgia, Indiana, Louisiana, Missouri, New York, South Carolina, Vermont.

1824

Popular vote, at large: Alabama, Connecticut, Indiana, Massachusetts, Mississippi, New Hampshire, New Jersey, North Carolina, Ohio, Pennsylvania, Rhode Island, Virginia.

Popular vote, by district: Illinois, Kentucky, Maine, Maryland, Missouri, Tennessee.

State legislature: Delaware, Georgia, Louisiana, New York, South Carolina, Vermont.

1828

Popular vote, at large: Alabama, Connecticut, Georgia, Illinois, Indiana, Kentucky, Louisiana, Massachusetts, Mississippi, Missouri, New Hampshire, New Jersey, North Carolina, Ohio, Pennsylvania, Rhode Island, Vermont, Virginia.

Popular vote, by district: Maine, Maryland, New York, Tennessee.

State legislature: Delaware, South Carolina.

1832

Popular vote, at large: All states except Maryland and South Carolina.

Popular vote, by district: Maryland.

State legislature: South Carolina.

By 1836 Maryland switched to the system of choosing its electors by statewide popular vote. This left only South Carolina selecting its electors through the state legislature. The state continued this practice through the election of

1860. Only after the Civil War was popular voting for presidential electors instituted in South Carolina.

Thus, since 1836 the statewide, winner-take-all popular vote for electors has been the almost universal practice. Exceptions include the following:

Massachusetts, 1848. Three slates of electors ran — Whig, Democratic, and Free Soil — none of which received a majority of the popular vote. Under the law then in force, the state legislature was to choose in such a case. It chose the Whig electors.

Florida, 1868. The state legislature chose the electors.

Colorado, 1876. The state legislature chose the electors because the state had just been admitted to the Union, had held state elections in August and did not want to go to the trouble and expense of holding a popular vote for the presidential election so soon thereafter.

Michigan, 1892. Republicans had been predominant in the state since the 1850s. However, in 1890 the Democrats gained control of the legislature and the governorship and enacted a districting system of choosing presidential electors in the expectation that the Democrats could carry some districts and thus some electoral votes in 1892. They were correct; the Republicans won nine and the Democrats five electoral votes that year. But the Republicans soon regained control of the state and reenacted the at-large system for the 1896 election.

Maine, 1972. In 1969 the Maine legislature enacted a district system for choosing presidential electors. Two of the state's four electors were selected on the basis of the statewide vote, and the other two were determined by which party carried each of the state's two congressional districts. The system is still in force.

Historical Anomalies

The complicated and indirect system of electing the president has led to anomalies from time to time. In 1836, for example, the Whigs sought to take advantage of the electoral system by running different presidential candidates in different parts of the country. William Henry Harrison ran in most of New England, the mid-Atlantic states and the Midwest; Daniel Webster ran in Massachusetts; Hugh White of Tennessee ran in the South.

The theory was that each candidate could capture electoral votes for the Whig Party in the region where he was strongest. Then the Whig electors could combine on one candidate or, alternatively, throw the election into the House, whichever seemed to their advantage. However, the scheme did not work because Martin Van Buren, the Democratic nominee, captured a majority of the electoral vote.

Another quirk in the system surfaced in 1872. The Democratic presidential nominee, Horace Greeley, died between the time of the popular vote and the meeting of the presidential electors. The Democratic electors had no party nominee to vote for, and each was left to his own judgment. Forty-two of the 66 Democratic electors chose to vote for the Democratic governor-elect of Indiana, Thomas Hendricks. The rest of the electors split their votes among three other politicians: 18 for B. Gratz Brown of Missouri, the Democratic vice presidential nominee; two for Charles J. Jenkins of Georgia, and one for David Davis of Illinois. Three Georgia electors insisted on casting their votes for Greeley, but Congress refused to count them.

In three elections the Electoral College has chosen presidents who ran behind their opponents in the popular vote. In two of these instances — Republican Rutherford B.

Hayes in 1876 and Republican Benjamin Harrison in 1888 — the winning candidate carried a number of key states by close margins, while losing other states by wide margins. In the third instance — Democratic-Republican John Quincy Adams in 1924 — the House of Representatives chose the new president after no candidate had achieved a majority in the Electoral College. *("Minority" Presidents, box, p. 81)*

Election by Congress

Under the Constitution, Congress has two major responsibilities relating to the election of the president and vice president. First, it is directed to receive and, in joint session, count the electoral votes certified by the states. Second, if no candidate has a majority of the electoral vote, the House of Representatives must elect the president and the Senate the vice president.

Although many of the Framers of the Constitution apparently thought that most elections would be decided by Congress, the House actually has chosen a president only twice, in 1801 and 1825. But a number of campaigns have been deliberately designed to throw elections into the House, where each state has one vote and a majority of states is needed to elect.

In modern times the formal counting of electoral votes has been largely a ceremonial function, but the congressional role can be decisive when votes are contested. The preeminent example is the Hayes-Tilden contest of 1876, when congressional decisions on disputed electoral votes from four states gave the election to Republican Hayes despite the fact that Democrat Samuel J. Tilden had a majority of the popular vote. *(Hayes-Tilden election, p. 16)* From the beginning, the constitutional provisions governing the selection of the president have had few defenders, and many efforts at Electoral College reform have been undertaken. Although prospects for reform seemed favorable after the close 1968 presidential election, the 91st Congress (1969-1971) did not take final action on a proposed constitutional amendment that would have provided for direct popular election of the president and eliminated the existing provision for contingent election by the House. Reform legislation was reintroduced in the Senate during the 94th Congress (1975-1977) and 95th Congress (1977-1979).

In addition to its role in electing the president, Congress bears responsibility in the related areas of presidential succession and disability. The 12th Amendment empowers Congress to decide what to do if the president-elect and the vice president-elect both fail to qualify by the date prescribed for commencement of their terms; it also gives Congress authority to settle problems arising from the death of candidates in cases where the election devolves upon Congress. Under the 25th Amendment, Congress has ultimate responsibility for resolving disputes over presidential disability. It also must confirm presidential nominations to fill a vacancy in the vice presidency.

Jefferson-Burr Deadlock

The election of 1800 was the first in which the contingent election procedures of the Constitution were put to the test and the president was elected by the House.

The Federalists, a declining but still potent political force, nominated John Adams for a second term and chose Charles Cotesworth Pinckney as his running mate. A Democratic-Republican congressional caucus chose Vice President

Presidential Election by the House

The following rules, reprinted from Hinds' Precedents of the House of Representatives, were adopted by the House in 1825 for use in deciding the presidential election of 1824. They would provide a precedent for any future House election of a president, although the House could change them.

1. In the event of its appearing, on opening all the certificates, and counting the votes given by the electors of the several States for President, that no person has a majority of the votes of the whole number of electors appointed, the same shall be entered on the Journals of this House.

2. The roll of the House shall then be called by States; and, on its appearing that a Member or Members from two-thirds of the States are present, the House shall immediately proceed, by ballot, to choose a President from the persons having the highest numbers, not exceeding three, on the list of those voted for as President; and, in case neither of those persons shall receive the votes of a majority of all the states on the first ballot, the House shall continue to ballot for a President, without interruption by other business, until a President be chosen.

3. The doors of the Hall shall be closed during the balloting, except against the Members of the Senate, stenographers, and the officers of the House.

4. From the commencement of the balloting until an election is made no proposition to adjourn shall be received, unless on the motion of one State, seconded by another State, and the question shall be decided by States. The same rule shall be observed in regard to any motion to change the usual hour for the meeting of the House.

5. In balloting the following mode shall be observed, to wit:

The Representatives of each State shall be arranged and seated together, beginning with the seats at the right hand of the Speaker's chair, with the Members from the State of Maine; thence, proceeding with the Members from the States, in the order the States are usually named for receiving petitions[1] around the Hall of the House, until all are seated.

A ballot box shall be provided for each State.

The Representatives of each State shall, in the first instance, ballot among themselves, in order to ascertain the vote of their State; and they may, if necessary, appoint tellers of their ballots.

After the vote of each State is ascertained, duplicates thereof shall be made out; and in case any one of the persons from whom the choice is to be made shall receive a majority of the votes given, on any one balloting by the Representatives of a State, the name of that person shall be written on each of the duplicates; and in case the votes so given shall be divided so that neither of said persons shall have a majority of the whole number of votes given by such State, on any one balloting, then the word "divided" shall be written on each duplicate.

After the delegation from each State shall have ascertained the vote of their State, the Clerk shall name the States in the order they are usually named for receiving petitions; and as the name of each is called the Sergeant-at-Arms shall present to the delegation of each two ballot boxes, in each of which shall be deposited, by some Representative of the State, one of the duplicates made as aforesaid of the vote of said State, in the presence and subject to the examination of all the Members from said State then present; and where there is more than one Representative from a State, the duplicates shall not both be deposited by the same person.

When the votes of the States are thus all taken in, the Sergeant-at-Arms shall carry one of said ballot boxes to one table and the other to a separate and distinct table.

One person from each State represented in the balloting shall be appointed by the Representatives to tell off said ballots; but, in case the Representatives fail to appoint a teller, the Speaker shall appoint.

The said tellers shall divide themselves into two sets, as nearly equal in number as can be, and one of the said sets of tellers shall proceed to count the votes in one of said boxes, and the other set the votes in the other box.

When the votes are counted by the different sets of tellers, the result shall be reported to the House; and if the reports agree, the same shall be accepted as the true votes of the States; but if the reports disagree, the States shall proceed, in the same manner as before, to a new ballot.

6. All questions arising after the balloting commences, requiring the decision of the House, which shall be decided by the House, voting per capita, to be incidental to the power of choosing a President, shall be decided by States without debate; and in case of an equal division of the votes of States, the question shall be lost.

7. When either of the persons from whom the choice is to be made shall have received a majority of all the States, the Speaker shall declare the same, and that that person is elected President of the United States.

8. The result shall be immediately communicated to the Senate by message, and a committee of three persons shall be appointed to inform the President of the United States and the President-elect of said election.

On Feb. 9, 1825, the election of John Quincy Adams took place in accordance with these rules.

---

1. Petitions are no longer introduced in this way. This old procedure of calling the states beginning with Maine proceeded through the original 13 states and then through the remaining states in the order of their admission to the Union.

Jefferson for president and Burr, who had been instrumental in winning the New York legislature for the Democratic-Republicans earlier in 1800, for vice president.

The electors met in each state on December 4, with the following results: Jefferson and Burr, 73 electoral votes each; Adams, 65; Pinckney, 64; and John Jay, 1. The Federalists had lost, but because the Democratic-Republicans had neglected to withhold one electoral vote from Burr, their presidential and vice presidential candidates were tied, and the election was thrown into the House.

The lame-duck Congress, with a partisan Federalist majority, was still in office for the electoral count, and the possibilities for intrigue were only too apparent. After toying with and rejecting a proposal to block any election until March 4, when Adams' term expired, the Federalists decided to support Burr and thus elect a relatively pliant politician over a man they considered a "dangerous radical." Alexander Hamilton opposed this move. "I trust the Federalists will not finally be so mad as to vote for Burr," he wrote. "I speak with intimate and accurate knowledge of his character. His elevation can only promote the purposes of the desperate and the profligate. If there be a man in the world I ought to hate, it is Jefferson. With Burr I have always been personally well. But the public good must be paramount to every private consideration."

On Feb. 11, 1801, Congress met in joint session — with Jefferson, the outgoing vice president, in the chair — to count the electoral vote. This ritual ended, the House retired to its own chamber to elect a president. When the House met, it became apparent that Hamilton's advice had been rejected; a majority of Federalists insisted on backing Burr over Jefferson, the man they despised more. Indeed, if Burr had given clear assurances that he would run the country as a Federalist, he might have been elected. But Burr was unwilling to make those assurances; and, as one chronicler put it, "No one knows whether it was honor or a wretched indecision which gagged Burr's lips."

In all, there were 106 members of the House at the time, 58 Federalists and 48 Democratic-Republicans. If the ballots had been cast per capita Burr would have been elected, but the Constitution provided that each state should cast a single vote and that a majority of states was necessary for election.

On the first ballot Jefferson received the votes of eight states, one short of a majority of the 16 states then in the Union. Six states backed Burr. The representatives of Vermont and Maryland were equally divided and, therefore, could not cast their states' votes. By midnight of the first day of voting, 19 ballots had been taken, and the deadlock remained.

In all, 36 ballots were taken before the House came to a decision on February 17. Predictably, there were men who sought to exploit the situation for personal gain. Jefferson wrote: "Many attempts have been made to obtain terms and promises from me. I have declared to them unequivocally that I would not receive the Government on capitulation; that I would not go in with my hands tied."

The impasse was broken finally when Vermont and Maryland switched to support Jefferson. Delaware and South Carolina also withdrew their support from Burr by casting blank ballots. The final vote: 10 states for Jefferson, four (all in New England) for Burr. Jefferson became president, and Burr, under the Constitution as it then stood, automatically became vice president.

Federalist James A. Bayard of Delaware, who had played an important role in breaking the deadlock, wrote to Hamilton: "The means existed of electing Burr, but this required his cooperation. By deceiving one man (a great blockhead) and tempting two (not incorruptible), he might have secured a majority of the states. He will never have another chance of being president of the United States; and the little use he has made of the one which has occurred gives me but an humble opinion of the talents of an unprincipled man."

The Jefferson-Burr contest clearly illustrated the dangers of the double-balloting system established by the original Constitution, and pressure began to build for an amendment requiring separate votes for president and vice president. Congress approved the 12th Amendment in December 1803, and the states — acting with unexpected speed — ratified it in time for the 1804 election.

John Quincy Adams Election

The only other time the House of Representatives elected a president was in 1825. There were many contenders in the 1824 election, but four predominated: John Quincy Adams, Henry Clay, William H. Crawford and Andrew Jackson. Crawford, secretary of the Treasury under President James Monroe, was the early frontrunner, but his candidacy faltered after he suffered an incapacitating illness in 1823.

When the electoral votes were counted, Jackson had 99, Adams 84, Crawford 41 and Clay 37. With 18 of the 24 states choosing their electors by popular vote, Jackson also led in the popular voting, although the significance of the popular vote was open to challenge. Under the 12th Amendment, the names of the three top contenders — Jackson, Adams and the ailing Crawford — were placed before the House. Clay's support was vital to either of the two front-runners.

From the start, Clay apparently intended to support Adams as the lesser of two evils. But before the House voted, a great scandal erupted. A Philadelphia newspaper published an anonymous letter alleging that Clay had agreed to support Adams in return for being made secretary of state. The letter alleged also that Clay would have been willing to make the same deal with Jackson. Clay immediately denied the charge and pronounced the writer of the letter "a base and infamous character, a dastard and a liar."

When the House met to vote, Adams was supported by the six New England states and New York and, in large part through Clay's backing, by Maryland, Ohio, Kentucky, Illinois, Missouri and Louisiana. Thus a majority of 13 delegations voted for him — the bare minimum he needed for election, since there were 24 states in the Union at the time. The election was accomplished on the first ballot, but Adams took office under a cloud from which his administration never emerged.

Jackson had believed the charges and found his suspicions vindicated when Adams, after the election, did appoint Clay as secretary of state. "Was there ever witnessed such a bare-faced corruption in any country before?" Jackson wrote to a friend. Jackson's successful 1828 campaign made much of his contention that the House of Representatives had thwarted the will of the people by denying him the presidency in 1825, even though he had been the leader in the popular and electoral votes.

Other Anomalies

The Senate has chosen the vice president only once. That was in 1837, when Van Buren was elected president with 170 of the 294 electoral votes while his vice presidential running mate, Richard M. Johnson, received only 147 elec-

Splitting of States' Electoral Votes . . .

Throughout the history of presidential elections, there have been numerous cases where the electoral votes of a state have been divided between two candidates. The split electoral votes occurred for a variety of reasons.

Electoral Vote Splits, 1789-1836

Splits of a state's electoral votes cast for president before 1836 occurred for these reasons:

● For the first four presidential elections (1789-1800) held under Article II, Section 1 of the Constitution, each elector cast two votes without designating which vote was for president and which for vice president. As a result, electoral votes for each state were often scattered among several candidates. The 12th Amendment, ratified in 1804, required electors to vote separately for president and vice president.

● The district system of choosing electors, in which different candidates each could carry several districts. This system is the explanation for the split electoral votes in Maryland in 1804, 1808, 1812, 1824, 1828 and 1832; North Carolina in 1808; Illinois in 1824; and Maine in 1828; and New York in 1828.

● The selection of electors by the legislatures of some states. This system sometimes led to party factionalism or political deals that resulted in the choice of electors loyal to more than one candidate. This was the cause for the division of electoral votes in New York in 1808 and 1824, Delaware in 1824 and Louisiana in 1824.

● The vote of an individual elector for someone other than his party's candidate. This happened in New Hampshire in 1820 when one Democratic-Republican elector voted for John Quincy Adams instead of the party nominee, James Monroe.

Voting for Individual Electors

By 1836 all states except South Carolina, which selected its electors by the state legislature until after the Civil War, had established a system of statewide popular election of electors. The new system limited the frequency of electoral vote splits. Nevertheless, a few states on occasion still divided their electoral votes among different presidential candidates. This occurred because of the practice of listing on the ballot the names of all electors and allowing voters to cross off the names of any particular electors they did not like, or, alternatively, requiring voters to vote for each individual elector. In a close election, electors of different parties sometimes were chosen. An example occurred in California in 1880, when one Democratic elector ran behind the Republican thus:

Winning Votes	Party	Losing Electors	Party
80,443	Democratic	80,282	Republican
80,426	Democratic	80,252	Republican
80,420	Democratic	80,242	Republican
80,413	Democratic	80,228	Republican
80,348	Republican	79,885	Democratic

Other similar occurrences include the following:

New Jersey, 1860. Four Republican and three Douglas Democratic electors won.
California, 1892. Eight Democratic electors and one Republican won.

toral votes — 1 less than a majority. This discrepancy occurred because Van Buren electors from Virginia boycotted Johnson, reportedly in protest against his social behavior. The Senate elected Johnson, 33-16, over Francis Granger of New York, the runner-up in the electoral vote for vice president.

Although only two presidential elections actually have been decided by the House, a number of others — including those of 1836, 1856, 1860, 1892, 1948, 1960 and 1968 — could have been thrown into the House by only a small shift in the popular vote.

The threat of House election was most clearly evident in 1968, when Democrat George C. Wallace of Alabama ran as a strong third-party candidate. Wallace frequently asserted that he could win an outright majority in the Electoral College by the addition of key Midwestern and Mountain states to his hoped-for base in the South and Border states. In reality, the Wallace campaign had a narrower goal: to win the balance of power in Electoral College voting, thus depriving either major party of the clear electoral majority required for election. Wallace made it clear that he then would expect one of the major party candidates to make concessions in return for enough votes from Wallace electors to win the election. Wallace indicated that he expected the election to be settled in the Electoral College and not in the House of Representatives. At the end of the campaign it was disclosed that Wallace had obtained written affidavits from all of his electors in which they promised to vote for Wallace "or whomsoever he may direct" in the Electoral College.

In response to the Wallace challenge, both major party candidates, Republican Richard Nixon and Democrat Hubert H. Humphrey, maintained that they would refuse to bargain with Wallace for his electoral votes. Nixon asserted that the House, if the decision rested there, should elect the popular-vote winner. Humphrey said the representatives should select "the president they believe would be best for the country." Bipartisan efforts to obtain advance agreements from House candidates to vote for the national popular-vote winner if the election should go to the House ended in failure. Neither Nixon nor Humphrey replied to suggestions that they pledge before the election to swing enough electoral votes to the popular-vote winner to ensure his election without help from Wallace.

In the end Wallace received only 13.5 percent of the popular vote and 46 electoral votes (including the vote of one Republican defector), all from Southern states. He failed to win the balance of power in the Electoral College, which he had hoped to use to wring policy concessions from

...Factionalism and ''Faithless Electors''

North Dakota, 1892. Two Fusionists (Democrats and Populists) and one Republican won. One of the Fusion electors voted for Democrat Grover Cleveland, and the other voted for Populist James B. Weaver, while the Republican elector voted for Benjamin Harrison, thus splitting the state's electoral vote three ways.

Ohio, 1892. Twenty-two Republicans and one Democratic elector won.

Oregon, 1892. Three Republicans and one Populist with Democratic support won.

California, 1896. Eight Republicans and one Democratic elector won.

Kentucky, 1896. Twelve Republicans and one Democratic elector won.

Maryland, 1904. Seven Democratic electors and one Republican won.

Maryland, 1908. Six Democratic and two Republican electors won.

California, 1912. Eleven Progressive and two Democratic electors won.

West Virginia, 1916. Seven Republicans and one Democratic elector won.

The increasing use of voting machines and straight-ticket voting — where the pull of a lever or the marking of an "X" results in automatically casting a vote for every elector — led to the decline in split electoral votes.

'Faithless Electors'

Yet another cause for occasional splits in a state's electoral vote is the so-called "faithless elector." Legally, electors are not bound to vote for any particular candidate; they may cast their ballots any way they wish. But in reality electors are almost always faithful to the candidate of the party with which they are affiliated.

But at times in American political history electors have broken ranks to vote for candidates not supported by their parties. In 1796 a Pennsylvania Federalist elector voted for Democratic-Republican Thomas Jefferson instead of Federalist John Adams. And some historians and political scientists claim that three Democratic-Republican electors voted for Adams. However, the fluidity of political party lines at that early date and the well-known personal friendship between Adams and at least one of the electors make the claim of their being faithless electors one of continuing controversy. In 1820 a New Hampshire Democratic-Republican elector voted for John Quincy Adams instead of the party nominee, James Monroe.

There was no further occurrence until 1948, when Preston Parks, a Truman elector in Tennessee, voted for Gov. Strom Thurmond of South Carolina, the States Rights Democratic Party (Dixiecrat) presidential nominee. Since then, there have been the following instances:

- In 1956 W. F. Turner, a Stevenson elector in Alabama, voted for a local judge, Walter B. Jones.
- In 1960 Henry D. Irwin, a Nixon elector in Oklahoma, voted for Sen. Harry F. Byrd, D-Va.
- In 1968 Dr. Lloyd W. Bailey, a Nixon elector in North Carolina, voted for George C. Wallace, the American Independent Party candidate.
- In 1972 Roger L. MacBride, a Nixon elector in Virginia, voted for John Hospers, the Libertarian Party candidate.
- In 1976 Mike Padden, a Ford elector in the state of Washington, voted for former governor Ronald Reagan of California.
- In 1988 Margaret Leach, a Dukakis elector in West Virginia, voted for Dukakis's running mate, Sen. Lloyd Bentsen of Texas.

one of the major party candidates. If Wallace had won a few Border states, or if a few thousand more Democratic votes had been cast in Northern states barely carried by Nixon, thus reducing Nixon's electoral vote below 270, Wallace would have been in a position to bargain off his electoral votes or to throw the election into the House for final settlement.

Counting the Electoral Vote

Over the years Congress has mandated a variety of dates for the casting of popular votes, the meeting of the electors to cast ballots in the various states and the official counting of the electoral votes before both houses of Congress.

The Continental Congress made the provisions for the first election. On Sept. 13, 1788, it directed that each state choose its electors on the first Wednesday in January 1789. It further directed these electors to cast their ballots on the first Wednesday in February 1789.

In 1792 the Second Congress passed legislation setting up a permanent calendar for choosing electors. Allowing some flexibility in dates, the law directed that states choose their electors within the 34 days preceding the first Wednes-

day in December of each presidential election year. Then the electors would meet in their various states and cast their ballots on the first Wednesday in December. On the second Wednesday of the following February, the votes were to be opened and counted before a joint session of Congress. Provision also was made for a special presidential election in case of the removal, death, resignation or disability of both the president and vice president.

Under that system, states chose presidential electors at various times. For instance, in 1840 the popular balloting for electors began in Pennsylvania and Ohio on Oct. 30 and ended in North Carolina on Nov. 12. South Carolina, the only state still choosing presidential electors through its state legislature, appointed its electors on Nov. 26.

Congress modified the system in 1845, providing that each state choose its electors on the same day — the Tuesday next after the first Monday in November — a provision that still remains in force. Otherwise, the days for casting and counting the electoral votes remained the same.

The next change occurred in 1887, when Congress provided that electors were to meet and cast their ballots on the second Monday in January instead of the first Wednesday in December. Congress also dropped the provision for a special presidential election.

In 1934 Congress again revised the law. The new arrangements, still in force, directed the electors to meet on the first Monday after the second Wednesday in December. The ballots are opened and counted before Congress on Jan. 6 (the next day if Jan. 6 falls on a Sunday).

The Constitution states: "The President of the Senate shall, in the presence of the Senate and House of Representatives, open all the certificates, and the votes shall then be counted." It gives no guidance on disputed ballots.

Before counting the electoral votes in 1865, Congress adopted the 22nd Joint Rule, which provided that no electoral votes objected to in joint session could be counted except by the concurrent votes of both the Senate and House. The rule was pushed by congressional Republicans to ensure rejection of the electoral votes from the newly reconstructed states of Louisiana and Tennessee. Under this rule, Congress in 1873 also threw out the electoral votes of Louisiana and Arkansas and three from Georgia.

However, the rule lapsed at the beginning of 1876, when the Senate refused to readopt it because the House was under Democratic control. Thus, following the 1876 Hayes-Tilden election, when it became apparent that for the first time the outcome of an election would be determined by decisions on disputed electoral votes, Congress had no rules to guide it.

Hayes-Tilden Contest

The 1876 campaign pitted Republican Hayes against Democrat Tilden. Early returns indicated that Tilden had been elected. He had won the swing states of Indiana, New York, Connecticut and New Jersey; those states plus his expected Southern support would give him the election. However, by the following morning it became apparent that if the Republicans could hold South Carolina, Florida and Louisiana, Hayes would be elected with 185 electoral votes to 184 for Tilden. But if a single elector in any of these states voted for Tilden, he would throw the election to the Democrats. Tilden led in the popular-vote count by more than a quarter million votes.

The situation was much the same in each of the three contested states. Historian Eugene H. Roseboom described it as follows: "The Republicans controlled the state governments and the election machinery, had relied upon the Negro masses for votes, and had practiced frauds as in the past. The Democrats used threats, intimidation, and even violence when necessary, to keep Negroes from the polls; and where they were in a position to do so they resorted to fraud also. The firm determination of the whites to overthrow carpetbag rule contributed to make a full and fair vote impossible; carpetbag hold on the state governments made a fair count impossible. Radical reconstruction was reaping its final harvest."

Both parties pursued the votes of the three states with a fine disregard for propriety or legality, and in the end double sets of elector returns were sent to Congress from all three. Oregon also sent two sets of returns. Although Hayes carried that state, the Democratic governor discovered that one of the Hayes electors was a postmaster and therefore ineligible under the Constitution, so he certified the election of the top-polling Democratic elector. However, the Republican electors met, received the resignation of their ineligible colleague, then reappointed him to the vacancy because he had in the meantime resigned his postmastership.

Had the 22nd Joint Rule remained in effect, the Democratic House of Representatives could have objected to any of Hayes' disputed votes. But since the rule had lapsed, Con-

gress had to find a new method of resolving electoral disputes. A joint committee was created to work out a plan, and the resulting Electoral Commission Law was approved by large majorities and signed into law Jan. 29, 1877 — only days before the date scheduled for counting the electoral votes.

The law, which applied only to the 1876 electoral vote count, established a 15-member commission that was to have final authority over disputed electoral votes, unless both houses of Congress agreed to overrule it. The commission was to consist of five senators, five representatives and five Supreme Court justices. Each chamber was to appoint its own members of the commission, with the understanding that the majority party would have three members and the minority two. Four justices, two from each party, were named in the bill, and these four were to select the fifth. It was expected that they would choose Justice David Davis, who was considered a political independent, but he disqualified himself when the Illinois legislature named him to a seat in the Senate. Justice Joseph P. Bradley, a Republican, then was named to the fifteenth seat. The Democrats supported his selection because they considered him the most independent of the remaining justices, all of whom were Republicans. However, he was to vote with the Republicans on every dispute and thus ensure the victory of Hayes.

The electoral count began in Congress Feb. 1 (moved up from the second Wednesday in February for this one election), and the proceedings continued until March 2. States were called in alphabetical order, and as each disputed state was reached objections were raised to both the Hayes and Tilden electors. The question was then referred to the electoral commission, which in every case voted 8-7 for Hayes. In each case, the Democratic House rejected the commission's decision, but the Republican Senate upheld it, so the decision stood.

As the count went on, Democrats in the House threatened to launch a filibuster to block resumption of joint sessions so that the count could not be completed before Inauguration Day. The threat was never carried out because of an agreement reached between the Hayes forces and Southern conservatives. The southerners agreed to let the electoral count continue without obstruction. In return Hayes agreed that, as president, he would withdraw federal troops from the South, end Reconstruction and make other concessions. The southerners, for their part, pledged to respect Negro rights, a pledge they did not carry out.

Thus, at 4 a.m. March 2, 1877, the president of the Senate was able to announce that Hayes had been elected president with 185 electoral votes, as against 184 for Tilden. Later that day Hayes arrived in Washington. The next evening he took the oath of office privately at the White House, because March 4 fell on a Sunday. His formal inauguration followed on Monday. The country acquiesced. Thus ended a crisis that could have resulted in civil war.

Not until 1887 did Congress enact permanent legislation on the handling of disputed electoral votes. The Electoral Count Act of that year gave each state final authority in determining the legality of its choice of electors and required a concurrent majority of both the Senate and House to reject any electoral votes. It also established procedures for counting electoral votes in Congress. *(Law for Counting Electoral Votes in Congress, box, p. 17)*

Application of 1887 Law in 1969

The procedures relating to disputed electoral votes were used for the first time after the election of 1968. When Congress met in joint session Jan. 6, 1969, to count the

Law for Counting Electoral Votes in Congress

Following is the complete text of Title 3, section 15 of the U.S. Code, enacted originally in 1887, governing the counting of electoral votes in Congress:

Congress shall be in session on the sixth day of January succeeding every meeting of the electors. The Senate and House of Representatives shall meet in the Hall of the House of Representatives at the hour of 1 o'clock in the afternoon on that day, and the President of the Senate shall be their presiding officer. Two tellers shall be previously appointed on the part of the Senate and two on the part of the House of Representatives, to whom shall be handed, as they are opened by the President of the Senate, all the certificates and papers purporting to be certificates of the electoral votes, which certificates and papers shall be opened, presented, and acted upon in the alphabetical order of the States, beginning with the letter A; and said tellers, having then read the same in the presence and hearing of the two Houses, shall make a list of the votes as they shall appear from the said certificates; and the votes having been ascertained and counted according to the rules in this subchapter provided, the result of the same shall be delivered to the President of the Senate, who shall thereupon announce the state of the vote, which announcement shall be deemed a sufficient declaration of the persons, if any, elected President and Vice President of the United States, and, together with a list of votes, be entered on the Journals of the two Houses. Upon such reading of any such certificate or paper, the President of the Senate shall call for objections, if any. Every objection shall be made in writing, and shall state clearly and concisely, and without argument, the ground thereof, and shall be signed by at least one Senator and one Member of the House of Representatives before the same shall be received. When all objections so made to any vote or paper from a State shall have been received and read, the Senate shall thereupon withdraw, and such objections shall be submitted to the Senate for its decision; and the Speaker of the House of Representatives shall, in like manner, submit such objections to the House of Representatives for its decision; and no electoral vote or votes from any State which shall have been regularly given by electors whose appointment has been lawfully certified to according to section 6* of this title from which but one return has been received shall be rejected, but the two Houses concurrently may reject the vote or votes when they agree that such vote or votes have not been so regularly given by electors whose appointment has been so certified. If more than one return or paper purporting to be a return from a State shall have been received by the President of the Senate, those votes, and those only, shall be counted which shall have been regularly given by the electors who are shown by the determination mentioned in section 5† of this title to have been appointed, if the determination in said section provided for shall have been made, or by such successors or substitutes, in case of a vacancy in the board of electors so ascertained, as have been appointed to fill such vacancy in the mode provided by the laws of the State; but in case there shall arise the question which of two or more of such State authorities determining what electors have been appointed, as mentioned in section 5 of this title, is the lawful tribunal of such State, the votes regularly given of those electors, and those only, of such State shall be counted whose title as electors the two Houses, acting separately, shall concurrently decide is supported by the decision of such State so authorized by its law; and in such case of more than one return or paper purporting to be a return from a State, if there shall have been no such determination of the question in the State aforesaid, then those votes, and those only, shall be counted which the two Houses shall concurrently decide were cast by lawful electors appointed in accordance with the laws of the State, unless the two Houses, acting separately, shall concurrently decide such votes not to be the lawful votes of the legally appointed electors of such State. But if the two Houses shall disagree in respect of the counting of such votes, then, and in that case, the votes of the electors whose appointment shall have been certified by the executive of the State, under the seal thereof, shall be counted. When the two Houses have voted, they shall immediately again meet, and the presiding officer shall then announce the decision of the questions submitted. No votes or papers from any other State shall be acted upon until the objections previously made to the votes or papers from any State shall have been finally disposed of.

* Section 6 provides for certification of votes by electors by state governors.

†Section 5 provides that if state law specifies a method for resolving disputes concerning the vote for presidential electors, Congress must respect any determination so made by a state.

electoral votes, Sen. Edmund S. Muskie, D-Maine, and Rep. James G. O'Hara, D-Mich., joined by six other senators and 37 other representatives, filed a written objection to the vote cast by a North Carolina elector, Lloyd W. Bailey of Rocky Mount. He had been elected as a Republican but chose to vote for George Wallace and Curtis LeMay, the candidates of the American Independent party, instead of Republican Nixon and his running mate, Spiro T. Agnew.

Acting under the 1887 law, Muskie and O'Hara objected to Bailey's vote on the grounds that it was "not properly given" because a plurality of the popular votes in North Carolina were cast for Nixon-Agnew and the state's voters had chosen electors to vote for Nixon and Agnew only.

Muskie and O'Hara asked that Bailey's vote not be counted at all by Congress.

The 1887 statute stipulated that "no electoral vote or votes from any state which shall have been regularly given by electors whose appointment has been lawfully certified ... from which but one return has been received shall be rejected, but the two Houses concurrently may reject the vote or votes when they agree that such vote or votes have not been so regularly given by electors whose appointment has been so certified." The statute did not define the term "regularly given," although at the time of its adoption chief concern centered on problems of dual sets of electoral vote returns from a state, votes cast on an improper day, or votes disputed because of uncertainty about whether a state lawfully was in the Union when the vote was cast.

The 1887 statute provided that if written objection to any state's vote was received from at least one member of both the Senate and House, the two legislative bodies were to retire immediately to separate sessions, debate for two hours with a five-minute limitation on speeches, and each decide the issue by vote before resuming the joint session. The statute made clear that both the Senate and House had to reject a challenged electoral vote (or votes) for such action to prevail.

At the Jan. 6 joint session, with Senate President Pro Tempore Richard B. Russell, D-Ga., presiding, the counting of the electoral vote proceeded smoothly through the alphabetical order of states until the North Carolina result was announced, at which time O'Hara rose to announce filing of the complaint. The two houses then reassembled in joint session at which the results of the separate deliberations were announced and the count of the electoral vote by state proceeded without event. At the conclusion, Russell announced the vote and declared Nixon and Agnew elected.

Reform Proposals

Since Jan. 6, 1797, when Rep. William L. Smith, F-S.C., introduced in Congress the first proposed constitutional amendment for reform of the Electoral College system, hardly a session of Congress has passed without the introduction of one or more resolutions of this nature. But only one — the 12th Amendment, ratified in 1804 — ever has been approved.

In recent years, public interest in a change in the Electoral College system was spurred by the close 1960 and 1968 elections, by a series of Supreme Court rulings relating to apportionment and districting and by introduction of unpledged elector systems in the Southern states.

House Approval of Amendment

Early in 1969, President Nixon asked Congress to take prompt action on Electoral College reform. He said he would support any plan that would eliminate individual electors and distribute among the presidential candidates the electoral vote of every state and the District of Columbia in a manner more closely approximating the popular vote.

Later that year the House approved, 338-70, a resolution proposing a constitutional amendment to eliminate the Electoral College and to provide instead for direct popular election of the president and vice president. The measure set a minimum of 40 percent of the popular vote as sufficient for election and provided for a runoff election between the two top candidates for the presidency if no candidate received 40 percent. Under this plan the House of Representatives could no longer be called upon to select a president. The proposed amendment also authorized Congress to provide a method of filling vacancies caused by the death, resignation or disability of presidential nominees before the election and a method of filling post-election vacancies caused by the death of the president-elect or vice president-elect.

Nixon, who previously had favored a proportional plan of allocating each state's electoral votes, endorsed the House resolution and urged the Senate to adopt it. To become effective, the proposed amendment had to be approved by a two-thirds majority in both the Senate and House and be ratified by the legislatures of three-fourths of the states. When the proposal reached the Senate floor in September

1970, senators from small states and the South succeeded in blocking final action. The resolution was laid aside Oct. 5, after two unsuccessful efforts to cut off debate by invoking cloture.

Carter Endorsement of Plan

Another major effort to eliminate the Electoral College occurred in 1977, when President Jimmy Carter included such a proposal in his election reform package, unveiled March 22. Carter endorsed the amendment approved by the House in 1969 to replace the Electoral College with direct popular election of the president and vice president, and provide for a runoff if no candidate received at least 40 percent of the vote. Because the Senate again was seen as the major stumbling block, the House waited to see what the Senate would do before beginning any deliberation of its own.

After several months of deadlock, the Senate Judiciary Committee approved Sept. 15 the direct presidential election plan by a 9-8 vote. But Senate opponents threatened a filibuster, and the Senate leadership decided it could not spare the time or effort to try to break it. The measure was never brought to the floor and died when the 95th Congress adjourned in 1978.

On Jan. 15, 1979, the opening day of the 96th Congress, Sen. Birch Bayh, D-Ind., began another effort to abolish the Electoral College through a constitutional amendment. In putting off action in the previous Congress, Senate leaders had agreed to try for early action in the 96th.

A proposed constitutional amendment to abolish the Electoral College and elect the president by popular vote did reach the Senate floor in July 1979. The Senate voted in favor of the measure, 51-48 — 15 votes short of the required two-thirds majority of those present and voting needed to approve a constitutional amendment.

Supporters of the resolution blamed defections by several Northern liberals for the margin of defeat. Major Jewish and black groups extensively lobbied the Northern senators, arguing that the voting strength of black and Jewish voters is maximized under the Electoral College system because both groups are concentrated in urban areas of the large electoral vote states.

Presidential Disability

A decade of congressional concern over the question of presidential disability was eased in 1967 by ratification of the 25th Amendment to the Constitution. The amendment for the first time provided for continuity in carrying out the functions of the presidency in the event of presidential disability and for filling a vacancy in the vice presidency. The amendment was approved by the Senate and House in 1965 and took effect Feb. 10, 1967, after ratification by 38 states. *(Amendment XXV, p. 263)* Congressional consideration of the problem of presidential disability had been prompted by President Dwight D. Eisenhower's heart attack in 1955. The ambiguity of the language of the disability clause (Article II, Section 1, Clause 5) of the Constitution had provoked occasional debate ever since the Constitutional Convention of 1787. But it never had been decided how far the term *disability* extended or who would be the judge of it.

Clause 5 provided that Congress should decide who was to succeed to the presidency if both the president and the vice president died, resigned, or became disabled. Congress enacted succession laws three times. By the Act of March 1,

1792, it provided for succession (after the vice president) of the president pro tempore of the Senate, then of the House Speaker; if those offices were vacant, states were to send electors to Washington to choose a new president.

That law stood until passage of the Presidential Succession Act of Jan. 19, 1886, which changed the line of succession to run from the vice president to the secretary of state, secretary of the Treasury and so on through the cabinet in order of rank. Sixty-one years later the Presidential Succession Act of July 18, 1947, (still in force) placed the Speaker of the House and the president pro tempore of the Senate ahead of cabinet officers in succession after the vice president.

Before ratification of the 25th Amendment, no procedures had been laid down to govern situations arising in the event of presidential incapacity or of a vacancy in the office of vice president. Two presidents had had serious disabilities — James A. Garfield, shot in 1881 and confined to his bed until he died two and a half months later, and Woodrow Wilson, who suffered a stroke in 1919. In each case the vice president did not assume any duties of the presidency for fear he would appear to be usurping the powers of that office. As for a vice presidential vacancy, the United States has been without a vice president 18 times for a total of 40 years through 1996, after the elected vice president suceeded to the presidency, died or resigned.

Ratification of the 25th Amendment established procedures that clarified these areas of uncertainty in the Constitution. The amendment provided that the vice president should become acting president under either one of two circumstances: (1) if the president informed Congress that he was unable to perform his duties, the vice president would become acting president until the president could resume his responsibilities; (2) if the vice president and a majority of the cabinet, or another body designated by Congress, found the president to be incapacitated, the vice president would become acting president until the president informed Congress that his disability had ended. Congress was given 21 days to resolve any dispute over the president's disability; a two-thirds vote of both chambers was required to overrule the president's declaration that he was no longer incapacitated.

Vacancy in the Vice Presidency

Whenever a vacancy occurred in the office of the vice president, either by death, succession to the presidency or resignation, the president was to nominate a vice president, and the nomination was to be confirmed by a majority vote of both houses of Congress.

Within only eight years, the power of the president to appoint a new vice president under the terms of the 25th Amendment was used twice. In 1973 when Vice President Agnew resigned, President Nixon nominated Gerald R. Ford as the new vice president. Ford was confirmed by both houses of Congress and sworn in Dec. 6, 1973. On Nixon's resignation Aug. 9, 1974, Ford succeeded to the presidency, becoming the first president in American history who was elected neither to the presidency nor to the vice presidency. President Ford chose as his new vice president Nelson A. Rockefeller, former governor of New York, who was sworn in Dec. 19, 1974.

With both the president and vice president holding office through appointment rather than election, members of Congress and the public expressed concern about the power of a president to appoint, in effect, his own successor. Accordingly, Sen. John O. Pastore, D-R.I., introduced a proposed constitutional amendment Feb. 3, 1975, to provide for a special national election for president when more than one year remained in a presidential term. Hearings were held before the Senate Judiciary Subcommittee on Constitutional Amendments, but no action was taken.

Confusion After Reagan Shooting

In the aftermath of the attempted assassination of President Ronald Reagan in 1981, there was no need to invoke the presidential disability provisions of the 25th Amendment. However, some of the public statements made by administration officials immediately after the president was shot by John W. Hinckley Jr., reflected continuing confusion over the issue of who is in charge when the president temporarily is unable to function. Soon after news of the shooting became known, the members of the Reagan cabinet gathered in the White House, ready to invoke the amendment's procedures, if necessary. Vice President George Bush was on an Air Force jet returning to Washington from Texas.

At a televised press briefing later that afternoon, Secretary of State Alexander M. Haig Jr., confirmed that Reagan was in surgery and under anesthesia. It was clear that he temporarily was unable to make presidential decisions should the occasion — such as a foreign attack or other national emergency — require them. Attempting to reassure the country, Haig stated that he was in control in the White House pending the return of Vice President Bush, with whom he was in contact.

This assertion was followed by a question from the press about who was making administration decisions. Haig responded, "Constitutionally, gentlemen, you have the president, the vice president and the secretary of state in that order, and should the president decide he wants to transfer the helm to the vice president, he will do so. He has not done that." Haig's response reflected the law in effect before the Presidential Succession Act of 1947. The law applicable in the 1981 shooting incident was the 1947 act, which specifies that the line of succession is the vice president, the Speaker of the House, the president pro tempore of the Senate and then the cabinet officials in order of rank.

Distribution of House Seats and Electoral Votes

(Based on Censuses of 1950, 1960, 1970, 1980 and 1990)

State	U.S. House Seats									Electoral Votes				
	1953–1963	1960 Census Changes	1963–1973	1970 Census Changes	1973–1983	1980 Census Changes	1983–1993	1990 Census Changes	1993–2003	1952, 1956, 1960	1964, 1968	1972, 1976, 1980	1984, 1988	1992, 1996, 2000
Alabama	9	−1	8	−1	7	—	7	—	7	11	10	9	9	9
Alaska	1	—	1	—	1	—	1	—	1	3	3	3	3	3
Arizona	2	+1	3	+1	4	+1	5	+1	6	4	5	6	7	8
Arkansas	6	−2	4	—	4	—	4	—	4	8	6	6	6	6
California	30	+8	38	+5	43	+2	45	+7	52	32	40	45	47	54
Colorado	4	—	4	+1	5	+1	6	—	6	6	6	7	8	8
Connecticut	6	—	6	—	6	—	6	—	6	8	8	8	8	8
Delaware	1	—	1	—	1	—	1	—	1	3	3	3	3	3
District of Columbia	—	—	—	—	—	—	—	—	—	—	3	3	3	3
Florida	8	+4	12	+3	15	+4	19	+4	23	10	14	17	21	25
Georgia	10	—	10	—	10	—	10	+1	11	12	12	12	12	13
Hawaii	1	+1	2	—	2	—	2	—	2	3	4	4	4	4
Idaho	2	—	2	—	2	—	2	—	2	4	4	4	4	4
Illinois	25	−1	24	—	24	−2	22	−2	20	27	26	26	24	22
Indiana	11	—	11	—	11	−1	10	—	10	13	13	13	12	12
Iowa	8	−1	7	−1	6	—	6	−1	5	10	9	8	8	7
Kansas	6	−1	5	—	5	—	5	−1	4	8	7	7	7	6
Kentucky	8	−1	7	—	7	—	7	−1	6	10	9	9	9	8
Louisiana	8	—	8	—	8	—	8	−1	7	10	10	10	10	9
Maine	3	−1	2	—	2	—	2	—	2	5	4	4	4	4
Maryland	7	+1	8	—	8	—	8	—	8	9	10	10	10	10
Massachusetts	14	−2	12	—	12	−1	11	−1	10	16	14	14	13	12
Michigan	18	+1	19	—	19	−1	18	−2	16	20	21	21	20	18
Minnesota	9	−1	8	—	8	—	8	—	8	11	10	10	10	10
Mississippi	6	−1	5	—	5	—	5	—	5	8	7	7	7	7
Missouri	11	−1	10	—	10	−1	9	—	9	13	12	12	11	11
Montana	2	—	2	—	2	—	2	−1	1	4	4	4	4	3
Nebraska	4	−1	3	—	3	—	3	—	3	6	5	5	5	5
Nevada	1	—	1	—	1	+1	2	—	2	3	3	3	4	4
New Hampshire	2	—	2	—	2	—	2	—	2	4	4	4	4	4
New Jersey	14	+1	15	—	15	−1	14	−1	13	16	17	17	16	15
New Mexico	2	—	2	—	2	+1	3	—	3	4	4	4	5	5
New York	43	−2	41	−2	39	−5	34	−3	31	45	43	41	36	33
North Carolina	12	−1	11	—	11	—	11	+1	12	14	13	13	13	14
North Dakota	2	—	2	−1	1	—	1	—	1	4	4	3	3	3
Ohio	23	+1	24	−1	23	−2	21	−2	19	25	26	25	23	21
Oklahoma	6	—	6	—	6	—	6	—	6	8	8	8	8	8
Oregon	4	—	4	—	4	+1	5	—	5	6	6	6	7	7
Pennsylvania	30	−3	27	−2	25	−2	23	−2	21	32	29	27	25	23
Rhode Island	2	—	2	—	2	—	2	—	2	4	4	4	4	4
South Carolina	6	—	6	—	6	—	6	—	6	8	8	8	8	8
South Dakota	2	—	2	—	2	−1	1	—	1	4	4	4	3	3
Tennessee	9	—	9	−1	8	+1	9	—	9	11	11	10	11	11
Texas	22	+1	23	+1	24	+3	27	+3	30	24	25	26	29	32
Utah	2	—	2	—	2	+1	3	—	3	4	4	4	5	5
Vermont	1	—	1	—	1	—	1	—	1	3	3	3	3	3
Virginia	10	—	10	—	10	—	10	+1	11	12	12	12	12	13
Washington	7	—	7	—	7	+1	8	+1	9	9	9	9	10	11
West Virginia	6	−1	5	−1	4	—	4	−1	3	8	7	6	6	5
Wisconsin	10	—	10	−1	9	—	9	—	9	12	12	11	11	11
Wyoming	1	—	1	—	1	—	1	—	1	3	3	3	3	3

Electoral Votes for President, 1789-1996

Sources: Electoral College Votes

The sources for electoral votes cast for presidential candidates are the *Senate Manual* (Washington, D.C., U.S. Government Printing Office, 1995), pp.1027-1071, and *Congressional Quarterly Weekly Report.*

Total electoral votes for each state through the 1996 election were compiled from a chart of each apportionment of the House of Representatives, published in Kenneth C. Martis and Gregory A. Elmes, *The Historical Atlas of State Power in Congress, 1790-1990* (Washington, D.C., Congressional Quarterly, 1993), pp. 6-7.

Article II, Section 1 of the Constitution gives each state a number of electors equal to the number of senators and representatives to which it is entitled.

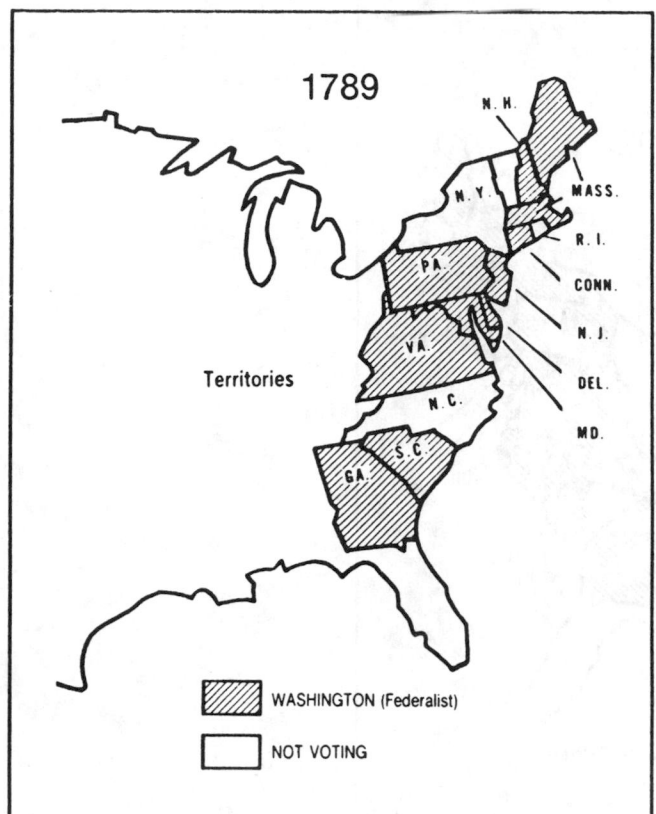

1789

Territories

WASHINGTON (Federalist)

NOT VOTING

Electoral Votes 1789-1996

Under Article II, Section 1, of the Constitution, each presidential elector had two votes and was required to cast each vote for a different person. The person receiving the highest number of votes from a majority of electors was elected president; the person receiving the second highest total became vice president. Since there were 69 electors in 1789, Washington's 69 votes constituted a unanimous election. After ratification of the 12th Amendment in 1804, electors were required to designate which of their two votes was for president and which was for vice president. The Electoral College tables on pages 23-75 show *all* electoral votes cast in the elections of 1788, 1792, 1796 and 1800; the charts for 1804 and thereafter show electoral votes cast only for president. For electoral votes totals for vice president, see table on pages 76-78.

States	Electoral Votes [1]	Washington	Adams	Jay	Harrison	Rutledge	Hancock	Clinton	Huntington	Milton	Armstrong	Lincoln	Telfair
Connecticut [2]	(14)	7	5	-	-	-	-	-	2	-	-	-	-
Delaware	(6)	3	-	3	-	-	-	-	-	-	-	-	-
Georgia [2]	(10)	5	-	-	-	-	-	-	-	2	1	1	1
Maryland [3]	(16)	6	-	-	6	-	-	-	-	-	-	-	-
Massachusetts	(20)	10	10	-	-	-	-	-	-	-	-	-	-
New Hampshire	(10)	5	5	-	-	-	-	-	-	-	-	-	-
New Jersey [2]	(12)	6	1	5	-	-	-	-	-	-	-	-	-
New York [4]	(16)	-	-	-	-	-	-	-	-	-	-	-	-
North Carolina [5]	(14)	-	-	-	-	-	-	-	-	-	-	-	-
Pennsylvania [2]	(20)	10	8	-	-	-	2	-	-	-	-	-	-
Rhode Island [5]	(6)	-	-	-	-	-	-	-	-	-	-	-	-
South Carolina [2]	(14)	7	-	-	-	6	1	-	-	-	-	-	-
Virginia [6]	(24)	10	5	1	-	-	1	3	-	-	-	-	-
Totals	(182)	**69**	**34**	**9**	**6**	**6**	**4**	**3**	**2**	**2**	**1**	**1**	**1**

1. Two votes for each elector; see text above.
2. For explanation of split electoral votes, see p. 14.
3. Two Maryland electors did not vote.
4. Not voting. For explanation, see p. 9.

5. Not voting because had not yet ratified Constitution.
6. Two Virginia electors did not vote. For explanation of split electoral votes, see p. 14.

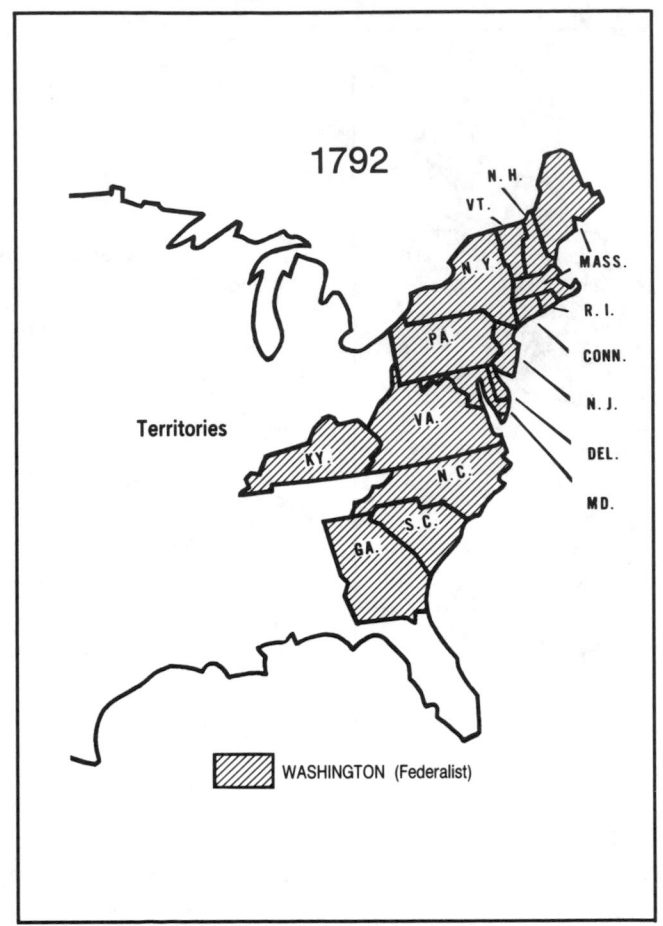

States	Electoral Votes [1]	Washington	Adams	Clinton	Jefferson	Burr
Connecticut	(18)	9	9	-	-	-
Delaware	(6)	3	3	-	-	-
Georgia	(8)	4	-	4	-	-
Kentucky	(8)	4	-	-	4	-
Maryland [2]	(20)	8	8	-	-	-
Massachusetts	(32)	16	16	-	-	-
New Hampshire	(12)	6	6	-	-	-
New Jersey	(14)	7	7	-	-	-
New York	(24)	12	-	12	-	-
North Carolina	(24)	12	-	12	-	-
Pennsylvania [3]	(30)	15	14	1	-	-
Rhode Island	(8)	4	4	-	-	-
South Carolina [3]	(16)	8	7	-	-	1
Vermont [2]	(8)	3	3	-	-	-
Virginia	(42)	21	-	21	-	-
Totals	**(270)**	**132**	**77**	**50**	**4**	**1**

1. Two votes for each elector; see page 23.
2. Two Maryland electors and one Vermont elector did not vote.
3. For explanation of split electoral votes, see p. 14.

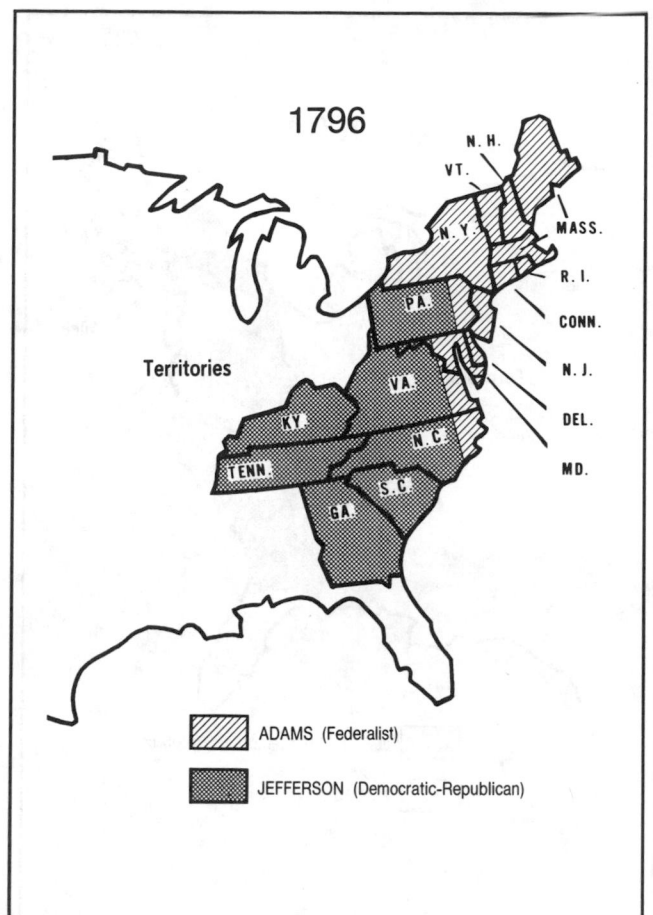

States	Electoral Votes [1]	J. Adams	Jefferson	T. Pinckney	Burr	S. Adams	Ellsworth	Clinton	Jay	Iredell	Henry	Johnston	Washington	C. Pinckney
Connecticut [2]	(18)	9	-	4	-	-	-	-	5	-	-	-	-	-
Delaware	(6)	3	-	3	-	-	-	-	-	-	-	-	-	-
Georgia	(8)	-	4	-	-	-	-	4	-	-	-	-	-	-
Kentucky	(8)	-	4	-	4	-	-	-	-	-	-	-	-	-
Maryland [2]	(20)	7	4	4	3	-	-	-	-	2	-	-	-	-
Massachusetts [2]	(32)	16	-	13	-	-	1	-	-	-	-	2	-	-
New Hampshire	(12)	6	-	-	-	-	6	-	-	-	-	-	-	-
New Jersey	(14)	7	-	7	-	-	-	-	-	-	-	-	-	-
New York	(24)	12	-	12	-	-	-	-	-	-	-	-	-	-
North Carolina [2]	(24)	1	11	1	6	-	-	-	-	3	-	-	1	1
Pennsylvania [2]	(30)	1	14	2	13	-	-	-	-	-	-	-	-	-
Rhode Island	(8)	4	-	-	-	-	4	-	-	-	-	-	-	-
South Carolina	(16)	-	8	8	-	-	-	-	-	-	-	-	-	-
Tennessee	(6)	-	3	-	3	-	-	-	-	-	-	-	-	-
Vermont	(8)	4	-	4	-	-	-	-	-	-	-	-	-	-
Virginia [2]	(42)	1	20	1	1	15	-	3	-	-	-	-	1	-
Totals	**(276)**	**71**	**68**	**59**	**30**	**15**	**11**	**7**	**5**	**3**	**2**	**2**	**2**	**1**

1. *Two votes for each elector; see page 23.*
2. *For explanation of split electoral votes, see p. 14.*

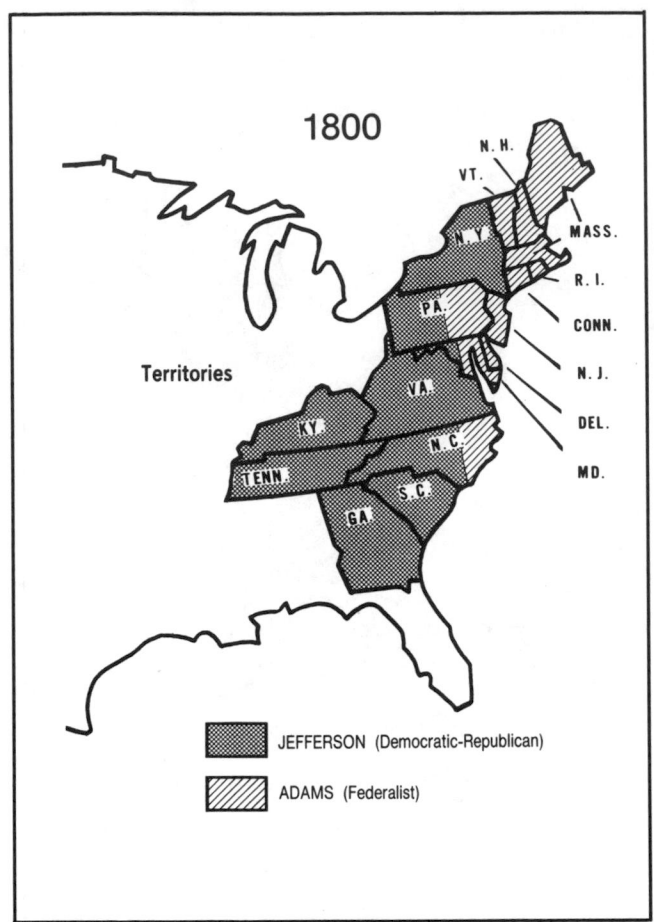

States	Electoral Votes [1]	Jefferson [2]	Burr [2]	Adams	Pinckney	Jay
Connecticut	(18)	-	-	9	9	-
Delaware	(6)	-	-	3	3	-
Georgia	(8)	4	4	-	-	-
Kentucky	(8)	4	4	-	-	-
Maryland [3]	(20)	5	5	5	5	-
Massachusetts	(32)	-	-	16	16	-
New Hampshire	(12)	-	-	6	6	-
New Jersey	(14)	-	-	7	7	-
New York	(24)	12	12	-	-	-
North Carolina [3]	(24)	8	8	4	4	-
Pennsylvania [3]	(30)	8	8	7	7	-
Rhode Island [3]	(8)	-	-	4	3	1
South Carolina [1]	(16)	8	8	-	-	-
Tennessee	(6)	3	3	-	-	-
Vermont	(8)	-	-	4	4	-
Virginia	(42)	21	21	-	-	-
Totals	**(276)**	**73**	**73**	**65**	**64**	**1**

1. Two votes for each elector; see page 23.
2. For explanation and result of tie vote, see p. 11.
3. For explanation of split electoral votes, see p. 14.

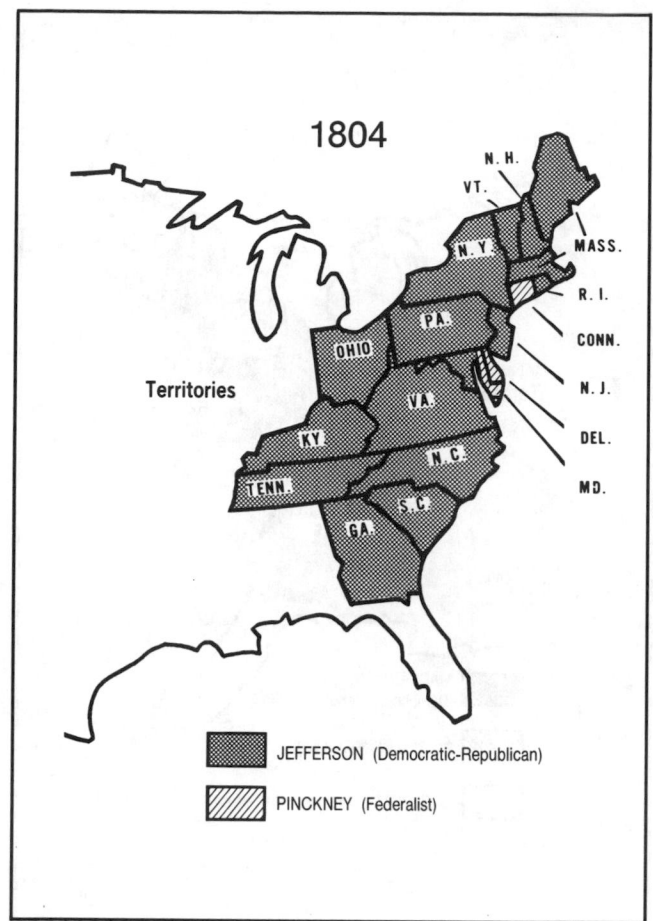

States	Electoral Votes	Jefferson	Pinckney
Connecticut	(9)	-	9
Delaware	(3)	-	3
Georgia	(6)	6	-
Kentucky	(8)	8	-
Maryland [1]	(11)	9	2
Massachusetts	(19)	19	-
New Hampshire	(7)	7	-
New Jersey	(8)	8	-
New York	(19)	19	-
North Carolina	(14)	14	-
Ohio	(3)	3	-
Pennsylvania	(20)	20	-
Rhode Island	(4)	4	-
South Carolina	(10)	10	-
Tennessee	(5)	5	-
Vermont	(6)	6	-
Virginia	(24)	24	-
Totals	**(176)**	**162**	**14**

1. For explanation of split electoral votes, see p. 14.

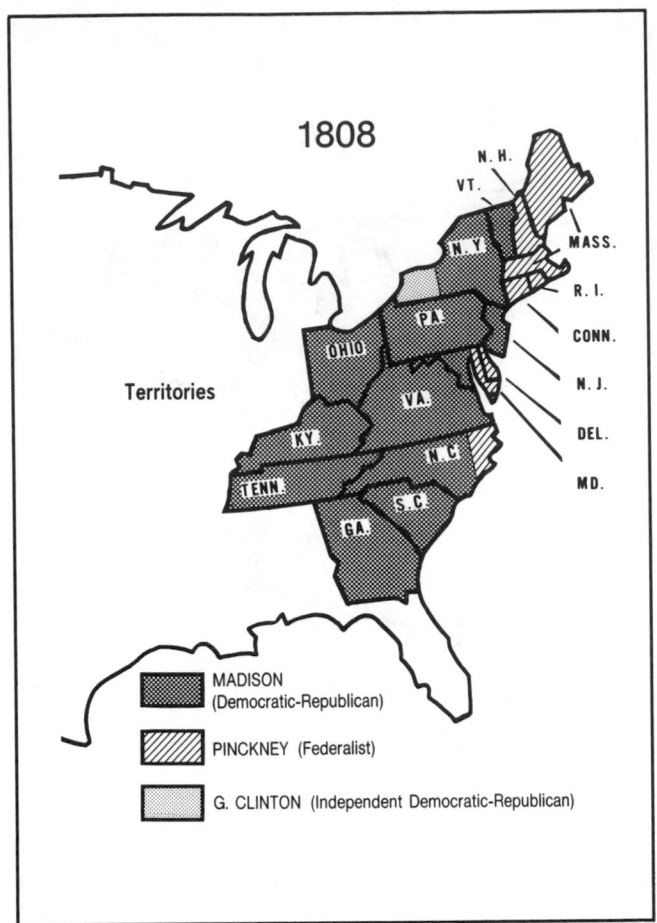

States	Electoral Votes	Madison	Pinckney	Clinton
Connecticut	(9)	-	9	-
Delaware	(3)	-	3	-
Georgia	(6)	6	-	-
Kentucky [1]	(8)	7	-	-
Maryland [2]	(11)	9	2	-
Massachusetts	(19)	-	19	-
New Hampshire	(7)	-	7	-
New Jersey	(8)	8	-	-
New York [2]	(19)	13	-	6
North Carolina [2]	(14)	11	3	-
Ohio	(3)	3	-	-
Pennsylvania	(20)	20	-	-
Rhode Island	(4)	-	4	-
South Carolina	(10)	10	-	-
Tennessee	(5)	5	-	-
Vermont	(6)	6	-	-
Virginia	(24)	24	-	-
Totals	**(176)**	**122**	**47**	**6**

1. *One Kentucky elector did not vote.*
2. *For explanation of split electoral votes, see p. 14.*

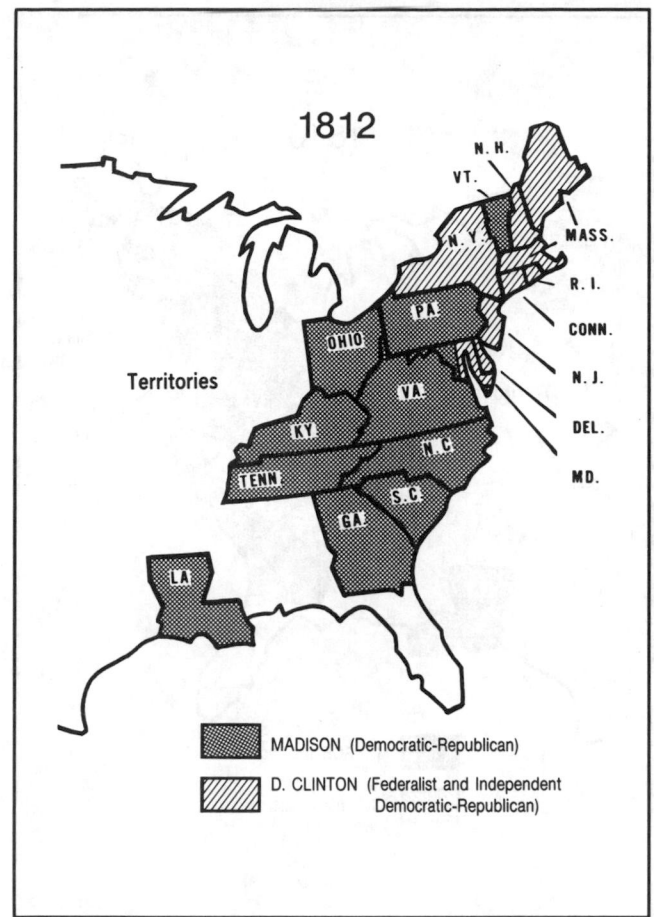

1812

Territories

| | MADISON (Democratic-Republican) |
| | D. CLINTON (Federalist and Independent Democratic-Republican) |

States	Electoral Votes	Madison	Clinton
Connecticut	(9)	-	9
Delaware	(4)	-	4
Georgia	(8)	8	-
Kentucky	(12)	12	-
Louisiana	(3)	3	-
Maryland [1]	(11)	6	5
Massachusetts	(22)	-	22
New Hampshire	(8)	-	8
New Jersey	(8)	-	8
New York	(29)	-	29
North Carolina	(15)	15	-
Ohio [2]	(8)	7	-
Pennsylvania	(25)	25	-
Rhode Island	(4)	-	4
South Carolina	(11)	11	-
Tennessee	(8)	8	-
Vermont	(8)	8	-
Virginia	(25)	25	-
Totals	**(218)**	**128**	**89**

1. *For explanation of split electoral votes, see p. 14.*
2. *One Ohio elector did not vote.*

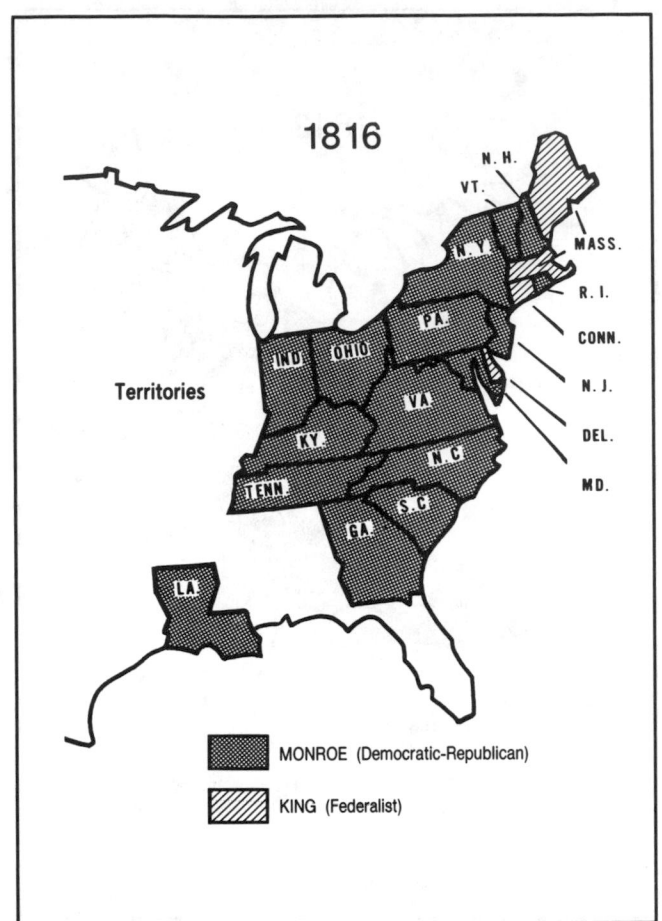

States	Electoral Votes	Monroe	King
Connecticut	(9)	-	9
Delaware [1]	(4)	-	3
Georgia	(8)	8	-
Indiana	(3)	3	-
Kentucky	(12)	12	-
Louisiana	(3)	3	-
Maryland [1]	(11)	8	-
Massachusetts	(22)	-	22
New Hampshire	(8)	8	-
New Jersey	(8)	8	-
New York	(29)	29	-
North Carolina	(15)	15	-
Ohio	(8)	8	-
Pennsylvania	(25)	25	-
Rhode Island	(4)	4	-
South Carolina	(11)	11	-
Tennessee	(8)	8	-
Vermont	(8)	8	-
Virginia	(25)	25	-
Totals	**(221)**	**183**	**34**

1. One Delaware and three Maryland electors did not vote.

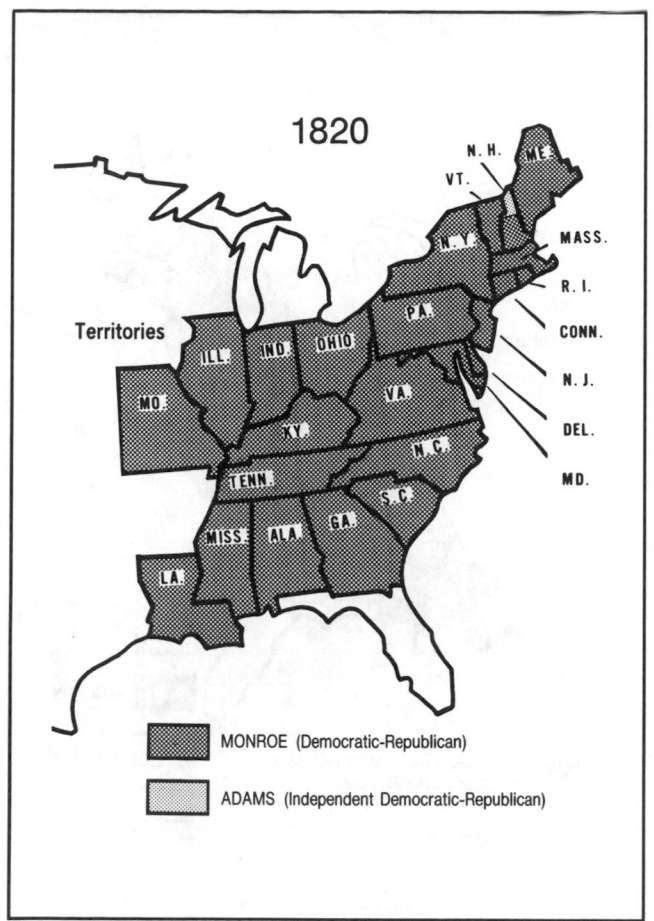

States	Electoral Votes	Monroe	Adams
Alabama	(3)	3	-
Connecticut	(9)	9	-
Delaware	(4)	4	-
Georgia	(8)	8	-
Illinois	(3)	3	-
Indiana	(3)	3	-
Kentucky	(12)	12	-
Louisiana	(3)	3	-
Maine	(9)	9	-
Maryland	(11)	11	-
Massachusetts	(15)	15	-
Mississippi [1]	(3)	2	-
Missouri	(3)	3	-
New Hampshire [2]	(8)	7	1
New Jersey	(8)	8	-
New York	(29)	29	-
North Carolina	(15)	15	-
Ohio	(8)	8	-
Pennsylvania [1]	(25)	24	-
Rhode Island	(4)	4	-
South Carolina	(11)	11	-
Tennessee [1]	(8)	7	-
Vermont	(8)	8	-
Virginia	(25)	25	-
Totals	**(235)**	**231**	**1**

1. One elector each from Mississippi, Pennsylvania and Tennessee did not vote.
2. For explanation of split electoral votes, see p. 14.

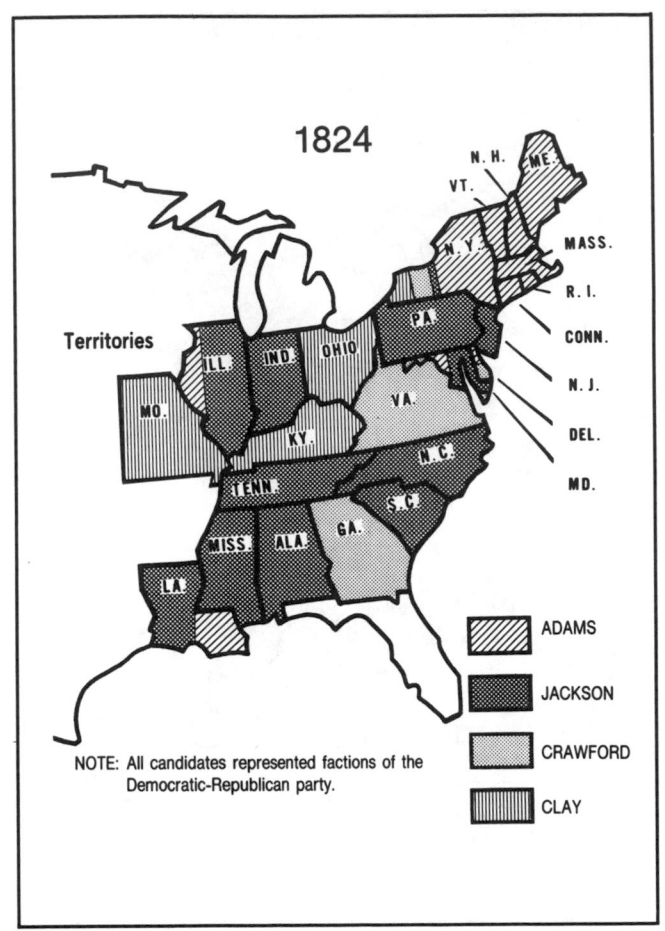

NOTE: All candidates represented factions of the Democratic-Republican party.

States	Electoral Votes	Jackson	Adams	Crawford	Clay
Alabama	(5)	5	-	-	-
Connecticut	(8)	-	8	-	-
Delaware [1]	(3)	-	1	2	-
Georgia	(9)	-	-	9	-
Illinois [1]	(3)	2	1	-	-
Indiana	(5)	5	-	-	-
Kentucky	(14)	-	-	-	14
Louisiana [1]	(5)	3	2	-	-
Maine	(9)	-	9	-	-
Maryland [1]	(11)	7	3	1	-
Massachusetts	(15)	-	15	-	-
Mississippi	(3)	3	-	-	-
Missouri	(3)	-	-	-	3
New Hampshire	(8)	-	8	-	-
New Jersey	(8)	8	-	-	-
New York [1]	(36)	1	26	5	4
North Carolina	(15)	15	-	-	-
Ohio	(16)	-	-	-	16
Pennsylvania	(28)	28	-	-	-
Rhode Island	(4)	-	4	-	-
South Carolina	(11)	11	-	-	-
Tennessee	(11)	11	-	-	-
Vermont	(7)	-	7	-	-
Virginia	(24)	-	-	24	-
Totals	**(261)**	**99 [2]**	**84**	**41**	**37**

1. For explanation of split electoral votes, see p. 14.
2. As no candidate received a majority of the electoral votes, the election was decided by the House of Representatives. See p. 13.

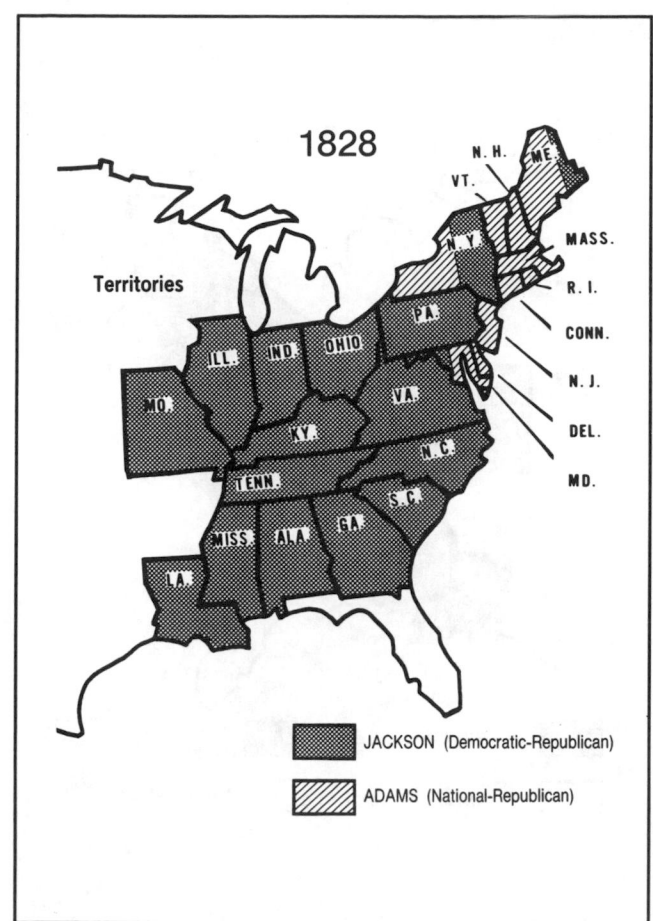

States	Electoral Votes	Jackson	Adams
Alabama	(5)	5	-
Connecticut	(8)	-	8
Delaware	(3)	-	3
Georgia	(9)	9	-
Illinois	(3)	3	-
Indiana	(5)	5	-
Kentucky	(14)	14	-
Louisiana	(5)	5	-
Maine [1]	(9)	1	8
Maryland [1]	(11)	5	6
Massachusetts	(15)	-	15
Mississippi	(3)	3	-
Missouri	(3)	3	-
New Hampshire	(8)	-	8
New Jersey	(8)	-	8
New York [1]	(36)	20	16
North Carolina	(15)	15	-
Ohio	(16)	16	-
Pennsylvania	(28)	28	-
Rhode Island	(4)	-	4
South Carolina	(11)	11	-
Tennessee	(11)	11	-
Vermont	(7)	-	7
Virginia	(24)	24	-
Totals	**(261)**	**178**	**83**

1. For explanation of split electoral votes, see p. 14.

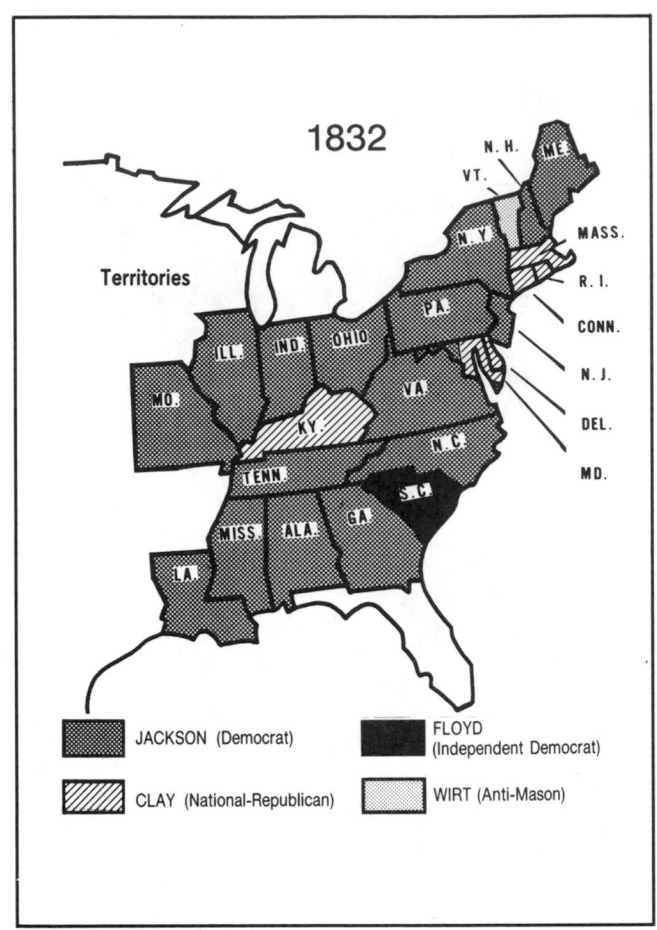

States	Electoral Votes	Jackson	Clay	Floyd	Wirt
Alabama	(7)	7	-	-	-
Connecticut	(8)	-	8	-	-
Delaware	(3)	-	3	-	-
Georgia	(11)	11	-	-	-
Illinois	(5)	5	-	-	-
Indiana	(9)	9	-	-	-
Kentucky	(15)	-	15	-	-
Louisiana	(5)	5	-	-	-
Maine	(10)	10	-	-	-
Maryland [1]	(10)	3	5	-	-
Massachusetts	(14)	-	14	-	-
Mississippi	(4)	4	-	-	-
Missouri	(4)	4	-	-	-
New Hampshire	(7)	7	-	-	-
New Jersey	(8)	8	-	-	-
New York	(42)	42	-	-	-
North Carolina	(15)	15	-	-	-
Ohio	(21)	21	-	-	-
Pennsylvania	(30)	30	-	-	-
Rhode Island	(4)	-	4	-	-
South Carolina	(11)	-	-	11	-
Tennessee	(15)	15	-	-	-
Vermont	(7)	-	-	-	7
Virginia	(23)	23	-	-	-
Totals	**(288)**	**219**	**49**	**11**	**7**

1. *Two Maryland electors did not vote. For explanation of split electoral votes, see p. 14.*

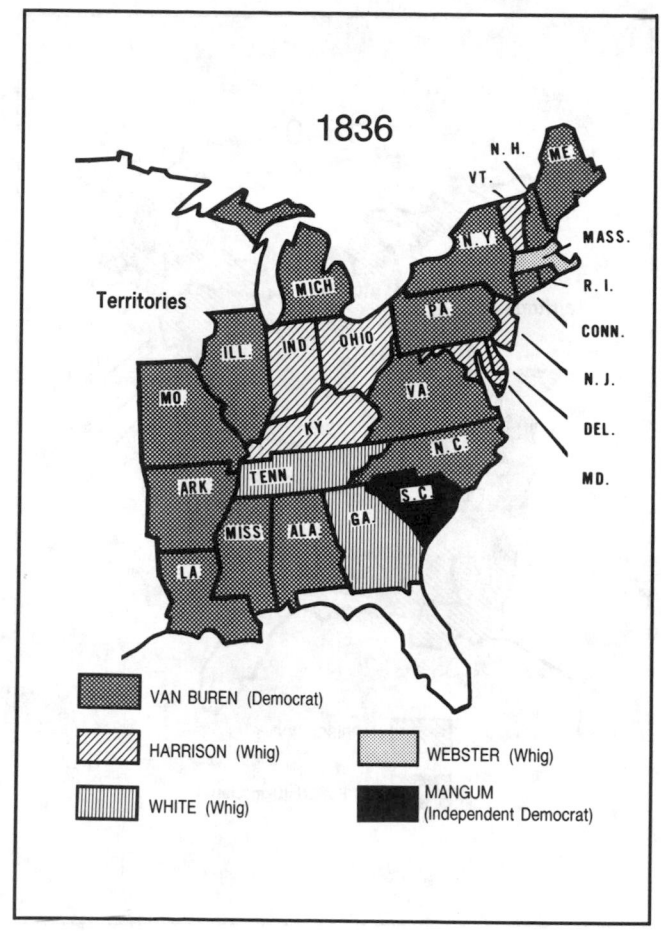

States	Electoral Votes	Van Buren	Harrison [1]	White [1]	Webster [1]	Mangum
Alabama	(7)	7	-	-	-	-
Arkansas	(3)	3	-	-	-	-
Connecticut	(8)	8	-	-	-	-
Delaware	(3)	-	3	-	-	-
Georgia	(11)	-	-	11	-	-
Illinois	(5)	5	-	-	-	-
Indiana	(9)	-	9	-	-	-
Kentucky	(15)	-	15	-	-	-
Louisiana	(5)	5	-	-	-	-
Maine	(10)	10	-	-	-	-
Maryland	(10)	-	10	-	-	-
Massachusetts	(14)	-	-	-	14	-
Michigan	(3)	3	-	-	-	-
Mississippi	(4)	4	-	-	-	-
Missouri	(4)	4	-	-	-	-
New Hampshire	(7)	7	-	-	-	-
New Jersey	(8)	-	8	-	-	-
New York	(42)	42	-	-	-	-
North Carolina	(15)	15	-	-	-	-
Ohio	(21)	-	21	-	-	-
Pennsylvania	(30)	30	-	-	-	-
Rhode Island	(4)	4	-	-	-	-
South Carolina	(11)	-	-	-	-	11
Tennessee	(15)	-	-	15	-	-
Vermont	(7)	-	7	-	-	-
Virginia	(23)	23	-	-	-	-
Totals	(294)	170	73	26	14	11

1. For explanation of three Whig presidential candidates, see p. 11.

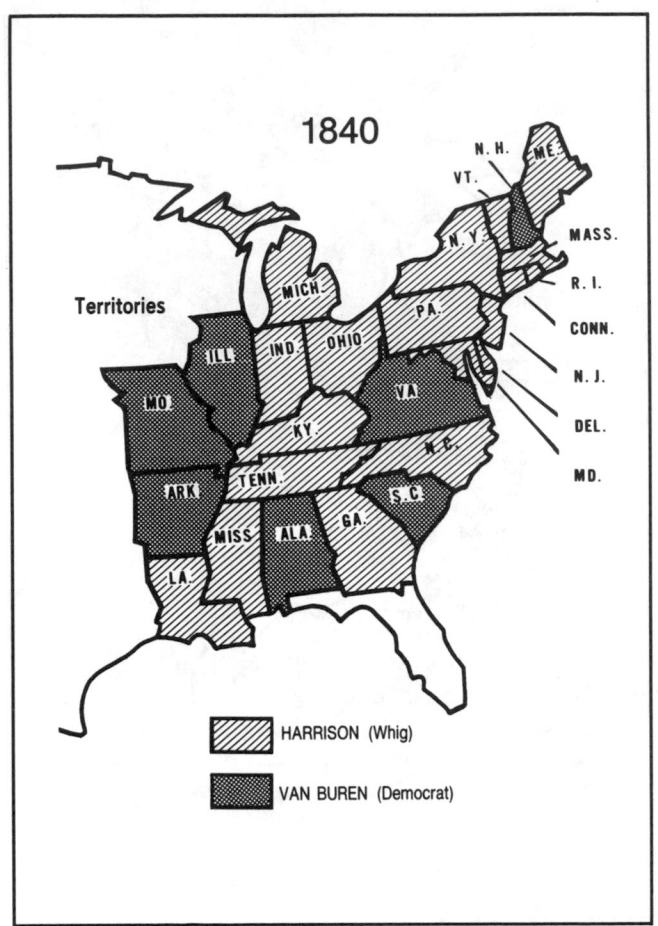

States	Electoral Votes	Harrison	Van Buren
Alabama	(7)	-	7
Arkansas	(3)	-	3
Connecticut	(8)	8	-
Delaware	(3)	3	-
Georgia	(11)	11	-
Illinois	(5)	-	5
Indiana	(9)	9	-
Kentucky	(15)	15	-
Louisiana	(5)	5	-
Maine	(10)	10	-
Maryland	(10)	10	-
Massachusetts	(14)	14	-
Michigan	(3)	3	-
Mississippi	(4)	4	-
Missouri	(4)	-	4
New Hampshire	(7)	-	7
New Jersey	(8)	8	-
New York	(42)	42	-
North Carolina	(15)	15	-
Ohio	(21)	21	-
Pennsylvania	(30)	30	-
Rhode Island	(4)	4	-
South Carolina	(11)	-	11
Tennessee	(15)	15	-
Vermont	(7)	7	-
Virginia	(23)	-	23
Totals	**(294)**	**234**	**60**

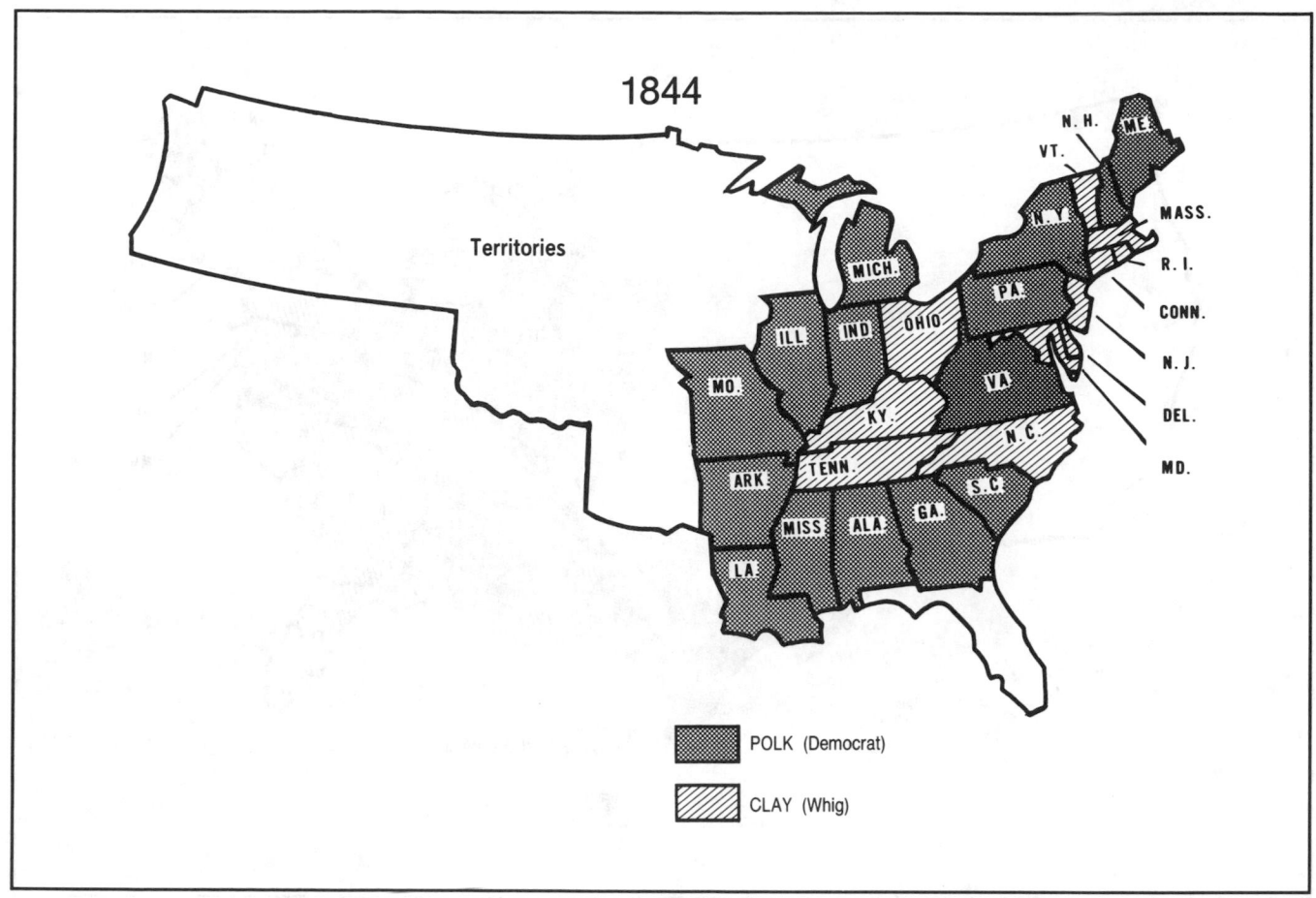

1844

Territories

POLK (Democrat)

CLAY (Whig)

States	Electoral Votes	Polk	Clay
Alabama	(9)	9	-
Arkansas	(3)	3	-
Connecticut	(6)	-	6
Delaware	(3)	-	3
Georgia	(10)	10	-
Illinois	(9)	9	-
Indiana	(12)	12	-
Kentucky	(12)	-	12
Louisiana	(6)	6	-
Maine	(9)	9	-
Maryland	(8)	-	8
Massachusetts	(12)	-	12
Michigan	(5)	5	-
Mississippi	(6)	6	-
Missouri	(7)	7	-
New Hampshire	(6)	6	-
New Jersey	(7)	-	7
New York	(36)	36	-
North Carolina	(11)	-	11
Ohio	(23)	-	23
Pennsylvania	(26)	26	-
Rhode Island	(4)	-	4
South Carolina	(9)	9	-
Tennessee	(13)	-	13
Vermont	(6)	-	6
Virginia	(17)	17	-
Totals	**(275)**	**170**	**105**

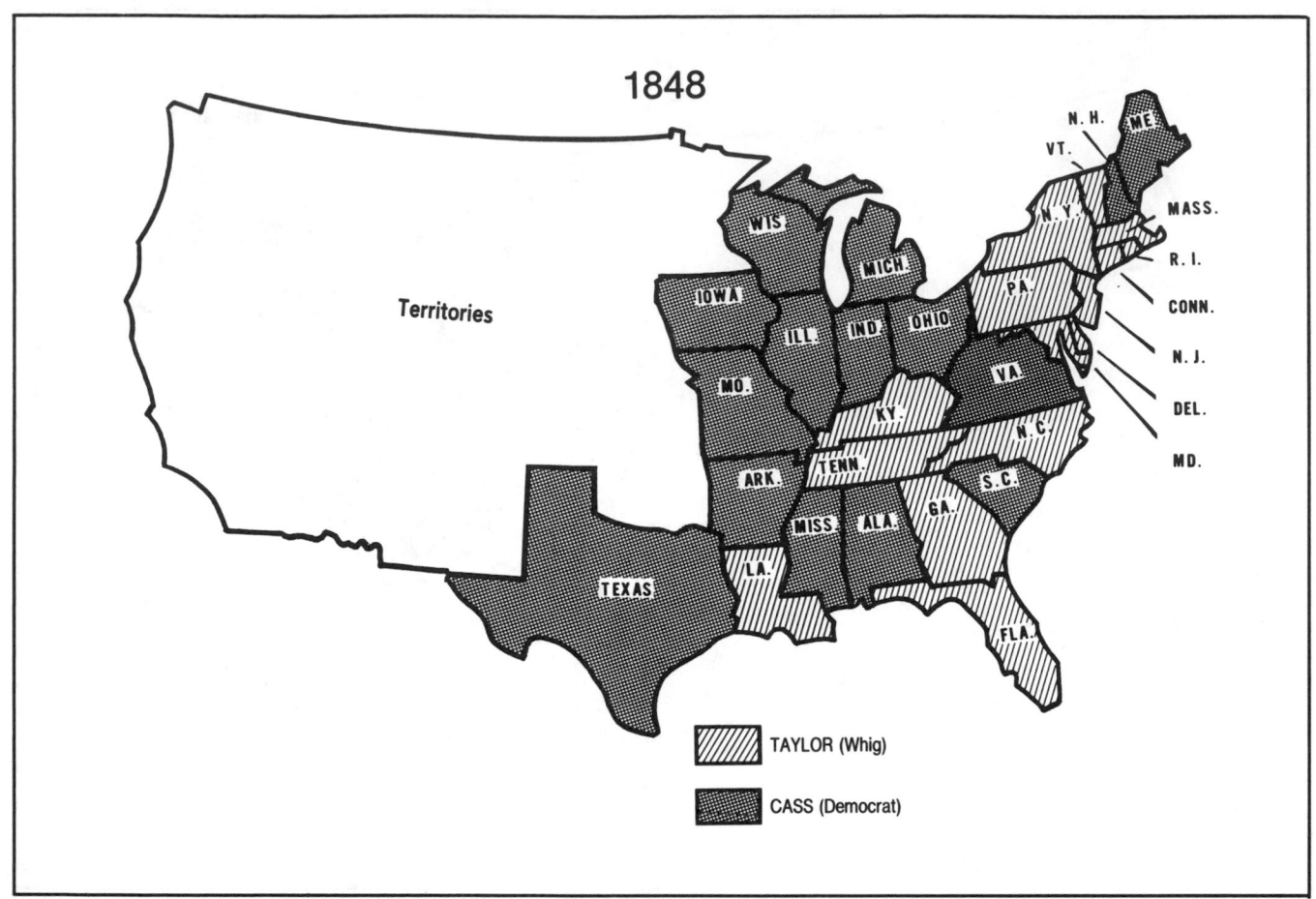

1848

Territories

TAYLOR (Whig)

CASS (Democrat)

States	Electoral Votes	Taylor	Cass	States	Electoral Votes	Taylor	Cass
Alabama	(9)	-	9	Mississippi	(6)	-	6
Arkansas	(3)	-	3	Missouri	(7)	-	7
Connecticut	(6)	6	-	New Hampshire	(6)	-	6
Delaware	(3)	3	-	New Jersey	(7)	7	-
Florida	(3)	3	-	New York	(36)	36	-
Georgia	(10)	10	-	North Carolina	(11)	11	-
Illinois	(9)	-	9	Ohio	(23)	-	23
Indiana	(12)	-	12	Pennsylvania	(26)	26	-
Iowa	(4)	-	4	Rhode Island	(4)	4	-
Kentucky	(12)	12	-	South Carolina	(9)	-	9
Louisiana	(6)	6	-	Tennessee	(13)	13	-
Maine	(9)	-	9	Texas	(4)	-	4
Maryland	(8)	8	-	Vermont	(6)	6	-
Massachusetts	(12)	12	-	Virginia	(17)	-	17
Michigan	(5)	-	5	Wisconsin	(4)	-	4
				Totals	**(290)**	**163**	**127**

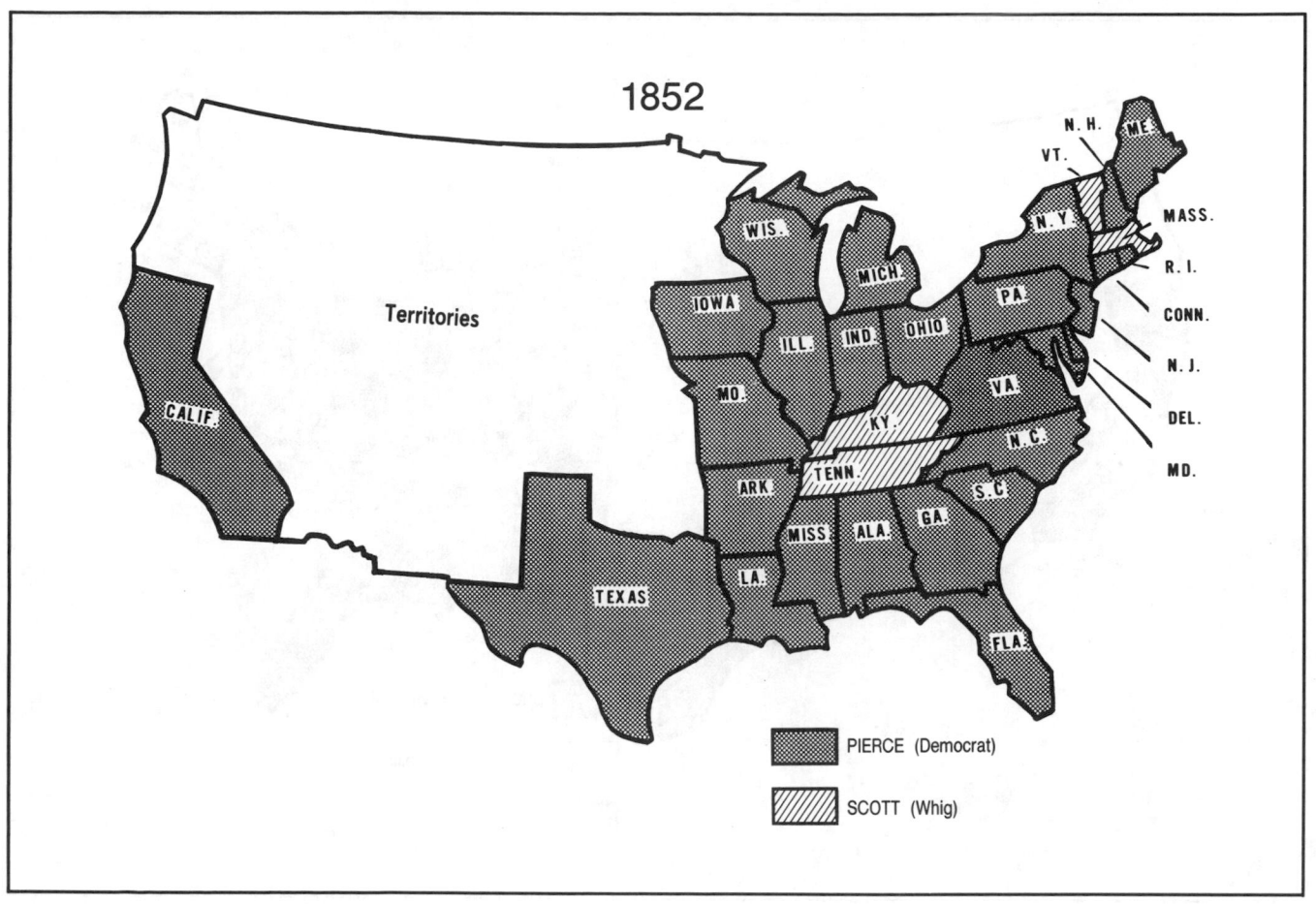

States	Electoral Votes	Pierce	Scott	States	Electoral Votes	Pierce	Scott
Alabama	(9)	9	-	Mississippi	(7)	7	-
Arkansas	(4)	4	-	Missouri	(9)	9	-
California	(4)	4	-	New Hampshire	(5)	5	-
Connecticut	(6)	6	-	New Jersey	(7)	7	-
Delaware	(3)	3	-	New York	(35)	35	-
Florida	(3)	3	-	North Carolina	(10)	10	-
Georgia	(10)	10	-	Ohio	(23)	23	-
Illinois	(11)	11	-	Pennsylvania	(27)	27	-
Indiana	(13)	13	-	Rhode Island	(4)	4	-
Iowa	(4)	4	-	South Carolina	(8)	8	-
Kentucky	(12)	-	12	Tennessee	(12)	-	12
Louisiana	(6)	6	-	Texas	(4)	4	-
Maine	(8)	8	-	Vermont	(5)	-	5
Maryland	(8)	8	-	Virginia	(15)	15	-
Massachusetts	(13)	-	13	Wisconsin	(5)	5	-
Michigan	(6)	6	-	**Totals**	**(296)**	**254**	**42**

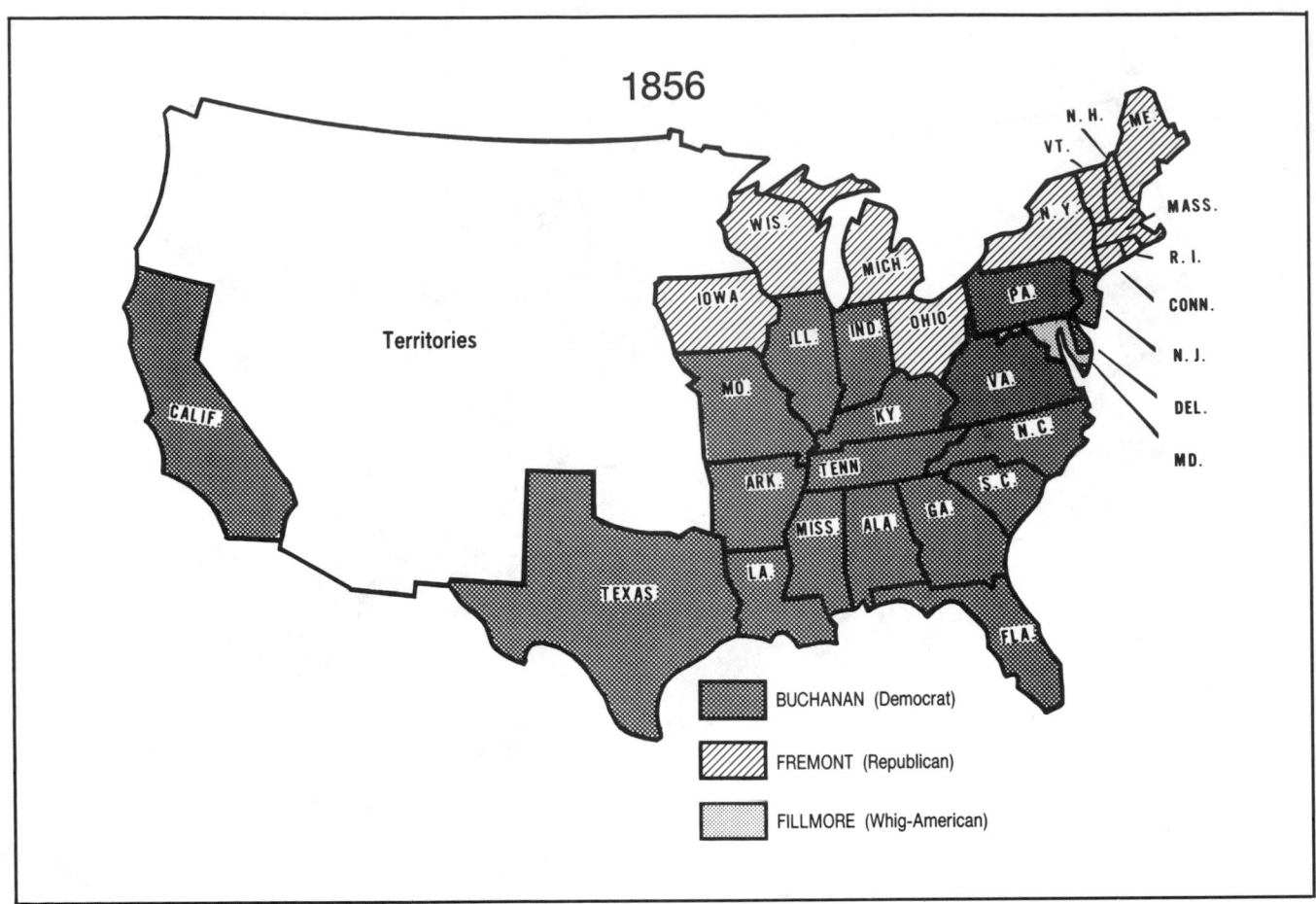

1856

Territories

BUCHANAN (Democrat)

FREMONT (Republican)

FILLMORE (Whig-American)

States	Electoral Votes	Buchanan	Fremont	Fillmore	States	Electoral Votes	Buchanan	Fremont	Fillmore
Alabama	(9)	9	-	-	Mississippi	(7)	7	-	-
Arkansas	(4)	4	-	-	Missouri	(9)	9	-	-
California	(4)	4	-	-	New Hampshire	(5)	-	5	-
Connecticut	(6)	-	6	-	New Jersey	(7)	7	-	-
Delaware	(3)	3	-	-	New York	(35)	-	35	-
Florida	(3)	3	-	-	North Carolina	(10)	10	-	-
Georgia	(10)	10	-	-	Ohio	(23)	-	23	-
Illinois	(11)	11	-	-	Pennsylvania	(27)	27	-	-
Indiana	(13)	13	-	-	Rhode Island	(4)	-	4	-
Iowa	(4)	-	4	-	South Carolina	(8)	8	-	-
Kentucky	(12)	12	-	-	Tennessee	(12)	12	-	-
Louisiana	(6)	6	-	-	Texas	(4)	4	-	-
Maine	(8)	-	8	-	Vermont	(5)	-	5	-
Maryland	(8)	-	-	8	Virginia	(15)	15	-	-
Massachusetts	(13)	-	13	-	Wisconsin	(5)	-	5	-
Michigan	(6)	-	6	-	**Totals**	**(296)**	**174**	**114**	**8**

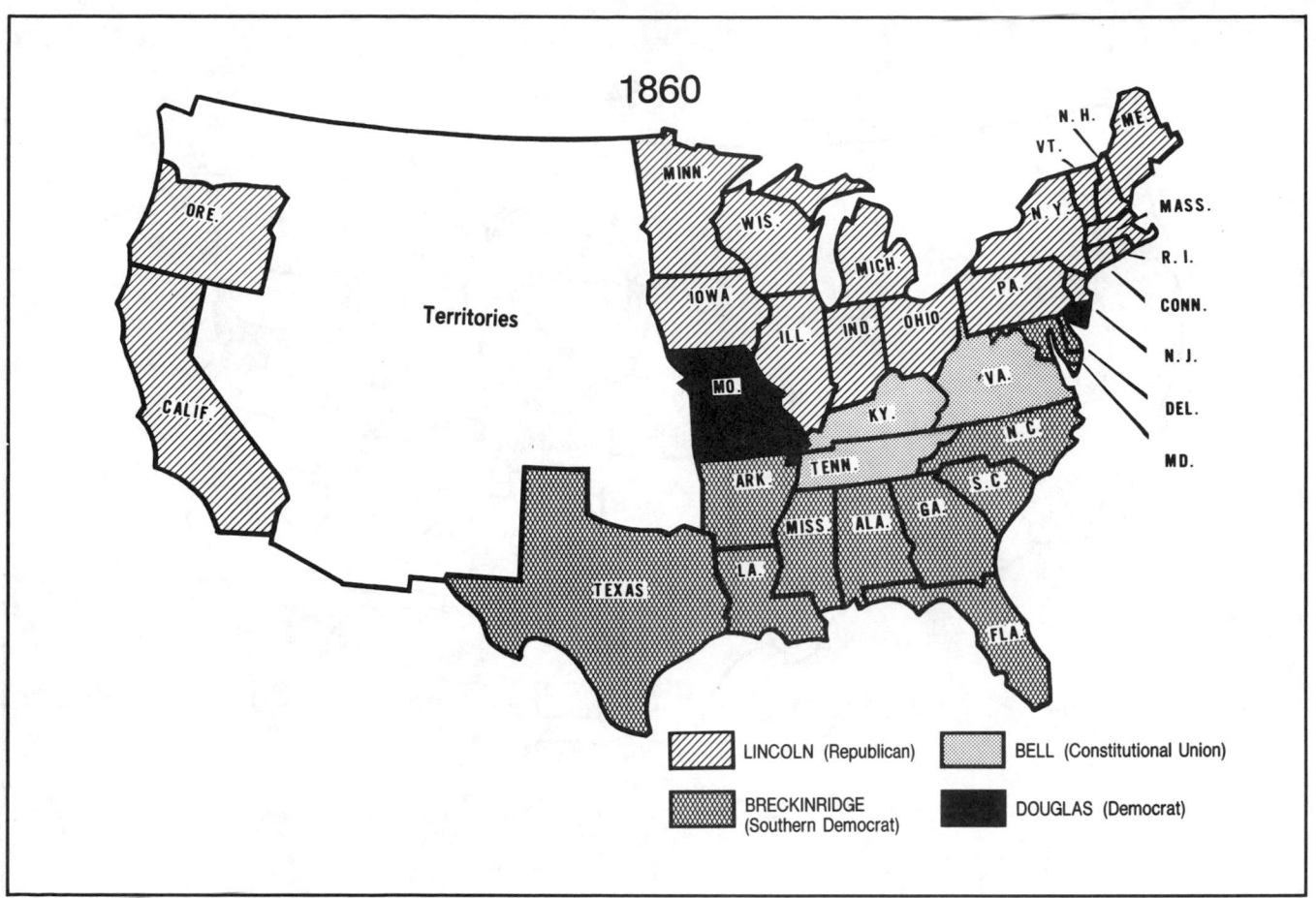

1860

States	Electoral Votes	Lincoln	Breckinridge	Bell	Douglas	States	Electoral Votes	Lincoln	Breckinridge	Bell	Douglas
Alabama	(9)	-	9	-	-	Mississippi	(7)	-	7	-	-
Arkansas	(4)	-	4	-	-	Missouri	(9)	-	-	-	9
California	(4)	4	-	-	-	New Hampshire	(5)	5	-	-	-
Connecticut	(6)	6	-	-	-	New Jersey [1]	(7)	4	-	-	3
Delaware	(3)	-	3	-	-	New York	(35)	35	-	-	-
Florida	(3)	-	3	-	-	North Carolina	(10)	-	10	-	-
Georgia	(10)	-	10	-	-	Ohio	(23)	23	-	-	-
Illinois	(11)	11	-	-	-	Oregon	(3)	3	-	-	-
Indiana	(13)	13	-	-	-	Pennsylvania	(27)	27	-	-	-
Iowa	(4)	4	-	-	-	Rhode Island	(4)	4	-	-	-
Kentucky	(12)	-	-	12	-	South Carolina	(8)	-	8	-	-
Louisiana	(6)	-	6	-	-	Tennessee	(12)	-	-	12	-
Maine	(8)	8	-	-	-	Texas	(4)	-	4	-	-
Maryland	(8)	-	8	-	-	Vermont	(5)	5	-	-	-
Massachusetts	(13)	13	-	-	-	Virginia	(15)	-	-	15	-
Michigan	(6)	6	-	-	-	Wisconsin	(5)	5	-	-	-
Minnesota	(4)	4	-	-	-	**Totals**	**(303)**	**180**	**72**	**39**	**12**

1. For explanation of split electoral votes, see p. 14.

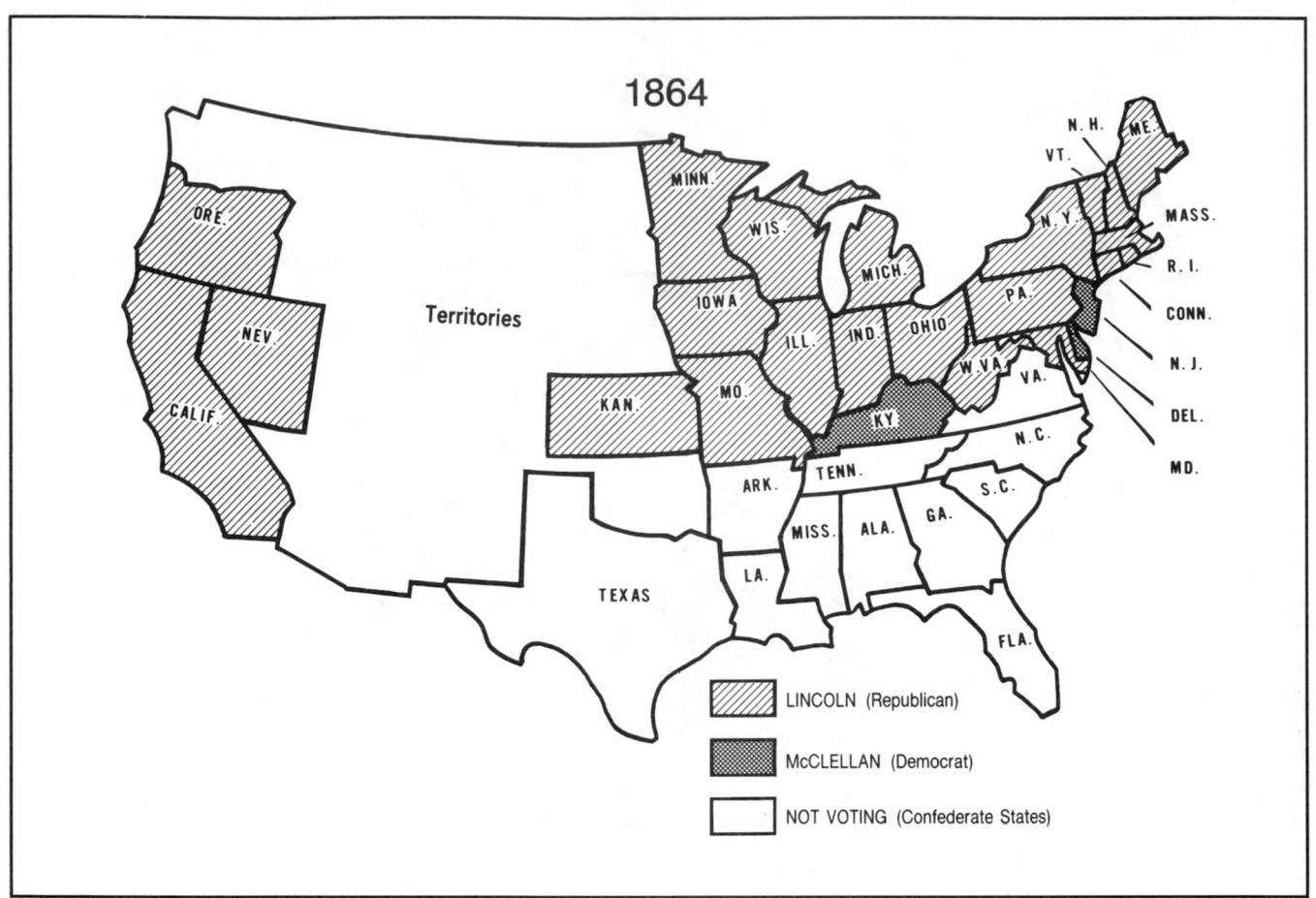

1864

LINCOLN (Republican)

McCLELLAN (Democrat)

NOT VOTING (Confederate States)

States [1]	Electoral Votes	Lincoln	McClellan	States [1]	Electoral Votes	Lincoln	McClellan
California	(5)	5	-	Missouri	(11)	11	-
Connecticut	(6)	6	-	Nevada [2]	(3)	2	-
Delaware	(3)	-	3	New Hampshire	(5)	5	-
Illinois	(16)	16	-	New Jersey	(7)	-	7
Indiana	(13)	13	-	New York	(33)	33	-
Iowa	(8)	8	-	Ohio	(21)	21	-
Kansas	(3)	3	-	Oregon	(3)	3	-
Kentucky	(11)	-	11	Pennsylvania	(26)	26	-
Maine	(7)	7	-	Rhode Island	(4)	4	-
Maryland	(7)	7	-	Vermont	(5)	5	-
Massachusetts	(12)	12	-	West Virginia	(5)	5	-
Michigan	(8)	8	-	Wisconsin	(8)	8	-
Minnesota	(4)	4	-	**Totals**	**(234)**	**212**	**21**

1. Eleven Southern States — Alabama, Arkansas, Florida, Georgia, Louisiana, Mississippi, North Carolina, South Carolina, Tennessee, Texas and Virginia — had seceded from the Union and did not vote.
2. One Nevada elector did not vote.

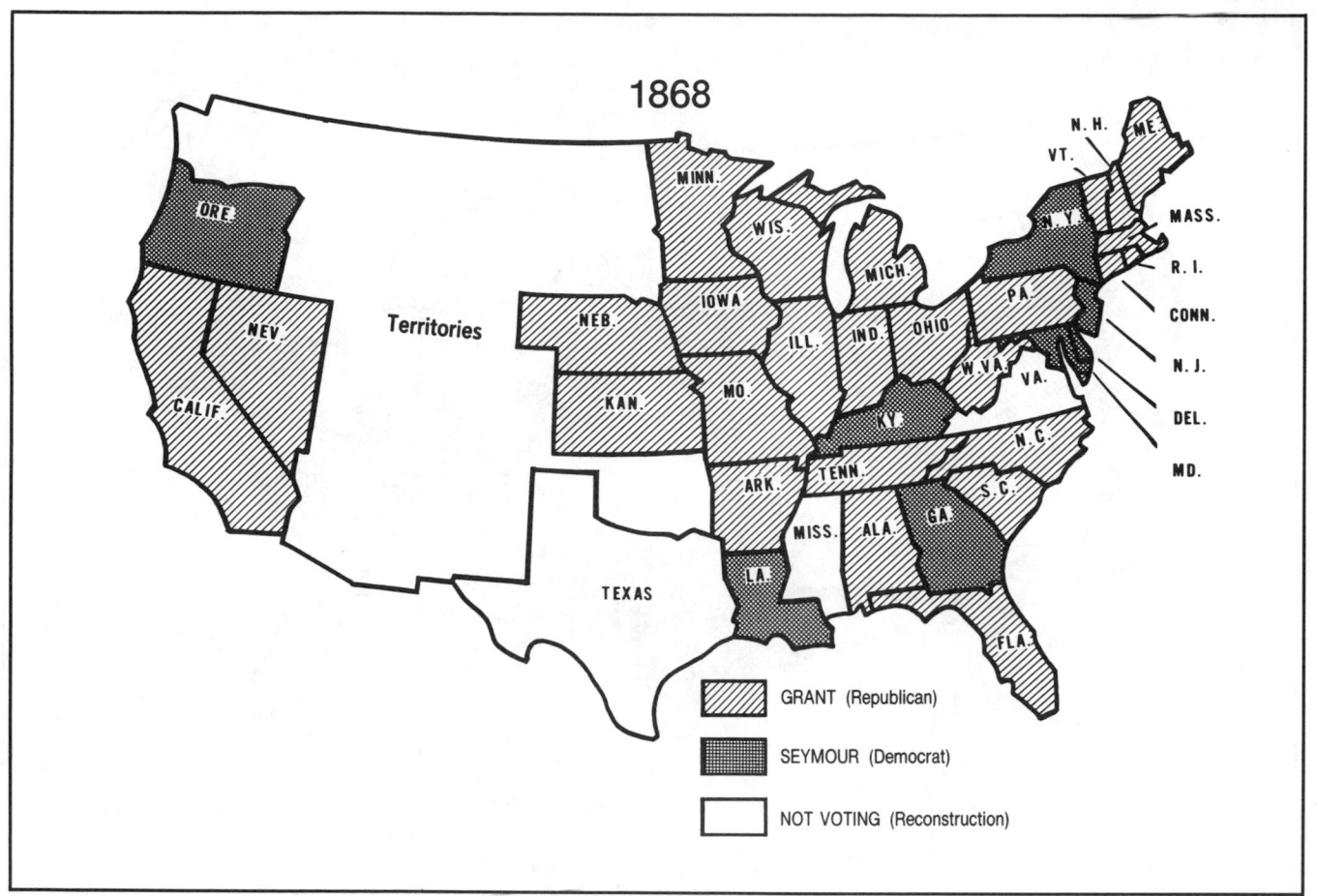

1868

States [1]	Electoral Votes	Grant	Seymour
Alabama	(8)	8	-
Arkansas	(5)	5	-
California	(5)	5	-
Connecticut	(6)	6	-
Delaware	(3)	-	3
Florida	(3)	3	-
Georgia	(9)	-	9
Illinois	(16)	16	-
Indiana	(13)	13	-
Iowa	(8)	8	-
Kansas	(3)	3	-
Kentucky	(11)	-	11
Louisiana	(7)	-	7
Maine	(7)	7	-
Maryland	(7)	-	7
Massachusetts	(12)	12	-
Michigan	(8)	8	-
Minnesota	(4)	4	-

States [1]	Electoral Votes	Grant	Seymour
Missouri	(11)	11	-
Nebraska	(3)	3	-
Nevada	(3)	3	-
New Hampshire	(5)	5	-
New Jersey	(7)	-	7
New York	(33)	-	33
North Carolina	(9)	9	-
Ohio	(21)	21	-
Oregon	(3)	-	3
Pennsylvania	(26)	26	-
Rhode Island	(4)	4	-
South Carolina	(6)	6	-
Tennessee	(10)	10	-
Vermont	(5)	5	-
West Virginia	(5)	5	-
Wisconsin	(8)	8	-
Totals	(294)	214	80

1. Mississippi, Texas, and Virginia were not yet readmitted to the Union and did not participate in the election.

Electoral Votes, 1872

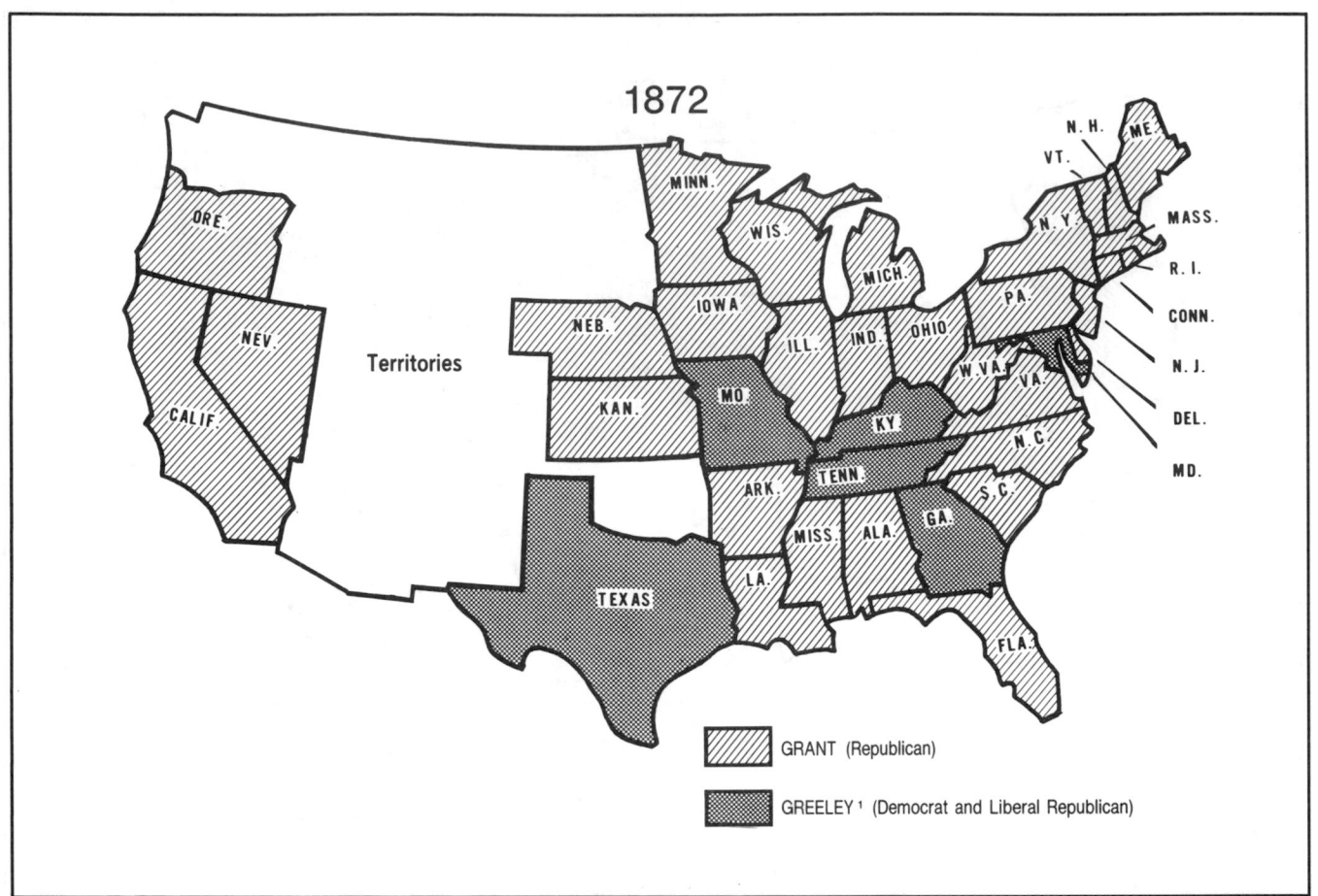

1872

Territories

GRANT (Republican)

GREELEY [1] (Democrat and Liberal Republican)

States	Electoral Votes	Grant	Hendricks [1]	Brown [1]	Jenkins [1]	Davis [1]	States	Electoral Votes	Grant	Hendricks [1]	Brown [1]	Jenkins [1]	Davis [1]
Alabama	(10)	10	-	-	-	-	Nebraska	(3)	3	-	-	-	-
Arkansas [2]	(6)	-	-	-	-	-	Nevada	(3)	3	-	-	-	-
California	(6)	6	-	-	-	-	New Hampshire	(5)	5	-	-	-	-
Connecticut	(6)	6	-	-	-	-	New Jersey	(9)	9	-	-	-	-
Delaware	(3)	3	-	-	-	-	New York	(35)	35	-	-	-	-
Florida	(4)	4	-	-	-	-	North Carolina	(10)	10	-	-	-	-
Georgia [3]	(11)	-	-	6	2	-	Ohio	(22)	22	-	-	-	-
Illinois	(21)	21	-	-	-	-	Oregon	(3)	3	-	-	-	-
Indiana	(15)	15	-	-	-	-	Pennsylvania	(29)	29	-	-	-	-
Iowa	(11)	11	-	-	-	-	Rhode Island	(4)	4	-	-	-	-
Kansas	(5)	5	-	-	-	-	South Carolina	(7)	7	-	-	-	-
Kentucky	(12)	-	8	4	-	-	Tennessee	(12)	-	12	-	-	-
Louisiana [2]	(8)	-	-	-	-	-	Texas	(8)	-	8	-	-	-
Maine	(7)	7	-	-	-	-	Vermont	(5)	5	-	-	-	-
Maryland	(8)	-	8	-	-	-	Virginia	(11)	11	-	-	-	-
Massachusetts	(13)	13	-	-	-	-	West Virginia	(5)	5	-	-	-	-
Michigan	(11)	11	-	-	-	-	Wisconsin	(10)	10	-	-	-	-
Minnesota	(5)	5	-	-	-	-	**Totals**	**(366)**	**286**	**42**	**18**	**2**	**1**
Mississippi	(8)	8	-	-	-	-							
Missouri	(15)	-	6	8	-	1							

1. For explanation of Democratic electoral vote, cast after Greeley's death, see p. 11.
2. Congress refused to accept electoral votes of Arkansas and Louisiana because of disruptive conditions during Reconstruction.
3. Three Georgia electoral votes cast for Greeley were not counted.

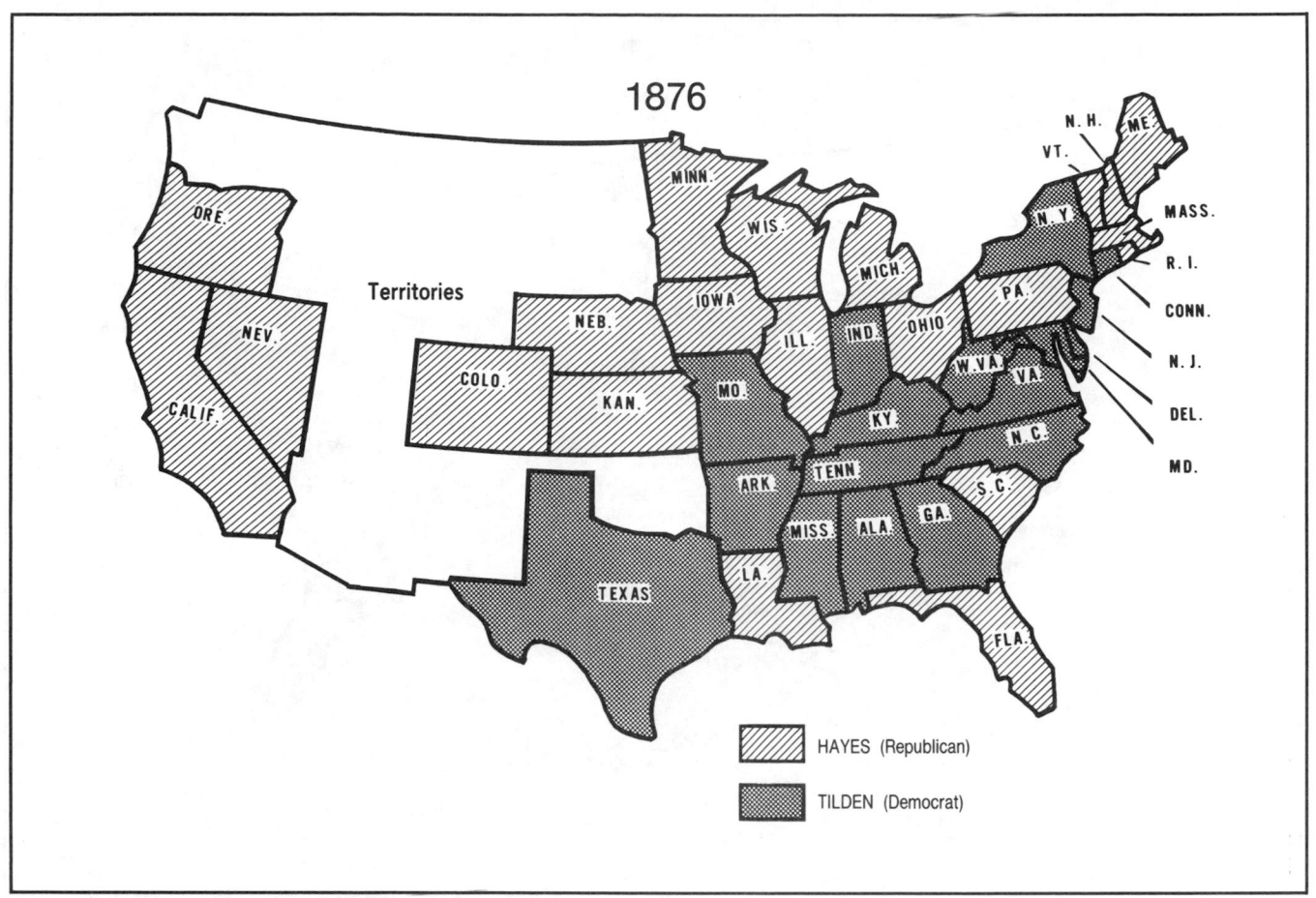

1876

Territories

HAYES (Republican)

TILDEN (Democrat)

States	Electoral Votes	Hayes	Tilden	States	Electoral Votes	Hayes	Tilden
Alabama	(10)	-	10	Missouri	(15)	-	15
Arkansas	(6)	-	6	Nebraska	(3)	3	-
California	(6)	6	-	Nevada	(3)	3	-
Colorado	(3)	3	-	New Hampshire	(5)	5	-
Connecticut	(6)	-	6	New Jersey	(9)	-	9
Delaware	(3)	-	3	New York	(35)	-	35
Florida [1]	(4)	4	-	North Carolina	(10)	-	10
Georgia	(11)	-	11	Ohio	(22)	22	-
Illinois	(21)	21	-	Oregon [1]	(3)	3	-
Indiana	(15)	-	15	Pennsylvania	(29)	29	-
Iowa	(11)	11	-	Rhode Island	(4)	4	-
Kansas	(5)	5	-	South Carolina [1]	(7)	7	-
Kentucky	(12)	-	12	Tennessee	(12)	-	12
Louisiana [1]	(8)	8	-	Texas	(8)	-	8
Maine	(7)	7	-	Vermont	(5)	5	-
Maryland	(8)	-	8	Virginia	(11)	-	11
Massachusetts	(13)	13	-	West Virginia	(5)	-	5
Michigan	(11)	11	-	Wisconsin	(10)	10	-
Minnesota	(5)	5	-	**Totals**	(369)	185	184
Mississippi	(8)	-	8				

1. For explanation of disputed electoral votes of Florida, Louisiana, Oregon and South Carolina, see p. 16.

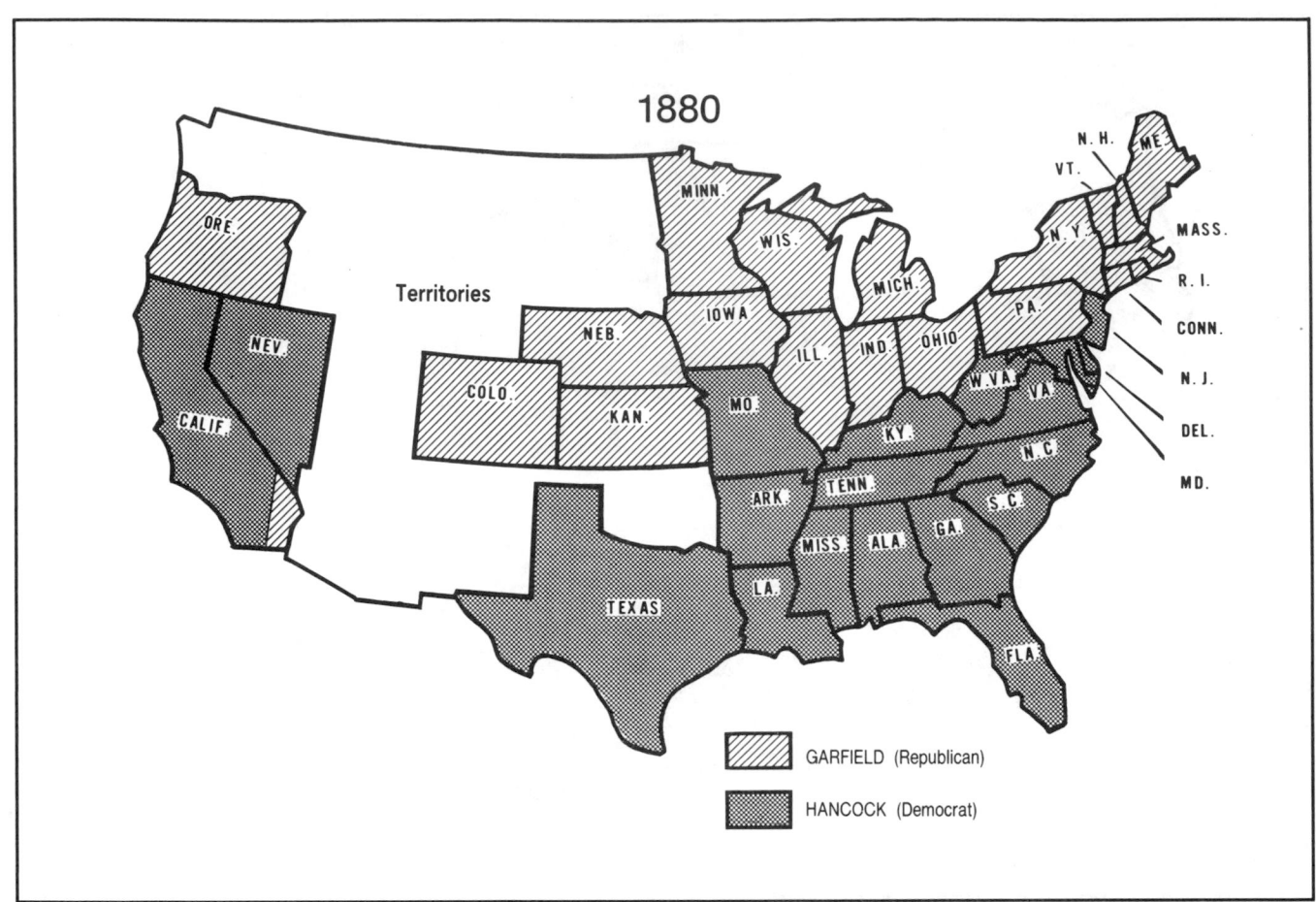

1880

GARFIELD (Republican)

HANCOCK (Democrat)

States	Electoral Votes	Garfield	Hancock	States	Electoral Votes	Garfield	Hancock
Alabama	(10)	-	10	Mississippi	(8)	-	8
Arkansas	(6)	-	6	Missouri	(15)	-	15
California [1]	(6)	1	5	Nebraska	(3)	3	-
Colorado	(3)	3	-	Nevada	(3)	-	3
Connecticut	(6)	6	-	New Hampshire	(5)	5	-
Delaware	(3)	-	3	New Jersey	(9)	-	9
Florida	(4)	-	4	New York	(35)	35	-
Georgia	(11)	-	11	North Carolina	(10)	-	10
Illinois	(21)	21	-	Ohio	(22)	22	-
Indiana	(15)	15	-	Oregon	(3)	3	-
Iowa	(11)	11	-	Pennsylvania	(29)	29	-
Kansas	(5)	5	-	Rhode Island	(4)	4	-
Kentucky	(12)	-	12	South Carolina	(7)	-	7
Louisiana	(8)	-	8	Tennessee	(12)	-	12
Maine	(7)	7	-	Texas	(8)	-	8
Maryland	(8)	-	8	Vermont	(5)	5	-
Massachusetts	(13)	13	-	Virginia	(11)	-	11
Michigan	(11)	11	-	West Virginia	(5)	-	5
Minnesota	(5)	5	-	Wisconsin	(10)	10	-
				Totals	**(369)**	**214**	**155**

1. For explanation of split electoral votes, see p. 14.

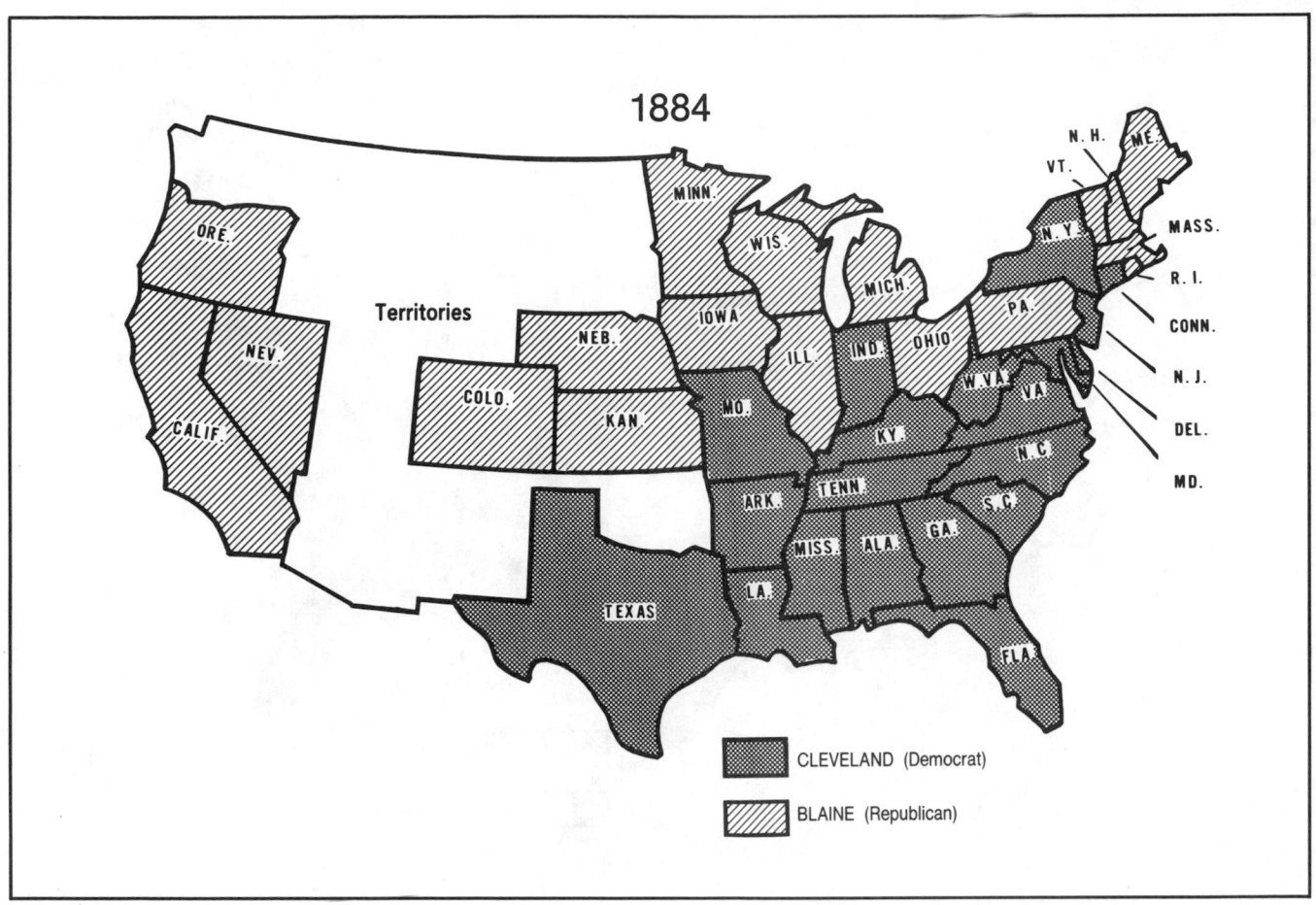

1884

Territories

CLEVELAND (Democrat)

BLAINE (Republican)

States	Electoral Votes	Cleveland	Blaine	States	Electoral Votes	Cleveland	Blaine
Alabama	(10)	10	-	Mississippi	(9)	9	-
Arkansas	(7)	7	-	Missouri	(16)	16	-
California	(8)	-	8	Nebraska	(5)	-	5
Colorado	(3)	-	3	Nevada	(3)	-	3
Connecticut	(6)	6	-	New Hampshire	(4)	-	4
Delaware	(3)	3	-	New Jersey	(9)	9	-
Florida	(4)	4	-	New York	(36)	36	-
Georgia	(12)	12	-	North Carolina	(11)	11	-
Illinois	(22)	-	22	Ohio	(23)	-	23
Indiana	(15)	15	-	Oregon	(3)	-	3
Iowa	(13)	-	13	Pennsylvania	(30)	-	30
Kansas	(9)	-	9	Rhode Island	(4)	-	4
Kentucky	(13)	13	-	South Carolina	(9)	9	-
Louisiana	(8)	8	-	Tennessee	(12)	12	-
Maine	(6)	-	6	Texas	(13)	13	-
Maryland	(8)	8	-	Vermont	(4)	-	4
Massachusetts	(14)	-	14	Virginia	(12)	12	-
Michigan	(13)	-	13	West Virginia	(6)	6	-
Minnesota	(7)	-	7	Wisconsin	(11)	-	11
				Totals	**(401)**	**219**	**182**

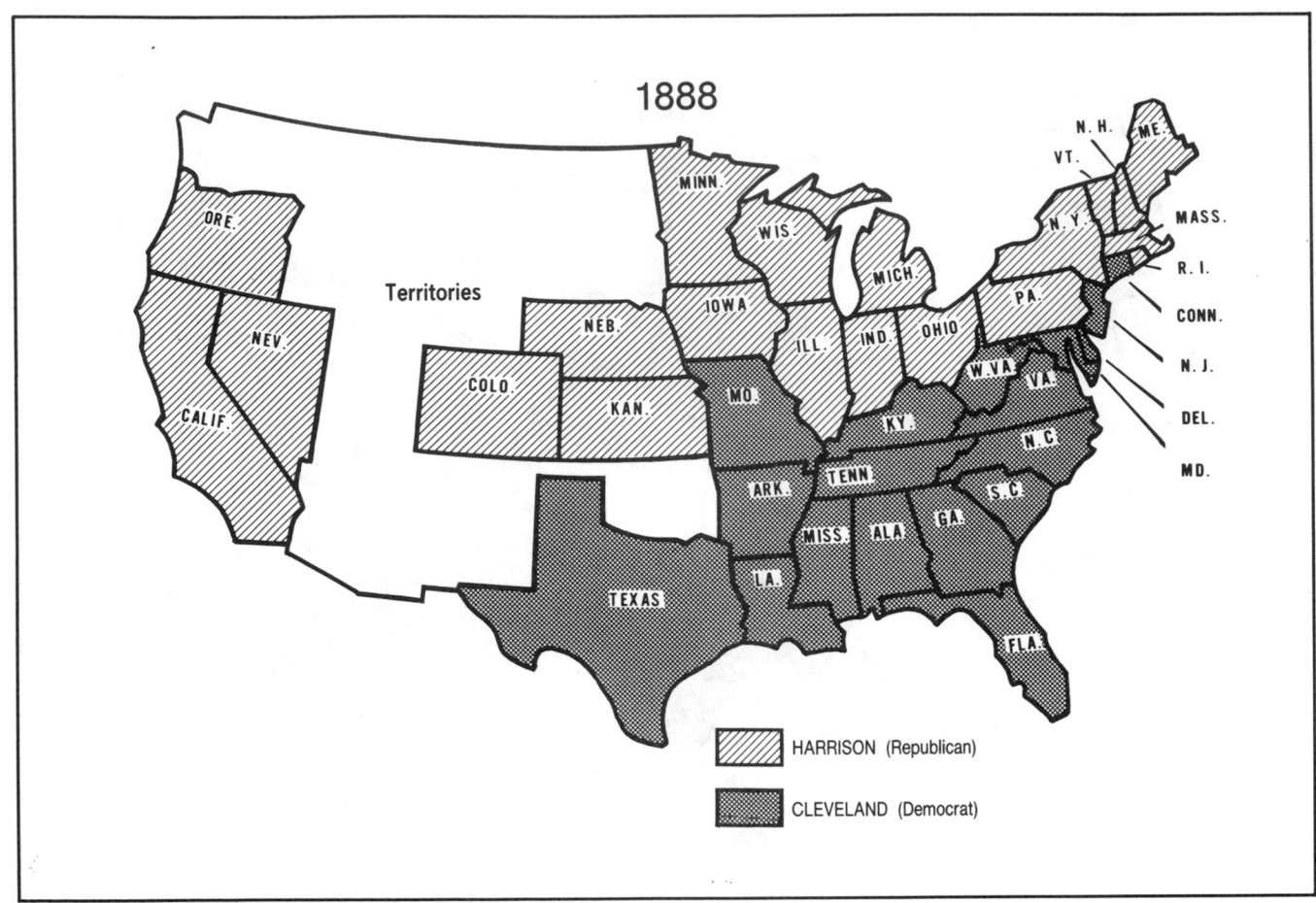

States	Electoral Votes	Harrison	Cleveland	States	Electoral Votes	Harrison	Cleveland
Alabama	(10)	-	10	**Mississippi**	(9)	-	9
Arkansas	(7)	-	7	**Missouri**	(16)	-	16
California	(8)	8	-	**Nebraska**	(5)	5	-
Colorado	(3)	3	-	**Nevada**	(3)	3	-
Connecticut	(6)	-	6	**New Hampshire**	(4)	4	-
Delaware	(3)	-	3	**New Jersey**	(9)	-	9
Florida	(4)	-	4	**New York**	(36)	36	-
Georgia	(12)	-	12	**North Carolina**	(11)	-	11
Illinois	(22)	22	-	**Ohio**	(23)	23	-
Indiana	(15)	15	-	**Oregon**	(3)	3	-
Iowa	(13)	13	-	**Pennsylvania**	(30)	30	-
Kansas	(9)	9	-	**Rhode Island**	(4)	4	-
Kentucky	(13)	-	13	**South Carolina**	(9)	-	9
Louisiana	(8)	-	8	**Tennessee**	(12)	-	12
Maine	(6)	6	-	**Texas**	(13)	-	13
Maryland	(8)	-	8	**Vermont**	(4)	4	-
Massachusetts	(14)	14	-	**Virginia**	(12)	-	12
Michigan	(13)	13	-	**West Virginia**	(6)	-	6
Minnesota	(7)	7	-	**Wisconsin**	(11)	11	-
				Totals	**(401)**	**233**	**168**

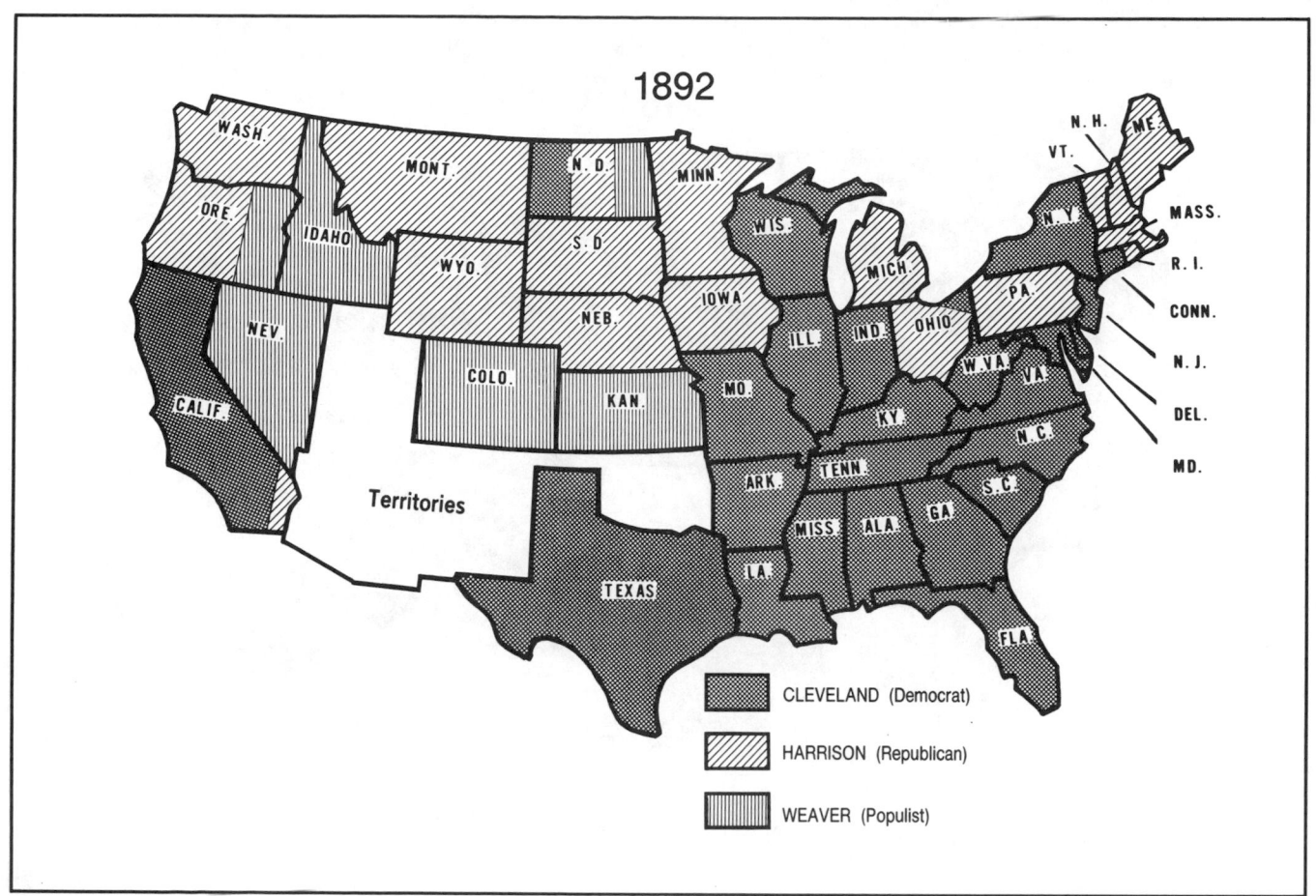

1892

CLEVELAND (Democrat)

HARRISON (Republican)

WEAVER (Populist)

States	Electoral Votes	Cleveland	Harrison	Weaver	States	Electoral Votes	Cleveland	Harrison	Weaver
Alabama	(11)	11	-	-	Montana	(3)	-	3	-
Arkansas	(8)	8	-	-	Nebraska	(8)	-	8	-
California[1]	(9)	8	1	-	Nevada	(3)	-	-	3
Colorado	(4)	-	-	4	New Hampshire	(4)	-	4	-
Connecticut	(6)	6	-	-	New Jersey	(10)	10	-	-
Delaware	(3)	3	-	-	New York	(36)	36	-	-
Florida	(4)	4	-	-	North Carolina	(11)	11	-	-
Georgia	(13)	13	-	-	North Dakota[1]	(3)	1	1	1
Idaho	(3)	-	-	3	Ohio[1]	(23)	1	22	-
Illinois	(24)	24	-	-	Oregon[1]	(4)	-	3	1
Indiana	(15)	15	-	-	Pennsylvania	(32)	-	32	-
Iowa	(13)	-	13	-	Rhode Island	(4)	-	4	-
Kansas	(10)	-	-	10	South Carolina	(9)	9	-	-
Kentucky	(13)	13	-	-	South Dakota	(4)	-	4	-
Louisiana	(8)	8	-	-	Tennessee	(12)	12	-	-
Maine	(6)	-	6	-	Texas	(15)	15	-	-
Maryland	(8)	8	-	-	Vermont	(4)	-	4	-
Massachusetts	(15)	-	15	-	Virginia	(12)	12	-	-
Michigan[1]	(14)	5	9	-	Washington	(4)	-	4	-
Minnesota	(9)	-	9	-	West Virginia	(6)	6	-	-
Mississippi	(9)	9	-	-	Wisconsin	(12)	12	-	-
Missouri	(17)	17	-	-	Wyoming	(3)	-	3	-
					Totals	**(444)**	**277**	**145**	**22**

1. For explanation of split electoral votes, see p. 14.

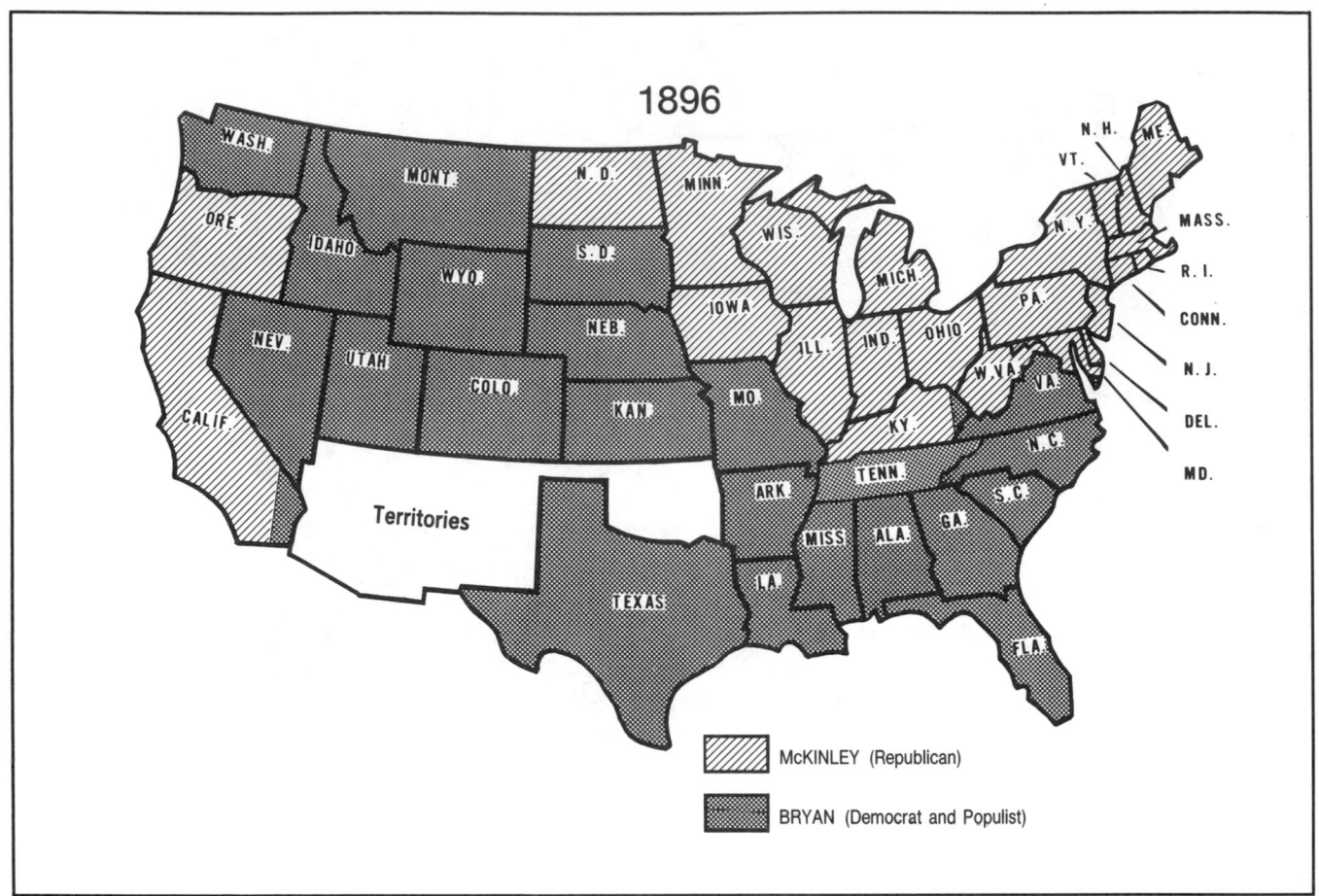

1896

McKINLEY (Republican)

BRYAN (Democrat and Populist)

States	Electoral Votes	McKinley	Bryan	States	Electoral Votes	McKinley	Bryan
Alabama	(11)	-	11	Nebraska	(8)	-	8
Arkansas	(8)	-	8	Nevada	(3)	-	3
California [1]	(9)	8	1	New Hampshire	(4)	4	-
Colorado	(4)	-	4	New Jersey	(10)	10	-
Connecticut	(6)	6	-	New York	(36)	36	-
Delaware	(3)	3	-	North Carolina	(11)	-	11
Florida	(4)	-	4	North Dakota	(3)	3	-
Georgia	(13)	-	13	Ohio	(23)	23	-
Idaho	(3)	-	3	Oregon	(4)	4	-
Illinois	(24)	24	-	Pennsylvania	(32)	32	-
Indiana	(15)	15	-	Rhode Island	(4)	4	-
Iowa	(13)	13	-	South Carolina	(9)	-	9
Kansas	(10)	-	10	South Dakota	(4)	-	4
Kentucky [1]	(13)	12	1	Tennessee	(12)	-	12
Louisiana	(8)	-	8	Texas	(15)	-	15
Maine	(6)	6	-	Utah	(3)	-	3
Maryland	(8)	8	-	Vermont	(4)	4	-
Massachusetts	(15)	15	-	Virginia	(12)	-	12
Michigan	(14)	14	-	Washington	(4)	-	4
Minnesota	(9)	9	-	West Virginia	(6)	6	-
Mississippi	(9)	-	9	Wisconsin	(12)	12	-
Missouri	(17)	-	17	Wyoming	(3)	-	3
Montana	(3)	-	3	**Totals**	**(447)**	**271**	**176**

1. For explanation of split electoral votes, see p. 14.

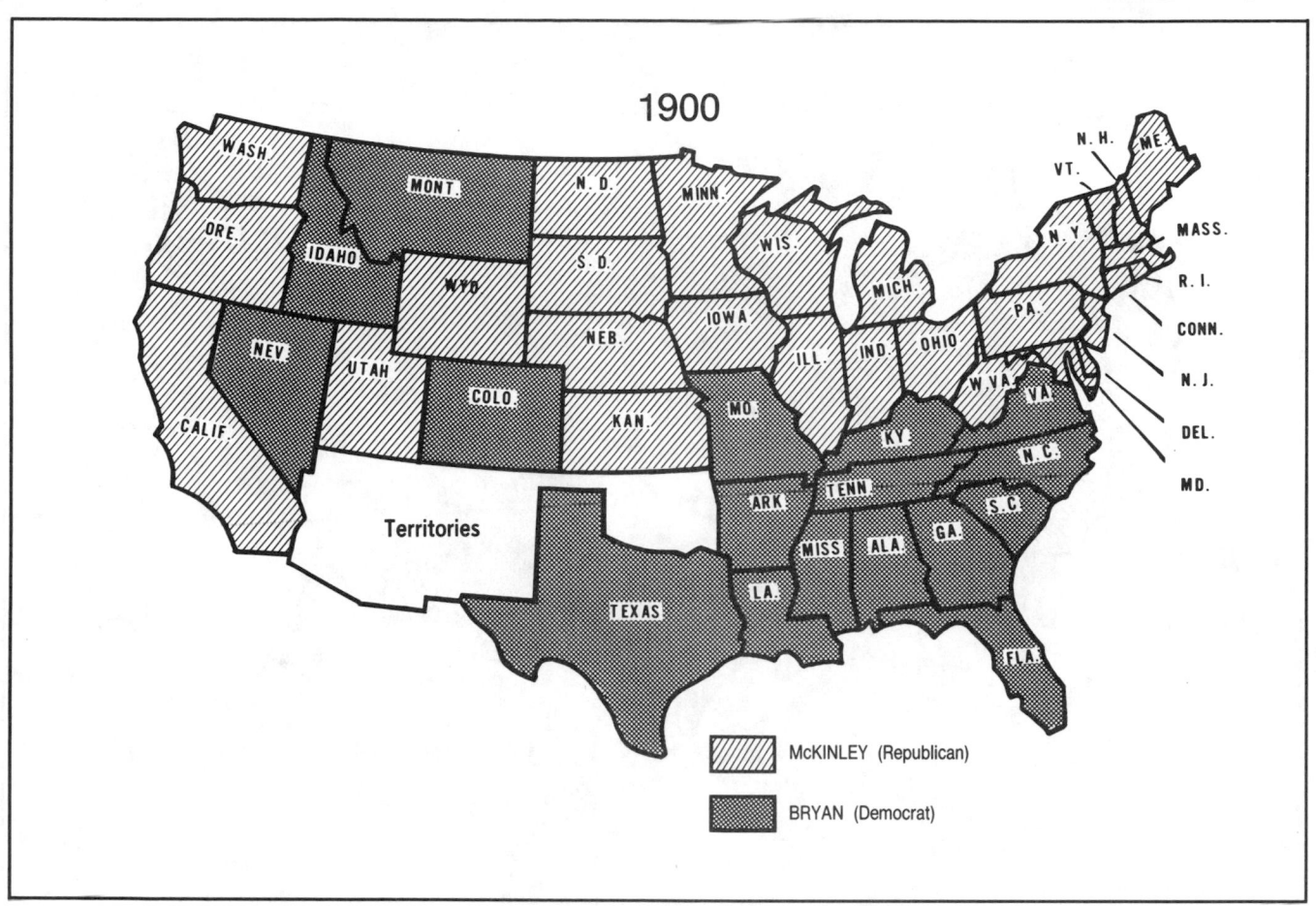

1900

Territories

McKINLEY (Republican)

BRYAN (Democrat)

States	Electoral Votes	McKinley	Bryan	States	Electoral Votes	McKinley	Bryan
Alabama	(11)	-	11	Nebraska	(8)	8	-
Arkansas	(8)	-	8	Nevada	(3)	-	3
California	(9)	9	-	New Hampshire	(4)	4	-
Colorado	(4)	-	4	New Jersey	(10)	10	-
Connecticut	(6)	6	-	New York	(36)	36	-
Delaware	(3)	3	-	North Carolina	(11)	-	11
Florida	(4)	-	4	North Dakota	(3)	3	-
Georgia	(13)	-	13	Ohio	(23)	23	-
Idaho	(3)	-	3	Oregon	(4)	4	-
Illinois	(24)	24	-	Pennsylvania	(32)	32	-
Indiana	(15)	15	-	Rhode Island	(4)	4	-
Iowa	(13)	13	-	South Carolina	(9)	-	9
Kansas	(10)	10	-	South Dakota	(4)	4	-
Kentucky	(13)	-	13	Tennessee	(12)	-	12
Louisiana	(8)	-	8	Texas	(15)	-	15
Maine	(6)	6	-	Utah	(3)	3	-
Maryland	(8)	8	-	Vermont	(4)	4	-
Massachusetts	(15)	15	-	Virginia	(12)	-	12
Michigan	(14)	14	-	Washington	(4)	4	-
Minnesota	(9)	9	-	West Virginia	(6)	6	-
Mississippi	(9)	-	9	Wisconsin	(12)	12	-
Missouri	(17)	-	17	Wyoming	(3)	3	-
Montana	(3)	-	3	**Totals**	**(447)**	**292**	**155**

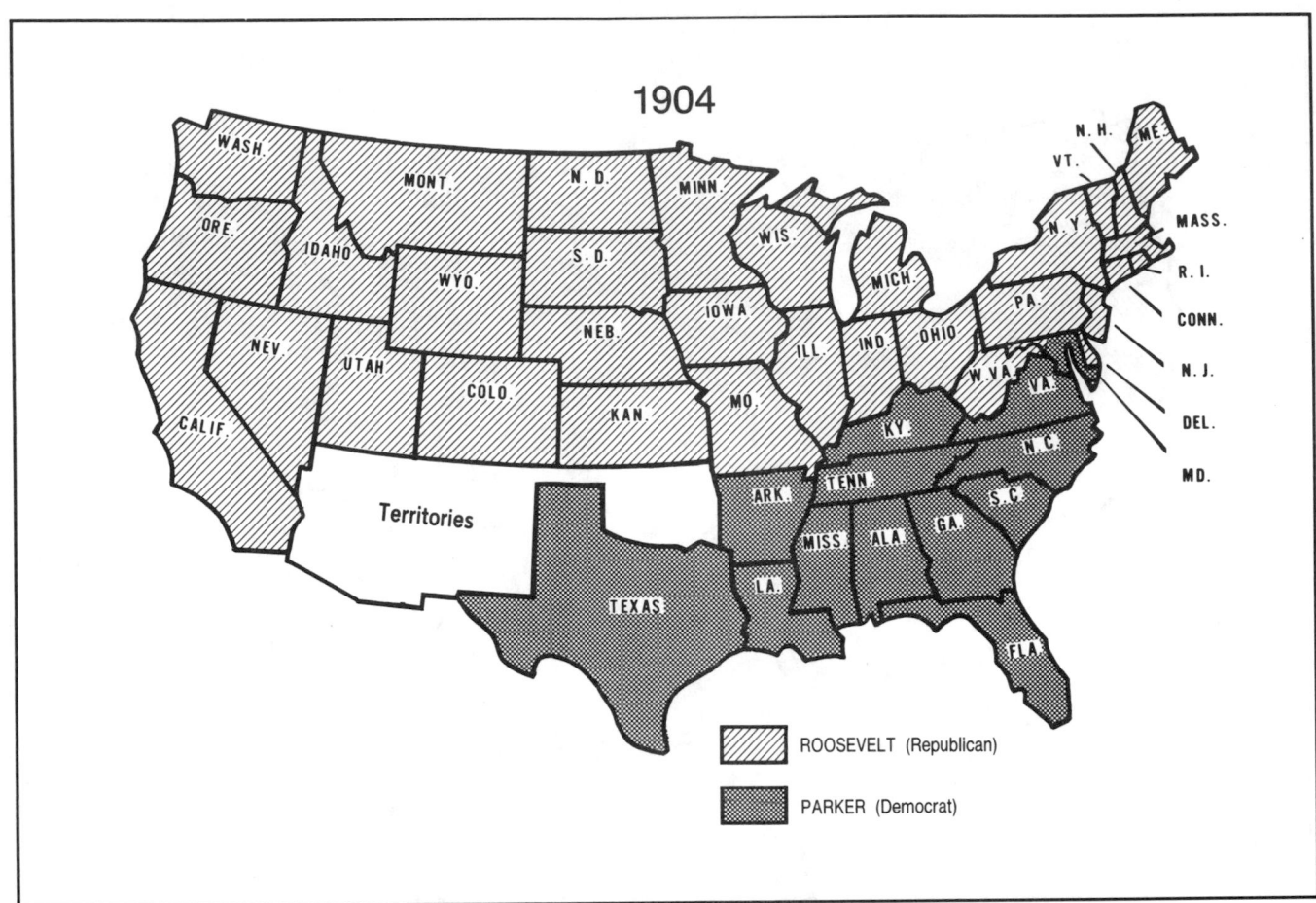

1904

ROOSEVELT (Republican)

PARKER (Democrat)

States	Electoral Votes	Roosevelt	Parker	States	Electoral Votes	Roosevelt	Parker
Alabama	(11)	-	11	Nebraska	(8)	8	-
Arkansas	(9)	-	9	Nevada	(3)	3	-
California	(10)	10	-	New Hampshire	(4)	4	-
Colorado	(5)	5	-	New Jersey	(12)	12	-
Connecticut	(7)	7	-	New York	(39)	39	-
Delaware	(3)	3	-	North Carolina	(12)	-	12
Florida	(5)	-	5	North Dakota	(4)	4	-
Georgia	(13)	-	13	Ohio	(23)	23	-
Idaho	(3)	3	-	Oregon	(4)	4	-
Illinois	(27)	27	-	Pennsylvania	(34)	34	-
Indiana	(15)	15	-	Rhode Island	(4)	4	-
Iowa	(13)	13	-	South Carolina	(9)	-	9
Kansas	(10)	10	-	South Dakota	(4)	4	-
Kentucky	(13)	-	13	Tennessee	(12)	-	12
Louisiana	(9)	-	9	Texas	(18)	-	18
Maine	(6)	6	-	Utah	(3)	3	-
Maryland [1]	(8)	1	7	Vermont	(4)	4	-
Massachusetts	(16)	16	-	Virginia	(12)	-	12
Michigan	(14)	14	-	Washington	(5)	5	-
Minnesota	(11)	11	-	West Virginia	(7)	7	-
Mississippi	(10)	-	10	Wisconsin	(13)	13	-
Missouri	(18)	18	-	Wyoming	(3)	3	-
Montana	(3)	3	-	**Totals**	**(476)**	**336**	**140**

1. For explanation of split electoral votes, see p. 14.

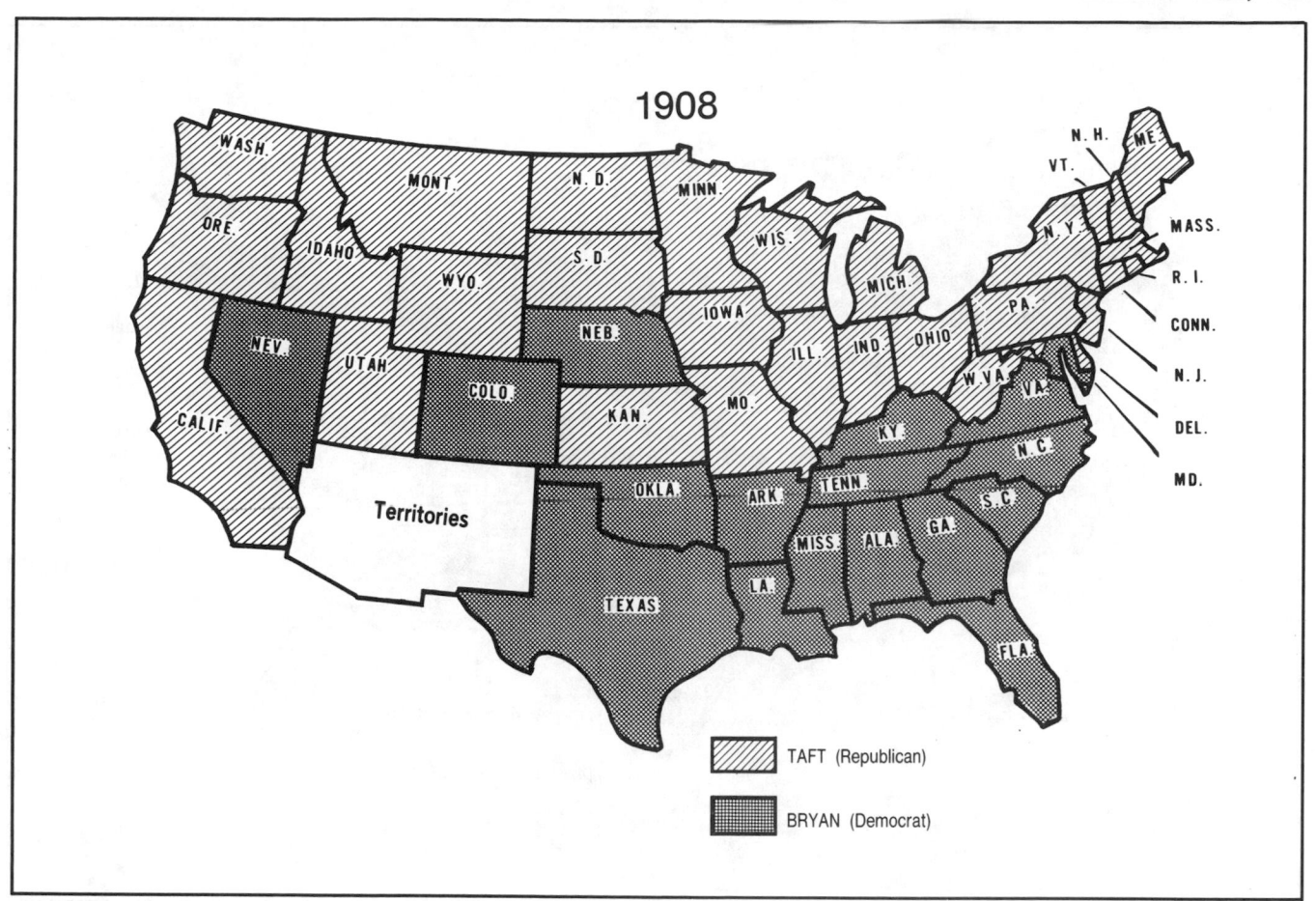

1908

TAFT (Republican)

BRYAN (Democrat)

States	Electoral Votes	Taft	Bryan	States	Electoral Votes	Taft	Bryan
Alabama	(11)	-	11	Nebraska	(8)	-	8
Arkansas	(9)	-	9	Nevada	(3)	-	3
California	(10)	10	-	New Hampshire	(4)	4	-
Colorado	(5)	-	5	New Jersey	(12)	12	-
Connecticut	(7)	7	-	New York	(39)	39	-
Delaware	(3)	3	-	North Carolina	(12)	-	12
Florida	(5)	-	5	North Dakota	(4)	4	-
Georgia	(13)	-	13	Ohio	(23)	23	-
Idaho	(3)	3	-	Oklahoma	(7)	-	7
Illinois	(27)	27	-	Oregon	(4)	4	-
Indiana	(15)	15	-	Pennsylvania	(34)	34	-
Iowa	(13)	13	-	Rhode Island	(4)	4	-
Kansas	(10)	10	-	South Carolina	(9)	-	9
Kentucky	(13)	-	13	South Dakota	(4)	4	-
Louisiana	(9)	-	9	Tennessee	(12)	-	12
Maine	(6)	6	-	Texas	(18)	-	18
Maryland [1]	(8)	2	6	Utah	(3)	3	-
Massachusetts	(16)	16	-	Vermont	(4)	4	-
Michigan	(14)	14	-	Virginia	(12)	-	12
Minnesota	(11)	11	-	Washington	(5)	5	-
Mississippi	(10)	-	10	West Virginia	(7)	7	-
Missouri	(18)	18	-	Wisconsin	(13)	13	-
Montana	(3)	3	-	Wyoming	(3)	3	-
				Totals	**(483)**	**321**	**162**

1. *For explanation of split electoral votes, see p. 14.*

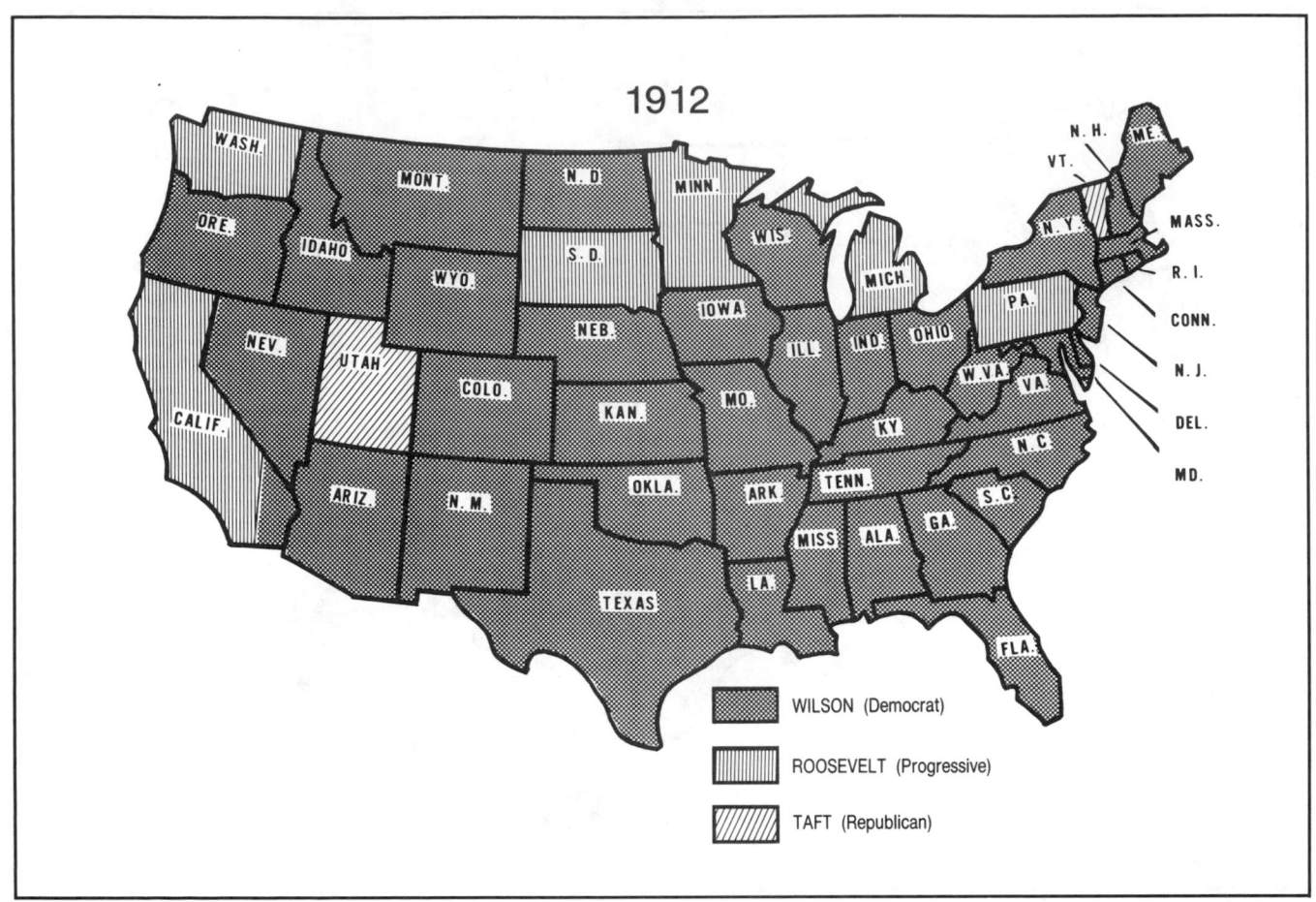

1912

WILSON (Democrat)

ROOSEVELT (Progressive)

TAFT (Republican)

States	Electoral Votes	Wilson	Roosevelt	Taft	States	Electoral Votes	Wilson	Roosevelt	Taft
Alabama	(12)	12	-	-	**Nebraska**	(8)	8	-	-
Arizona	(3)	3	-	-	**Nevada**	(3)	3	-	-
Arkansas	(9)	9	-	-	**New Hampshire**	(4)	4	-	-
California [1]	(13)	2	11	-	**New Jersey**	(14)	14	-	-
Colorado	(6)	6	-	-	**New Mexico**	(3)	3	-	-
Connecticut	(7)	7	-	-	**New York**	(45)	45	-	-
Delaware	(3)	3	-	-	**North Carolina**	(12)	12	-	-
Florida	(6)	6	-	-	**North Dakota**	(5)	5	-	-
Georgia	(14)	14	-	-	**Ohio**	(24)	24	-	-
Idaho	(4)	4	-	-	**Oklahoma**	(10)	10	-	-
Illinois	(29)	29	-	-	**Oregon**	(5)	5	-	-
Indiana	(15)	15	-	-	**Pennsylvania**	(38)	-	38	-
Iowa	(13)	13	-	-	**Rhode Island**	(5)	5	-	-
Kansas	(10)	10	-	-	**South Carolina**	(9)	9	-	-
Kentucky	(13)	13	-	-	**South Dakota**	(5)	-	5	-
Louisiana	(10)	10	-	-	**Tennessee**	(12)	12	-	-
Maine	(6)	6	-	-	**Texas**	(20)	20	-	-
Maryland	(8)	8	-	-	**Utah**	(4)	-	-	4
Massachusetts	(18)	18	-	-	**Vermont**	(4)	-	-	4
Michigan	(15)	-	15	-	**Virginia**	(12)	12	-	-
Minnesota	(12)	-	12	-	**Washington**	(7)	-	7	-
Mississippi	(10)	10	-	-	**West Virginia**	(8)	8	-	-
Missouri	(18)	18	-	-	**Wisconsin**	(13)	13	-	-
Montana	(4)	4	-	-	**Wyoming**	(3)	3	-	-
					Totals	(531)	435	88	8

1. For explanation of split electoral votes, see p. 14.

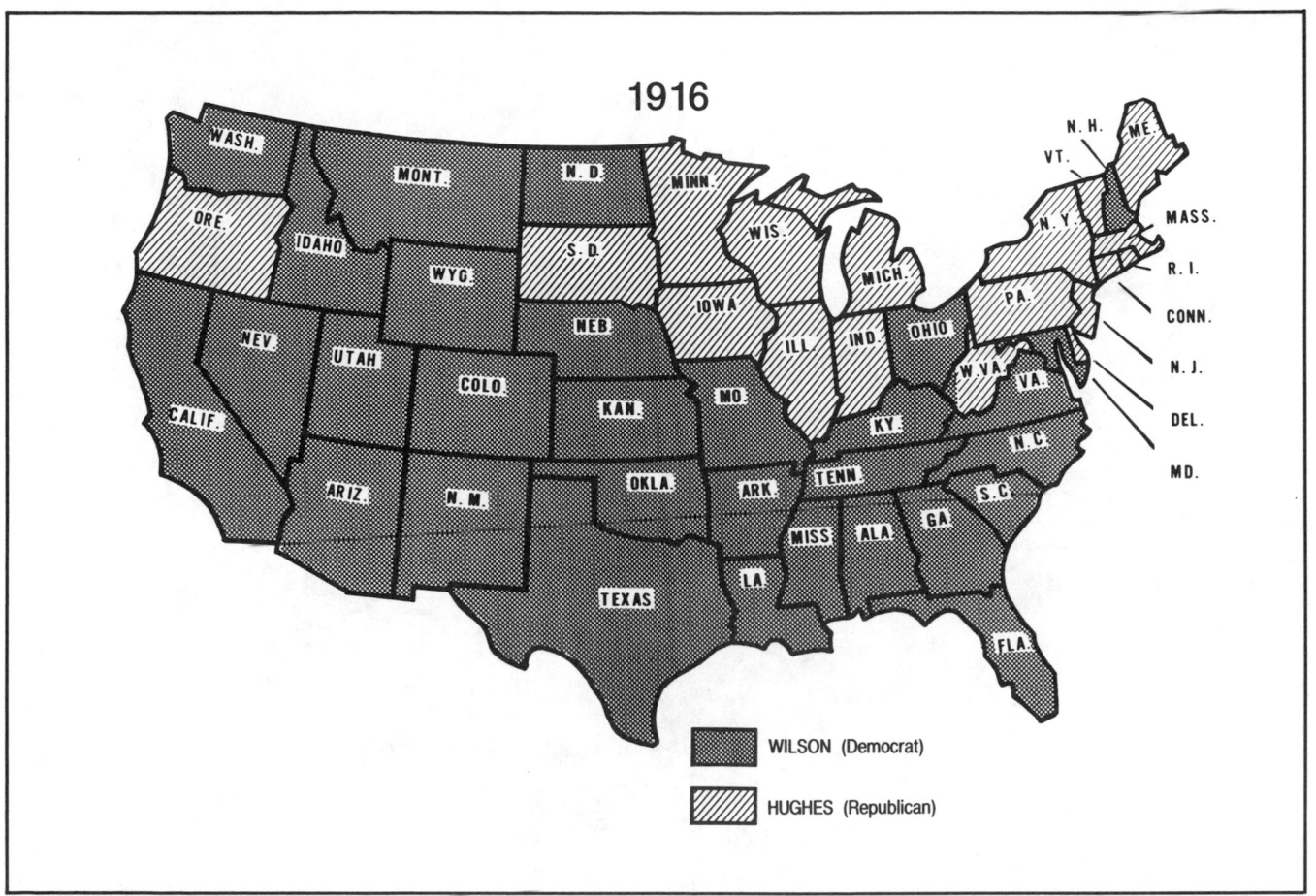

1916

WILSON (Democrat)

HUGHES (Republican)

States	Electoral Votes	Wilson	Hughes	States	Electoral Votes	Wilson	Hughes
Alabama	(12)	12	-	Nebraska	(8)	8	-
Arizona	(3)	3	-	Nevada	(3)	3	-
Arkansas	(9)	9	-	New Hampshire	(4)	4	-
California	(13)	13	-	New Jersey	(14)	-	14
Colorado	(6)	6	-	New Mexico	(3)	3	-
Connecticut	(7)	-	7	New York	(45)	-	45
Delaware	(3)	-	3	North Carolina	(12)	12	-
Florida	(6)	6	-	North Dakota	(5)	5	-
Georgia	(14)	14	-	Ohio	(24)	24	-
Idaho	(4)	4	-	Oklahoma	(10)	10	-
Illinois	(29)	-	29	Oregon	(5)	-	5
Indiana	(15)	-	15	Pennsylvania	(38)	-	38
Iowa	(13)	-	13	Rhode Island	(5)	-	5
Kansas	(10)	10	-	South Carolina	(9)	9	-
Kentucky	(13)	13	-	South Dakota	(5)	-	5
Louisiana	(10)	10	-	Tennessee	(12)	12	-
Maine	(6)	-	6	Texas	(20)	20	-
Maryland	(8)	8	-	Utah	(4)	4	-
Massachusetts	(18)	-	18	Vermont	(4)	-	4
Michigan	(15)	-	15	Virginia	(12)	12	-
Minnesota	(12)	-	12	Washington	(7)	7	-
Mississippi	(10)	10	-	West Virginia [1]	(8)	1	7
Missouri	(18)	18	-	Wisconsin	(13)	-	13
Montana	(4)	4	-	Wyoming	(3)	3	-
				Totals	**(531)**	**277**	**254**

1. *For explanation of split electoral votes, see p. 14.*

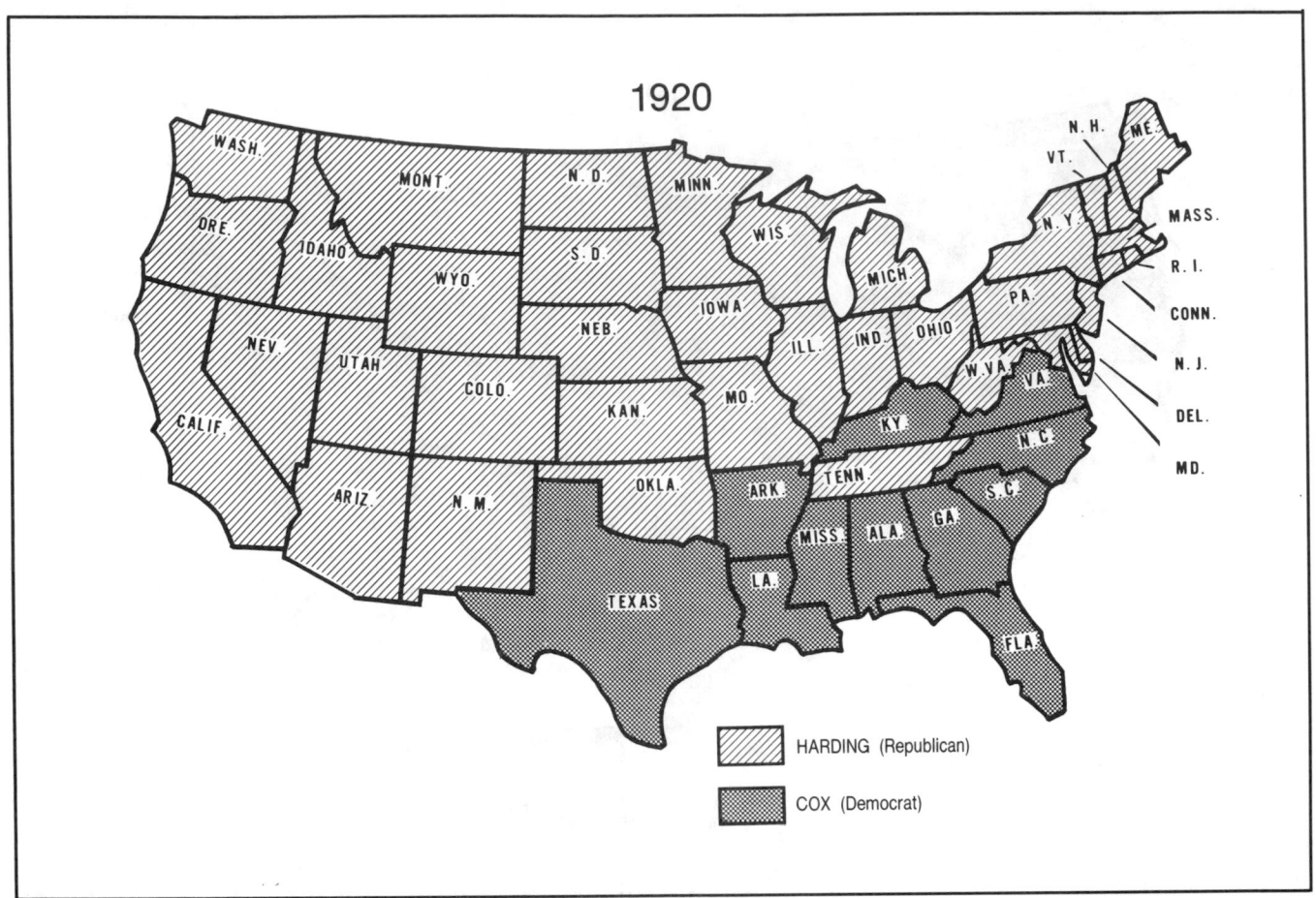

1920

HARDING (Republican)

COX (Democrat)

States	Electoral Votes	Harding	Cox	States	Electoral Votes	Harding	Cox
Alabama	(12)	-	12	Nebraska	(8)	8	-
Arizona	(3)	3	-	Nevada	(3)	3	-
Arkansas	(9)	-	9	New Hampshire	(4)	4	-
California	(13)	13	-	New Jersey	(14)	14	-
Colorado	(6)	6	-	New Mexico	(3)	3	-
Connecticut	(7)	7	-	New York	(45)	45	-
Delaware	(3)	3	-	North Carolina	(12)	-	12
Florida	(6)	-	6	North Dakota	(5)	5	-
Georgia	(14)	-	14	Ohio	(24)	24	-
Idaho	(4)	4	-	Oklahoma	(10)	10	-
Illinois	(29)	29	-	Oregon	(5)	5	-
Indiana	(15)	15	-	Pennsylvania	(38)	38	-
Iowa	(13)	13	-	Rhode Island	(5)	5	-
Kansas	(10)	10	-	South Carolina	(9)	-	9
Kentucky	(13)	-	13	South Dakota	(5)	5	-
Louisiana	(10)	-	10	Tennessee	(12)	12	-
Maine	(6)	6	-	Texas	(20)	-	20
Maryland	(8)	8	-	Utah	(4)	4	-
Massachusetts	(18)	18	-	Vermont	(4)	4	-
Michigan	(15)	15	-	Virginia	(12)	-	12
Minnesota	(12)	12	-	Washington	(7)	7	-
Mississippi	(10)	-	10	West Virginia	(8)	8	-
Missouri	(18)	18	-	Wisconsin	(13)	13	-
Montana	(4)	4	-	Wyoming	(3)	3	-
				Totals	**(531)**	**404**	**127**

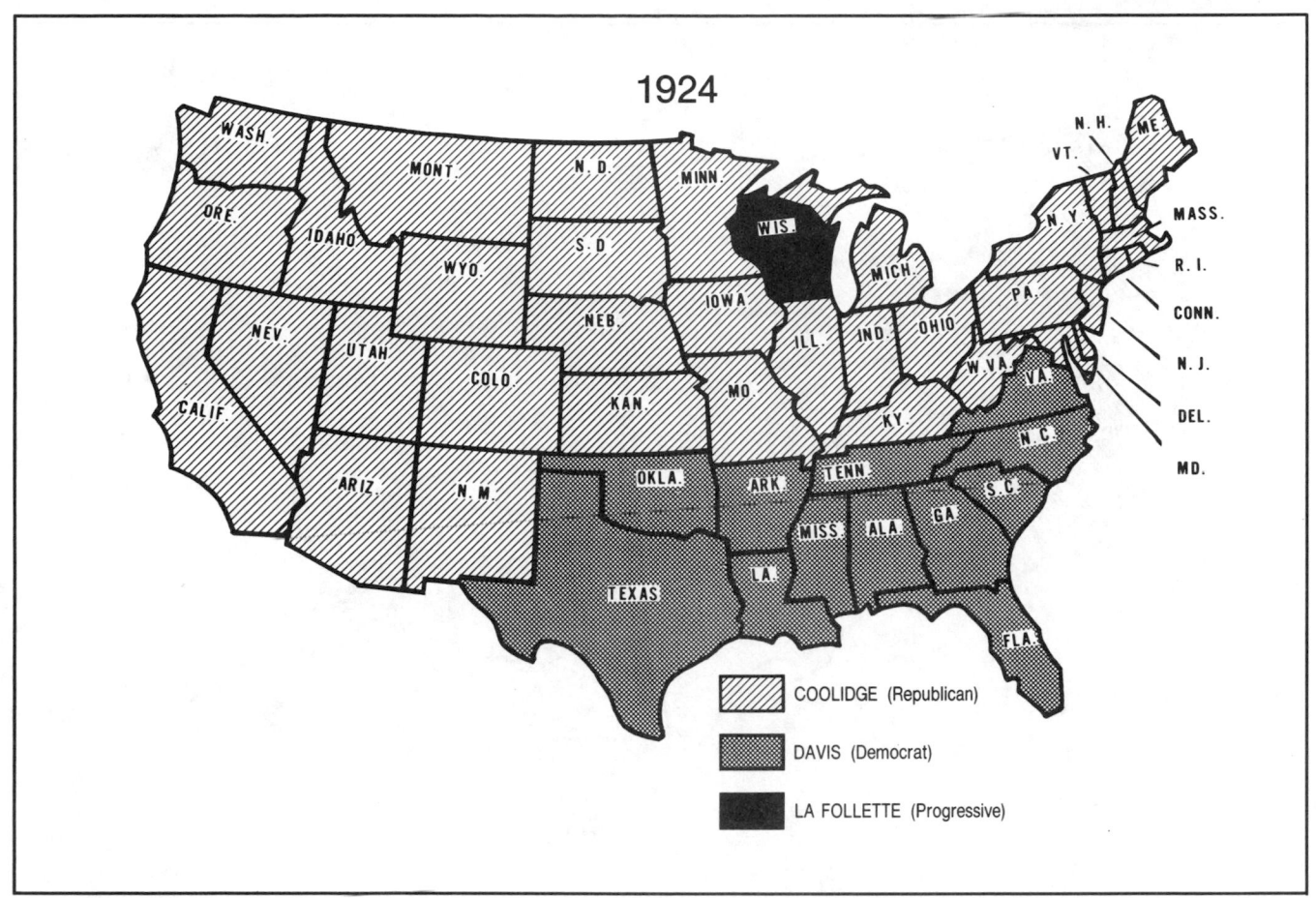

1924

COOLIDGE (Republican)

DAVIS (Democrat)

LA FOLLETTE (Progressive)

States	Electoral Votes	Coolidge	Davis	La Follette	States	Electoral Votes	Coolidge	Davis	La Follette
Alabama	(12)	-	12	-	Nebraska	(8)	8	-	-
Arizona	(3)	3	-	-	Nevada	(3)	3	-	-
Arkansas	(9)	-	9	-	New Hampshire	(4)	4	-	-
California	(13)	13	-	-	New Jersey	(14)	14	-	-
Colorado	(6)	6	-	-	New Mexico	(3)	3	-	-
Connecticut	(7)	7	-	-	New York	(45)	45	-	-
Delaware	(3)	3	-	-	North Carolina	(12)	-	12	-
Florida	(6)	-	6	-	North Dakota	(5)	5	-	-
Georgia	(14)	-	14	-	Ohio	(24)	24	-	-
Idaho	(4)	4	-	-	Oklahoma	(10)	-	10	-
Illinois	(29)	29	-	-	Oregon	(5)	5	-	-
Indiana	(15)	15	-	-	Pennsylvania	(38)	38	-	-
Iowa	(13)	13	-	-	Rhode Island	(5)	5	-	-
Kansas	(10)	10	-	-	South Carolina	(9)	-	9	-
Kentucky	(13)	13	-	-	South Dakota	(5)	5	-	-
Louisiana	(10)	-	10	-	Tennessee	(12)	-	12	-
Maine	(6)	6	-	-	Texas	(20)	-	20	-
Maryland	(8)	8	-	-	Utah	(4)	4	-	-
Massachusetts	(18)	18	-	-	Vermont	(4)	4	-	-
Michigan	(15)	15	-	-	Virginia	(12)	-	12	-
Minnesota	(12)	12	-	-	Washington	(7)	7	-	-
Mississippi	(10)	-	10	-	West Virginia	(8)	8	-	-
Missouri	(18)	18	-	-	Wisconsin	(13)	-	-	13
Montana	(4)	4	-	-	Wyoming	(3)	3	-	-
					Totals	**(531)**	**382**	**136**	**13**

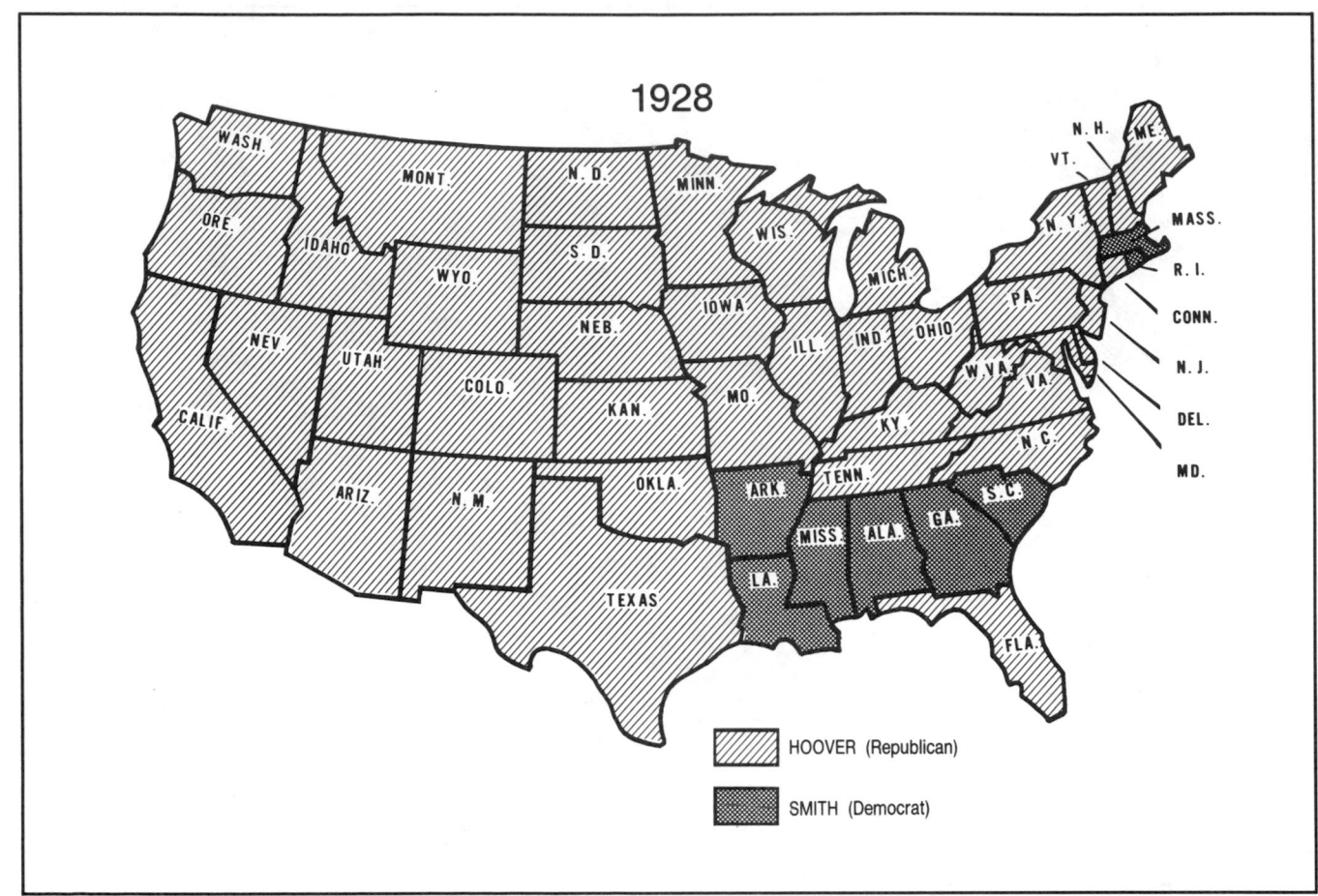

1928

| | | HOOVER (Republican) |
| | | SMITH (Democrat) |

States	Electoral Votes	Hoover	Smith	States	Electoral Votes	Hoover	Smith
Alabama	(12)	-	12	Nebraska	(8)	8	-
Arizona	(3)	3	-	Nevada	(3)	3	-
Arkansas	(9)	-	9	New Hampshire	(4)	4	-
California	(13)	13	-	New Jersey	(14)	14	-
Colorado	(6)	6	-	New Mexico	(3)	3	-
Connecticut	(7)	7	-	New York	(45)	45	-
Delaware	(3)	3	-	North Carolina	(12)	12	-
Florida	(6)	6	-	North Dakota	(5)	5	-
Georgia	(14)	-	14	Ohio	(24)	24	-
Idaho	(4)	4	-	Oklahoma	(10)	10	-
Illinois	(29)	29	-	Oregon	(5)	5	-
Indiana	(15)	15	-	Pennsylvania	(38)	38	-
Iowa	(13)	13	-	Rhode Island	(5)	-	5
Kansas	(10)	10	-	South Carolina	(9)	-	9
Kentucky	(13)	13	-	South Dakota	(5)	5	-
Louisiana	(10)	-	10	Tennessee	(12)	12	-
Maine	(6)	6	-	Texas	(20)	20	-
Maryland	(8)	8	-	Utah	(4)	4	-
Massachusetts	(18)	-	18	Vermont	(4)	4	-
Michigan	(15)	15	-	Virginia	(12)	12	-
Minnesota	(12)	12	-	Washington	(7)	7	-
Mississippi	(10)	-	10	West Virginia	(8)	8	-
Missouri	(18)	18	-	Wisconsin	(13)	13	-
Montana	(4)	4	-	Wyoming	(3)	3	-
				Totals	**(531)**	**444**	**87**

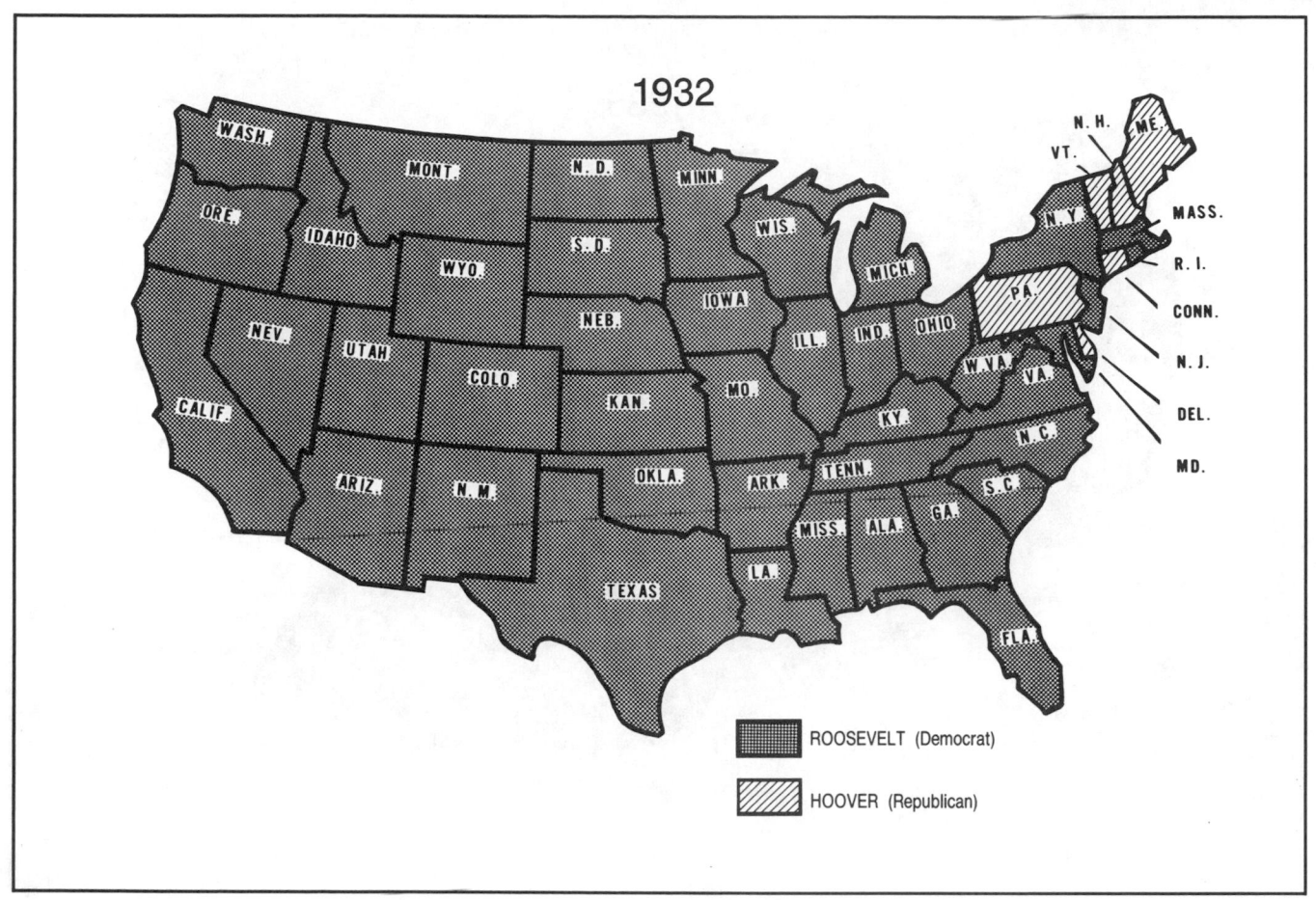

1932

ROOSEVELT (Democrat)

HOOVER (Republican)

States	Electoral Votes	Roosevelt	Hoover	States	Electoral Votes	Roosevelt	Hoover
Alabama	(11)	11	-	Nebraska	(7)	7	-
Arizona	(3)	3	-	Nevada	(3)	3	-
Arkansas	(9)	9	-	New Hampshire	(4)	-	4
California	(22)	22	-	New Jersey	(16)	16	-
Colorado	(6)	6	-	New Mexico	(3)	3	-
Connecticut	(8)	-	8	New York	(47)	47	-
Delaware	(3)	-	3	North Carolina	(13)	13	-
Florida	(7)	7	-	North Dakota	(4)	4	-
Georgia	(12)	12	-	Ohio	(26)	26	-
Idaho	(4)	4	-	Oklahoma	(11)	11	-
Illinois	(29)	29	-	Oregon	(5)	5	-
Indiana	(14)	14	-	Pennsylvania	(36)	-	36
Iowa	(11)	11	-	Rhode Island	(4)	4	-
Kansas	(9)	9	-	South Carolina	(8)	8	-
Kentucky	(11)	11	-	South Dakota	(4)	4	-
Louisiana	(10)	10	-	Tennessee	(11)	11	-
Maine	(5)	-	5	Texas	(23)	23	-
Maryland	(8)	8	-	Utah	(4)	4	-
Massachusetts	(17)	17	-	Vermont	(3)	-	3
Michigan	(19)	19	-	Virginia	(11)	11	-
Minnesota	(11)	11	-	Washington	(8)	8	-
Mississippi	(9)	9	-	West Virginia	(8)	8	-
Missouri	(15)	15	-	Wisconsin	(12)	12	-
Montana	(4)	4	-	Wyoming	(3)	3	-
				Totals	**(531)**	**472**	**59**

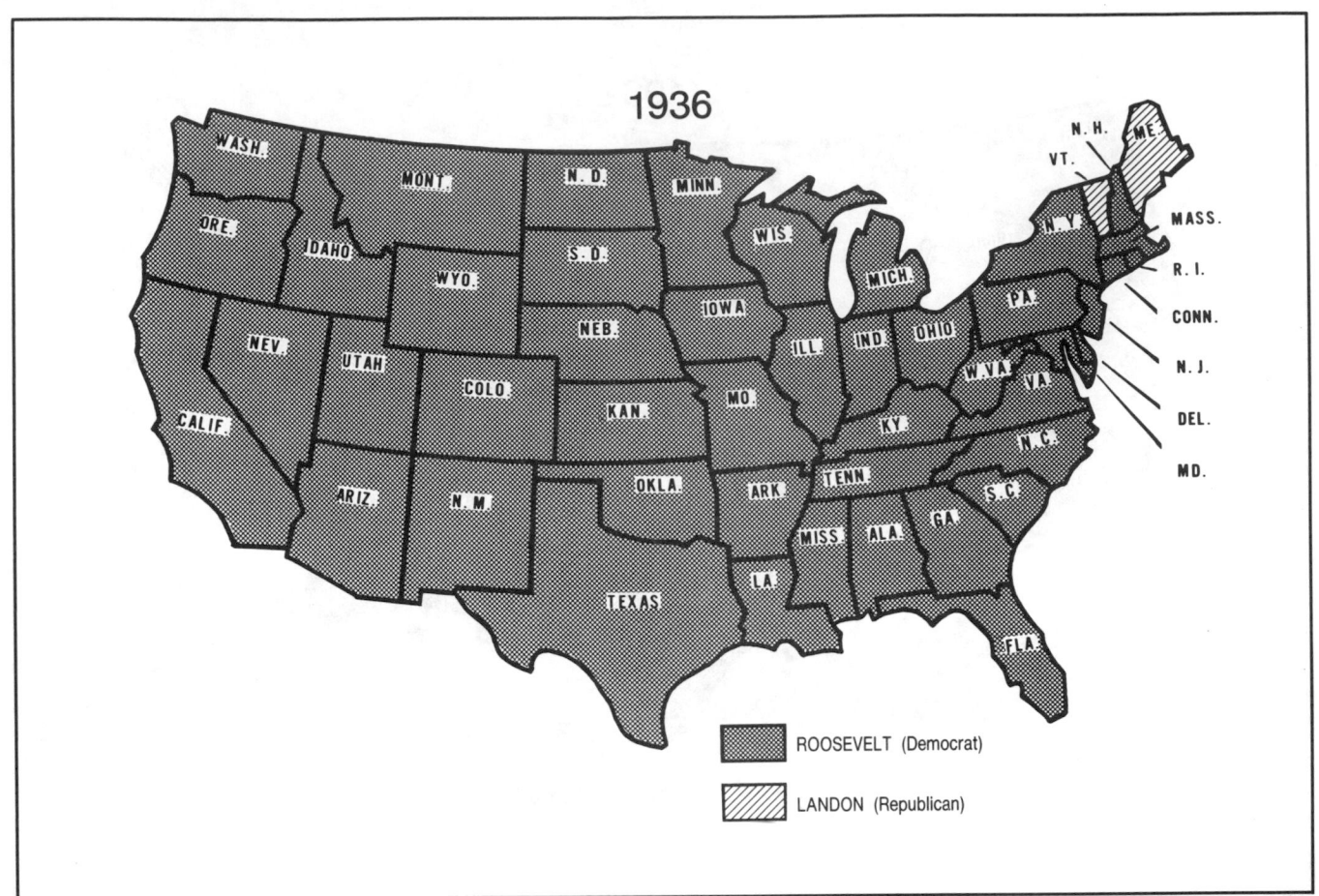

1936

ROOSEVELT (Democrat)

LANDON (Republican)

States	Electoral Votes	Roosevelt	Landon	States	Electoral Votes	Roosevelt	Landon
Alabama	(11)	11	-	Nebraska	(7)	7	-
Arizona	(3)	3	-	Nevada	(3)	3	-
Arkansas	(9)	9	-	New Hampshire	(4)	4	-
California	(22)	22	-	New Jersey	(16)	16	-
Colorado	(6)	6	-	New Mexico	(3)	3	-
Connecticut	(8)	8	-	New York	(47)	47	-
Delaware	(3)	3	-	North Carolina	(13)	13	-
Florida	(7)	7	-	North Dakota	(4)	4	-
Georgia	(12)	12	-	Ohio	(26)	26	-
Idaho	(4)	4	-	Oklahoma	(11)	11	-
Illinois	(29)	29	-	Oregon	(5)	5	-
Indiana	(14)	14	-	Pennsylvania	(36)	36	-
Iowa	(11)	11	-	Rhode Island	(4)	4	-
Kansas	(9)	9	-	South Carolina	(8)	8	-
Kentucky	(11)	11	-	South Dakota	(4)	4	-
Louisiana	(10)	10	-	Tennessee	(11)	11	-
Maine	(5)	-	5	Texas	(23)	23	-
Maryland	(8)	8	-	Utah	(4)	4	-
Massachusetts	(17)	17	-	Vermont	(3)	-	3
Michigan	(19)	19	-	Virginia	(11)	11	-
Minnesota	(11)	11	-	Washington	(8)	8	-
Mississippi	(9)	9	-	West Virginia	(8)	8	-
Missouri	(15)	15	-	Wisconsin	(12)	12	-
Montana	(4)	4	-	Wyoming	(3)	3	-
				Totals	(531)	523	8

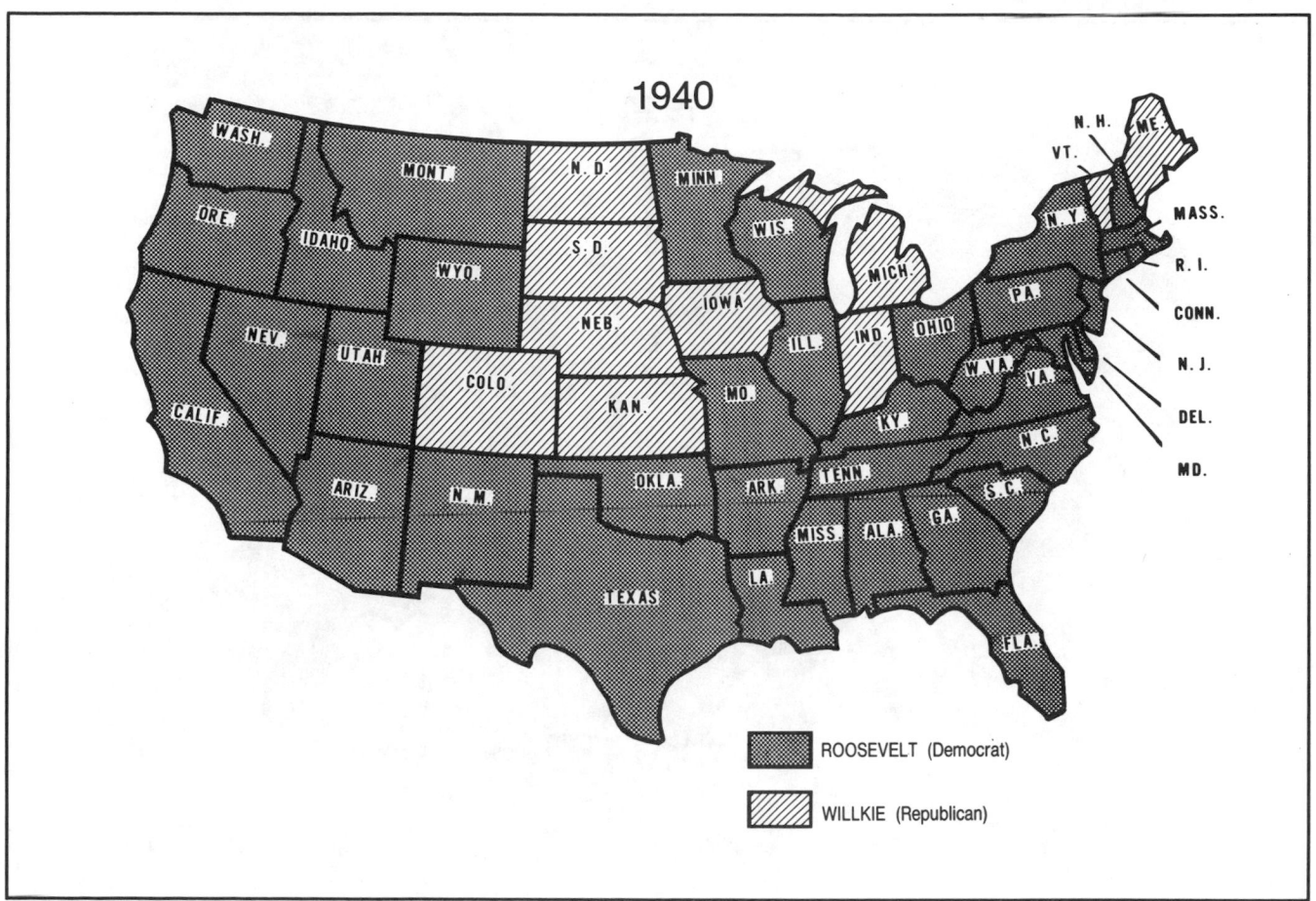

1940

ROOSEVELT (Democrat)

WILLKIE (Republican)

States	Electoral Votes	Roosevelt	Willkie	States	Electoral Votes	Roosevelt	Willkie
Alabama	(11)	11	-	Nebraska	(7)	-	7
Arizona	(3)	3	-	Nevada	(3)	3	-
Arkansas	(9)	9	-	New Hampshire	(4)	4	-
California	(22)	22	-	New Jersey	(16)	16	-
Colorado	(6)	-	6	New Mexico	(3)	3	-
Connecticut	(8)	8	-	New York	(47)	47	-
Delaware	(3)	3	-	North Carolina	(13)	13	-
Florida	(7)	7	-	North Dakota	(4)	-	4
Georgia	(12)	12	-	Ohio	(26)	26	-
Idaho	(4)	4	-	Oklahoma	(11)	11	-
Illinois	(29)	29	-	Oregon	(5)	5	-
Indiana	(14)	-	14	Pennsylvania	(36)	36	-
Iowa	(11)	-	11	Rhode Island	(4)	4	-
Kansas	(9)	-	9	South Carolina	(8)	8	-
Kentucky	(11)	11	-	South Dakota	(4)	-	4
Louisiana	(10)	10	-	Tennessee	(11)	11	-
Maine	(5)	-	5	Texas	(23)	23	-
Maryland	(8)	8	-	Utah	(4)	4	-
Massachusetts	(17)	17	-	Vermont	(3)	-	3
Michigan	(19)	-	19	Virginia	(11)	11	-
Minnesota	(11)	11	-	Washington	(8)	8	-
Mississippi	(9)	9	-	West Virginia	(8)	8	-
Missouri	(15)	15	-	Wisconsin	(12)	12	-
Montana	(4)	4	-	Wyoming	(3)	3	-
				Totals	**(531)**	**449**	**82**

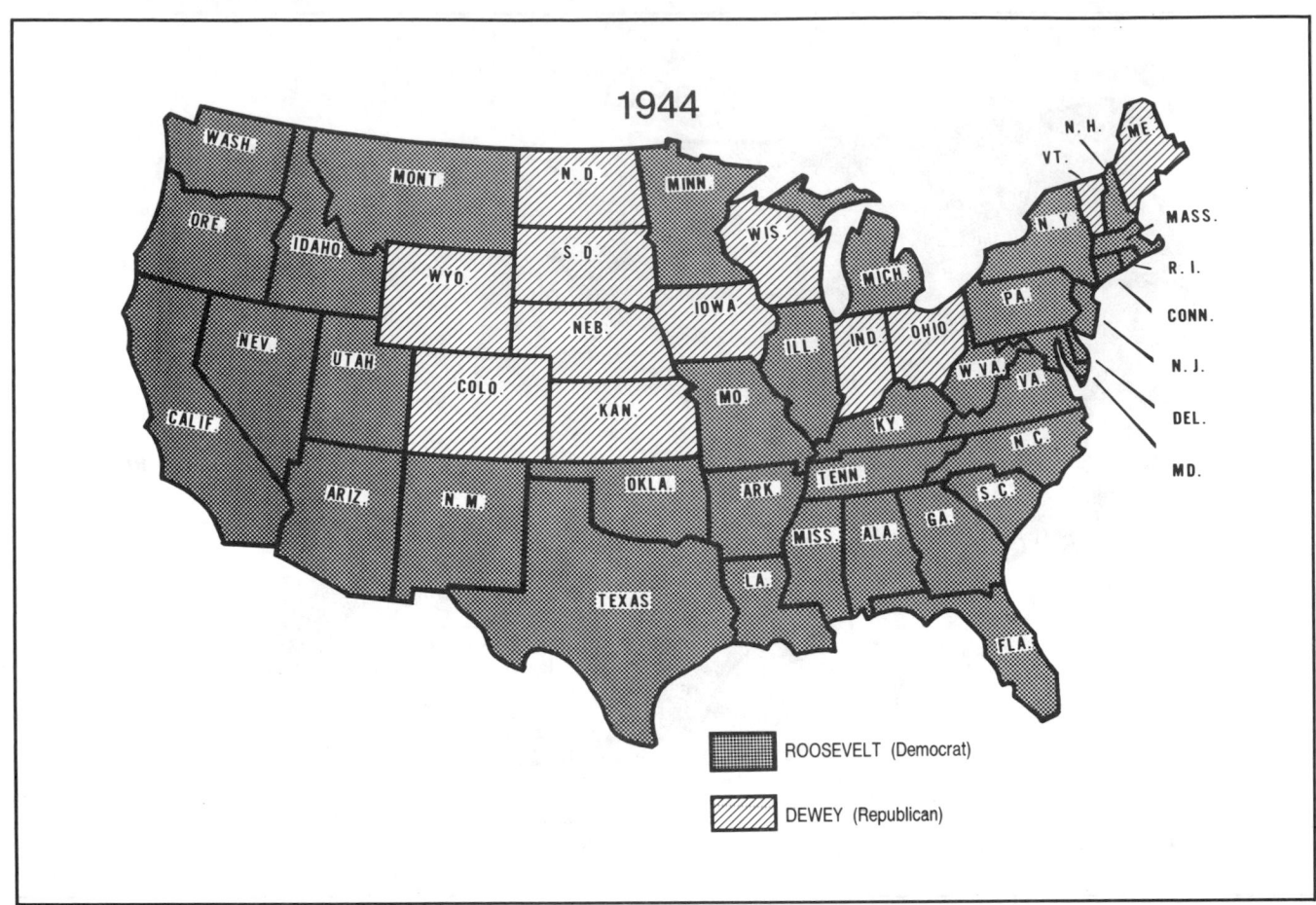

1944

ROOSEVELT (Democrat)

DEWEY (Republican)

States	Electoral Votes	Roosevelt	Dewey	States	Electoral Votes	Roosevelt	Dewey
Alabama	(11)	11	-	Nebraska	(6)	-	6
Arizona	(4)	4	-	Nevada	(3)	3	-
Arkansas	(9)	9	-	New Hampshire	(4)	4	-
California	(25)	25	-	New Jersey	(16)	16	-
Colorado	(6)	-	6	New Mexico	(4)	4	-
Connecticut	(8)	8	-	New York	(47)	47	-
Delaware	(3)	3	-	North Carolina	(14)	14	-
Florida	(8)	8	-	North Dakota	(4)	-	4
Georgia	(12)	12	-	Ohio	(25)	-	25
Idaho	(4)	4	-	Oklahoma	(10)	10	-
Illinois	(28)	28	-	Oregon	(6)	6	-
Indiana	(13)	-	13	Pennsylvania	(35)	35	-
Iowa	(10)	-	10	Rhode Island	(4)	4	-
Kansas	(8)	-	8	South Carolina	(8)	8	-
Kentucky	(11)	11	-	South Dakota	(4)	-	4
Louisiana	(10)	10	-	Tennessee	(12)	12	-
Maine	(5)	-	5	Texas	(23)	23	-
Maryland	(8)	8	-	Utah	(4)	4	-
Massachusetts	(16)	16	-	Vermont	(3)	-	3
Michigan	(19)	19	-	Virginia	(11)	11	-
Minnesota	(11)	11	-	Washington	(8)	8	-
Mississippi	(9)	9	-	West Virginia	(8)	8	-
Missouri	(15)	15	-	Wisconsin	(12)	-	12
Montana	(4)	4	-	Wyoming	(3)	-	3
				Totals	**(531)**	**432**	**99**

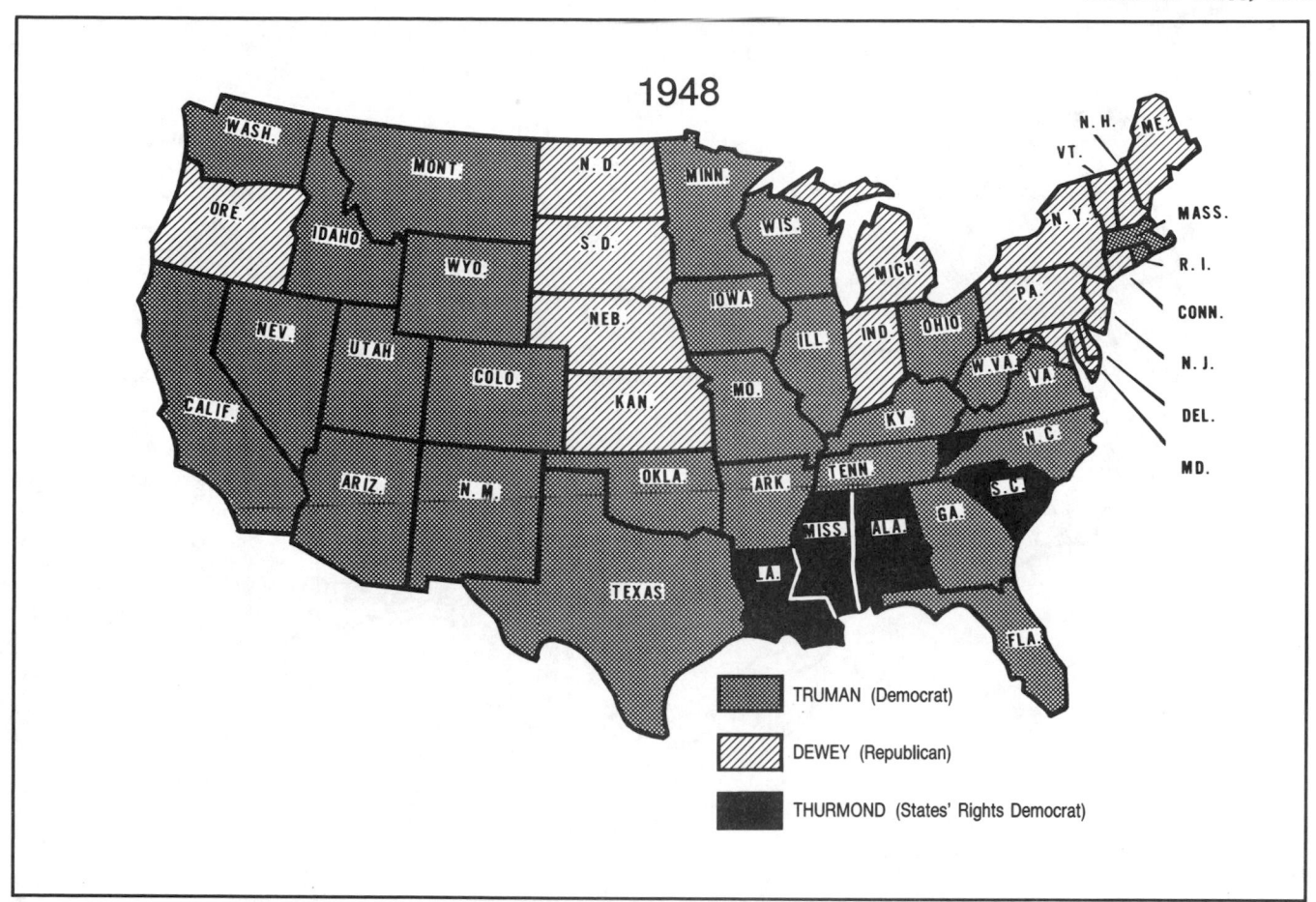

1948

TRUMAN (Democrat)

DEWEY (Republican)

THURMOND (States' Rights Democrat)

States	Electoral Votes	Truman	Dewey	Thurmond	States	Electoral Votes	Truman	Dewey	Thurmond
Alabama	(11)	-	-	11	**Nebraska**	(6)	-	6	-
Arizona	(4)	4	-	-	**Nevada**	(3)	3	-	-
Arkansas	(9)	9	-	-	**New Hampshire**	(4)	-	4	-
California	(25)	25	-	-	**New Jersey**	(16)	-	16	-
Colorado	(6)	6	-	-	**New Mexico**	(4)	4	-	-
Connecticut	(8)	-	8	-	**New York**	(47)	-	47	-
Delaware	(3)	-	3	-	**North Carolina**	(14)	14	-	-
Florida	(8)	8	-	-	**North Dakota**	(4)	-	4	-
Georgia	(12)	12	-	-	**Ohio**	(25)	25	-	-
Idaho	(4)	4	-	-	**Oklahoma**	(10)	10	-	-
Illinois	(28)	28	-	-	**Oregon**	(6)	-	6	-
Indiana	(13)	-	13	-	**Pennsylvania**	(35)	-	35	-
Iowa	(10)	10	-	-	**Rhode Island**	(4)	4	-	-
Kansas	(8)	-	8	-	**South Carolina**	(8)	-	-	8
Kentucky	(11)	11	-	-	**South Dakota**	(4)	-	4	-
Louisiana	(10)	-	-	10	**Tennessee** [1]	(12)	11	-	1
Maine	(5)	-	5	-	**Texas**	(23)	23	-	-
Maryland	(8)	-	8	-	**Utah**	(4)	4	-	-
Massachusetts	(16)	16	-	-	**Vermont**	(3)	-	3	-
Michigan	(19)	-	19	-	**Virginia**	(11)	11	-	-
Minnesota	(11)	11	-	-	**Washington**	(8)	8	-	-
Mississippi	(9)	-	-	9	**West Virginia**	(8)	8	-	-
Missouri	(15)	15	-	-	**Wisconsin**	(12)	12	-	-
Montana	(4)	4	-	-	**Wyoming**	(3)	3	-	-
					Totals	**(531)**	**303**	**189**	**39**

1. For explanation of split electoral votes, see p. 14.

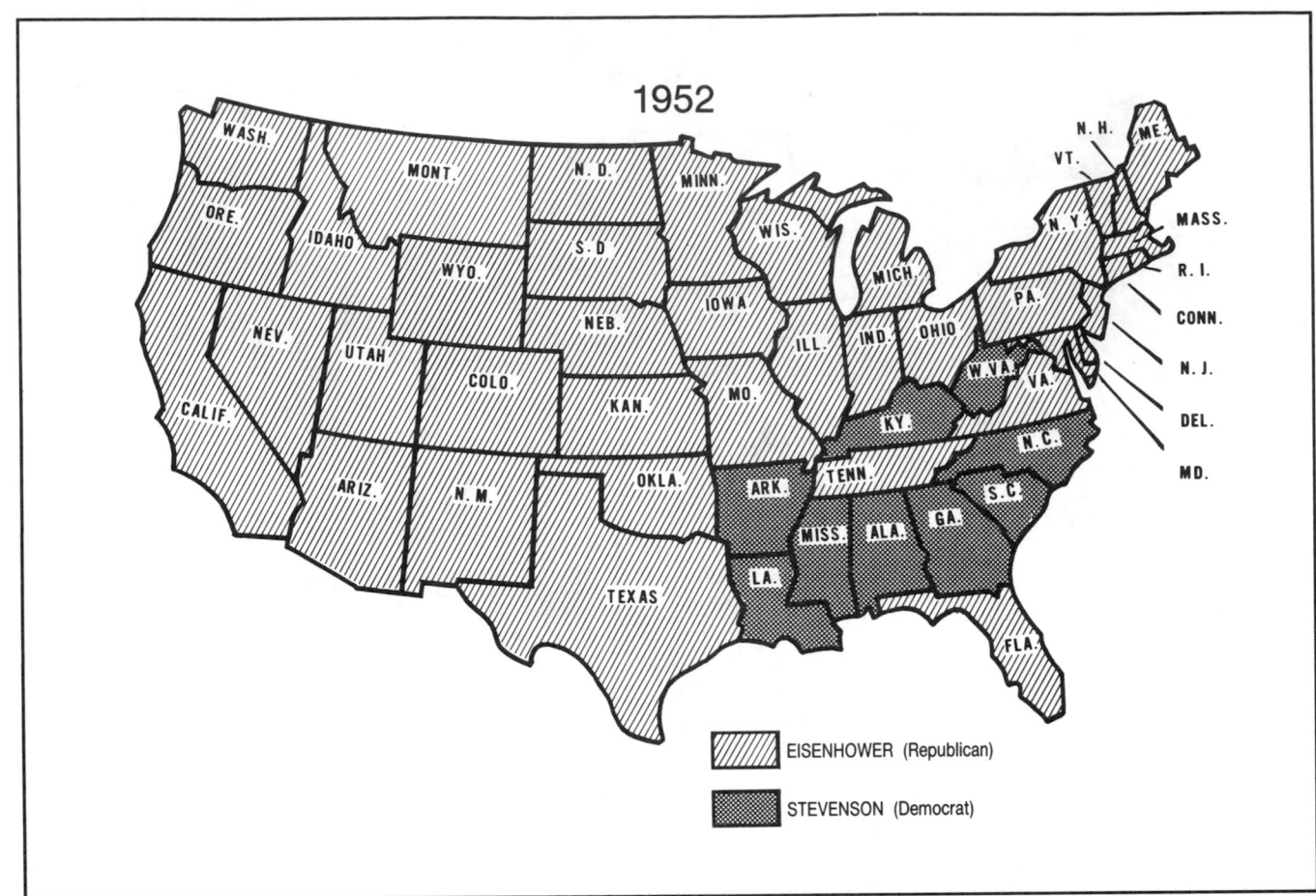

1952

EISENHOWER (Republican)

STEVENSON (Democrat)

States	Electoral Votes	Eisenhower	Stevenson	States	Electoral Votes	Eisenhower	Stevenson
Alabama	(11)	-	11	Nebraska	(6)	6	-
Arizona	(4)	4	-	Nevada	(3)	3	-
Arkansas	(8)	-	8	New Hampshire	(4)	4	-
California	(32)	32	-	New Jersey	(16)	16	-
Colorado	(6)	6	-	New Mexico	(4)	4	-
Connecticut	(8)	8	-	New York	(45)	45	-
Delaware	(3)	3	-	North Carolina	(14)	-	14
Florida	(10)	10	-	North Dakota	(4)	4	-
Georgia	(12)	-	12	Ohio	(25)	25	-
Idaho	(4)	4	-	Oklahoma	(8)	8	-
Illinois	(27)	27	-	Oregon	(6)	6	-
Indiana	(13)	13	-	Pennsylvania	(32)	32	-
Iowa	(10)	10	-	Rhode Island	(4)	4	-
Kansas	(8)	8	-	South Carolina	(8)	-	8
Kentucky	(10)	-	10	South Dakota	(4)	4	-
Louisiana	(10)	-	10	Tennessee	(11)	11	-
Maine	(5)	5	-	Texas	(24)	24	-
Maryland	(9)	9	-	Utah	(4)	4	-
Massachusetts	(16)	16	-	Vermont	(3)	3	-
Michigan	(20)	20		Virginia	(12)	12	-
Minnesota	(11)	11	-	Washington	(9)	9	-
Mississippi	(8)	-	8	West Virginia	(8)	-	8
Missouri	(13)	13	-	Wisconsin	(12)	12	-
Montana	(4)	4	-	Wyoming	(3)	3	-
				Totals	(531)	442	89

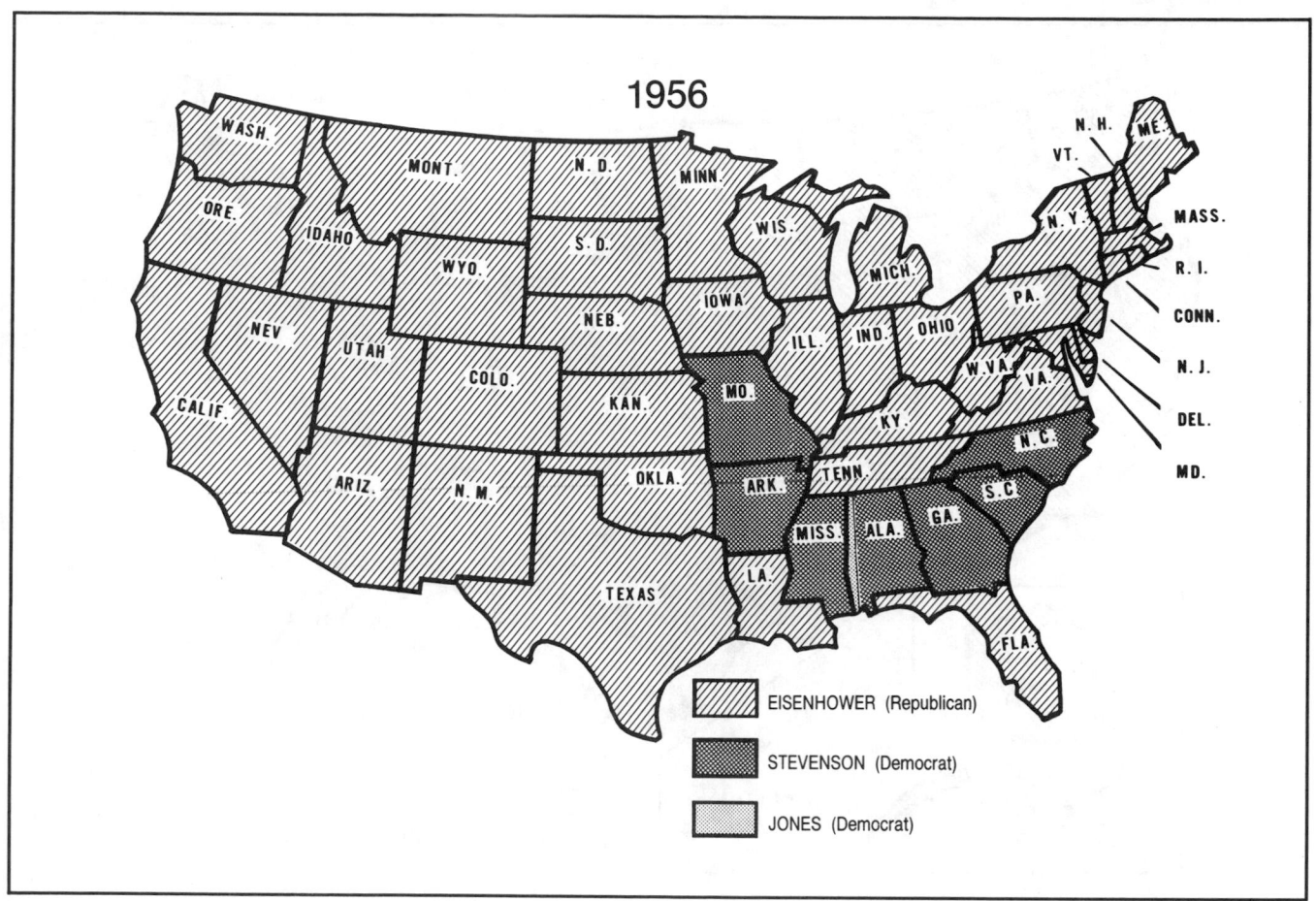

1956

EISENHOWER (Republican)

STEVENSON (Democrat)

JONES (Democrat)

States	Electoral Votes	Eisenhower	Stevenson	Jones	States	Electoral Votes	Eisenhower	Stevenson	Jones
Alabama [1]	(11)	-	10	1	Nebraska	(6)	6	-	-
Arizona	(4)	4	-	-	Nevada	(3)	3	-	-
Arkansas	(8)	-	8	-	New Hampshire	(4)	4	-	-
California	(32)	32	-	-	New Jersey	(16)	16	-	-
Colorado	(6)	6	-	-	New Mexico	(4)	4	-	-
Connecticut	(8)	8	-	-	New York	(45)	45	-	-
Delaware	(3)	3	-	-	North Carolina	(14)	-	14	-
Florida	(10)	10	-	-	North Dakota	(4)	4	-	-
Georgia	(12)	-	12	-	Ohio	(25)	25	-	-
Idaho	(4)	4	-	-	Oklahoma	(8)	8	-	-
Illinois	(27)	27	-	-	Oregon	(6)	6	-	-
Indiana	(13)	13	-	-	Pennsylvania	(32)	32	-	-
Iowa	(10)	10	-	-	Rhode Island	(4)	4	-	-
Kansas	(8)	8	-	-	South Carolina	(8)	-	8	-
Kentucky	(10)	10	-	-	South Dakota	(4)	4	-	-
Louisiana	(10)	10	-	-	Tennessee	(11)	11	-	-
Maine	(5)	5	-	-	Texas	(24)	24	-	-
Maryland	(9)	9	-	-	Utah	(4)	4	-	-
Massachusetts	(16)	16	-	-	Vermont	(3)	3	-	-
Michigan	(20)	20	-	-	Virginia	(12)	12	-	-
Minnesota	(11)	11	-	-	Washington	(9)	9	-	-
Mississippi	(8)	-	8	-	West Virginia	(8)	8	-	-
Missouri	(13)	-	13	-	Wisconsin	(12)	12	-	-
Montana	(4)	4	-	-	Wyoming	(3)	3	-	-
					Totals	**(531)**	**457**	**73**	**1**

1. For explanation of split electoral votes, see p. 14.

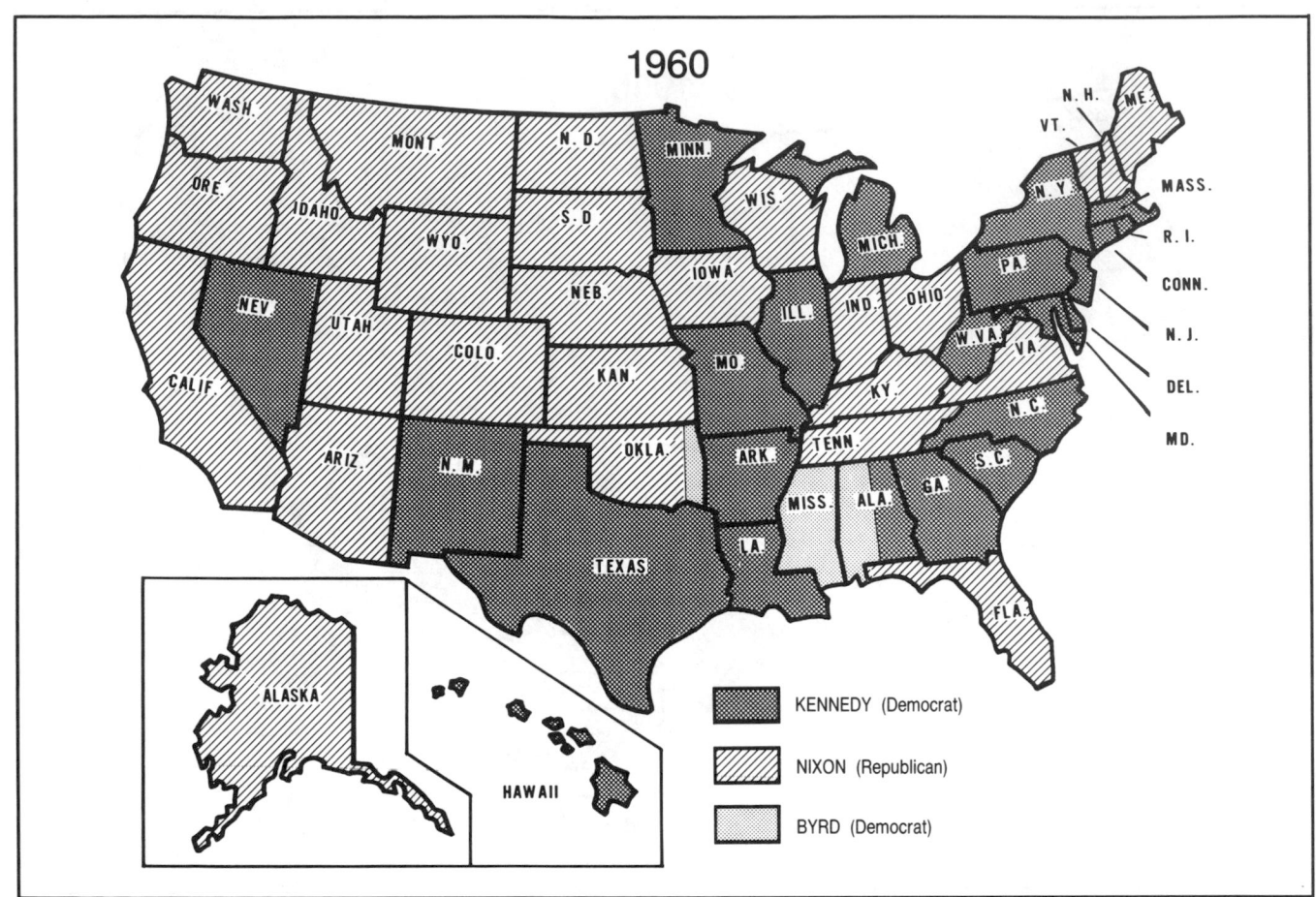

1960

KENNEDY (Democrat)

NIXON (Republican)

BYRD (Democrat)

States	Electoral Votes	Kennedy	Nixon	Byrd	States	Electoral Votes	Kennedy	Nixon	Byrd
Alabama [1]	(11)	5	-	6	Montana	(4)	-	4	-
Alaska	(3)	-	3	-	Nebraska	(6)	-	6	-
Arizona	(4)	-	4	-	Nevada	(3)	3	-	-
Arkansas	(8)	8	-	-	New Hampshire	(4)	-	4	-
California	(32)	-	32	-	New Jersey	(16)	16	-	-
Colorado	(6)	-	6	-	New Mexico	(4)	4	-	-
Connecticut	(8)	8	-	-	New York	(45)	45	-	-
Delaware	(3)	3	-	-	North Carolina	(14)	14	-	-
Florida	(10)	-	10	-	North Dakota	(4)	-	4	-
Georgia	(12)	12	-	-	Ohio	(25)	-	25	-
Hawaii	(3)	3	-	-	Oklahoma [2]	(8)	-	7	1
Idaho	(4)	-	4	-	Oregon	(6)	-	6	-
Illinois	(27)	27	-	-	Pennsylvania	(32)	32	-	-
Indiana	(13)	-	13	-	Rhode Island	(4)	4	-	-
Iowa	(10)	-	10	-	South Carolina	(8)	8	-	-
Kansas	(8)	-	8	-	South Dakota	(4)	-	4	-
Kentucky	(10)	-	10	-	Tennessee	(11)	-	11	-
Louisiana	(10)	10	-	-	Texas	(24)	24	-	-
Maine	(5)	-	5	-	Utah	(4)	-	4	-
Maryland	(9)	9	-	-	Vermont	(3)	-	3	-
Massachusetts	(16)	16	-	-	Virginia	(12)	-	12	-
Michigan	(20)	20	-	-	Washington	(9)	-	9	-
Minnesota	(11)	11	-	-	West Virginia	(8)	8	-	-
Mississippi [1]	(8)	-	-	8	Wisconsin	(12)	-	12	-
Missouri	(13)	13	-	-	Wyoming	(3)	-	3	-
					Totals	**(537)**	**303**	**219**	**15**

1. *Six Alabama electors and all eight Mississippi electors, elected as "unpledged Democrats," cast their votes for Byrd.*
2. *One Republican elector voted for Byrd.*

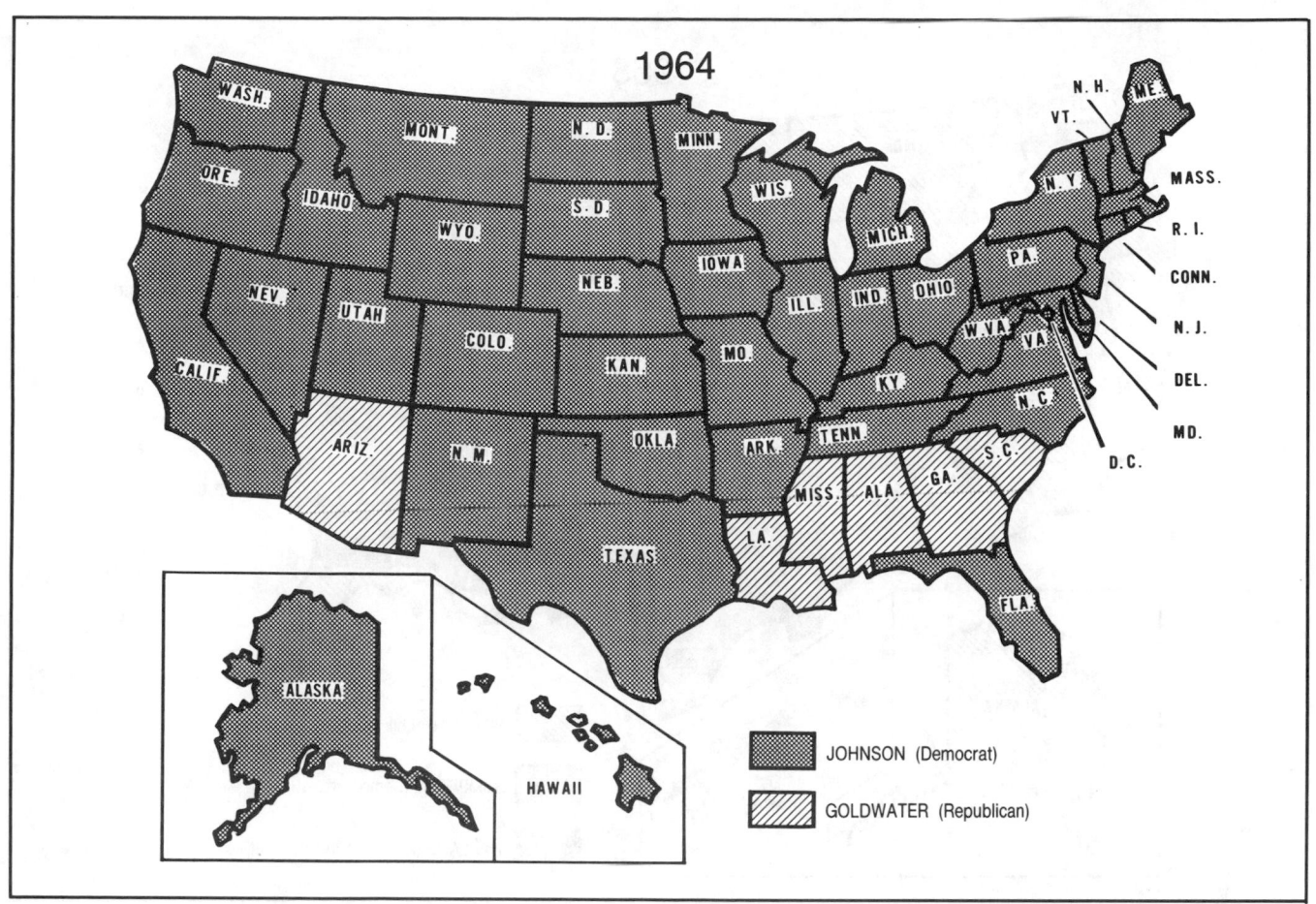

1964

JOHNSON (Democrat)

GOLDWATER (Republican)

States	Electoral Votes	Johnson	Goldwater	States	Electoral Votes	Johnson	Goldwater
Alabama	(10)	-	10	Montana	(4)	4	-
Alaska	(3)	3	-	Nebraska	(5)	5	-
Arizona	(5)	-	5	Nevada	(3)	3	-
Arkansas	(6)	6	-	New Hampshire	(4)	4	-
California	(40)	40	-	New Jersey	(17)	17	-
Colorado	(6)	6	-	New Mexico	(4)	4	-
Connecticut	(8)	8	-	New York	(43)	43	-
Delaware	(3)	3	-	North Carolina	(13)	13	-
District of Columbia	(3)	3	-	North Dakota	(4)	4	-
Florida	(14)	14	-	Ohio	(26)	26	-
Georgia	(12)	-	12	Oklahoma	(8)	8	-
Hawaii	(4)	4	-	Oregon	(6)	6	-
Idaho	(4)	4	-	Pennsylvania	(29)	29	-
Illinois	(26)	26	-	Rhode Island	(4)	4	-
Indiana	(13)	13	-	South Carolina	(8)	-	8
Iowa	(9)	9	-	South Dakota	(4)	4	-
Kansas	(7)	7	-	Tennessee	(11)	11	-
Kentucky	(9)	9	-	Texas	(25)	25	-
Louisiana	(10)	-	10	Utah	(4)	4	-
Maine	(4)	4	-	Vermont	(3)	3	-
Maryland	(10)	10	-	Virginia	(12)	12	-
Massachusetts	(14)	14	-	Washington	(9)	9	-
Michigan	(21)	21	-	West Virginia	(7)	7	-
Minnesota	(10)	10	-	Wisconsin	(12)	12	-
Mississippi	(7)	-	7	Wyoming	(3)	3	-
Missouri	(12)	12	-	**Totals**	**(538)**	**486**	**52**

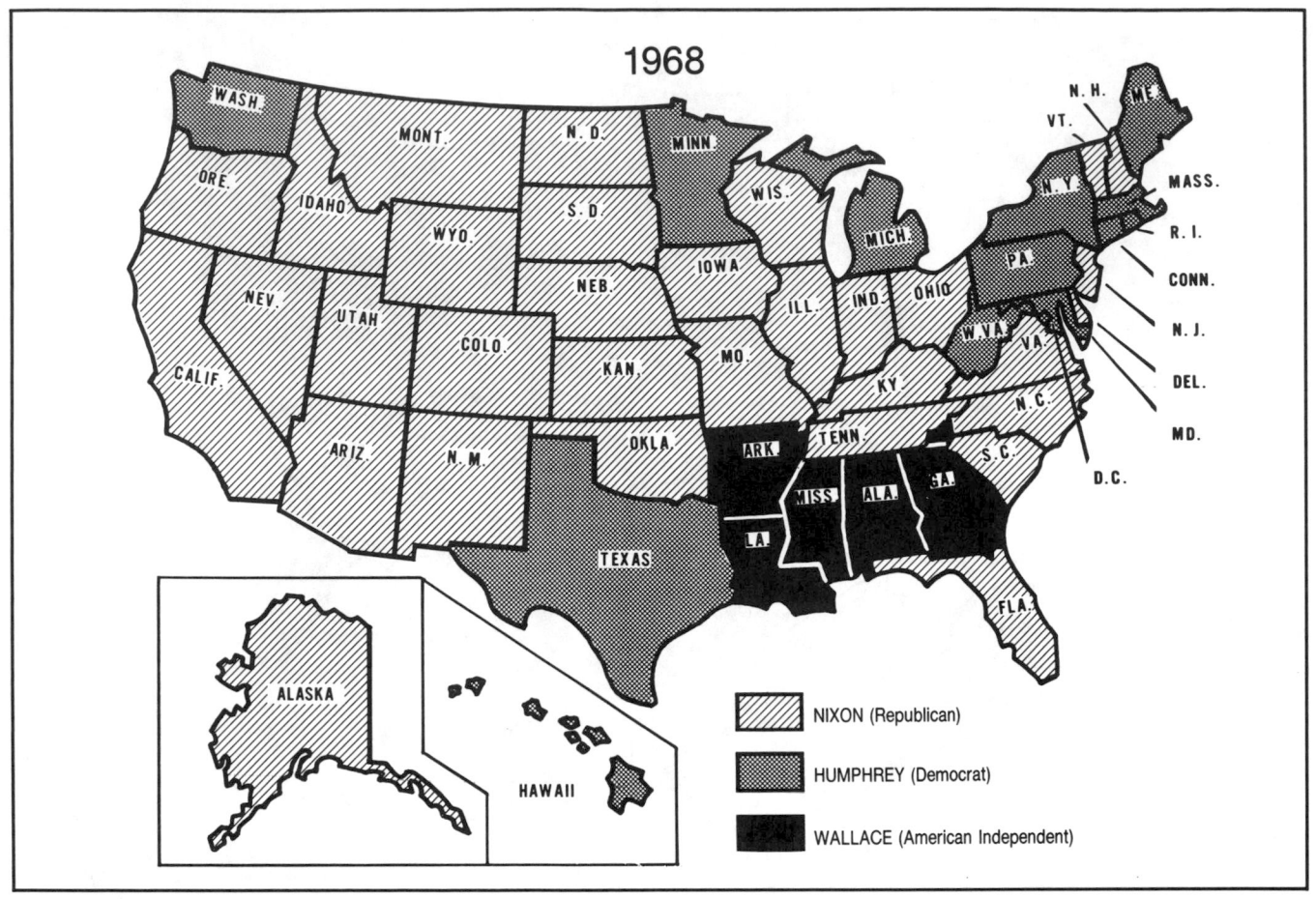

1968

NIXON (Republican)

HUMPHREY (Democrat)

WALLACE (American Independent)

States	Electoral Votes	Nixon	Humphrey	Wallace
Alabama	(10)	-	-	10
Alaska	(3)	3	-	-
Arizona	(5)	5	-	-
Arkansas	(6)	-	-	6
California	(40)	40	-	-
Colorado	(6)	6	-	-
Connecticut	(8)	-	8	-
Delaware	(3)	3	-	-
District of Columbia	(3)	-	3	-
Florida	(14)	14	-	-
Georgia	(12)	-	-	12
Hawaii	(4)	-	4	-
Idaho	(4)	4	-	-
Illinois	(26)	26	-	-
Indiana	(13)	13	-	-
Iowa	(9)	9	-	-
Kansas	(7)	7	-	-
Kentucky	(9)	9	-	-
Louisiana	(10)	-	-	10
Maine	(4)	-	4	-
Maryland	(10)	-	10	-
Massachusetts	(14)	-	14	-
Michigan	(21)	-	21	-
Minnesota	(10)	-	10	-
Mississippi	(7)	-	-	7
Missouri	(12)	12	-	-
Montana	(4)	4	-	-
Nebraska	(5)	5	-	-
Nevada	(3)	3	-	-
New Hampshire	(4)	4	-	-
New Jersey	(17)	17	-	-
New Mexico	(4)	4	-	-
New York	(43)	-	43	-
North Carolina [1]	(13)	12	-	1
North Dakota	(4)	4	-	-
Ohio	(26)	26	-	-
Oklahoma	(8)	8	-	-
Oregon	(6)	6	-	-
Pennsylvania	(29)	-	29	-
Rhode Island	(4)	-	4	-
South Carolina	(8)	8	-	-
South Dakota	(4)	4	-	-
Tennessee	(11)	11	-	-
Texas	(25)	-	25	-
Utah	(4)	4	-	-
Vermont	(3)	3	-	-
Virginia	(12)	12	-	-
Washington	(9)	-	9	-
West Virginia	(7)	-	7	-
Wisconsin	(12)	12	-	-
Wyoming	(3)	3	-	-
Totals	**(538)**	**301**	**191**	**46**

1. For explanation of split electoral votes, see p. 14.

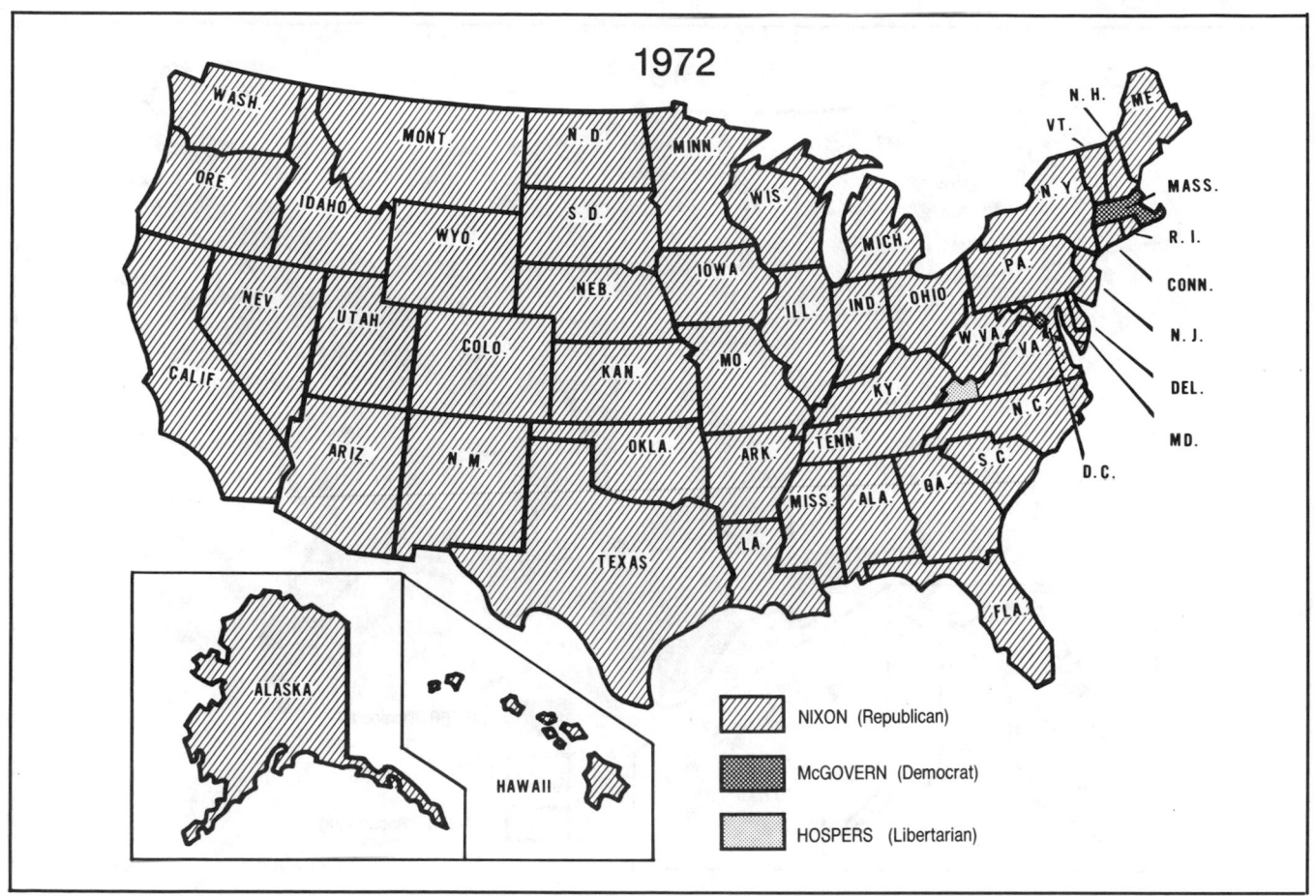

1972

NIXON (Republican)

McGOVERN (Democrat)

HOSPERS (Libertarian)

States	Electoral Votes	Nixon	McGovern	Hospers	States	Electoral Votes	Nixon	McGovern	Hospers
Alabama	(9)	9	-	-	Montana	(4)	4	-	-
Alaska	(3)	3	-	-	Nebraska	(5)	5	-	-
Arizona	(6)	6	-	-	Nevada	(3)	3	-	-
Arkansas	(6)	6	-	-	New Hampshire	(4)	4	-	-
California	(45)	45	-	-	New Jersey	(17)	17	-	-
Colorado	(7)	7	-	-	New Mexico	(4)	4	-	-
Connecticut	(8)	8	-	-	New York	(41)	41	-	-
Delaware	(3)	3	-	-	North Carolina	(13)	13	-	-
District of Columbia	(3)	-	3	-	North Dakota	(3)	3	-	-
Florida	(17)	17	-	-	Ohio	(25)	25	-	-
Georgia	(12)	12	-	-	Oklahoma	(8)	8	-	-
Hawaii	(4)	4	-	-	Oregon	(6)	6	-	-
Idaho	(4)	4	-	-	Pennsylvania	(27)	27	-	-
Illinois	(26)	26	-	-	Rhode Island	(4)	4	-	-
Indiana	(13)	13	-	-	South Carolina	(8)	8	-	-
Iowa	(8)	8	-	-	South Dakota	(4)	4	-	-
Kansas	(7)	7	-	-	Tennessee	(10)	10	-	-
Kentucky	(9)	9	-	-	Texas	(26)	26	-	-
Louisiana	(10)	10	-	-	Utah	(4)	4	-	-
Maine	(4)	4	-	-	Vermont	(3)	3	-	-
Maryland	(10)	10	-	-	Virginia [1]	(12)	11	-	1
Massachusetts	(14)	-	14	-	Washington	(9)	9	-	-
Michigan	(21)	21	-	-	West Virginia	(6)	6	-	-
Minnesota	(10)	10	-	-	Wisconsin	(11)	11	-	-
Mississippi	(7)	7	-	-	Wyoming	(3)	3	-	-
Missouri	(12)	12	-	-	**Totals**	**(538)**	**520**	**17**	**1**

1. For explanation of split electoral votes, see p. 14.

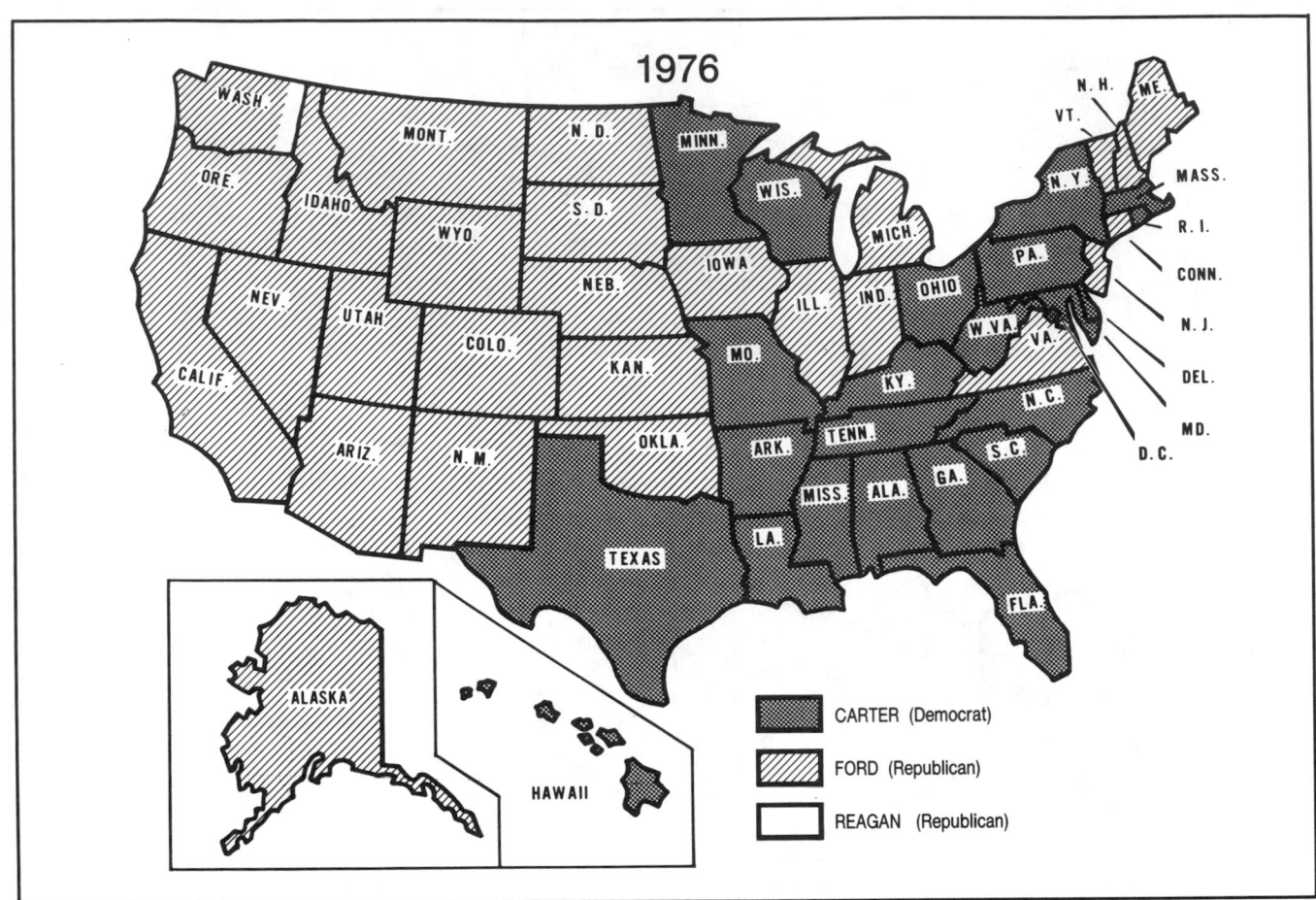

States	Electoral Votes	Carter	Ford	Reagan
Alabama	(9)	9	-	-
Alaska	(3)	-	3	-
Arizona	(6)	-	6	-
Arkansas	(6)	6	-	-
California	(45)	-	45	-
Colorado	(7)	-	7	-
Connecticut	(8)	-	8	-
Delaware	(3)	3	-	-
District of Columbia	(3)	3	-	-
Florida	(17)	17	-	-
Georgia	(12)	12	-	-
Hawaii	(4)	4	-	-
Idaho	(4)	-	4	-
Illinois	(26)	-	26	-
Indiana	(13)	-	13	-
Iowa	(8)	-	8	-
Kansas	(7)	-	7	-
Kentucky	(9)	9	-	-
Louisiana	(10)	10	-	-
Maine	(4)	-	4	-
Maryland	(10)	10	-	-
Massachusetts	(14)	14	-	-
Michigan	(21)	-	21	-
Minnesota	(10)	10	-	-
Mississippi	(7)	7	-	-
Missouri	(12)	12	-	-
Montana	(4)	-	4	-
Nebraska	(5)	-	5	-
Nevada	(3)	-	3	-
New Hampshire	(4)	-	4	-
New Jersey	(17)	-	17	-
New Mexico	(4)	-	4	-
New York	(41)	41	-	-
North Carolina	(13)	13	-	-
North Dakota	(3)	-	3	-
Ohio	(25)	25	-	-
Oklahoma	(8)	-	8	-
Oregon	(6)	-	6	-
Pennsylvania	(27)	27	-	-
Rhode Island	(4)	4	-	-
South Carolina	(8)	8	-	-
South Dakota	(4)	-	4	-
Tennessee	(10)	10	-	-
Texas	(26)	26	-	-
Utah	(4)	-	4	-
Vermont	(3)	-	3	-
Virginia	(12)	-	12	-
Washington [1]	(9)	-	8	1
West Virginia	(6)	6	-	-
Wisconsin	(11)	11	-	-
Wyoming	(3)	-	3	-
Totals	(538)	297	240	1

1. *For explanation of split electoral votes, see p. 14.*

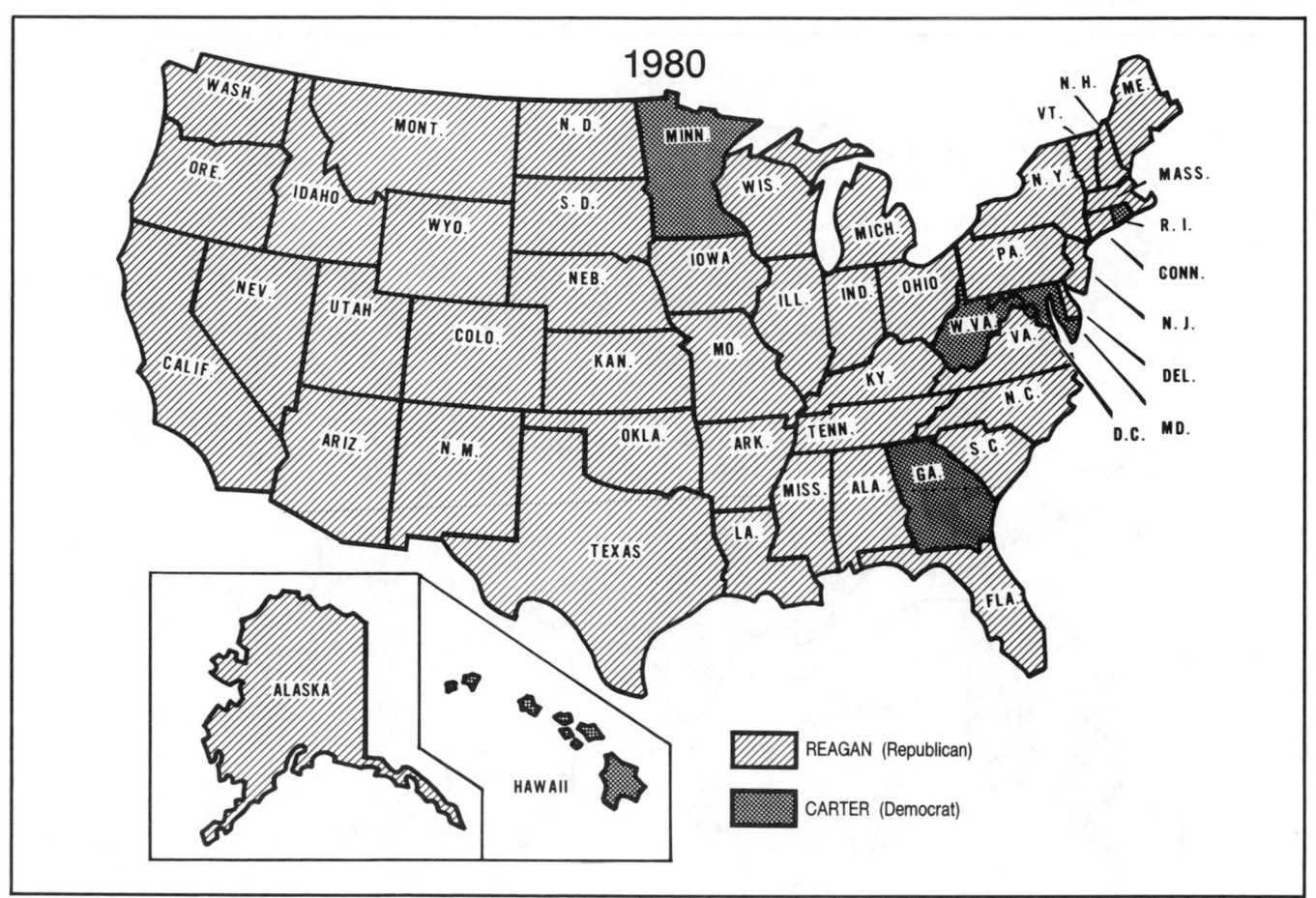

1980

REAGAN (Republican)

CARTER (Democrat)

States	Electoral Votes	Reagan	Carter	States	Electoral Votes	Reagan	Carter
Alabama	(9)	9	-	Montana	(4)	4	-
Alaska	(3)	3	-	Nebraska	(5)	5	-
Arizona	(6)	6	-	Nevada	(3)	3	-
Arkansas	(6)	6	-	New Hampshire	(4)	4	-
California	(45)	45	-	New Jersey	(17)	17	-
Colorado	(7)	7	-	New Mexico	(4)	4	-
Connecticut	(8)	8	-	New York	(41)	41	-
Delaware	(3)	3	-	North Carolina	(13)	13	-
District of Columbia	(3)	-	3	North Dakota	(3)	3	-
Florida	(17)	17	-	Ohio	(25)	25	-
Georgia	(12)	-	12	Oklahoma	(8)	8	-
Hawaii	(4)	-	4	Oregon	(6)	6	-
Idaho	(4)	4	-	Pennsylvania	(27)	27	-
Illinois	(26)	26	-	Rhode Island	(4)	-	4
Indiana	(13)	13	-	South Carolina	(8)	8	-
Iowa	(8)	8	-	South Dakota	(4)	4	-
Kansas	(7)	7	-	Tennessee	(10)	10	-
Kentucky	(9)	9	-	Texas	(26)	26	-
Louisiana	(10)	10	-	Utah	(4)	4	-
Maine	(4)	4	-	Vermont	(3)	3	-
Maryland	(10)	-	10	Virginia	(12)	12	-
Massachusetts	(14)	14	-	Washington	(9)	9	-
Michigan	(21)	21	-	West Virginia	(6)	-	6
Minnesota	(10)	-	10	Wisconsin	(11)	11	-
Mississippi	(7)	7	-	Wyoming	(3)	3	-
Missouri	(12)	12	-	**Totals**	**(538)**	**489**	**49**

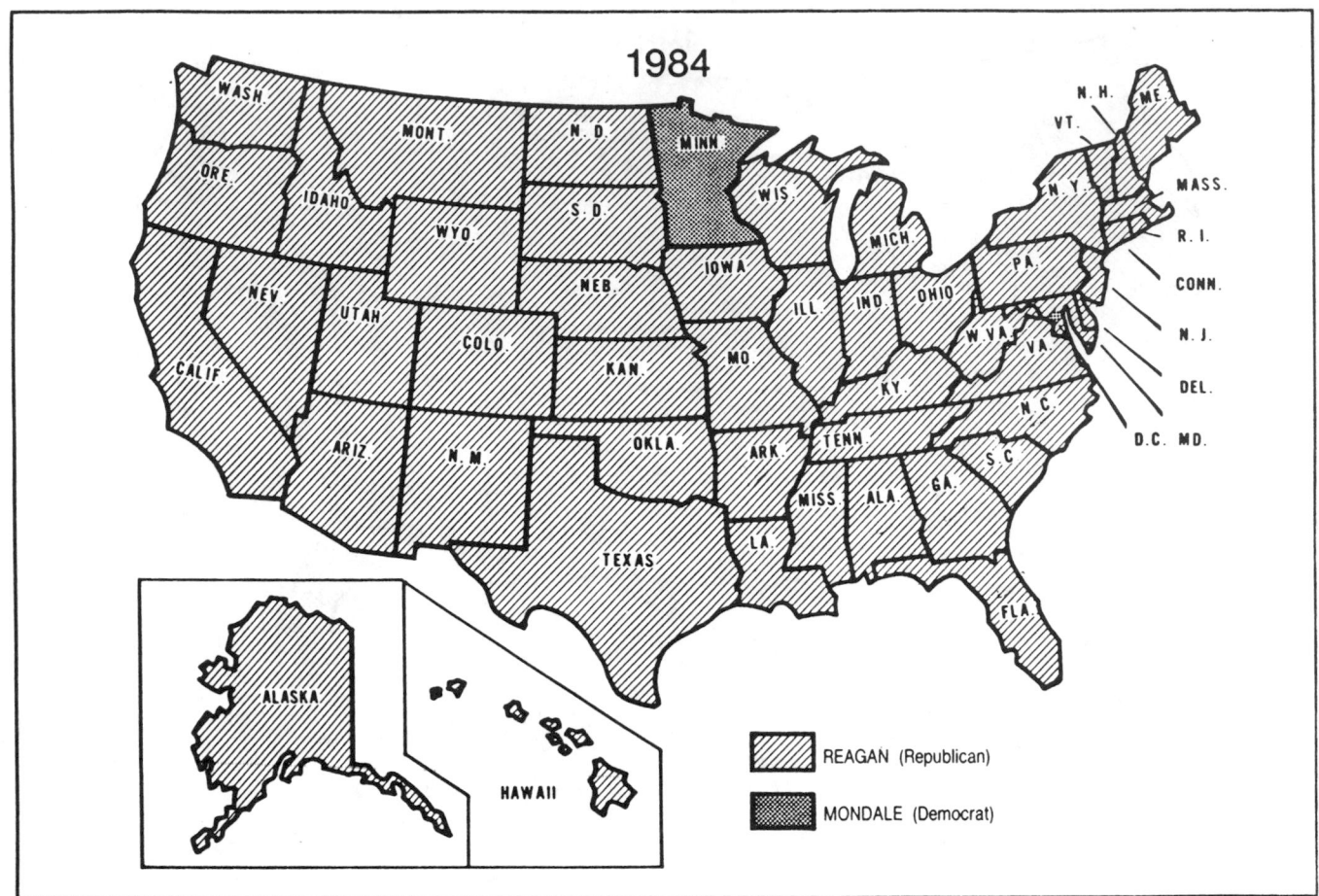

1984

REAGAN (Republican)

MONDALE (Democrat)

States	Electoral Votes	Reagan	Mondale	States	Electoral Votes	Reagan	Mondale
Alabama	(9)	9	-	Montana	(4)	4	-
Alaska	(3)	3	-	Nebraska	(5)	5	-
Arizona	(7)	7	-	Nevada	(4)	4	-
Arkansas	(6)	6	-	New Hampshire	(4)	4	-
California	(47)	47	-	New Jersey	(16)	16	-
Colorado	(8)	8	-	New Mexico	(5)	5	-
Connecticut	(8)	8	-	New York	(36)	36	-
Delaware	(3)	3	-	North Carolina	(13)	13	-
District of Columbia	(3)	-	3	North Dakota	(3)	3	-
Florida	(21)	21	-	Ohio	(23)	23	-
Georgia	(12)	12	-	Oklahoma	(8)	8	-
Hawaii	(4)	4	-	Oregon	(7)	7	-
Idaho	(4)	4	-	Pennsylvania	(25)	25	-
Illinois	(24)	24	-	Rhode Island	(4)	4	-
Indiana	(12)	12	-	South Carolina	(8)	8	-
Iowa	(8)	8	-	South Dakota	(3)	3	-
Kansas	(7)	7	-	Tennessee	(11)	11	-
Kentucky	(9)	9	-	Texas	(29)	29	-
Louisiana	(10)	10	-	Utah	(5)	5	-
Maine	(4)	4	-	Vermont	(3)	3	-
Maryland	(10)	10	-	Virginia	(12)	12	-
Massachusetts	(13)	13	-	Washington	(10)	10	-
Michigan	(20)	20	-	West Virginia	(6)	6	-
Minnesota	(10)	-	10	Wisconsin	(11)	11	-
Mississippi	(7)	7	-	Wyoming	(3)	3	-
Missouri	(11)	11	-	**Totals**	**(538)**	**525**	**13**

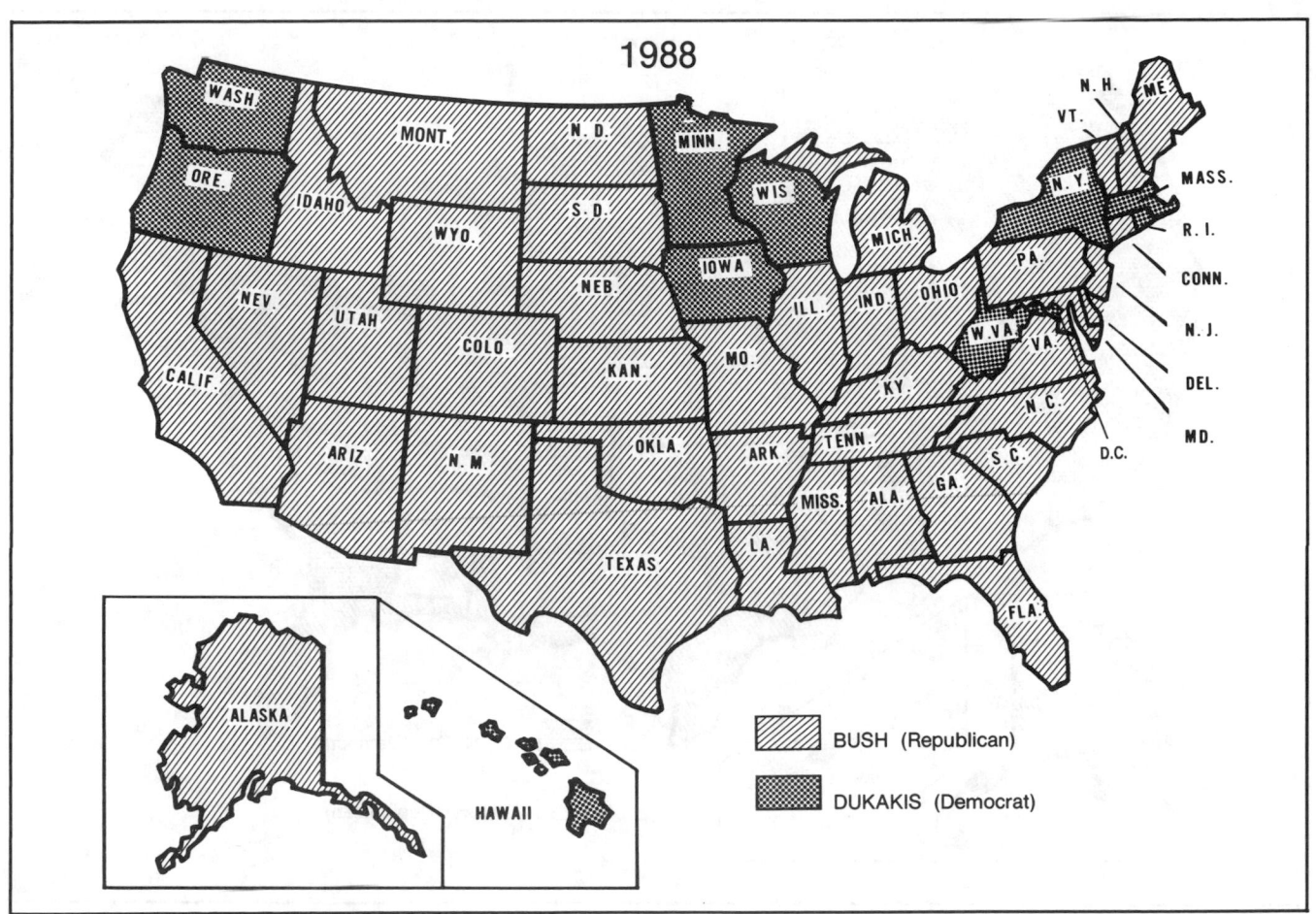

1988

BUSH (Republican)

DUKAKIS (Democrat)

States	Electoral Votes	Bush	Dukakis	Bentsen	States	Electoral Votes	Bush	Dukakis	Bentsen
Alabama	(9)	9	-	-	Montana	(4)	4	-	-
Alaska	(3)	3	-	-	Nebraska	(5)	5	-	-
Arizona	(7)	7	-	-	Nevada	(4)	4	-	-
Arkansas	(6)	6	-	-	New Hampshire	(4)	4	-	-
California	(47)	47	-	-	New Jersey	(16)	16	-	-
Colorado	(8)	8	-	-	New Mexico	(5)	5	-	-
Connecticut	(8)	8	-	-	New York	(36)	-	36	-
Delaware	(3)	3	-	-	North Carolina	(13)	13	-	-
District of Columbia	(3)	-	3	-	North Dakota	(3)	3	-	-
Florida	(21)	21	-	-	Ohio	(23)	23	-	-
Georgia	(12)	12	-	-	Oklahoma	(8)	8	-	-
Hawaii	(4)	-	4	-	Oregon	(7)	-	7	-
Idaho	(4)	4	-	-	Pennsylvania	(25)	25	-	-
Illinois	(24)	24	-	-	Rhode Island	(4)	-	4	-
Indiana	(12)	12	-	-	South Carolina	(8)	8	-	-
Iowa	(8)	-	8	-	South Dakota	(3)	3	-	-
Kansas	(7)	7	-	-	Tennessee	(11)	11	-	-
Kentucky	(9)	9	-	-	Texas	(29)	29	-	-
Louisiana	(10)	10	-	-	Utah	(5)	5	-	-
Maine	(4)	4	-	-	Vermont	(3)	3	-	-
Maryland	(10)	10	-	-	Virginia	(12)	12	-	-
Massachusetts	(13)	-	13	-	Washington	(10)	-	10	-
Michigan	(20)	20	-	-	West Virginia [1]	(6)	-	5	1
Minnesota	(10)	-	10	-	Wisconsin	(11)	-	11	-
Mississippi	(7)	7	-	-	Wyoming	(3)	3	-	-
Missouri	(11)	11	-	-	**Totals**	**(538)**	**426**	**111**	**1**

1. *Margaret Leach, a Dukakis elector, voted for Dukakis's running mate, Sen. Lloyd Bentsen of Texas.*

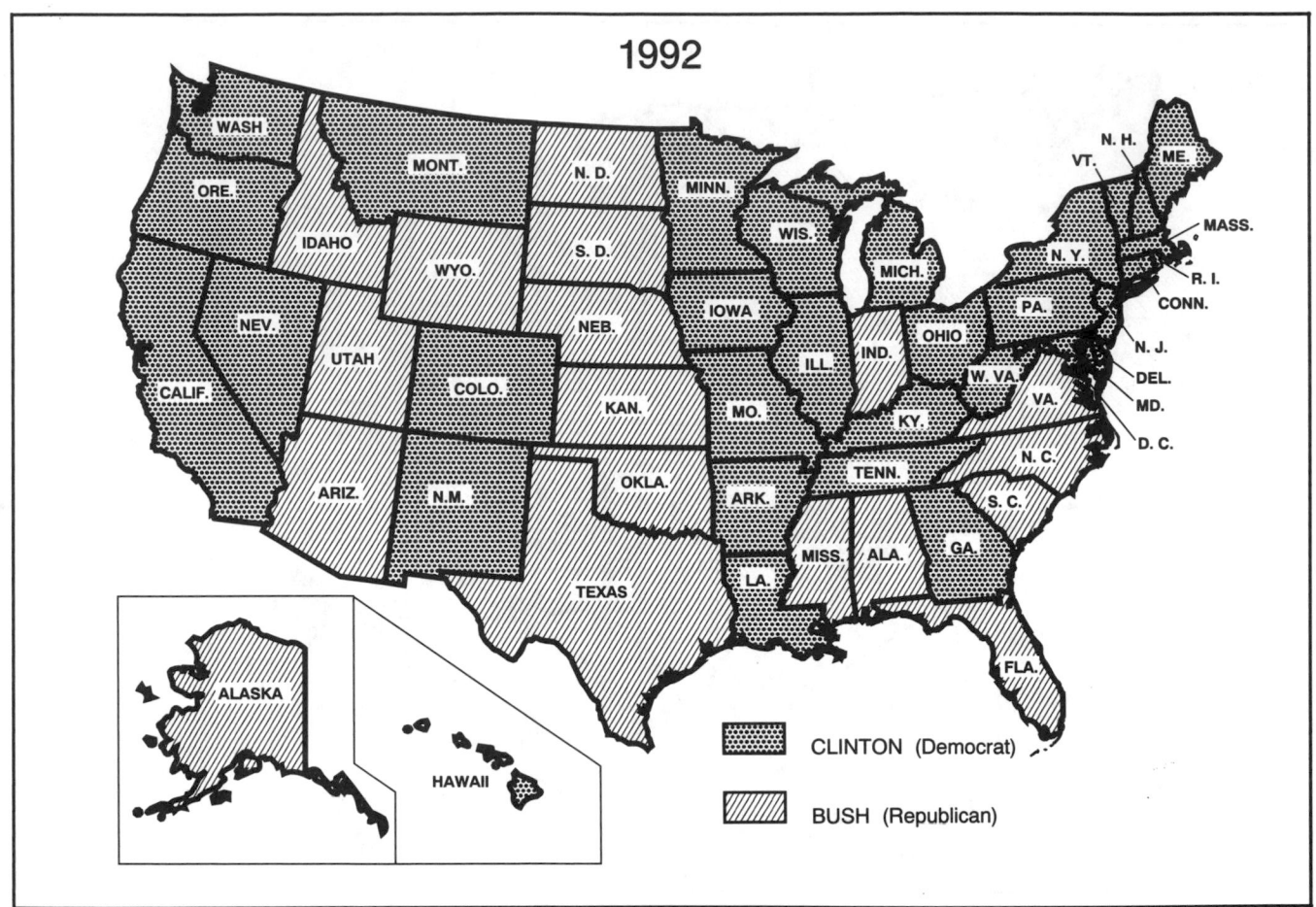

1992

CLINTON (Democrat)

BUSH (Republican)

States	Electoral Votes	Clinton	Bush	States	Electoral Votes	Clinton	Bush
Alabama	(9)	-	9	Montana	(3)	3	-
Alaska	(3)	-	3	Nebraska	(5)	-	5
Arizona	(8)	-	8	Nevada	(4)	4	-
Arkansas	(6)	6	-	New Hampshire	(4)	4	-
California	(54)	54	-	New Jersey	(15)	15	-
Colorado	(8)	8	-	New Mexico	(5)	5	-
Connecticut	(8)	8	-	New York	(33)	33	-
Delaware	(3)	3	-	North Carolina	(14)	-	14
District of Columbia	(3)	3	-	North Dakota	(3)	-	3
Florida	(25)	-	25	Ohio	(21)	21	-
Georgia	(13)	13	-	Oklahoma	(8)	-	8
Hawaii	(4)	4	-	Oregon	(7)	7	-
Idaho	(4)	-	4	Pennsylvania	(23)	23	-
Illinois	(22)	22	-	Rhode Island	(4)	4	-
Indiana	(12)	-	12	South Carolina	(8)	-	8
Iowa	(7)	7	-	South Dakota	(3)	-	3
Kansas	(6)	-	6	Tennessee	(11)	11	-
Kentucky	(8)	8	-	Texas	(32)	-	32
Louisiana	(9)	9	-	Utah	(5)	-	5
Maine	(4)	4	-	Vermont	(3)	3	-
Maryland	(10)	10	-	Virginia	(13)	-	13
Massachusetts	(12)	12	-	Washington	(11)	11	-
Michigan	(18)	18	-	West Virginia	(5)	5	-
Minnesota	(10)	10	-	Wisconsin	(11)	11	-
Mississippi	(7)	-	7	Wyoming	(3)	-	3
Missouri	(11)	11	-	**Totals**	**(538)**	**370**	**168**

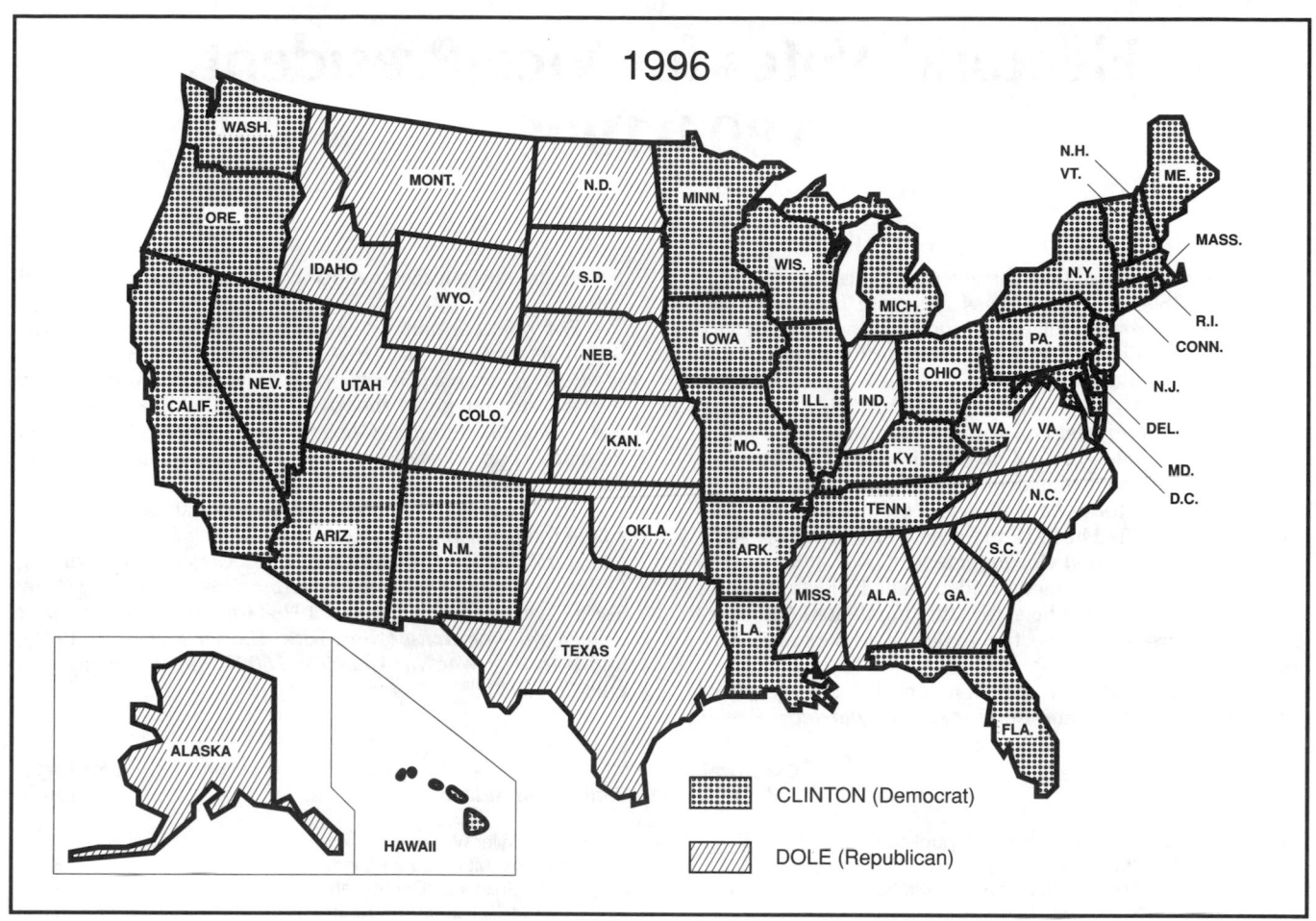

1996

| | CLINTON (Democrat) |
| | DOLE (Republican) |

States	Electoral Votes	Clinton	Dole	States	Electoral Votes	Clinton	Dole
Alabama	(9)	-	9	Montana	(3)	-	3
Alaska	(3)	-	3	Nebraska	(5)	-	5
Arizona	(8)	8	-	Nevada	(4)	4	-
Arkansas	(6)	6	-	New Hampshire	(4)	4	-
California	(54)	54	-	New Jersey	(15)	15	-
Colorado	(8)	-	8	New Mexico	(5)	5	-
Connecticut	(8)	8	-	New York	(33)	33	-
Delaware	(3)	3	-	North Carolina	(14)	-	14
District of Columbia	(3)	3	-	North Dakota	(3)	-	3
Florida	(25)	25	-	Ohio	(21)	21	-
Georgia	(13)	-	13	Oklahoma	(8)	-	8
Hawaii	(4)	4	-	Oregon	(7)	7	-
Idaho	(4)	-	4	Pennsylvania	(23)	23	-
Illinois	(22)	22	-	Rhode Island	(4)	4	-
Indiana	(12)	-	12	South Carolina	(8)	-	8
Iowa	(7)	7	-	South Dakota	(3)	-	3
Kansas	(6)	-	6	Tennessee	(11)	11	-
Kentucky	(8)	8	-	Texas	(32)	-	32
Louisiana	(9)	9	-	Utah	(5)	-	5
Maine	(4)	4	-	Vermont	(3)	3	-
Maryland	(10)	10	-	Virginia	(13)	-	13
Massachusetts	(12)	12	-	Washington	(11)	11	-
Michigan	(18)	18	-	West Virginia	(5)	5	-
Minnesota	(10)	10	-	Wisconsin	(11)	11	-
Mississippi	(7)	-	7	Wyoming	(3)	-	3
Missouri	(11)	11	-	**Totals**	**(538)**	**379**	**159**

Electoral Votes for Vice President, 1804-1996

The following list gives the electoral votes for vice president from 1804 to 1996. Unless indicated by a note, the state-by-state breakdown of electoral votes for each vice presidential candidate was the same as for his or her party's presidential candidate.

Prior to 1804, under Article II, Section 1 of the Constitution, each elector cast two votes — each vote for a different person. The electors did not distinguish between votes for president and vice president. The candidate receiving the second highest total became vice president. The 12th Amendment, ratified in 1804, required electors to vote separately for president and vice president.

In some cases, persons had received electoral votes although they had never been formally nominated. The word *candidate* is used in this section to designate persons receiving electoral votes.

The *Senate Manual* (Washington, D.C.: Government Printing Office, 1995) and *Congressional Quarterly Weekly Report* are the sources used for vice presidential electoral votes.

For political party designation, the basic source was Svend Petersen, *A Statistical History of the American Presidential Elections* (Westport, Conn.: Greenwood Press, 1981). Petersen gives the party designation of *presidential candidates only*. Congressional Quarterly adopted Petersen's party designations for the running mates of presidential candidates.

To supplement Petersen, Congressional Quarterly consulted the *Biographical Directory of the United States Congress, 1774-1989* (Washington, D.C.: Government Printing Office, 1989); the *Dictionary of American Biography* (New York: Charles Scribner's Sons, 1928-36); the *Encyclopedia of American Biography* (New York: Harper and Row, 1974); and *Who Was Who in America, 1607-1968* (Chicago: Marquis Co., 1943-68).

Year	Candidate	Electoral Votes
1804	George Clinton (Democratic-Republican)	162
	Rufus King (Federalist)	14
1808	George Clinton (Democratic-Republican)[1]	113
	John Langdon (Democratic-Republican)	9
	James Madison (Democratic-Republican)	3
	James Monroe (Democratic-Republican)	3
	Rufus King (Federalist)	47
1812	Elbridge Gerry (Democratic-Republican)[2]	131
	Jared Ingersoll (Federalist)	86
1816	Daniel D. Tompkins (Democratic-Republican)	183
	John E. Howard (Federalist)[3]	22
	James Ross (Federalist)	5
	John Marshall (Federalist)	4
	Robert G. Harper (Federalist)	3
1820	Daniel D. Tompkins (Democratic-Republican)[4]	218
	Richard Rush (Democratic-Republican)	1
	Richard Stockton (Federalist)	8
	Daniel Rodney (Federalist)	4
	Robert G. Harper (Federalist)	1
1824	John C. Calhoun (Democratic-Republican)[5]	182
	Nathan Sanford (Democratic-Republican)	30
	Nathaniel Macon (Democratic-Republican)	24
	Andrew Jackson (Democratic-Republican)	13
	Martin Van Buren (Democratic-Republican)	9
	Henry Clay (Democratic-Republican)	2
1828	John C. Calhoun (Democratic-Republican)[6]	171
	William Smith (Independent Democratic-Republican)	7
	Richard Rush (National Republican)	83
1832	Martin Van Buren (Democrat)[7]	189
	William Wilkins (Democrat)	30
	Henry Lee (Independent Democrat)	11
	John Sergeant (National Republican)	49
	Amos Ellmaker (Anti-Mason)	7
1836	Richard M. Johnson (Democrat)[8]	147
	William Smith (Independent Democrat)	23
	Francis Granger (Whig)	77
	John Tyler (Whig)	47

Year	Candidate	Electoral Votes
1840	John Tyler (Whig)	234
	Richard M. Johnson (Democrat)[9]	48
	L. W. Tazewell (Democrat)	11
	James K. Polk (Democrat)	1
1844	George M. Dallas (Democrat)	170
	Theodore Frelinghuysen (Whig)	105
1848	Millard Fillmore (Whig)	163
	William Orlando Butler (Democrat)	127
1852	William R. King (Democrat)	254
	William Alexander Graham (Whig)	42
1856	John C. Breckinridge (Democrat)	174
	William L. Dayton (Republican)	114
	Andrew Jackson Donelson (Whig-American)	8
1860	Hannibal Hamlin (Republican)	180
	Joseph Lane (Southern Democrat)	72
	Edward Everett (Constitutional Union)	39
	Herschel V. Johnson (Democrat)	12
1864	Andrew Johnson (Republican)	212
	George H. Pendleton (Democrat)	21
1868	Schuyler Colfax (Republican)	214
	Francis P. Blair (Democrat)	80
1872	Henry Wilson (Republican)	286
	Benjamin Gratz Brown (Democrat)[10]	47
	Alfred H. Colquitt (Democrat)	5
	John M. Palmer (Democrat)	3
	Thomas E. Bramlette (Democrat)	3
	William S. Groesbeck (Democrat)	1
	Willis B. Machen (Democrat)	1
	George W. Julian (Liberal Republican)	5
	Nathaniel P. Banks (Liberal Republican)	1
1876	William A. Wheeler (Republican)	185
	Thomas A. Hendricks (Democrat)	184
1880	Chester A. Arthur (Republican)	214
	William H. English (Democrat)	155
1884	Thomas A. Hendricks (Democrat)	219
	John A. Logan (Republican)	182
1888	Levi P. Morton (Republican)	233
	Allen G. Thurman (Democrat)	168

Year	Candidate	Electoral Votes
1892	Adlai E. Stevenson (Democrat)	277
	Whitelaw Reid (Republican)	145
	James G. Field (Populist)	22
1896	Garret A. Hobart (Republican)	271
	Arthur Sewall (Democrat)[11]	149
	Thomas E. Watson (Populist)	27
1900	Theodore Roosevelt (Republican)	292
	Adlai E. Stevenson (Democrat)	155
1904	Charles W. Fairbanks (Republican)	336
	Henry G. Davis (Democrat)	140
1908	James S. Sherman (Republican)	321
	John W. Kern (Democrat)	162
1912	Thomas R. Marshall (Democrat)	435
	Hiram W. Johnson (Progressive)	88
	Nicholas Murray Butler (Republican)[12]	8
1916	Thomas R. Marshall (Democrat)	277
	Charles W. Fairbanks (Republican)	254
1920	Calvin Coolidge (Republican)	404
	Franklin D. Roosevelt (Democrat)	127
1924	Charles G. Dawes (Republican)	382
	Charles W. Bryan (Democrat)	136
	Burton K. Wheeler (Progressive)	13
1928	Charles Curtis (Republican)	444
	Joseph T. Robinson (Democrat)	87
1932	John N. Garner (Democrat)	472
	Charles Curtis (Republican)	59
1936	John N. Garner (Democrat)	523
	Frank Knox (Republican)	8
1940	Henry A. Wallace (Democrat)	449
	Charles L. McNary (Republican)	82
1944	Harry S. Truman (Democrat)	432
	John W. Bricker (Republican)	99

Year	Candidate	Electoral Votes
1948	Alben W. Barkley (Democrat)	303
	Earl Warren (Republican)	189
	Fielding L. Wright (States' Rights Democrat)	39
1952	Richard Nixon (Republican)	442
	John J. Sparkman (Democrat)	89
1956	Richard Nixon (Republican)	457
	Estes Kefauver (Democrat)	73
	Herman Talmadge (Democrat)	1
1960	Lyndon B. Johnson (Democrat)	303
	Strom Thurmond (Democrat)[13]	14
	Henry Cabot Lodge (Republican)	219
	Barry Goldwater (Republican)	1
1964	Hubert H. Humphrey (Democrat)	486
	William E. Miller (Republican)	52
1968	Spiro T. Agnew (Republican)	301
	Edmund S. Muskie (Democrat)	191
	Curtis E. LeMay (American Independent)	46
1972	Spiro T. Agnew (Republican)	520
	R. Sargent Shriver (Democrat)	17
	Theodora Nathan (Libertarian)	1
1976	Walter F. Mondale (Democrat)	297
	Robert Dole (Republican)[14]	241
1980	George Bush (Republican)	489
	Walter F. Mondale (Democrat)	49
1984	George Bush (Republican)	525
	Geraldine A. Ferraro (Democrat)	13
1988	Dan Quayle (Republican)	426
	Lloyd Bentsen (Democrat)[15]	111
	Michael S. Dukakis (Democrat)	1
1992	Al Gore (Democrat)	370
	Dan Quayle (Republican)	168
1996	Al Gore (Democrat)	379
	Jack Kemp (Republican)	159

Notes

1. New York cast 13 presidential electoral votes for Democratic-Republican James Madison and 6 votes for Clinton; for vice president, New York cast 13 votes for Clinton, 3 votes for Madison, and 3 votes for Monroe. Langdon received Ohio's 3 votes and Vermont's 6 votes.

2. The state-by-state vote for Gerry was the same as for Democratic-Republican presidential candidate Madison, except for Massachusetts and New Hampshire. Massachusetts cast 2 votes for Gerry and 20 votes for Ingersoll; New Hampshire cast 1 vote for Gerry and 7 votes for Ingersoll.

3. Four Federalists received vice-presidential electoral votes: Howard — Massachusetts, 22 votes; Ross — Connecticut, 5 votes; Marshall — Connecticut, 4 votes; Harper — Delaware, 3 votes.

4. The state-by-state vote for Tompkins was the same as for Democratic-Republican presidential candidate Monroe, except for Delaware, Maryland, and Massachusetts. Delaware cast 4 votes for Rodney; Maryland cast 10 votes for Tompkins and 1 for Harper; Massachusetts cast 7 votes for Tompkins and 8 for Stockton.

New Hampshire, which cast 7 presidential electoral votes for Monroe and 1 vote for John Quincy Adams, cast 7 vice-presidential electoral votes for Tompkins and 1 vote for Rush.

5. The state-by-state vice-presidential electoral vote was as follows:

Calhoun — Alabama, 5 votes; Delaware, 1 vote; Illinois, 3 votes; Indiana, 5 votes; Kentucky, 7 votes; Louisiana, 5 votes; Maine, 9 votes; Maryland, 10 votes; Massachusetts, 15 votes; Mississippi, 3 votes; New Hampshire, 7 votes; New Jersey, 8 votes; New York, 29 votes; North Carolina, 15 votes; Pennsylvania, 28 votes; Rhode Island, 3 votes; South Carolina, 11 votes; Tennessee, 11 votes; Vermont, 7 votes.

Sanford — Kentucky, 7 votes; New York, 7 votes; Ohio, 16 votes.

Macon — Virginia, 24 votes.

Jackson — Connecticut, 8 votes; Maryland, 1 vote; Missouri, 3 votes; New Hampshire, 1 vote.

Van Buren — Georgia, 9 votes.

Clay — Delaware, 2 votes.

6. The state-by-state vote for Calhoun was the same as for Democratic-Republican presidential candidate Jackson, except for Georgia, which cast 2 votes for Calhoun and 7 votes for Smith.

7. The state-by-state vote for Van Buren was the same as for Democratic-Republican presidential candidate Jackson, except for Pennsylvania, which cast 30 votes for Wilkins.

South Carolina cast 11 presidential electoral votes for Independent Democratic presidential candidate Floyd and 11 votes for Independent Democratic vice-presidential candidate Lee.

Vermont cast 7 presidential electoral votes for Anti-Masonic candidate Wirt and 7 vice-presidential electoral votes for Wirt's running mate, Ellmaker.

8. The state-by-state vote for Johnson was the same as for Democratic presidential candidate Van Buren, except for Virginia, which cast 23 votes for Smith.

Granger's state-by-state vote was the same as for Whig presidential candidate Harrison, except for Maryland and Massachusetts. Maryland cast 10 presidential electoral votes for Harrison and 10 vice-presidential votes for Tyler; Massachusetts cast 14 presidential electoral votes for Whig candidate Webster and 14 vice-presidential votes over Granger.

Tyler received 11 votes from Georgia, 10 from Maryland, 11 from South Carolina, and 15 from Tennessee.

No vice-presidential candidate received a majority of the electoral vote. As a result the Senate, for the only time in history, selected the vice president under the provisions of the Twelfth Amendment. Johnson was elected vice president by a vote of 33 to 16 over Granger.

9. The Democratic party did not nominate a vice-presidential candidate in 1840. Johnson's state-by-state vote was the same as for presidential candidate Van Buren, except for South Carolina and Virginia. South Carolina cast 11 votes for Tazewell. Virginia cast 23 presidential electoral votes for Van Buren, 22 vice-presidential votes for Johnson, and 1 vice-presidential vote for Polk.

10. Liberal Republican and Democratic presidential candidate Horace Greeley died November 29, 1872. As a result eighteen electors pledged to Greeley cast their presidential electoral votes for Brown, Greeley's running mate.

Electoral Votes for Vice President

The vice-presidential vote was as follows:

Brown — Georgia, 5 votes; Kentucky, 8 votes; Maryland, 8 votes; Missouri, 6 votes; Tennessee, 12 votes; Texas, 8 votes.

Colquitt — Georgia, 5 votes.

Palmer — Missouri, 3 votes.

Bramlette — Kentucky, 3 votes.

Groesbeck — Missouri, 1 vote.

Machen — Kentucky, 1 vote.

Julian — Missouri, 5 votes.

Banks — Georgia, 1 vote.

11. The state-by-state vote for Sewall was the same as for Democratic-Populist candidate William Jennings Bryan, except for the following states, which cast electoral votes for Watson: Arkansas, 3 votes; Louisiana, 4; Missouri, 4; Montana, 1; Nebraska, 4; North Carolina, 5; South Dakota, 2; Utah, 1; Washington, 2; Wyoming, 1.

12. Butler received the 8 electoral votes of Vice President James Sherman, who died Oct. 30, 1912, after being renominated on the Republican ticket. Butler was named as the substitute candidate.

13. Democratic electors carried Alabama's 11 electoral votes. Five of the electors were pledged to the national Democratic ticket of Kennedy and Johnson. Six electors ran unpledged and voted for Harry F. Byrd for president and Strom Thurmond for vice president.

Mississippi's eight electors voted for Byrd and Thurmond.

In Oklahoma the Republican ticket of Nixon and Lodge carried the state, but Henry D. Irwin, 1 of the state's 8 electors voted for Byrd for president and Goldwater for vice president.

14. Mike Padden, a Republican elector from the state of Washington cast his presidential electoral vote for Reagan instead of the Republican nominee, Ford. But he voted for Dole, Ford's running mate, for vice president. Dole thus received one more electoral vote than Ford.

15. Margaret Leach, a Democratic elector from West Virginia, cast her vice presidential electoral vote for Dukakis, the Democratic nominee for president, and her presidential vote for his running mate, Bentsen.

The Popular Vote

Few elements of the American political system have changed so markedly over the years as has the electorate. Since the early days of the nation, when the voting privilege was limited to the upper economic class of males, one voting barrier after another has fallen to pressures for wider suffrage. First non-property-holding males, then women, then African Americans and finally young people pushed for the franchise. By the early 1970s almost every restriction on voting had been removed, and virtually every adult citizen 18 years of age and older had won the right to vote.

Actions to expand the electorate have taken place at both the state and federal levels. Voting qualifications have varied widely because the U.S. Constitution (Article I, Section 2) permits the states to set their own voting standards. Early in the nation's history, the states dropped their property qualifications for voting, but some retained literacy tests as late as 1970.

On the federal level the Constitution has been amended five times to circumvent state qualifications denying the franchise to certain categories of people. The 14th Amendment, ratified in 1868, directed Congress to reduce the number of representatives from any state that disfranchised adult male citizens for any reason other than commission of a crime. However, no such reduction was ever made. The 15th Amendment, ratified in 1870, prohibited denial of the right to vote "on account of race, color or previous condition of servitude," and the 19th Amendment in 1920 prohibited denial of that right "on account of sex." The 24th Amendment, which came into effect in 1964, barred denial of the right to vote in any federal election "by reason of failure to pay any poll tax or other tax." Finally, in 1971 the 26th Amendment lowered the voting age to 18 in federal, state and local elections. *(U.S. Constitution on Presidential Selection, p. 262)*

Congress in the 1950s and 1960s enacted a series of statutes to enforce the 15th Amendment's guarantee against racial discrimination in voting. A law passed in 1970 nullified state residence requirements of longer than 30 days for voting in presidential elections, suspended literacy tests for a five-year period (the suspension was made permanent in 1975) and lowered the minimum voting age to 18 years from 21, the requirement then in effect in most states. A 1970 Supreme Court ruling upheld the voting-age change for federal elections but invalidated it for state and local elections. In the same decision the Court upheld the provision on residence requirements and sustained the suspension of literacy tests with respect to both state and local elections. The 26th Amendment was ratified six months after the Court's decision.

The right to vote in presidential elections was extended to citizens of the District of Columbia by the 23rd Amendment, ratified in 1961. District residents had been disfranchised from national elections except for a brief period in the 1870s when they elected a non-voting delegate to the House of Representatives. In 1970 Congress took another step toward full suffrage for District residents by again authorizing the election of a non-voting delegate to the House.

Broadening the Franchise

During the first few decades of the Republic, all 13 of the original states limited the franchise to property holders and taxpayers. Seven of the states required ownership of land or a life estate as opposed to a leased estate as a qualification for voting, and the other six permitted persons to qualify by substituting either evidence of ownership of certain amounts of personal property or payment of taxes.

The Framers of the Constitution apparently were content to have the states limit the right to vote to adult males who had a real stake in good government. This meant, in most cases, persons in the upper economic levels. Not wishing to discriminate against any particular type of property owner (uniform federal voting standards inevitably would have conflicted with some of the state standards), the Constitutional Convention adopted without dissent the recommendation of its Committee of Detail providing that qualifications for the electors of the House of Representatives "shall be the same . . . as those of the electors in the several states of the most numerous branch of their own legislatures."

Under this provision fewer than half of the adult white men in the United States were eligible to vote in federal elections. Because no state made women eligible (although states were not forbidden to do so), only one white adult in four qualified to go to the polls. Slaves and most blacks and Indians were ineligible, and they formed almost one-fifth of the American population as enumerated in the census of 1790. Also ineligible were white indentured servants, whose status was little better than that of the slaves.

Actually, these early state practices represented a liberalization of restrictions on voting that had prevailed at one time in the colonial period. Roman Catholics had been disfranchised in almost every colony, Jews in most colonies, Quakers and Baptists in some. In Rhode Island Jews remained legally ineligible to vote until 1842.

For half a century before the Civil War there was a steady broadening of the electorate. The new Western settlements supplied a stimulus to the principle of universal male suffrage, and Jacksonian democracy encouraged its acceptance. Gradually, the seven states making property ownership a condition for voting substituted a taxpaying requirement: Delaware in 1792, Maryland in 1810, Connecticut in 1818, Massachusetts in 1821, New York in 1821, Rhode Island in 1842 and Virginia in 1850. By the middle of the 19th century most states had removed even the taxpaying qualifications, although some jurisdictions persisted in this practice into the 20th century.

Another 19th century development, one that made it easier to vote, was the introduction of the *Australian ballot*, which is produced by the government and lists candidates from all parties. Previously, parties offered their own ballots listing only their own candidates. Introduced in the United States in 1888, the Australian ballot was adopted by almost all states by 1896. Variations introduced later were the *Indiana ballot*, which facilitates straight-ticket voting by listing candidates under their party name, and the *Massachusetts ballot*, which lists candidates of all parties under the office they are seeking.

The trend toward a broadened franchise continued in the 20th century with women obtaining the vote and with barriers to black voting slowly falling. Once Congress acted, the Supreme Court steadily backed its power to ensure the right to vote. In general, by the 200th anniversary of the nation, the only remaining restrictions prevented voting by the insane, convicted felons and otherwise eligible voters who were unable to meet short residence requirements.

Voting Trends

Statistics show that each major liberalization of election laws resulted in a sharp increase in the number of people voting. From 1824 to 1856, a period in which states gradually relaxed their property and taxpaying qualifications, voter participation in presidential elections increased from 3.8 percent to 16.7 percent of the total population. In 1920, when the 19th Amendment giving women the franchise went into effect, voter participation increased to 25.1 percent. In 1928 presidential election, participation of the voting age population topped 50 percent for the first time.

Between 1932 and 1976 both the voting-age population and the number of voters in presidential elections doubled. Voter turnout in the postwar years through 1968 was approximately 60 percent, according to Census Bureau surveys. This relatively high percentage was due largely to passage of new civil rights laws encouraging blacks to vote.

Despite a steady increase in the number of persons voting in the 1970s, voter turnout actually declined as a percentage of eligible voters. Voter participation reached a modern peak of 62.8 percent in the 1960 presidential election. It declined steadily over the next two decades, falling to 61.9 percent in 1964, 55.2 percent in 1972 and 52.8 percent in 1980. Voting in the off-year congressional elections, always lower than in presidential years, also declined during this period.

Despite the get-out-the-vote drives in 1984, voter participation in that year's presidential election rose only slightly to 53.3 percent. In 1988 both major parties cut back their voter registration drives, and turnout dropped to 50.3 percent. Between 1960 and 1988, the turnout of the eligible voting age population declined 12.5 percentage points.

Changes in the age distribution of the electorate figured prominently in the decline during the 1970s and 1980s. Since the surge in the birth rate beginning in 1947, youth has been the most rapidly growing group. However, young adults have tended to vote in much smaller proportions than the rest of the voting-age population. Approximately 11 million young voters entered the electorate in 1972 when the voting age was lowered to 18; even though the total number of voters who cast ballots for president rose to 77,718,554, 4.5 million more than in 1968, the percentage of eligible Americans who voted dropped sharply. (*Growing Franchise in the United States, 1930-1996*, table, p. 81)

Voter turnout increased dramatically in 1992. A total of 104.4 million voters cast ballots, easily surpassing the previous record of 92.7 million in 1984. Turnout was 55.1 percent of the estimated voting age population of 189.5 million, the highest turnout rate for any national election since 1972.

In 1996, however, the decline in voter turnout resumed. Only 49.1 percent of the eligible voting age population went to the polls, a decrease of 6 percentage points from 1992 and the lowest turnout since 1924. It was the first time since 1924 that the turnout for a presidential election was under 50 percent.

Clinton retained the presidency in 1996 by garnering the 47.4 million votes — 24.1 percent of the voting age population — one of the lowest turnouts for winners in the twenty presidential elections held 1920-1996. Lyndon B. Johnson won the highest percentage of the voting age population in these elections with 37.8 percent in 1964. Calvin Coolidge, with just 23.7 of the voting age population, won with the least support.

The 47.4 million votes cast for Bill Clinton in 1996 were the most that a Democratic candidate had ever received, surpassing the 44.9 million cast for Clinton in 1992 and the 43.1 million cast for Lyndon B. Johnson in 1964. The 39.2 million votes for former Republican senator Bob Dole of Kansas were 15.3 million fewer than the record 54.5 million won in 1984 by Ronald Reagan, the first and only presidential candidate to date to receive more than 50 million votes.

Winning 49.2 percent of the popular vote in 1996, Clinton once again won the presidency without securing a majority of the popular vote. In 1992 Clinton won 42.0 percent of the popular vote — only John Quincy Adams (1824), Abraham Lincoln (1860) and Woodrow Wilson (1912) won with lower percentages. (*"Minority" Presidents*, table, p. 82)

Clinton's low shares of the popular vote in 1992 and 1996 were due in part to the presence of a strong third party candidate. Independent candidate Ross Perot won 19.7 million votes in 1992 — 18.9 percent of the total vote and the highest percentage for any third-party candidate since former president Theodore Roosevelt ran in 1912. Perot, running under the Reform Party banner in 1996, took only 8.4 percent of the vote.

In recent years, political activists have argued for simplifying the voter registration process in hopes of reversing the decline in voter turnout. By the late 1980s, the majority of U.S. citizens lived in states that allowed postcard registration. Oregon and Wisconsin allow registration on the day of the election, which may explain why the participation rate in those states is about 10 percentage points higher than the national rate.

In 1993 President Clinton signed the "motor-voter" bill into law. The measure required all states to provide voter registration forms in government offices such as motor vehicle bureaus and public assistance agencies. It also required states to allow voters to send in registration forms by mail. From 1993 to 1996, a record numbers of new voters —10 million—were registered.

In 1996 the states reported a total of 146,211,960 registered voters nationwide, amounting to 74.4 percent of the

Growing Franchise in the United States, 1930-1996

Year	Estimated Population of Voting Age	Vote Cast for Presidential Electors		Vote Cast for U.S. Representatives	
		Number	Percent	Number	Percent
1930	73,623,000	—	—	24,777,000	33.7
1932	75,768,000	39,758,759	52.5	37,657,000	49.7
1934	77,997,000	—	—	32,256,000	41.4
1936	80,174,000	45,654,763	56.9	42,886,000	53.5
1938	82,354,000	—	—	36,236,000	44.0
1940	84,728,000	49,900,418	58.9	46,951,000	55.4
1942	86,465,000	—	—	28,074,000	32.5
1944	85,654,000	47,976,670	56.0	45,103,000	52.7
1946	92,659,000	—	—	34,398,000	37.1
1948	95,573,000	48,793,826	51.1	45,933,000	48.1
1950	98,134,000	—	—	40,342,000	41.1
1952	99,929,000	61,550,918	61.6	57,571,000	57.6
1954	102,075,000	—	—	42,580,000	41.7
1956	104,515,000	62,026,908	59.3	58,426,000	55.9
1958	106,447,000	—	—	45,818,000	43.0
1960	109,672,000	68,838,219	62.8	64,133,000	58.5
1962	112,952,000	—	—	51,267,000	45.4
1964	114,090,000	70,644,592	61.9	65,895,000	57.8
1966	116,638,000	—	—	52,908,000	45.4
1968	120,285,000	73,211,875	60.9	66,288,000	55.1
1970	124,498,000	—	—	54,173,000	43.5
1972	140,777,000	77,718,554	55.2	71,430,000	50.7
1974	146,338,000	—	—	52,495,000	35.9
1976	152,308,000	81,555,889	53.5	74,422,000	48.9
1978	158,369,000	—	—	55,332,000	34.9
1980	163,945,000	86,515,221	52.8	77,995,000	47.6
1982	169,643,000	—	—	64,514,000	38.0
1984	173,995,000	92,652,842	53.3	83,231,000	47.8
1986	177,922,000	—	—	59,619,000	33.5
1988	181,956,000	91,594,809	50.3	81,786,000	44.9
1990	185,812,000	—	—	61,513,000	33.1
1992	189,524,000	104,425,014	55.1	96,239,000	50.8
1994	193,650,000	—	—	69,770,000	36.0
1996	196,511,000	96,277,223	49.0	92,272,000	47.0

Sources: Bureau of the Census, *Statistical Abstract of the United States 1996* (Washington, D.C.: U.S. Government Printing Office, 1996); Federal Election Commission, *Federal Elections 96* (Washington, D.C.: Federal Election Commission, 1997).

voting age population. *(Voter Turnout, table, p. 83)* This was the highest percentage of voter registration since reliable records were first available in 1960. Much to the consternation of motor-voter supporters, however, this increase in voter registration did not translate into an increase in voters on election day. The disappointing turnout in 1996 marked the first time since 1972 that voter registration rose while turnout declined.

Voting Behavior

The Survey Research Center-Center for Political Studies at the University of Michigan analyzes voting behavior in surveys referred to as the National Election Studies (NES).

The Census Bureau also attempts to measure voting behavior by surveying a cross section of eligible voters, defined as all adult civilians of voting age — 18 and older, registered and unregistered — every election year, a practice the bureau began in 1964. These surveys cannot be precise because they are based on people's responses. Estimates made from the survey differ from the actual ballot count because people frequently report that they or members of their families voted when in fact they did not. For example, 61.3 percent of adults eligible to vote reported that they went to the polls in 1992 (the most recent presidential election for which Census Bureau data was available), but the number of ballots cast indicates that only 50.8 percent actually voted.

"Minority" Presidents

Under the U.S. electoral system, there have been 17 presidential elections (decided by either by the Electoral College itself or by the House of Representatives) where the victor did not receive a majority of the popular votes cast in the election. Three of these future presidents — John Quincy Adams in 1824, Rutherford B. Hayes in 1876 and Benjamin Harrison in 1888 — actually trailed their opponents in the popular vote.

The following table shows the percentage of the popular vote received by candidates in the 17 elections in which a "minority" president (designated by boldface type) was elected:

Year Elected	Candidate	Percentage of Popular Vote	Candidate	Percentage of Popular Vote	Candidate	Percentage of Popular Vote	Candidate	Percentage of Popular Vote
1824	Jackson	41.34	**Adams**	30.92	Clay	12.99	Crawford	11.17
1844	**Polk**	49.54	Clay	48.08	Birney	2.30		
1848	**Taylor**	47.28	Cass	42.49	Van Buren	10.12		
1856	**Buchanan**	45.28	Fremont	33.11	Fillmore	21.53		
1860	**Lincoln**	39.82	Douglas	29.46	Breckenridge	18.09	Bell	12.61
1876	Tilden	50.97	**Hayes**	47.95	Cooper	0.97		
1880	**Garfield**	48.27	Hancock	48.25	Weaver	3.32	Others	0.15
1884	**Cleveland**	48.50	Blaine	48.25	Butler	1.74	St. John	1.47
1888	Cleveland	48.62	**Harrison**	47.82	Fisk	2.19	Streeter	1.29
1892	Cleveland	46.05	Harrison	42.96	Weaver	8.50	Others	2.25
1912	**Wilson**	41.84	T. Roosevelt	27.39	Taft	23.18	Debs	5.99
1916	**Wilson**	49.24	Hughes	46.11	Benson	3.18	Others	1.46
1948	**Truman**	49.52	Dewey	45.12	Thurmond	2.40	Wallace	2.38
1960	**Kennedy**	49.72	Nixon	49.55	Others	0.72		
1968	**Nixon**	43.42	Humphrey	42.72	Wallace	13.53	Others	0.33
1992	**Clinton**	43.01	Bush	37.45	Perot	18.91	Others	0.64
1996	**Clinton**	49.24	Dole	40.71	Perot	8.40	Others	1.65

In the *Statistical Abstract of the United States, 1996,* the Census Bureau reported that 68.2 percent of the voting-age population said they were registered to vote in 1992. Of the white voting-age population, 63.6 percent reported they voted in 1992 (59.1 percent in 1988), compared with 54.0 percent (51.5 percent in 1988) of the black population, and 28.9 (28.8 percent in 1988) percent of the Hispanic population.

About 40 percent of Hispanics (who according to the Census Bureau may be of any race) in the United States are not citizens. Omitting non-citizens raises the Hispanic turnout rate to about 48 percent. In 1992 for the first time the Census Bureau tabulated voting among Asians and Pacific Islanders, about 45 percent of whom are not citizens. Their turnout rates were 27.3 percent overall and about 50 percent with non-citizens omitted.

Women outvoted men by almost 2 percentage points in 1992. Of the male voting-age population, 60.2 percent voted, while 62.3 percent of the females voted. The Census Bureau reported 8.5 million more females than males of voting age in 1992, however. The youngest group of voters continued to lag far behind others in participation. Only 38.5 percent of voters aged 18 to 20 reported voting in 1992. The oldest voters (over age 65) had the best participation rate with 70.1 percent, barely topping the 45-64 age group (70.0 percent).

The Midwest continued to lead the rest of the country in 1992 as it had in modern presidential elections, with a reported turnout of 67.2 percent. The West, with 58.5 percent in 1992 had the lowest rate, according to the Census Bureau. The South with a 59.0 percent turnout in 1992 had the lowest rate in 1988 (54.5 percent). In the Northeast, 61.2 percent reported voting in 1992.

Turnout in 1992 was highest among the best-educated Americans. Of those with four or more years of college, 81.0 percent voted in 1992, up from 77.6 percent in 1988. The numbers declined with fewer years of education; 35.1 percent of those with less than an eighth grade education reported voting in 1992 (down from 36.7 percent in 1988). Employed persons had a much higher turnout (63.8 percent) compared with the unemployed (46.2 percent).

Several reasons have been advanced to explain the drop in turnout in modern elections. In addition to the growth of a younger electorate mentioned above, some political scientists point to the growing weakness of party identification for much of the electorate. The major political parties, which voters in the 19th and early 20th century found as the best mechanisms for defining political issues and mobilizing the strength to make a particular policy through to enactment and execution, have been declining in favor. In 1995, for the first time ever, a plurality of voters surveyed by the Gallup poll identified themselves as "other" (36 percent) rather than Republican or Democrat (32 percent each). The lack of party loyalty makes voting decisions more difficult and time-consuming.

Other political scientists have attributed the decline in the percentage of Americans voting to several factors: a growing sense of powerlessness among the electorate — a feeling that one vote was not important and that it made no difference which party won; the lack of appeal of some candidates; the predictable outcome of many races; and long periods of political and economic stability.

Voter Turnout, 1996 Presidential Election

State	Resident Voting Age Population[1]	1996 Voter Registration[2]	Total Vote for President	% of Voting Age Who Registered	% of Voting Age Who Voted	% of Registered Who Voted
Alabama	3,220,000	2,470,766	1,534,349	76.7	47.7	62.5
Alaska	425,000	414,815	241,620	97.6	56.9	58.2
Arizona	3,145,000	2,244,672	1,404,405	71.4	44.7	62.7
Arkansas	1,873,000	1,369,459	884,262	73.1	47.2	64.6
California	22,826,000	15,662,075	10,019,484	68.6	43.9	64.0
Colorado	2,862,000	2,346,253	1,510,704	82.0	52.8	64.4
Connecticut	2,479,000	1,881,323	1,392,614	75.9	56.2	74.0
Delaware	548,000	421,710	270,845	77.0	49.4	64.2
Florida	11,043,000	8,077,877	5,303,794	73.1	48.0	65.7
Georgia	5,418,000	3,811,284	2,299,071	70.3	42.4	60.3
Hawaii	890,000	544,916	360,120	61.2	40.5	66.1
Idaho	858,000	700,430	491,719	81.6	57.3	70.2
Illinois	8,754,000	6,663,301	4,311,391	76.1	49.3	64.7
Indiana	4,374,000	3,488,088	2,135,431	79.7	48.8	61.2
Iowa	2,138,000	1,776,433	1,234,075	83.1	57.7	69.4
Kansas	1,897,000	1,436,418	1,074,300	75.7	56.6	74.8
Kentucky	2,928,000	2,396,086	1,388,708	81.8	44.4	58.0
Louisiana	3,131,000	2,559,352	1,783,959	81.7	57.0	69.7
Maine	945,000	1,001,292	605,897	106.0	64.1	60.5
Maryland	3,820,000	2,587,978	1,780,870	67.7	46.6	68.8
Massachusetts	4,649,000	3,459,193	2,556,786	74.4	55.0	73.9
Michigan	7,072,000	6,677,079	3,848,844	94.4	54.4	57.6
Minnesota	3,422,000	3,067,802	2,192,640	89.6	64.1	71.5
Mississippi	1,967,000	1,715,913	893,857	87.2	45.4	52.1
Missouri	3,995,000	3,342,849	2,158,065	83.7	54.0	64.6
Montana	656,000	590,751	407,261	90.1	62.1	86.9
Nebraska	1,211,000	1,015,056	677,415	83.8	55.9	66.7
Nevada	1,212,000	778,092	464,279	64.2	38.3	59.7
New Hampshire	871,000	754,771	499,175	86.7	57.3	66.1
New Jersey	6,034,000	4,320,866	3,075,807	71.6	51.0	71.2
New Mexico	1,224,000	851,479	556,074	69.6	45.4	65.3
New York	13,564,000	10,162,156	6,316,129	74.9	46.6	62.1
North Carolina	5,519,000	4,318,008	2,515,807	78.2	45.6	58.2
North Dakota[3]	476,000	—	266,411	—	56.0	—
Ohio	8,347,000	6,879,687	4,534,434	82.4	54.3	65.9
Oklahoma	2,426,000	1,979,017	1,206,713	81.6	49.7	61.0
Oregon	2,411,000	1,962,155	1,377,760	81.4	57.1	70.2
Pennsylvania	9,197,000	6,805,612	4,506,118	74.0	49.0	66.2
Rhode Island	751,000	602,692	390,284	80.3	52.0	64.8
South Carolina	2,771,000	1,814,777	1,151,689	65.4	41.6	63.5
South Dakota	535,000	459,971	323,826	86.0	60.5	70.4
Tennessee	4,035,000	2,849,910	1,894,105	70.6	46.9	66.5
Texas	13,597,000	10,540,678	5,611,644	77.5	41.3	53.2
Utah	1,333,000	1,050,452	665,629	78.8	49.9	63.4
Vermont	445,000	385,328	258,449	86.6	58.1	67.1
Virginia	5,083,000	3,322,135	2,416,642	65.4	47.5	72.7
Washington	4,115,000	3,078,128	2,253,837	74.8	54.8	73.2
West Virginia	1,417,000	970,745	636,459	68.5	44.9	65.6
Wisconsin[3]	3,824,000	—	2,196,169	—	57.4	—
Wyoming	356,000	240,711	211,571	67.6	59.4	87.9
District of Columbia	422,000	361,419	185,726	85.6	44.0	51.4
United States	196,511,000	146,211,960	96,277,223	74.4	49.0	66.0

1. Bureau of Census estimate of all persons over the age of 18 (includes a significant number of people not allowed to vote in U.S. elections).
2. The total number of registered voters in 1996 as reported by the states.
3. North Dakota has no formal voter registration system; Wisconsin has election day registration at the polls.

Sources: Bureau of Census, Federal Election Commission, Government Division of the Congressional Research Service, and state election offices.

Victorious Party in Presidential Races, 1860-1996

State	1860	1864	1868	1872	1876	1880	1884	1888	1892	1896	1900	1904	1908	1912	1916	1920	1924	1928	1932	1936	1940	1944	1948	1952	1956	1960	1964	1968	1972	1976	1980	1984	1988	1992	1996	Dem.	Rep.	Other
Ala.	SD	[b]	R	R	D	D	D	D	D	D	D	D	D	D	D	D	D	D	D	D	D	D	SR	D	D[r]	D[s]	R	AI	R	D	R	R	R	R	R	22	9	3
Alaska																										R	D	R	R	R	R	R	R	R	R	1	9	0
Ariz.														D	D	R	R	R	D	D	D	D	D	R	R	R	R	R	R	R	R	R	R	R	D	8	14	0
Ark.	SD	[b]	R	[d]	D	D	D	D	D	D	D	D	D	D	D	D	D	D	D	D	D	D	D	D	D	D	AI	R	D	R	R	R	R	D	D	26	5	2
Calif.	R	R	R	R	R	R	D[f]	R	R	D[g]	R[l]	R	R	R	PR	D	R	R	R	D	D	D	D	R	R	D	R	R	R	D	R	R	R	D	D	11	23	1
Colo.					R	R	R	R	PP	D	D	D	D	D	R	R	R	D	R	D	R	R	R	D	R	R	R	R	D	R	10	20	1
Conn.		R	R	R	R	D	D	D	D	R	R	R	R	D	R	R	R	R	D	D	D	D	R	R	D	R	D	R	R	D	R	R	D	D		13	22	1
Del.	SD	D	D	R	D	D	D	D	D	D	R	R	R	R	D	R	R	R	D	D	D	D	R	R	D	R	D	R	R	D	R	R	R	D	D	16	18	1
D.C.																											D	D	D	D	D	D	D	D	D	9	0	0
Fla.	SD	[b]	R	R	D	D	D	D	D	D	D	D	D	D	D	D	D	D	D	D	D	D	D	R	D	D	D	R	R	D	R	R	R	D	R	20	13	1
Ga.	SD	[b]	D	D[e]	D	D	D	D	D	D	D	D	D	D	D	D	D	D	D	D	D	D	D	D	R	D	R	AI	R	D	R	R	R	D	R	27	5	2
Hawaii																										D	D	D	R	D	D	R	D	D	D	8	2	0
Idaho									PP	D	R	R	D	D	R	R	D	R	R	R	D	R	D	R	R	R	D	R	R	R	R	D	R	R		10	16	1
Ill.	R	R	R	R	R	R	R	R	R	D	R	R	R	D	R	R	R	R	D	D	D	D	R	R	R	D	D	R	R	R	R	R	D	D	D	11	24	0
Ind.	R	R	R	D	R	D	D	R	D	R	R	R	R	D	R	R	R	R	D	D	R	R	R	R	R	R	R	R	R	R	R	R	R	R	R	7	28	0
Iowa	R	R	R	R	R	R	R	R	R	R	R	R	R	D	R	R	R	R	D	D	D	R	R	R	R	R	D	R	R	R	R	R	R	D	D	8	27	0
Kan.		R	R	R	R	R	R	R	PP	D	R	R	R	D	R	R	R	R	D	R	R	R	R	R	R	R	D	R	R	R	R	R	R	R	R	6	27	1
Ky.	CU	D	D	D	D	D	D	D	D	D	R[m]	D	D	D	D	D	D	R	D	D	D	D	D	R	D	R	D	R	R	D	R	R	R	D	D	24	10	1
La.	SD	[b]	D	[d]	R	D	D	D	D	D	D	D	D	D	D	D	D	D	D	D	D	D	SR	D	D	R	D	R	AI	R	D	R	R	R	D	D	23	7	3
Maine	R	R	R	R	R	R	R	R	R	R	R	R	R	R	R	R	R	R	R	R	R	R	R	R	R	D	D	R	R	R	R	R	D	D	D	5	30	0
Md.	SD	R	D	D	D	D	D	D	D	R	R	D[n]	D[o]	D	D	R	R	R	D	D	D	D	R	R	R	D	D	R	R	D	R	R	R	D	D	22	12	1
Mass.	R	R	R	R	R	R	R	R	R	R	R	R	R	D	R	R	R	D	R	D	D	D	D	D	R	D	D	D	R	R	R	R	D	D	D	15	20	0
Mich.	R	R	R	R	R	R	R	R	R[h]	R	R	R	R	PR	R	R	R	R	R	D	D	D	R	R	R	D	D	R	R	R	R	R	D	D	D	8	26	1
Minn.	R	R	R	R	R	R	R	R	R	R	R	R	R	PR	R	R	R	R	D	D	D	D	D	R	R	D	D	D	R	D	D	R	D	D	D	14	20	1
Miss.	SD	[b]	[c]	R	D	D	D	D	D	D	D	D	D	D	D	D	D	D	D	D	D	D	SR	D	D	D	R	AI	R	D	R	R	R	R	R	21	8	3
Mo.	D	R	R	D	D	D	D	D	D	D	D	D	D	D	D	R	R	R	D	D	D	D	D	R	R	D	D	R	R	D	R	R	R	D	D	22	13	0
Mont.									R	D	R	R	D	D	R	R	D	R	R	R	D	R	D	R	R	R	D	R	R	R	R	D	R	R		11	16	0
Neb.		R	R	R	R	R	R	R	D	R	R	R	R	D	R	R	R	R	D	R	R	R	R	R	R	R	D	R	R	R	R	R	R	R	R	7	26	0
Nev.		R	R	R	D	R	R	R	PP	D	D	R	D	R	D	R	R	R	D	D	D	D	R	R	R	D	D	R	R	D	R	R	R	D	D	15	18	1
N.H.	R	R	R	R	R	R	R	R	R	R	R	R	R	D	R	R	R	R	D	D	R	R	R	R	R	D	D	R	R	R	R	R	R	D	R	8	27	0
N.J.	R[a]	D	R	D	D	D	D	D	D	R	R	R	R	D	R	R	R	R	D	D	D	D	R	R	R	D	D	R	R	R	R	R	R	D	D	16	19	0
N.M.														D	D	R	R	R	D	D	D	D	D	R	R	R	R	R	R	R	R	R	R	D	D	11	11	0
N.Y.	R	R	D	R	D	D	D	D	R	R	R	R	R	D	R	R	R	D	D	D	D	D	D	R	R	D	D	R	R	R	R	R	D	D	D	16	19	0
N.C.	SD	[b]	R	R	D	D	D	D	D	D	D	D	D	D	D	D	D	D	D	D	D	D	D	R	D	D	D	R[v]	R	D	R	R	R	R	R	23	10	1
N.D.									[i]	R	R	R	D	R	R	R	R	D	R	R	R	D	R	D	R	R	R	R	R	R	R	R	D	R	R	5	21	1
Ohio	R	R	R	R	R	R	R	R	R	R[j]	R	R	R	D	R	R	R	R	D	D	D	R	R	R	R	D	D	R	R	R	R	R	R	D	D	10	25	0
Okla.													D	D	R	D	D	R	R	D	D	D	D	R	R	R	R	D	R	R[u]	R	D	R	R	R	10	13	0
Ore.	R	R	D	R	R	R	R	R	R	R[k]	R	R	R	D	R	R	R	R	D	D	D	D	R	R	R	D	D	R	R	R	R	R	D	D	D	10	25	0
Pa.	R	R	R	R	R	R	R	R	R	R	R	R	R	PR	R	R	R	R	D	D	D	R	R	R	R	D	D	R	R	R	R	R	D	D	D	9	25	1
R.I.	R	R	R	R	R	R	R	R	R	R	R	R	R	D	R	R	R	D	D	D	D	D	D	R	R	D	D	D	R	D	R	R	D	D	D	15	20	0
S.C.	SD	[b]	R	R	R	D	D	D	D	D	D	D	D	D	D	D	D	D	D	D	D	D	SR	D	D	D	R	R	R	D	R	R	R	R	R	21	8	2
S.D.									R	D	R	R	R	PR	R	R	R	R	D	R	R	R	R	D	R	R	R	R	R	R	R	R	R	D	R	4	22	1
Tenn.	CU	[b]	R	D	D	D	D	D	D	D	D	D	D	D	R	D	R	R	D	D	D	D	D	R	R	R	D[q]	R	R	D	R	R	R	D	R	22	11	1
Texas	SD	[b]	[c]	D	D	D	D	D	D	D	D	D	D	D	D	D	D	D	D	D	D	D	D	R	D	D	D	R	R	D	R	R	R	R	R	23	9	1
Utah										D	R	R	R	R	D	D	D	D	D	R	R	R	R	R	R	R	R	R	R	R	R	R	R	R	R	8	18	0
Vt.	R	R	R	R	R	R	R	R	R	R	R	R	R	R	R	R	R	R	R	R	R	R	R	R	R	R	D	R	R	R	R	R	R	D	D	3	32	0
Va.	CU	[b]	[c]	R	D	D	D	D	D	D	D	D	D	D	D	D	D	D	D	R	R	R	R	R	R	D	D	R	R	R[w]	R	R	R	R	R	19	13	1
Wash.									R	D	R	R	PR	D	R	R	R	D	R	R	R	D	D	D	D	R	R	R	D	D	R[x]	R	R	D	D	12	14	1
W.Va.		R	R	D	D	D	D	D	R	R	R	R	D	R[p]	R	R	R	D	D	D	D	D	D	R	R	D	D	R	R	D	R	D[y]	D			20	14	0
Wis.	R	R	R	R	R	R	R	R	R	D	R	R	R	D	R	R	R	R	PR	R	R	D	R	R	R	D	D	R	R	R	R	R	D	D	D	11	23	1
Wyo.									R	D	R	R	D	R	R	R	D	R	R	R	D	R	D	R	R	R	R	R	R	R	R	D	R	R		8	19	0
Winning Party	R	R	R	R	R	R	D	R	D	R	R	R	R	D	D	R	R	R	D	D	D	D	D	R	R	D	D	R	R	D	R	R	R	D	D	14	21	0

Note: With the exception of the District of Columbia, blanks indicate states not yet admitted to the Union. The District of Columbia received the presidential vote in 1961.

Key: AI—American Independent Party; CU—Constitutional Union Party; D—Democratic Party; PP—People's Party; PR—Progressive (Bull Moose) Party; R—Republican Party; SD—Southern Democratic Party; SR—States' Rights Democratic Party.

a Four electors voted Republican; three, Democratic.
b Confederate states did not vote in 1864.
c Did not vote in 1868.
d Votes were not counted.
e Three votes for Greeley not counted.
f Five electors voted Democratic; one, Republican.
g Eight electors voted Democratic; one, Republican.
h Nine electors voted Republican; five, Democratic.
i One vote each for Democratic, Republican and People's parties.
j Twenty-two electors voted Republican; one, Democratic.
k Three electors voted Republican; one, People's Party.
l Eight electors voted Republican; one, Democratic.
m Twelve electors voted Republican; one, Democratic.
n Seven electors voted Democratic; one, Republican.
o Six electors voted Democratic; two, Republican.
p Seven electors voted Republican; one, Democratic.
q Eleven electors voted Democratic; one, States' Rights.
r One elector voted for Walter B. Jones.
s Six of eleven electors voted for Harry F. Byrd.
t Eight independent electors voted for Byrd.
u One vote cast for Byrd.
v Twelve electors voted Republican; one, American Independent.
w One elector voted Libertarian.
x One elector voted for Ronald Reagan.
y One elector voted for Lloyd Bentsen.

Popular Vote Returns for
President, 1824-1996

Sources for Presidential Returns

The presidential election popular returns presented in this section (pages 87-127), except where indicated by a footnote, were obtained from the following sources. The returns for 1824 to 1916 are from Inter-University Consortium for Political and Social Research (ICPSR) at the University of Michigan. The returns from 1920 to 1992 are from Richard M. Scammon and Alice V. McGillivray, *America at the Polls* (Washington, D.C.: Congressional Quarterly, 1994); the returns for 1996 are from *Federal Elections 96* (Washington, D.C.: Federal Election Commission, 1997).

The 1824 starting date for the ICPSR collection was based on factors such as the pronounced trend by 1824 for the election of presidential electors by popular vote, as well as the availability, accessibility and quality of the returns. The bulk of the ICPSR election data collection consists of returns at the county level in computer-readable form.

The collection of ICPSR presidential returns — part of a larger project involving gubernatorial, House and Senate returns — began in 1962 under grants from the Social Science Research Council and the National Science Foundation. Scholars searched state and local archives, newspaper files and other sources for the data. In as many cases as possible, multiple sources were consulted. Although general preference was given to official sources, these scholars were charged with evaluating the quality and completeness of all available sources.

Table Organization

For each presidential election from 1824 to 1996, the following information is provided in the tables for the popular returns:
- Names and party affiliations of major candidates.
- Total state-by-state popular vote for president.
- State-by-state breakdown of the popular vote and the percentage of the vote received by each candidate.
- The aggregate vote and percentage of the total vote received in each state by minor party candidates, minor parties running unpledged electors or unidentified votes. These figures appear in the column designated "Other"; a complete breakdown of these votes appears on pages 128-138.
- The plurality received by the candidate who carried each state, along with the candidate's party designation.
- The total national popular vote for president, the total national popular vote and percentage of the vote received by each candidate and the nationwide plurality of the candidate who received the greatest number of votes.

The omission of popular vote returns for a state *after 1824* indicates an absence of popular voting for that election. The South Carolina legislature, for example, chose the state's presidential electors until 1860, and the state did not participate in the 1864 presidential election because of the Civil War. Thus, the first popular vote returns shown for South Carolina are for the 1868 election.

Party Designation

In many cases presidential candidates appeared on state ballots under different, even *multiple* party designations. Thus, in the returns for 1968, George C. Wallace ran for president under a variety of party designations in different states: Democratic, American, American Independent, Independent, George Wallace Party, Conservative, American Party of Missouri, Independent American, Courage, and George Wallace and Independent.

To provide one party designation for presidential candidates for the elections 1824 through 1916, Congressional Quarterly has aggregated under a single party designation the votes of candidates who are listed in the ICPSR data as receiving votes under more than one party designation. The source used for assigning party designation for these years is Svend Petersen, *A Statistical History of the American Presidential Elections* (Westport, Conn.: Greenwood Press, 1981). For the 1920 to 1992 elections, the source for party designation is Scammon and McGillivray, *America at the Polls* (Washington, D.C.: Congressional Quarterly, 1994). For 1968, Scammon lists Wallace as an American Independent, and Congressional Quarterly follows this usage. For the 1996 election, the sources for party designation is *Federal Elections 96* (Washington, D.C.: Federal Election Commission, 1997).

Vote Totals and Percentages

The total popular vote for each candidate in a given election was determined by adding the votes received by that candidate in each state (including write-in votes where available), even though the vote totals for some states may have come from sources other than ICPSR, Scammon or the Federal Election Commission.

The percentages of the vote received in each state and nationally by any candidate or party has been calculated to two decimal places and rounded to one place; thus, 0.05 percent is listed as 0.1 percent. Due to rounding, state and national percentages do not always equal 100 percent.

Pluralities

The plurality column represents the differences between the vote received by the first- and second-place finishers in each state and in the nation. In most cases, most notably in 1912 and 1924, a losing major party candidate finished in third place in a state. In those few cases where votes from the "Other" column were needed to calculate the plurality, a footnote provides an explanation. (For a breakdown of "Other" votes, see Popular Vote Returns: Minor Candidates and Parties, pp. 128-138.)

1824 Presidential Election

STATE	TOTAL VOTE	JOHN Q. ADAMS (Democratic-Republican)		ANDREW JACKSON (Democratic-Republican)		HENRY CLAY (Democratic-Republican)		WILLIAM H. CRAWFORD (Democratic-Republican)		OTHER [1]		PLURALITY [2]	
		Votes	%	Votes	%	Votes	%	Votes	%	Votes	%		
Alabama	13,603	2,422	17.8	9,429	69.3	96	0.7	1,656	12.2	—		7,007	AJ
Connecticut	10,647	7,494	70.4	—				1,965	18.5	1,188	11.2	5,529	JQA
Illinois	4,671	1,516	32.5	1,272	27.2	1,036	22.2	847	18.1	—		244	JQA
Indiana	15,838	3,071	19.4	7,444	47.0	5,316	33.6	—		7		2,128	AJ
Kentucky	23,338	—		6,356	27.2	16,982	72.8	—		—		10,626	HC
Maine [3]	12,625	10,289	81.5	—		—		2,336	18.5	—		7,953	JQA
Maryland [3]	33,214	14,632	44.1	14,523	43.7	695	2.1	3,364	10.1	—		109	JQA
Massachusetts	42,056	30,687	73.0	—		—		—		11,369	27.0	24,071	JQA [4]
Mississippi	4,894	1,654	33.8	3,121	63.8			119	2.4	—		1,467	AJ
Missouri	3,432	159	4.6	1,166	34.0	2,042	59.5	32	0.9	33	1.0	876	HC
New Hampshire [3]	10,032	9,389	93.6	—		—		643	6.4	—		8,746	JQA
New Jersey	19,837	8,309	41.9	10,332	52.1	—		1,196	6.0	—		2,023	AJ
North Carolina	36,109	—		20,231	56.0	—		15,622	43.3	256	0.7	4,609	AJ
Ohio [3]	50,024	12,280	24.5	18,489	37.0	19,255	38.5	—		—		766	HC
Pennsylvania	47,073	5,441	11.6	35,736	75.9	1,690	3.6	4,206	8.9	—		30,295	AJ
Rhode Island	2,344	2,144	91.5	—		—		—		200	8.5	1,944	JQA
Tennessee [3]	20,725	216	1.0	20,197	97.5	—		312	1.5	—		19,885	AJ
Virginia	15,371	3,419	22.2	2,975	19.4	419	2.7	8,558	55.7			5,139	WHC
Totals	**365,833**	**113,122**	**30.9**	**151,271**	**41.3**	**47,531**	**13.0**	**40,856**	**11.2**	**13,053**	**3.6**	**38,149**	**AJ**

1828 Presidential Election

STATE	TOTAL VOTE	ANDREW JACKSON (Democratic-Republican)		JOHN Q. ADAMS (National Republican)		OTHER [1]		PLURALITY	
		Votes	%	Votes	%	Votes	%		
Alabama	18,618	16,736	89.9	1,878	10.1	4		14,858	DR
Connecticut	19,378	4,448	23.0	13,829	71.4	1,101	5.7	9,381	NR
Georgia [5]	20,004	19,362	96.8	642	3.2	—		18,720	DR
Illinois	14,222	9,560	67.2	4,662	32.8	—		4,898	DR
Indiana	39,210	22,201	56.6	17,009	43.4	—		5,192	DR
Kentucky	70,776	39,308	55.5	31,468	44.5	—		7,840	DR
Louisiana	8,687	4,605	53.0	4,082	47.0	—		523	DR
Maine	34,789	13,927	40.0	20,773	59.7	89	0.3	6,846	NR
Maryland	45,796	22,782	49.7	23,014	50.3	—		232	NR
Massachusetts	39,074	6,012	15.4	29,836	76.4	3,226	8.3	23,824	NR
Mississippi	8,344	6,763	81.1	1,581	18.9	—		5,182	DR
Missouri	11,654	8,232	70.6	3,422	29.4	—		4,810	DR
New Hampshire	44,035	20,212	45.9	23,823	54.1	—		3,611	NR
New Jersey	45,570	21,809	47.9	23,753	52.1	8		1,944	NR
New York	270,975	139,412	51.4	131,563	48.6	—		7,849	DR
North Carolina	51,747	37,814	73.1	13,918	26.9	15		23,896	DR
Ohio	131,049	67,596	51.6	63,453	48.4	—		4,143	DR
Pennsylvania	152,220	101,457	66.7	50,763	33.3	—		50,694	DR
Rhode Island	3,580	820	22.9	2,755	77.0	5	0.1	1,935	NR
Tennessee [5]	46,533	44,293	95.2	2,240	4.8	—		42,053	DR
Vermont	32,833	8,350	25.4	24,363	74.2	120	0.4	16,013	NR
Virginia	38,924	26,854	69.0	12,070	31.0	—		14,784	DR
Totals	**1,148,018**	**642,553**	**56.0**	**500,897**	**43.6**	**4,568**	**0.4**	**141,656**	**DR**

1. For breakdown of "Other" vote, see minor candidate vote totals, p. 128.
2. For the 1824 plurality winner the designations are JQA (John Quincy Adams), AJ (Andrew Jackson), WHC (William H. Crawford) and H (Henry Clay). Adams was elected president by the House of Representatives.
3. Figures from Svend Petersen, A Statistical History of the American Presidential Elections, (Westport, Conn. 1981), p. 18.
4. Plurality of 24,071 votes is calculated on the basis of 6,616 for unpledged electors.
5. Figures from Petersen, op. cit., p. 20.

1832 Presidential Election

STATE	TOTAL VOTE	ANDREW JACKSON (Democrat)		HENRY CLAY (National Republican)		WILLIAM WIRT (Anti-Mason)		OTHER [1]		PLURALITY	
		Votes	%	Votes	%	Votes	%	Votes	%		
Alabama	14,291	14,286	100.0	5		—		—		14,281	D
Connecticut	32,833	11,269	34.3	18,155	55.3	3,409	10.4	—		6,886	NR
Delaware	8,386	4,110	49.0	4,276	51.0	—		—		166	NR
Georgia [2]	20,750	20,750	100.0	—		—		—		20,750	D
Illinois	21,481	14,609	68.0	6,745	31.4	97	0.5	30	0.1	7,864	D
Indiana	57,152	31,652	55.4	25,473	44.6	27		—		6,179	D
Kentucky	79,741	36,292	45.5	43,449	54.5	—		—		7,157	NR
Louisiana	6,337	3,908	61.7	2,429	38.3	—		—		1,479	D
Maine	62,153	33,978	54.7	27,331	44.0	844	1.4	—		6,647	D
Maryland	38,316	19,156	50.0	19,160	50.0	—		—		4	NR
Massachusetts	67,619	13,933	20.6	31,963	47.3	14,692	21.7	7,031	10.4	17,271	NR
Mississippi	5,750	5,750	100.0	—		—		—		5,750	D
Missouri [2]	5,192	5,192	100.0	—		—		—		5,192	D
New Hampshire	43,793	24,855	56.8	18,938	43.2	—		—		5,917	D
New Jersey	47,760	23,826	49.9	23,466	49.1	468	1.0	—		360	D
New York	323,393	168,497	52.1	154,896	47.9	—		—		13,601	D
North Carolina	29,799	25,261	84.8	4,538	15.2	—		—		20,723	D
Ohio	158,350	81,246	51.3	76,566	48.4	538	0.3	—		4,680	D
Pennsylvania	157,679	90,973	57.7	—		66,706	42.3	—		24,267	D
Rhode Island	5,747	2,051	35.7	2,871	50.0	819	14.3	6	0.1	820	NR
Tennessee	29,425	28,078	95.4	1,347	4.6	—		—		26,731	D
Vermont	32,344	7,865	24.3	11,161	34.5	13,112	40.5	206	0.6	1,951	AM
Virginia	45,682	34,243	75.0	11,436	25.0	3		—		22,807	D
Totals	1,293,973	701,780	54.2	484,205	37.4	100,715	7.8	7,273	0.6	217,575	D

1836 Presidential Election

STATE	TOTAL VOTE	MARTIN VAN BUREN (Democrat)		WILLIAM H. HARRISON (Whig)		HUGH L. WHITE (Whig)		DANIEL WEBSTER (Whig)		OTHER [1]		PLURALITY [3]	
		Votes	%	Votes	%	Votes	%	Votes	%	Votes	%		
Alabama	37,296	20,638	55.3	—		16,658	44.7	—		—		3,980	MVB
Arkansas	3,714	2,380	64.1	—		1,334	35.9	—		—		1,046	MVB
Connecticut	38,093	19,294	50.6	18,799	49.4	—		—		—		495	MVB
Delaware	8,895	4,154	46.7	4,736	53.2	—		—		5	0.1	582	WHH
Georgia	47,259	22,778	48.2	—		24,481	51.8	—		—		1,703	HLW
Illinois	33,589	18,369	54.7	15,220	45.3	—		—		—		3,149	MVB
Indiana	74,423	33,084	44.5	41,339	55.5	—		—		—		8,255	WHH
Kentucky	70,090	33,229	47.4	36,861	52.6	—		—		—		3,632	WHH
Louisiana	7,425	3,842	51.7	—		3,583	48.3	—		—		259	MVB
Maine	38,740	22,825	58.9	14,803	38.2	—		—		1,112	2.9	8,022	MVB
Maryland	48,119	22,267	46.3	25,852	53.7	—		—		—		3,585	WHH
Massachusetts	74,732	33,486	44.8	—		—		41,201	55.1	45	0.1	33,486	DW
Michigan	12,052	6,507	54.0	5,545	46.0	—		—		—		962	MVB
Mississippi	20,079	10,297	51.3	—		9,782	48.7	—		—		515	MVB
Missouri [4]	18,332	10,995	60.0	—		7,337	40.0	—		—		3,658	MVB
New Hampshire	24,925	18,697	75.0	6,228	25.0	—		—		—		12,469	MVB
New Jersey	51,729	25,592	49.5	26,137	50.5	—		—		—		545	WHH
New York	305,343	166,795	54.6	138,548	45.4	—		—		—		28,247	MVB
North Carolina	50,153	26,631	53.1	—		23,521	46.9	—		1		3,110	MVB
Ohio	202,931	97,122	47.9	105,809	52.1	—		—		—		8,687	WHH
Pennsylvania	178,701	91,466	51.2	87,235	48.8	—		—		—		4,231	MVB
Rhode Island	5,673	2,962	52.2	2,710	47.8	—		—		1		252	MVB
Tennessee	62,197	26,170	42.1	—		36,027	57.9	—		—		9,857	HLW
Vermont	35,099	14,040	4	20,994	59.8	—		—		65	0.2	6,954	WHH
Virginia	53,945	30,556	56.6	—		23,384	43.3	—		5		7,172	MVB
Totals	1,503,534	764,176	50.8	550,816	36.6	146,107	9.7	41,201	2.7	1,234	0.1	213,360	MVB

1. For breakdown of "Other" vote, see minor candidate vote totals, p. 128.
2. Figures from Petersen, op. cit., p. 21.
3. For the 1836 plurality winner, the designations are MVB (Martin Van Buren), WHH (William Henry Harrison), HLW (Hugh L. White) and DW (Daniel Webster).
4. Figures from Petersen, op. cit., p. 22.

1840 Presidential Election

STATE	TOTAL VOTE	WILLIAM H. HARRISON (Whig)		MARTIN VAN BUREN (Democrat)		JAMES G. BIRNEY (Liberty)		OTHER [1]		PLURALITY	
		Votes	%	Votes	%	Votes	%	Votes	%		
Alabama	62,511	28,515	45.6	33,996	54.4	—		—		5,481	D
Arkansas	11,839	5,160	43.6	6,679	56.4	—		—		1,519	D
Connecticut	56,879	31,598	55.6	25,281	44.4	—		—		6,317	W
Delaware	10,852	5,967	55.0	4,872	44.9	—		13	0.1	1,095	W
Georgia	72,322	40,339	55.8	31,983	44.2	—		—		8,356	W
Illinois	93,175	45,574	48.9	47,441	50.9	160	0.2	—		1,867	D
Indiana	117,605	65,280	55.5	51,696	44.0	30		599	0.5	13,584	W
Kentucky	91,104	58,488	64.2	32,616	35.8	—		—		25,872	W
Louisiana	18,912	11,296	59.7	7,616	40.3	—		—		3,680	W
Maine	92,802	46,612	50.2	46,190	49.8	—		—		422	W
Maryland	62,280	33,528	53.8	28,752	46.2	—		—		4,776	W
Massachusetts	126,825	72,852	57.4	52,355	41.3	1,618	1.3	—		20,497	W
Michigan	44,029	22,933	52.1	21,096	47.9	—		—		1,837	W
Mississippi	36,525	19,515	53.4	17,010	46.6	—		—		2,505	W
Missouri	52,923	22,954	43.4	29,969	56.6	—		—		7,015	D
New Hampshire	59,956	26,310	43.9	32,774	54.7	872	1.5	—		6,464	D
New Jersey	64,454	33,351	51.7	31,034	48.1	69	0.1	—		2,317	W
New York	441,543	226,001	51.2	212,733	48.2	2,809	0.6	—		13,268	W
North Carolina	80,735	46,567	57.7	34,168	42.3	—		—		12,399	W
Ohio	272,890	148,043	54.3	123,944	45.4	903	0.3	—		24,099	W
Pennsylvania	287,695	144,023	50.1	143,672	49.9	—		—		351	W
Rhode Island	8,631	5,213	60.4	3,263	37.8	19	0.2	136	1.6	1,950	W
Tennessee	108,145	60,194	55.7	47,951	44.3	—		—		12,243	W
Vermont	50,782	32,440	63.9	18,006	35.5	317	0.6	19		14,434	W
Virginia	86,394	42,637	49.4	43,757	50.6	—		—		1,120	D
Totals	**2,411,808**	**1,275,390**	**52.9**	**1,128,854**	**46.8**	**6,797**	**0.3**	**767**		**146,536**	**W**

1844 Presidential Election

STATE	TOTAL VOTE	JAMES K. POLK (Democrat)		HENRY CLAY (Whig)		JAMES G. BIRNEY (Liberty)		OTHER [1]		PLURALITY	
		Votes	%	Votes	%	Votes	%	Votes	%		
Alabama	63,403	37,401	59.0	26,002	41.0	—		—		11,399	D
Arkansas	15,150	9,546	63.0	5,604	37.0	—		—		3,942	D
Connecticut	64,616	29,841	46.2	32,832	50.8	1,943	3.0	—		2,991	W
Delaware	12,247	5,970	48.7	6,271	51.2	—		6		301	W
Georgia	86,247	44,147	51.2	42,100	48.8	—		—		2,047	D
Illinois	109,057	58,795	53.9	45,854	42.0	3,469	3.2	939	0.9	12,941	D
Indiana	140,157	70,183	50.1	67,866	48.4	2,108	1.5	—		2,317	D
Kentucky	113,237	51,988	45.9	61,249	54.1	—		—		9,261	W
Louisiana	26,865	13,782	51.3	13,083	48.7	—		—		699	D
Maine	84,933	45,719	53.8	34,378	40.5	4,836	5.7	—		11,341	D
Maryland	68,690	32,706	47.6	35,984	52.4	—		—		3,278	W
Massachusetts	132,037	53,039	40.2	67,062	50.8	10,830	8.2	1,106	0.8	14,023	W
Michigan	55,560	27,737	49.9	24,185	43.5	3,638	6.5	—		3,552	D
Mississippi	45,004	25,846	57.4	19,158	42.6	—		—		6,688	D
Missouri	72,522	41,322	57.0	31,200	43.0	—		—		10,122	D
New Hampshire	49,187	27,160	55.2	17,866	36.3	4,161	8.5	—		9,294	D
New Jersey	75,944	37,495	49.4	38,318	50.5	131	0.2	—		823	W
New York	485,882	237,588	48.9	232,482	47.8	15,812	3.3	—		5,106	D
North Carolina	82,521	39,287	47.6	43,232	52.4	—		2		3,945	W
Ohio	312,300	149,127	47.8	155,091	49.7	8,082	2.6	—		5,964	W
Pennsylvania	331,645	167,311	50.4	161,195	48.6	3,139	0.9	—		6,116	D
Rhode Island	12,194	4,867	39.9	7,322	60.0	—		5		2,455	W
Tennessee	119,957	59,917	49.9	60,040	50.1	—		—		123	W
Vermont	48,765	18,041	37.0	26,770	54.9	3,954	8.1	—		8,729	W
Virginia	95,539	50,679	53.0	44,860	47.0	—		—		5,819	D
Totals	**2,703,659**	**1,339,494**	**49.5**	**1,300,004**	**48.1**	**62,103**	**2.3**	**2,058**	**0.1**	**39,490**	**D**

1. For breakdown of "Other" vote, see minor candidate vote totals, p. 128.

1848 Presidential Election

STATE	TOTAL VOTE	ZACHARY TAYLOR (Whig)		LEWIS CASS (Democrat)		MARTIN VAN BUREN (Free Soil)		OTHER [1]		PLURALITY	
		Votes	%	Votes	%	Votes	%	Votes	%		
Alabama	61,659	30,482	49.4	31,173	50.6	—		4		691	D
Arkansas	16,888	7,587	44.9	9,301	55.1	—		—		1,714	D
Connecticut	62,398	30,318	48.6	27,051	43.4	5,005	8.0	24		3,267	W
Delaware	12,432	6,440	51.8	5,910	47.5	82	0.7	—		530	W
Florida	7,203	4,120	57.2	3,083	42.8	—		—		1,037	W
Georgia	92,317	47,532	51.5	44,785	48.5	—		—		2,747	W
Illinois	124,596	52,853	42.4	55,952	44.9	15,702	12.6	89	0.1	3,099	D
Indiana	152,394	69,668	45.7	74,695	49.0	8,031	5.3	—		5,027	D
Iowa	22,271	9,930	44.6	11,238	50.5	1,103	5.0	—		1,308	D
Kentucky	116,865	67,145	57.5	49,720	42.5	—		—		17,425	W
Louisiana	33,866	18,487	54.6	15,379	45.4	—		—		3,108	W
Maine	87,625	35,273	40.3	40,195	45.9	12,157	13.9	—		4,922	D
Maryland	72,359	37,702	52.1	34,528	47.7	129	0.2	—		3,174	W
Massachusetts	134,748	61,072	45.3	35,281	26.2	38,333	28.4	62		22,739	W
Michigan	65,082	23,947	36.8	30,742	47.2	10,393	16.0	—		6,795	D
Mississippi	52,456	25,911	49.4	26,545	50.6	—		—		634	D
Missouri	72,748	32,671	44.9	40,077	55.1	—		—		7,406	D
New Hampshire	50,104	14,781	29.5	27,763	55.4	7,560	15.1	—		12,982	D
New Jersey	77,745	40,015	51.5	36,901	47.5	829	1.1	—		3,114	W
New York	455,944	218,583	47.9	114,319	25.1	120,497	26.4	2,545	0.6	98,086	W
North Carolina	79,826	44,054	55.2	35,772	44.8	—		—		8,282	W
Ohio	328,987	138,656	42.1	154,782	47.0	35,523	10.8	26		16,126	D
Pennsylvania	369,092	185,730	50.3	172,186	46.7	11,176	3.0	—		13,544	W
Rhode Island	11,049	6,705	60.7	3,613	32.7	726	6.6	5		3,092	W
Tennessee	122,463	64,321	52.5	58,142	47.5	—		—		6,179	W
Texas	17,000	5,281	31.1	11,644	68.5	—		75	0.4	6,363	D
Vermont	47,897	23,117	48.3	10,943	22.8	13,837	28.9	—		9,280	W
Virginia	92,004	45,265	49.2	46,739	50.8	—		—		1,474	D
Wisconsin	39,166	13,747	35.1	15,001	38.3	10,418	26.6	—		1,254	D
Totals	**2,879,184**	**1,361,393**	**47.3**	**1,223,460**	**42.5**	**291,501**	**10.1**	**2,830**	**0.1**	**137,933**	**W**

1. For breakdown of "Other" vote, see minor candidate vote totals, p. 128.

1852 Presidential Election

STATE	TOTAL VOTE	FRANKLIN PIERCE (Democrat)		WINFIELD SCOTT (Whig)		JOHN P. HALE (Free Soil)		OTHER [1]		PLURALITY	
		Votes	%	Votes	%	Votes	%	Votes	%		
Alabama	44,147	26,881	60.9	15,061	34.1	—		2,205	5.0	11,820	D
Arkansas	19,577	12,173	62.2	7,404	37.8	—		—		4,769	D
California	76,810	40,721	53.0	35,972	46.8	61	0.1	56	0.1	4,749	D
Connecticut	66,781	33,249	49.8	30,359	45.5	3,161	4.7	12		2,890	D
Delaware	12,673	6,318	49.9	6,293	49.7	62	0.5	—		25	D
Florida	7,193	4,318	60.0	2,875	40.0	—		—		1,443	D
Georgia [2]	62,626	40,516	64.7	16,660	26.6	—		5,450	8.7	23,856	D
Illinois	154,974	80,378	51.9	64,733	41.8	9,863	6.4	—		15,645	D
Indiana	183,176	95,340	52.0	80,907	44.2	6,929	3.8	—		14,433	D
Iowa	35,364	17,763	50.2	15,856	44.8	1,606	4.5	139	0.4	1,907	D
Kentucky	111,643	53,949	48.3	57,428	51.4	266	0.2	—		3,479	W
Louisiana	35,902	18,647	51.9	17,255	48.1	—		—		1,392	D
Maine	82,182	41,609	50.6	32,543	39.6	8,030	9.8	—		9,066	D
Maryland	75,120	40,022	53.3	35,077	46.7	21		—		4,945	D
Massachusetts	127,103	44,569	35.1	52,683	41.4	28,023	22.0	1,828	1.4	8,114	W
Michigan	82,939	41,842	50.4	33,860	40.8	7,237	8.7	—		7,982	D
Mississippi	44,454	26,896	60.5	17,558	39.5	—		—		9,338	D
Missouri	68,801	38,817	56.4	29,984	43.6	—		—		8,833	D
New Hampshire	50,535	28,503	56.4	15,486	30.6	6,546	13.0	—		13,017	D
New Jersey	83,926	44,301	52.8	38,551	45.9	336	0.4	738	0.9	5,750	D
New York	522,294	262,083	50.2	234,882	45.0	25,329	4.8	—		27,201	D
North Carolina	78,891	39,788	50.4	39,043	49.5	—		60	0.1	745	D
Ohio	352,903	169,193	47.9	152,577	43.2	31,133	8.8	—		16,616	D
Pennsylvania	387,920	198,568	51.2	179,182	46.2	8,500	2.2	1,670	0.4	19,386	D
Rhode Island	17,005	8,735	51.4	7,626	44.8	644	3.8	—		1,109	D
Tennessee	115,486	56,900	49.3	58,586	50.7	—		—		1,686	W
Texas	20,223	14,857	73.5	5,356	26.5	—		10		9,501	D
Vermont	43,838	13,044	29.8	22,173	50.6	8,621	19.7	—		9,129	W
Virginia	132,604	73,872	55.7	58,732	44.3	—		—		15,140	D
Wisconsin	64,740	33,658	52.0	22,240	34.4	8,842	13.7	—		11,418	D
Totals	3,161,830	1,607,510	50.8	1,386,942	43.9	155,210	4.9	12,168	0.4	220,568	D

1. For breakdown of "Other" vote, see minor candidate vote totals, p. 128.
2. Figures from Petersen, op. cit., p. 31.

1856 Presidential Election

STATE	TOTAL VOTE	JAMES BUCHANAN (Democrat)		JOHN C. FREMONT (Republican)		MILLARD FILLMORE (Whig-American)		OTHER [1]		PLURALITY	
		Votes	%	Votes	%	Votes	%	Votes	%		
Alabama	75,291	46,739	62.1	—		28,552	37.9	—		18,187	D
Arkansas	32,642	21,910	67.1	—		10,732	32.9	—		11,178	D
California	110,255	53,342	48.4	20,704	18.8	36,195	32.8	14		17,147	D
Connecticut	80,360	35,028	43.6	42,717	53.2	2,615	3.3	—		7,689	R
Delaware	14,598	8,004	54.8	310	2.1	6,275	43.0	9	0.1	1,729	D
Florida	11,191	6,358	56.8	—		4,833	43.2	—		1,525	D
Georgia	99,020	56,581	57.1	—		42,439	42.9	—		14,142	D
Illinois	239,334	105,528	44.1	96,275	40.2	37,531	15.7	—		9,253	D
Indiana	235,401	118,670	50.4	94,375	40.1	22,356	9.5	—		24,295	D
Iowa	92,310	37,568	40.7	45,073	48.8	9,669	10.5	—		7,505	R
Kentucky	142,058	74,642	52.5	—		67,416	47.5	—		7,226	D
Louisiana	42,873	22,164	51.7	—		20,709	48.3	—		1,455	D
Maine	109,689	39,140	35.7	67,279	61.3	3,270	3.0	—		28,139	R
Maryland	86,860	39,123	45.0	285	0.3	47,452	54.6	—		8,329	WA
Massachusetts	170,048	39,244	23.1	108,172	63.6	19,626	11.5	3,006	1.8	68,928	R
Michigan	125,558	52,136	41.5	71,762	57.2	1,660	1.3	—		19,626	R
Mississippi	59,647	35,456	59.4	—		24,191	40.6	—		11,265	D
Missouri	106,486	57,964	54.4	—		48,522	45.6	—		9,442	D
New Hampshire	69,774	31,891	45.7	37,473	53.7	410	0.6	—		5,582	R
New Jersey	99,396	46,943	47.2	28,338	28.5	24,115	24.3	—		18,605	D
New York	596,486	195,878	32.8	276,004	46.3	124,604	20.9	—		80,126	R
North Carolina	84,963	48,243	56.8	—		36,720	43.2	—		11,523	D
Ohio	386,640	170,874	44.2	187,497	48.5	28,121	7.3	148		16,623	R
Pennsylvania	460,937	230,772	50.1	147,963	32.1	82,202	17.8	—		82,809	D
Rhode Island	19,822	6,680	33.7	11,467	57.8	1,675	8.5	—		4,787	R
Tennessee	133,582	69,704	52.2	—		63,878	47.8	—		5,826	D
Texas	48,005	31,995	66.6	—		16,010	33.4	—		15,985	D
Vermont	50,675	10,569	20.9	39,561	78.1	545	1.1	—		28,992	R
Virginia	150,233	90,083	60.0	—		60,150	40.0	—		29,933	D
Wisconsin	120,513	52,843	43.8	67,090	55.7	580	0.5	—		14,247	R
Totals	**4,054,647**	**1,836,072**	**45.3**	**1,342,345**	**33.1**	**873,053**	**21.5**	**3,177**	**0.1**	**493,727**	**D**

1. For breakdown of "Other" vote, see minor candidate vote totals, p. 129.

1860 Presidential Election

STATE	TOTAL VOTE	ABRAHAM LINCOLN (Republican)		STEPHEN A. DOUGLAS (Democrat)		JOHN C. BRECKINRIDGE (Southern Democrat)		JOHN BELL (Constitutional Union)		OTHER [1]		PLURALITY	
		Votes	%	Votes	%	Votes	%	Votes	%	Votes	%		
Alabama	90,122	—		13,618	15.1	48,669	54.0	27,835	30.9	—		20,834	SD
Arkansas	54,152	—		5,357	9.9	28,732	53.1	20,063	37.0	—		8,669	SD
California	119,827	38,733	32.3	37,999	31.7	33,969	28.3	9,111	7.6	15		734	R
Connecticut	74,819	43,488	58.1	15,431	20.6	14,372	19.2	1,528	2.0	—		28,057	R
Delaware	16,115	3,822	23.7	1,066	6.6	7,339	45.5	3,888	24.1	—		3,451	SD
Florida	13,301	—		223	1.7	8,277	62.2	4,801	36.1	—		3,476	SD
Georgia	106,717	—		11,581	10.9	52,176	48.9	42,960	40.3	—		9,216	SD
Illinois	339,666	172,171	50.7	160,215	47.2	2,331	0.7	4,914	1.4	35		11,956	R
Indiana	272,143	139,033	51.1	115,509	42.4	12,295	4.5	5,306	1.9	—		23,524	R
Iowa	128,739	70,302	54.6	55,639	43.2	1,035	0.8	1,763	1.4	—		14,663	R
Kentucky [2]	146,216	1,364	0.9	25,651	17.5	53,143	36.3	66,058	45.2	—		12,915	CU
Louisiana	50,510	—		7,625	15.1	22,681	44.9	20,204	40.0	—		2,477	SD
Maine	100,918	62,811	62.2	29,693	29.4	6,368	6.3	2,046	2.0	—		33,118	R
Maryland	92,502	2,294	2.5	5,966	6.4	42,482	45.9	41,760	45.1	—		722	SD
Massachusetts	169,876	106,684	62.8	34,370	20.2	6,163	3.6	22,331	13.1	328	0.2	72,314	R
Michigan	154,758	88,481	57.2	65,057	42.0	805	0.5	415	0.3	—		23,424	R
Minnesota	34,804	22,069	63.4	11,920	34.2	748	2.1	50	0.1	17		10,149	R
Mississippi	69,095	—		3,282	4.7	40,768	59.0	25,045	36.2	—		15,723	SD
Missouri	165,563	17,028	10.3	58,801	35.5	31,362	18.9	58,372	35.3	—		429	D
New Hampshire	65,943	37,519	56.9	25,887	39.3	2,125	3.2	412	0.6	—		11,632	R
New Jersey [2]	121,215	58,346	48.1	62,869	51.9	—		—		—		4,523	D
New York	675,156	362,646	53.7	312,510	46.3	—		—		—		50,136	R
North Carolina	96,712	—		2,737	2.8	48,846	50.5	45,129	46.7	—		3,717	SD
Ohio	442,866	231,709	52.3	187,421	42.3	11,406	2.6	12,194	2.8	136		44,288	R
Oregon	14,758	5,329	36.1	4,136	28.0	5,075	34.4	218	1.5	—		254	R
Pennsylvania	476,442	268,030	56.3	16,765	3.5	178,871	37.5	12,776	2.7	—		89,159	R
Rhode Island	19,951	12,244	61.4	7,707	38.6	—		—		—		4,537	R
Tennessee	146,106	—		11,281	7.7	65,097	44.6	69,728	47.7	—		4,631	CU
Texas	62,855	—		18		47,454	75.5	15,383	24.5	—		32,071	SD
Vermont	44,644	33,808	75.7	8,649	19.4	218	0.5	1,969	4.4	—		25,159	R
Virginia	166,891	1,887	1.1	16,198	9.7	74,325	44.5	74,481	44.6	—		156	CU
Wisconsin	152,179	86,110	56.6	65,021	42.7	887	0.6	161	0.1	—		21,089	R
Totals	4,685,561	1,865,908	39.9	1,380,202	29.5	848,019	18.1	590,901	12.6	531		485,706	R

1. For breakdown of "Other" vote, see minor candidate vote totals, p. 129.
2. Figures from Petersen, op. cit., p. 37.

1864 Presidential Election

STATE [1]	TOTAL VOTE	ABRAHAM LINCOLN (Republican)		GEORGE B. McCLELLAN (Democrat)		OTHER [2]		PLURALITY	
		Votes	%	Votes	%	Votes	%		
California	105,890	62,053	58.6	43,837	41.4	—		18,216	R
Connecticut	86,958	44,673	51.4	42,285	48.6	—		2,388	R
Delaware	16,922	8,155	48.2	8,767	51.8	—		612	D
Illinois	348,236	189,512	54.4	158,724	45.6	—		30,788	R
Indiana	280,117	149,887	53.5	130,230	46.5	—		19,657	R
Iowa	132,947	83,858	63.1	49,089	36.9	—		34,769	R
Kansas	21,580	17,089	79.2	3,836	17.8	655	3.0	13,253	R
Kentucky	92,088	27,787	30.2	64,301	69.8	—		36,514	D
Maine	114,797	67,805	59.1	46,992	40.9	—		20,813	R
Maryland	72,892	40,153	55.1	32,739	44.9	—		7,414	R
Massachusetts	175,493	126,742	72.2	48,745	27.8	6		77,997	R
Michigan	165,279	91,133	55.1	74,146	44.9	—		16,987	R
Minnesota	42,433	25,031	59.0	17,376	40.9	26	0.1	7,655	R
Missouri	104,346	72,750	69.7	31,596	30.3	—		41,154	R
Nevada	16,420	9,826	59.8	6,594	40.2	—		3,232	R
New Hampshire	69,630	36,596	52.6	33,034	47.4	—		3,562	R
New Jersey	128,744	60,724	47.2	68,020	52.8	—		7,296	D
New York	730,721	368,735	50.5	361,986	49.5	—		6,749	R
Ohio	471,283	265,674	56.4	205,609	43.6	—		60,065	R
Oregon	18,350	9,888	53.9	8,457	46.1	5		1,431	R
Pennsylvania	573,735	296,292	51.6	277,443	48.4	—		18,849	R
Rhode Island	23,067	14,349	62.2	8,718	37.8	—		5,631	R
Vermont	55,740	42,419	76.1	13,321	23.9	—		29,098	R
West Virginia	34,877	23,799	68.2	11,078	31.8	—		12,721	R
Wisconsin	149,342	83,458	55.9	65,884	44.1	—		17,574	R
Totals	**4,031,887**	**2,218,388**	**55.0**	**1,812,807**	**45.0**	**692**		**405,581**	**R**

1. Eleven Confederate states did not participate in election because of the Civil War.
2. For breakdown of "Other" vote, see minor candidate vote totals, p. 129.

1868 Presidential Election

STATE [1]	TOTAL VOTE	ULYSSES S. GRANT (Republican)		HORATIO SEYMOUR (Democrat)		OTHER [2]		PLURALITY	
		Votes	%	Votes	%	Votes	%		
Alabama	149,594	76,667	51.3	72,921	48.7	6		3,746	R
Arkansas	41,190	22,112	53.7	19,078	46.3	—		3,034	R
California	108,656	54,588	50.2	54,068	49.8	—		520	R
Connecticut	98,570	50,789	51.5	47,781	48.5	—		3,008	R
Delaware	18,571	7,614	41.0	10,957	59.0	—		3,343	D
Georgia	159,816	57,109	35.7	102,707	64.3	—		45,598	D
Illinois	449,420	250,304	55.7	199,116	44.3	—		51,188	R
Indiana	343,528	176,548	51.4	166,980	48.6	—		9,568	R
Iowa	194,439	120,399	61.9	74,040	38.1	—		46,359	R
Kansas	43,630	30,027	68.8	13,600	31.2	3		16,427	R
Kentucky	155,455	39,566	25.5	115,889	74.5	—		76,323	D
Louisiana	113,488	33,263	29.3	80,225	70.7	—		46,962	D
Maine	112,962	70,502	62.4	42,460	37.6	—		28,042	R
Maryland	92,795	30,438	32.8	62,357	67.2	—		31,919	D
Massachusetts	195,508	136,379	69.8	59,103	30.2	26		77,276	R
Michigan	225,632	128,563	57.0	97,069	43.0	—		31,494	R
Minnesota	71,620	43,545	60.8	28,075	39.2	—		15,470	R
Missouri	152,488	86,860	57.0	65,628	43.0	—		21,232	R
Nebraska	15,291	9,772	63.9	5,519	36.1	—		4,253	R
Nevada	11,689	6,474	55.4	5,215	44.6	—		1,259	R
New Hampshire	68,304	37,718	55.2	30,575	44.8	11		7,143	R
New Jersey	163,133	80,132	49.1	83,001	50.9	—		2,869	D
New York	849,771	419,888	49.4	429,883	50.6	—		9,995	D
North Carolina	181,498	96,939	53.4	84,559	46.6	—		12,380	R
Ohio	518,665	280,159	54.0	238,506	46.0	—		41,653	R
Oregon	22,086	10,961	49.6	11,125	50.4	—		164	D
Pennsylvania	655,662	342,280	52.2	313,382	47.8	—		28,898	R
Rhode Island	19,511	13,017	66.7	6,494	33.3	—		6,523	R
South Carolina	107,538	62,301	57.9	45,237	42.1	—		17,064	R
Tennessee	82,757	56,628	68.4	26,129	31.6	—		30,499	R
Vermont	56,224	44,173	78.6	12,051	21.4	—		32,122	R
West Virginia	49,321	29,015	58.8	20,306	41.2	—		8,709	R
Wisconsin	193,628	108,920	56.3	84,708	43.7	—		24,212	R
Totals	5,722,440	3,013,650	52.7	2,708,744	47.3	46		304,906	R

1. Mississippi, Texas and Virginia did not participate in the election due to Reconstruction. In Florida the state legislature cast the electoral vote.
2. For breakdown of "Other" vote, see minor candidate vote totals, p. 129.

1872 Presidential Election

STATE	TOTAL VOTE	ULYSSES S. GRANT (Republican)		HORACE GREELEY (Democrat, Liberal Republican)		CHARLES O'CONOR (Straight Out Democrat)		OTHER [1]		PLURALITY	
		Votes	%	Votes	%	Votes	%	Votes	%		
Alabama	169,716	90,272	53.2	79,444	46.8	—		—		10,828	R
Arkansas	79,300	41,373	52.2	37,927	47.8	—		—		3,446	R
California	95,785	54,007	56.4	40,717	42.5	1,061	1.1	—		13,290	R
Connecticut	95,992	50,307	52.4	45,685	47.6	—		—		4,622	R
Delaware	21,822	11,129	51.0	10,205	46.8	488	2.2	—		924	R
Florida	33,190	17,763	53.5	15,427	46.5	—		—		2,336	R
Georgia	138,906	62,550	45.0	76,356	55.0	—		—		13,806	D
Illinois	429,971	241,936	56.3	184,884	43.0	3,151	0.7	—		57,052	R
Indiana	349,779	186,147	53.2	163,632	46.8	—		—		22,515	R
Iowa	216,365	131,566	60.8	71,189	32.9	2,221	1.0	11,389	5.3	60,377	R
Kansas	100,512	66,805	66.5	32,970	32.8	156	0.2	581	0.6	33,835	R
Kentucky	191,135	88,766	46.4	99,995	52.3	2,374	1.2	—		11,229	D
Louisiana	128,692	71,663	55.7	57,029	44.3	—		—		14,634	R
Maine	90,523	61,426	67.9	29,097	32.1	—		—		32,329	R
Maryland	134,447	66,760	49.7	67,687	50.3	—		—		927	D
Massachusetts	192,650	133,455	69.3	59,195	30.7	—		—		74,260	R
Michigan	221,569	138,768	62.6	78,651	35.5	2,879	1.3	1,271	0.6	60,117	R
Minnesota	91,339	56,040	61.4	35,131	38.5	—		168	0.2	20,909	R
Mississippi	129,457	82,175	63.5	47,282	36.5	—		—		34,893	R
Missouri	273,059	119,196	43.7	151,434	55.5	2,429	0.9	—		32,238	D
Nebraska	25,932	18,329	70.7	7,603	29.3	—		—		10,726	R
Nevada	14,649	8,413	57.4	6,236	42.6	—		—		2,177	R
New Hampshire	68,906	37,168	53.9	31,425	45.6	—		313	0.5	5,743	R
New Jersey	168,112	91,656	54.5	76,456	45.5	—		—		15,200	R
New York	828,020	440,738	53.2	387,282	46.8	—		—		53,456	R
North Carolina	165,163	94,772	57.4	70,130	42.5	261	0.2	—		24,642	R
Ohio	529,435	281,852	53.2	244,320	46.1	1,163	0.2	2,100	0.4	37,532	R
Oregon	20,107	11,818	58.8	7,742	38.5	547	2.7	—		4,076	R
Pennsylvania	561,629	349,589	62.2	212,040	37.8	—		—		137,549	R
Rhode Island	18,994	13,665	71.9	5,329	28.1	—		—		8,336	R
South Carolina	95,452	72,290	75.7	22,699	23.8	204	0.2	259	0.3	49,591	R
Tennessee	179,046	85,655	47.8	93,391	52.2	—		—		7,736	D
Texas	115,700	47,910	41.4	67,675	58.5	115	0.1	—		19,765	D
Vermont	52,408	41,481	79.2	10,927	20.8	—		—		30,554	R
Virginia	185,195	93,463	50.5	91,647	49.5	85		—		1,816	R
West Virginia	62,467	32,320	51.7	29,532	47.3	615	1.0	—		2,788	R
Wisconsin	192,255	105,012	54.6	86,390	44.9	853	0.4	—		18,622	R
Totals	6,467,679	3,598,235	55.6	2,834,761	43.8	18,602	0.3	16,081	0.3	763,474	R

1. For breakdown of "Other" vote, see minor candidate vote totals, p. 129.

1876 Presidential Election

STATE	TOTAL VOTE	RUTHERFORD B. HAYES [1] (Republican)		SAMUEL J. TILDEN [1] (Democrat)		PETER COOPER (Greenback)		OTHER [2]		PLURALITY	
		Votes	%	Votes	%	Votes	%	Votes	%		
Alabama	171,699	68,708	40.0	102,989	60.0	—		2		34,281	D
Arkansas	96,946	38,649	39.9	58,086	59.9	211	0.2	—		19,437	D
California	155,784	79,258	50.9	76,460	49.1	47		19		2,798	R
Connecticut	122,134	59,033	48.3	61,927	50.7	774	0.6	400	0.3	2,894	D
Delaware	24,133	10,752	44.6	13,381	55.4	—		—		2,629	D
Florida	46,776	23,849	51.0	22,927	49.0	—		—		922	R
Georgia	180,690	50,533	28.0	130,157	72.0	—		—		79,624	D
Illinois	554,368	278,232	50.2	258,611	46.6	17,207	3.1	318	0.1	19,621	R
Indiana	431,073	208,011	48.3	213,529	49.5	9,533	2.2	—		5,518	D
Iowa	293,398	171,326	58.4	112,121	38.2	9,431	3.2	520	0.2	59,205	R
Kansas	124,134	78,324	63.1	37,902	30.5	7,770	6.3	138	0.1	40,422	R
Kentucky	260,626	97,568	37.4	160,060	61.4	—		2,998	1.2	62,492	D
Louisiana	145,823	75,315	51.6	70,508	48.4	—		—		4,807	R
Maine	117,045	66,300	56.6	49,917	42.6	—		828	0.7	16,383	R
Maryland	163,759	71,980	44.0	91,779	56.0	—		—		19,799	D
Massachusetts	259,619	150,063	57.8	108,777	41.9	—		779	0.3	41,286	R
Michigan	318,426	166,901	52.4	141,665	44.5	9,023	2.8	837	0.3	25,236	R
Minnesota	124,160	72,962	58.8	48,799	39.3	2,399	1.9	—		24,163	R
Mississippi	164,776	52,603	31.9	112,173	68.1	—		—		59,570	D
Missouri	350,610	145,027	41.4	202,086	57.6	3,497	1.0	—		57,059	D
Nebraska	49,258	31,915	64.8	17,343	35.2	—		—		14,572	R
Nevada	19,691	10,383	52.7	9,308	47.3	—		—		1,075	R
New Hampshire	80,143	41,540	51.8	38,510	48.1	—		93	0.1	3,030	R
New Jersey	220,193	103,517	47.0	115,962	52.7	714	0.3	—		12,445	D
New York	1,015,503	489,207	48.2	521,949	51.4	1,978	0.2	2,369	0.2	32,742	D
North Carolina	233,911	108,484	46.4	125,427	53.6	—		—		16,943	D
Ohio	658,650	330,698	50.2	323,182	49.1	3,058	0.5	1,712	0.3	7,516	R
Oregon	29,873	15,207	50.9	14,157	47.4	509	1.7	—		1,050	R
Pennsylvania	758,973	384,157	50.6	366,204	48.2	7,209	0.9	1,403	0.2	17,953	R
Rhode Island	26,499	15,787	59.6	10,712	40.4	—		—		5,075	R
South Carolina	182,683	91,786	50.2	90,897	49.8	—		—		889	R
Tennessee	222,743	89,566	40.2	133,177	59.8	—		—		43,611	D
Texas	151,431	45,013	29.7	106,372	70.2	—		46		61,359	D
Vermont	64,460	44,092	68.4	20,254	31.4	—		114	0.2	23,838	R
Virginia	236,288	95,518	40.4	140,770	59.6	—		—		45,252	D
West Virginia	99,647	41,997	42.1	56,546	56.7	1,104	1.1	—		14,549	D
Wisconsin	257,176	130,050	50.6	123,922	48.2	1,509	0.6	1,695	0.7	6,128	R
Totals	8,413,101	4,034,311	48.0	4,288,546	51.0	75,973	0.9	14,271	0.2	254,235	D

1. Hayes won the election. For resolution of disputed 1876 election, see p. 16.
2. For breakdown of "Other" vote, see minor candidate vote totals, p. 129.

1880 Presidential Election

STATE	TOTAL VOTE	JAMES A. GARFIELD (Republican)		WINFIELD S. HANCOCK (Democrat)		JAMES B. WEAVER (Greenback)		OTHER [1]		PLURALITY	
		Votes	%	Votes	%	Votes	%	Votes	%		
Alabama	151,902	56,350	37.1	91,130	60.0	4,422	2.9	—		34,780	D
Arkansas	107,772	41,661	38.7	60,489	56.1	4,079	3.8	1,543	1.4	18,828	D
California	164,218	80,282	48.9	80,426	49.0	3,381	2.1	129	0.1	144	D
Colorado	53,546	27,450	51.3	24,647	46.0	1,435	2.7	14		2,803	R
Connecticut	132,798	67,071	50.5	64,411	48.5	868	0.7	448	0.3	2,660	R
Delaware	29,458	14,148	48.0	15,181	51.5	129	0.4	—		1,033	D
Florida	51,618	23,654	45.8	27,964	54.2	—		—		4,310	D
Georgia	157,451	54,470	34.6	102,981	65.4	—		—		48,511	D
Illinois	622,305	318,036	51.1	277,321	44.6	26,358	4.2	590	0.1	40,715	R
Indiana	470,758	232,169	49.3	225,523	47.9	13,066	2.8	—		6,646	R
Iowa	323,140	183,904	56.9	105,845	32.8	32,327	10.0	1,064	0.3	78,059	R
Kansas	201,054	121,520	60.4	59,789	29.7	19,710	9.8	35		61,731	R
Kentucky	267,104	106,490	39.9	148,875	55.7	11,506	4.3	233	0.1	42,385	D
Louisiana	104,462	38,978	37.3	65,047	62.3	437	0.4	—		26,069	D
Maine	143,903	74,052	51.5	65,211	45.3	4,409	3.1	231	0.2	8,841	R
Maryland	172,221	78,515	45.6	93,706	54.4	—		—		15,191	D
Massachusetts	282,505	165,198	58.5	111,960	39.6	4,548	1.6	799	0.3	53,238	R
Michigan	353,076	185,335	52.5	131,596	37.3	34,895	9.9	1,250	0.4	53,739	R
Minnesota	150,806	93,939	62.3	53,314	35.4	3,267	2.2	286	0.2	40,625	R
Mississippi	117,068	34,844	29.8	75,750	64.7	5,797	5.0	677	0.6	40,906	D
Missouri	397,289	153,647	38.7	208,600	52.5	35,042	8.8	—		54,953	D
Nebraska	87,355	54,979	62.9	28,523	32.7	3,853	4.4	—		26,456	R
Nevada	18,343	8,732	47.6	9,611	52.4	—		—		879	D
New Hampshire	86,361	44,856	51.9	40,797	47.2	528	0.6	180	0.2	4,059	R
New Jersey	245,928	120,555	49.0	122,565	49.8	2,617	1.1	191	0.1	2,010	D
New York	1,103,945	555,544	50.3	534,511	48.4	12,373	1.1	1,517	0.1	21,033	R
North Carolina	240,946	115,616	48.0	124,204	51.5	1,126	0.5	—		8,588	D
Ohio	724,984	375,048	51.7	340,867	47.0	6,456	0.9	2,613	0.4	34,181	R
Oregon	40,841	20,619	50.5	19,955	48.9	267	0.7	—		664	R
Pennsylvania	874,783	444,704	50.8	407,428	46.6	20,667	2.4	1,984	0.2	37,276	R
Rhode Island	29,235	18,195	62.2	10,779	36.9	236	0.8	25	0.1	7,416	R
South Carolina	169,793	57,954	34.1	111,236	65.5	567	0.3	36		53,282	D
Tennessee	243,263	107,677	44.3	129,569	53.3	6,017	2.5	—		21,892	D
Texas	233,632	50,217	21.5	156,010	66.8	27,405	11.7	—		105,793	D
Vermont	65,098	45,567	70.0	18,316	28.1	1,215	1.9	—		27,251	R
Virginia	211,616	83,533	39.5	128,083	60.5	—		—		44,550	D
West Virginia	112,641	46,243	41.1	57,390	50.9	9,008	8.0	—		11,147	D
Wisconsin	267,202	144,406	54.0	114,650	42.9	7,986	3.0	160	0.1	29,756	R
Totals	9,210,420	4,446,158	48.3	4,444,260	48.3	305,997	3.3	14,005	0.2	1,898	R

1. For breakdown of "Other" vote, see minor candidate vote totals, p. 129.

1884 Presidential Election

STATE	TOTAL VOTE	GROVER CLEVELAND (Democrat)		JAMES G. BLAINE (Republican)		BENJAMIN F. BUTLER (Greenback)		JOHN P. ST. JOHN (Prohibition)		OTHER [1]		PLURALITY	
		Votes	%	Votes	%	Votes	%	Votes	%	Votes	%		
Alabama	153,624	92,736	60.4	59,444	38.7	762	0.5	610	0.4	72		33,292	D
Arkansas	125,779	72,734	57.8	51,198	40.7	1,847	1.5	—		—		21,536	D
California	196,988	89,288	45.3	102,369	52.0	2,037	1.0	2,965	1.5	329	0.2	13,081	R
Colorado	66,519	27,723	41.7	36,084	54.2	1,956	2.9	756	1.1	—		8,361	R
Connecticut	137,221	67,167	48.9	65,879	48.0	1,682	1.2	2,493	1.8	—		1,288	D
Delaware	29,984	16,957	56.6	12,953	43.2	10		64	0.2	—		4,004	D
Florida	59,990	31,769	53.0	28,031	46.7	—		72	0.1	118	0.2	3,738	D
Georgia	143,610	94,667	65.9	48,603	33.8	145	0.1	195	0.1	—		46,064	D
Illinois	672,670	312,351	46.4	337,469	50.2	10,776	1.6	12,074	1.8	—		25,118	R
Indiana	491,649	244,989	49.8	238,466	48.5	8,194	1.7	—		—		6,523	D
Iowa	393,542	177,316	45.1	197,089	50.1	16,341	4.2	1,499	0.4	1,297	0.3	19,773	R
Kansas	250,991	90,111	35.9	154,410	61.5	1,691	0.7	4,311	1.7	468	0.2	64,299	R
Kentucky	274,910	152,961	55.6	118,690	43.2	120		3,139	1.1	—		34,271	D
Louisiana	113,234	62,594	55.3	46,347	40.9	3,955	3.5	338	0.3	—		16,247	D
Maine	127,114	52,153	41.0	72,217	56.8	578	0.5	2,160	1.7	6		20,064	R
Maryland	209,823	96,866	46.2	85,748	40.9	24,382	11.6	2,827	1.3	—		11,118	D
Massachusetts	321,253	122,352	38.1	146,724	45.7	42,252	13.2	9,923	3.1	2		24,372	R
Michigan	364,490	149,835	41.1	192,669	52.9	3,583	1.0	18,403	5.0	—		42,834	R
Minnesota	186,434	70,065	37.6	111,685	59.9	—		4,684	2.5	—		41,620	R
Mississippi	120,688	77,653	64.3	43,035	35.7	—		—		—		34,618	D
Missouri	441,268	236,023	53.5	203,081	46.0	—		2,164	0.5	—		32,942	D
Nebraska	134,202	54,391	40.5	76,912	57.3	—		2,899	2.2	—		22,521	R
Nevada	12,779	5,577	43.6	7,176	56.2	26	0.2	—		—		1,599	R
New Hampshire	84,586	39,198	46.3	43,254	51.1	554	0.7	1,580	1.9	—		4,056	R
New Jersey	260,853	127,747	49.0	123,436	47.3	3,486	1.3	6,156	2.4	28		4,311	D
New York	1,167,003	563,048	48.2	562,001	48.2	16,955	1.5	24,999	2.1	—		1,047	D
North Carolina	268,356	142,905	53.3	125,021	46.6	—		430	0.2	—		17,884	D
Ohio	784,620	368,280	46.9	400,092	51.0	5,179	0.7	11,069	1.4	—		31,812	R
Oregon	52,683	24,598	46.7	26,845	51.0	726	1.4	479	0.9	35	0.1	2,247	R
Pennsylvania	899,710	394,772	43.9	472,792	52.5	16,992	1.9	15,154	1.7	—		78,020	R
Rhode Island	32,771	12,391	37.8	19,030	58.1	422	1.3	928	2.8	—		6,639	R
South Carolina	92,812	69,845	75.3	21,730	23.4	—		—		1,237	1.3	48,115	D
Tennessee	259,978	133,770	51.5	124,101	47.7	957	0.4	1,150	0.4	—		9,669	D
Texas	321,242	223,209	69.5	91,234	28.4	3,310	1.0	3,489	1.1	—		131,975	D
Vermont	59,409	17,331	29.2	39,514	66.5	785	1.3	1,752	2.9	27		22,183	R
Virginia	284,977	145,491	51.1	139,356	48.9	—		130		—		6,135	D
West Virginia	132,145	67,311	50.9	63,096	47.7	799	0.6	939	0.7	—		4,215	D
Wisconsin	319,847	146,447	45.8	161,155	50.4	4,594	1.4	7,651	2.4	—		14,708	R
Totals	10,049,754	4,874,621	48.5	4,848,936	48.2	175,096	1.7	147,482	1.5	3,619		25,685	D

1. For breakdown of "Other" vote, see minor candidate vote totals, p. 129.

1888 Presidential Election

STATE	TOTAL VOTE	BENJAMIN HARRISON [1] (Republican)		GROVER CLEVELAND [1] (Democrat)		CLINTON B. FISK (Prohibition)		ALSON J. STREETER (Union Labor)		OTHER [2]		PLURALITY	
		Votes	%	Votes	%	Votes	%	Votes	%	Votes	%		
Alabama	175,085	57,177	32.7	117,314	67.0	594	0.3	—		—		60,137	D
Arkansas	157,058	59,752	38.0	86,062	54.8	614	0.4	10,630	6.8	—		26,310	D
California	251,339	124,816	49.7	117,729	46.8	5,761	2.3	—		3,033	1.2	7,087	R
Colorado	91,946	50,772	55.2	37,549	40.8	2,182	2.4	1,266	1.4	177	0.2	13,223	R
Connecticut	153,978	74,584	48.4	74,920	48.7	4,234	2.7	240	0.2	—		336	D
Delaware	29,764	12,950	43.5	16,414	55.1	399	1.3	—		1		3,464	D
Florida	66,500	26,529	39.9	39,557	59.5	414	0.6	—		—		13,028	D
Georgia	142,936	40,499	28.3	100,493	70.3	1,808	1.3	136	0.1	—		59,994	D
Illinois	747,813	370,475	49.5	348,351	46.6	21,703	2.9	7,134	1.0	150		22,124	R
Indiana	536,988	263,366	49.0	260,990	48.6	9,939	1.9	2,693	0.5	—		2,376	R
Iowa	404,694	211,607	52.3	179,876	44.4	3,550	0.9	9,105	2.2	556	0.1	31,731	R
Kansas	331,133	182,845	55.2	102,739	31.0	6,774	2.0	37,838	11.4	937	0.3	80,106	R
Kentucky	344,868	155,138	45.0	183,830	53.3	5,223	1.5	677	0.2	—		28,692	D
Louisiana	115,891	30,660	26.5	85,032	73.4	160	0.1	39		—		54,372	D
Maine	128,253	73,730	57.5	50,472	39.4	2,691	2.1	1,344	1.0	16		23,258	R
Maryland	210,941	99,986	47.4	106,188	50.3	4,767	2.3	—		—		6,202	D
Massachusetts	344,243	183,892	53.4	151,590	44.0	8,701	2.5	—		60		32,302	R
Michigan	475,356	236,387	49.7	213,469	44.9	20,945	4.4	4,555	1.0	—		22,918	R
Minnesota	263,162	142,492	54.1	104,372	39.7	15,201	5.8	1,097	0.4	—		38,120	R
Mississippi	115,786	30,095	26.0	85,451	73.8	240	0.2	—		—		55,356	D
Missouri	521,359	236,252	45.3	261,943	50.2	4,539	0.9	18,625	3.6	—		25,691	D
Nebraska	202,630	108,417	53.5	80,552	39.8	9,435	4.7	4,226	2.1	—		27,865	R
Nevada	12,573	7,229	57.5	5,303	42.2	41	0.3	—		—		1,926	R
New Hampshire	90,770	45,734	50.4	43,382	47.8	1,596	1.8	—		58	0.1	2,352	R
New Jersey	303,634	144,347	47.5	151,493	49.9	7,794	2.6	—		—		7,146	D
New York	1,319,748	650,338	49.3	635,965	48.2	30,231	2.3	627		2,587	0.2	14,373	R
North Carolina	285,563	134,784	47.2	147,902	51.8	2,840	1.0	—		37		13,118	D
Ohio	839,357	416,054	49.6	395,456	47.1	24,356	2.9	3,491	0.4	—		20,598	R
Oregon	61,889	33,291	53.8	26,518	42.8	1,676	2.7	—		404	0.7	6,773	R
Pennsylvania	997,568	526,091	52.7	446,633	44.8	20,947	2.1	3,873	0.4	24		79,458	R
Rhode Island	40,775	21,969	53.9	17,530	43.0	1,251	3.1	18		7		4,439	R
South Carolina	79,997	13,736	17.2	65,824	82.3	—		—		437	0.5	52,088	D
Tennessee	303,694	138,978	45.8	158,699	52.3	5,969	2.0	48		—		19,721	D
Texas	354,412	88,604	25.0	232,189	65.5	4,739	1.3	28,880	8.1	—		143,585	D
Vermont	63,476	45,193	71.2	16,788	26.4	1,460	2.3	—		35	0.1	28,405	R
Virginia	304,087	150,399	49.5	152,004	50.0	1,684	0.6	—		—		1,605	D
West Virginia	159,440	78,171	49.0	78,677	49.3	1,084	0.7	1,508	0.9	—		506	D
Wisconsin	354,614	176,553	49.8	155,232	43.8	14,277	4.0	8,552	2.4	—		21,321	R
Totals	11,383,320	5,443,892	47.8	5,534,488	48.6	249,819	2.2	146,602	1.3	8,519	0.1	90,596	D

1. Harrison won the election. See p. 48.
2. For breakdown of "Other" vote, see minor candidate vote totals, p. 129.

1892 Presidential Election

STATE	TOTAL VOTE	GROVER CLEVELAND (Democrat)		BENJAMIN HARRISON (Republican)		JAMES B. WEAVER (Populist)		JOHN BIDWELL (Prohibition)		OTHER [1]		PLURALITY	
		Votes	%	Votes	%	Votes	%	Votes	%	Votes	%		
Alabama	232,543	138,135	59.4	9,184	3.9	84,984	36.5	240	0.1	—		53,151	D
Arkansas	148,117	87,834	59.3	47,072	31.8	11,831	8.0	113	0.1	1,267	0.9	40,762	D
California	269,585	118,151	43.8	118,027	43.8	25,311	9.4	8,096	3.0	—		124	D
Colorado	93,881	—		38,620	41.1	53,584	57.1	1,677	1.8	—		14,964	POP
Connecticut	164,593	82,395	50.1	77,030	46.8	809	0.5	4,026	2.4	333	0.2	5,365	D
Delaware	37,235	18,581	49.9	18,077	48.5	—		564	1.5	13		504	D
Florida	35,471	30,153	85.0	—		4,843	13.7	475	1.3	—		25,310	D
Georgia	223,126	129,446	58.0	48,408	21.7	41,939	18.8	988	0.4	2,345	1.1	81,038	D
Idaho	19,407	—		8,599	44.3	10,520	54.2	288	1.5	—		1,921	POP
Illinois	873,667	426,281	48.8	399,308	45.7	22,207	2.5	25,871	3.0	—		26,973	D
Indiana	553,613	262,740	47.5	255,615	46.2	22,208	4.0	13,050	2.4	—		7,125	D
Iowa	443,159	196,367	44.3	219,795	49.6	20,595	4.6	6,402	1.4	—		23,428	R
Kansas	323,591	—		156,134	48.3	162,888	50.3	4,569	1.4	—		6,754	POP
Kentucky	340,864	175,461	51.5	135,462	39.7	23,500	6.9	6,441	1.9	—		39,999	D
Louisiana	114,889	87,926	76.5	26,963	23.5	—		—		—		60,963	D
Maine	116,451	48,049	41.3	62,936	54.0	2,396	2.1	3,066	2.6	4		14,887	R
Maryland	213,275	113,866	53.4	92,736	43.5	796	0.4	5,877	2.8	—		21,130	D
Massachusetts	391,028	176,813	45.2	202,814	51.9	3,210	0.8	7,539	1.9	652	0.2	26,001	R
Michigan	466,917	202,396	43.3	222,708	47.7	20,031	4.3	20,857	4.5	925	0.2	20,312	R
Minnesota	267,841	100,589	37.6	122,736	45.8	30,399	11.3	14,117	5.3	—		22,147	R
Mississippi	52,519	40,030	76.2	1,398	2.7	10,118	19.3	973	1.9	—		29,912	D
Missouri	541,583	268,400	49.6	227,646	42.0	41,204	7.6	4,333	0.8	—		40,754	D
Montana	44,461	17,690	39.8	18,871	42.4	7,338	16.5	562	1.3	—		1,181	R
Nebraska	200,205	24,956	12.5	87,213	43.6	83,134	41.5	4,902	2.4	—		4,079	R
Nevada	10,826	703	6.5	2,811	26.0	7,226	66.7	86	0.8	—		4,415	POP
New Hampshire	89,328	42,081	47.1	45,658	51.1	292	0.3	1,297	1.5	—		3,577	R
New Jersey	337,485	170,987	50.7	156,059	46.2	969	0.3	8,133	2.4	1,337	0.4	14,928	D
New York	1,336,793	654,868	49.0	609,350	45.6	16,429	1.2	38,190	2.9	17,956	1.3	45,518	D
North Carolina	280,270	132,951	47.4	100,346	35.8	44,336	15.8	2,637	0.9	—		32,605	D
North Dakota [2]	36,118	—		17,519	48.5	17,700	49.0	899	2.5	—		181	POP
Ohio	850,164	404,115	47.5	405,187	47.7	14,850	1.7	26,012	3.1	—		1,072	R
Oregon	78,378	14,243	18.2	35,002	44.7	26,875	34.3	2,258	2.9	—		8,127	R
Pennsylvania	1,003,000	452,264	45.1	516,011	51.4	8,714	0.9	25,123	2.5	888	0.1	63,747	R
Rhode Island	53,196	24,336	45.7	26,975	50.7	228	0.4	1,654	3.1	3		2,639	R
South Carolina	70,504	54,680	77.6	13,345	18.9	2,407	3.4	—		72	0.1	41,335	D
South Dakota	70,160	8,894	12.7	34,714	49.5	26,552	37.8	—		—		8,162	R
Tennessee	265,732	136,468	51.4	100,537	37.8	23,918	9.0	4,809	1.8	—		35,931	D
Texas	410,860	236,979	57.7	70,982	17.3	96,649	23.5	2,164	0.5	4,086	1.0	140,330	D
Vermont	55,793	16,325	29.3	37,992	68.1	42	0.1	1,424	2.6	10		21,667	R
Virginia	292,238	164,136	56.2	113,098	38.7	12,275	4.2	2,729	0.9	—		51,038	D
Washington	87,968	29,802	33.9	36,459	41.4	19,165	21.8	2,542	2.9	—		6,657	R
West Virginia	171,079	84,467	49.4	80,292	46.9	4,167	2.4	2,153	1.3	—		4,175	D
Wisconsin	371,481	177,325	47.7	171,101	46.1	9,919	2.7	13,136	3.5	—		6,224	D
Wyoming	16,703	—		8,454	50.6	7,722	46.2	498	3.0	29	0.2	732	R
Totals	12,056,097	5,551,883	46.1	5,179,244	43.0	1,024,280	8.5	270,770	2.2	29,920	0.2	372,639	D

1. For breakdown of "Other" vote, see minor candidate vote totals, p. 129.
2. Figures from Petersen, op. cit., p. 60.

1896 Presidential Election

STATE	TOTAL VOTE	WILLIAM McKINLEY (Republican)		WILLIAM J. BRYAN (Democrat, Populist)		JOHN M. PALMER (National Democrat)		JOSHUA LEVERING (Prohibition)		OTHER [1]		PLURALITY	
		Votes	%	Votes	%	Votes	%	Votes	%	Votes	%		
Alabama	194,580	55,673	28.6	130,298	67.0	6,375	3.3	2,234	1.1	—		74,625	D
Arkansas	149,396	37,512	25.1	110,103	73.7	—		889	0.6	892	0.6	72,591	D
California	298,598	146,756	49.1	144,877	48.5	1,730	0.6	2,573	0.9	2,662	0.9	1,879	R
Colorado	189,539	26,271	13.9	161,005	84.9	1		1,717	0.9	545	0.3	134,734	D
Connecticut	174,394	110,285	63.2	56,740	32.5	4,336	2.5	1,806	1.0	1,227	0.7	53,545	R
Delaware	38,456	20,450	53.2	16,574	43.1	966	2.5	466	1.2	—		3,876	R
Florida	46,488	11,298	24.3	32,756	70.5	1,778	3.8	656	1.4	—		21,458	D
Georgia	162,480	59,395	36.6	93,885	57.8	3,670	2.3	5,483	3.4	47		34,490	D
Idaho	29,631	6,324	21.3	23,135	78.1	—		172	0.6	—		16,811	D
Illinois	1,090,766	607,130	55.7	465,593	42.7	6,307	0.6	9,796	0.9	1,940	0.2	141,537	R
Indiana	637,089	323,754	50.8	305,538	48.0	2,145	0.3	3,061	0.5	2,591	0.4	18,216	R
Iowa	521,550	289,293	55.5	223,744	42.9	4,516	0.9	3,192	0.6	805	0.2	65,549	R
Kansas	336,085	159,484	47.5	173,049	51.5	1,209	0.4	1,723	0.5	620	0.2	13,565	D
Kentucky	445,928	218,171	48.9	217,894	48.9	5,084	1.1	4,779	1.1	—		277	R
Louisiana	101,046	22,037	21.8	77,175	76.4	1,834	1.8	—		—		55,138	D
Maine	118,419	80,403	67.9	34,587	29.2	1,867	1.6	1,562	1.3	—		45,816	R
Maryland	250,249	136,959	54.7	104,150	41.6	2,499	1.0	5,918	2.4	723	0.3	32,809	R
Massachusetts	401,269	278,976	69.5	105,414	26.3	11,749	2.9	2,998	0.7	2,132	0.5	173,562	R
Michigan	545,583	293,336	53.8	237,164	43.5	6,923	1.3	4,978	0.9	3,182	0.6	56,172	R
Minnesota	341,762	193,503	56.6	139,735	40.9	3,222	0.9	4,348	1.3	954	0.3	53,768	R
Mississippi	69,591	4,819	6.9	63,355	91.0	1,021	1.5	396	0.6	—		58,536	D
Missouri	674,032	304,940	45.2	363,667	54.0	2,365	0.4	2,169	0.3	891	0.1	58,727	D
Montana	53,330	10,509	19.7	42,628	79.9	—		193	0.4	—		32,119	D
Nebraska	223,181	103,064	46.2	115,007	51.5	2,885	1.3	1,242	0.6	983	0.4	11,943	D
Nevada	10,286	1,938	18.8	8,348	81.2	—		—		—		6,410	D
New Hampshire	83,670	57,444	68.7	21,650	25.9	3,520	4.2	779	0.9	277	0.3	35,794	R
New Jersey	371,014	221,367	59.7	133,675	36.0	6,373	1.7	—		9,599	2.6	87,692	R
New York	1,423,876	819,838	57.6	551,369	38.7	18,950	1.3	16,052	1.1	17,667	1.2	268,469	R
North Carolina	331,337	155,122	46.8	174,408	52.6	578	0.2	635	0.2	594	0.2	19,286	D
North Dakota	47,391	26,335	55.6	20,686	43.6	—		358	0.8	12		5,649	R
Ohio	1,014,295	525,991	51.9	477,497	47.1	1,858	0.2	5,068	0.5	3,881	0.4	48,494	R
Oregon	97,335	48,700	50.0	46,739	48.0	977	1.0	919	0.9	—		1,961	R
Pennsylvania	1,194,355	728,300	61.0	433,228	36.3	11,000	0.9	19,274	1.6	2,553	0.2	295,072	R
Rhode Island	54,785	37,437	68.3	14,459	26.4	1,166	2.1	1,160	2.1	563	1.0	22,978	R
South Carolina	68,938	9,313	13.5	58,801	85.3	824	1.2	—		—		49,488	D
South Dakota	82,937	41,040	49.5	41,225	49.7	—		672	0.8	—		185	D
Tennessee	320,903	148,683	46.3	167,168	52.1	1,953	0.6	3,099	1.0	—		18,485	D
Texas	541,018	163,894	30.3	370,308	68.4	5,022	0.9	1,794	0.3	—		206,414	D
Utah	78,098	13,491	17.3	64,607	82.7	—		—		—		51,116	D
Vermont	63,568	51,127	80.4	10,367	16.3	1,341	2.1	733	1.2	—		40,760	R
Virginia	294,674	135,379	45.9	154,708	52.5	2,129	0.7	2,350	0.8	108		19,329	D
Washington	93,583	39,153	41.8	53,314	57.0	—		968	1.0	148	0.2	14,161	D
West Virginia	201,757	105,379	52.2	94,480	46.8	678	0.3	1,220	0.6	—		10,899	R
Wisconsin	447,409	268,135	59.9	165,523	37.0	4,584	1.0	7,507	1.7	1,660	0.4	102,612	R
Wyoming	21,067	10,072	47.8	10,862	51.6	—		133	0.6	—		790	D
Totals	**13,935,738**	**7,108,480**	**51.0**	**6,511,495**	**46.7**	**133,435**	**1.0**	**125,072**	**0.9**	**57,256**	**0.4**	**596,985**	**R**

1. For breakdown of "Other" vote, see minor candidate vote totals, p. 129.

1900 Presidential Election

STATE	TOTAL VOTE	WILLIAM McKINLEY (Republican)		WILLIAM J. BRYAN (Democrat)		JOHN G. WOOLEY (Prohibition)		EUGENE V. DEBS (Socialist)		OTHER [1]		PLURALITY	
		Votes	%	Votes	%	Votes	%	Votes	%	Votes	%		
Alabama	159,692	55,612	34.8	97,129	60.8	2,763	1.7	—		4,188	2.6	41,517	D
Arkansas	127,966	44,800	35.0	81,242	63.5	584	0.5	—		1,340	1.0	36,442	D
California	302,318	164,755	54.5	124,985	41.3	5,024	1.7	—		7,554	2.5	39,770	R
Colorado	220,895	92,701	42.0	122,705	55.5	3,790	1.7	686	0.3	1,013	0.5	30,004	D
Connecticut	180,195	102,572	56.9	74,014	41.1	1,617	0.9	1,029	0.6	963	0.5	28,558	R
Delaware	41,989	22,535	53.7	18,852	44.9	546	1.3	56	0.1	—		3,683	R
Florida	39,649	7,355	18.6	28,273	71.3	2,244	5.7	634	1.6	1,143	2.9	20,918	D
Georgia	121,410	34,260	28.2	81,180	66.9	1,402	1.2	—		4,568	3.8	46,920	D
Idaho	57,984	27,198	46.9	29,484	50.8	857	1.5	—		445	0.8	2,286	D
Illinois	1,131,898	597,985	52.8	503,061	44.4	17,626	1.6	9,687	0.9	3,539	0.3	94,924	R
Indiana	664,094	336,063	50.6	309,584	46.6	13,718	2.1	2,374	0.4	2,355	0.4	26,479	R
Iowa	530,345	307,799	58.0	209,261	39.5	9,502	1.8	2,743	0.5	1,040	0.2	98,538	R
Kansas [2]	353,766	185,955	52.6	162,601	46.0	3,605	1.0	1,605	0.5	—		23,354	R
Kentucky	468,265	227,132	48.5	235,126	50.2	2,890	0.6	766	0.2	2,351	0.5	7,994	D
Louisiana	67,906	14,234	21.0	53,668	79.0	—		—		4		39,434	D
Maine	105,693	65,412	61.9	36,822	34.8	2,581	2.4	878	0.8	—		28,590	R
Maryland	264,386	136,151	51.5	122,237	46.2	4,574	1.7	900	0.3	524	0.2	13,914	R
Massachusetts	414,804	238,866	57.6	156,997	37.8	6,202	1.5	9,607	2.3	3,132	0.8	81,869	R
Michigan	543,789	316,014	58.1	211,432	38.9	11,804	2.2	2,820	0.5	1,719	0.3	104,582	R
Minnesota	316,311	190,461	60.2	112,901	35.7	8,555	2.7	3,065	1.0	1,329	0.4	77,560	R
Mississippi	59,055	5,707	9.7	51,706	87.6	—		—		1,642	2.8	45,999	D
Missouri	683,658	314,092	45.9	351,922	51.5	5,965	0.9	6,139	0.9	5,540	0.8	37,830	D
Montana	63,856	25,409	39.8	37,311	58.4	306	0.5	711	1.1	119	0.2	11,902	D
Nebraska	241,430	121,835	50.5	114,013	47.2	3,655	1.5	823	0.3	1,104	0.5	7,822	R
Nevada	10,196	3,849	37.8	6,347	62.2	—		—		—		2,498	D
New Hampshire	92,364	54,799	59.3	35,489	38.4	1,270	1.4	790	0.9	16		19,310	R
New Jersey	401,050	221,707	55.3	164,808	41.1	7,183	1.8	4,609	1.1	2,743	0.7	56,899	R
New York	1,548,043	822,013	53.1	678,462	43.8	22,077	1.4	12,869	0.8	12,622	0.8	143,551	R
North Carolina	292,518	132,997	45.5	157,733	53.9	990	0.3	—		798	0.3	24,736	D
North Dakota	57,783	35,898	62.1	20,524	35.5	735	1.3	517	0.9	109	0.2	15,374	R
Ohio	1,040,073	543,918	52.3	474,882	45.7	10,203	1.0	4,847	0.5	6,223	0.6	69,036	R
Oregon	83,251	46,172	55.5	32,810	39.4	2,536	3.0	1,464	1.8	269	0.3	13,362	R
Pennsylvania	1,173,210	712,665	60.7	424,232	36.2	27,908	2.4	4,831	0.4	3,574	0.3	288,433	R
Rhode Island	56,548	33,784	59.7	19,812	35.0	1,529	2.7	—		1,423	2.5	13,972	R
South Carolina	50,698	3,525	7.0	47,173	93.0	—		—		—		43,648	D
South Dakota	96,169	54,574	56.7	39,538	41.1	1,541	1.6	176	0.2	340	0.4	15,036	R
Tennessee	273,860	123,108	45.0	145,240	53.0	3,844	1.4	346	0.1	1,322	0.5	22,132	D
Texas	424,334	131,174	30.9	267,945	63.1	2,642	0.6	1,846	0.4	20,727	4.9	136,771	D
Utah	93,071	47,089	50.6	44,949	48.3	205	0.2	717	0.8	111	0.1	2,140	R
Vermont	56,212	42,569	75.7	12,849	22.9	383	0.7	39	0.1	372	0.7	29,720	R
Virginia	264,208	115,769	43.8	146,079	55.3	2,130	0.8	—		230	0.1	30,310	D
Washington	107,523	57,455	53.4	44,833	41.7	2,363	2.2	2,006	1.9	866	0.8	12,622	R
West Virginia	220,796	119,829	54.3	98,807	44.8	1,628	0.7	286	0.1	246	0.1	21,022	R
Wisconsin	442,501	265,760	60.1	159,163	36.0	10,027	2.3	7,048	1.6	503	0.1	106,597	R
Wyoming	24,708	14,482	58.6	10,164	41.1	—		21	0.1	41	0.2	4,318	R
Totals	13,970,470	7,218,039	51.7	6,358,345	45.5	209,004	1.5	86,935	0.6	98,147	0.7	859,694	R

1. For breakdown of "Other" vote, see minor candidate vote totals, p. 130.
2. Figures from Petersen, op. cit., p. 67.

1904 Presidential Election

STATE	TOTAL VOTE	THEODORE ROOSEVELT (Republican)		ALTON B. PARKER (Democrat)		EUGENE V. DEBS (Socialist)		SILAS C. SWALLOW (Prohibition)		OTHER [1]		PLURALITY	
		Votes	%	Votes	%	Votes	%	Votes	%	Votes	%		
Alabama	108,785	22,472	20.7	79,797	73.4	853	0.8	612	0.6	5,051	4.6	57,325	D
Arkansas	116,328	46,760	40.2	64,434	55.4	1,816	1.6	992	0.9	2,326	2.0	17,674	D
California	331,768	205,226	61.9	89,294	26.9	29,535	8.9	7,380	2.2	333	0.1	115,932	R
Colorado	243,667	134,661	55.3	100,105	41.1	4,304	1.8	3,438	1.4	1,159	0.5	34,556	R
Connecticut	191,136	111,089	58.1	72,909	38.1	4,543	2.4	1,506	0.8	1,089	0.6	38,180	R
Delaware	43,856	23,705	54.1	19,347	44.1	146	0.3	607	1.4	51	0.1	4,358	R
Florida	38,705	8,314	21.5	26,449	68.3	2,337	6.0	—		1,605	4.1	18,135	D
Georgia	130,986	24,004	18.3	83,466	63.7	196	0.1	685	0.5	22,635	17.3	59,462	D
Idaho	72,577	47,783	65.8	18,480	25.5	4,949	6.8	1,013	1.4	352	0.5	29,303	R
Illinois	1,076,495	632,645	58.8	327,606	30.4	69,225	6.4	34,770	3.2	12,249	1.1	305,039	R
Indiana	682,206	368,289	54.0	274,356	40.2	12,023	1.8	23,496	3.4	4,042	0.6	93,933	R
Iowa	485,703	307,907	63.4	149,141	30.7	14,847	3.1	11,601	2.4	2,207	0.5	158,766	R
Kansas	329,047	213,455	64.9	86,164	26.2	15,869	4.8	7,306	2.2	6,253	1.9	127,291	R
Kentucky	435,946	205,457	47.1	217,170	49.8	3,599	0.8	6,603	1.5	3,117	0.7	11,713	D
Louisiana	53,908	5,205	9.7	47,708	88.5	995	1.8	—		—		42,503	D
Maine	97,023	65,432	67.4	27,642	28.5	2,102	2.2	1,510	1.6	337	0.3	37,790	R
Maryland	224,229	109,497	48.8	109,446	48.8	2,247	1.0	3,034	1.4	5		51	R
Massachusetts	445,100	257,813	57.9	165,746	37.2	13,604	3.1	4,279	1.0	3,658	0.8	92,067	R
Michigan	520,443	361,863	69.5	134,163	25.8	8,942	1.7	13,312	2.6	2,163	0.4	227,700	R
Minnesota	292,860	216,651	74.0	55,187	18.8	11,692	4.0	6,253	2.1	3,077	1.1	161,464	R
Mississippi	58,721	3,280	5.6	53,480	91.1	462	0.8	—		1,499	2.6	50,200	D
Missouri	643,861	321,449	49.9	296,312	46.0	13,009	2.0	7,191	1.1	5,900	0.9	25,137	R
Montana	63,568	33,994	53.5	21,816	34.3	5,675	8.9	339	0.5	1,744	2.7	12,178	R
Nebraska	225,732	138,558	61.4	52,921	23.4	7,412	3.3	6,323	2.8	20,518	9.1	85,637	R
Nevada	12,115	6,864	56.7	3,982	32.9	925	7.6	—		344	2.8	2,882	R
New Hampshire	90,151	54,157	60.1	34,071	37.8	1,090	1.2	750	0.8	83	0.1	20,086	R
New Jersey	432,247	245,164	56.7	164,566	38.1	9,587	2.2	6,845	1.6	6,085	1.4	80,598	R
New York	1,617,765	859,533	53.1	683,981	42.3	36,883	2.3	20,787	1.3	16,581	1.0	175,552	R
North Carolina	207,818	82,442	39.7	124,091	59.7	124	0.1	342	0.2	819	0.4	41,649	D
North Dakota	70,014	52,595	75.1	14,273	20.4	2,009	2.9	1,137	1.6	—		38,322	R
Ohio	1,004,395	600,095	59.7	344,674	34.3	36,260	3.6	19,339	1.9	4,027	0.4	255,421	R
Oregon	89,656	60,309	67.3	17,327	19.3	7,479	8.3	3,795	4.2	746	0.8	42,982	R
Pennsylvania	1,236,738	840,949	68.0	337,998	27.3	21,863	1.8	33,717	2.7	2,211	0.2	502,951	R
Rhode Island	68,656	41,605	60.6	24,839	36.2	956	1.4	768	1.1	488	0.7	16,766	R
South Carolina	55,890	2,570	4.6	53,320	95.4	—		—		—		50,750	D
South Dakota	101,395	72,083	71.1	21,969	21.7	3,138	3.1	2,965	2.9	1,240	1.2	50,114	R
Tennessee	242,750	105,363	43.4	131,653	54.2	1,354	0.6	1,889	0.8	2,491	1.0	26,290	D
Texas	233,609	51,307	22.0	167,088	71.5	2,788	1.2	3,933	1.7	8,493	3.6	115,781	D
Utah	101,626	62,446	61.4	33,413	32.9	5,767	5.7	—		—		29,033	R
Vermont	51,888	40,459	78.0	9,777	18.8	859	1.7	792	1.5	1		30,682	R
Virginia	130,410	48,180	36.9	80,649	61.8	202	0.2	1,379	1.1	—		32,469	D
Washington	145,151	101,540	70.0	28,098	19.4	10,023	6.9	3,229	2.2	2,261	1.6	73,442	R
West Virginia	239,986	132,620	55.3	100,855	42.0	1,573	0.7	4,599	1.9	339	0.1	31,765	R
Wisconsin	443,440	280,314	63.2	124,205	28.0	28,240	6.4	9,872	2.2	809	0.2	156,109	R
Wyoming	30,614	20,489	66.9	8,930	29.2	987	3.2	208	0.7	—		11,559	R
Totals	**13,518,964**	**7,626,593**	**56.4**	**5,082,898**	**37.6**	**402,489**	**3.0**	**258,596**	**1.9**	**148,388**	**1.1**	**2,543,695**	**R**

1. For breakdown of "Other" vote, see minor candidate vote totals, p. 130.

1908 Presidential Election

STATE	TOTAL VOTE	WILLIAM H. TAFT (Republican)		WILLIAM J. BRYAN (Democrat)		EUGENE V. DEBS (Socialist)		EUGENE W. CHAFIN (Prohibition)		OTHER [1]		PLURALITY	
		Votes	%	Votes	%	Votes	%	Votes	%	Votes	%		
Alabama	105,152	25,561	24.3	74,391	70.7	1,450	1.4	690	0.7	3,060	2.9	48,830	D
Arkansas	151,845	56,684	37.3	87,020	57.3	5,842	3.8	1,026	0.7	1,273	0.8	30,336	D
California	386,625	214,398	55.5	127,492	33.0	28,659	7.4	11,770	3.0	4,306	1.1	86,906	R
Colorado	263,858	123,693	46.9	126,644	48.0	7,960	3.0	5,559	2.1	2		2,951	D
Connecticut	189,903	112,815	59.4	68,255	35.9	5,113	2.7	2,380	1.3	1,340	0.7	44,560	R
Delaware	48,007	25,014	52.1	22,055	45.9	239	0.5	670	1.4	29	0.1	2,959	R
Florida	49,360	10,654	21.6	31,104	63.0	3,747	7.6	1,356	2.7	2,499	5.1	20,450	D
Georgia	132,504	41,355	31.2	72,350	54.6	584	0.4	1,452	1.1	16,763	12.7	30,995	D
Idaho	97,293	52,621	54.1	36,162	37.2	6,400	6.6	1,986	2.0	124	0.1	16,459	R
Illinois	1,155,254	629,932	54.5	450,810	39.0	34,711	3.0	29,364	2.5	10,437	0.9	179,122	R
Indiana	721,117	348,993	48.4	338,262	46.9	13,476	1.9	18,036	2.5	2,350	0.3	10,731	R
Iowa	494,770	275,210	55.6	200,771	40.6	8,287	1.7	9,837	2.0	665	0.1	74,439	R
Kansas	376,043	197,316	52.5	161,209	42.9	12,420	3.3	5,030	1.3	68		36,107	R
Kentucky	490,719	235,711	48.0	244,092	49.7	4,093	0.8	5,885	1.2	938	0.2	8,381	D
Louisiana	75,117	8,958	11.9	63,568	84.6	2,514	3.3	—		77	0.1	54,610	D
Maine	106,335	66,987	63.0	35,403	33.3	1,758	1.7	1,487	1.4	700	0.7	31,584	R
Maryland	238,531	116,513	48.8	115,908	48.6	2,323	1.0	3,302	1.4	485	0.2	605	R
Massachusetts	456,905	265,966	58.2	155,533	34.0	10,778	2.4	4,373	1.0	20,255	4.4	110,433	R
Michigan	538,124	333,313	61.9	174,619	32.4	11,527	2.1	16,785	3.1	1,880	0.3	158,694	R
Minnesota	330,254	195,843	59.3	109,401	33.1	14,472	4.4	10,114	3.1	424	0.1	86,442	R
Mississippi	66,904	4,363	6.5	60,287	90.1	978	1.5	—		1,276	1.9	55,924	D
Missouri	715,841	347,203	48.5	346,574	48.4	15,431	2.2	4,209	0.6	2,424	0.3	629	R
Montana	69,233	32,471	46.9	29,511	42.6	5,920	8.6	838	1.2	493	0.7	2,960	R
Nebraska	266,799	126,997	47.6	131,099	49.1	3,524	1.3	5,179	1.9	—		4,102	D
Nevada	24,526	10,775	43.9	11,212	45.7	2,103	8.6	—		436	1.8	437	D
New Hampshire	89,595	53,144	59.3	33,655	37.6	1,299	1.4	905	1.0	592	0.7	19,489	R
New Jersey	467,111	265,298	56.8	182,522	39.1	10,249	2.2	4,930	1.1	4,112	0.9	82,776	R
New York	1,638,350	870,070	53.1	667,468	40.7	38,451	2.3	22,667	1.4	39,694	2.4	202,602	R
North Carolina	252,554	114,887	45.5	136,928	54.2	372	0.1	354	0.1	13		22,041	D
North Dakota	94,524	57,680	61.0	32,884	34.8	2,421	2.6	1,496	1.6	43		24,796	R
Ohio	1,121,552	572,312	51.0	502,721	44.8	33,795	3.0	11,402	1.0	1,322	0.1	69,591	R
Oklahoma	254,260	110,473	43.4	122,362	48.1	21,425	8.4	—		—		11,889	D
Oregon	110,539	62,454	56.5	37,792	34.2	7,322	6.6	2,682	2.4	289	0.3	24,662	R
Pennsylvania	1,267,450	745,779	58.8	448,782	35.4	33,914	2.7	36,694	2.9	2,281	0.2	296,997	R
Rhode Island	72,317	43,942	60.8	24,706	34.2	1,365	1.9	1,016	1.4	1,288	1.8	19,236	R
South Carolina	66,379	3,945	5.9	62,288	93.8	100	0.2	—		46	0.1	58,343	D
South Dakota	114,775	67,536	58.8	40,266	35.1	2,846	2.5	4,039	3.5	88	0.1	27,270	R
Tennessee	257,180	117,977	45.9	135,608	52.7	1,870	0.7	301	0.1	1,424	0.6	17,631	D
Texas	292,913	65,605	22.4	216,662	74.0	7,779	2.7	1,626	0.6	1,241	0.4	151,057	D
Utah	108,757	61,165	56.2	42,610	39.2	4,890	4.5	—		92	0.1	18,555	R
Vermont	52,680	39,552	75.1	11,496	21.8	—		799	1.5	833	1.6	28,056	R
Virginia	137,065	52,572	38.4	82,946	60.5	255	0.2	1,111	0.8	181	0.1	30,374	D
Washington	183,570	106,062	57.8	58,383	31.8	14,177	7.7	4,700	2.6	248	0.1	47,679	R
West Virginia	258,098	137,869	53.4	111,410	43.2	3,679	1.4	5,140	2.0	—		26,459	R
Wisconsin	454,438	247,744	54.5	166,662	36.7	28,147	6.2	11,565	2.5	320	0.1	81,082	R
Wyoming	37,608	20,846	55.4	14,918	39.7	1,715	4.6	66	0.2	63	0.2	5,928	R
Totals	14,882,734	7,676,258	51.6	6,406,801	43.0	420,380	2.8	252,821	1.7	126,474	0.8	1,269,457	R

1. For breakdown of "Other" vote, see minor candidate vote totals, p. 130.

1912 Presidential Election

STATE	TOTAL VOTE	WOODROW WILSON (Democrat)		THEODORE ROOSEVELT (Progressive)		WILLIAM H. TAFT (Republican)		EUGENE V. DEBS (Socialist)		OTHER [1]		PLURALITY	
		Votes	%	Votes	%	Votes	%	Votes	%	Votes	%		
Alabama	117,959	82,438	69.9	22,680	19.2	9,807	8.3	3,029	2.6	5		59,758	D
Arizona	23,687	10,324	43.6	6,949	29.3	2,986	12.6	3,163	13.4	265	1.1	3,375	D
Arkansas	125,104	68,814	55.0	21,644	17.3	25,585	20.5	8,153	6.5	908	0.7	43,229	D
California	677,877	283,436	41.8	283,610	41.8	3,847	0.6	79,201	11.7	27,783	4.1	174	PR
Colorado	265,954	113,912	42.8	71,752	27.0	58,386	22.0	16,366	6.2	5,538	2.1	42,160	D
Connecticut	190,404	74,561	39.2	34,129	17.9	68,324	35.9	10,056	5.3	3,334	1.8	6,237	D
Delaware	48,690	22,631	46.5	8,886	18.3	15,997	32.9	556	1.1	620	1.3	6,634	D
Florida	50,837	35,343	69.5	4,555	9.0	4,279	8.4	4,806	9.5	1,854	3.6	30,788	D
Georgia	121,470	93,087	76.6	21,985	18.1	5,191	4.3	1,058	0.9	149	0.1	71,102	D
Idaho	105,754	33,921	32.1	25,527	24.1	32,810	31.0	11,960	11.3	1,536	1.5	1,111	D
Illinois	1,146,173	405,048	35.3	386,478	33.7	253,593	22.1	81,278	7.1	19,776	1.7	18,570	D
Indiana	654,474	281,890	43.1	162,007	24.8	151,267	23.1	36,931	5.6	22,379	3.4	119,883	D
Iowa	492,353	185,322	37.6	161,819	32.9	119,805	24.3	16,967	3.4	8,440	1.7	23,503	D
Kansas	365,560	143,663	39.3	120,210	32.9	74,845	20.5	26,779	7.3	63		23,453	D
Kentucky	452,714	219,484	48.5	101,766	22.5	115,510	25.5	11,646	2.6	4,308	1.0	103,974	D
Louisiana	79,248	60,871	76.8	9,283	11.7	3,833	4.8	5,261	6.6	—		51,588	D
Maine	129,641	51,113	39.4	48,495	37.4	26,545	20.5	2,541	2.0	947	0.7	2,618	D
Maryland	231,981	112,674	48.6	57,789	24.9	54,956	23.7	3,996	1.7	2,566	1.1	54,885	D
Massachusetts	488,056	173,408	35.5	142,228	29.1	155,948	32.0	12,616	2.6	3,856	0.8	17,460	D
Michigan	547,971	150,201	27.4	213,243	38.9	151,434	27.6	23,060	4.2	10,033	1.8	61,809	PR
Minnesota	334,219	106,426	31.8	125,856	37.7	64,334	19.2	27,505	8.2	10,098	3.0	19,430	PR
Mississippi	64,483	57,324	88.9	3,549	5.5	1,560	2.4	2,050	3.2	—		53,775	D
Missouri	698,566	330,746	47.3	124,375	17.8	207,821	29.7	28,466	4.1	7,158	1.0	122,925	D
Montana	80,256	28,129	35.0	22,709	28.3	18,575	23.1	10,811	13.5	32		5,420	D
Nebraska	249,483	109,008	43.7	72,681	29.1	54,226	21.7	10,185	4.1	3,383	1.4	36,327	D
Nevada	20,115	7,986	39.7	5,620	27.9	3,196	15.9	3,313	16.5	—		2,366	D
New Hampshire	87,961	34,724	39.5	17,794	20.2	32,927	37.4	1,981	2.3	535	0.6	1,797	D
New Jersey	433,663	178,638	41.2	145,679	33.6	89,066	20.5	15,948	3.7	4,332	1.0	32,959	D
New Mexico	48,807	20,437	41.9	8,347	17.1	17,164	35.2	2,859	5.9	—		3,273	D
New York	1,588,315	655,573	41.3	390,093	24.6	455,487	28.7	63,434	4.0	23,728	1.5	200,086	D
North Carolina	243,776	144,407	59.2	69,135	28.4	29,129	11.9	987	0.4	118		75,272	D
North Dakota	86,474	29,549	34.2	25,726	29.7	22,990	26.6	6,966	8.1	1,243	1.4	3,823	D
Ohio	1,037,114	424,834	41.0	229,807	22.2	278,168	26.8	90,164	8.7	14,141	1.4	146,666	D
Oklahoma	253,694	119,143	47.0	—		90,726	35.8	41,630	16.4	2,195	0.9	28,417	D
Oregon	137,040	47,064	34.3	37,600	27.4	34,673	25.3	13,343	9.7	4,360	3.2	9,464	D
Pennsylvania	1,217,736	395,637	32.5	444,894	36.5	273,360	22.4	83,614	6.9	20,231	1.7	49,257	PR
Rhode Island	77,894	30,412	39.0	16,878	21.7	27,703	35.6	2,049	2.6	852	1.1	2,709	D
South Carolina	50,403	48,355	95.9	1,293	2.6	536	1.1	164	0.3	55	0.1	47,062	D
South Dakota	116,327	48,942	42.1	58,811	50.6	—		4,664	4.0	3,910	3.4	9,869	PR
Tennessee	251,933	133,021	52.8	54,041	21.5	60,475	24.0	3,564	1.4	832	0.3	72,546	D
Texas	300,961	218,921	72.7	26,715	8.9	28,310	9.4	24,884	8.3	2,131	0.7	190,611	D
Utah	112,272	36,576	32.6	24,174	21.5	42,013	37.4	8,999	8.0	510	0.5	5,437	R
Vermont	62,804	15,350	24.4	22,129	35.2	23,303	37.1	928	1.5	1,094	1.7	1,174	R
Virginia	136,975	90,332	65.9	21,776	15.9	23,288	17.0	820	0.6	759	0.6	67,044	D
Washington	322,799	86,840	26.9	113,698	35.2	70,445	21.8	40,134	12.4	11,682	3.6	26,858	PR
West Virginia	268,728	113,097	42.1	79,112	29.4	56,754	21.1	15,248	5.7	4,517	1.7	33,985	D
Wisconsin	399,975	164,230	41.1	62,448	15.6	130,596	32.7	33,476	8.4	9,225	2.3	33,634	D
Wyoming	42,283	15,310	36.2	9,232	21.8	14,560	34.4	2,760	6.5	421	1.0	750	D
Totals	15,040,963	6,293,152	41.8	4,119,207	27.4	3,486,333	23.2	900,369	6.0	241,902	1.6	2,173,945	D

1. For breakdown of "Other" vote, see minor candidate vote totals, p. 130.

1916 Presidential Election

STATE	TOTAL VOTE	WOODROW WILSON (Democrat)		CHARLES E. HUGHES (Republican)		ALLAN L. BENSON (Socialist)		J. FRANK HANLY (Prohibition)		OTHER [1]		PLURALITY	
		Votes	%	Votes	%	Votes	%	Votes	%	Votes	%		
Alabama	130,435	99,116	76.0	28,662	22.0	1,916	1.5	741	0.6	—		70,454	D
Arizona	58,019	33,170	57.2	20,522	35.4	3,174	5.5	1,153	2.0	—		12,648	D
Arkansas	170,104	112,211	66.0	48,879	28.7	6,999	4.1	2,015	1.2	—		63,332	D
California	999,250	465,936	46.6	462,516	46.3	42,898	4.3	27,713	2.8	187		3,420	D
Colorado	292,037	177,496	60.8	101,388	34.7	9,951	3.4	2,793	1.0	409	0.1	76,108	D
Connecticut	213,874	99,786	46.7	106,514	49.8	5,179	2.4	1,789	0.8	606	0.3	6,728	R
Delaware	51,810	24,753	47.8	26,011	50.2	480	0.9	566	1.1	—		1,258	R
Florida	80,734	55,984	69.3	14,611	18.1	5,353	6.6	4,786	5.9	—		41,373	D
Georgia	160,681	127,754	79.5	11,294	7.0	941	0.6	—		20,692	12.9	107,062	D [2]
Idaho	134,615	70,054	52.0	55,368	41.1	8,066	6.0	1,127	0.8	—		14,686	D
Illinois	2,192,707	950,229	43.3	1,152,549	52.6	61,394	2.8	26,047	1.2	2,488	0.1	202,320	R
Indiana	718,853	334,063	46.5	341,005	47.4	21,860	3.0	16,368	2.3	5,557	0.8	6,942	R
Iowa	518,738	221,699	42.7	280,439	54.1	10,976	2.1	3,371	0.6	2,253	0.4	58,740	R
Kansas	629,813	314,588	49.9	277,658	44.1	24,685	3.9	12,882	2.0	—		36,930	D
Kentucky	520,078	269,990	51.9	241,854	46.5	4,734	0.9	3,039	0.6	461	0.1	28,136	D
Louisiana	92,974	79,875	85.9	6,466	7.0	284	0.3	—		6,349	6.8	73,409	D
Maine	136,314	64,033	47.0	69,508	51.0	2,177	1.6	596	0.4	—		5,475	R
Maryland	262,039	138,359	52.8	117,347	44.8	2,674	1.0	2,903	1.1	756	0.3	21,012	D
Massachusetts	531,822	247,885	46.6	268,784	50.5	11,058	2.1	2,993	0.6	1,102	0.2	20,899	R
Michigan	646,873	283,993	43.9	337,952	52.2	16,012	2.5	8,085	1.2	831	0.1	53,959	R
Minnesota	387,367	179,155	46.2	179,544	46.3	20,117	5.2	7,793	2.0	758	0.2	389	R
Mississippi	86,679	80,422	92.8	4,253	4.9	1,484	1.7	—		520	0.6	76,169	D
Missouri	786,773	398,032	50.6	369,339	46.9	14,612	1.9	3,887	0.5	903	0.1	28,693	D
Montana	178,009	101,104	56.8	66,933	37.6	9,634	5.4	—		338	0.2	34,171	D
Nebraska	287,315	158,827	55.3	117,771	41.0	7,141	2.5	2,952	1.0	624	0.2	41,056	D
Nevada	33,314	17,776	53.4	12,127	36.4	3,065	9.2	346	1.0	—		5,649	D
New Hampshire	89,127	43,781	49.1	43,725	49.1	1,318	1.5	303	0.3	—		56	D
New Jersey	494,442	211,018	42.7	268,982	54.4	10,405	2.1	3,182	0.6	855	0.2	57,964	R
New Mexico	66,879	33,693	50.4	31,097	46.5	1,977	3.0	112	0.2	—		2,596	D
New York	1,706,305	759,426	44.5	879,238	51.5	45,944	2.7	19,031	1.1	2,666	0.2	119,812	R
North Carolina	289,837	168,383	58.1	120,890	41.7	509	0.2	55		—		47,493	D
North Dakota	115,390	55,206	47.8	53,471	46.3	5,716	5.0	997	0.9	—		1,735	D
Ohio	1,165,091	604,161	51.9	514,753	44.2	38,092	3.3	8,085	0.7	—		89,408	D
Oklahoma	292,327	148,123	50.7	97,233	33.3	45,091	15.4	1,646	0.6	234	0.1	50,890	D
Oregon	261,650	120,087	45.9	126,813	48.5	9,711	3.7	4,729	1.8	310	0.1	6,726	R
Pennsylvania	1,297,189	521,784	40.2	703,823	54.3	42,638	3.3	28,525	2.2	419		182,039	R
Rhode Island	87,816	40,394	46.0	44,858	51.1	1,914	2.2	470	0.5	180	0.2	4,464	R
South Carolina	63,950	61,845	96.7	1,550	2.4	135	0.2	—		420	0.7	60,295	D
South Dakota	128,942	59,191	45.9	64,217	49.8	3,760	2.9	1,774	1.4	—		5,026	R
Tennessee	272,190	153,280	56.3	116,223	42.7	2,542	0.9	145	0.1	—		37,057	D
Texas	373,310	287,415	77.0	64,999	17.4	18,960	5.1	1,936	0.5	—		222,416	D
Utah	143,145	84,145	58.8	54,137	37.8	4,460	3.1	149	0.1	254	0.2	30,008	D
Vermont	64,475	22,708	35.2	40,250	62.4	798	1.2	709	1.1	10		17,542	R
Virginia	152,025	101,840	67.0	48,384	31.8	1,056	0.7	678	0.4	67		53,456	D
Washington	380,994	183,388	48.1	167,208	43.9	22,800	6.0	6,868	1.8	730	0.2	16,180	D
West Virginia	289,671	140,403	48.5	143,124	49.4	6,144	2.1	—		—		2,721	R
Wisconsin	447,134	191,363	42.8	220,822	49.4	27,631	6.2	7,318	1.6	—		29,459	R
Wyoming	51,906	28,376	54.7	21,698	41.8	1,459	2.8	373	0.7	—		6,678	D
Totals	18,535,022	9,126,300	49.2	8,546,789	46.1	589,924	3.2	221,030	1.2	50,979	0.3	579,511	D

1. For breakdown of "Other" vote, see minor candidate vote totals, p. 130.
2. Plurality of 107,062 votes is calculated on the basis of 20,692 votes cast for the Progressive Party.

1920 Presidential Election

STATE	TOTAL VOTE	WARREN G. HARDING (Republican)		JAMES M. COX (Democrat)		EUGENE V. DEBS (Socialist)		PARLEY P. CHRISTENSEN (Farmer-Labor)		OTHER [1]		PLURALITY
		Votes	%	Votes	%	Votes	%	Votes	%	Votes	%	
Alabama	233,951	74,719	31.9	156,064	66.7	2,402	1.0	—		766	0.3	81,345 D
Arizona	66,803	37,016	55.4	29,546	44.2	222	0.3	15		4		7,470 R
Arkansas	183,871	72,316	39.3	106,427	57.9	5,128	2.8	—		—		34,111 D
California	943,463	624,992	66.2	229,191	24.3	64,076	6.8	—		25,204	2.7	395,801 R
Colorado	292,053	173,248	59.3	104,936	35.9	8,046	2.8	3,016	1.0	2,807	1.0	68,312 R
Connecticut	365,518	229,238	62.7	120,721	33.0	10,350	2.8	1,947	0.5	3,262	0.9	108,517 R
Delaware	94,875	52,858	55.7	39,911	42.1	988	1.0	93	0.1	1,025	1.1	12,947 R
Florida	145,684	44,853	30.8	90,515	62.1	5,189	3.6	—		5,127	3.5	45,662 D
Georgia	149,558	42,981	28.7	106,112	71.0	465	0.3	—		—		63,131 D
Idaho	138,281	91,351	66.1	46,930	33.9	—		—		—		44,421 R
Illinois	2,094,714	1,420,480	67.8	534,395	25.5	74,747	3.6	49,630	2.4	15,462	0.7	886,085 R
Indiana	1,262,974	696,370	55.1	511,364	40.5	24,713	2.0	16,499	1.3	14,028	1.1	185,006 R
Iowa	894,959	634,674	70.9	227,804	25.5	16,981	1.9	10,321	1.2	5,179	0.6	406,870 R
Kansas	570,243	369,268	64.8	185,464	32.5	15,511	2.7	—		—		183,804 R
Kentucky	918,636	452,480	49.3	456,497	49.7	6,409	0.7	—		3,250	0.4	4,017 D
Louisiana	126,397	38,539	30.5	87,519	69.2	—		—		339	0.3	48,980 D
Maine	197,840	136,355	68.9	58,961	29.8	2,214	1.1	—		310	0.2	77,394 R
Maryland	428,443	236,117	55.1	180,626	42.2	8,876	2.1	1,645	0.4	1,179	0.3	55,491 R
Massachusetts	993,718	681,153	68.5	276,691	27.8	32,267	3.2	—		3,607	0.4	404,462 R
Michigan	1,048,411	762,865	72.8	233,450	22.3	28,947	2.8	10,480	1.0	12,669	1.2	529,415 R
Minnesota	735,838	519,421	70.6	142,994	19.4	56,106	7.6	—		17,317	2.4	376,427 R
Mississippi	82,351	11,576	14.1	69,136	84.0	1,639	2.0	—		—		57,560 D
Missouri	1,332,140	727,252	54.6	574,699	43.1	20,342	1.5	3,108	0.2	6,739	0.5	152,553 R
Montana	179,006	109,430	61.1	57,372	32.1	—		12,204	6.8	—		52,058 R
Nebraska	382,743	247,498	64.7	119,608	31.3	9,600	2.5	—		6,037	1.6	127,890 R
Nevada	27,194	15,479	56.9	9,851	36.2	1,864	6.9	—		—		5,628 R
New Hampshire	159,092	95,196	59.8	62,662	39.4	1,234	0.8	—		—		32,534 R
New Jersey	910,251	615,333	67.6	258,761	28.4	27,385	3.0	2,264	0.2	6,508	0.7	356,572 R
New Mexico	105,412	57,634	54.7	46,668	44.3	2		1,104	1.0	4		10,966 R
New York	2,898,513	1,871,167	64.6	781,238	27.0	203,201	7.0	18,413	0.6	24,494	0.8	1,089,929 R
North Carolina	538,649	232,819	43.2	305,367	56.7	446	0.1	—		17		72,548 D
North Dakota	205,786	160,082	77.8	37,422	18.2	8,282	4.0	—		—		122,660 R
Ohio	2,021,653	1,182,022	58.5	780,037	38.6	57,147	2.8	—		2,447	0.1	401,985 R
Oklahoma	485,678	243,840	50.2	216,122	44.5	25,716	5.3	—		—		27,718 R
Oregon	238,522	143,592	60.2	80,019	33.5	9,801	4.1	—		5,110	2.1	63,573 R
Pennsylvania	1,851,248	1,218,215	65.8	503,202	27.2	70,021	3.8	15,642	0.8	44,168	2.4	715,013 R
Rhode Island	167,981	107,463	64.0	55,062	32.8	4,351	2.6	—		1,105	0.7	52,401 R
South Carolina	66,808	2,610	3.9	64,170	96.1	28		—		—		61,560 D
South Dakota	182,237	110,692	60.7	35,938	19.7	—		34,707	19.0	900	0.5	74,754 R
Tennessee	428,036	219,229	51.2	206,558	48.3	2,249	0.5	—		—		12,671 R
Texas	486,109	114,658	23.6	287,920	59.2	8,124	1.7	—		75,407	15.5	173,262 D
Utah	145,828	81,555	55.9	56,639	38.8	3,159	2.2	4,475	3.1	—		24,916 R
Vermont	89,961	68,212	75.8	20,919	23.3	—		—		830	0.9	47,293 R
Virginia	231,000	87,456	37.9	141,670	61.3	808	0.3	240	0.1	826	0.4	54,214 D
Washington	398,715	223,137	56.0	84,298	21.1	8,913	2.2	77,246	19.4	5,121	1.3	138,839 R
West Virginia	509,936	282,007	55.3	220,785	43.3	5,618	1.1	—		1,526	0.3	61,222 R
Wisconsin	701,281	498,576	71.1	113,422	16.2	80,635	11.5	—		8,648	1.2	385,154 R
Wyoming	56,253	35,091	62.4	17,429	31.0	1,288	2.3	2,180	3.9	265	0.5	17,662 R
Totals	26,768,613	16,153,115	60.3	9,133,092	34.1	915,490	3.4	265,229	1.0	301,687	1.1	7,020,023 R

1. For breakdown of "Other" vote, see minor candidate vote totals, p. 131.

1924 Presidential Election

STATE	TOTAL VOTE	CALVIN COOLIDGE (Republican)		JOHN W. DAVIS (Democrat)		ROBERT M. LA FOLLETTE (Progressive)		HERMAN P. FARIS (Prohibition)		OTHER [1]		PLURALITY	
		Votes	%	Votes	%	Votes	%	Votes	%	Votes	%		
Alabama	164,563	42,823	26.0	113,138	68.8	8,040	4.9	562	0.3	—		70,315	D
Arizona	73,961	30,516	41.3	26,235	35.5	17,210	23.3	—		—		4,281	R
Arkansas	138,540	40,583	29.3	84,790	61.2	13,167	9.5	—		—		44,207	D
California	1,281,778	733,250	57.2	105,514	8.2	424,649	33.1	18,365	1.4	—		308,601	R
Colorado	342,261	195,171	57.0	75,238	22.0	69,946	20.4	966	0.3	940	0.3	119,933	R
Connecticut	400,396	246,322	61.5	110,184	27.5	42,416	10.6	—		1,474	0.4	136,138	R
Delaware	90,885	52,441	57.7	33,445	36.8	4,979	5.5	—		20		18,996	R
Florida	109,158	30,633	28.1	62,083	56.9	8,625	7.9	5,498	5.0	2,319	2.1	31,450	D
Georgia	166,635	30,300	18.2	123,262	74.0	12,687	7.6	231	0.1	155	0.1	92,962	D
Idaho	147,690	69,791	47.3	23,951	16.2	53,948	36.5	—		—		15,843	R
Illinois	2,470,067	1,453,321	58.8	576,975	23.4	432,027	17.5	2,367	0.1	5,377	0.2	876,346	R
Indiana	1,272,390	703,042	55.3	492,245	38.7	71,700	5.6	4,416	0.3	987	0.1	210,797	R
Iowa	976,770	537,458	55.0	160,382	16.4	274,448	28.1	—		4,482	0.5	263,010	R
Kansas	662,456	407,671	61.5	156,320	23.6	98,461	14.9	—		4		251,351	R
Kentucky	813,843	396,758	48.8	375,593	46.2	38,465	4.7	—		3,027	0.4	21,165	R
Louisiana	121,951	24,670	20.2	93,218	76.4	—		—		4,063	3.3	68,548	D
Maine	192,192	138,440	72.0	41,964	21.8	11,382	5.9	—		406	0.2	96,476	R
Maryland	358,630	162,414	45.3	148,072	41.3	47,157	13.1	—		987	0.3	14,342	R
Massachusetts	1,129,837	703,476	62.3	280,831	24.9	141,225	12.5	—		4,305	0.4	422,645	R
Michigan	1,160,419	874,631	75.4	152,359	13.1	122,014	10.5	6,085	0.5	5,330	0.5	722,272	R
Minnesota	822,146	420,759	51.2	55,913	6.8	339,192	41.3	—		6,282	0.8	81,567	R
Mississippi	112,442	8,494	7.6	100,474	89.4	3,474	3.1	—		—		91,980	D
Missouri	1,310,095	648,488	49.5	574,962	43.9	83,996	6.4	1,418	0.1	1,231	0.1	73,526	R
Montana	174,425	74,138	42.5	33,805	19.4	66,124	37.9	—		358	0.2	8,014	R
Nebraska	463,559	218,985	47.2	137,299	29.6	105,681	22.8	1,594	0.3	—		81,686	R
Nevada	26,921	11,243	41.8	5,909	21.9	9,769	36.3	—		—		1,474	R
New Hampshire	164,769	98,575	59.8	57,201	34.7	8,993	5.5	—		—		41,374	R
New Jersey	1,088,054	676,277	62.2	298,043	27.4	109,028	10.0	1,660	0.2	3,046	0.3	378,234	R
New Mexico	112,830	54,745	48.5	48,542	43.0	9,543	8.5	—		—		6,203	R
New York	3,263,939	1,820,058	55.8	950,796	29.1	474,913	14.6	—		18,172	0.6	869,262	R
North Carolina	481,608	190,754	39.6	284,190	59.0	6,651	1.4	13		—		93,436	D
North Dakota	199,081	94,931	47.7	13,858	7.0	89,922	45.2	—		370	0.2	5,009	R
Ohio	2,016,296	1,176,130	58.3	477,887	23.7	358,008	17.8	—		4,271	0.2	698,243	R
Oklahoma	527,828	225,756	42.8	255,798	48.5	46,274	8.8	—		—		30,042	D
Oregon	279,488	142,579	51.0	67,589	24.2	68,403	24.5	—		917	0.3	74,176	R
Pennsylvania	2,144,850	1,401,481	65.3	409,192	19.1	307,567	14.3	9,779	0.5	16,831	0.8	992,289	R
Rhode Island	210,115	125,286	59.6	76,606	36.5	7,628	3.6	—		595	0.3	48,680	R
South Carolina	50,755	1,123	2.2	49,008	96.6	623	1.2	—		1		47,885	D
South Dakota	203,868	101,299	49.7	27,214	13.3	75,355	37.0	—		—		25,944	R
Tennessee	301,030	130,831	43.5	159,339	52.9	10,666	3.5	94		100		28,508	D
Texas	657,054	130,794	19.9	483,381	73.6	42,879	6.5	—		—		352,587	D
Utah	156,990	77,327	49.3	47,001	29.9	32,662	20.8	—		—		30,326	R
Vermont	102,917	80,498	78.2	16,124	15.7	5,964	5.8	326	0.3	5		64,374	R
Virginia	223,603	73,328	32.8	139,717	62.5	10,369	4.6	—		189	0.1	66,389	D
Washington	421,549	220,224	52.2	42,842	10.2	150,727	35.8	—		7,756	1.8	69,497	R
West Virginia	583,662	288,635	49.5	257,232	44.1	36,723	6.3	—		1,072	0.2	31,403	R
Wisconsin	840,827	311,614	37.1	68,115	8.1	453,678	54.0	2,918	0.3	4,502	0.5	142,064	P
Wyoming	79,900	41,858	52.4	12,868	16.1	25,174	31.5	—		—		16,684	R
Totals	29,095,023	15,719,921	54.0	8,386,704	28.8	4,832,532	16.6	56,292	0.2	99,574	0.3	7,333,217	R

1. For breakdown of "Other" vote, see minor candidate vote totals, p. 131.

1928 Presidential Election

STATE	TOTAL VOTE	HERBERT C. HOOVER (Republican)		ALFRED E. SMITH (Democrat)		NORMAN M. THOMAS (Socialist)		WILLIAM Z. FOSTER (Communist)		OTHER [1]		PLURALITY	
		Votes	%	Votes	%	Votes	%	Votes	%	Votes	%		
Alabama	248,981	120,725	48.5	127,796	51.3	460	0.2	—		—		7,071	D
Arizona	91,254	52,533	57.6	38,537	42.2	—		184	0.2	—		13,996	R
Arkansas	197,726	77,784	39.3	119,196	60.3	429	0.2	317	0.2	—		41,412	D
California	1,796,656	1,162,323	64.7	614,365	34.2	19,595	1.1	—		373		547,958	R
Colorado	392,242	253,872	64.7	133,131	33.9	3,472	0.9	675	0.2	1,092	0.3	120,741	R
Connecticut	553,118	296,641	53.6	252,085	45.6	3,029	0.5	738	0.1	625	0.1	44,556	R
Delaware	104,602	68,860	65.8	35,354	33.8	329	0.3	59	0.1	—		33,506	R
Florida	252,068	145,860	57.9	101,764	40.4	2,284	0.9	2,160	0.9	—		44,096	R
Georgia	231,592	101,800	44.0	129,604	56.0	124	0.1	64		—		27,804	D
Idaho	151,541	97,322	64.2	52,926	34.9	1,293	0.9	—		—		44,396	R
Illinois	3,107,489	1,769,141	56.9	1,313,817	42.3	19,138	0.6	3,581	0.1	1,812	0.1	455,324	R
Indiana	1,421,314	848,290	59.7	562,691	39.6	3,871	0.3	321		6,141	0.4	285,599	R
Iowa	1,009,189	623,570	61.8	379,011	37.6	2,960	0.3	328		3,320	0.3	244,559	R
Kansas	713,200	513,672	72.0	193,003	27.1	6,205	0.9	320		—		320,669	R
Kentucky	940,521	558,064	59.3	381,070	40.5	783	0.1	288		316		176,994	R
Louisiana	215,833	51,160	23.7	164,655	76.3	—		—		18		113,495	D
Maine	262,170	179,923	68.6	81,179	31.0	1,068	0.4	—		—		98,744	R
Maryland	528,348	301,479	57.1	223,626	42.3	1,701	0.3	636	0.1	906	0.2	77,853	R
Massachusetts	1,577,823	775,566	49.2	792,758	50.2	6,262	0.4	2,461	0.2	776		17,192	D
Michigan	1,372,082	965,396	70.4	396,762	28.9	3,516	0.3	2,881	0.2	3,527	0.3	568,634	R
Minnesota	970,976	560,977	57.8	396,451	40.8	6,774	0.7	4,853	0.5	1,921	0.2	164,526	R
Mississippi	151,568	27,030	17.8	124,538	82.2	—		—		—		97,508	D
Missouri	1,500,845	834,080	55.6	662,684	44.2	3,739	0.2	—		342		171,396	R
Montana	194,108	113,300	58.4	78,578	40.5	1,667	0.9	563	0.3	—		34,722	R
Nebraska	547,128	345,745	63.2	197,950	36.2	3,433	0.6	—		—		147,795	R
Nevada	32,417	18,327	56.5	14,090	43.5	—		—		—		4,237	R
New Hampshire	196,757	115,404	58.7	80,715	41.0	465	0.2	173	0.1	—		34,689	R
New Jersey	1,549,381	926,050	59.8	616,517	39.8	4,897	0.3	1,257	0.1	660		309,533	R
New Mexico	118,077	69,708	59.0	48,211	40.8	—		158	0.1	—		21,497	R
New York	4,405,626	2,193,344	49.8	2,089,863	47.4	107,332	2.4	10,876	0.2	4,211	0.1	103,481	R
North Carolina	635,150	348,923	54.9	286,227	45.1	—		—		—		62,696	R
North Dakota	239,845	131,419	54.8	106,648	44.5	936	0.4	842	0.4	—		24,771	R
Ohio	2,508,346	1,627,546	64.9	864,210	34.5	8,683	0.3	2,836	0.1	5,071	0.2	763,336	R
Oklahoma	618,427	394,046	63.7	219,174	35.4	3,924	0.6	—		1,283	0.2	174,872	R
Oregon	319,942	205,341	64.2	109,223	34.1	2,720	0.9	1,094	0.3	1,564	0.5	96,118	R
Pennsylvania	3,150,612	2,055,382	65.2	1,067,586	33.9	18,647	0.6	4,726	0.2	4,271	0.1	987,796	R
Rhode Island	237,194	117,522	49.5	118,973	50.2	—		283	0.1	416	0.2	1,451	D
South Carolina	68,605	5,858	8.5	62,700	91.4	47	0.1	—		—		56,842	D
South Dakota	261,857	157,603	60.2	102,660	39.2	443	0.2	224	0.1	927	0.4	54,943	R
Tennessee	353,192	195,388	55.3	157,143	44.5	567	0.2	94		—		38,245	R
Texas	717,733	372,324	51.9	344,542	48.0	658	0.1	209		—		27,782	R
Utah	176,603	94,618	53.6	80,985	45.9	954	0.5	46		—		13,633	R
Vermont	135,191	90,404	66.9	44,440	32.9	—		—		347	0.3	45,964	R
Virginia	305,364	164,609	53.9	140,146	45.9	249	0.1	179	0.1	181	0.1	24,463	R
Washington	500,840	335,844	67.1	156,772	31.3	2,615	0.5	1,541	0.3	4,068	0.8	179,072	R
West Virginia	642,752	375,551	58.4	263,784	41.0	1,313	0.2	401	0.1	1,703	0.3	111,767	R
Wisconsin	1,016,831	544,205	53.5	450,259	44.3	18,213	1.8	1,528	0.2	2,626	0.3	93,946	R
Wyoming	82,835	52,748	63.7	29,299	35.4	788	1.0	—		—		23,449	R
Totals	**36,805,951**	**21,437,277**	**58.2**	**15,007,698**	**40.8**	**265,583**	**0.7**	**46,896**	**0.1**	**48,497**	**0.1**	**6,429,579**	**R**

1. For breakdown of "Other" vote, see minor candidate vote totals, p. 131.

1932 Presidential Election

STATE	TOTAL VOTE	FRANKLIN D. ROOSEVELT (Democrat)		HERBERT C. HOOVER (Republican)		NORMAN M. THOMAS (Socialist)		WILLIAM Z. FOSTER (Communist)		OTHER [1]		PLURALITY	
		Votes	%	Votes	%	Votes	%	Votes	%	Votes	%		
Alabama	245,303	207,910	84.8	34,675	14.1	2,030	0.8	675	0.3	13		173,235	D
Arizona	118,251	79,264	67.0	36,104	30.5	2,618	2.2	256	0.2	9		43,160	D
Arkansas	216,569	186,829	86.3	27,465	12.7	1,166	0.5	157	0.1	952	0.4	159,364	D
California	2,266,972	1,324,157	58.4	847,902	37.4	63,299	2.8	1,023		30,591	1.3	476,255	D
Colorado	457,696	250,877	54.8	189,617	41.4	13,591	3.0	787	0.2	2,824	0.6	61,260	D
Connecticut	594,183	281,632	47.4	288,420	48.5	20,480	3.4	1,364	0.2	2,287	0.4	6,788	R
Delaware	112,901	54,319	48.1	57,073	50.6	1,376	1.2	133	0.1	—		2,754	R
Florida	276,943	206,307	74.5	69,170	25.0	775	0.3	—		691	0.2	137,137	D
Georgia	255,590	234,118	91.6	19,863	7.8	461	0.2	23		1,125	0.4	214,255	D
Idaho	186,520	109,479	58.7	71,312	38.2	526	0.3	491	0.3	4,712	2.5	38,167	D
Illinois	3,407,926	1,882,304	55.2	1,432,756	42.0	67,258	2.0	15,582	0.5	10,026	0.3	449,548	D
Indiana	1,576,927	862,054	54.7	677,184	42.9	21,388	1.4	2,187	0.1	14,114	0.9	184,870	D
Iowa	1,036,687	598,019	57.7	414,433	40.0	20,467	2.0	559	0.1	3,209	0.3	183,586	D
Kansas	791,978	424,204	53.6	349,498	44.1	18,276	2.3	—		—		74,706	D
Kentucky	983,059	580,574	59.1	394,716	40.2	3,853	0.4	271		3,645	0.4	185,858	D
Louisiana	268,804	249,418	92.8	18,853	7.0	—		—		533	0.2	230,565	D
Maine	298,444	128,907	43.2	166,631	55.8	2,489	0.8	162	0.1	255	0.1	37,724	R
Maryland	511,054	314,314	61.5	184,184	36.0	10,489	2.1	1,031	0.2	1,036	0.2	130,130	D
Massachusetts	1,580,114	800,148	50.6	736,959	46.6	34,305	2.2	4,821	0.3	3,881	0.2	63,189	D
Michigan	1,664,765	871,700	52.4	739,894	44.4	39,205	2.4	9,318	0.6	4,648	0.3	131,806	D
Minnesota	1,002,843	600,806	59.9	363,959	36.3	25,476	2.5	6,101	0.6	6,501	0.6	236,847	D
Mississippi	146,034	140,168	96.0	5,180	3.5	686	0.5	—		—		134,988	D
Missouri	1,609,894	1,025,406	63.7	564,713	35.1	16,374	1.0	568		2,833	0.2	460,693	D
Montana	216,479	127,286	58.8	78,078	36.1	7,891	3.6	1,775	0.8	1,449	0.7	49,208	D
Nebraska	570,135	359,082	63.0	201,177	35.3	9,876	1.7	—		—		157,905	D
Nevada	41,430	28,756	69.4	12,674	30.6	—		—		—		16,082	D
New Hampshire	205,520	100,680	49.0	103,629	50.4	947	0.5	264	0.1	—		2,949	R
New Jersey	1,630,063	806,630	49.5	775,684	47.6	42,998	2.6	2,915	0.2	1,836	0.1	30,946	D
New Mexico	151,606	95,089	62.7	54,217	35.8	1,776	1.2	135	0.1	389	0.3	40,872	D
New York	4,688,614	2,534,959	54.1	1,937,963	41.3	177,397	3.8	27,956	0.6	10,339	0.2	596,996	D
North Carolina	711,498	497,566	69.9	208,344	29.3	5,588	0.8	—		—		289,222	D
North Dakota	256,290	178,350	69.6	71,772	28.0	3,521	1.4	830	0.3	1,817	0.7	106,578	D
Ohio	2,609,728	1,301,695	49.9	1,227,319	47.0	64,094	2.5	7,231	0.3	9,389	0.4	74,376	D
Oklahoma	704,633	516,468	73.3	188,165	26.7	—		—		—		328,303	D
Oregon	368,751	213,871	58.0	136,019	36.9	15,450	4.2	1,681	0.5	1,730	0.5	77,852	D
Pennsylvania	2,859,021	1,295,948	45.3	1,453,540	50.8	91,119	3.2	5,658	0.2	12,756	0.4	157,592	R
Rhode Island	266,170	146,604	55.1	115,266	43.3	3,138	1.2	546	0.2	616	0.2	31,338	D
South Carolina	104,407	102,347	98.0	1,978	1.9	82	0.1	—		—		100,369	D
South Dakota	288,438	183,515	63.6	99,212	34.4	1,551	0.5	364	0.1	3,796	1.3	84,303	D
Tennessee	390,273	259,473	66.5	126,752	32.5	1,796	0.5	254	0.1	1,998	0.5	132,721	D
Texas	874,382	771,109	88.2	98,218	11.2	4,414	0.5	207		434		672,891	D
Utah	206,578	116,750	56.5	84,795	41.0	4,087	2.0	946	0.5	—		31,955	D
Vermont	136,980	56,266	41.1	78,984	57.7	1,533	1.1	195	0.1	2		22,718	R
Virginia	297,942	203,979	68.5	89,637	30.1	2,382	0.8	86		1,858	0.6	114,342	D
Washington	614,814	353,260	57.5	208,645	33.9	17,080	2.8	2,972	0.5	32,857	5.3	144,615	D
West Virginia	743,774	405,124	54.5	330,731	44.5	5,133	0.7	444	0.1	2,342	0.3	74,393	D
Wisconsin	1,114,814	707,410	63.5	347,741	31.2	53,379	4.8	3,105	0.3	3,179	0.3	359,669	D
Wyoming	96,962	54,370	56.1	39,583	40.8	2,829	2.9	180	0.2	—		14,787	D
Totals	39,758,759	22,829,501	57.4	15,760,684	39.6	884,649	2.2	103,253	0.3	180,672	0.5	7,068,817	D

1. For breakdown of "Other" vote, see minor candidate vote totals, p. 131.

1936 Presidential Election

STATE	TOTAL VOTE	FRANKLIN D. ROOSEVELT (Democrat)		ALFRED M. LANDON (Republican)		WILLIAM LEMKE (Union)		NORMAN M. THOMAS (Socialist)		OTHER [1]		PLURALITY	
		Votes	%	Votes	%	Votes	%	Votes	%	Votes	%		
Alabama	275,744	238,196	86.4	35,358	12.8	551	0.2	242	0.1	1,397	0.5	202,838	D
Arizona	124,163	86,722	69.8	33,433	26.9	3,307	2.7	317	0.3	384	0.3	53,289	D
Arkansas	179,431	146,765	81.8	32,049	17.9	4		446	0.2	167	0.1	114,716	D
California	2,638,882	1,766,836	67.0	836,431	31.7	—		11,331	0.4	24,284	0.9	930,405	D
Colorado	488,685	295,021	60.4	181,267	37.1	9,962	2.0	1,594	0.3	841	0.2	113,754	D
Connecticut	690,723	382,129	55.3	278,685	40.3	21,805	3.2	5,683	0.8	2,421	0.4	103,444	D
Delaware	127,603	69,702	54.6	57,236	44.9	442	0.3	172	0.1	51		12,466	D
Florida	327,436	249,117	76.1	78,248	23.9	—		—		71		170,869	D
Georgia	293,170	255,363	87.1	36,943	12.6	136		68		660	0.2	218,420	D
Idaho	199,617	125,683	63.0	66,256	33.2	7,678	3.8	—		—		59,427	D
Illinois	3,956,522	2,282,999	57.7	1,570,393	39.7	89,439	2.3	7,530	0.2	6,161	0.2	712,606	D
Indiana	1,650,897	934,974	56.6	691,570	41.9	19,407	1.2	3,856	0.2	1,090	0.1	243,404	D
Iowa	1,142,737	621,756	54.4	487,977	42.7	29,687	2.6	1,373	0.1	1,944	0.2	133,779	D
Kansas	865,507	464,520	53.7	397,727	46.0	494	0.1	2,766	0.3	—		66,793	D
Kentucky	926,214	541,944	58.5	369,702	39.9	12,501	1.3	627	0.1	1,440	0.2	172,242	D
Louisiana	329,778	292,894	88.8	36,791	11.2	—		—		93		256,103	D
Maine	304,240	126,333	41.5	168,823	55.5	7,581	2.5	783	0.3	720	0.2	42,490	R
Maryland	624,896	389,612	62.3	231,435	37.0	—		1,629	0.3	2,220	0.4	158,177	D
Massachusetts	1,840,357	942,716	51.2	768,613	41.8	118,639	6.4	5,111	0.3	5,278	0.3	174,103	D
Michigan	1,805,098	1,016,794	56.3	699,733	38.8	75,795	4.2	8,208	0.5	4,568	0.3	317,061	D
Minnesota	1,129,975	698,811	61.8	350,461	31.0	74,296	6.6	2,872	0.3	3,535	0.3	348,350	D
Mississippi	162,142	157,333	97.0	4,467	2.8	—		342	0.2	—		152,866	D
Missouri	1,828,635	1,111,043	60.8	697,891	38.2	14,630	0.8	3,454	0.2	1,617	0.1	413,152	D
Montana	230,502	159,690	69.3	63,598	27.6	5,539	2.4	1,066	0.5	609	0.3	96,092	D
Nebraska	608,023	347,445	57.1	247,731	40.7	12,847	2.1	—		—		99,714	D
Nevada	43,848	31,925	72.8	11,923	27.2	—		—		—		20,002	D
New Hampshire	218,114	108,460	49.7	104,642	48.0	4,819	2.2	—		193	0.1	3,818	D
New Jersey	1,820,437	1,083,850	59.5	720,322	39.6	9,407	0.5	3,931	0.2	2,927	0.2	363,528	D
New Mexico	169,135	106,037	62.7	61,727	36.5	924	0.5	343	0.2	104	0.1	44,310	D
New York	5,596,398	3,293,222	58.8	2,180,670	39.0	—		86,897	1.6	35,609	0.6	1,112,552	D
North Carolina	839,475	616,141	73.4	223,294	26.6	2		21		17		392,847	D
North Dakota	273,716	163,148	59.6	72,751	26.6	36,708	13.4	552	0.2	557	0.2	90,397	D
Ohio	3,012,660	1,747,140	58.0	1,127,855	37.4	132,212	4.4	167		5,286	0.2	619,285	D
Oklahoma	749,740	501,069	66.8	245,122	32.7	—		2,221	0.3	1,328	0.2	255,947	D
Oregon	414,021	266,733	64.4	122,706	29.6	21,831	5.3	2,143	0.5	608	0.1	144,027	D
Pennsylvania	4,138,105	2,353,788	56.9	1,690,300	40.8	67,467	1.6	14,375	0.3	12,175	0.3	663,488	D
Rhode Island	310,278	164,338	53.0	125,031	40.3	19,569	6.3	—		1,340	0.4	39,307	D
South Carolina	115,437	113,791	98.6	1,646	1.4	—		—		—		112,145	D
South Dakota	296,452	160,137	54.0	125,977	42.5	10,338	3.5	—		—		34,160	D
Tennessee	477,086	328,083	68.8	147,055	30.8	296	0.1	692	0.1	960	0.2	181,028	D
Texas	849,701	739,952	87.1	104,661	12.3	3,187	0.4	1,122	0.1	779	0.1	635,291	D
Utah	216,679	150,248	69.3	64,555	29.8	1,121	0.5	432	0.2	323	0.1	85,693	D
Vermont	143,689	62,124	43.2	81,023	56.4	—		—		542	0.4	18,899	R
Virginia	334,590	234,980	70.2	98,336	29.4	233	0.1	313	0.1	728	0.2	136,644	D
Washington	692,338	459,579	66.4	206,892	29.9	17,463	2.5	3,496	0.5	4,908	0.7	252,687	D
West Virginia	829,945	502,582	60.6	325,358	39.2	—		832	0.1	1,173	0.1	177,224	D
Wisconsin	1,258,560	802,984	63.8	380,828	30.3	60,297	4.8	10,626	0.8	3,825	0.3	422,156	D
Wyoming	103,382	62,624	60.6	38,739	37.5	1,653	1.6	200	0.2	166	0.2	23,885	D
Totals	45,654,763	27,757,333	60.8	16,684,231	36.5	892,267	2.0	187,833	0.4	133,099	0.3	11,073,102	D

1. For breakdown of "Other" vote, see minor candidate vote totals, p. 131.

1940 Presidential Election

STATE	TOTAL VOTE	FRANKLIN D. ROOSEVELT (Democrat)		WENDELL WILLKIE (Republican)		NORMAN M. THOMAS (Socialist)		ROGER W. BABSON (Prohibition)		OTHER [1]		PLURALITY	
		Votes	%	Votes	%	Votes	%	Votes	%	Votes	%		
Alabama	294,219	250,726	85.2	42,184	14.3	100		700	0.2	509	0.2	208,542	D
Arizona	150,039	95,267	63.5	54,030	36.0	—		742	0.5	—		41,237	D
Arkansas	200,429	157,213	78.4	42,122	21.0	301	0.2	793	0.4	—		115,091	D
California	3,268,791	1,877,618	57.4	1,351,419	41.3	16,506	0.5	9,400	0.3	13,848	0.4	526,199	D
Colorado	549,004	265,554	48.4	279,576	50.9	1,899	0.3	1,597	0.3	378	0.1	14,022	R
Connecticut	781,502	417,621	53.4	361,819	46.3	—		—		2,062	0.3	55,802	D
Delaware	136,374	74,599	54.7	61,440	45.1	115	0.1	220	0.2	—		13,159	D
Florida	485,640	359,334	74.0	126,158	26.0	—		—		148		233,176	D
Georgia	312,686	265,194	84.8	46,495	14.9	—		983	0.3	14		218,699	D
Idaho	235,168	127,842	54.4	106,553	45.3	497	0.2	—		276	0.1	21,289	D
Illinois	4,217,935	2,149,934	51.0	2,047,240	48.5	10,914	0.3	9,190	0.2	657		102,694	D
Indiana	1,782,747	874,063	49.0	899,466	50.5	2,075	0.1	6,437	0.4	706		25,403	R
Iowa	1,215,432	578,802	47.6	632,370	52.0	—		2,284	0.2	1,976	0.2	53,568	R
Kansas	860,297	364,725	42.4	489,169	56.9	2,347	0.3	4,056	0.5	—		124,444	R
Kentucky	970,163	557,322	57.4	410,384	42.3	1,014	0.1	1,443	0.1	—		146,938	D
Louisiana	372,305	319,751	85.9	52,446	14.1	—		—		108		267,305	D
Maine	320,840	156,478	48.8	163,951	51.1	—		—		411	0.1	7,473	R
Maryland	660,104	384,546	58.3	269,534	40.8	4,093	0.6	—		1,931	0.3	115,012	D
Massachusetts	2,026,993	1,076,522	53.1	939,700	46.4	4,091	0.2	1,370	0.1	5,310	0.3	136,822	D
Michigan	2,085,929	1,032,991	49.5	1,039,917	49.9	7,593	0.4	1,795	0.1	3,633	0.2	6,926	R
Minnesota	1,251,188	644,196	51.5	596,274	47.7	5,454	0.4	—		5,264	0.4	47,922	D
Mississippi	175,824	168,267	95.7	7,364	4.2	193	0.1	—		209		160,903	D
Missouri	1,833,729	958,476	52.3	871,009	47.5	2,226	0.1	1,809	0.1	209		87,467	D
Montana	247,873	145,698	58.8	99,579	40.2	1,443	0.6	664	0.3	489	0.2	46,119	D
Nebraska	615,878	263,677	42.8	352,201	57.2	—		—		—		88,524	R
Nevada	53,174	31,945	60.1	21,229	39.9	—		—		—		10,716	D
New Hampshire	235,419	125,292	53.2	110,127	46.8	—		—		—		15,165	D
New Jersey	1,972,552	1,016,808	51.5	945,475	47.9	2,433	0.1	873		6,963	0.4	71,333	D
New Mexico	183,258	103,699	56.6	79,315	43.3	144	0.1	100	0.1	—		24,384	D
New York	6,301,596	3,251,918	51.6	3,027,478	48.0	18,950	0.3	3,250	0.1	—		224,440	D
North Carolina	822,648	609,015	74.0	213,633	26.0	—		—		—		395,382	D
North Dakota	280,775	124,036	44.2	154,590	55.1	1,279	0.5	325	0.1	545	0.2	30,554	R
Ohio	3,319,912	1,733,139	52.2	1,586,773	47.8	—		—		—		146,366	D
Oklahoma	826,212	474,313	57.4	348,872	42.2	—		3,027	0.4	—		125,441	D
Oregon	481,240	258,415	53.7	219,555	45.6	398	0.1	154		2,718	0.6	38,860	D
Pennsylvania	4,078,714	2,171,035	53.2	1,889,848	46.3	10,967	0.3	—		6,864	0.2	281,187	D
Rhode Island	321,152	182,181	56.7	138,654	43.2	—		74		243	0.1	43,527	D
South Carolina	99,830	95,470	95.6	4,360	4.4	—		—		—		91,110	D
South Dakota	308,427	131,362	42.6	177,065	57.4	—		—		—		45,703	R
Tennessee	522,823	351,601	67.3	169,153	32.4	463	0.1	1,606	0.3	—		182,448	D
Texas	1,124,437	909,974	80.9	212,692	18.9	628	0.1	928	0.1	215		697,282	D
Utah	247,819	154,277	62.3	93,151	37.6	200	0.1	—		191	0.1	61,126	D
Vermont	143,062	64,269	44.9	78,371	54.8	—		—		422	0.3	14,102	R
Virginia	346,608	235,961	68.1	109,363	31.6	282	0.1	882	0.3	120		126,598	D
Washington	793,833	462,145	58.2	322,123	40.6	4,586	0.6	1,686	0.2	3,293	0.4	140,022	D
West Virginia	868,076	495,662	57.1	372,414	42.9	—		—		—		123,248	D
Wisconsin	1,405,522	704,821	50.1	679,206	48.3	15,071	1.1	2,148	0.2	4,276	0.3	25,615	D
Wyoming	112,240	59,287	52.8	52,633	46.9	148	0.1	172	0.2	—		6,654	D
Totals	49,900,418	27,313,041	54.7	22,348,480	44.8	116,410	0.2	58,708	0.1	63,779	0.1	4,964,561	D

1. For breakdown of "Other" vote, see minor candidate vote totals, p. 132.

1944 Presidential Election

STATE	TOTAL VOTE	FRANKLIN D. ROOSEVELT (Democrat)		THOMAS E. DEWEY (Republican)		NORMAN M. THOMAS (Socialist)		CLAUDE A. WATSON (Prohibition)		OTHER [1]		PLURALITY	
		Votes	%	Votes	%	Votes	%	Votes	%	Votes	%		
Alabama	244,743	198,918	81.3	44,540	18.2	190	0.1	1,095	0.4	—		154,378	D
Arizona	137,634	80,926	58.8	56,287	40.9	—		421	0.3	—		24,639	D
Arkansas	212,954	148,965	70.0	63,551	29.8	438	0.2	—		—		85,414	D
California	3,520,875	1,988,564	56.5	1,512,965	43.0	2,515	0.1	14,770	0.4	2,061	0.1	475,599	D
Colorado	505,039	234,331	46.4	268,731	53.2	1,977	0.4	—		—		34,400	R
Connecticut	831,990	435,146	52.3	390,527	46.9	5,097	0.6	—		1,220	0.1	44,619	D
Delaware	125,361	68,166	54.4	56,747	45.3	154	0.1	294	0.2	—		11,419	D
Florida	482,803	339,377	70.3	143,215	29.7	—		—		211		196,162	D
Georgia	328,129	268,187	81.7	59,900	18.3	6		36		—		208,287	D
Idaho	208,321	107,399	51.6	100,137	48.1	282	0.1	503	0.2	—		7,262	D
Illinois	4,036,061	2,079,479	51.5	1,939,314	48.0	180		7,411	0.2	9,677	0.2	140,165	D
Indiana	1,672,091	781,403	46.7	875,891	52.4	2,223	0.1	12,574	0.8	—		94,488	R
Iowa	1,052,599	499,876	47.5	547,267	52.0	1,511	0.1	3,752	0.4	193		47,391	R
Kansas	733,776	287,458	39.2	442,096	60.2	1,613	0.2	2,609	0.4	—		154,638	R
Kentucky	867,924	472,589	54.5	392,448	45.2	535	0.1	2,023	0.2	329		80,141	D
Louisiana	349,383	281,564	80.6	67,750	19.4	—		—		69		213,814	D
Maine	296,400	140,631	47.4	155,434	52.4	—		—		335	0.1	14,803	R
Maryland	608,439	315,490	51.9	292,949	48.1	—		—		—		22,541	D
Massachusetts	1,960,665	1,035,296	52.8	921,350	47.0	—		973		3,046	0.2	113,946	D
Michigan	2,205,223	1,106,899	50.2	1,084,423	49.2	4,598	0.2	6,503	0.3	2,800	0.1	22,476	D
Minnesota	1,125,504	589,864	52.4	527,416	46.9	5,048	0.4	—		3,176	0.3	62,448	D
Mississippi	180,234	168,621	93.6	11,613	6.4	—		—		—		157,008	D
Missouri	1,571,697	807,356	51.4	761,175	48.4	1,751	0.1	1,195	0.1	220		46,181	D
Montana	207,355	112,556	54.3	93,163	44.9	1,296	0.6	340	0.2	—		19,393	D
Nebraska	563,126	233,246	41.4	329,880	58.6	—		—		—		96,634	R
Nevada	54,234	29,623	54.6	24,611	45.4	—		—		—		5,012	D
New Hampshire	229,625	119,663	52.1	109,916	47.9	46		—		—		9,747	D
New Jersey	1,963,761	987,874	50.3	961,335	49.0	3,358	0.2	4,255	0.2	6,939	0.4	26,539	D
New Mexico	152,225	81,389	53.5	70,688	46.4	—		148	0.1	—		10,701	D
New York	6,316,790	3,304,238	52.3	2,987,647	47.3	10,553	0.2	—		14,352	0.2	316,591	D
North Carolina	790,554	527,399	66.7	263,155	33.3	—		—		—		264,244	D
North Dakota	220,182	100,144	45.5	118,535	53.8	954	0.4	549	0.2	—		18,391	R
Ohio	3,153,056	1,570,763	49.8	1,582,293	50.2	—		—		—		11,530	R
Oklahoma	722,636	401,549	55.6	319,424	44.2	—		1,663	0.2	—		82,125	D
Oregon	480,147	248,635	51.8	225,365	46.9	3,785	0.8	2,362	0.5	—		23,270	D
Pennsylvania	3,794,793	1,940,479	51.1	1,835,054	48.4	11,721	0.3	5,750	0.2	1,789		105,425	D
Rhode Island	299,276	175,356	58.6	123,487	41.3	—		433	0.1	—		51,869	D
South Carolina	103,382	90,601	87.6	4,617	4.5	—		365	0.4	7,799	7.5	82,802	D [2]
South Dakota	232,076	96,711	41.7	135,365	58.3	—		—		—		38,654	R
Tennessee	510,692	308,707	60.4	200,311	39.2	792	0.2	882	0.2	—		108,396	D
Texas	1,150,334	821,605	71.4	191,423	16.6	594	0.1	1,018	0.1	135,694	11.8	630,182	D
Utah	248,319	150,088	60.4	97,891	39.4	340	0.1	—		—		52,197	D
Vermont	125,361	53,820	42.9	71,527	57.1	—		—		14		17,707	R
Virginia	388,485	242,276	62.4	145,243	37.4	417	0.1	459	0.1	90		97,033	D
Washington	856,328	486,774	56.8	361,689	42.2	3,824	0.4	2,396	0.3	1,645	0.2	125,085	D
West Virginia	715,596	392,777	54.9	322,819	45.1	—		—		—		69,958	D
Wisconsin	1,339,152	650,413	48.6	674,532	50.4	13,205	1.0	—		1,002	0.1	24,119	R
Wyoming	101,340	49,419	48.8	51,921	51.2	—		—		—		2,502	R
Totals	47,976,670	25,612,610	53.4	22,017,617	45.9	79,003	0.2	74,779	0.2	192,661	0.4	3,594,993	D

1. For breakdown of "Other" vote, see minor candidate vote totals, p. 132.
2. Plurality of 82,802 votes is calculated on the basis of 7,799 votes cast for Southern Democratic electors.

1948 Presidential Election

STATE	TOTAL VOTE	HARRY S. TRUMAN (Democrat)		THOMAS E. DEWEY (Republican)		J. STROM THURMOND (States' Rights Democrat)		HENRY A. WALLACE (Progressive)		OTHER [1]		PLURALITY	
		Votes	%	Votes	%	Votes	%	Votes	%	Votes	%		
Alabama	214,980	—		40,930	19.0	171,443	79.7	1,522	0.7	1,085	0.5	130,513	SR
Arizona	177,065	95,251	53.8	77,597	43.8	—		3,310	1.9	907	0.5	17,654	D
Arkansas	242,475	149,659	61.7	50,959	21.0	40,068	16.5	751	0.3	1,038	0.4	98,700	D
California	4,021,538	1,913,134	47.6	1,895,269	47.1	1,228		190,381	4.7	21,526	0.5	17,865	D
Colorado	515,237	267,288	51.9	239,714	46.5	—		6,115	1.2	2,120	0.4	27,574	D
Connecticut	883,518	423,297	47.9	437,754	49.5	—		13,713	1.6	8,754	1.0	14,457	R
Delaware	139,073	67,813	48.8	69,588	50.0	—		1,050	0.8	622	0.4	1,775	R
Florida	577,643	281,988	48.8	194,280	33.6	89,755	15.5	11,620	2.0	—		87,708	D
Georgia	418,844	254,646	60.8	76,691	18.3	85,135	20.3	1,636	0.4	736	0.2	169,511	D
Idaho	214,816	107,370	50.0	101,514	47.3	—		4,972	2.3	960	0.4	5,856	D
Illinois	3,984,046	1,994,715	50.1	1,961,103	49.2	—		—		28,228	0.7	33,612	D
Indiana	1,656,212	807,831	48.8	821,079	49.6	—		9,649	0.6	17,653	1.1	13,248	R
Iowa	1,038,264	522,380	50.3	494,018	47.6	—		12,125	1.2	9,741	0.9	28,362	D
Kansas	788,819	351,902	44.6	423,039	53.6	—		4,603	0.6	9,275	1.2	71,137	R
Kentucky	822,658	466,756	56.7	341,210	41.5	10,411	1.3	1,567	0.2	2,714	0.3	125,546	D
Louisiana	416,336	136,344	32.7	72,657	17.5	204,290	49.1	3,035	0.7	10		67,946	SR
Maine	264,787	111,916	42.3	150,234	56.7	—		1,884	0.7	753	0.3	38,318	R
Maryland	596,748	286,521	48.0	294,814	49.4	2,489	0.4	9,983	1.7	2,941	0.5	8,293	R
Massachusetts	2,107,146	1,151,788	54.7	909,370	43.2	—		38,157	1.8	7,831	0.4	242,418	D
Michigan	2,109,609	1,003,448	47.6	1,038,595	49.2	—		46,515	2.2	21,051	1.0	35,147	R
Minnesota	1,212,226	692,966	57.2	483,617	39.9	—		27,866	2.3	7,777	0.6	209,349	D
Mississippi	192,190	19,384	10.1	5,043	2.6	167,538	87.2	225	0.1	—		148,154	SR
Missouri	1,578,628	917,315	58.1	655,039	41.5	—		3,998	0.3	2,276	0.1	262,276	D
Montana	224,278	119,071	53.1	96,770	43.1	—		7,313	3.3	1,124	0.5	22,301	D
Nebraska	488,940	224,165	45.8	264,774	54.2	—		—		1		40,609	R
Nevada	62,117	31,291	50.4	29,357	47.3	—		1,469	2.4	—		1,934	D
New Hampshire	231,440	107,995	46.7	121,299	52.4	7		1,970	0.9	169	0.1	13,304	R
New Jersey	1,949,555	895,455	45.9	981,124	50.3	—		42,683	2.2	30,293	1.6	85,669	R
New Mexico	187,063	105,464	56.4	80,303	42.9	—		1,037	0.6	259	0.1	25,161	D
New York	6,177,337	2,780,204	45.0	2,841,163	46.0	—		509,559	8.2	46,411	0.8	60,959	R
North Carolina	791,209	459,070	58.0	258,572	32.7	69,652	8.8	3,915	0.5	—		200,498	D
North Dakota	220,716	95,812	43.4	115,139	52.2	374	0.2	8,391	3.8	1,000	0.5	19,327	R
Ohio	2,936,071	1,452,791	49.5	1,445,684	49.2	—		37,596	1.3	—		7,107	D
Oklahoma	721,599	452,782	62.7	268,817	37.3	—		—		—		183,965	D
Oregon	524,080	243,147	46.4	260,904	49.8	—		14,978	2.9	5,051	1.0	17,757	R
Pennsylvania	3,735,348	1,752,426	46.9	1,902,197	50.9	—		55,161	1.5	25,564	0.7	149,771	R
Rhode Island	327,702	188,736	57.6	135,787	41.4	—		2,619	0.8	560	0.2	52,949	D
South Carolina	142,571	34,423	24.1	5,386	3.8	102,607	72.0	154	0.1	1		68,184	SR
South Dakota	250,105	117,653	47.0	129,651	51.8	—		2,801	1.1	—		11,998	R
Tennessee	550,283	270,402	49.1	202,914	36.9	73,815	13.4	1,864	0.3	1,288	0.2	67,488	D
Texas	1,249,577	824,235	66.0	303,467	24.3	113,920	9.1	3,918	0.3	4,037	0.3	520,768	D
Utah	276,306	149,151	54.0	124,402	45.0	—		2,679	1.0	74		24,749	D
Vermont	123,382	45,557	36.9	75,926	61.5	—		1,279	1.0	620	0.5	30,369	R
Virginia	419,256	200,786	47.9	172,070	41.0	43,393	10.4	2,047	0.5	960	0.2	28,716	D
Washington	905,058	476,165	52.6	386,314	42.7	—		31,692	3.5	10,887	1.2	89,851	D
West Virginia	748,750	429,188	57.3	316,251	42.2	—		3,311	0.4	—		112,937	D
Wisconsin	1,276,800	647,310	50.7	590,959	46.3	—		25,282	2.0	13,249	1.0	56,351	D
Wyoming	101,425	52,354	51.6	47,947	47.3	—		931	0.9	193	0.2	4,407	D
Totals	48,793,826	24,179,345	49.6	21,991,291	45.1	1,176,125	2.4	1,157,326	2.4	289,739	0.6	2,188,054	D

1. For breakdown of "Other" vote, see minor candidate vote totals, p. 132.

1952 Presidential Election

STATE	TOTAL VOTE	DWIGHT D. EISENHOWER (Republican)		ADLAI E. STEVENSON (Democrat)		VINCENT HALLINAN (Progressive)		STUART HAMBLEN (Prohibition)		OTHER [1]		PLURALITY	
		Votes	%	Votes	%	Votes	%	Votes	%	Votes	%		
Alabama	426,120	149,231	35.0	275,075	64.6	—		1,814	0.4	—		125,844	D
Arizona	260,570	152,042	58.3	108,528	41.7	—		—		—		43,514	R
Arkansas	404,800	177,155	43.8	226,300	55.9	—		886	0.2	459	0.1	49,145	D
California	5,141,849	2,897,310	56.3	2,197,548	42.7	24,106	0.5	15,653	0.3	7,232	0.1	699,762	R
Colorado	630,103	379,782	60.3	245,504	39.0	1,919	0.3	—		2,898	0.5	134,278	R
Connecticut	1,096,911	611,012	55.7	481,649	43.9	1,466	0.1	—		2,784	0.3	129,363	R
Delaware	174,025	90,059	51.8	83,315	47.9	155	0.1	234	0.1	262	0.2	6,744	R
Florida	989,337	544,036	55.0	444,950	45.0	—		—		351		99,086	R
Georgia	655,785	198,961	30.3	456,823	69.7	—		—		1		257,862	D
Idaho	276,254	180,707	65.4	95,081	34.4	443	0.2	—		23		85,626	R
Illinois	4,481,058	2,457,327	54.8	2,013,920	44.9	—		—		9,811	0.2	443,407	R
Indiana	1,955,049	1,136,259	58.1	801,530	41.0	1,085	0.1	15,335	0.8	840		334,729	R
Iowa	1,268,773	808,906	63.8	451,513	35.6	5,085	0.4	2,882	0.2	387		357,393	R
Kansas	896,166	616,302	68.8	273,296	30.5	—		6,038	0.7	530	0.1	343,006	R
Kentucky	993,148	495,029	49.8	495,729	49.9	336		1,161	0.1	893	0.1	700	D
Louisiana	651,952	306,925	47.1	345,027	52.9	—		—		—		38,102	D
Maine	351,786	232,353	66.0	118,806	33.8	332	0.1	—		295	0.1	113,547	R
Maryland	902,074	499,424	55.4	395,337	43.8	7,313	0.8	—		—		104,087	R
Massachusetts	2,383,398	1,292,325	54.2	1,083,525	45.5	4,636	0.2	886		2,026	0.1	208,800	R
Michigan	2,798,592	1,551,529	55.4	1,230,657	44.0	3,922	0.1	10,331	0.4	2,153	0.1	320,872	R
Minnesota	1,379,483	763,211	55.3	608,458	44.1	2,666	0.2	2,147	0.2	3,001	0.2	154,753	R
Mississippi	285,532	112,966	39.6	172,566	60.4	—		—		—		59,600	D
Missouri	1,892,062	959,429	50.7	929,830	49.1	987	0.1	885		931		29,599	R
Montana	265,037	157,394	59.4	106,213	40.1	723	0.3	548	0.2	159	0.1	51,181	R
Nebraska	609,660	421,603	69.2	188,057	30.8	—		—		—		233,546	R
Nevada	82,190	50,502	61.4	31,688	38.6	—		—		—		18,814	R
New Hampshire	272,950	166,287	60.9	106,663	39.1	—		—		—		59,624	R
New Jersey	2,418,554	1,373,613	56.8	1,015,902	42.0	5,589	0.2	989		22,461	0.9	357,711	R
New Mexico	238,608	132,170	55.4	105,661	44.3	225	0.1	297	0.1	255	0.1	26,509	R
New York	7,128,239	3,952,813	55.5	3,104,601	43.6	64,211	0.9	—		6,614	0.1	848,212	R
North Carolina	1,210,910	558,107	46.1	652,803	53.9	—		—		—		94,696	D
North Dakota	270,127	191,712	71.0	76,694	28.4	344	0.1	302	0.1	1,075	0.4	115,018	R
Ohio	3,700,758	2,100,391	56.8	1,600,367	43.2	—		—		—		500,024	R
Oklahoma	948,984	518,045	54.6	430,939	45.4	—		—		—		87,106	R
Oregon	695,059	420,815	60.5	270,579	38.9	3,665	0.5	—		—		150,236	R
Pennsylvania	4,580,969	2,415,789	52.7	2,146,269	46.9	4,222	0.1	8,951	0.2	5,738	0.1	269,520	R
Rhode Island	414,498	210,935	50.9	203,293	49.0	187		—		83		7,642	R
South Carolina	341,087	168,082	49.3	173,004	50.7	—		1		—		4,922	D
South Dakota	294,283	203,857	69.3	90,426	30.7	—		—		—		113,431	R
Tennessee	892,553	446,147	50.0	443,710	49.7	885	0.1	1,432	0.2	379		2,437	R
Texas	2,075,946	1,102,878	53.1	969,228	46.7	294		1,983	0.1	1,563	0.1	133,650	R
Utah	329,554	194,190	58.9	135,364	41.1	—		—		—		58,826	R
Vermont	153,557	109,717	71.5	43,355	28.2	282	0.2	—		203	0.1	66,362	R
Virginia	619,689	349,037	56.3	268,677	43.4	311	0.1	—		1,664	0.3	80,360	R
Washington	1,102,708	599,107	54.3	492,845	44.7	2,460	0.2	—		8,296	0.8	106,262	R
West Virginia	873,548	419,970	48.1	453,578	51.9	—		—		—		33,608	D
Wisconsin	1,607,370	979,744	61.0	622,175	38.7	2,174	0.1	—		3,277	0.2	357,569	R
Wyoming	129,253	81,049	62.7	47,934	37.1	—		194	0.2	76	0.1	33,115	R
Totals	61,550,918	33,936,234	55.1	27,314,992	44.4	140,023	0.2	72,949	0.1	86,720	0.1	6,621,242	R

1. For breakdown of "Other" vote, see minor candidate vote totals, p. 132.

1956 Presidential Election

STATE	TOTAL VOTE	DWIGHT D. EISENHOWER (Republican)		ADLAI E. STEVENSON (Democrat)		T. COLEMAN ANDREWS (Constitution)		ERIC HASS (Socialist Labor)		OTHER [1]		PLURALITY	
		Votes	%	Votes	%	Votes	%	Votes	%	Votes	%		
Alabama	496,861	195,694	39.4	280,844	56.5	—		—		20,323	4.1	85,150	D
Arizona	290,173	176,990	61.0	112,880	38.9	303	0.1	—		—		64,110	R
Arkansas	406,572	186,287	45.8	213,277	52.5	7,008	1.7	—		—		26,990	D
California	5,466,355	3,027,668	55.4	2,420,135	44.3	6,087	0.1	300		12,165	0.2	607,533	R
Colorado	657,074	394,479	60.0	257,997	39.3	759	0.1	3,308	0.5	531	0.1	136,482	R
Connecticut	1,117,121	711,837	63.7	405,079	36.3	—		—		205		306,758	R
Delaware	177,988	98,057	55.1	79,421	44.6	—		110	0.1	400	0.2	18,636	R
Florida	1,125,762	643,849	57.2	480,371	42.7	—		—		1,542	0.1	163,478	R
Georgia	669,655	222,778	33.3	444,688	66.4	2,096	0.3	—		93		221,910	D
Idaho	272,989	166,979	61.2	105,868	38.8	126		—		16		61,111	R
Illinois	4,407,407	2,623,327	59.5	1,775,682	40.3	—		8,342	0.2	56		847,645	R
Indiana	1,974,607	1,182,811	59.9	783,908	39.7	—		1,334	0.1	6,554	0.3	398,903	R
Iowa	1,234,564	729,187	59.1	501,858	40.7	3,202	0.3	125		192		227,329	R
Kansas	866,243	566,878	65.4	296,317	34.2	—		—		3,048	0.4	270,561	R
Kentucky	1,053,805	572,192	54.3	476,453	45.2	—		358		4,802	0.5	95,739	R
Louisiana	617,544	329,047	53.3	243,977	39.5	—		—		44,520	7.2	85,070	R
Maine	351,706	249,238	70.9	102,468	29.1	—		—		—		146,770	R
Maryland	932,827	559,738	60.0	372,613	39.9	—		—		476	0.1	187,125	R
Massachusetts	2,348,506	1,393,197	59.3	948,190	40.4	—		5,573	0.2	1,546	0.1	445,007	R
Michigan	3,080,468	1,713,647	55.6	1,359,898	44.1	—		—		6,923	0.2	353,749	R
Minnesota	1,340,005	719,302	53.7	617,525	46.1	—		2,080	0.2	1,098	0.1	101,777	R
Mississippi	248,104	60,685	24.5	144,453	58.2	—		—		42,966	17.3	83,768	D
Missouri	1,832,562	914,289	49.9	918,273	50.1	—		—		—		3,984	D
Montana	271,171	154,933	57.1	116,238	42.9	—		—		—		38,695	R
Nebraska	577,137	378,108	65.5	199,029	34.5	—		—		—		179,079	R
Nevada	96,689	56,049	58.0	40,640	42.0	—		—		—		15,409	R
New Hampshire	266,994	176,519	66.1	90,364	33.8	111		—		—		86,155	R
New Jersey	2,484,312	1,606,942	64.7	850,337	34.2	5,317	0.2	6,736	0.3	14,980	0.6	756,605	R
New Mexico	253,926	146,788	57.8	106,098	41.8	364	0.1	69		607	0.2	40,690	R
New York	7,095,971	4,345,506	61.2	2,747,944	38.7	1,027		150		1,344		1,597,562	R
North Carolina	1,165,592	575,062	49.3	590,530	50.7	—		—		—		15,468	D
North Dakota	253,991	156,766	61.7	96,742	38.1	483	0.2	—		—		60,024	R
Ohio	3,702,265	2,262,610	61.1	1,439,655	38.9	—		—		—		822,955	R
Oklahoma	859,350	473,769	55.1	385,581	44.9	—		—		—		88,188	R
Oregon	736,132	406,393	55.2	329,204	44.7	—		—		535	0.1	77,189	R
Pennsylvania	4,576,503	2,585,252	56.5	1,981,769	43.3	—		7,447	0.2	2,035		603,483	R
Rhode Island	387,609	225,819	58.3	161,790	41.7	—		—		—		64,029	R
South Carolina	300,583	75,700	25.2	136,372	45.4	2		—		88,509	29.4	47,863	D [2]
South Dakota	293,857	171,569	58.4	122,288	41.6	—		—		—		49,281	R
Tennessee	939,404	462,288	49.2	456,507	48.6	19,820	2.1	—		789	0.1	5,781	R
Texas	1,955,168	1,080,619	55.3	859,958	44.0	14,591	0.7	—		—		220,661	R
Utah	333,995	215,631	64.6	118,364	35.4	—		—		—		97,267	R
Vermont	152,978	110,390	72.2	42,549	27.8	—		—		39		67,841	R
Virginia	697,978	386,459	55.4	267,760	38.4	42,964	6.2	351	0.1	444	0.1	118,699	R
Washington	1,150,889	620,430	53.9	523,002	45.4	—		7,457	0.6	—		97,428	R
West Virginia	830,831	449,297	54.1	381,534	45.9	—		—		—		67,763	R
Wisconsin	1,550,558	954,844	61.6	586,768	37.8	6,918	0.4	710		1,318	0.1	368,076	R
Wyoming	124,127	74,573	60.1	49,554	39.9	—		—		—		25,019	R
Totals	62,026,908	35,590,472	57.4	26,022,752	42.0	111,178	0.2	44,450	0.1	258,056	0.4	9,567,720	R

1. For breakdown of "Other" vote, see minor candidate vote totals, p. 133.
2. Plurality of 47,863 votes is calculated on the basis of Stevenson's vote and the 88,509 votes cast for unpledged electors.

1960 Presidential Election

STATE	TOTAL VOTE	JOHN F. KENNEDY (Democrat)		RICHARD M. NIXON (Republican)		ERIC HASS (Socialist Labor)		UNPLEDGED		OTHER [1]		PLURALITY	
		Votes	%	Votes	%	Votes	%	Votes	%	Votes	%		
Alabama	570,225	324,050	56.8	237,981	41.7	—		—		8,194	1.4	86,069	D
Alaska	60,762	29,809	49.1	30,953	50.9	—		—		—		1,144	R
Arizona	398,491	176,781	44.4	221,241	55.5	469	0.1	—		—		44,460	R
Arkansas	428,509	215,049	50.2	184,508	43.1	—		—		28,952	6.8	30,541	D
California	6,506,578	3,224,099	49.6	3,259,722	50.1	1,051		—		21,706	0.3	35,623	R
Colorado	736,236	330,629	44.9	402,242	54.6	2,803	0.4	—		562	0.1	71,613	R
Connecticut	1,222,883	657,055	53.7	565,813	46.3	—		—		15		91,242	D
Delaware	196,683	99,590	50.6	96,373	49.0	82		—		638	0.3	3,217	D
Florida	1,544,176	748,700	48.5	795,476	51.5	—		—		—		46,776	R
Georgia	733,349	458,638	62.5	274,472	37.4	—		—		239		184,166	D
Hawaii	184,705	92,410	50.0	92,295	50.0	—		—		—		115	D
Idaho	300,450	138,853	46.2	161,597	53.8	—		—		—		22,744	R
Illinois	4,757,409	2,377,846	50.0	2,368,988	49.8	10,560	0.2	—		15		8,858	D
Indiana	2,135,360	952,358	44.6	1,175,120	55.0	1,136	0.1	—		6,746	0.3	222,762	R
Iowa	1,273,810	550,565	43.2	722,381	56.7	230		—		634		171,816	R
Kansas	928,825	363,213	39.1	561,474	60.4	—		—		4,138	0.4	198,261	R
Kentucky	1,124,462	521,855	46.4	602,607	53.6	—		—		—		80,752	R
Louisiana	807,891	407,339	50.4	230,980	28.6	—		—		169,572	21.0	176,359	D
Maine	421,767	181,159	43.0	240,608	57.0	—		—		—		59,449	R
Maryland	1,055,349	565,808	53.6	489,538	46.4	—		—		3		76,270	D
Massachusetts	2,469,480	1,487,174	60.2	976,750	39.6	3,892	0.2	—		1,664	0.1	510,424	D
Michigan	3,318,097	1,687,269	50.9	1,620,428	48.8	1,718	0.1	—		8,682	0.3	66,841	D
Minnesota	1,541,887	779,933	50.6	757,915	49.2	962	0.1	—		3,077	0.2	22,018	D
Mississippi	298,171	108,362	36.3	73,561	24.7	—		116,248 [2]	39.0	—		7,886	U
Missouri	1,934,422	972,201	50.3	962,221	49.7	—		—		—		9,980	D
Montana	277,579	134,891	48.6	141,841	51.1	—		—		847	0.3	6,950	R
Nebraska	613,095	232,542	37.9	380,553	62.1	—		—		—		148,011	R
Nevada	107,267	54,880	51.2	52,387	48.8	—		—		—		2,493	D
New Hampshire	295,761	137,772	46.6	157,989	53.4	—		—		—		20,217	R
New Jersey	2,773,111	1,385,415	50.0	1,363,324	49.2	4,262	0.2	—		20,110	0.7	22,091	D
New Mexico	311,107	156,027	50.2	153,733	49.4	570	0.2	—		777	0.2	2,294	D
New York	7,291,079	3,830,085	52.5	3,446,419	47.3	—		—		14,575	0.2	383,666	D
North Carolina	1,368,556	713,136	52.1	655,420	47.9	—		—		—		57,716	D
North Dakota	278,431	123,963	44.5	154,310	55.4	—		—		158	0.1	30,347	R
Ohio	4,161,859	1,944,248	46.7	2,217,611	53.3	—		—		—		273,363	R
Oklahoma	903,150	370,111	41.0	533,039	59.0	—		—		—		162,928	R
Oregon	776,421	367,402	47.3	408,060	52.6	—		—		959	0.1	40,658	R
Pennsylvania	5,006,541	2,556,282	51.1	2,439,956	48.7	7,185	0.1	—		3,118	0.1	116,326	D
Rhode Island	405,535	258,032	63.6	147,502	36.4	—		—		1		110,530	D
South Carolina	386,688	198,129	51.2	188,558	48.8	—		—		1		9,571	D
South Dakota	306,487	128,070	41.8	178,417	58.2	—		—		—		50,347	R
Tennessee	1,051,792	481,453	45.8	556,577	52.9	—		—		13,762	1.3	75,124	R
Texas	2,311,084	1,167,567	50.5	1,121,310	48.5	—		—		22,207	1.0	46,257	D
Utah	374,709	169,248	45.2	205,361	54.8	—		—		100		36,113	R
Vermont	167,324	69,186	41.3	98,131	58.6	—		—		7		28,945	R
Virginia	771,449	362,327	47.0	404,521	52.4	397	0.1	—		4,204	0.5	42,194	R
Washington	1,241,572	599,298	48.3	629,273	50.7	10,895	0.9	—		2,106	0.2	29,975	R
West Virginia	837,781	441,786	52.7	395,995	47.3	—		—		—		45,791	D
Wisconsin	1,729,082	830,805	48.0	895,175	51.8	1,310	0.1	—		1,792	0.1	64,370	R
Wyoming	140,782	63,331	45.0	77,451	55.0	—		—		—		14,120	R
Totals	68,838,219	34,226,731	49.7	34,108,157	49.5	47,522	0.1	116,248	0.2	339,561	0.5	118,574	D

1. For breakdown of "Other" vote, see minor candidate vote totals, p. 133.
2. Votes for unpledged electors who carried the state and cast electoral votes for Harry F. Byrd (D Va.).

1964 Presidential Election

STATE	TOTAL VOTE	LYNDON B. JOHNSON (Democrat)		BARRY M. GOLDWATER (Republican)		ERIC HASS (Socialist Labor)		CLIFTON DeBERRY (Socialist Workers)		OTHER [1]		PLURALITY	
		Votes	%	Votes	%	Votes	%	Votes	%	Votes	%		
Alabama	689,818	—		479,085	69.5	—		—		210,733	30.5	268,353	R [2]
Alaska	67,259	44,329	65.9	22,930	34.1	—		—		—		21,399	D
Arizona	480,770	237,753	49.5	242,535	50.4	482	0.1	—		—		4,782	R
Arkansas	560,426	314,197	56.1	243,264	43.4	—		—		2,965	0.5	70,933	D
California	7,057,586	4,171,877	59.1	2,879,108	40.8	489		378		5,734	0.1	1,292,769	D
Colorado	776,986	476,024	61.3	296,767	38.2	302		2,537	0.3	1,356	0.2	179,257	D
Connecticut	1,218,578	826,269	67.8	390,996	32.1	—		—		1,313	0.1	435,273	D
Delaware	201,320	122,704	60.9	78,078	38.8	113	0.1	—		425	0.2	44,626	D
Florida	1,854,481	948,540	51.1	905,941	48.9	—		—		—		42,599	D
Georgia	1,139,335	522,556	45.9	616,584	54.1	—		—		195		94,028	R
Hawaii	207,271	163,249	78.8	44,022	21.2	—		—		—		119,227	D
Idaho	292,477	148,920	50.9	143,557	49.1	—		—		—		5,363	D
Illinois	4,702,841	2,796,833	59.5	1,905,946	40.5	—		—		62		890,887	D
Indiana	2,091,606	1,170,848	56.0	911,118	43.6	1,374	0.1	—		8,266	0.4	259,730	D
Iowa	1,184,539	733,030	61.9	449,148	37.9	182		159		2,020	0.2	283,882	D
Kansas	857,901	464,028	54.1	386,579	45.1	1,901	0.2	—		5,393	0.6	77,449	D
Kentucky	1,046,105	669,659	64.0	372,977	35.7	—		—		3,469	0.3	296,682	D
Louisiana	896,293	387,068	43.2	509,225	56.8	—		—		—		122,157	R
Maine	380,965	262,264	68.8	118,701	31.2	—		—		—		143,563	D
Maryland	1,116,457	730,912	65.5	385,495	34.5	—		—		50		345,417	D
Massachusetts	2,344,798	1,786,422	76.2	549,727	23.4	4,755	0.2	—		3,894	0.2	1,236,695	D
Michigan	3,203,102	2,136,615	66.7	1,060,152	33.1	1,704	0.1	3,817	0.1	814		1,076,463	D
Minnesota	1,554,462	991,117	63.8	559,624	36.0	2,544	0.2	1,177	0.1	—		431,493	D
Mississippi	409,146	52,618	12.9	356,528	87.1	—		—		—		303,910	R
Missouri	1,817,879	1,164,344	64.0	653,535	36.0	—		—		—		510,809	D
Montana	278,628	164,246	58.9	113,032	40.6	—		332	0.1	1,018	0.4	51,214	D
Nebraska	584,154	307,307	52.6	276,847	47.4	—		—		—		30,460	D
Nevada	135,433	79,339	58.6	56,094	41.4	—		—		—		23,245	D
New Hampshire	288,093	184,064	63.9	104,029	36.1	—		—		—		80,035	D
New Jersey	2,847,663	1,868,231	65.6	964,174	33.9	7,075	0.2	8,183	0.3	—		904,057	D
New Mexico	328,645	194,015	59.0	132,838	40.4	1,217	0.4	—		575	0.2	61,177	D
New York	7,166,275	4,913,102	68.6	2,243,559	31.3	6,118	0.1	3,228		268		2,669,543	D
North Carolina	1,424,983	800,139	56.2	624,844	43.8	—		—		—		175,295	D
North Dakota	258,389	149,784	58.0	108,207	41.9	—		224	0.1	174	0.1	41,577	D
Ohio	3,969,196	2,498,331	62.9	1,470,865	37.1	—		—		—		1,027,466	D
Oklahoma	932,499	519,834	55.7	412,665	44.3	—		—		—		107,169	D
Oregon	786,305	501,017	63.7	282,779	36.0	—		—		2,509	0.3	218,238	D
Pennsylvania	4,822,690	3,130,954	64.9	1,673,657	34.7	5,092	0.1	10,456	0.2	2,531	0.1	1,457,297	D
Rhode Island	390,091	315,463	80.9	74,615	19.1	—		—		13		240,848	D
South Carolina	524,779	215,723	41.1	309,048	58.9	—		—		8		93,325	R
South Dakota	293,118	163,010	55.6	130,108	44.4	—		—		—		32,902	D
Tennessee	1,143,946	634,947	55.5	508,965	44.5	—		—		34		125,982	D
Texas	2,626,811	1,663,185	63.3	958,566	36.5	—		—		5,060	0.2	704,619	D
Utah	401,413	219,628	54.7	181,785	45.3	—		—		—		37,843	D
Vermont	163,089	108,127	66.3	54,942	33.7	—		—		20		53,185	D
Virginia	1,042,267	558,038	53.5	481,334	46.2	2,895	0.3	—		—		76,704	D
Washington	1,258,556	779,881	62.0	470,366	37.4	7,772	0.6	537		—		309,515	D
West Virginia	792,040	538,087	67.9	253,953	32.1	—		—		—		284,134	D
Wisconsin	1,691,815	1,050,424	62.1	638,495	37.7	1,204	0.1	1,692	0.1	—		411,929	D
Wyoming	142,716	80,718	56.6	61,998	43.4	—		—		—		18,720	D
Dist. of Col.	198,597	169,796	85.5	28,801	14.5	—		—		—		140,995	D
Totals	70,644,592	43,129,566	61.1	27,178,188	38.5	45,219	0.1	32,720		258,899	0.4	15,951,378	D

1. For breakdown of "Other" vote, see minor candidate vote totals, p. 133.
2. Plurality of 268,353 votes is calculated on the basis of Goldwater's vote and the 210,732 votes cast for the unpledged Democratic elector ticket.

1968 Presidential Election

STATE	TOTAL VOTE	RICHARD M. NIXON (Republican)		HUBERT H. HUMPHREY (Democrat)		GEORGE C. WALLACE (American Independent)		HENNING A. BLOMEN (Socialist Labor)		OTHER [1]		PLURALITY	
		Votes	%	Votes	%	Votes	%	Votes	%	Votes	%		
Alabama	1,049,922	146,923	14.0	196,579	18.7	691,425	65.9	—		14,995	1.4	494,846	A
Alaska	83,035	37,600	45.3	35,411	42.6	10,024	12.1	—		—		2,189	R
Arizona	486,936	266,721	54.8	170,514	35.0	46,573	9.6	75		3,053	0.6	96,207	R
Arkansas	619,969	190,759	30.8	188,228	30.4	240,982	38.9	—		—		50,223	A
California	7,251,587	3,467,664	47.8	3,244,318	44.7	487,270	6.7	341		51,994	0.7	223,346	R
Colorado	811,199	409,345	50.5	335,174	41.3	60,813	7.5	3,016	0.4	2,851	0.4	74,171	R
Connecticut	1,256,232	556,721	44.3	621,561	49.5	76,650	6.1	—		1,300	0.1	64,840	D
Delaware	214,367	96,714	45.1	89,194	41.6	28,459	13.3	—		—		7,520	R
Florida	2,187,805	886,804	40.5	676,794	30.9	624,207	28.5	—		—		210,010	R
Georgia	1,250,266	380,111	30.4	334,440	26.7	535,550	42.8	—		165		155,439	A
Hawaii	236,218	91,425	38.7	141,324	59.8	3,469	1.5	—		—		49,899	D
Idaho	291,183	165,369	56.8	89,273	30.7	36,541	12.5	—		—		76,096	R
Illinois	4,619,749	2,174,774	47.1	2,039,814	44.2	390,958	8.5	13,878	0.3	325		134,960	R
Indiana	2,123,597	1,067,885	50.3	806,659	38.0	243,108	11.4	—		5,945	0.3	261,226	R
Iowa	1,167,931	619,106	53.0	476,699	40.8	66,422	5.7	241		5,463	0.5	142,407	R
Kansas	872,783	478,674	54.8	302,996	34.7	88,921	10.2	—		2,192	0.3	175,678	R
Kentucky	1,055,893	462,411	43.8	397,541	37.6	193,098	18.3	—		2,843	0.3	64,870	R
Louisiana	1,097,450	257,535	23.5	309,615	28.2	530,300	48.3	—		—		220,685	A
Maine	392,936	169,254	43.1	217,312	55.3	6,370	1.6	—		—		48,058	D
Maryland	1,235,039	517,995	41.9	538,310	43.6	178,734	14.5	—		—		20,315	D
Massachusetts	2,331,752	766,844	32.9	1,469,218	63.0	87,088	3.7	6,180	0.3	2,422	0.1	702,374	D
Michigan	3,306,250	1,370,665	41.5	1,593,082	48.2	331,968	10.0	1,762	0.1	8,773	0.3	222,417	D
Minnesota	1,588,506	658,643	41.5	857,738	54.0	68,931	4.3	285		2,909	0.2	199,095	D
Mississippi	654,509	88,516	13.5	150,644	23.0	415,349	63.5	—		—		264,705	A
Missouri	1,809,502	811,932	44.9	791,444	43.7	206,126	11.4	—		—		20,488	R
Montana	274,404	138,835	50.6	114,117	41.6	20,015	7.3	—		1,437	0.5	24,718	R
Nebraska	536,851	321,163	59.8	170,784	31.8	44,904	8.4	—		—		150,379	R
Nevada	154,218	73,188	47.5	60,598	39.3	20,432	13.2	—		—		12,590	R
New Hampshire	297,298	154,903	52.1	130,589	43.9	11,173	3.8	—		633	0.2	24,314	R
New Jersey	2,875,395	1,325,467	46.1	1,264,206	44.0	262,187	9.1	6,784	0.2	16,751	0.6	61,261	R
New Mexico	327,350	169,692	51.8	130,081	39.7	25,737	7.9	—		1,840	0.6	39,611	R
New York	6,791,688	3,007,932	44.3	3,378,470	49.7	358,864	5.3	8,432	0.1	37,990	0.6	370,538	D
North Carolina	1,587,493	627,192	39.5	464,113	29.2	496,188	31.3	—		—		131,004	R
North Dakota	247,882	138,669	55.9	94,769	38.2	14,244	5.7	—		200	0.1	43,900	R
Ohio	3,959,698	1,791,014	45.2	1,700,586	42.9	467,495	11.8	120		483		90,428	R
Oklahoma	943,086	449,697	47.7	301,658	32.0	191,731	20.3	—		—		148,039	R
Oregon	819,622	408,433	49.8	358,866	43.8	49,683	6.1	—		2,640	0.3	49,567	R
Pennsylvania	4,747,928	2,090,017	44.0	2,259,405	47.6	378,582	8.0	4,977	0.1	14,947	0.3	169,388	D
Rhode Island	385,000	122,359	31.8	246,518	64.0	15,678	4.1	—		445	0.1	124,159	D
South Carolina	666,978	254,062	38.1	197,486	29.6	215,430	32.3	—		—		38,632	R
South Dakota	281,264	149,841	53.3	118,023	42.0	13,400	4.8	—		—		31,818	R
Tennessee	1,248,617	472,592	37.8	351,233	28.1	424,792	34.0	—		—		47,800	R
Texas	3,079,216	1,227,844	39.9	1,266,804	41.1	584,269	19.0	—		299		38,960	D
Utah	422,568	238,728	56.5	156,665	37.1	26,906	6.4	—		269	0.1	82,063	R
Vermont	161,404	85,142	52.8	70,255	43.5	5,104	3.2	—		903	0.6	14,887	R
Virginia	1,361,491	590,319	43.4	442,387	32.5	321,833	23.6	4,671	0.3	2,281	0.2	147,932	R
Washington	1,304,281	588,510	45.1	616,037	47.2	96,990	7.4	488		2,256	0.2	27,527	D
West Virginia	754,206	307,555	40.8	374,091	49.6	72,560	9.6	—		—		66,536	D
Wisconsin	1,691,538	809,997	47.9	748,804	44.3	127,835	7.6	1,338	0.1	3,564	0.2	61,193	R
Wyoming	127,205	70,927	55.8	45,173	35.5	11,105	8.7	—		—		25,754	R
Dist. of Col.	170,578	31,012	18.2	139,566	81.8	—		—		—		108,554	D
Totals	73,211,875	31,785,480	43.4	31,275,166	42.7	9,906,473	13.5	52,588	0.1	192,168	0.3	510,314	R

1. For breakdown of "Other" vote, see minor candidate vote totals, p. 133.

1972 Presidential Election

STATE	TOTAL VOTE	RICHARD M. NIXON (Republican)		GEORGE S. McGOVERN (Democrat)		JOHN G. SCHMITZ (American)		BENJAMIN SPOCK (People's)		OTHER [1]		PLURALITY	
		Votes	%	Votes	%	Votes	%	Votes	%	Votes	%		
Alabama	1,006,111	728,701	72.4	256,923	25.5	11,928	1.2	—		8,559	0.9	471,778	R
Alaska	95,219	55,349	58.1	32,967	34.6	6,903	7.2	—		—		22,382	R
Arizona	622,926	402,812	64.7	198,540	31.9	21,208	3.4	—		366	0.1	204,272	R
Arkansas	651,320	448,541	68.9	199,892	30.7	2,887	0.4	—		—		248,649	R
California	8,367,862	4,602,096	55.0	3,475,847	41.5	232,554	2.8	55,167	0.7	2,198		1,126,249	R
Colorado	953,884	597,189	62.6	329,980	34.6	17,269	1.8	2,403	0.3	7,043	0.7	267,209	R
Connecticut	1,384,277	810,763	58.6	555,498	40.1	17,239	1.2	—		777	0.1	255,265	R
Delaware	235,516	140,357	59.6	92,283	39.2	2,638	1.1	—		238	0.1	48,074	R
Florida	2,583,283	1,857,759	71.9	718,117	27.8	—		—		7,407	0.3	1,139,642	R
Georgia	1,174,772	881,496	75.0	289,529	24.6	812	0.1	—		2,935	0.2	591,967	R
Hawaii	270,274	168,865	62.5	101,409	37.5	—		—		—		67,456	R
Idaho	310,379	199,384	64.2	80,826	26.0	28,869	9.3	903	0.3	397	0.1	118,558	R
Illinois	4,723,236	2,788,179	59.0	1,913,472	40.5	2,471	0.1	—		19,114	0.4	874,707	R
Indiana	2,125,529	1,405,154	66.1	708,568	33.3	—		4,544	0.2	7,263	0.3	696,586	R
Iowa	1,225,944	706,207	57.6	496,206	40.5	22,056	1.8	—		1,475	0.1	210,001	R
Kansas	916,095	619,812	67.7	270,287	29.5	21,808	2.4	—		4,188	0.5	349,525	R
Kentucky	1,067,499	676,446	63.4	371,159	34.8	17,627	1.7	1,118	0.1	1,149	0.1	305,287	R
Louisiana	1,051,491	686,852	65.3	298,142	28.4	52,099	5.0	—		14,398	1.4	388,710	R
Maine	417,042	256,458	61.5	160,584	38.5	—		—		—		95,874	R
Maryland	1,353,812	829,305	61.3	505,781	37.4	18,726	1.4	—		—		323,524	R
Massachusetts	2,458,756	1,112,078	45.2	1,332,540	54.2	2,877	0.1	101		11,160	0.5	220,462	D
Michigan	3,489,727	1,961,721	56.2	1,459,435	41.8	63,321	1.8	—		5,250	0.2	502,286	R
Minnesota	1,741,652	898,269	51.6	802,346	46.1	31,407	1.8	2,805	0.2	6,825	0.4	95,923	R
Mississippi	645,963	505,125	78.2	126,782	19.6	11,598	1.8	—		2,458	0.4	378,343	R
Missouri	1,855,803	1,153,852	62.2	697,147	37.6	—		—		4,804	0.3	456,705	R
Montana	317,603	183,976	57.9	120,197	37.8	13,430	4.2	—		—		63,779	R
Nebraska	576,289	406,298	70.5	169,991	29.5	—		—		—		236,307	R
Nevada	181,766	115,750	63.7	66,016	36.3	—		—		—		49,734	R
New Hampshire	334,055	213,724	64.0	116,435	34.9	3,386	1.0	—		510	0.2	97,289	R
New Jersey	2,997,229	1,845,502	61.6	1,102,211	36.8	34,378	1.1	5,355	0.2	9,783	0.3	743,291	R
New Mexico	386,241	235,606	61.0	141,084	36.5	8,767	2.3	—		784	0.2	94,522	R
New York	7,165,919	4,192,778	58.5	2,951,084	41.2	—		—		22,057	0.3	1,241,694	R
North Carolina	1,518,612	1,054,889	69.5	438,705	28.9	25,018	1.6	—		—		616,184	R
North Dakota	280,514	174,109	62.1	100,384	35.8	5,646	2.0	—		375	0.1	73,725	R
Ohio	4,094,787	2,441,827	59.6	1,558,889	38.1	80,067	2.0	—		14,004	0.3	882,938	R
Oklahoma	1,029,900	759,025	73.7	247,147	24.0	23,728	2.3	—		—		511,878	R
Oregon	927,946	486,686	52.4	392,760	42.3	46,211	5.0	—		2,289	0.2	93,926	R
Pennsylvania	4,592,106	2,714,521	59.1	1,796,951	39.1	70,593	1.5	—		10,041	0.2	917,570	R
Rhode Island	415,808	220,383	53.0	194,645	46.8	25		5		750	0.2	25,738	R
South Carolina	673,960	477,044	70.8	186,824	27.7	10,075	1.5	—		17		290,220	R
South Dakota	307,415	166,476	54.2	139,945	45.5	—		—		994	0.3	26,531	R
Tennessee	1,201,182	813,147	67.7	357,293	29.7	30,373	2.5	—		369		455,854	R
Texas	3,471,281	2,298,896	66.2	1,154,289	33.3	6,039	0.2	—		12,057	0.3	1,144,607	R
Utah	478,476	323,643	67.6	126,284	26.4	28,549	6.0	—		—		197,359	R
Vermont	186,947	117,149	62.7	68,174	36.5	—		1,010	0.5	614	0.3	48,975	R
Virginia	1,457,019	988,493	67.8	438,887	30.1	19,721	1.4	—		9,918	0.7	549,606	R
Washington	1,470,847	837,135	56.9	568,334	38.6	58,906	4.0	2,644	0.2	3,828	0.3	268,801	R
West Virginia	762,399	484,964	63.6	277,435	36.4	—		—		—		207,529	R
Wisconsin	1,852,890	989,430	53.4	810,174	43.7	47,525	2.6	2,701	0.1	3,060	0.2	179,256	R
Wyoming	145,570	100,464	69.0	44,358	30.5	748	0.5	—		—		56,106	R
Dist. of Col.	163,421	35,226	21.6	127,627	78.1	—		—		568	0.3	92,401	D
Totals	77,718,554	47,169,911	60.7	29,170,383	37.5	1,099,482	1.4	78,756	0.1	200,022	0.3	17,999,528	R

1. For breakdown of "Other" vote, see minor candidate vote totals, p. 134.

1976 Presidential Election

STATE	TOTAL VOTE	JIMMY CARTER (Democrat)		GERALD R. FORD (Republican)		EUGENE J. McCARTHY (Independent)		ROGER MacBRIDE (Libertarian)		OTHER [1]		PLURALITY	
		Votes	%	Votes	%	Votes	%	Votes	%	Votes	%		
Alabama	1,182,850	659,170	55.7	504,070	42.6	99		1,481	0.1	18,030	1.5	155,100	D
Alaska	123,574	44,058	35.7	71,555	57.9	—		6,785	5.5	1,176	1.0	27,497	R
Arizona	742,719	295,602	39.8	418,642	56.4	19,229	2.6	7,647	1.0	1,599	0.2	123,040	R
Arkansas	767,535	498,604	65.0	267,903	34.9	639	0.1	—		389	0.1	230,701	D
California	7,867,117	3,742,284	47.6	3,882,244	49.3	58,412	0.7	56,388	0.7	127,789	1.6	139,960	R
Colorado	1,081,554	460,353	42.6	584,367	54.0	26,107	2.4	5,330	0.5	5,397	0.5	124,014	R
Connecticut	1,381,526	647,895	46.9	719,261	52.1	3,759	0.3	209		10,402	0.8	71,366	R
Delaware	235,834	122,596	52.0	109,831	46.6	2,437	1.0	—		970	0.4	12,765	D
Florida	3,150,631	1,636,000	51.9	1,469,531	46.6	23,643	0.8	103		21,354	0.7	166,469	D
Georgia	1,467,458	979,409	66.7	483,743	33.0	991	0.1	175		3,140	0.2	495,666	D
Hawaii	291,301	147,375	50.6	140,003	48.1	—		3,923	1.3	—		7,372	D
Idaho	344,071	126,549	36.8	204,151	59.3	1,194	0.3	3,558	1.0	8,619	2.5	77,602	R
Illinois	4,718,914	2,271,295	48.1	2,364,269	50.1	55,939	1.2	8,057	0.2	19,354	0.4	92,974	R
Indiana	2,220,362	1,014,714	45.7	1,183,958	53.3	—		—		21,690	1.0	169,244	R
Iowa	1,279,306	619,931	48.5	632,863	49.5	20,051	1.6	1,452	0.1	5,009	0.4	12,932	R
Kansas	957,845	430,421	44.9	502,752	52.5	13,185	1.4	3,242	0.3	8,245	0.9	72,331	R
Kentucky	1,167,142	615,717	52.8	531,852	45.6	6,837	0.6	814	0.1	11,922	1.0	83,865	D
Louisiana	1,278,439	661,365	51.7	587,446	46.0	6,588	0.5	3,325	0.3	19,715	1.5	73,919	D
Maine	483,216	232,279	48.1	236,320	48.9	10,874	2.3	11		3,732	0.8	4,041	R
Maryland	1,439,897	759,612	52.8	672,661	46.7	4,541	0.3	255		2,828	0.2	86,951	D
Massachusetts	2,547,558	1,429,475	56.1	1,030,276	40.4	65,637	2.6	135		22,035	0.9	399,199	D
Michigan	3,653,749	1,696,714	46.4	1,893,742	51.8	47,905	1.3	5,406	0.1	9,982	0.3	197,028	R
Minnesota	1,949,931	1,070,440	54.9	819,395	42.0	35,490	1.8	3,529	0.2	21,077	1.1	251,045	D
Mississippi	769,361	381,309	49.6	366,846	47.7	4,074	0.5	2,788	0.4	14,344	1.9	14,463	D
Missouri	1,953,600	998,387	51.1	927,443	47.5	24,029	1.2	—		3,741	0.2	70,944	D
Montana	328,734	149,259	45.4	173,703	52.8	—		—		5,772	1.8	24,444	R
Nebraska	607,668	233,692	38.5	359,705	59.2	9,409	1.5	1,482	0.2	3,380	0.6	126,013	R
Nevada	201,876	92,479	45.8	101,273	50.2	—		1,519	0.8	6,605	3.3	8,794	R
New Hampshire	339,618	147,635	43.5	185,935	54.7	4,095	1.2	936	0.3	1,017	0.3	38,300	R
New Jersey	3,014,472	1,444,653	47.9	1,509,688	50.1	32,717	1.1	9,449	0.3	17,965	0.6	65,035	R
New Mexico	418,409	201,148	48.1	211,419	50.5	1,161	0.3	1,110	0.3	3,571	0.9	10,271	R
New York	6,534,170	3,389,558	51.9	3,100,791	47.5	4,303	0.1	12,197	0.2	27,321	0.4	288,767	D
North Carolina	1,678,914	927,365	55.2	741,960	44.2	780		2,219	0.1	6,590	0.4	185,405	D
North Dakota	297,188	136,078	45.8	153,470	51.6	2,952	1.0	253	0.1	4,435	1.5	17,392	R
Ohio	4,111,873	2,011,621	48.9	2,000,505	48.7	58,258	1.4	8,961	0.2	32,528	0.8	11,116	D
Oklahoma	1,092,251	532,442	48.7	545,708	50.0	14,101	1.3	—		—		13,266	R
Oregon	1,029,876	490,407	47.6	492,120	47.8	40,207	3.9	—		7,142	0.7	1,713	R
Pennsylvania	4,620,787	2,328,677	50.4	2,205,604	47.7	50,584	1.1	—		35,922	0.8	123,073	D
Rhode Island	411,170	227,636	55.4	181,249	44.1	479	0.1	715	0.2	1,091	0.3	46,387	D
South Carolina	802,583	450,807	56.2	346,149	43.1	289		53		5,285	0.7	104,658	D
South Dakota	300,678	147,068	48.9	151,505	50.4	—		1,619	0.5	486	0.2	4,437	R
Tennessee	1,476,345	825,879	55.9	633,969	42.9	5,004	0.3	1,375	0.1	10,118	0.7	191,910	D
Texas	4,071,884	2,082,319	51.1	1,953,300	48.0	20,118	0.5	189		15,958	0.4	129,019	D
Utah	541,198	182,110	33.6	337,908	62.4	3,907	0.7	2,438	0.5	14,835	2.7	155,798	R
Vermont	187,765	80,954	43.1	102,085	54.4	4,001	2.1	—		725	0.4	21,131	R
Virginia	1,697,094	813,896	48.0	836,554	49.3	—		4,648	0.3	41,996	2.5	22,658	R
Washington	1,555,534	717,323	46.1	777,732	50.0	36,986	2.4	5,042	0.3	18,451	1.2	60,409	R
West Virginia	750,964	435,914	58.0	314,760	41.9	113		16		161		121,154	D
Wisconsin	2,104,175	1,040,232	49.4	1,004,987	47.8	34,943	1.7	3,814	0.2	20,199	1.0	35,245	D
Wyoming	156,343	62,239	39.8	92,717	59.3	624	0.4	89	0.1	674	0.4	30,478	R
Dist. of Col.	168,830	137,818	81.6	27,873	16.5	—		274	0.2	2,865	1.7	109,945	D
Totals	**81,555,889**	**40,830,763**	**50.1**	**39,147,793**	**48.0**	**756,691**	**0.9**	**173,011**	**0.2**	**647,631**	**0.8**	**1,682,970**	**D**

1. For breakdown of "Other" vote, see minor candidate vote totals, p. 134.

1980 Presidential Election

STATE	TOTAL VOTE	RONALD REAGAN (Republican)		JIMMY CARTER (Democrat)		JOHN B. ANDERSON (Independent)		ED CLARK (Libertarian)		OTHER [1]		PLURALITY	
		Votes	%	Votes	%	Votes	%	Votes	%	Votes	%		
Alabama	1,341,929	654,192	48.8	636,730	47.4	16,481	1.2	13,318	1.0	21,208	1.6	17,462	R
Alaska	158,445	86,112	54.3	41,842	26.4	11,155	7.0	18,479	11.7	857	0.5	44,270	R
Arizona	873,945	529,688	60.6	246,843	28.2	76,952	8.8	18,784	2.1	1,678	0.2	282,845	R
Arkansas	837,582	403,164	48.1	398,041	47.5	22,468	2.7	8,970	1.1	4,939	0.6	5,123	R
California	8,587,063	4,524,858	52.7	3,083,661	35.9	739,833	8.6	148,434	1.7	90,277	1.1	1,441,197	R
Colorado	1,184,415	652,264	55.1	367,973	31.1	130,633	11.0	25,744	2.2	7,801	0.7	284,291	R
Connecticut	1,406,285	677,210	48.2	541,732	38.5	171,807	12.2	8,570	0.6	6,966	0.5	135,478	R
Delaware	235,900	111,252	47.2	105,754	44.8	16,288	6.9	1,974	0.8	632	0.3	5,498	R
Florida	3,686,930	2,046,951	55.5	1,419,475	38.5	189,692	5.1	30,524	0.8	288		627,476	R
Georgia	1,596,695	654,168	41.0	890,733	55.8	36,055	2.3	15,627	1.0	112		236,565	D
Hawaii	303,287	130,112	42.9	135,879	44.8	32,021	10.6	3,269	1.1	2,006	0.7	5,767	D
Idaho	437,431	290,699	66.5	110,192	25.2	27,058	6.2	8,425	1.9	1,057	0.2	180,507	R
Illinois	4,749,721	2,358,049	49.6	1,981,413	41.7	346,754	7.3	38,939	0.8	24,566	0.5	376,636	R
Indiana	2,242,033	1,255,656	56.0	844,197	37.7	111,639	5.0	19,627	0.9	10,914	0.5	411,459	R
Iowa	1,317,661	676,026	51.3	508,672	38.6	115,633	8.8	13,123	1.0	4,207	0.3	167,354	R
Kansas	979,795	566,812	57.9	326,150	33.3	68,231	7.0	14,470	1.5	4,132	0.4	240,662	R
Kentucky	1,294,627	635,274	49.1	616,417	47.6	31,127	2.4	5,531	0.4	6,278	0.5	18,857	R
Louisiana	1,548,591	792,853	51.2	708,453	45.7	26,345	1.7	8,240	0.5	12,700	0.8	84,400	R
Maine	523,011	238,522	45.6	220,974	42.3	53,327	10.2	5,119	1.0	5,069	1.0	17,548	R
Maryland	1,540,496	680,606	44.2	726,161	47.1	119,537	7.8	14,192	0.9	—		45,555	D
Massachusetts	2,524,298	1,057,631	41.9	1,053,802	41.7	382,539	15.2	22,038	0.9	8,288	0.3	3,829	R
Michigan	3,909,725	1,915,225	49.0	1,661,532	42.5	275,223	7.0	41,597	1.1	16,148	0.4	253,693	R
Minnesota	2,051,980	873,268	42.6	954,174	46.5	174,990	8.5	31,592	1.5	17,956	0.9	80,906	D
Mississippi	892,620	441,089	49.4	429,281	48.1	12,036	1.3	5,465	0.6	4,749	0.5	11,808	R
Missouri	2,099,824	1,074,181	51.2	931,182	44.3	77,920	3.7	14,422	0.7	2,119	0.1	142,999	R
Montana	363,952	206,814	56.8	118,032	32.4	29,281	8.0	9,825	2.7	—		88,782	R
Nebraska	640,854	419,937	65.5	166,851	26.0	44,993	7.0	9,073	1.4	—		253,086	R
Nevada	247,885	155,017	62.5	66,666	26.9	17,651	7.1	4,358	1.8	4,193	1.7	88,351	R
New Hampshire	383,990	221,705	57.7	108,864	28.4	49,693	12.9	2,064	0.5	1,664	0.4	112,841	R
New Jersey	2,975,684	1,546,557	52.0	1,147,364	38.6	234,632	7.9	20,652	0.7	26,479	0.9	399,193	R
New Mexico	456,971	250,779	54.9	167,826	36.7	29,459	6.4	4,365	1.0	4,542	1.0	82,953	R
New York	6,201,959	2,893,831	46.7	2,728,372	44.0	467,801	7.5	52,648	0.8	59,307	1.0	165,459	R
North Carolina	1,855,833	915,018	49.3	875,635	47.2	52,800	2.8	9,677	0.5	2,703	0.1	39,383	R
North Dakota	301,545	193,695	64.2	79,189	26.3	23,640	7.8	3,743	1.2	1,278	0.4	114,506	R
Ohio	4,283,603	2,206,545	51.5	1,752,414	40.9	254,472	5.9	49,033	1.1	21,139	0.5	454,131	R
Oklahoma	1,149,708	695,570	60.5	402,026	35.0	38,284	3.3	13,828	1.2	—		293,544	R
Oregon	1,181,516	571,044	48.3	456,890	38.7	112,389	9.5	25,838	2.2	15,355	1.3	114,154	R
Pennsylvania	4,561,501	2,261,872	49.6	1,937,540	42.5	292,921	6.4	33,263	0.7	35,905	0.8	324,332	R
Rhode Island	416,072	154,793	37.2	198,342	47.7	59,819	14.4	2,458	0.6	660	0.2	43,549	D
South Carolina	894,071	441,841	49.4	430,385	48.1	14,153	1.6	5,139	0.6	2,553	0.3	11,456	R
South Dakota	327,703	198,343	60.5	103,855	31.7	21,431	6.5	3,824	1.2	250	0.1	94,488	R
Tennessee	1,617,616	787,761	48.7	783,051	48.4	35,991	2.2	7,116	0.4	3,697	0.2	4,710	R
Texas	4,541,636	2,510,705	55.3	1,881,147	41.4	111,613	2.5	37,643	0.8	528		629,558	R
Utah	604,222	439,687	72.8	124,266	20.6	30,284	5.0	7,226	1.2	2,759	0.5	315,421	R
Vermont	213,299	94,628	44.4	81,952	38.4	31,761	14.9	1,900	0.9	3,058	1.4	12,676	R
Virginia	1,866,032	989,609	53.0	752,174	40.3	95,418	5.1	12,821	0.7	16,010	0.9	237,435	R
Washington	1,742,394	865,244	49.7	650,193	37.3	185,073	10.6	29,213	1.7	12,671	0.7	215,051	R
West Virginia	737,715	334,206	45.3	367,462	49.8	31,691	4.3	4,356	0.6	—		33,256	D
Wisconsin	2,273,221	1,088,845	47.9	981,584	43.2	160,657	7.1	29,135	1.3	13,000	0.6	107,261	R
Wyoming	176,713	110,700	62.6	49,427	28.0	12,072	6.8	4,514	2.6	—		61,273	R
Dist. of Col.	175,237	23,545	13.4	131,113	74.8	16,337	9.3	1,114	0.6	3,128	1.8	107,568	D
Totals	**86,515,221**	**43,904,153**	**50.7**	**35,483,883**	**41.0**	**5,720,060**	**6.6**	**921,299**	**1.1**	**485,826**	**0.6**	**8,420,270**	**R**

1. For breakdown of "Other" vote, see minor candidate vote totals, p. 135.

1984 Presidential Election

STATE	TOTAL VOTE	RONALD REAGAN (Republican) Votes	%	WALTER F. MONDALE (Democrat) Votes	%	DAVID BERGLAND (Libertarian) Votes	%	LYNDON H. LaROUCHE JR. (Independent) Votes	%	OTHER [1] Votes	%	PLURALITY	
Alabama	1,441,713	872,849	60.5	551,899	38.3	9,504	0.7	—		7,461	0.5	320,950	R
Alaska	207,605	138,377	66.7	62,007	29.9	6,378	3.1	—		843	0.4	76,370	R
Arizona	1,025,897	681,416	66.4	333,854	32.5	10,585	1.0	—		42		347,562	R
Arkansas	884,406	534,774	60.5	338,646	38.3	2,221	0.3	1,890	0.2	6,875	0.8	196,128	R
California	9,505,423	5,467,009	57.5	3,922,519	41.3	49,951	0.5	—		65,944	0.7	1,544,490	R
Colorado	1,295,380	821,817	63.4	454,975	35.1	11,257	0.9	4,662	0.4	2,669	0.2	366,842	R
Connecticut	1,466,900	890,877	60.7	569,597	38.8	204		—		6,222	0.4	321,280	R
Delaware	254,572	152,190	59.8	101,656	39.9	268	0.1	—		458	0.2	50,534	R
Florida	4,180,051	2,730,350	65.3	1,448,816	34.7	754		—		131		1,281,534	R
Georgia	1,776,120	1,068,722	60.2	706,628	39.8	152		34		584		362,094	R
Hawaii	335,846	185,050	55.1	147,154	43.8	2,167	0.6	654	0.2	821	0.2	37,896	R
Idaho	411,144	297,523	72.4	108,510	26.4	2,823	0.7	—		2,288	0.6	189,013	R
Illinois	4,819,088	2,707,103	56.2	2,086,499	43.3	10,086	0.2	—		15,400	0.3	620,604	R
Indiana	2,233,069	1,377,230	61.7	841,481	37.7	6,741	0.3	—		7,617	0.3	535,749	R
Iowa	1,319,805	703,088	53.3	605,620	45.9	1,844	0.1	6,248	0.5	3,005	0.2	97,468	R
Kansas	1,021,991	677,296	66.3	333,149	32.6	3,329	0.3	—		8,217	0.8	344,147	R
Kentucky	1,369,345	821,702	60.0	539,539	39.4	—		1,776	0.1	6,328	0.5	282,163	R
Louisiana	1,706,822	1,037,299	60.8	651,586	38.2	1,876	0.1	3,552	0.2	12,509	0.7	385,713	R
Maine	553,144	336,500	60.8	214,515	38.8	—		—		2,129	0.4	121,985	R
Maryland	1,675,873	879,918	52.5	787,935	47.0	5,721	0.3	—		2,299	0.1	91,983	R
Massachusetts	2,559,453	1,310,936	51.2	1,239,606	48.4	—		—		8,911	0.3	71,330	R
Michigan	3,801,658	2,251,571	59.2	1,529,638	40.2	10,055	0.3	3,862	0.1	6,532	0.2	721,933	R
Minnesota	2,084,449	1,032,603	49.5	1,036,364	49.7	2,996	0.1	3,865	0.2	8,621	0.4	3,761	D
Mississippi	941,104	582,377	61.9	352,192	37.4	2,336	0.2	1,001	0.1	3,198	0.3	230,185	R
Missouri	2,122,783	1,274,188	60.0	848,583	40.0	—		—		12		425,605	R
Montana	384,377	232,450	60.5	146,742	38.2	5,185	1.3	—		—		85,708	R
Nebraska	652,090	460,054	70.6	187,866	28.8	2,079	0.3	—		2,091	0.3	272,188	R
Nevada	286,667	188,770	65.8	91,655	32.0	2,292	0.8	—		3,950	1.4	97,115	R
New Hampshire	389,066	267,051	68.6	120,395	30.9	735	0.2	467	0.1	418	0.1	146,656	R
New Jersey	3,217,862	1,933,630	60.1	1,261,323	39.2	6,416	0.2	—		16,493	0.5	672,307	R
New Mexico	514,370	307,101	59.7	201,769	39.2	4,459	0.9	—		1,041	0.2	105,332	R
New York	6,806,810	3,664,763	53.8	3,119,609	45.8	11,949	0.2	—		10,489	0.2	545,154	R
North Carolina	2,175,361	1,346,481	61.9	824,287	37.9	3,794	0.2	—		799		522,194	R
North Dakota	308,971	200,336	64.8	104,429	33.8	703	0.2	1,278	0.4	2,225	0.7	95,907	R
Ohio	4,547,619	2,678,560	58.9	1,825,440	40.1	5,886	0.1	10,693	0.2	27,040	0.6	853,120	R
Oklahoma	1,255,676	861,530	68.6	385,080	30.7	9,066	0.7	—		—		476,450	R
Oregon	1,226,527	685,700	55.9	536,479	43.7	—		—		4,348	0.4	149,221	R
Pennsylvania	4,844,903	2,584,323	53.3	2,228,131	46.0	6,982	0.1	—		25,467	0.5	356,192	R
Rhode Island	410,492	212,080	51.7	197,106	48.0	277	0.1	—		1,029	0.3	14,974	R
South Carolina	968,529	615,539	63.6	344,459	35.6	4,359	0.5	—		4,172	0.4	271,080	R
South Dakota	317,867	200,267	63.0	116,113	36.5	—		—		1,487	0.5	84,154	R
Tennessee	1,711,994	990,212	57.8	711,714	41.6	3,072	0.2	1,852	0.1	5,144	0.3	278,498	R
Texas	5,397,571	3,433,428	63.6	1,949,276	36.1	—		14,613	0.3	254		1,484,152	R
Utah	629,656	469,105	74.5	155,369	24.7	2,447	0.4	—		2,735	0.4	313,736	R
Vermont	234,561	135,865	57.9	95,730	40.8	1,002	0.4	423	0.2	1,541	0.7	40,135	R
Virginia	2,146,635	1,337,078	62.3	796,250	37.1	—		13,307	0.6	—		540,828	R
Washington	1,883,910	1,051,670	55.8	807,352	42.9	8,844	0.5	4,712	0.3	11,332	0.6	244,318	R
West Virginia	735,742	405,483	55.1	328,125	44.6	—		—		2,134	0.3	77,358	R
Wisconsin	2,211,689	1,198,584	54.2	995,740	45.0	4,883	0.2	3,791	0.2	8,691	0.4	202,844	R
Wyoming	188,968	133,241	70.5	53,370	28.2	2,357	1.2	—		—		79,871	R
Dist. of Col.	211,288	29,009	13.7	180,408	85.4	279	0.1	127	0.1	1,465	0.7	151,399	D
Totals	92,652,842	54,455,075	58.8	37,577,185	40.6	228,314	0.2	78,807	0.1	313,461	0.3	16,877,890	R

1. For breakdown of "Other" vote, see minor candidate vote totals, p. 135.

1988 Presidential Election

STATE	TOTAL VOTE	GEORGE BUSH (Republican)		MICHAEL S. DUKAKIS (Democrat)		RON PAUL (Libertarian)		LENORA B. FULANI (New Alliance)		OTHER [1]		PLURALITY
		Votes	%	Votes	%	Votes	%	Votes	%	Votes	%	
Alabama	1,378,476	815,576	59.2	549,506	39.9	8,460	0.6	3,311	0.2	1,623	0.1	266,070 R
Alaska	200,116	119,251	59.6	72,584	36.3	5,484	2.7	1,024	0.5	1,773	0.9	46,667 R
Arizona	1,171,873	702,541	60.0	454,029	38.7	13,351	1.1	1,662	0.1	290		248,512 R
Arkansas	827,738	466,578	56.4	349,237	42.2	3,297	0.4	2,161	0.3	6,465	0.8	117,341 R
California	9,887,065	5,054,917	51.1	4,702,233	47.6	70,105	0.7	31,181	0.3	28,629	0.3	352,684 R
Colorado	1,372,394	728,177	53.1	621,453	45.3	15,482	1.1	2,539	0.2	4,743	0.3	106,724 R
Connecticut	1,443,394	750,241	52.0	676,584	46.9	14,071	1.0	2,491	0.2	7		73,657 R
Delaware	249,891	139,639	55.9	108,647	43.5	1,162	0.5	443	0.2	—		30,992 R
Florida	4,302,313	2,618,885	60.9	1,656,701	38.5	19,796	0.5	6,655	0.2	276		962,184 R
Georgia	1,809,672	1,081,331	59.8	714,792	39.5	8,435	0.5	5,099	0.3	15		366,539 R
Hawaii	354,461	158,625	44.8	192,364	54.3	1,999	0.6	1,003	0.3	470	0.1	33,739 D
Idaho	408,968	253,881	62.1	147,272	36.0	5,313	1.3	2,502	0.6	—		106,609 R
Illinois	4,559,120	2,310,939	50.7	2,215,940	48.6	14,944	0.3	10,276	0.2	7,021	0.2	94,999 R
Indiana	2,168,621	1,297,763	59.8	860,643	39.7	—		10,215	0.5	—		437,120 R
Iowa	1,225,614	545,355	44.5	670,557	54.7	2,494	0.2	540		6,668	0.5	125,202 D
Kansas	993,044	554,049	55.8	422,636	42.6	12,553	1.3	3,806	0.4	—		131,413 R
Kentucky	1,322,517	734,281	55.5	580,368	43.9	2,118	0.2	1,256	0.1	4,494	0.3	153,913 R
Louisiana	1,628,202	883,702	54.3	717,460	44.1	4,115	0.3	2,355	0.1	20,570	1.3	166,242 R
Maine	555,035	307,131	55.3	243,569	43.9	2,700	0.5	1,405	0.3	230		63,562 R
Maryland	1,714,358	876,167	51.1	826,304	48.2	6,748	0.4	5,115	0.3	24		49,863 R
Massachusetts	2,632,805	1,194,635	45.4	1,401,415	53.2	24,251	0.9	9,561	0.4	2,943	0.1	206,780 D
Michigan	3,669,163	1,965,486	53.6	1,675,783	45.7	18,336	0.5	2,513	0.1	7,045	0.2	289,703 R
Minnesota	2,096,790	962,337	45.9	1,109,471	52.9	5,109	0.2	1,734	0.1	18,139	0.9	147,134 D
Mississippi	931,527	557,890	59.9	363,921	39.1	3,329	0.4	2,155	0.2	4,232	0.5	193,969 R
Missouri	2,093,713	1,084,953	51.8	1,001,619	47.8	434		6,656	0.3	51		83,334 R
Montana	365,674	190,412	52.1	168,936	46.2	5,047	1.4	1,279	0.3	—		21,476 R
Nebraska	661,465	397,956	60.2	259,235	39.2	2,534	0.4	1,740	0.3	—		138,721 R
Nevada	350,067	206,040	58.9	132,738	37.9	3,520	1.0	835	0.2	6,934	2.0	73,302 R
New Hampshire	451,074	281,537	62.4	163,696	36.3	4,502	1.0	790	0.2	549	0.1	117,841 R
New Jersey	3,099,553	1,743,192	56.2	1,320,352	42.6	8,421	0.3	5,139	0.2	22,449	0.7	422,840 R
New Mexico	521,287	270,341	51.9	244,497	46.9	3,268	0.6	2,237	0.4	944	0.2	25,844 R
New York	6,485,683	3,081,871	47.5	3,347,882	51.6	12,109	0.2	15,845	0.2	27,976	0.4	266,011 D
North Carolina	2,134,370	1,237,258	58.0	890,167	41.7	1,263	0.1	5,682	0.3	—		347,091 R
North Dakota	297,261	166,559	56.0	127,739	43.0	1,315	0.4	396	0.1	1,252	0.4	38,820 R
Ohio	4,393,699	2,416,549	55.0	1,939,629	44.1	11,989	0.3	12,017	0.3	13,515	0.3	476,920 R
Oklahoma	1,171,036	678,367	57.9	483,423	41.3	6,261	0.5	2,985	0.3	—		194,944 R
Oregon	1,201,694	560,126	46.6	616,206	51.3	14,811	1.2	6,487	0.5	4,064	0.3	56,080 D
Pennsylvania	4,536,251	2,300,087	50.7	2,194,944	48.4	12,051	0.3	4,379	0.1	24,790	0.5	105,143 R
Rhode Island	404,620	177,761	43.9	225,123	55.6	825	0.2	280	0.1	631	0.2	47,362 D
South Carolina	986,009	606,443	61.5	370,554	37.6	4,935	0.5	4,077	0.4	—		235,889 R
South Dakota	312,991	165,415	52.8	145,560	46.5	1,060	0.3	730	0.2	226	0.1	19,855 R
Tennessee	1,636,250	947,233	57.9	679,794	41.5	2,041	0.1	1,334	0.1	5,848	0.4	267,439 R
Texas	5,427,410	3,036,829	56.0	2,352,748	43.3	30,355	0.6	7,208	0.1	270		684,081 R
Utah	647,008	428,442	66.2	207,343	32.0	7,473	1.2	455	0.1	3,295	0.5	221,099 R
Vermont	243,328	124,331	51.1	115,775	47.6	1,000	0.4	205	0.1	2,017	0.8	8,556 R
Virginia	2,191,609	1,309,162	59.7	859,799	39.2	8,336	0.4	14,312	0.7	—		449,363 R
Washington	1,865,253	903,835	48.5	933,516	50.0	17,240	0.9	3,520	0.2	7,142	0.4	29,681 D
West Virginia	653,311	310,065	47.5	341,016	52.2	—		2,230	0.3	—		30,951 D
Wisconsin	2,191,608	1,047,499	47.8	1,126,794	51.4	5,157	0.2	1,953	0.1	10,205	0.5	79,295 D
Wyoming	176,551	106,867	60.5	67,113	38.0	2,026	1.1	545	0.3	—		39,754 R
Dist. of Col.	192,877	27,590	14.3	159,407	82.6	554	0.3	2,901	1.5	2,425	1.3	131,817 D
Totals	91,594,809	48,886,097	53.4	41,809,074	45.6	432,179	0.5	217,219	0.2	250,240	0.3	7,077,023 R

1. For breakdown of "Other" vote, see minor candidate vote totals, p. 136.

1992 Presidential Election

STATE	TOTAL VOTE	BILL CLINTON (Democrat)		GEORGE BUSH (Republican)		ROSS PEROT (Independent)		ANDRE V. MARROU (Libertarian)		OTHER [1]		PLURALITY	
		Votes	%	Votes	%	Votes	%	Votes	%	Votes	%		
Alabama	1,688,060	690,080	40.9	804,283	47.6	183,109	10.8	5,737	0.3	4,851	0.3	114,203	R
Alaska	258,506	78,294	30.3	102,000	39.5	73,481	28.4	1,378	0.5	3,353	1.3	23,706	R
Arizona	1,486,975	543,050	36.5	572,086	38.5	353,741	23.8	6,759	0.5	11,339	0.8	29,036	R
Arkansas	950,653	505,823	53.2	337,324	35.5	99,132	10.4	1,261	0.1	7,113	0.7	168,499	D
California	11,131,721	5,121,325	46.0	3,630,574	32.6	2,296,006	20.6	48,139	0.4	35,677	0.3	1,490,751	D
Colorado	1,569,180	629,681	40.1	562,850	35.9	366,010	23.3	8,669	0.6	1,970	0.1	66,831	D
Connecticut	1,616,332	682,318	42.2	578,313	35.8	348,771	21.6	5,391	0.3	1,539	0.1	104,005	D
Delaware	289,735	126,054	43.5	102,313	35.3	59,213	20.4	935	0.3	1,220	0.4	23,741	D
Florida	5,314,392	2,072,698	39.0	2,173,310	40.9	1,053,067	19.8	15,079	0.3	238		100,612	R
Georgia	2,321,125	1,008,966	43.5	995,252	42.9	309,657	13.3	7,110	0.3	140		13,714	D
Hawaii	372,842	179,310	48.1	136,822	36.7	53,003	14.2	1,119	0.3	2,588	0.7	42,488	D
Idaho	482,142	137,013	28.4	202,645	42.0	130,395	27.0	1,167	0.2	10,922	2.3	65,632	R
Illinois	5,050,157	2,453,350	48.6	1,734,096	34.3	840,515	16.6	9,218	0.2	12,978	0.3	719,254	D
Indiana	2,305,871	848,420	36.8	989,375	42.9	455,934	19.8	7,936	0.3	4,206	0.2	140,955	R
Iowa	1,354,607	586,353	43.3	504,891	37.3	253,468	18.7	1,076	0.1	8,819	0.7	81,462	D
Kansas	1,157,335	390,434	33.7	449,951	38.9	312,358	27.0	4,314	0.4	278		59,517	R
Kentucky	1,492,900	665,104	44.6	617,178	41.3	203,944	13.7	4,513	0.3	2,161	0.1	47,926	D
Louisiana	1,790,017	815,971	45.6	733,386	41.0	211,478	11.8	3,155	0.2	26,027	1.5	82,585	D
Maine	679,499	263,420	38.8	206,504	30.4	206,820	30.4	1,681	0.2	1,074	0.2	56,600	D
Maryland	1,985,046	988,571	49.8	707,094	35.6	281,414	14.2	4,715	0.2	3,252	0.2	281,477	D
Massachusetts	2,773,700	1,318,662	47.5	805,049	29.0	630,731	22.7	9,024	0.3	10,234	0.4	513,613	D
Michigan	4,274,673	1,871,182	43.8	1,554,940	36.4	824,813	19.3	10,175	0.2	13,563	0.3	316,242	D
Minnesota	2,347,948	1,020,997	43.5	747,841	31.9	562,506	24.0	3,374	0.1	13,230	0.6	273,156	D
Mississippi	981,793	400,258	40.8	487,793	49.7	85,626	8.7	2,154	0.2	5,962	0.6	87,535	R
Missouri	2,391,565	1,053,873	44.1	811,159	33.9	518,741	21.7	7,497	0.3	295		242,714	D
Montana	410,611	154,507	37.6	144,207	35.1	107,225	26.1	986	0.2	3,686	0.9	10,300	D
Nebraska	737,546	216,864	29.4	343,678	46.6	174,104	23.6	1,340	0.2	1,560	0.2	126,814	R
Nevada	506,318	189,148	37.4	175,828	34.7	132,580	26.2	1,835	0.4	6,927	1.4	13,320	D
New Hampshire	537,943	209,040	38.9	202,484	37.6	121,337	22.6	3,548	0.7	1,534	0.3	6,556	D
New Jersey	3,343,594	1,436,206	43.0	1,356,865	40.6	521,829	15.6	6,822	0.2	21,872	0.7	79,341	D
New Mexico	569,986	261,617	45.9	212,824	37.3	91,895	16.1	1,615	0.3	2,035	0.4	48,793	D
New York	6,926,925	3,444,450	49.7	2,346,649	33.9	1,090,721	15.7	13,451	0.2	31,654	0.5	1,097,801	D
North Carolina	2,611,850	1,114,042	42.7	1,134,661	43.4	357,864	13.7	5,171	0.2	112		20,619	R
North Dakota	308,133	99,168	32.2	136,244	44.2	71,084	23.1	416	0.1	1,221	0.4	37,076	R
Ohio	4,939,967	1,984,942	40.2	1,894,310	38.3	1,036,426	21.0	7,252	0.1	17,037	0.3	90,632	D
Oklahoma	1,390,359	473,066	34.0	592,929	42.6	319,878	23.0	4,486	0.3	—		119,863	R
Oregon	1,462,643	621,314	42.5	475,757	32.5	354,091	24.2	4,277	0.3	7,204	0.5	145,557	D
Pennsylvania	4,959,810	2,239,164	45.1	1,791,841	36.1	902,667	18.2	21,477	0.4	4,661	0.1	447,323	D
Rhode Island	453,477	213,299	47.0	131,601	29.0	105,045	23.2	571	0.1	2,961	0.7	81,698	D
South Carolina	1,202,527	479,514	39.9	577,507	48.0	138,872	11.5	2,719	0.2	3,915	0.3	97,993	R
South Dakota	336,254	124,888	37.1	136,718	40.7	73,295	21.8	814	0.2	539	0.2	11,830	R
Tennessee	1,982,638	933,521	47.1	841,300	42.4	199,968	10.1	1,847	0.1	6,002	0.3	92,221	D
Texas	6,154,018	2,281,815	37.1	2,496,071	40.6	1,354,781	22.0	19,699	0.3	1,652		214,256	R
Utah	743,999	183,429	24.7	322,632	43.4	203,400	27.3	1,900	0.3	32,638	4.4	119,232	R
Vermont	289,701	133,592	46.1	88,122	30.4	65,991	22.8	501	0.2	1,495	0.5	45,470	D
Virginia	2,558,665	1,038,650	40.6	1,150,517	45.0	348,639	13.6	5,730	0.2	15,129	0.6	111,867	R
Washington	2,288,230	993,037	43.4	731,234	32.0	541,780	23.7	7,533	0.3	14,646	0.6	261,803	D
West Virginia	683,762	331,001	48.4	241,974	35.4	108,829	15.9	1,873	0.3	85		89,027	D
Wisconsin	2,531,114	1,041,066	41.1	930,855	36.8	544,479	21.5	2,877	0.1	11,837	0.5	110,211	D
Wyoming	200,598	68,160	34.0	79,347	39.6	51,263	25.6	844	0.4	984	0.5	11,187	R
Dist. of Col.	227,572	192,619	84.6	20,698	9.1	9,681	4.3	467	0.2	4,107	1.8	171,921	D
Totals	104,425,014	44,909,326	43.0	39,103,882	37.4	19,741,657	18.9	291,627	0.3	378,522	0.4	5,805,444	D

1. For breakdown of "Other" vote, see minor candidate vote totals, p. 136.

1996 Presidential Election

STATE	TOTAL VOTE	BILL CLINTON (Democrat)		BOB DOLE (Republican)		ROSS PEROT (Reform)		RALPH NADER (Green)		OTHER[1]		PLURALITY	
		Votes	%	Votes	%	Votes	%	Votes	%	Votes	%		
Alabama	1,534,349	662,165	43.2	769,044	50.1	92,149	6.0	—		10,991	0.7	106,879	R
Alaska	241,620	80,380	33.3	122,746	50.8	26,333	10.9	7,597	3.1	4,564	1.9	42,366	R
Arizona	1,404,405	653,288	46.5	622,073	44.3	112,072	8.0	2,062	0.1	14,910	1.1	31,215	D
Arkansas	884,262	475,171	53.7	325,416	36.8	69,884	7.9	3,649	0.4	10,142	1.1	149,755	D
California	10,019,484	5,119,835	51.1	3,828,380	38.2	697,847	7.0	237,016	2.4	136,406	1.4	1,291,455	D
Colorado	1,510,704	671,152	44.4	691,848	45.8	99,629	6.6	25,070	1.7	23,005	1.5	20,696	R
Connecticut	1,392,614	735,740	52.8	483,109	34.7	139,523	10.0	24,321	1.7	9,921	0.7	252,631	D
Delaware	270,845	140,355	51.8	99,062	36.6	28,719	10.6	18		2,691	1.0	41,293	D
Florida	5,303,794	2,546,870	48.0	2,244,536	42.3	483,870	9.1	4,101	0.1	24,417	0.5	302,334	D
Georgia	2,299,071	1,053,849	45.8	1,080,843	47.0	146,337	6.4	—		18,042	0.8	26,994	R
Hawaii	360,120	205,012	56.9	113,943	31.6	27,358	7.6	10,386	2.9	3,421	0.9	91,069	D
Idaho	491,719	165,443	33.6	256,595	52.2	62,518	12.7	—		7,163	1.5	91,152	R
Illinois	4,311,391	2,341,744	54.3	1,587,021	36.8	346,408	8.0	1,447		34,771	0.8	754,723	D
Indiana	2,135,431	887,424	41.6	1,006,693	47.1	224,299	10.5	895		16,120	0.8	119,269	R
Iowa	1,234,075	620,258	50.3	492,644	39.9	105,159	8.5	6,550	0.5	9,464	0.8	127,614	D
Kansas	1,074,300	387,659	36.1	583,245	54.3	92,639	8.6	914	0.1	9,843	0.9	195,586	R
Kentucky	1,388,708	636,614	45.8	623,283	44.9	120,396	8.7	701	0.1	7,714	0.6	13,331	D
Louisiana	1,783,959	927,837	52.0	712,586	39.9	123,293	6.9	4,719	0.3	15,524	0.9	215,251	D
Maine	605,897	312,788	51.6	186,378	30.8	85,970	14.2	15,279	2.5	5,482	0.9	126,410	D
Maryland	1,780,870	966,207	54.3	681,530	38.3	115,812	6.5	2,606	0.1	14,715	0.8	284,677	D
Massachusetts	2,556,786	1,571,763	61.5	718,107	28.1	227,217	8.9	4,565	0.2	35,134	1.4	853,656	D
Michigan	3,848,844	1,989,653	51.7	1,481,212	38.5	336,670	8.7	2,322	0.1	38,987	1.0	508,441	D
Minnesota	2,192,640	1,120,438	51.1	766,476	35.0	257,704	11.8	24,908	1.1	23,114	1.1	353,962	D
Mississippi	893,857	394,022	44.1	439,838	49.2	52,222	5.8	—		7,775	0.9	45,816	R
Missouri	2,158,065	1,025,935	47.5	890,016	41.2	217,188	10.1	534		24,392	1.1	135,919	D
Montana	407,261	167,922	41.3	179,652	44.1	55,229	13.6	—		4,458	1.1	11,730	R
Nebraska	677,415	236,761	35.0	363,467	53.7	71,278	10.5	—		5,909	0.9	126,706	R
Nevada	464,279	203,974	43.9	199,244	42.9	43,986	9.5	4,730	1.0	12,345	2.7	4,730	D
New Hampshire	499,175	246,214	49.3	196,532	39.4	48,390	9.7	—		8,039	1.6	49,682	D
New Jersey	3,075,807	1,652,329	53.7	1,103,078	35.9	262,134	8.5	32,465	1.1	25,801	0.8	549,251	D
New Mexico	556,074	273,495	49.2	232,751	41.9	32,257	5.8	13,218	2.4	4,353	0.8	40,744	D
New York	6,316,129	3,756,177	59.5	1,933,492	30.6	503,458	8.0	75,956	1.2	47,046	0.7	1,822,685	D
North Carolina	2,515,807	1,107,849	44.0	1,225,938	48.7	168,059	6.7	2,108	0.1	11,853	0.4	118,089	R
North Dakota	266,411	106,905	40.1	125,050	46.9	32,515	12.2	—		1,941	0.7	18,145	R
Ohio	4,534,434	2,148,222	47.4	1,859,883	41.0	483,207	10.7	2,962	0.1	40,160	0.9	288,339	D
Oklahoma	1,206,713	488,105	40.4	582,315	48.3	130,788	10.8	—		5,505	0.5	94,210	R
Oregon	1,377,760	649,641	47.2	538,152	39.1	121,221	8.8	49,415	3.6	19,331	1.4	111,489	D
Pennsylvania	4,506,118	2,215,819	49.2	1,801,169	40.0	430,984	9.6	3,086	0.1	55,060	1.2	414,650	D
Rhode Island	390,284	233,050	59.7	104,683	26.8	43,723	11.2	6,040	1.5	2,788	0.7	128,367	D
South Carolina	1,151,689	506,283	44.0	573,458	49.8	64,386	5.6	—		7,562	0.7	67,175	R
South Dakota	323,826	139,333	43.0	150,543	46.5	31,250	9.7	—		2,700	0.8	11,210	R
Tennessee	1,894,105	909,146	48.0	863,530	45.6	105,918	5.6	6,427	0.3	9,084	0.4	45,616	D
Texas	5,611,644	2,459,683	43.8	2,736,167	48.8	378,537	6.7	4,810	0.1	32,447	0.6	276,484	R
Utah	665,629	221,633	33.3	361,911	54.4	66,461	10.0	4,615	0.7	11,009	1.7	140,278	R
Vermont	258,449	137,894	53.4	80,352	31.1	31,024	12.0	5,585	2.2	3,594	1.4	57,542	D
Virginia	2,416,642	1,091,060	45.1	1,138,350	47.1	159,861	6.6	—		27,371	1.1	47,290	R
Washington	2,253,837	1,123,323	49.8	840,712	37.3	201,003	8.9	60,322	2.7	28,477	1.3	282,611	D
West Virginia	636,459	327,812	51.5	233,946	36.8	71,639	11.3	—		3,062	0.5	93,866	D
Wisconsin	2,196,169	1,071,971	48.8	845,029	38.5	227,339	10.4	28,723	1.3	23,107	1.1	226,942	D
Wyoming	211,571	77,934	36.8	105,388	49.8	25,928	12.3	—		2,321	1.1	27,454	R
Dist. of Col.	185,726	158,220	85.2	17,339	9.3	3,611	1.9	4,780	2.6	1,776	1.0	140,881	D
Totals	96,277,223	47,402,357	49.2	39,198,755	40.7	8,085,402	8.4	684,902	0.7	905,807	0.9	8,203,602	D

1. For breakdown of "Other" votes, see minor candidate vote totals, p. 138.

Popular Vote Returns:
Minor Candidates and Parties

This section contains popular vote returns for all minor candidates and parties that were aggregated in the columns labeled "Other" in the presidential election returns found on pages 87-127. The source for these data for 1824-1916, except where indicated by a footnote, is the Inter-University Consortium for Political and Social Research (ICPSR). For 1920-1992 the source is Richard M. Scammon and Alice V. McGillivray, *America at the Polls* (Washington, D.C.: Congressional Quarterly, 1994). For 1996 the source is *Federal Elections 96* (Washington, D.C.: Federal Election Commission, 1997).

The material is presented in the following order:

• Year of presidential election.

• Name of candidate and party, if available from the ICPSR and Scammon data. "Scattered write-ins" is used where votes were recorded but neither the candidate nor a party was known. In nearly all cases, these figures were the total write-in vote.

• State name and number of votes. Percentages may be calculated by using the state vote totals from the presidential election tables found on pages 87-127.

• Nationwide vote totals. Percentages may be calculated by using the national vote total from the presidential election tables.

In the ICPSR data, the distinct party designations appearing in the original sources are preserved. Thus, in the ICPSR returns for 1880, John W. Phelps received votes under the following four party designations: "Anti-Masonic" — California, 5 votes, Illinois, 150 votes, and Pennsylvania, 44 votes; "Anti-Secret" — Kansas, 25 votes; "National American" — Michigan, 312 votes; and "American" — Rhode Island, 4 votes, and Wisconsin, 91 votes.

To provide one party designation for each minor candidate for the elections 1824 to 1916, Congressional Quarterly has aggregated under a single party designation the votes of minor candidates who are listed in the ICPSR data as receiving votes under more than one party designation. The source used for assigning party designations for these years is Svend Petersen, *A Statistical History of the American Presidential Elections* (Westport, Conn.: Greenwood Press, 1981) where Petersen gives a party designation. In the 1880 election cited above, Peterson lists John W. Phelps as an American Party candidate. Where Petersen lists no party designation, Congressional Quarterly selected the party designation for a candidate that appeared most frequently in the ICPSR returns. For the 1920 to 1992 elections, the source for party designations is Scammon and McGillivray, *America at the Polls* (Washington, D.C.: Congressional Quarterly, 1994). For 1996 the source for party designations is *Federal Elections 96* (Washington, D.C.: Federal Election Commission, 1997).

1824 Election

Unpledged Republican
Massachusetts, 6,616 votes.
Scattered write-ins
Connecticut, 1,188 votes; Indiana, 7; Massachusetts, 4,753; Missouri, 33; North Carolina, 256; Rhode Island, 200.
Total: 6,437

1828 Election

Scattered write-ins
Alabama, 4 votes; Connecticut, 1,101; Maine, 89; Massachusetts, 3,226; New Jersey, 8; North Carolina, 15; Rhode Island, 5; Vermont, 120.
Total: 4,568

1832 Election

Scattered write-ins
Illinois, 30 votes; Massachusetts, 7,031; Rhode Island, 6; Vermont, 206.
Total: 7,273

1836 Election

Scattered write-ins
Delaware, 5 votes; Maine, 1,112; Massachusetts, 45; North Carolina, 1; Rhode Island, 1; Vermont, 65; Virginia, 5.
Total: 1,234

1840 Election

Scattered write-ins
Delaware, 13 votes; Indiana, 599; Rhode Island, 136; Vermont, 19.
Total: 767

1844 Election

Scattered write-ins
Delaware, 6 votes; Illinois, 939; Massachusetts, 1,106; North Carolina, 2; Rhode Island, 5.
Total: 2,058

1848 Election

Gerrit Smith (Liberty)
New York, 2,545 votes.
Henry Clay (Clay Whig)
Illinois, 89 votes.
Scattered write-ins
Alabama, 4 votes; Connecticut, 24; Massachusetts, 62; North Carolina, 26; Rhode Island, 5; Texas, 75.
Total: 196

1852 Election

Daniel Webster (Whig)[1]
Georgia, 5,324 votes; Massachusetts, 1,670.
Total: 6,994
—Broome (Native American)
Massachusetts, 158 votes; New Jersey, 738; Pennsylvania, 1,670.
Total: 2,566
George Michael Troup (Southern Rights)[2]
Alabama, 2,205 votes; Georgia, 126.
Total: 2,331
Scattered write-ins
California, 56 votes; Connecticut, 12; Iowa, 139; North Carolina, 60; Texas, 10.
Total: 272

1856 Election

Scattered write-ins
California, 14 votes; Delaware, 9; Massachusetts, 3,006; Ohio, 148.
Total: 3,177

1860 Election

Gerrit Smith (Union)
Illinois, 35 votes; Ohio, 136.
Scattered write-ins
California, 15 votes; Massachusetts, 328; Minnesota, 17.
Total: 360

1864 Election

E. Cheeseborough
Kansas, 543 votes.
vote text:Kansas, 112 votes; Massachusetts, 6; Minnesota, 26; Oregon, 5.
Total: 149

1868 Election

Scattered write-ins
Alabama, 6 votes; Kansas, 3; Massachusetts, 26; New Hampshire, 11.
Total: 46

1872 Election

James Black (Prohibition)
Michigan, 1,271 votes; Ohio, 2,100.
Total: 3,371
Liberal Republican Elector
Iowa, 10,447 votes.
Scattered write-ins
Iowa, 942 votes; Kansas, 581; Minnesota, 168; New Hampshire, 313; South Carolina, 259.
Total: 2,263

1876 Election

Green Clay Smith (Prohibition)
Connecticut, 374 votes; Illinois, 141; Kansas, 110; Michigan, 766; New York, 2,369; Ohio, 1,636; Pennsylvania, 1,320; Wisconsin, 27.
Total: 6,743
James B. Walker (American)
Illinois, 177 votes; Kansas, 23; Michigan, 71; Ohio, 76; Pennsylvania, 83; Wisconsin, 29.
Total: 459
Communist
Wisconsin, 32 votes.
Scattered write-ins
Alabama, 2 votes; California, 19; Connecticut, 26; Iowa, 520; Kansas, 5; Kentucky, 2,998; Maine, 828; Massachusetts, 779; New Hampshire, 93; Texas, 46; Vermont, 114; Wisconsin, 1,607.
Total: 7,037

1880 Election

Neal Dow (Prohibition)
California, 54 votes; Connecticut, 409; Illinois, 440; Kansas, 10; Kentucky, 233; Maine, 92; Massachusetts, 682; Michigan, 938; Minnesota, 286; New Hampshire, 180; New Jersey, 191; New York,

1,517; Ohio, 2,613; Pennsylvania, 1,940; Rhode Island, 20; Wisconsin, 69.
Total: 9,674
John W. Phelps (American)
California, 5 votes; Illinois, 150; Kansas, 25; Michigan, 312; Pennsylvania, 44; Rhode Island, 4; Wisconsin, 91.
Total: 631
A. C. Brewer (Independent Democrat)
Arkansas, 322 votes.
Scattered write-ins
Arkansas, 1,221 votes; California, 70; Colorado, 14; Connecticut, 39; Iowa, 1,064; Maine, 139; Massachusetts, 117; Mississippi, 677; Rhode Island, 1; South Carolina, 36.
Total: 3,378

1884 Election

Scattered write-ins
Alabama, 72 votes; California, 329; Florida, 118; Iowa, 1,297; Kansas, 468; Maine, 6; Massachusetts, 2; New Jersey, 28; Oregon, 35; South Carolina, 1,237; Vermont, 27.
Total: 3,619

1888 Election

Robert H. Cowdrey (United Labor)
Illinois, 150 votes; New York, 519; Oregon, 351.
Total: 1,020
Socialist Labor
New York, 2,068 votes.
Total: 2,068
James Langdon Curtis (American)
California, 1,591 votes; Pennsylvania, 24.
Total: 1,615
Scattered write-ins
California, 1,442 votes; Colorado, 177; Delaware, 1; Iowa, 556; Kansas, 937; Maine, 16; Massachusetts, 60; New Hampshire, 58; North Carolina, 37; Oregon, 53; Rhode Island, 7; South Carolina, 437; Vermont, 35.
Total: 3,816

1892 Election

Simon Wing (Socialist Labor)
Connecticut, 333 votes; Massachusetts, 649; New Jersey, 1,337; New York, 17,956; Pennsylvania, 888.
Total: 21,163
Scattered write-ins
Arkansas, 1,267 votes; Delaware, 13; Georgia, 2,345; Maine, 4; Massachusetts, 3; Michigan, 925; Rhode Island, 3; South Carolina, 72; Texas, 4,086; Vermont, 10; Wyoming, 29.
Total: 8,757

1896 Election

Charles Horatio Matchett (Socialist Labor)
California, 1,611 votes; Colorado, 159; Connecticut, 1,223; Illinois, 1,147; Indiana, 324; Iowa, 453; Maryland, 587; Massachusetts, 2,112; Michigan, 293; Minnesota, 954; Missouri, 599; Nebraska, 186; New Hampshire, 228; New Jersey, 3,985; New York, 17,667; Ohio, 1,165; Pennsylvania, 1,683; Rhode Island, 558; Virginia, 108; Wisconsin, 1,314
Total: 36,356
Charles Eugene Bentley (National Prohibition)
Arkansas, 892 votes; California, 1,047; Colorado, 386; Illinois, 793; Indiana, 2,267; Iowa, 352; Kansas, 620; Maryland, 136; Michigan, 1,816; Missouri, 292; Nebraska, 797; New Hampshire, 49; New Jersey, 5,614; North Carolina, 222; Ohio, 2,716; Pennsylvania, 870; Washington, 148; Wisconsin, 346.
Total: 19,363

Scattered write-ins

California, 4 votes; Connecticut, 4; Georgia, 47; Massachusetts, 20; Michigan, 1,073; North Carolina, 372; North Dakota, 12; Rhode Island, 5.

Total: 1,537

1900 Election

Wharton Barker (Populist)

Alabama, 4,188 votes; Arkansas, 972; Colorado, 333; Florida, 1,143; Georgia, 4,568; Idaho, 445; Illinois, 1,141; Indiana, 1,438; Iowa, 615; Kentucky, 1,961; Michigan, 889; Mississippi, 1,642; Missouri, 4,244; Nebraska, 1,104; New Jersey, 669; North Carolina, 798; North Dakota, 109; Ohio, 251; Oregon, 269; Pennsylvania, 638; South Dakota, 340; Tennessee, 1,322; Texas, 20,565; Vermont, 367; Virginia, 63; West Virginia, 246; Wyoming, 20.

Total: 50,340

Joseph P. Malloney (Socialist Labor)

California, 7,554 votes; Colorado, 654; Connecticut, 908; Illinois, 1,374; Indiana, 663; Iowa, 259; Kentucky, 390; Maryland, 382; Massachusetts, 2,599; Michigan, 830; Minnesota, 1,329; Missouri, 1,296; Montana, 119; New Jersey, 2,074; New York, 12,622; Ohio, 1,688; Pennsylvania, 2,936; Rhode Island, 1,423; Texas, 162; Utah, 102; Virginia, 167; Washington, 866; Wisconsin, 503.

Total: 40,900

Seth Hockett Ellis (Union Reform)

Arkansas, 341 votes; Illinois, 672; Indiana, 254; Maryland, 142; Ohio, 4,284.

Total: 5,693

Jonah Fitz Randolph Leonard (United Christian)

Illinois, 352 votes; Iowa, 166.

Total: 518

Anti-Imperialist

Connecticut, 45 votes.

Scattered write-ins

Arkansas, 27 votes; Colorado, 26; Connecticut, 10; Louisiana, 4; Massachusetts, 533, New Hampshire, 16; Utah, 9; Vermont, 5; Wyoming, 21.

Total: 651

1904 Election

Thomas E. Watson (Populist)

Alabama, 5,051 votes; Arkansas, 2,326; Colorado, 824; Connecticut, 495; Delaware, 51; Florida, 1,605; Georgia, 22,635; Idaho, 352; Illinois, 6,725; Indiana, 2,444; Iowa, 2,207; Kansas, 6,253; Kentucky, 2,521; Maine, 337; Maryland, 1; Massachusetts, 1,294; Michigan, 1,145; Minnesota, 2,103; Mississippi, 1,499; Missouri, 4,226; Montana, 1,531; Nebraska, 20,518; Nevada, 344; New Hampshire, 82; New Jersey, 3,705; New York, 7,459; North Carolina, 819; Ohio, 1,392; Oregon, 746; South Dakota, 1,240; Tennessee, 2,491; Texas, 8,062; Washington, 669; West Virginia, 339; Wisconsin, 560.

Total: 114,051

Charles Hunter Corregan (Socialist Labor)

Colorado, 335 votes; Connecticut, 583; Illinois, 4,698; Indiana, 1,598; Kentucky, 596; Massachusetts, 2,359; Michigan, 1,018; Minnesota, 974; Missouri, 1,674; Montana, 213; New Jersey, 2,380; New York, 9,122; Ohio, 2,635; Pennsylvania, 2,211; Rhode Island, 488; Texas, 431; Washington, 1,592; Wisconsin, 249.

Total: 33,156

Austin Holcomb (Continental)

Illinois, 826 votes.

Scattered write-ins

California, 333 votes; Connecticut, 11; Maryland, 4; Massachusetts, 5; New Hampshire, 1; Vermont, 1.

Total: 355

1908 Election

Thomas L. Hisgen (Independence)

Alabama, 497 votes; Arkansas, 286; California, 4,278; Connecticut, 728; Delaware, 29; Florida, 553; Georgia, 76; Idaho, 124;

Illinois; 7,724; Indiana, 514; Iowa, 404; Kansas, 68; Kentucky, 200; Louisiana, 77; Maine, 700; Maryland, 485; Massachusetts, 19,235; Michigan, 734; Minnesota, 424; Missouri, 392; Montana, 493; Nevada, 436; New Hampshire, 584; New Jersey, 2,916; New York, 35,817; North Dakota, 43; Ohio, 439; Oregon, 289; Pennsylvania, 1,057; Rhode Island, 1,105; South Carolina, 46; South Dakota, 88; Tennessee, 332; Texas, 106; Utah, 92; Vermont, 804; Virginia, 51; Washington, 248; Wyoming, 63.

Total: 82,537

Thomas E. Watson (Populist)

Alabama, 1,576 votes; Arkansas, 987; Florida, 1,946; Georgia, 16,687; Illinois, 633; Indiana, 1,193; Iowa, 261; Kentucky, 333; Mississippi, 1,276; Missouri, 1,165; Ohio, 162; Tennessee, 1,092; Texas, 960; Virginia, 105.

Total: 28,376

August Gillhaus (Socialist Labor)

Connecticut, 608 votes; Illinois, 1,680; Indiana, 643; Kentucky, 405; Massachusetts, 1,011; Michigan, 1,085; Missouri, 867; New Jersey, 1,196; New York, 3,877; Ohio, 721; Pennsylvania, 1,224; Rhode Island, 183; Texas, 175; Virginia, 25; Wisconsin, 318.

Total: 14,018

Daniel Braxton Turney (United Christian)

Illinois, 400 votes; Michigan, 61.

Republican (Davidson Faction)

Alabama, 987 votes.

Scattered write-ins

California, 28 votes; Colorado, 2; Connecticut, 4; Massachusetts, 9; New Hampshire, 8; North Carolina, 13; Vermont, 29; Wisconsin, 2.

Total: 95

1912 Election

Eugene W. Chafin (Prohibition)

Arizona, 265 votes; Arkansas, 908; California, 23,366; Colorado, 5,063; Connecticut, 2,068; Delaware, 620; Florida, 1,854; Georgia, 149; Idaho, 1,536; Illinois, 15,710; Indiana, 19,249; Iowa, 8,440; Kentucky, 3,253; Maine, 947; Maryland, 2,244; Massachusetts, 2,753; Michigan, 8,794; Minnesota, 7,886; Missouri, 5,380; Montana, 32; Nebraska, 3,383; New Hampshire, 535; New Jersey, 2,936; New York, 19,455; North Carolina, 118; North Dakota, 1,243; Ohio, 11,511; Oklahoma, 2,195; Oregon, 4,360; Pennsylvania, 19,525; Rhode Island, 616; South Dakota, 3,910; Tennessee, 832; Texas, 1,701; Vermont, 1,094; Virginia, 709; Washington, 9,810; West Virginia, 4,517; Wisconsin, 8,584; Wyoming, 421.

Total: 207,972

Arthur E. Reimer (Socialist Labor)

Colorado, 475 votes; Connecticut, 1,260; Illinois, 4,066; Indiana, 3,130; Kentucky, 1,055; Maryland, 322; Massachusetts, 1,102; Michigan, 1,239; Minnesota, 2,212; Missouri, 1,778; New Jersey, 1,396; New York, 4,273; Ohio, 2,630; Pennsylvania, 706; Rhode Island, 236; Texas, 430; Utah, 510; Virginia, 50; Washington, 1,872; Wisconsin, 632.

Total: 29,374

Scattered write-ins

Alabama, 5 votes; California, 4,417; Connecticut, 6; Kansas, 63; Massachusetts, 1; South Carolina, 55; Wisconsin, 9.

Total: 4,556

1916 Election

Arthur E. Reimer (Socialist Labor)

Connecticut, 606 votes; Illinois, 2,488; Indiana, 1,659; Iowa, 460; Kentucky, 332; Maryland, 756; Massachusetts, 1,096; Michigan, 831; Minnesota, 468; Missouri, 903; Nebraska, 624; New Jersey, 855; New York; 2,666; Pennsylvania, 419; Rhode Island, 180; Utah, 144; Virginia, 67; Washington, 730.

Total: 15,284

Progressive[3]

Colorado, 409 votes; Georgia, 20,692; Indiana, 3,898; Iowa, 1,793; Kentucky, 129; Louisiana, 6,349; Minnesota, 290; Mississip-

pi, 520; Montana, 338; Oklahoma, 234; Oregon, 310; South Carolina, 162; Utah, 110.
Total: 35,234

Scattered write-ins
California, 187 votes; Massachusetts, 6; South Carolina, 258; Vermont, 10.
Total: 461

1920 Election

Aaron Sherman Watkins (Prohibition)
Alabama, 766 votes; Arizona, 4; California, 25,204; Colorado, 2,807; Connecticut, 1,771; Delaware, 986; Florida, 5,127; Illinois, 11,216; Indiana, 13,462; Iowa, 4,197; Kentucky, 3,250; Michigan, 9,646; Minnesota, 11,489; Missouri, 5,152; Nebraska, 5,947; New Jersey, 4,895; New York, 19,653; North Carolina, 17; Ohio, 294; Oregon, 3,595; Pennsylvania, 42,612; Rhode Island, 510; South Dakota, 900; Vermont, 774; Virginia, 826; Washington, 3,800; West Virginia, 1,526; Wisconsin, 8,648; Wyoming, 265.
Total: 189,339

James Edward Ferguson (American)
Texas, 48,098 votes.

William W. Cox (Socialist Labor)
Connecticut, 1,491 votes; Illinois, 3,471; Iowa, 982; Maryland, 1,178; Massachusetts, 3,583; Michigan, 2,539; Minnesota, 5,828; Missouri, 1,587; New Jersey, 1,010; New York, 4,841; Oregon, 1,515; Pennsylvania, 753; Rhode Island, 495; Washington, 1,321.
Total: 30,594

Robert Colvin Macauley (Single Tax)
Delaware, 39 votes; Illinois, 775; Indiana, 566; Maine, 310; Michigan, 484; New Jersey, 603; Ohio, 2,153; Pennsylvania, 803; Rhode Island, 100.
Total: 5,833

Black and Tan Republican
Texas, 27,309 votes.

Scattered write-ins
Louisiana, 339 votes; Maryland, 1; Massachusetts, 24; Nebraska, 90; New Mexico, 4; Vermont, 56.
Total: 514

1924 Election

Frank T. Johns (Socialist Labor)
Colorado, 378 votes; Connecticut, 1,373; Illinois, 2,334; Kentucky, 1,501; Maine, 406; Maryland, 987; Massachusetts, 1,668; Michigan, 5,330; Minnesota, 1,855; Missouri, 1,066; New Jersey, 853; New York, 9,928; Ohio, 3,025; Oregon, 917; Pennsylvania, 634; Rhode Island, 268; Virginia, 189; Washington, 1,004; Wisconsin, 458.
Total: 34,174

William Z. Foster (Communist)
Colorado, 562 votes; Illinois, 2,622; Indiana, 987; Iowa, 4,037; Massachusetts, 2,635; Minnesota, 4,427; Montana, 358; New Jersey, 1,560; New York, 8,244; North Dakota, 370; Pennsylvania, 2,735; Rhode Island, 289; Washington, 761; Wisconsin, 3,773.
Total: 33,360

Gilbert Owen Nations (American)
Florida, 2,319 votes; Georgia, 155; Kentucky, 1,300; New Jersey, 368; Pennsylvania, 13,035; Tennessee, 100; Washington, 5,991; West Virginia, 1,072.
Total: 24,340

William J. Wallace (Commonwealth Land)
Delaware, 20 votes; Illinois, 421; Kentucky, 226; Missouri, 165; New Jersey, 265; Ohio, 1,246, Pennsylvania, 296; Rhode Island, 38; Wisconsin, 271.
Total: 2,948

Scattered write-ins
Connecticut, 101 votes; Iowa, 445; Kansas, 4; Louisiana, 4,063; Pennsylvania, 131; South Carolina, 1; Vermont, 5.
Total: 4,752

1928 Election

Verne L. Reynolds (Socialist Labor)
Connecticut, 625 votes; Illinois, 1,812; Indiana, 645; Iowa, 230; Kentucky, 316; Maryland, 906; Massachusetts, 772; Michigan, 799; Minnesota, 1,921; Missouri, 342; New Jersey, 500; New York, 4,211; Ohio, 1,515; Oregon, 1,564; Pennsylvania, 382; Rhode Island, 416; Virginia, 181; Washington, 4,068; Wisconsin, 381.
Total: 21,586

William Frederick Varney (Prohibition)
Indiana, 5,496 votes; Michigan, 2,728; New Jersey, 160; Ohio, 3,556; Pennsylvania, 3,875; Vermont, 338; West Virginia, 1,703; Wisconsin, 2,245.
Total: 20,101

Frank Elbridge Webb (Farmer Labor)
Colorado, 1,092 votes; Iowa, 3,088; Oklahoma, 1,283; South Dakota, 927.
Total: 6,390

Scattered write-ins
California, 373 votes; Iowa, 2; Massachusetts, 4; Pennsylvania, 14; Vermont, 9.
Total: 420

1932 Election

William David Upshaw (Prohibition)
Alabama, 13 votes; California, 20,637; Colorado, 1,928; Georgia, 1,125; Illinois, 6,388; Indiana, 10,399; Iowa, 2,111; Kentucky, 2,252; Massachusetts, 1,142; Michigan, 2,893; Missouri, 2,429; New Jersey, 774; Ohio, 7,421; Pennsylvania, 11,319; Rhode Island, 183; South Dakota, 463; Tennessee, 1,998; Virginia, 1,843; Washington, 1,540; West Virginia, 2,342; Wisconsin, 2,672.
Total: 81,872

William Hope Harvey (Liberty)
Arkansas, 952 votes; California, 9,827; Idaho, 4,712; Michigan, 217; Montana, 1,449; New Mexico, 389; North Dakota, 1,817; South Dakota, 3,333; Texas, 243; Washington, 30,308.
Total: 53,247

Verne L. Reynolds (Socialist Labor)
Colorado, 427 votes; Connecticut, 2,287; Illinois, 3,638; Indiana, 2,070; Kentucky, 1,393; Maine, 255; Maryland, 1,036; Massachusetts, 2,668; Michigan, 1,401; Minnesota, 770; Missouri, 404; New Jersey, 1,062; New York, 10,339; Ohio, 1,968; Oregon, 1,730; Pennsylvania, 659; Rhode Island, 433; Washington, 1,009; Wisconsin, 494.
Total: 34,043

Jacob S. Coxey (Farmer Labor)
Colorado, 469 votes; Iowa, 1,094; Michigan, 137; Minnesota, 5,731.
Total: 7,431

John Zahnd (National)
Indiana, 1,645 votes.

James R. Cox (Jobless)
Pennsylvania, 725 votes; Virginia, 15.
Total: 740.

Jacksonian
Texas, 157 votes.

Arizona Progressive Democrat
Arizona, 9 votes.

Scattered write-ins
California, 127 votes; Florida, 691; Iowa, 4; Louisiana, 533; Massachusetts, 71; Pennsylvania, 53; Texas, 34; Vermont, 2; Wisconsin, 13.
Total: 1,528

1936 Election

Earl Browder (Communist)
Alabama, 678 votes; Arkansas, 167; California, 10,877; Colorado, 497; Connecticut, 1,193; Delaware, 51; Illinois, 801; Indiana, 1,090; Iowa, 506; Kentucky, 207; Maine, 257; Maryland, 915; Mass-

achusetts, 2,930; Michigan, 3,384; Minnesota, 2,574; Missouri, 417; Montana, 385; New Hampshire, 193; New Jersey, 1,639; New Mexico, 43; New York, 35,609; North Carolina, 11; North Dakota, 360; Ohio, 5,251; Oregon, 104; Pennsylvania, 4,060; Rhode Island, 411; Tennessee, 326; Texas, 257; Utah, 280; Vermont, 405; Virginia, 98; Washington, 1,907; Wisconsin, 2,197; Wyoming, 91.

Total: 80,171

D. Leigh Colvin (Prohibition)

Alabama, 719 votes; Arizona, 384; California, 12,917; Georgia, 660; Illinois, 3,439; Iowa, 1,182; Kentucky, 939; Maine, 334; Massachusetts, 1,032; Michigan, 579; Missouri, 908; Montana, 224; New Jersey, 926; New Mexico, 61; North Dakota, 197; Oklahoma, 1,328; Oregon, 4; Pennsylvania, 6,691; Tennessee, 634; Texas, 522; Utah, 43; Virginia, 594; Washington, 1,041; West Virginia, 1,173; Wisconsin, 1,071; Wyoming, 75.

Total: 37,677

John W. Aiken (Socialist Labor)

Colorado, 344 votes; Connecticut, 1,228; Illinois, 1,921; Iowa, 252, Kentucky, 294; Maine, 129; Maryland, 1,305; Massachusetts, 1,305; Michigan, 600; Minnesota, 961; Missouri, 292; New Jersey, 362; Ohio, 28; Oregon, 500; Pennsylvania, 1,424; Rhode Island, 929; Virginia, 36; Washington, 362; Wisconsin, 557.

Total: 12,829

William Dudley Pelley (Christian)

Washington, 1,598 votes.

Scattered write-ins

California, 490 votes; Florida, 71; Iowa, 4; Louisiana, 93; Massachusetts, 11; Michigan, 5; North Carolina, 6; Ohio, 7; Oregon, 108; Vermont, 137.

Total: 824

1940 Election

Earl Browder (Communist)

Alabama, 509 votes; California, 13,586; Colorado, 378; Connecticut, 1,091; Idaho, 276; Iowa, 1,524; Maine, 411; Maryland, 1,274; Massachusetts, 3,806; Michigan, 2,834; Minnesota, 2,711; Montana, 489; New Jersey, 6,508; Oregon, 191; Pennsylvania, 4,519; Rhode Island, 243; Texas, 215; Utah, 191; Vermont, 411; Virginia, 72; Washington, 2,626; Wisconsin, 2,394.

Total: 46,259

John W. Aiken (Socialist Labor)

Connecticut, 971 votes; Indiana, 706; Iowa, 452; Maryland, 657; Massachusetts, 1,492; Michigan, 795; Minnesota, 2,553; Missouri, 209; New Jersey, 455; Oregon, 2,487; Pennsylvania, 1,518; Virginia, 48; Washington, 667; Wisconsin, 1,882.

Total: 14,892

Alfred Knutson (Independent)

North Dakota, 545 votes.

Scattered write-ins

California, 262 votes; Florida, 148; Georgia, 14; Illinois, 657; Louisiana, 108; Massachusetts, 12; Michigan, 4; Oregon, 40: Pennsylvania, 827; Vermont, 11.

Total: 2,083

1944 Election

Edward A. Teichert (Socialist Labor)

California, 180 votes; Connecticut, 1,220; Illinois, 9,677; Iowa, 193; Kentucky, 329; Maine, 335; Massachusetts, 2,780; Michigan, 1,264; Minnesota, 3,176; Missouri, 220; New Jersey, 6,939; New York, 14,352; Pennsylvania, 1,789; Virginia, 90; Washington, 1,645; Wisconsin, 1,002.

Total: 45,191

Gerald L. K. Smith (America First)

Michigan, 1,530 votes; Texas, 250.

Total: 1,780

Texas Regulars

Texas, 135,444 votes.

Southern Democrat

South Carolina, 7,799.

Scattered write-ins

California, 1,881 votes; Florida, 211; Louisiana, 69; Massachusetts, 266; Michigan, 6; Vermont, 14.

Total: 2,447

1948 Election

Norman M. Thomas (Socialist)

Arkansas, 1,037 votes; California, 3,459; Colorado, 1,678; Connecticut, 6,964; Delaware, 250; Georgia, 3; Idaho, 332; Illinois, 11,522; Indiana, 2,179; Iowa, 1,829; Kansas, 2,807; Kentucky, 1,284; Maine, 547; Maryland, 2,941; Michigan, 6,063; Minnesota, 4,646; Missouri, 2,222; Montana, 695; New Hampshire, 86; New Jersey, 10,521; New Mexico, 83; New York, 40,879; North Dakota; 1,000; Oregon, 5,051; Pennsylvania, 11,325; Rhode Island, 429; South Carolina, 1; Tennessee, 1,288; Texas, 922; Vermont, 585; Virginia, 726; Washington, 3,534; Wisconsin, 12,547; Wyoming, 137.

Total: 139,572

Claude A. Watson (Prohibition)

Alabama, 1,085 votes; Arizona, 786; Arkansas, 1; California, 16,926; Delaware, 343; Georgia, 732; Idaho, 628; Illinois, 11,959; Indiana, 14,711; Iowa, 3,382; Kansas, 6,468; Kentucky, 1,245; Massachusetts, 1,663; Michigan, 13,052; Montana, 429; New Jersey, 10,593; New Mexico, 127; Pennsylvania, 10,538; Texas, 3,115; Washington, 6,117.

Total: 103,900

Edward A. Teichert (Socialist Labor)

Arizona, 121 votes; California, 195; Colorado, 214; Connecticut, 1,184; Delaware, 29; Illinois, 3,118; Indiana, 763; Iowa, 4,274; Kentucky, 185; Maine, 206; Massachusetts, 5,535; Michigan, 1,263; Minnesota, 2,525; New Hampshire, 83; New Jersey, 3,354; New Mexico, 49; New York, 2,729; Pennsylvania, 1,461; Rhode Island, 131; Virginia, 234; Washington, 1,133; Wisconsin, 399; Wyoming, 56.

Total: 29,241

Farrell Dobbs (Socialist Workers)

California, 133 votes; Colorado, 228; Connecticut, 606; Iowa, 256; Michigan, 672; Minnesota, 606; New Jersey, 5,825; New York, 2,675; Pennsylvania, 2,133; Utah, 74; Washington, 103; Wisconsin, 303.

Total: 13,614

Scattered write-ins

California, 813 votes; Geoergia, 1; Illinois, 1,629; Louisiana, 10; Massachusetts, 633; Michigan, 1; Missouri, 54; Nebraska, 1; New York, 128; Pennsylvania, 107; Vermont, 35.

Total: 3,412

1952 Election

Eric Hass (Socialist Labor)

Arkansas, 1 vote; California, 273; Colorado, 352; Connecticut, 535; Delaware, 242; Illinois, 9,363; Indiana, 840; Iowa, 139; Kentucky, 893; Maine, 156; Massachusetts, 1,957; Michigan, 1,495; Minnesota, 2,383; Missouri, 169; New Jersey, 5,815; New Mexico, 35; New York, 1,560; Pennsylvania, 1,377; Rhode Island, 83; Virginia, 1,160; Washington, 633; Wisconsin, 770; Wyoming, 36.

Total: 30,267

Darlington Hoopes (Socialist)

California, 206 votes; Colorado, 365; Connecticut, 2,244; Delaware, 20; Iowa, 219; Kansas, 530; Maine, 138; Missouri, 227; Montana, 159; New Jersey, 8,593; New York, 2,664; Pennsylvania, 2,698; Vermont, 185; Virginia, 504; Washington, 254; Wisconsin, 1,157; Wyoming, 40.

Total: 20,203

Douglas MacArthur (Constitution)[4]

Arkansas, 458 votes; California, 3,504; Colorado, 2,181; Missouri, 535; New Mexico; 220; North Dakota, 1,075; Tennessee, 379; Texas, 1,563; Washington, 7,290.

Total: 17,205

Farrell Dobbs (Socialist Workers)
Michigan, 655 votes; Minnesota, 618; New Jersey, 3,850; New York, 2,212; Pennsylvania, 1,508; Washington, 119; Wisconsin, 1,350.
Total: 10,312

Henry Krajewski (Poor Man's)
New Jersey, 4,203 votes.

Scattered write-ins
California, 3,249 votes; Connecticut, 5; Florida, 351; Georgia, 1; Idaho, 23; Illinois, 448; Iowa, 29; Maine, 1; Massachusetts, 69; Michigan, 3; New York, 178; Pennsylvania, 155; Vermont, 18.
Total: 4,530

1956 Election

Enoch A. Holtwick (Prohibition)
California, 11,119 votes; Delaware, 400; Indiana, 6,554; Kansas, 3,048; Kentucky, 2,145; Massachusetts, 1,205; Michigan, 6,923; New Jersey, 9,147; New Mexico, 607; Tennessee, 789.
Total: 41,937

Farrell Dobbs (Socialist Workers)
California, 96 votes; Minnesota, 1,098; New Jersey, 4,004; Pennsylvania, 2,035; Wisconsin, 564.
Total: 7,797

Harry F. Byrd (States' Rights)
Kentucky, 2,657 votes.

Darlington Hoopes (Socialist)
California, 123 votes; Colorado, 531; Iowa, 192; New York, 82; Virginia, 444; Wisconsin, 754.
Total: 2,126

Henry Krajewski (American Third Party)
New Jersey, 1,829 votes.

Gerald L. K. Smith (Christian Nationalist)
California, 8 votes.

Independent Electors
Alabama, 20,323 votes; Louisiana, 44,520; Mississippi, 42,966; South Carolina, 88,509.
Total: 196,318

Scattered write-ins
California, 819 votes; Connecticut, 205; Florida, 1,542; Georgia, 93; Idaho, 16; Illinois, 56; Maryland, 476; Massachusetts, 341; New York, 1,262; Oregon, 535; Vermont, 39.
Total: 5,384

1960 Election

Rutherford L. Decker (Prohibition)
Alabama, 2,106 votes; California, 21,706; Delaware, 284; Indiana, 6,746; Kansas, 4,138; Massachusetts, 1,633; Michigan, 2,029; Montana, 456; New Mexico, 777; Tennessee, 2,458; Texas, 3,870.
Total: 46,203

Orval E. Faubus (National States' Rights)
Alabama, 4,367 votes; Arkansas, 28,952; Delaware, 354; Tennessee, 11,296.
Total: 44,977

Farrell Dobbs (Socialist Workers)
Colorado, 562 votes; Iowa, 634; Michigan, 4,347; Minnesota, 3,077; Montana, 391; New Jersey, 11,402; New York, 14,319; North Dakota, 158; Pennsylvania, 2,678; Utah, 100; Washington, 705; Wisconsin, 1,792.
Total: 40,165

Charles L. Sullivan (Constitutional)
Texas, 18,162 votes.

J. Bracken Lee (Conservative)
New Jersey, 8,708 votes.

C. Benton Coiner (Virginia Conservative)
Virginia, 4,204 votes.

Lar Daly (Tax Cut)
Michigan, 1,767 votes.

Clennon King (Independent Afro-American Unity)
Alabama, 1,485 votes.

Merritt B. Curtis (Constitution)
Washington, 1,401 votes.

Independent Electors
Louisiana, 169,572 votes; Michigan, 539.
Total: 170,111

Scattered write-ins
Alabama, 236 votes; Connecticut, 15; Georgia, 239; Illinois, 15; Maryland, 3; Massachusetts, 31; Oregon, 959; Pennsylvania, 440; South Carolina, 1; Texas, 175; Vermont, 7.
Total: 2,378

1964 Election

E. Harold Munn (Prohibition)
California, 305 votes; Colorado, 1,356; Delaware, 425; Indiana, 8,266; Iowa, 1,902; Kansas, 5,393; Massachusetts, 3,735; Michigan, 669; Montana, 499; New Mexico, 543; North Dakota, 174.
Total: 23,267

John Kasper (National States' Rights)
Arkansas, 2,965 votes; Kentucky, 3,469; Montana, 519.
Total: 6,953

Joseph B. Lightburn (Constitution)
Texas, 5,060 votes.

James Hensley (Universal Party)
California, 19 votes.

Unpledged Democrat
Alabama, 210,732 votes.

Scattered write-ins
Alabama, 1 vote; California, 5,410; Connecticut, 1,313; Georgia, 195; Illinois, 62; Iowa, 118; Maryland, 50; Massachusetts, 159; Michigan, 145; New York, 268; Oregon, 2,509; Pennsylvania, 2,531; Rhode Island, 13; South Carolina, 8; Tennessee, 34; Vermont, 20.
Total: 12,868

1968 Election

Dick Gregory (Freedom and Peace)
California, 3,230 votes; Colorado, 1,393; Indiana, 36; New Jersey, 8,084; New York, 24,517; Ohio, 372; Pennsylvania, 7,821; Virginia, 1,680.
Total: 47,133

Fred Halstead (Socialist Workers)
Arizona, 85 votes; Colorado, 235; Indiana, 1,293; Iowa, 3,377; Kentucky, 2,843; Michigan, 4,099; Minnesota, 807; Montana, 457; New Hampshire, 104; New Jersey, 8,667; New Mexico, 252; New York, 11,851; North Dakota, 128; Ohio, 69; Pennsylvania, 4,862; Rhode Island, 383; Utah, 89; Vermont, 295; Washington, 270; Wisconsin, 1,222.
Total: 41,388

Eldridge Cleaver (Peace and Freedom)
Arizona, 217 votes; California, 27,707; Iowa, 1,332; Michigan, 4,585; Minnesota, 933; Utah, 180; Washington, 1,609.
Total: 36,563

Eugene J. McCarthy
Arizona, 2,751 votes; California, 20,721; Minnesota, 584; Oregon, 1,496.
Total: 25,552

E. Harold Munn (Prohibition)
Alabama, 4,022 votes; California, 59; Colorado, 275; Indiana, 4,616; Iowa, 362; Kansas, 2,192; Massachusetts, 2,369; Michigan, 60; Montana, 510; North Dakota, 38; Ohio, 19; Virginia, 601.
Total: 15,123

Ventura Chavez (People's Constitution)
New Mexico, 1,519 votes.

Charlene Mitchell (Communist)
California, 260 votes; Minnesota, 415; Ohio, 23; Washington, 377.
Total: 1,075

James Hensley (Universal)
Iowa, 142 votes.

Richard K. Troxell (Constitution)
North Dakota, 34 votes.

Kent M. Soeters (Berkeley Defense Group)
    California, 17 votes.
American Independent Democrat
    Alabama, 10,960 votes.
New Party
    New Hampshire, 421 votes; Vermont, 579.
    Total: 1,000
New Reform
    Montana, 470 votes.
Scattered write-ins
    Alabama, 13 votes; Colorado, 948; Connecticut, 1,300; Georgia, 165; Illinois, 325; Iowa, 250; Massachusetts, 53; Michigan, 29; Minnesota, 170; New Hampshire, 108; New Mexico, 69; New York, 1,622; Oregon, 1,144; Pennsylvania, 2,264; Rhode Island, 62; Texas, 299; Vermont, 29; Wisconsin, 2,342.
    Total: 11,192

1972 Election

Louis Fisher (Socialist Labor)
    California, 197 votes; Colorado, 4,361; Georgia, 3; Illinois, 12,344; Indiana, 1,688; Iowa, 195; Massachusetts, 129; Michigan, 2,437; Minnesota, 4,261; New Jersey, 4,544; New York, 4,530; Ohio, 7,107; Virginia, 9,918; Washington, 1,102; Wisconsin, 998.
    Total: 53,814
Linda Jenness (Socialist Workers)
    Arizona, 366 votes; California, 574; Colorado, 666; District of Columbia, 316; Idaho, 397; Iowa, 488; Kentucky, 685; Louisiana, 14,398; Massachusetts, 10,600; Michigan, 1,603; Minnesota, 940; Mississippi, 2,458; New Hampshire, 368; New Jersey, 2,233; New Mexico, 474; North Dakota, 288; Pennsylvania, 4,639; Rhode Island, 729; South Dakota, 994; Texas, 8,664; Vermont, 296; Washington, 623.
    Total: 52,799
Gus Hall (Communist)
    California, 373 votes; Colorado, 432; District of Columbia, 252; Illinois, 4,541; Iowa, 272; Kentucky, 464; Massachusetts, 46; Michigan, 1,210; Minnesota, 662; New Jersey, 1,263; New York, 5,641; North Dakota, 87; Ohio, 6,437; Pennsylvania, 2,686; Washington, 566; Wisconsin, 663.
    Total: 25,595
Evelyn Reed (Socialist Workers)
    Indiana, 5,575 votes; New York, 7,797; Wisconsin, 506.
    Total: 13,878
E. Harold Munn (Prohibition)
    Alabama, 8,559 votes; California, 53; Colorado, 467; Delaware, 238; Kansas, 4,188.
    Total: 13,505
John Hospers (Libertarian)
    California, 980 votes; Colorado, 1,111; Massachusetts, 43; Rhode Island, 2; Washington, 1,537.
    Total: 3,673
John V. Mahalchik (America First)
    New Jersey, 1,743 votes.
Gabriel Green (Universal)
    California, 21 votes; Iowa, 199.
    Total: 220
Scattered write-ins
    Colorado, 6 votes; Connecticut, 777; Florida, 7,407; Georgia, 2,932; Illinois, 2,229; Iowa, 321; Massachusetts, 342; Minnesota, 962; Missouri, 4,804; New Hampshire, 142; New Mexico, 1; New York, 4,089; Ohio, 460; Oregon, 2,289; Pennsylvania, 2,716; Rhode Island, 19; South Carolina, 17; Tennessee, 369; Texas, 3,393; Vermont, 318; Wisconsin, 893.
    Total: 34,795

1976 Election

Lester Maddox (American Independent)
    Alabama, 9,198 votes; Arizona, 85; California, 51,098; Connecticut, 7,101; Georgia, 1,071; Idaho, 5,935; Kansas, 2,118; Ken-

tucky, 2,328; Louisiana, 10,058; Maine, 8; Maryland, 171; Mississippi, 4,861; Nebraska, 3,380; Nevada, 1,497; New Jersey, 7,716; New Mexico, 31; New York, 97; North Dakota, 269; Ohio, 15,529; Pennsylvania, 25,344; Rhode Island, 1; South Carolina, 1,950; Tennessee, 2,303; Texas, 41; Utah, 1,162; Washington, 8,585; West Virginia, 12; Wisconsin, 8,552; Wyoming; 30.
    Total: 170,531
Thomas J. Anderson (American)
    Alabama, 70 votes; Arizona, 564; Arkansas, 389; California, 4,565; Colorado, 397; Connecticut, 155; Delaware, 645; Florida, 21,325; Georgia, 1,168; Idaho, 493; Illinois, 387; Indiana, 14,048; Iowa, 3,040; Kansas, 4,724; Kentucky, 8,308; Maine, 28; Maryland, 321; Massachusetts, 7,555; Minnesota, 13,592; Mississippi, 6,678; Montana, 5,772; New Mexico, 106; New York, 451; North Carolina, 5,607; North Dakota, 3,796; Oregon, 1,035; Rhode Island, 24; South Carolina, 2,996; Tennessee, 5,769; Texas, 11,442; Utah, 13,284; Virginia, 16,686; Washington, 5,046; West Virginia, 17; Wyoming, 290.
    Total: 160,773
Peter Camejo (Socialist Workers)
    Alabama, 1 vote; Arizona, 928; California, 17,259; Colorado, 1,126; Connecticut, 42; District of Columbia, 545; Georgia, 43; Idaho, 14; Illinois, 3,615; Indiana, 5,695; Iowa, 267; Kentucky, 350; Louisiana, 2,240; Maine, 1; Maryland, 261; Massachusetts, 8,138; Michigan, 1,804; Minnesota, 4,149; Mississippi, 2,805; New Hampshire, 161; New Jersey, 1,184; New Mexico, 2,462; New York, 6,996; North Dakota, 43; Ohio, 4,717; Pennsylvania, 3,009; Rhode Island, 462; South Carolina, 8; South Dakota, 168; Texas, 1,723; Utah, 268; Vermont, 430; Virginia, 17,802; Washington, 905; West Virginia, 2; Wisconsin, 1,691.
    Total: 91,314
Gus Hall (Communist)
    Alabama, 1,954 votes; California, 12,766; Colorado, 403; Connecticut, 186; District of Columbia, 219; Georgia, 3; Idaho, 5; Illinois, 9,250; Iowa, 554; Kentucky, 426; Louisiana, 7,417; Maine, 14; Maryland, 68; Minnesota, 1,092; New Jersey, 1,662; New Mexico, 19; New York, 10,270; North Dakota, 84; Ohio, 7,817; Pennsylvania, 1,891; Rhode Island, 334; South Carolina, 1; South Dakota, 318; Tennessee, 547; Utah, 121; Washington, 817; West Virginia, 5; Wisconsin, 749.
    Total: 58,992
Margaret Wright (People's Party)
    California, 41,731 votes; Connecticut, 1; Idaho, 1; Maryland, 8; Massachusetts, 33; Michigan, 3,504; Minnesota, 635; New Jersey, 1,044; Washington, 1,124; Wisconsin, 943.
    Total: 49,024
Lyndon H. LaRouche Jr. (U.S. Labor)
    Alabama, 1 vote; Colorado, 567; Connecticut, 1,789; Delaware, 136; District of Columbia, 157; Georgia, 1; Idaho, 739; Illinois, 2,018; Indiana, 1,947; Iowa, 241; Kentucky, 510; Maryland, 21; Massachusetts, 4,922; Michigan, 1,366; Minnesota, 543; New Hampshire, 186; New Jersey, 1,650; New Mexico, 1; New York, 5,413; North Carolina, 755; North Dakota, 142; Ohio, 4,335; Pennsylvania, 2,744; South Carolina, 2; Tennessee, 512; Vermont, 196; Virginia, 7,508; Washington, 903; Wisconsin, 738.
    Total: 40,043
Benjamin C. Bubar (Prohibition)
    Alabama, 6,669 votes; California, 34; Colorado, 2,882; Delaware, 103; Kansas, 1,403; Maine, 3,495; Maryland, 2; Massachusetts, 14; New Jersey, 554; New Mexico, 211; North Dakota, 63; Ohio, 62; Tennessee, 442.
    Total: 15,934
Jules Levin (Socialist Labor)
    California, 222 votes; Colorado, 14; Connecticut, 1; Delaware, 86; Florida, 19; Georgia, 2; Illinois, 2,422; Iowa, 167; Maine, 1; Maryland, 7; Massachusetts, 19; Michigan, 1,148; Minnesota, 370; New Hampshire, 66; New Jersey, 3,686; New York, 28; Ohio, 68; Rhode Island, 188; Washington, 713; Wisconsin, 389.
    Total: 9,616
Frank P. Zeidler (Socialist)
    Connecticut, 5 votes; Florida, 8; Georgia, 2; Idaho, 2; Iowa, 234; Maryland, 16; Minnesota, 354; New Jersey, 469; New Mexico,

240; New York, 14; North Dakota, 38; Washington, 358; Wisconsin, 4,298.

Total: 6,038

Ernest L. Miller (Restoration)

California, 26 votes; Colorado, 6; Florida, 2; Georgia, 3; Maryland, 8; Tennessee, 316.

Total: 361

Frank Taylor (United American)

Arizona, 22 votes; California, 14.

Total: 36

Scattered write-ins

Alabama, 137 votes; Alaska, 1,176; California, 74; Colorado, 2; Connecticut, 1,122; District of Columbia, 1,944, 1.2; Georgia, 847; Idaho, 1,430; Illinois, 1,662; Iowa, 506; Maine, 185; Maryland, 1,945; Massachusetts, 1,354; Michigan, 2,160; Minnesota, 342; Missouri, 3,741; Nevada, 5,108 (none of the above), 2.5; New Hampshire, 604; New Mexico, 501; New York, 4,052; North Carolina, 228; Oregon, 6,107; Pennsylvania, 2,934; Rhode Island, 82; South Carolina, 328; Tennessee, 229; Texas, 2,752; Vermont, 99; West Virginia, 125; Wisconsin, 2,839; Wyoming, 354.

Total: 44,969

1980 Election

Barry Commoner (Citizens)

Alabama, 517 votes; Arizona, 551; Arkansas, 2,345; California, 61,063; Colorado, 5,614; Connecticut, 6,130; Delaware, 103; District of Columbia, 1,840; Georgia, 104; Hawaii, 1,548; Illinois, 10,692; Indiana, 4,852; Iowa, 2,273; Kentucky, 1,304; Louisiana, 1,584; Maine, 4,394; Massachusetts, 2,056; Michigan, 11,930; Minnesota, 8,407; Missouri, 573; New Hampshire, 1,320; New Jersey, 8,203; New Mexico, 2,202; New York, 23,186; North Carolina, 2,287; North Dakota, 429; Ohio, 8,564; Oregon, 13,642; Pennsylvania, 10,430; Rhode Island, 67; Tennessee, 1,112; Texas, 453; Utah, 1,009; Vermont, 2,316; Virginia, 14,024; Washington, 9,403; Wisconsin, 7,767.

Total: 234,294

Gus Hall (Communist)

Alabama, 1,629 votes; Arizona, 25; Arkansas, 1,244; California, 847; Colorado, 487; Delaware, 13; District of Columbia, 371; Florida, 123; Hawaii, 458; Illinois, 9,711; Indiana, 702; Iowa, 298; Kansas, 967; Kentucky, 348; Maine, 591; Michigan, 3,262; Minnesota, 1,184; Missouri, 26; New Hampshire, 129; New Jersey, 2,555; New York, 7,414; North Dakota, 93; Pennsylvania, 5,184; Rhode Island, 218; Tennessee, 503; Texas, 49; Utah, 139; Vermont, 118; Washington, 834; Wisconsin, 772.

Total: 45,023

John R. Rarick (American Independent)

Alabama, 15,010 votes; California, 9,856; Idaho, 1,057; Kansas, 789; Louisiana, 10,333; Michigan, 5; South Carolina, 2,177; Utah, 522; Wisconsin, 1,519.

Total: 41,268

Clifton DeBerry (Socialist Workers)

Alabama, 1,303 votes; Arizona, 1,100; District of Columbia, 173; Florida, 41; Illinois, 1,302; Indiana, 610; Iowa, 244; Louisiana, 783; Massachusetts, 5,143; Minnesota, 711; Missouri, 1,515; New Hampshire, 71; New York, 2,068; North Carolina, 416; North Dakota, 89; Pennsylvania, 20,291; Rhode Island, 90; Tennessee, 490; Utah, 124; Vermont, 75; Virginia, 1,986; Washington, 1,137.

Total: 38,737

Ellen McCormack (Right to Life)

Delaware, 3 votes; Kentucky, 4,233; Missouri, 5; New Jersey, 3,927; New York, 24,159; Rhode Island, 1.

Total: 32,327

Maureen Smith (Peace and Freedom)

California, 18,116 votes.

Deirdre Griswold (Workers World)

California, 15 votes; Delaware, 3; District of Columbia, 52; Florida, 8; Georgia, 1; Illinois, 2,257; Massachusetts, 19; Michigan, 30; Minnesota, 698; Mississippi, 2,402; New Hampshire, 76; New Jersey, 1,288; Ohio, 3,790; Rhode Island, 77; Tennessee, 400; Texas, 11; Washington, 341; Wisconsin, 414.

Total: 13,300

Benjamin C. Bubar (Statesman)

Alabama, 1,743 votes; Arkansas, 1,350; California, 36; Colorado, 1,180; Delaware, 6; Iowa, 150; Kansas, 821; Massachusetts, 34; Michigan, 9; New Mexico, 1,281; North Dakota, 54; Ohio, 27; Tennessee, 521.

Total: 7,212

David McReynolds (Socialist)

Alabama, 1,006 votes; Florida, 116; Iowa, 534; Massachusetts, 62; Minnesota, 536; New Jersey, 1,973; North Dakota, 82; Rhode Island, 170; Tennessee, 519; Vermont, 136; Washington, 956; Wisconsin, 808.

Total: 6,898

Percy L. Greaves (American)

California, 87 votes; Delaware, 400; Indiana, 4,750; Iowa, 189; Michigan, 21; North Dakota, 235; Utah, 965.

Total: 6,647

Andrew Pulley (Socialist Workers)

California, 231 votes; Colorado, 520; Delaware, 4; Georgia, 4; Kentucky, 393; Mississippi, 2,347; New Jersey, 2,198; New Mexico, 325; South Dakota, 250.

Total: 6,272

Richard Congress (Socialist Workers)

Ohio, 4,029 votes.

Kurt Lynen (Middle Class)

New Jersey, 3,694 votes.

Bill Gahres (Down With Lawyers)

New Jersey, 1,718 votes.

Frank W. Shelton (American)

Kansas, 1,555 votes.

Martin E. Wendelken, (Independent)

New Jersey, 923 votes.

Harley McLain (Natural Peoples League)

North Dakota, 296 votes.

Scattered write-ins

Alaska, 857 votes; California, 1,242; Connecticut, 836; Delaware, 101; District of Columbia, 690; Georgia, 112; Illinois, 604; Iowa, 519; Maine, 84; Massachusetts, 2,382; Michigan, 891; Minnesota, 6,139 (American Party, with no candidate specified); Missouri, 604; Nevada, 4,193 (none of the above); New Hampshire, 68; New Mexico, 734; New York, 1,064; Oregon, 1,713; Rhode Island, 37; South Carolina, 376; Tennessee, 152; Vermont, 413; Wisconsin, 1,337.

Total: 23,517

1984 Election

Sonia Johnson (Citizens)

Arizona, 18 votes; Arkansas, 960; California, 26,297; Colorado, 23; Connecticut, 14; Delaware, 121; Florida, 58; Georgia, 4; Illinois, 2,716; Kentucky, 599; Louisiana, 9,502; Massachusetts, 18; Michigan, 1,191; Minnesota, 1,219; Missouri, 2; New Jersey, 1,247; New Mexico, 455; North Dakota, 368; Pennsylvania, 21,628; Rhode Island, 240; Tennessee, 978; Texas, 87; Utah, 844; Vermont, 264; Washington, 1,891; Wisconsin, 1,456.

Total: 72,200

Bob Richards (Populist)

Alabama, 1,401 votes; Arkansas, 1,461; California, 39,265; Georgia, 95; Idaho, 2,288; Kansas, 3,564; Louisiana, 1,310; Minnesota, 2,377; Mississippi, 641; North Dakota, 1,077; Rhode Island, 10; Tennessee, 1,763; Washington, 5,724; West Virginia, 996; Wisconsin, 3,864.

Total: 66,336

Dennis L. Serrette (Independent Alliance)

Alabama, 659 votes; Arkansas, 1,291; California, 16; Colorado, 978; Connecticut, 1,374; Delaware, 68; District of Columbia, 165; Georgia, 2; Illinois, 2,386; Iowa, 463; Kansas, 2,544; Kentucky, 365; Louisiana, 533; Maine, 755; Maryland, 656; Massachusetts, 7,998; Michigan, 665; Minnesota, 232; Mississippi, 356; Nebraska, 1,025; New Hampshire, 305; New Jersey, 2,293; New Mexico, 155; New York, 3,200; North Dakota, 152; Ohio, 12,090; Rhode Island,

49; South Carolina, 682; South Dakota, 1,150; Tennessee, 524; Texas, 41; Utah, 220; Vermont, 323; Washington, 1,654; West Virginia, 493; Wisconsin, 1,006.

Total: 46,868

Gus Hall (Communist)

Alabama, 4,671 votes; Arkansas, 1,499; Connecticut, 4,826; District of Columbia, 257; Georgia, 1; Hawaii, 821; Illinois, 4,672; Iowa, 286; Kentucky, 328; Maine, 1,292; Maryland, 898; Michigan, 1,048; Minnesota, 630; New Jersey, 1,564; New York, 4,226; North Dakota, 169; Ohio, 4,438; Pennsylvania, 1,780; Rhode Island, 75; Tennessee, 1,036; Texas, 126; Utah, 184; Vermont, 115; Washington, 814; Wisconsin, 596.

Total: 36,386

Mel Mason (Socialist Workers)

Alabama, 730 votes; Colorado, 810; District of Columbia, 127; Florida, 7; Georgia, 10; Illinois, 2,132; Iowa, 313; Kentucky, 3,129; Louisiana, 1,164; Michigan, 1,049; Minnesota, 3,180; Mississippi, 1,032; Missouri, 8; Nebraska, 1,066; New Jersey, 1,264; New Mexico, 224; North Carolina, 799; North Dakota, 239; Ohio, 4,344; Rhode Island, 61; South Dakota, 337; Tennessee, 715; Utah, 142; Vermont, 127; Washington, 608; West Virginia, 645; Wisconsin, 444.

Total: 24,706

Larry Holmes (Workers World)

District of Columbia, 107 votes; Georgia, 2; Maryland, 745; Michigan, 1,416; Mississippi, 1,169; New Jersey, 8,404; New York, 2,226; Washington, 641; Wisconsin, 619.

Total: 15,329

Delmar Dennis (American)

Delaware, 269 votes; Georgia, 4; Indiana, 7,617; Kentucky, 428; Missouri, 1; South Carolina, 3,490; Tennessee, 7; Utah, 1,345.

Total: 13,161

Ed Winn (Workers League)

Arizona, 3 votes; Illinois, 2,632 ; Michigan, 561; Minnesota, 260; New Jersey, 1,721; Ohio, 3,565; Pennsylvania, 2,059.

Total: 10,801

Earl F. Dodge (Prohibition)

Arkansas, 842 votes; Colorado, 858; Kansas, 2,109; Massachusetts, 3; New Mexico, 206; North Dakota, 220; Ohio, 4.

Total: 4,242

Gavrielle Holmes (Workers World)

Ohio, 2,565 votes; Rhode Island, 91.

Total: 2,656

John B. Anderson (National Unity Party of Kentucky)

Georgia, 3 votes; Kentucky, 1,479; Tennessee, 4.

Total: 1,486

Gerald Baker (Big Deal)

Iowa, 892 votes.

Arthur J. Lowery (United Sovereign Citizens)

Arkansas, 822 votes; Georgia, 3.

Total: 825

Scattered write-ins

Alaska, 843 votes; Arizona, 21; California, 366; Connecticut, 8; District of Columbia, 809; Florida, 32; Georgia, 460; Illinois, 862; Iowa, 1,051; Maine, 82; Massachusetts, 892; Michigan, 602; Minnesota, 723; Montana, 1; Nevada, 3,950 (none of the above); New Hampshire, 113; New Mexico, 1; New York, 837; Ohio, 34; Oregon, 4,348; Rhode Island, 3; Tennessee, 117; Vermont, 712; Wisconsin, 706.

Total: 17,573

1988 Election

David E. Duke (Populist)

Arizona, 113 votes; Arkansas, 5,146; California, 483; Colorado, 139; Florida, 249; Iowa, 755; Kentucky, 4,494; Louisiana, 18,612; Michigan, 60; Minnesota, 1,529; Mississippi, 4,232; Missouri, 44; New Jersey, 2,446; Oregon, 90; Pennsylvania, 3,444; Rhode Island, 159; Tennessee, 1,807; Vermont, 189; Wisconsin, 3,056.

Total: 47,047

Eugene J. McCarthy (Consumer)

Arizona, 159 votes; California, 234; Michigan, 2,497; Minnesota, 5,403; New Jersey, 3,454; Pennsylvania, 19,158.

Total: 30,905

James C. Griffin (American Independent)

California, 27,818 votes.

Lyndon H. LaRouche Jr. (National Economic Recovery)

Alaska, 816 votes; Hawaii, 470; Iowa, 3,526; Louisiana, 1,958; Minnesota, 1,702; North Dakota, 905; Ohio, 7,733; Tennessee, 873; Utah, 427; Vermont, 275; Washington, 4,412; Wisconsin, 2,302; District of Columbia, 163.

Total: 25,562

William A. Marra (Right to Life)

Connecticut, 7 votes; New York, 20,497.

Total: 20,504

Ed Winn (Workers League)

Alabama, 461 votes; Illinois, 7,021; Iowa, 235; Michigan, 1,958; Minnesota, 489; New Jersey, 691; New York, 10; Ohio, 5,432; Pennsylvania, 2,188; District of Columbia, 208.

Total: 18,693

James Warren (Socialist Workers)

Alabama, 656 votes; Iowa, 205; Michigan, 819; Minnesota, 2,155; New Jersey, 2,298; New Mexico, 344; New York, 3,287 0.1; North Dakota, 347; Rhode Island, 130; South Dakota, 226; Tennessee, 718; Texas, 110; Utah, 209; Vermont, 113; Washington, 1,290; Wisconsin, 2,574; District of Columbia, 123.

Total: 15,604

Herbert Lewin (Peace and Freedom)

California, 58 votes; New Jersey, 9,953; Rhode Island, 195; Vermont, 164.

Total: 10,370

Earl F. Dodge (Prohibition)

Arkansas, 1,319 votes; Colorado, 4,604; Massachusetts, 18; Michigan, 5; New Mexico, 249; Tennessee, 1,807.

Total: 8,002

Larry Holmes (Workers World)

California, 11 votes; Michigan, 804; New Jersey, 1,020; New Mexico, 258; New York 4,179; Ohio, 134; Washington, 1,440.

Total: 7,846

Willa Kenoyer (Socialist)

Florida, 14 votes; Iowa, 334; Massachusetts, 15; New Jersey, 2,587; New York, 3; Rhode Island, 96; Tennessee, 358; Texas, 62; Utah, 129; Vermont, 142; District of Columbia, 142.

Total: 3,882

Delmar Dennis (American)

Arizona, 18 votes; Minnesota, 1,298; Missouri, 1; Utah, 2,158.

Total: 3,475

Jack E. Herer (Grassroots)

Minnesota, 1,949 votes.

Louie G. Youngkeit (Independent)

Utah, 372 votes.

John G. Martin (Third World Assembly)

District of Columbia, 236 votes.

Scattered write-ins

Alabama, 506 votes; Alaska, 957; California, 25; Florida, 13; Georgia, 15; Iowa, 1,613; Maine, 230; Maryland, 24; Massachusetts, 2,910; Michigan, 902; Minnesota, 3,614; Missouri, 6; Nevada, 6,934 (none of the above); New Hampshire, 549; New Mexico, 93; Ohio, 216; Oregon, 3,974; Rhode Island, 51; Tennessee, 285; Texas, 98; Vermont, 1,134; Wisconsin, 2,273; District of Columbia, 1,553.

Total: 27,975

1992 Election

James "Bo" Gritz (Populist)

Alaska, 1,379 votes; Arizona, 8,141; Arkansas, 819; California, 3,077; Colorado, 274; Connecticut, 72; Delaware, 9; Georgia, 78; Hawaii, 1,452; Idaho, 10,281; Illinois, 3,577; Indiana, 1,467; Iowa, 1,177; Kansas, 79; Kentucky, 47; Louisiana, 18,545; Maryland, 41; Michigan, 168; Minnesota, 3,363; Mississippi, 545; Missouri, 180; Montana, 3,658; Nevada, 2,892; New Jersey, 1,867; New York, 23;

Ohio, 4,699; Oregon, 1,470; Rhode Island, 3; Tennessee, 756; Texas, 505; Utah, 28,602, 3.8; Washington, 4,854; West Virginia, 34; Wisconsin, 2,311; Wyoming, 569.

Total: 107,014

Lenora B. Fulani (New Alliance)

Alabama, 2,161 votes; Alaska, 330; Arizona, 923; Arkansas, 1,022; Colorado, 1,608; Connecticut, 1,363; Delaware, 1,105; District of Columbia, 1,459; Georgia, 44; Hawaii, 720; Idaho, 613; Illinois, 5,267; Indiana, 2,583; Iowa, 197; Kansas, 10; Kentucky, 430; Louisiana, 1,434; Maine, 519; Maryland, 2,786; Massachusetts, 3,172; Michigan, 21; Minnesota, 958; Mississippi, 2,625; Missouri, 17; Montana, 8; Nebraska, 846; Nevada, 483; New Hampshire, 512; New Jersey, 3,513; New Mexico, 369; New York, 11,318; North Carolina, 59; North Dakota, 143; Ohio, 6,413; Oregon, 3,030; Pennsylvania, 4,661; Rhode Island, 1,878; South Carolina, 1,235; South Dakota, 110; Tennessee, 727; Texas, 301; Utah, 414; Vermont, 429; Virginia, 3,192; Washington, 1,776; West Virginia, 6; Wisconsin, 654; Wyoming, 270.

Total: 73,714

Howard Phillips (U.S. Taxpayers)

Alaska, 377 votes; Arkansas, 1,437; California, 12,711; Connecticut, 20; Delaware, 2; Georgia, 7; Iowa, 480; Kansas, 55; Kentucky, 989; Louisiana, 1,552; Maine, 464; Maryland, 22; Massachusetts, 2,218; Michigan, 8,263; Minnesota, 733; Mississippi, 1,652; Nevada, 677; New Jersey, 2,670; New Mexico, 620; Rhode Island, 215; South Carolina, 2,680; Tennessee, 579; Texas, 359; Utah, 393; Vermont, 124; Washington, 2,354; West Virginia, 2; Wisconsin, 1,772; Wyoming, 7.

Total: 43,434

John Hagelin (Natural Law)

Alabama, 495 votes; Alaska, 433; Arizona, 2,267; Arkansas, 764; California, 836; Colorado, 47; Connecticut, 75; Delaware, 6; District of Columbia, 230; Florida, 214; Hawaii, 416; Idaho, 24; Illinois, 2,751; Indiana, 126; Iowa, 3,079; Kansas, 77; Kentucky, 695; Louisiana, 889; Maryland, 191; Massachusetts, 1,812; Michigan, 2,954; Minnesota, 1,406; Mississippi, 1,140; Missouri, 64; Montana, 20; Nebraska, 714; Nevada, 338; New Hampshire, 292; New Jersey, 1,353; New Mexico, 562; New York, 4,420; North Carolina, 41; North Dakota, 240; Ohio, 3,437; Oregon, 91; Rhode Island, 262; South Dakota, 429; Tennessee, 599; Texas, 217; Utah, 1,319; Vermont, 315; Washington, 2,456; West Virginia, 2; Wisconsin, 1,070; Wyoming, 11.

Total: 39,179

Ron Daniels (Peace and Freedom)

California, 18,597 votes; District of Columbia, 1,186; Iowa, 212; Louisiana, 1,663; Maryland, 167; Missouri, 12; New Jersey, 1,996; New York, 385; Rhode Island, 1; Tennessee, 511; Utah, 177; Washington, 1,171; Wisconsin, 1,883.

Total: 27,961

Lyndon H. LaRouche Jr. (Economic Recovery)

Alabama, 641 votes; Alaska, 469; Arizona, 8; Arkansas, 762; California, 180; Colorado, 20; Connecticut, 4; Delaware, 9; District of Columbia, 260; Idaho, 1; Indiana, 14; Iowa, 238; Louisiana, 1,136; Maryland, 18; Massachusetts, 1,027; Michigan, 14; Minnesota, 622; Missouri, 13; New Jersey, 2,095; New York, 20; North Dakota, 642; Ohio, 2,446; Rhode Island, 494; Tennessee, 460; Texas, 169; Utah, 1,089; Vermont, 57; Virginia, 11,937; Washington, 855; Wisconsin, 633.

Total: 26,333

James Warren (Socialist Workers)

Alabama, 831 votes; California, 115; Connecticut, 5; Delaware, 3; District of Columbia, 105; Georgia, 9; Illinois, 1,361; Iowa, 273; Maryland, 25; Minnesota, 990; Missouri, 6; New Jersey, 2,011; New Mexico, 183; New York, 15,472; North Carolina, 12; North Dakota, 193; Ohio, 32; Tennessee, 277; Utah, 200; Vermont, 82; Washington, 515; West Virginia, 6; Wisconsin, 390.

Total: 23,096

Drew Bradford (Independent)

New Jersey, 4,749 votes.

Jack E. Herer (Grassroots)

Iowa, 669 votes; Minnesota, 2,659; Wisconsin, 547.

Total: 3,875

J. Quinn Brisben (Socialist)

District of Columbia, 191 votes; Florida, 16; Idaho, 3; Indiana, 16; Massachusetts, 13; New York, 16; Oregon, 4; Rhode Island, 2; Tennessee, 1,356; Texas, 78; Utah, 151; Wisconsin, 1,211.

Total: 3,057

Helen Halyard (Workers League)

Michigan, 1,432 votes; New Jersey, 1,618.

Total: 3,050

John Yiamouyiannas (Take Back America)

Arkansas, 554 votes; Iowa, 604; Louisiana, 808; Tennessee, 233.

Total: 2,199

Delbert L. Ehlers (Independent)

Iowa, 1,149 votes.

Earl F. Dodge (Prohibition)

Arkansas, 472 votes; Colorado, 21; Massachusetts, 2; New Mexico, 120; North Dakota, 3; Tennessee, 343.

Total: 961

Jim Boren (Apathy)

Arkansas, 956 votes.

Eugene A. Hem (Third)

Wisconsin, 405 votes.

Isabell Masters (Looking Back)

Arkansas, 327 votes; California, 12.

Total: 339

Robert J. Smith (American)

Utah, 292 votes.

Gloria La Riva (Workers World)

New Mexico, 181 votes.

Scattered write-ins

Alabama, 723 votes; Alaska, 365; California, 149; Delaware, 86; District of Columbia, 676; Florida, 8; Georgia, 2; Illinois, 22; Iowa, 741; Kansas, 57; Maine, 91; Maryland, 2; Massachusetts, 1,990; Michigan, 711; Minnesota, 2,499; Missouri, 3; Nevada (None of these candidates), 2,537; New Hampshire, 730; Ohio, 10; Oregon, 2,609; Rhode Island, 106; Tennessee, 161; Texas, 23; Utah, 1; Vermont, 488; Washington, 665; West Virginia, 35; Wisconsin, 961; Wyoming, 127.

Total: 16,578

1996 Election

Harry Browne (Libertarian)

Alabama, 5,290 votes; Alaska, 2,276; Arizona, 14,358; Arkansas, 3,076; California, 73,600; Colorado, 12,392; Connecticut, 5,788; Delaware, 2,052; District of Columbia, 588; Florida, 23,965; Georgia, 17,870; Hawaii, 2,493; Idaho, 3,325; Illinois, 22,548; Indiana, 15,632; Iowa, 2,315; Kansas, 4,557; Kentucky, 4,009; Louisiana, 7,499; Maine, 2,996; Maryland, 8,765; Massachusetts, 20,426; Michigan, 27,670; Minnesota, 8,271; Mississippi, 2,809; Missouri, 10,522; Montana, 2,526; Nebraska, 2,792; Nevada, 4,460; New Hampshire, 4,237; New Jersey, 14,763; New Mexico, 2,996; New York, 12,220; North Carolina, 8,740; North Dakota, 847; Ohio, 12,851; Oklahoma, 5,505; Oregon, 8,903; Pennsylvania, 28,000; Rhode Island, 1,109; South Carolina, 4,271; South Dakota, 1,472; Tennessee, 5,020; Texas, 20,256; Utah, 4,129; Vermont, 1,183; Virginia, 9,174; Washington, 12,522; West Virginia, 3,062; Wisconsin, 7,929; Wyoming, 1,739.

Total: 485,798

Howard Phillips (U.S. Taxpayers)

Alabama, 2,365 votes; Alaska, 925; Arizona, 347; Arkansas, 2,065; California, 21,202; Colorado, 2,813; Connecticut, 2,425; Delaware, 348; Georgia, 145; Hawaii, 358; Idaho, 2,230; Illinois, 7,606; Indiana, 291; Iowa, 2,229; Kansas, 3,519; Kentucky, 2,204; Louisiana, 3,366; Maine, 1,517; Maryland, 3,402; Michigan, 539; Minnesota, 3,416; Mississippi, 2,314; Missouri, 11,521; Montana, 152; Nebraska, 1,928; Nevada, 1,732; New Hampshire, 1,346; New Jersey, 3,440; New Mexico, 713; New York, 23,580; North Carolina, 258; North Dakota, 745; Ohio, 7,361; Oregon, 3,379; Pennsylvania, 19,552; Rhode Island, 1,021; South Carolina, 2,043; South Dakota,

912; Tennessee, 1,818; Texas, 7,472; Utah, 2,601; Vermont, 382; Virginia, 13,687; Washington, 4,578; Wisconsin, 8,811.

Total: 184,658

John Hagelin (Natural Law)

Alabama, 1,697 votes; Alaska, 729; Arizona, 153; Arkansas, 729; California, 15,403; Colorado, 2,547; Connecticut, 1,703; Delaware, 274; District of Columbia, 283; Florida, 418; Hawaii, 570; Idaho, 1,600; Illinois, 4,606; Indiana, 118; Iowa, 3,349; Kansas, 1,655; Kentucky, 1,493; Louisiana, 2,981; Maine, 825; Maryland, 2,517; Massachusetts, 5,184; Michigan, 4,254; Minnesota, 1,808; Mississippi, 1,447; Missouri, 2,287; Montana, 1,754; Nebraska, 1,189; Nevada, 545; New Jersey, 3,887; New Mexico, 644; New York, 5,011; North Carolina, 2,771; North Dakota, 349; Ohio, 9,120; Oregon, 2,798; Pennsylvania, 5,783; Rhode Island, 435; South Carolina, 1,248; South Dakota, 316; Tennessee, 636; Texas, 4,422; Utah, 1,085; Vermont, 498; Virginia, 4,510; Washington, 6,076; Wisconsin, 1,379; Wyoming, 582.

Total: 113,668

Monica Moorehead (Workers World)

Arkansas, 747 votes; Colorado, 599; Louisiana, 1,678; Massachusetts, 3,277; Michigan, 3,153; New Jersey, 1,337; New York, 3,473; Ohio, 10,813; Rhode Island, 186; Utah, 298; Washington, 2,189; Wisconsin, 1,333.

Total: 29,083

Marsha Feinland (Peace and Freedom)

California, 25,332 votes.

Charles E. Collins (Independent)

Arizona, 36 votes; Arkansas, 823; California, 765; Colorado, 2,809; Georgia, 15; Idaho, 7; Indiana, 11; Kansas, 112; Maryland, 6; Mississippi, 1,205; Missouri, 62; Montana, 20; Tennessee, 688; Utah, 8; Washington, 2,374.

Total: 8,941

James E. Harris (Socialist Workers)

Alabama, 516 votes; California, 77; Colorado, 244; Connecticut, 4; District of Columbia, 257; Florida, 13; Georgia, 12; Iowa, 331; Minnesota, 684; New Jersey, 1,837; New York, 2,762; North Carolina, 84; Utah, 235; Vermont, 199; Washington, 738; Wisconsin, 483.

Total: 8,476

"None of These Candidates"

Nevada, 5,608 votes.

Dennis Peron (Grassroots)

Minnesota, 4,898 votes; Vermont 480.

Total: 5,378

Mary Cal Hollis (Socialist)

Arkansas, 538 votes; Colorado, 669; Florida, 21; Indiana, 59; Maryland, 4; Massachusetts, 61; Montana, 1; Oregon, 1,922; Texas, 297; Utah, 53; Vermont, 292; Wisconsin, 848.

Total: 4,765

Jerome White (Socialist Equality)

Michigan, 1,554 votes; Minnesota, 347, New Jersey, 537.

Total: 2,438

Diane Beall Templin (American)

Colorado, 557 votes; Utah, 1,290.

Total: 1,847

Earl F. Dodge (Prohibition)

Arkansas, 483 votes; Colorado, 375; Illinois, 1; Massachusetts, 4; Tennessee, 324; Utah, 111.

Total: 1,298

A. Peter Crane (Independent Party of Utah)

Utah, 1,101 votes.

Ralph Forbes (America First)

Arkansas, 932 votes.

John Birrenbach (Independent Grassroots)

Minnesota, 787 votes.

Isabell Masters (Looking Back)

Arkansas, 749 votes; California, 2; Maryland 1.

Total: 752

Steve Michael (Independent)

Tennessee, 408 votes.

Scattered write-ins[5]

Alabama, 1,123 votes; Alaska, 634; Arizona, 16; California, 25; Connecticut, 1; Delaware, 17; District of Columbia 648; Idaho, 1; Illinois, 10; Indiana, 9; Iowa, 1,240; Kentucky, 8; Maine, 144; Maryland, 20; Massachusetts, 6,182; Michigan, 1,817; Minnesota, 2,903; Montana, 5; New Hampshire, 2,456; Ohio, 15; Oregon, 2,329; Pennsylvania, 1,725; Rhode Island, 37; Tennessee, 190; Utah, 98; Vermont, 560; Wisconsin, 2,324.

Total: 24,537

---

1. *Georgia figures for Webster obtained from Svend Petersen, A Statistical History of the American Presidential Elections, Westport, Conn.: Greenwood Press, 1981, 31.*

2. *Troup figures obtained from Petersen, A Statistical History, 31.*

3. *Iowa and Mississippi figures from Petersen, A Statistical History, 81. Petersen lists these votes, as well as Progressive votes in all other states, for Theodore Roosevelt. In the ICPSR data for 1916, votes are listed for Progressive electors; Roosevelt's name does not appear. Since Roosevelt*

declined to be a candidate, *Congressional Quarterly* followed ICPSR in listing these votes as Progressive.

4. *MacArthur ran under a variety of party designations: Christian Nationalist in Arkansas, New Mexico, Tennessee, North Dakota and Washington; Christian Nationalist—Constitution in California and Texas; Constitution in Colorado; and Christian Nationalist—America First in Missouri.*

5. *Total does not include the 123,000 write-in and blank votes that were compiled as one total in New York.*

Presidential Primaries

After temporarily losing some popularity in the mid-1980s, presidential primaries today stand undisputed as the favored method of showing voter preferences among candidates for the major party nominations. The two parties combined held record numbers of primaries (including those in the District of Columbia and Puerto Rico) in 1992 and 1996: 79 each year. The Democrats held a record 40 primaries in 1992, while the Republicans bettered that with a record 43 in 1996 (when the incumbent president Bill Clinton faced no major challenge for renomination).

In most cases, the convention delegates were bound to vote for the candidates who received the most votes in their states, thus giving primary voters a direct and important role in the nominating of American presidential candidates. Not since George S. McGovern won the Democratic nomination in 1972 has a candidate obtained a major party nomination without first winning at least a plurality in the party's total primary vote.

Yet, entrenched as they now are in the electoral process, primaries are still relatively recent replacements for the old smoke-filled rooms where party bosses once dictated the choice of presidential nominees. Presidential primaries originated as an outgrowth of the Progressive movement in the early 20th century. Progressives, populists and reformers in general were fighting state and municipal corruption. They objected to the links between political bosses and big business and advocated returning the government to the people.

Part of this "return to the people" movement was a turn away from what were looked upon as boss-dominated political party conventions. It was only a matter of time before the primary idea spread from state and local elections to presidential contests. Because there was no provision for a nation-wide primary, state primaries were initiated to choose delegates to the national party conventions (delegate-selection primaries) and to register voters' preferences on their parties' eventual presidential nominees (preference primaries).

Florida enacted the first presidential primary law in 1901 (which went into effect for the 1904 nominating season). The law gave party officials an option of holding a party primary to choose any party candidate for public office, as well as delegates to the national conventions. However, there was no provision for placing names of presidential candidates on the ballot — either in the form of a preference vote or with information indicating the preference of the candidates for convention delegates.

Progressive Era to Modern Day

Wisconsin's Progressive Republican politician, Gov. Robert M. La Follette, gave a major boost to the presidential primary following the 1904 Republican National Convention. It was at that convention that the credentials of La Follette's Progressive delegation were rejected and a regular Republican delegation from Wisconsin was seated. Angered by what he considered his unfair treatment, La Follette returned to his home state and began pushing for a presidential primary law. The result was the Wisconsin law of 1905 mandating the direct election of national convention delegates. The law, however, did not include a provision for indicating the delegates' presidential preference.

Pennsylvania followed Wisconsin in 1906 with a statute providing that each candidate for delegate to a national convention could have printed beside his name on the official primary ballot the name of the presidential candidate he would support at the convention. However, no member of either party exercised this option in the 1908 primary.

La Follette's sponsorship of the delegate-selection primary helped make the concept a part of the Progressive political program. The growth of the Progressive movement rapidly resulted in the enactment of presidential primary laws in other states.

The next step in presidential primaries — the preferential vote for president — took place in Oregon. There, in

Sources

Cook, Rhodes. *U.S. Primary Elections 1995-1996*. Washington, D.C.: Congressional Quarterly, 1997.

Davis, James W. *Presidential Primaries: Road to the White House*. 1967. Reprint. Westport, Conn.: Greenwood Press, 1980.

Scammon, Richard M. *America Votes 1956-57*. New York: Macmillan, 1958. *America Votes*. Vol. 4. Pittsburgh: University of Pittsburgh Press, 1962. *America Votes*. Vols. 6, 8, 10. Washington, D.C.: Congressional Quarterly, 1966-1973.

Scammon, Richard M., and Alice V. McGillivray. *America Votes*. Vols. 12, 14, 16, 18, 20. Washington, D.C.: Congressional Quarterly, 1977-1993.

Types of Primaries and Procedures

There are two basic types of presidential primaries. One is the presidential preference primary in which voters vote directly for the person they wish to be nominated for president. The second is the type in which voters elect delegates to the national conventions.

States may use combinations of these methods:

- A state may have a preference vote but choose delegates at party conventions. The preference vote may or may not be binding on the delegates.

- A state may combine the preference and delegate-selection primaries by electing delegates pledged or favorable to a candidate named on the ballot. Under this system, however, state party organizations may run unpledged slates of delegates.

- A state may have an advisory preference vote and a separate delegate-selection vote in which delegates may be listed three ways: pledged to a candidate, favorable to a candidate or unpledged.

- A state may have a mandatory preference vote with a separate delegate-selection vote. In these cases, the delegates are required to reflect the preference primary vote.

Most primary states hold presidential preference votes, in which voters choose among the candidates who have qualified for the ballot in their states. Although preference votes may be binding or non-binding, in most states the vote is binding on the delegates, who are elected in the primary itself or chosen outside of it by a caucus process, by a state committee or by the candidates who have qualified to win delegates.

For those primaries in which the preference vote is binding upon delegates, state laws may vary as to the number of ballots through which delegates at the convention must remain committed. Delegates may be bound for as short as one ballot or as long as a candidate remains in the race. In 1980 national Democratic rules were changed to bind delegates for one ballot unless released by the candidate they were elected to support. The rule was dropped in subsequent elections. Until 1980 the Republicans had a rule requiring delegates bound to a specific candidate by state law in primary states to vote for that candidate at the convention regardless of their personal presidential preferences. That rule was repealed at the July 1980 convention.

Delegates from primary states are allocated to candidates in various ways. Most of the methods are based on the preference vote — proportional representation, statewide winner-take-all (in which the candidate winning the most votes statewide wins all the delegates), congressional district and statewide winner-take-all (in which the high vote-getter in a district wins that district's delegates and the high vote-getter statewide wins all the at-large delegates), or some combination of the three. Still another method is the selection of individual delegates in a "loophole," or direct election, primary. Then the preference vote is either nonbinding or there is no preference vote at all.

In the proportional representation system, the qualifying threshold for candidates to win delegates can vary. After a decade of intensive debate, Democratic leaders voted to require proportional representation in all primary and caucus states in 1980. This was made optional in 1984 and 1988. For 1992 and 1996 the Democrats again made proportional allocation mandatory, with candidates awarded delegates if they received 15 percent of the vote. Along with winner-take-all systems, the Democrats in the 1990s also banned winner-reward systems that gave extra delegates to primary or caucus victors.

The Republicans allow the primary states to set their own qualifying thresholds, which in many states were lower than the Democrats'. In Massachusetts in 1992, for example, a GOP candidate had to receive only 2.631 percent of the vote to win a delegate.

In nearly half the primary states, major candidates are placed on the ballot by the secretary of state or a special nominating committee. The consent of the candidate is required in only three states — Kentucky, Michigan and North Carolina. Elsewhere, candidates must take the initiative to get on the ballot. The filing requirements range from sending a letter of candidacy to election officials — the case in Puerto Rico — to filing petitions signed by a specified number of registered voters and paying a filing fee — the case in Alabama.

On many primary ballots, voters have the opportunity to choose a "uncommitted" category if they do not prefer any of the candidates. In 1996, 647,000 voters in Republican and Democratic primaries made such a choice.

1910, Sen. Jonathan Bourne, a Progressive Republican colleague of La Follette (then a senator), sponsored a referendum to establish a presidential preference primary, with delegates legally bound to support the primary winner. By 1912, with Oregon in the lead, 12 states had enacted presidential primary laws that provided for either direct election of delegates, a preferential vote, or both. The number had expanded to 26 states by 1916.

Primaries and Conventions

The first major test of the impact of presidential primary laws — in 1912 — demonstrated that victories in the primaries did not ensure a candidate's nomination. Former president Theodore Roosevelt, campaigning in 12 Republican primaries, won nine of them, including a defeat of incumbent Republican president William Howard Taft in Ohio, Taft's home state. Roosevelt lost to Taft by a narrow margin in Massachusetts and to La Follette in North Dakota and Wisconsin.

Despite this impressive string of primary victories, the convention rejected Roosevelt in favor of Taft. Taft supporters dominated the Republican National Committee, which ran the convention, and the convention's credentials committee, which ruled on contested delegates. Moreover, Taft was backed by many state organizations, especially in the South, where most delegates were chosen by caucuses or conventions dominated by party leaders.

On the Democratic side, the convention more closely reflected the primary results. Gov. Woodrow Wilson of New Jersey and Speaker of the House Champ Clark of Missouri were closely matched in total primary votes, with Wilson only 29,632 votes ahead of Clark. Wilson emerged with the nomination after a long convention struggle with Clark.

Votes Cast and Delegates Selected in Presidential Primaries, 1912-1996

	Democratic Party			Republican Party			Total	
Year	Number of Primaries	Votes Cast	Delegates Selected Through Primaries (%)	Number of Primaries	Votes Cast	Delegates Selected Through Primaries (%)	Votes Cast	Delegates Selected Through Primaries (%)
1912	12	974,775	32.9	13	2,261,240	41.7	3,236,015	37.3
1916	20	1,187,691	53.5	20	1,923,374	58.9	3,111,065	56.2
1920	16	571,671	44.6	20	3,186,248	57.8	3,757,919	51.2
1924	14	763,858	35.5	17	3,525,185	45.3	4,289,043	40.4
1928	16	1,264,220	42.2	15	4,110,288	44.9	5,374,508	43.5
1932	16	2,952,933	40.0	14	2,346,996	37.7	5,299,929	38.8
1936	14	5,181,808	36.5	12	3,319,810	37.5	8,501,618	37.0
1940	13	4,468,631	35.8	13	3,227,875	38.8	7,696,506	37.3
1944	14	1,867,609	36.7	13	2,271,605	38.7	4,139,214	37.7
1948	14	2,151,865	36.3	12	2,653,255	36.0	4,805,120	36.1
1952	16	4,928,006	38.7	13	7,801,413	39.0	12,729,419	38.8
1956	19	5,832,592	42.7	19	5,828,272	44.8	11,660,864	43.7
1960	16	5,686,664	38.3	15	5,537,967	38.6	11,224,631	38.5
1964	16	6,247,435	45.7	16	5,935,339	45.6	12,182,774	45.6
1968	15	7,535,069	40.2	15	4,473,551	38.1	12,008,620	39.1
1972	21	15,993,965	65.3	20	6,188,281	56.8	22,182,246	61.0
1976	27	16,052,652	76.0	26	10,374,125	71.0	26,426,777	73.5
1980	35	18,747,825	71.8	35	12,690,451	76.0	31,438,276	73.7
1984	30	18,009,217	52.4	25	6,575,651	71.0	24,584,868	59.6
1988	37	22,961,936	66.6	37	12,165,115	76.9	35,127,051	70.2
1992	40	20,239,385	66.9	39	12,696,547	83.9	32,935,932	72.7
1996	36	10,996,395	65.3	43	14,233,939	84.6	25,230,334	69.2

Source: Percentages of delegates selected are from *Selecting the President: From 1789-1996* (Washington, D.C.: Congressional Quarterly, 1997). 17.

Likewise, in 1916 Democratic primary results foreshadowed the winner of the nomination, although Wilson, who was then the incumbent, had no major opposition for renomination. But once again Republican presidential primaries had little impact upon the nominating process at the convention. The eventual nominee, Supreme Court justice Charles Evans Hughes, had won only two primaries.

In 1920, presidential primaries did not play a major role in determining the winner of either party's nomination. James M. Cox, the eventual Democratic nominee, ran in only one primary, his home state of Ohio. Most of the Democratic primaries featured favorite-son candidates or write-in votes. And at the convention Democrats took 44 ballots to settle on Cox.

Similarly, the main entrants in the Republican presidential primaries that year failed to capture their party's nomination. Sen. Warren G. Harding of Ohio, the compromise choice, won the primary in his home state but lost badly in Indiana and garnered only a handful of votes elsewhere. The three primary leaders — Sen. Hiram Johnson of California, Gen. Leonard Wood of New Hampshire and Gov. Frank O. Lowden of Illinois — lost out in the end.

After the first wave of enthusiasm for presidential primaries in the early years of the century, interest in them waned. By 1935, eight states had repealed their presidential primary laws. The diminution of reform zeal during the 1920s and the preoccupation of the country with the Great Depression in the 1930s and war in the 1940s appeared to have been leading factors in this decline. Also, party leaders were not enthusiastic about primaries; the cost of conducting them was relatively high, both for the candidates and the states. Many presidential candidates ignored the primaries, and voter participation often was low.

But after World War II interest picked up again. Some politicians with presidential ambitions, knowing the party leadership was not enthusiastic about their candidacies, entered the primaries to try to generate a bandwagon effect. In 1948 Harold Stassen, Republican governor of Minnesota from 1939 to 1943, entered presidential primaries in opposition to the Republican organization and made some headway before losing in Oregon to Gov. Thomas E. Dewey of New York. And in 1952 senator Estes Kefauver, D-Tenn., riding a wave of public recognition as head of the Senate Organized Crime Investigating Committee, challenged Democratic Party leaders by winning several primaries, including an upset of President Harry S. Truman in New Hampshire. The Eisenhower-Taft struggle for the Republican Party nomination that year also stimulated interest in the primaries.

In 1960, Sen. John F. Kennedy of Massachusetts challenged Sen. Hubert Humphrey of Minnesota in two primaries: Wisconsin, which bordered on Humphrey's home state, and West Virginia, a labor state with few Catholic voters. (Kennedy was Roman Catholic, and some questioned whether voters would elect a Catholic president.) After Kennedy won both primaries, Humphrey was forced to withdraw. Party leaders' efforts to draft an alternative to Kennedy

Selection by Caucus Method

In the current primary-dominated era of presidential politics, which began two decades ago, caucuses have survived in the quiet backwater of the nominating process.

The impact of caucuses decreased in the 1970s as the number of primaries grew dramatically. During the 1960s a candidate sought to run well in primary states mainly to have a bargaining chip with which to deal with powerful leaders in the caucus states. Republicans Barry M. Goldwater in 1964 and Richard Nixon in 1968 and Democrat Hubert H. Humphrey in 1968 all built up solid majorities among caucus state delegates that carried them to their parties' nominations. Humphrey did not even enter a primary in 1968.

After 1968 candidates placed their principal emphasis on primaries. First George McGovern in 1972 — and then incumbent Republican president Gerald R. Ford and Democratic challenger Jimmy Carter in 1976 — won nomination by securing large majorities of the primary state delegates. Neither McGovern nor Ford won a majority of the caucus state delegates. Carter was able to win a majority only after his opponents' campaigns collapsed.

Complex Method

Compared with a primary, the caucus system is complicated. Instead of focusing on a single primary election ballot, the caucus presents a multi-tiered system that involves meetings scheduled over several weeks, sometimes even months. There is mass participation at the first level only, with meetings often lasting several hours and attracting only the most enthusiastic and dedicated party members.

The operation of the caucus varies from state to state, and each party has its own set of rules. Most begin with precinct caucuses or some other type of local mass meeting open to all party voters. Participants, often publicly declaring their votes, elect delegates to the next stage in the process.

In smaller states such as Delaware and Hawaii, delegates are elected directly to a state convention, where the national convention delegates are chosen. In larger states such as Iowa, there is at least one more step. Most frequently, delegates are elected at the precinct caucuses to county conventions, where the national convention delegates are chosen.

Participation, even at the first level of the caucus process, is much lower than in primaries. Caucus participants usually are local party leaders and activists. Many rank-and-file voters find a caucus complex, confusing, or intimidating.

In a caucus state the focus is on one-on-one campaigning. Time, not money, is the most valuable resource. Because organization and personal campaigning are so important, an early start is far more crucial in a caucus state than in a primary. And because only a small segment of the electorate is targeted in most caucus states, candidates usually use media advertising sparingly.

Although the basic steps in the caucus process are the same for both parties, the rules that govern them are vastly different. Democratic rules have been revamped substantially since 1968, establishing national standards for grass-roots participation. Republican rules have remained largely unchanged, with the states given wide latitude in drawing up their delegate-selection plans.

Caucuses

For both the Republican and Democratic parties, the percentage of delegates elected from caucus states was on a sharp decline throughout the 1970s. But the Democrats broke the downward trend and elected more delegates by the caucus process in 1980 than in 1976.

Between 1980 and 1984 six states switched from a primary to a caucus system; none the other way. Since 1984 the trend has turned back toward primaries. In 1996 primaries were held in 41 states, the District of Columbia and Puerto Rico. The Democrats elected 65.3 percent of their national convention delegates in primaries, against only 16.8 percent in caucuses. (The remaining 17.9 percent were "superdelegate" party and elected officials.) The Republicans in 1992 chose 84.6 percent of delegates in primaries and the rest by caucus or state committee, with no superdelegates.

A strong showing in the caucuses by Walter F. Mondale in 1984 led many Democrats — and not only supporters of his chief rivals — to conclude that caucuses are inherently unfair. The mainstream Democratic coalition of party activists, labor union members and teachers dominated the caucuses in Mondale's behalf.

The caucus also came in for criticism in 1988. The Iowa Democratic caucuses were seen as an unrepresentative test dominated by liberal interest groups. And the credibility of the caucuses was shaken by the withdrawal from the race of the two winners — Democrat Richard A. Gephardt and Republican Robert Dole — within a month after the caucuses were held. Furthermore, several other state caucuses featured vicious infighting between supporters of various candidates.

In 1992 the presence of a favorite son, Sen. Tom Harkin, among the leading Democratic candidates for president further diminished the Iowa caucus' significance as a rival to the New Hampshire primary as an early indicator of the candidate to beat for the nomination. Harkin easily won his state's party caucus, but he soon dropped out after fading in the primaries elsewhere. By contrast, 20 years earlier, a surprise win in Iowa helped to propel Sen. George McGovern of South Dakota toward the Democratic nomination.

The major complaint about the caucus process is that it does not involve enough voters, and that the low turnouts are not so representative of voter sentiment as a higher-turnout primary.

Staunch defenders, however, believe a caucus has party-building attributes a primary cannot match. They note that several hours at a caucus can involve voters in a way that quickly casting a primary ballot does not. Following caucus meetings, the state party comes away with lists of thousands of voters who can be tapped to volunteer time or money, or even to run for local office. And, while the multi-tiered caucus process is often a chore for the state party to organize, a primary is substantially more expensive.

came to be viewed as undemocratic by rank-and-file voters. The primary had replaced approval by party leaders as the preferred route to the nomination.

Similarly, Sen. Barry M. Goldwater, R-Ariz., in 1964, former vice president Richard Nixon, R-Calif., in 1968 and Sen. George S. McGovern, D-S.D., in 1972 were able to use the primaries to show their vote-getting and organizational abilities on the way to becoming their party's presidential nominees.

The Democrats Begin to Tinker

Despite the growing importance of primaries, party leaders until 1968 maintained some control of the nominating process. With only a handful of the 15 to 20 primaries regularly contested, candidates could count on a short primary season. They began in New Hampshire in March, then tested their appeal during the spring in Wisconsin, Nebraska, Oregon and California before resuming their courtship of party leaders. In 1968 — admittedly an unusual year, with incumbent Democratic president Lyndon B. Johnson suddenly withdrawing from his race for re-election, and the leading Democratic candidate (Sen. Robert F. Kennedy of New York) assassinated a few weeks before the convention — Sen. Humphrey was able to gain the party's nomination without entering a single primary.

But after 1968 the Democrats began tinkering with the nominating rules, in an effort to reduce the alienation of liberals and minorities from the political system and to allow the people to choose their own leaders. The Republicans seldom made any changes in their rules. *(Democratic rules, box, p. 237; GOP rules, box, p. 238)* This era of grass-roots control produced for the Democrats presidential candidates such as McGovern, a liberal from South Dakota who lost in a landslide to Nixon in 1972, and Jimmy Carter, who beat incumbent president Gerald R. Ford in 1976 but lost to Ronald Reagan in 1980.

With a then-record high of 37 primaries held in 1980, the opportunity for mass participation in the nominating process was greater than ever before. President Carter and Republican nominee Reagan were the clear winners of the long 1980 primary season. Although Carter received a bare majority of the cumulative Democratic primary vote, he amassed a plurality of nearly 2.7 million votes over his major rival, Sen. Edward M. Kennedy of Massachusetts. With no opposition in the late primary contests, Reagan emerged as a more one-sided choice of GOP primary voters. He finished nearly 4.8 million votes ahead of his closest competitor, George Bush.

Disheartened by Carter's massive defeat in 1980, the Democrats revised their nominating rules for the 1984 election. The party created the so-called superdelegates; that is, delegate seats were reserved for party leaders who were not formally committed to any presidential candidate. This reform had two main goals. First, Democratic leaders wanted to ensure that the party's elected and appointed officials would participate at the convention. Second, they wanted to ensure that these uncommitted party leaders could play a major role in selecting the presidential nominee if no candidate was a clear front-runner.

While the reforms of the 1970s were designed to give more influence to grass-roots activists and less to party regulars, these revisions were intended to bring about a deliberative process in which experienced party leaders could help select a consensus Democratic nominee with a strong chance to win the presidency.

The Democrats' new rules had some expected, as well as unexpected, results. For the first time since 1968, the number of primaries declined and the number of caucuses increased. The Democrats held only 30 primaries in 1984. Yet, like McGovern in 1972 and Carter in 1976, Colorado senator Gary Hart used the primaries to pull ahead (temporarily) of former vice president Walter F. Mondale, an early front-runner whose strongest ties were to the party leadership and its traditional core elements. In 1984 the presence of superdelegates was important because about four out of five backed Mondale. (But Mondale did wind up with more primary votes than Hart.)

A few critics regarded the seating of superdelegates as undemocratic, and there were calls for reducing their numbers. Instead, the Democratic National Committee (DNC) set aside additional seats for party leaders, increasing the number of superdelegates from 14 percent of the delegates in 1984 to 18 percent in 1996. All members of the DNC are guaranteed convention seats, as are all Democratic governors. About 80 percent of the Democrats in Congress also are guaranteed seats.

The Republican Party does not guarantee delegate seats to its leaders, nor has the party created superdelegates. However, its rules permit less rigid pledging of delegates and generally have led to substantial participation by Republican leaders, despite the absence of such guarantees.

Regional Primaries and Super Tuesday

In addition to the Democrats' internal party concerns with the nominating process, other critics often cited the length of the primary season (nearly twice as long as the general election campaign), the expense, the physical strain on the candidates and the variations and complexities of state laws as problems of presidential primaries.

To deal with these problems, several states in 1974 and 1975 discussed the feasibility of creating regional primaries, in which individual states within a geographical region would hold their primaries on the same day. Supporters of the concept believed it would reduce candidate expenses and strain and would permit concentration on regional issues.

The idea achieved some limited success in 1976 when three Western states (Idaho, Nevada and Oregon) and three Southern states (Arkansas, Kentucky and Tennessee) — decided to organize regional primaries in each of their areas. However, the two groups chose May 25 to hold their primaries, thus defeating one of the main purposes of the plan by forcing candidates to shuttle across the country to cover both areas.

Attempts also were made in New England to construct a regional primary. But New Hampshire could not participate because its law requires the state to hold its primary at least one week before any other state. Hesitancy by the other New England state legislatures defeated the idea. Only Vermont joined Massachusetts, on March 2, in holding a simultaneous presidential primary, although New Hampshire voted only one week earlier.

In 1980 and 1984, limited regional primaries were held again in several areas of the country. In 1988, 36 states and the District of Columbia held presidential primaries. More and more states, hoping to increase their impact on the presidential campaign, decided to hold their primaries early. When South Dakota announced its Feb. 23 primary date, New Hampshire moved its date to Feb. 16.

Sixteen states — eleven from the South — held primaries on Super Tuesday, March 8, 1988. The parties' long-held goal of a regional primary was finally realized. Most of

Choosing a Running Mate: The Balancing Act

In modern times with presidential candidates wrapping up their party's nominations early in the primary season, the greatest suspense before a national convention has centered on the selection of a running mate. But this closely watched selection process is a recent development. During the country's first years, the runner-up for the presidency automatically took the second slot.

That system did not last long. In 1800 Thomas Jefferson and Aaron Burr found themselves in a tie for electoral votes. Neither man's supporters were willing to settle for the lesser office. The deadlock went to the House of Representatives, where Jefferson needed 36 ballots to clinch the presidency. It also led to the 12th Amendment to the U.S. Constitution, ratified in 1804, providing for separate Electoral College balloting for president and vice president. With the emergence of political parties after 1800, candidates ran as teams. Once party conventions began in 1831, delegates, with the guidance of party bosses, began to do the choosing.

In fact, it was only in 1940 that presidential nominees began regularly hand-picking their running mates. That year, after failing to persuade Secretary of State Cordell Hull to accept the vice presidency, Franklin D. Roosevelt forced Henry A. Wallace on a reluctant Democratic convention by threatening to not run a third time if Wallace was rejected. The only exception to the practice Roosevelt established came in 1956, when Democrat Adlai E. Stevenson left the choice up to the convention.

If the selection of a running mate often seemed like something of an afterthought, it could be because the position itself was not especially coveted. John Adams, the first to hold the job, once complained, "My country has in its wisdom contrived for me the most insignificant office that ever the intention of man contrived or his imagination conceived." More than a century later Thomas R. Marshall, Woodrow Wilson's vice president, expressed a similarly dismal view: "Once there were two brothers. One ran away to sea; the other was elected Vice President. And nothing was ever heard of either of them again."

Writing in *Atlantic* in 1974, historian Arthur Schlesinger Jr. suggested the office be done away with. "It is a doomed office," he commented. "The Vice President has only one serious thing to do: that is, to wait around for the President to die." But there is a reasonable chance that whoever fills the position will get a chance to move up, either by succession or election. As of 1997, 14 presidents had held the second-ranking post, seven in the 20th century.

Also, since the 1970s the vice presidency has evolved from the somnolent office it once was; during this period four vice presidents enjoyed responsibility their predecessors did not. Nelson A. Rockefeller, who served under Gerald R. Ford, was given considerable authority in domestic policy coordination. Walter F. Mondale and George Bush helped to set policy for their respective presidents. And Bill Clinton placed Al Gore in charge of a "reinventing government" task force. Many aspiring politicians now see the office as the premiere base from which to campaign for the presidency.

Yet whoever is selected is often scrutinized for how well the choice balances (or unbalances) the ticket. One important factor is geography, which Clinton of Arkansas used unconventionally in choosing Sen. Gore of Tennessee to form the first successful all-Southern ticket in 164 years. Other traditional factors weighed by nominees are religion and ethnicity. In modern national politics, however, those considerations seemed to be losing their place to race, gender and age. In 1984, for example, the Democrats chose Rep. Geraldine A. Ferraro of New York to be their vice presidential candidate, the first woman to receive a major party nomination.

Although no African American has so far been selected by either party, many Democrats thought that Jesse L. Jackson deserved second place on the ticket in 1988. Jackson had received 29 percent of the primary vote to 43 percent for Michael Dukakis. Instead, the 54-year-old Dukakis chose Sen. Lloyd Bentsen of Texas, then 67, balancing the Democratic ticket by age as well as geographically and philosophically.

In 1988 George Bush surprised many by selecting Sen. Dan Quayle of Indiana. Quayle was 41 years old and had a relatively brief career in politics — two terms in the House of Representatives before his election to the Senate in 1980. Because of Quayle's youth and good looks, it was even suggested by some critics that Bush had selected him to appeal to young voters and women. Some disturbing revelations about Quayle's education and National Guard service along with his tendency to misspeak fostered doubts that he was qualified to serve a "heartbeat" away from the presidency. But Bush vigorously defended his choice, and the two won in 1988. The ticket, however, lost a reelection bid in 1992 .

For his running mate, the 46-year-old Clinton, in another unbalancing act, selected someone in his own age group (Gore, 44) rather than an elder statesman such as Bentsen (who served as Clinton's first secretary of the Treasury). But what the Clinton-Gore ticket lacked in the traditional sense, it made up with a balance of the candidates' other attributes. As governor of Arkansas, Clinton lacked foreign policy experience and had a mixed environmental record. Gore had a strong foreign policy and environmental record during his House and Senate terms in Congress.

---

the GOP primaries were winner-take-all, and when George Bush swept every Republican primary on Super Tuesday, he effectively locked up the GOP nomination. His major opponent, Sen. Robert Dole, withdrew the following week. For the Democrats, Gov. Michael Dukakis also broke through on Super Tuesday, but the Rev. Jesse Jackson — the first serious black candidate for a major party presidential nomination — kept the contest going into June.

'March Madness'

In 1992, Super Tuesday had become part of a general rush among states to hold their primaries as early as possible and thus help to determine the ultimate nominees. Dubbed "March Madness," the early clustering of primaries — 17 states held primaries in February or March — was viewed with dismay by some political analysts. They said it could lead to nominees being locked in before most voters knew what was happening, resulting in less informed and deliberative voting in the general election.

As winner in the eight Super Tuesday primaries (six of which were again in the South) on March 10, 1992, President Bush was well on his way to his eventual GOP renomination. Although he lost the two New England primaries (Massachuestts and Rhode Island) that day, Bill Clinton by winning all six southern primaries (Florida, Louisiana, Mississippi, Oklahoma, Tennessee and Texas) established himself as the frontrunner. Most of his competitors dropped out of the race the following week. Former governor Jerry Brown of California held out till the Democratic convention, but Brown was never able to establish any sort of momentum to overtake Clinton.

In 1996, the process was even more heavily weighted in favor of early primaries with two-thirds of the primaries being held before the end of March. The idea of regional primaries also came the closest to fruition in 1996. "Junior Tuesday Week" (March 2-7) had 11 primaries (six of which were in New England); Super Tuesday (March 12) had seven primaries (six of which were in the South); and "Big Ten" Tuesday (March 19) had four primaries in important midwestern states. By the time California (which had moved it primary forward in hope of increasing its sway on the nominating process) had its primary on March 26 (along with two other Western states — Nevada and Washington), Kansas senator Bob Dole had all but clinched the Republican nomination.

Ballot Access and Third Parties

Despite the potential of third party presidential candidates to influence American politics, the electoral process continues to favor the two major parties' candidates for president. Since the advent of the so-called Australian ballot in the late 1800s, states — not parties — have compiled the official election ballots. Democratic and Republican candidates are now listed automatically, but for third party or independent candidates, getting on the ballot is an arduous and costly process.

The restrictions vary from state to state, but all states have requirements to keep the ballot from becoming unwieldy and to discourage frivolous or non-serious candidates. Usually the third party or independent must submit petitions with valid voters' signatures, which can vary from as few as 25 in Tennessee to 3 to 5 percent of the state's registered voters, which can run into several hundred thousand.

But starting with the American Independent Party candidacy of Gov. George Wallace in 1968, the year the movement to open up the major parties' presidential nominating process also began, a series of court cases has eased ballot access laws for third party presidential candidates. Wallace in 1968, John Anderson in 1980, Ross Perot in 1992 and 1996 (under Reform Party banner), and Libertarian and New Alliance Party candidates in recent years, have been able to get on the ballot in every state. Nevertheless, ballot access laws still serve as a considerable hurdle for third party and independent candidates, who must spend time gathering signatures for petitions and raising money, while major party candidates get easier access to the ballot, and public money up front. (Third party candidates do not qualify for federal matching funds until after they receive 5 percent of the vote in a contest.)

The major parties have an even stronger grip on ballot access for races below the presidential level. In Florida, for example, a third party or independent candidate for governor or senator needs signatures on petitions from at least 3 percent of the voters registered in the previous election —

Presidents' Re-election Chances

The record of 20th century U.S. presidential elections indicates that a smooth path to renomination is essential for incumbents seeking re-election. Every president who actively sought renomination this century was successful. And those who were virtually unopposed within their own party won another term. But all the presidents who faced significant opposition for renomination ended up losing in the general election.

The following chart shows the presidents who sought re-election to a second term since 1900, whether they had "clear sailing" or "tough sledding" for renomination and their fate in the general election.

A president with an asterisk (*) next to his name was, like Ronald Reagan in 1984, completing his first full four-year term when he sought re-election. A dash (—) indicates there were no presidential preference primaries. The primary vote for President Lyndon B. Johnson in 1964 included the vote for favorite sons and uncommitted delegate slates. George Bush in 1992 had to fight off a significant challenge by Patrick J. Buchanan in the primaries before he went on to win 95 percent of the convention delegates.

	Incumbent's Percentage of:		
	Primary Vote	Convention Delegates	General Election Result
'Clear Sailing'			
William McKinley (1900) *	—	100%	Won
Theodore Roosevelt (1904)	—	100	Won
Woodrow Wilson (1916) *	99%	99	Won
Calvin Coolidge (1924)	68	96	Won
Franklin D. Roosevelt (1936) *	93	100	Won
Franklin D. Roosevelt (1940)	72	86	Won
Franklin D. Roosevelt (1944)	71	92	Won
Harry S. Truman (1948)	64	75	Won
Dwight D. Eisenhower (1956) *	86	100	Won
Lyndon B. Johnson (1964)	88	100	Won
Richard Nixon (1972) *	87	99	Won
Ronald Reagan (1984) *	99	100	Won
Bill Clinton (1996) *	88	100	Won
'Tough Sledding'			
William H. Taft (1912) *	34%	52%	Lost
Herbert Hoover (1932) *	33	98	Lost
Gerald R. Ford (1976)	53	53	Lost
Jimmy Carter (1980) *	51	64	Lost
George Bush (1992) *	72	95	Lost

more than 200,000 signatures. Since this state law was adopted in the 1920s, no candidate other than a Democrat or Republican has ever been on the Florida ballot for governor or senator.

Moreover, in Florida and other states, third party and independent candidates must file earlier than the major party candidates — often months before they know who the major party candidates will be.

It should be noted, however, that independents were elected governors of Alaska and Connecticut in 1990 and Maine in 1994, and independent presidential candidate Perot

VPs Who Have Run For President

Fourteen men who served as vice president have become president: John Adams, Thomas Jefferson, Martin Van Buren, John Tyler, Millard Fillmore, Andrew Johnson, Chester A. Arthur, Theodore Roosevelt, Calvin Coolidge, Harry S. Truman, Richard Nixon, Lyndon B. Johnson, Gerald R. Ford and George Bush.

Of those, all but Adams, Jefferson, Van Buren, Nixon and Bush first became president on the death or resignation of their predecessor. Eight vice presidents since 1900 have run unsuccessfully for president:

• Thomas R. Marshall, Democratic vice president under Woodrow Wilson from 1913 to 1921, failed to win the nomination in 1920.

• Charles G. Dawes, Republican vice president under Coolidge from 1925 to 1929, unsuccessfully sought the nomination in 1928 and 1932.

• John Nance Garner, Democratic vice president under Franklin D. Roosevelt from 1933 to 1941, ran unsuccessfully for the nomination in 1940.

• Henry A. Wallace, Democratic vice president under Roosevelt from 1941 to 1945, was Progressive Party nominee in 1948.

• Alben W. Barkley, Democratic vice president under Truman from 1949 to 1953, failed to win the 1952 nomination.

• Nixon, Republican vice president under Dwight D. Eisenhower from 1953 to 1961, was the GOP nominee in 1960. (He won in 1968 and 1972.)

• Hubert H. Humphrey, Democratic vice president under Lyndon Johnson from 1965 to 1969, was the Democratic nominee in 1968.

• Walter F. Mondale, Democratic vice president under Jimmy Carter from 1977 to 1981, was the Democratic nominee in 1984.

received 18.9 percent of the popular vote in 1992 — the highest third party finish since the 27.4 percent that Theodore Roosevelt received as the Bull Moose candidate in 1912. The American voters will, occasionally, abandon the two party system — but they also seem to want to return to it after the issues that give rise to third party movements are resolved.

Approaches to Reform

After reviewing the 1996 primary season, some Republican leaders questioned the wisdom of rushing the nominating process. One advantage of having so many primaries clustered in the beginning of the year is that a party can unite early behind a nominee, so that the summer convention can focus on the November election instead of intraparty squabbles. However, many felt that the "front-loaded" primary schedule favored too heavily the best-known candidates who already have advantages in funding and endorsements. The Republican Party took steps to move primaries back for the election in 2000. One step was to grant bonus GOP delegates to those states that hold their primaries in May or June, rather than in March or April.

It is no accident that the last two times that dark horse candidates have successfully challenged front-runners were in the 1970s (George McGovern in 1972 and Jimmy Carter in 1976). In that era, the primary season started slowly, and little-known candidates had the time to raise money and momentum after doing well in the early rounds.

But change may not come easy. For a number of years, most states have assumed that attention from the candidates and media was worth more than delegates. And it has been axiomatic that a state's best chance of getting such attention was to schedule its primary as early as possible. In 1996 the advantages of having regional primaries may have been counterbalanced by the disadvantages of having all of them so close together in March. Both parties (especially the party that loses the White House) are likely to continue to refine the primary schedule in coming years.

In the past, various approaches to changing the primary system have been attempted at the national level. One suggested change was to establish a direct national primary. But a Democratic study commission as well as several academic groups that examined the idea rejected it. The consensus was that such a process would strip the party leadership of any role in the nominating process, enable presidential candidates to run factional or regional campaigns and increase the primacy of media "image" over serious discussion of the issues.

Since 1911 hundreds of bills have been introduced in Congress to reform the presidential primary system. Most of them appeared during sessions after the 1912, 1952 and 1968 nominating campaigns. These three campaigns produced the feeling among many voters that the will of the electorate, as expressed in the primaries, had been thwarted by national conventions. But since 1911, the only legislation enacted by Congress concerned the presidential primary in the District of Columbia.

No political leader wants, and no political scientist expects, an abandonment of primaries, or a return to the selection of candidates by party leaders. But as this discussion should have shown, our political system remains alive, and capable of significant change if the need for change should arise.

Presidential Primary Returns, 1912-1996

Sources: Presidential Primary Returns

The main source for the primary returns from 1912 through 1952 is James W. Davis, *Presidential Primaries: Road to the White House* (Westport, Conn.: Greenwood Press, 1980).

Congressional Quarterly has supplemented Davis' material with the following sources: Louise Overacker, *The Presidential Primary* (New York: Arno, 1974) — the source used by Davis for the 1912-24 returns; Walter Kravitz, "Presidential Preference Primaries, 1928-56," a 1960 Library of Congress study; Paul Davis, Malcolm Moos and Ralph Goldman, *Presidential Nominating Politics in 1952* (Baltimore: Johns Hopkins Press, 1954); the offices of the secretaries of state; and state handbooks and newspapers. All statistics and footnotes are from Davis, unless otherwise indicated.

The basic source for the primary returns from 1956 to 1992 is Richard M. Scammon and Alice V. McGillivray, *America Votes* series (Washington, D.C.: Congressional Quarterly, 1957-1993). All statistics and footnotes are from Scammon-McGillivray, unless otherwise indicated. The sources for the 1996 presidential primaries are Rhodes Cook, *U.S. Primary Elections: President, Congress, Governors: 1995-1996*, (Congressional Quarterly, 1997) and *Federal Elections 96* (Washington, D.C.: Federal Election Commission, 1997).

Figures in the following charts represent one of three types of votes:

- Votes cast directly for a presidential candidate.
- Votes cast for delegates whose candidate preference was indicated on the ballot.
- Votes cast for unpledged delegates. (Included in the "unpledged" category were delegates designated on the ballot as "uninstructed" and "no preference.")

For the delegate-at-large vote in 1912-24 primaries, Overacker listed the average vote for delegates at large. For the 1928-52 delegate-at-large vote, Davis listed the highest vote received by any one delegate at large. Congressional Quarterly followed Davis' style for subsequent years.

Percentages in the following tables have been calculated to two decimal points and then rounded; 0.05 percent appears as 0.1 percent. Therefore, columns of percentages do not always total 100 percent. Major presidential candidates, primary winners, favorite sons, members of Congress and prominent national and state political figures are included in the state-by-state primary results. Minor candidates, including most write-ins, have been grouped in the "Others" category.

The primary tables show only Republican and Democratic contests; other candidates receiving votes in third party presidential primaries are listed in the footnotes.

1912 Primaries

Republican			Democratic		
				Votes	%

March 19 North Dakota

Robert M. LaFollette (Wis.)	34,123	57.2	John Burke (N.D.)[1]	9,357	100.0
Theodore Roosevelt (N.Y.)	23,669	39.7			
William H. Taft (Ohio)	1,876	3.1			

March 26 New York[2]

April 2 Wisconsin

LaFollette	133,354	73.2	Woodrow Wilson (N.J.)	45,945	55.7
Taft	47,514	26.1	Champ Clark (Mo.)	36,464	44.2
Roosevelt	628	.3	Others	148	.2
Others	643	.4			

April 9 Illinois

Roosevelt	266,917	61.1	Clark	218,483	74.3
Taft	127,481	29.2	Wilson	75,527	25.7
LaFollette	42,692	9.8			

April 13 Pennsylvania

Roosevelt	282,853[3]	59.7	Wilson	98,000[3]	100.0
Taft	191,179[3]	40.3			

April 19 Nebraska

Roosevelt	45,795	58.7	Clark	21,027	41.0
LaFollette	16,785	21.5	Wilson	14,289	27.9
Taft	13,341	17.1	Judson Harmon (Ohio)	12,454	24.3
Others	2,036	2.6	Others	3,499	6.8

April 19 Oregon

Roosevelt	28,905	40.2	Wilson	9,588	53.0
LaFollette	22,491	31.3	Clark	7,857	43.4
Taft	20,517	28.5	Harmon	606	3.3
Others	14	—	Others	49	.3

April 30 Massachusetts

Taft	86,722	50.4	Clark	34,575	68.9
Roosevelt	83,099	48.3	Wilson	15,002	29.9
LaFollette	2,058	1.2	Others	627	1.2
Others	99	.1			

May 6 Maryland

Roosevelt	29,124	52.8	Clark	34,021	54.4
Taft	25,995	47.2	Wilson	21,490	34.3
			Harmon	7,070	11.3

May 14 California

Roosevelt	138,563	54.6	Clark	43,163	71.5
Taft	69,345	27.3	Wilson	17,214	28.5
LaFollette	45,876	18.1			

May 21 Ohio

Roosevelt	165,809	55.3	Harmon	96,164	51.7
Taft	118,362	39.5	Wilson	85,084	45.7
LaFollette	15,570	5.2	Clark	2,428	1.3
			Others	2,440	1.3

Republican

Democratic

	Votes	%		Votes	%
May 28 New Jersey					
Roosevelt	61,297	56.3	Wilson	48,336	98.9
Taft	44,034	40.5	Clark[4]	522	1.1
LaFollette	3,464	3.2			
June 4 South Dakota					
Roosevelt	38,106	55.2	Wilson[5]	4,694	35.2
Taft	19,960	28.9	Clark[5]	4,275	32.0
LaFollette	10,944	15.9	Clark[5]	2,722	20.4
			Others	1,655	12.4
TOTALS					
Roosevelt	1,164,765	51.5	Wilson	435,169	44.6
Taft	766,326	33.9	Clark	405,537	41.6
LaFollette	327,357	14.5	Harmon	116,294	11.9
Others	2,792	.1	Burke	9,357	1.0
			Others	8,418	.9
	2,261,240			974,775	

1. Burke was the "favorite son" candidate, according to the North Dakota secretary of state.
2. Primary law optional in 1912. Republicans elected pledged delegates but figures not available.
3. Unofficial figures.
4. Write-in.

5. No presidential preference. Three sets of delegates ran: one labelled "Wilson-Bryan" which came out openly for Wilson; one "Wilson-Clark-Bryan" which became identified with Clark; one Champ Clark which was accused by the Clark people of being a scheme to split the Clark vote. The "Wilson-Clark-Bryan" list polled 4,275 and the Champ Clark list 2,722. The delegates were given to Wilson by the convention.

1916 Primaries

	Republican			Democratic	
	Votes	%		Votes	%
March 7 Indiana					
Charles W. Fairbanks (Ind.)[1]	176,078	100.0	Woodrow Wilson (N.J.)	160,423	100.0
March 14 Minnesota					
Albert B. Cummins (Iowa)	54,214	76.8	Wilson	45,136	100.0
Others	16,403	23.2			
March 14 New Hampshire					
Unpledged delegates	9,687	100.0	Wilson	5,684	100.0
March 21 North Dakota					
Robert M. LaFollette (Wis.)	23,374[2]	70.4	Wilson	12,341	100.0
Others	9,851[2]	29.6			
April 3 Michigan					
Henry Ford (Mich.)	83,057	47.4	Wilson	84,972	100.0
William A. Smith (Mich.)	77,872	44.4			
William O. Simpson (Mich.)	14,365	8.2			
April 4 New York					
Unpledged delegates	147,038	100.0	Wilson	112,538	100.0
April 4 Wisconsin					
LaFollette[1]	110,052	98.8	Wilson	109,462	99.8
Others	1,347	1.2	Others	231	.2
April 11 Illinois					
Lawrence Y. Sherman (Ill.)[1]	155,945	90.2	Wilson	136,839	99.8
Theodore Roosevelt (N.Y.)[3]	15,348	8.9	Others	219	.2
Others	1,689	1.0			
April 18 Nebraska					
Cummins	29,850	33.7	Wilson	69,506	87.7
Ford	26,884	30.3	Others	9,744	12.3
Charles E. Hughes (N.Y.)[3]	15,837	17.9			
Roosevelt[3]	2,256	2.5			
Others	13,780	15.6			
April 21 Montana					
Cummins	10,415	89.9	Wilson	17,960	100.0
Others	1,173	10.1			
April 25 Iowa					
Cummins	40,257	100.0	Wilson	31,447	100.0
April 25 Massachusetts					
Unpledged delegates at large[4]	60,462	57.3	Wilson	19,580	100.0
Roosevelt[4]	45,117	42.7			
April 25 New Jersey					
Roosevelt[3]	1,076	73.7	Wilson	25,407	100.0
Hughes[3]	383	26.3			

	Republican			**Democratic**	
	Votes	%		Votes	%

April 25   Ohio

	Votes	%		Votes	%
Theodore E. Burton (Ohio)[1]	122,165	86.8	Wilson	82,688	97.2
Roosevelt[3]	1,932	1.4	Others	2,415	2.8
Ford[3]	1,683	1.2			
Hughes[3]	469	.3			
Others	14,428	10.3			

May 2   California

	Votes	%		Votes	%
Unpledged delegates	236,277	100.0	Wilson	75,085	100.0

May 16   Pennsylvania

	Votes	%		Votes	%
Martin G. Brumbaugh (Pa.)[1]	233,095	86.3	Wilson	142,202	98.7
Ford[3]	20,265	7.5	Others	1,839	1.3
Roosevelt[3]	12,359	4.6			
Hughes[3]	1,804	.7			
Others	2,682	1.0			

May 16   Vermont

	Votes	%		Votes	%
Hughes[3]	5,480	70.0	Wilson	3,711	99.4
Roosevelt[3]	1,931	24.6	Others	23	.6
Others	423	5.4			

May 19   Oregon

	Votes	%		Votes	%
Hughes	56,764	59.8	Wilson	27,898	100.0
Cummins	27,558	29.0			
Others	10,593	11.2			

May 23   South Dakota

	Votes	%		Votes	%
Cummins	29,656	100.0	Wilson	10,341	100.0

June 6   West Virginia

[5]			[5]		

TOTALS

	Votes	%		Votes	%
Unpledged delegates	453,464	23.6	Wilson	1,173,220	98.8
Brumbaugh	233,095	12.1	Others	14,471	1.2
Cummins	191,950	10.0			
Fairbanks	176,078	9.2		1,187,691	
Sherman	155,945	8.1			
LaFollette	133,426	6.9			
Ford	131,889	6.9			
Burton	122,165	6.4			
Hughes	80,737	4.2			
Roosevelt	80,019	4.2			
Smith	77,872	4.0			
Simpson	14,365	.7			
Others[6]	72,369	3.8			
	1,923,374				

1. Source for names of "favorite son" candidates: The New York Times.
2. Source for vote breakdown: North Dakota secretary of state.
3. Write-in.
4. No presidential preference vote but one set of delegates at large was for Roosevelt and the other set unpledged.

5. Figures not available. Republican winner was Sen. Theodore E. Burton (R Ohio) and Democratic winner was Woodrow Wilson, according to The New York Times.
6. In addition to scattered votes, "others" includes Robert G. Ross who received 5,-506 votes in the Nebraska primary; Henry D. Estabrook who received 9,851 in the North Dakota primary and 8,132 in the Nebraska primary.

1920 Primaries

Republican	Votes	%	Democratic	Votes	%
March 9 New Hampshire					
Leonard Wood (N.H.)[1]	8,591	53.0	Unpledged delegates[1]	7,103	100.0
Unpledged delegates	5,604	34.6			
Hiram Johnson (Calif.)[1]	2,000	12.3			
March 16 North Dakota					
Johnson[2]	30,573	96.1	William G. McAdoo (N.Y.)[2]	49	12.6
Leonard Wood[2]	987	3.1	Others[2]	340	87.4
Frank O. Lowden (Ill.)[2]	265	.8			
March 23 South Dakota					
Leonard Wood	31,265	36.5	Others	6,612	100.0
Lowden	26,981	31.5			
Johnson	26,301	30.7			
Others	1,144	1.3			
April 5 Michigan					
Johnson	156,939	38.4	McAdoo	18,665	21.1
Leonard Wood	112,568[3]	27.5	Edward I. Edwards (N.J.)	16,642	18.8
Lowden	62,418	15.3	A. Mitchell Palmer (Pa.)	11,187	12.6
Herbert C. Hoover (Calif.)	52,503	12.8	Others	42,000	47.5
Others	24,729	6.0			
April 6 New York					
Unpledged delegates	199,149	100.0	Unpledged delegates	113,300	100.0
April 6 Wisconsin[4]					
Leonard Wood[2]	4,505	15.0	James M. Cox (Ohio)[2]	76	2.2
Hoover[2]	3,910	13.0	Others	3,391	97.8
Johnson[2]	2,413	8.0			
Lowden[2]	921	3.1			
Others	18,350	60.9			
April 13 Illinois					
Lowden	236,802	51.1	Edwards[2]	6,933	32.3
Leonard Wood	156,719	33.8	McAdoo[2]	3,838	17.9
Johnson	64,201	13.8	Cox[2]	266	1.2
Hoover[2]	3,401	.7	Others	10,418	48.6
Others	2,674	.6			
April 20 Nebraska					
Johnson	63,161	46.2	Gilbert M. Hitchcock (Neb.)	37,452	67.3
Leonard Wood	42,385	31.0	Others	18,230	32.7
John J. Pershing (Mo.)	27,669	20.3			
Others	3,432	2.5			
April 23 Montana					
Johnson	21,034	52.4	Others[2]	2,994	100.0
Leonard Wood	6,804	17.0			
Lowden	6,503	16.2			
Hoover	5,076	12.6			
Warren G. Harding (Ohio)	723	1.8			
April 27 Massachusetts					
Unpledged delegates	93,356	100.0	Unpledged delegates	21,226	100.0

Republican			Democratic		
	Votes	%		Votes	%

April 27   New Jersey

Leonard Wood	52,909	50.2	Edwards	4,163	91.4
Johnson	51,685	49.0	McAdoo[3]	180	4.0
Hoover	900	.9	Others	213	4.7

April 27   Ohio

Harding	123,257	47.6	Cox	85,838	97.8
Leonard Wood	108,565	41.9	McAdoo[2]	292	.3
Johnson[2]	16,783	6.5	Others	1,647	1.9
Hoover[2]	10,467	4.0			

May 3   Maryland

Leonard Wood	15,900	66.4	[5]		
Johnson	8,059	33.6			

May 4   California

Johnson	369,853	63.9	Unpledged delegates	23,831	100.0
Hoover	209,009	36.1			

May 4   Indiana

Leonard Wood	85,708	37.9	[5]		
Johnson	79,840	35.3			
Lowden	39,627	17.5			
Harding	20,782	9.2			

May 18   Pennsylvania

Edward R. Wood (Pa.)	257,841	92.3	Palmer[6]	80,356	73.7
Johnson[2]	10,869	3.8	McAdoo	26,875	24.6
Leonard Wood[2]	3,878	1.4	Edwards[2]	674	.6
Hoover[2]	2,825	1.0	Others	1,132	1.0
Others[2]	4,059	1.5			

May 18   Vermont

Leonard Wood	3,451	66.1	McAdoo[2]	137	31.4
Hoover[2]	564	10.8	Edwards[2]	58	13.3
Johnson[2]	402	7.7	Cox[2]	14	3.2
Lowden[2]	29	.5	Others	227	52.1
Others	777	14.9			

May 21   Oregon

Johnson	46,163	38.4	McAdoo	24,951	98.6
Leonard Wood	43,770	36.5	Others	361	1.4
Lowden	15,581	13.0			
Hoover	14,557	12.1			

May 25   West Virginia

Leonard Wood	27,255	44.6	[5]		
Others	33,849 [7]	55.4			

	Republican				Democratic		
	Votes	%				Votes	%
June 5 North Carolina							
Johnson	15,375	73.3	[5]				
Leonard Wood	5,603	26.7					
TOTALS							
Johnson	965,651	30.3		Unpledged delegates		165,460	28.9
Leonard Wood	710,863	22.3		Palmer		91,543	16.0
Lowden	389,127	12.2		Cox		86,194	15.0
Hoover	303,212	9.5		McAdoo		74,987	13.1
Unpledged delegates	298,109	9.4		Hitchcock		37,452	6.6
Edward R. Wood	257,841	8.1		Edwards		28,470	5.0
Harding	144,762	4.5		Others [9]		87,565	15.3
Pershing	27,669	.9					
Others [8]	89,014	2.8				571,671	
	3,186,248						

1. Source: Louise Overacker, The Presidential Primaries (1926), p. 238-39. There was no preference vote. In the Republican primary, figures given were for delegates at large favoring Wood and Johnson. In the Democratic primary, although delegates were unpledged, the organization (Robert Charles Murchie) group was understood to be for Hoover. The highest Democratic Hoover delegate received 3,714 votes.

2. Write-in.

3. Source: Overacker, op. cit., p. 238.

4. No names entered for presidential preference in the Republican primary. The real contest lay between two lists of delegates, one headed by Robert M. La Follette and the other by Emanuel L. Philipp.

5. No names entered and no preference vote recorded.

6. Source for name of "favorite son" candidate: The New York Times.

7. Most of these votes were received by Sen. Howard Sutherland (R W.Va.). The figure is unofficial.

8. In addition to scattered votes, "others" includes Robert G. Ross who received 1,698 votes in the Nebraska primary.

9. In addition to scattered votes, "others" includes Robert G. Ross who received 13,179 in the Nebraska primary.

1924 Primaries

	Republican			Democratic		
	Votes	%		Votes	%	

March 11   New Hampshire

Calvin Coolidge (Mass.)	17,170	100.0	Unpledged delegates	6,687	100.0	

March 18   North Dakota

Coolidge	52,815	42.1	William G. McAdoo (Calif.)	11,273	100.0	
Robert M. LaFollette (Wis.)	40,252	32.1				
Hiram Johnson (Calif.)	32,363	25.8				

March 25   South Dakota

Johnson	40,935	50.7	McAdoo[1]	6,983	77.4	
Coolidge	39,791	49.3	Unpledged delegates[1]	2,040	22.6	

April 1   Wisconsin [2]

LaFollette[3]	40,738	62.5	McAdoo	54,922	68.2	
Coolidge[3]	23,324	35.8	Alfred E. Smith (N.Y.)[3]	5,774	7.2	
Johnson[3]	411	.6	Others	19,827	24.6	
Others	688	1.1				

April 7   Michigan

Coolidge	236,191	67.2	Henry Ford (Mich.)[4]	48,567	53.4	
Johnson	103,739	29.5	Woodbridge N. Ferris (Mich.)[4]	42,028	46.2	
Others	11,312	3.2	Others	435	.5	

April 8   Illinois

Coolidge	533,193	58.0	McAdoo	180,544	98.9	
Johnson	385,590	42.0	Smith[3]	235	.1	
LaFollette[3]	278	—	Others	1,724	.9	
Others	21	—				

April 8   Nebraska

Coolidge	79,676	63.6	McAdoo[3]	9,342	57.3	
Johnson	45,032	35.9	Smith[3]	700	4.3	
Others	627	.5	Others[3]	6,268	38.4	

April 22   New Jersey

Coolidge	111,739	89.1	George S. Silzer (N.J.)[5]	35,601	97.7	
Johnson	13,626	10.9	Smith[3]	721	2.0	
			McAdoo[3]	69	.2	
			Others	38	.1	

April 22   Pennsylvania

Coolidge[3]	117,262	87.9	McAdoo[3]	10,376	43.7	
Johnson[3]	4,345	3.3	Smith[3]	9,029	38.0	
LaFollette[3]	1,224	.9	Others[3]	4,341	18.3	
Others	10,523	7.9				

April 29   Massachusetts

Coolidge	84,840	100.0	Unpledged delegates at large[6]	30,341	100.0	

April 29   Ohio

Coolidge	173,613	86.3	James M. Cox (Ohio)[5]	74,183	71.7	
Johnson	27,578	13.7	McAdoo	29,267	28.3	

Republican
Democratic

	Votes	%		Votes	%
May 5 Maryland					
Coolidge	19,657	93.7	7		
Unpledged delegates	1,326	6.3			
Johnson [3]	3	—			
May 6 California					
Coolidge	310,618	54.3	McAdoo	110,235	85.6
Johnson	261,566	45.7	Unpledged delegates	18,586	14.4
May 6 Indiana					
Coolidge	330,045	84.1	7		
Johnson	62,603	15.9			
May 16 Oregon					
Coolidge	99,187	76.8	McAdoo	33,664	100.0
Johnson	30,042	23.2			
May 27 West Virginia					
Coolidge	162,042	100.0	7		
May 28 Montana					
Coolidge	19,200	100.0	McAdoo	10,058	100.0
TOTALS					
Coolidge	2,410,363	68.4	McAdoo	456,733	59.8
Johnson	1,007,833	28.6	Cox	74,183	9.7
LaFollette	82,492	2.3	Unpledged delegates	57,654	7.5
Unpledged delegates	1,326	—	Ford	48,567	6.4
Others	23,171	.7	Ferris	42,028	5.5
			Silzer	35,601	4.7
	3,525,185		Smith	16,459	2.2
			Others	32,633	4.3
				763,858	

1. No presidential preference vote, as McAdoo's was the only name entered, but a contest developed between "McAdoo" and "anti-McAdoo" lists of delegates. Figures are average votes cast for these lists.

2. In Wisconsin the real contest in the Republican primary was between two lists of delegates, one led by La Follette and one by Emanuel L. Philipp. In the Democratic primary, the real contest was between two lists of delegates, one favoring Smith and one favoring McAdoo.

3. Write-in.

4. Source for names of "favorite son" candidates: Michigan Manual, 1925.

5. Source for names of "favorite son" candidates: The New York Times.

6. No presidential preference vote provided for. There were nine candidates for the eight places as delegates at large, one of whom announced his preference for Smith during the campaign and received the second highest number of votes.

7. No names entered and no presidential preference vote taken.

1928 Primaries

	Republican			Democratic		
		Votes	%		Votes	%
March 13	**New Hampshire**					
	Unpledged delegates at large[1]	25,603	100.0	Unpledged delegates at large[1]	9,716	100.0
March 20	**North Dakota**					
	Frank O. Lowden (Ill.)	95,857	100.0	Alfred E. Smith (N.Y.)	10,822	100.0
April 2	**Michigan**					
	Herbert C. Hoover (Calif.)	282,809	97.6	Smith	77,276	98.3
	Lowden	5,349	1.8	Thomas Walsh (Mont.)	1,034	1.3
	Calvin Coolidge (Mass.)	1,666	.6	James A. Reed (Mo.)	324	.4
April 3	**Wisconsin**					
	George W. Norris (Neb.)	162,822	87.1	Reed	61,097	75.0
	Hoover	17,659	9.4	Smith	19,781	24.3
	Lowden	3,302	1.8	Walsh	541	.7
	Coolidge	680	.4			
	Charles G. Dawes (Ill.)	505	.3			
	Others	1,894	1.0			
April 10	**Illinois**					
	Lowden	1,172,278	99.3	Smith	44,212	91.7
	Hoover	4,368	.4	Reed	3,786	7.9
	Coolidge	2,420	.2	William G. McAdoo (Calif.)	213	.4
	Dawes	756	.1			
	Others	946	.1			
April 10	**Nebraska**					
	Norris	96,726	91.8	Gilbert M. Hitchcock (Neb.)	51,019	91.5
	Hoover	6,815	6.5	Smith	4,755	8.5
	Lowden	711	.7			
	Dawes	679	.7			
	Coolidge	452	.4			
April 24	**Ohio**					
	Hoover	217,430	68.1	Smith	42,365	65.9
	Frank B. Willis (Ohio)	84,461	26.5	Atlee Pomerene (Ohio)	13,957	21.7
	Dawes	4,311	1.4	Victor Donahey (Ohio)	7,935	12.3
	Lowden	3,676	1.2			
	Others	9,190	2.9			
April 24	**Pennsylvania**					
	[2]			[2]		
April 28	**Massachusetts**					
	Hoover[3]	100,279	85.2	Smith	38,081	98.1
	Coolidge[3]	7,767	6.6	Walsh	254	.7
	Alvan Fuller (Mass.)	1,686	1.4	Others	478	1.2
	Lowden[3]	1,040	.9			
	Others	6,950	5.9			
May 1	**California**					
	Hoover	567,219	100.0	Smith	134,471	54.1
				Reed	60,004	24.1
				Walsh	46,770	18.8
				Others	7,263	2.9

Republican			Democratic		
	Votes	%		Votes	%

May 7   Indiana

| James E. Watson (Ind.) | 228,795 | 53.0 | Evans Woollen (Ind.) | 146,934 | 100.0 |
| Hoover | 203,279 | 47.0 | | | |

May 7   Maryland[4]

| Hoover | 27,128 | 83.3 | [5] | | |
| Unpledged delegates | 5,426 | 16.7 | | | |

May 8   Alabama

| [5] | | | Unpledged delegates at large[6] | 138,957 | 100.0 |

May 15   New Jersey

| Hoover | 382,907 | 100.0 | Smith[3] | 28,506 | 100.0 |

May 18   Oregon

Hoover	101,129	98.7	Smith	17,444	48.5
Lowden	1,322	1.3	Walsh	11,272	31.3
			Reed	6,360	17.7
			Others	881	2.5

May 22   South Dakota

| Unpledged delegates at large[7] | 34,264 | 100.0 | Unpledged delegates at large[7] | 6,221 | 100.0 |

May 29   West Virginia

Guy D. Goff (W.Va.)	128,429	54.0	Smith	81,739	50.0
Hoover	109,303	46.0	Reed	75,796	46.4
			Others	5,789	3.5

June 5   Florida

| [5] | | | Unpledged delegates at large[8] | 108,167 | 100.00 |

TOTALS					
Hoover	2,020,325	49.2	Smith	499,452	39.5
Lowden	1,283,535	31.2	Unpledged delegates	263,061	20.8
Norris	259,548	6.3	Reed	207,367	16.4
Watson	228,795	5.6	Woollen	146,934	11.6
Goff	128,429	3.1	Walsh	59,871	4.7
Willis	84,461	2.1	Hitchcock	51,019	4.0
Unpledged delegates	65,293	1.6	Pomerene	13,957	1.1
Coolidge	12,985	.3	Donahey	7,935	.6
Dawes	6,251	.2	McAdoo	213	—
Fuller	1,686	—	Others[10]	14,411	1.1
Others[9]	18,980	.5			
	4,110,288			1,264,220	

1. *Winning Republican delegates were unofficially pledged to Hoover and winning Democratic delegates were unofficially pledged to Smith, according to Walter Kravitz, "Presidential Preferential Primaries: Results 1928-1956" (1960), p. 4.*
2. *No figures available.*
3. *Write-in.*
4. *Source: Kravitz, op. cit., p. 5.*
5. *No primary.*
6. *The Montgomery Advertiser of May 3, 1928, described the delegates as independent and anti-Smith.*

7. *Winning Republican delegates favored Lowden and winning Democratic delegates favored Smith, according to Kravitz, op. cit., p. 5.*
8. *The Miami Herald of June 6, 1928, described the delegates as unpledged and anti-Smith.*
9. *In addition to scattered votes, "others" includes Robert G. Ross who received 8,280 votes in the Ohio primary.*
10. *In addition to scattered votes, "others" includes Poling who received 7,263 votes in the California primary; and Workman who received 881 in the Oregon primary and 5,789 in the West Virginia primary.*

1932 Primaries

	Republican			Democratic		
		Votes	%		Votes	%
March 8 New Hampshire						
	Unpledged delegates at large[1]	22,903	100.0	Unpledged delegates at large[1]	15,401	100.0
March 15 North Dakota						
	Joseph I. France (Md.)	36,000[2]	59.0	Franklin D. Roosevelt (N.Y.)	52,000[2]	61.9
	Jacob S. Coxey (Ohio)	25,000[2]	41.0	William H. Murray (Okla.)	32,000[2]	38.1
March 23 Georgia						
	[3]			Roosevelt	51,498	90.3
				Others	5,541	9.7
April 5 Wisconsin						
	George W. Norris (Neb.)	139,514	95.5	Roosevelt	241,742	98.6
	Herbert C. Hoover (Calif.)	6,588	4.5	Alfred E. Smith (N.Y.)[4]	3,502	1.4
April 12 Nebraska						
	France	40,481	74.4	Roosevelt	91,393	63.5
	Hoover	13,934	25.6	John N. Garner (Texas)	27,359	19.0
				Murray	25,214	17.5
April 13 Illinois						
	France	345,498	98.7	James H. Lewis (Ill.)	590,130	99.8
	Hoover	4,368	1.2	Roosevelt	1,084	.2
	Charles G. Dawes (Ill.)	129	—	Smith	266	—
				Others[4]	72	—
April 26 Massachusetts						
	Unpledged delegates at large[5]	57,534	100.0	Smith[5]	153,465	73.1
				Roosevelt[5]	56,454	26.9
April 26 Pennsylvania						
	France	352,092	92.9	Roosevelt	133,002	56.6
	Hoover	20,662	5.5	Smith	101,227	43.1
	Others	6,126	1.6	Others	563	.2
May 2 Maryland						
	Hoover	27,324	60.0	[6]		
	France	17,008	37.3			
	Unpledged delegates	1,236	2.7			
May 3 Alabama						
	[3]			Unpledged delegates[7]	134,781	100.0
May 3 California						
	Hoover	657,420	100.0	Garner	222,385	41.3
				Roosevelt	175,008	32.5
				Smith	141,517	26.3
May 3 South Dakota						
	Johnson[8]	64,464	64.7	Roosevelt	35,370	100.0
	Others	35,133	35.3			

	Republican			**Democratic**		
		Votes	%		Votes	%
May 10 Ohio						
	Coxey	75,844	58.9	Murray	112,512	96.4
	France	44,853	34.8	Roosevelt[4]	1,999	1.7
	Hoover	8,154	6.3	Smith[4]	951	.8
				George White (Ohio)	834	.7
				Newton D. Baker (Ohio)	289	.2
				Garner[4]	72	—
May 10 West Virginia						
	France	88,005	100.0	Roosevelt	219,671	90.3
				Murray	19,826	8.2
				Others	3,727	1.5
May 17 New Jersey						
	France	141,330	93.3	Smith	5,234	61.9
	Hoover	10,116	6.7	Roosevelt	3,219	38.1
May 20 Oregon						
	France	72,681	69.0	Roosevelt	48,554	78.6
	Hoover	32,599	31.0	Murray	11,993	19.4
				Others	1,214	2.0
June 7 Florida						
[3]				Roosevelt	203,372	87.7
				Murray	24,847	10.7
				Others	3,645	1.6
TOTALS						
	France	1,137,948	48.5	Roosevelt	1,314,366	44.5
	Hoover	781,165	33.3	Lewis	590,130	20.0
	Norris	139,514	5.9	Smith	406,162	13.8
	Coxey	100,844	4.3	Garner	249,816	8.5
	Unpledged delegates	81,673	3.5	Murray	226,392	7.7
	Johnson	64,464	2.7	Unpledged delegates	150,182	5.1
	Dawes	129	—	White	834	—
	Others[9]	41,259	1.8	Baker	289	—
				Others[10]	14,762	.5
		2,346,996			2,952,933	

1. Hoover delegates won the Republican primary and Roosevelt delegates won the Democratic primary, according to Kravitz, op. cit., p. 6.
2. Unofficial figures.
3. No primary.
4. Write-in.
5. Delegate-at-large vote in Republican and Democratic primaries. Hoover delegates won the Republican primary, according to Kravitz, op. cit., p. 6. The New York Times of April 28, 1932, also reported that the Republican delegates were pledged to Hoover.
6. No names entered, according to the Maryland Record of Election Returns.

7. These were unpledged delegates who favored Roosevelt, according to Kravitz, op. cit., p. 6.
8. The winning Republican delegation supported Hoover, according to Kravitz, op. cit., p. 7.
9. In addition to scattered votes, "others" includes Bogue who received 35,133 in the South Dakota primary.
10. In addition to scattered votes, "others" includes Leo J. Chassee who received 3,645 in the Florida primary and 3,727 in the West Virginia primary; and Howard who received 5,541 votes in the Georgia primary.

1936 Primaries

	Republican			Democratic		
		Votes	%		Votes	%
March 10 New Hampshire						
Unpledged delegates at large[1]		32,992	100.0	Unpledged delegates at large[1]	15,752	100.0
April 7 Wisconsin						
William E. Borah (Idaho)		187,334	98.2	Franklin D. Roosevelt (N.Y.)	401,773	100.0
Alfred M. Landon (Kan.)		3,360	1.8	John N. Garner (Texas)	108	—
				Alfred E. Smith (N.Y.)	46	—
April 14 Illinois						
Frank Knox (Ill.)		491,575	53.7	Roosevelt	1,416,411	100.0
Borah		419,220	45.8	Others[2]	411	—
Landon		3,775	.4			
Others[2]		205	—			
April 14 Nebraska						
Borah		70,240	74.5	Roosevelt	139,743	100.0
Landon		23,117	24.5			
Others		973	1.0			
April 28 Massachusetts						
Landon[2]		76,862	80.6	Roosevelt[2]	51,924	85.9
Herbert C. Hoover (Calif.)[2]		7,276	7.6	Smith[2]	2,928	4.8
Borah[2]		4,259	4.5	Charles E. Coughlin (Mich.)[2]	2,854	4.7
Knox[2]		1,987	2.1	Others[2]	2,774	4.6
Others[2]		5,032	5.3			
April 28 Pennsylvania						
Borah		459,982	100.0	Roosevelt	720,309	95.3
				Henry Breckinridge (N.Y.)	35,351	4.7
May 4 Maryland						
[3]				Roosevelt	100,269	83.4
				Breckinridge	18,150	15.1
				Unpledged delegates	1,739	1.4
May 5 California						
Earl Warren (Calif.)		350,917	57.4	Roosevelt	790,235	82.5
Landon		260,170	42.6	Upton Sinclair (Calif.)	106,068	11.1
				John S. McGroarty (Calif.)	61,391	6.4
May 5 South Dakota						
Warren E. Green[4]		44,518	50.1	Roosevelt	48,262	100.0
Borah		44,261	49.9			
May 12 Ohio						
Stephen A. Day (Ohio)		155,732	93.4	Roosevelt	514,366	94.0
Landon		11,015	6.6	Breckinridge	32,950	6.0
May 12 West Virginia						
Borah		105,855	84.8	Roosevelt	288,799	97.3
Others		18,986	15.2	Others	8,162	2.7

Republican   # Democratic

May 15   Oregon

Borah	91,949	90.2	Roosevelt	88,305	99.8
Landon	4,467	4.4	Others	208	.2
Others	5,557	5.4			

May 19   New Jersey

Landon	347,142	79.2	Breckinridge	49,956	81.1
Borah	91,052	20.8	Roosevelt[2]	11,676	18.9

June 6   Florida

[3]			Roosevelt	242,906	89.7
			Others	27,982	10.3

TOTALS

Borah	1,474,152	44.4	Roosevelt	4,814,978	92.9
Landon	729,908	22.0	Breckinridge	136,407	2.6
Knox	493,562	14.9	Sinclair	106,068	2.0
Warren	350,917	10.6	McGroarty	61,391	1.2
Day	155,732	4.7	Unpledged delegates	17,491	.3
Green	44,518	1.3	Smith	2,974	.1
Unpledged delegates	32,992	1.0	Coughlin	2,854	.1
Hoover	7,276	.2	Garner	108	—
Others[5]	30,753	.9	Others[6]	39,537	.8
	3,319,810			5,181,808	

1. Delegates favorable to Knox won the Republican primary and Roosevelt delegates won the Democratic primary, according to Kravitz, op. cit., p. 8.
2. Write-in.
3. No preferential primary held.
4. These delegates were unpledged but favored Landon, according to Kravitz, op. cit., p. 9.

5. In addition to scattered votes, "others" includes Leo J. Chassee who received 18,986 votes in the West Virginia primary.
6. In addition to scattered votes, "others" includes Joseph A. Coutremarsh who received 27,982 votes in the Florida primary and 8,162 votes in the West Virginia primary.

1940 Primaries

Republican   **Democratic**

March 12   New Hampshire

Unpledged delegates at large	34,616	*100.0*	Unpledged delegates at large [1]	10,501	*100.0*

April 2   Wisconsin

Thomas E. Dewey (N.Y.)	70,168	*72.6*	Franklin D. Roosevelt (N.Y.)	322,991	*75.4*
Arthur Vandenberg (Mich.)	26,182	*27.1*	John N. Garner (Texas)	105,662	*24.6*
Robert A. Taft (Ohio)	341	*.4*			

April 9   Illinois

Dewey	977,225	*99.9*	Roosevelt	1,176,531	*86.0*
Others [2]	552	*.1*	Garner	190,801	*14.0*
			Others [2]	35	—

April 9   Nebraska

Dewey	102,915	*58.9*	Roosevelt	111,902	*100.0*
Vandenberg	71,798	*41.1*			

April 23   Pennsylvania

Dewey	52,661	*66.7*	Roosevelt	724,657	*100.0*
Franklin D. Roosevelt (N.Y.)	8,294	*10.5*			
Arthur H. James (Pa.)	8,172	*10.3*			
Taft	5,213	*6.6*			
Vandenberg	2,384	*3.0*			
Herbert C. Hoover (Calif.)	1,082	*1.4*			
Wendell Willkie (N.Y.)	707	*.9*			
Others	463	*.6*			

April 30   Massachusetts

Unpledged delegates at large [3]	98,975	*100.0*	Unpledged delegates at large [3]	76,919	*100.0*

May 5   South Dakota

Unpledged delegates	52,566	*100.0*	Unpledged delegates	27,636	*100.0*

May 6   Maryland

Dewey	54,802	*100.0*	[4]	

May 7   Alabama

[4]			Unpledged delegates at large [5]	196,508	*100.0*

May 7   California

Jerrold L. Seawell [6]	538,112	*100.0*	Roosevelt	723,782	*74.0*
			Garner	114,594	*11.7*
			Unpledged delegates [6]	139,055	*14.2*

May 14   Ohio

Taft	510,025	*99.5*	Unpledged delegates at large [7]	283,952	*100.0*
Dewey [2]	2,059	*.4*			
John W. Bricker (Ohio)	188	—			
Vandenberg [2]	83	—			
Willkie	53	—			
Others	69	—			

Republican

Democratic

	Votes	%		Votes	%
May 14 West Virginia					
R. N. Davis (W.Va.)	106,123	*100.0*	H. C. Allen (W.Va.)	102,729	*100.0*
May 17 Oregon					
Charles L. McNary (Ore.)	133,488	*95.9*	Roosevelt	109,913	*87.2*
Dewey	5,190	*3.7*	Garner	15,584	*12.4*
Taft	254	*.2*	Others	601	*.5*
Willkie	237	*.2*			
Vandenberg	36	—			
May 21 New Jersey					
Dewey	340,734	*93.9*	Roosevelt [2]	34,278	*100.0*
Willkie [2]	20,143	*5.6*			
Roosevelt [2]	1,202	*.3*			
Taft [2]	595	*.2*			
Vandenberg [2]	168	—			
TOTALS					
Dewey	1,605,754	*49.7*	Roosevelt	3,240,054	*71.7*
Seawell	538,112	*16.7*	Unpledged delegates	734,571	*16.4*
Taft	516,428	*16.0*	Garner	426,641	*9.5*
Unpledged delegates	186,157	*5.8*	Allen	102,729	*2.3*
McNary	133,488	*4.1*	Others	636	—
Davis	106,123	*3.3*			
Vandenberg	100,651	*3.1*			4,468,631
Willkie	21,140	*.7*			
Roosevelt	9,496	*.3*			
James	8,172	*.3*			
Hoover	1,082	—			
Bricker	188	—			
Others	1,084	—			
	3,227,875				

1. Roosevelt delegates won, according to Kravitz, op. cit., p. 10.
2. Write-in.
3. An unpledged Republican slate defeated a slate of delegates pledged to Dewey, according to Kravitz, op. cit., p. 10. Sixty-nine James A. Farley delegates and three unpledged delegates won in the Democratic primary, according to Kravitz, ibid. The New York Times of May 1, 1940, also reported that most Democratic delegates favored Farley.
4. No primary.
5. Winning delegates were pledged to "favorite son" candidate William B. Bankhead, then Speaker of the U.S. House of Representatives, according to Kravitz, op. cit., p. 10, and the Montgomery Advertiser of May 8, 1940.
6. The Los Angeles Times of May 8, 1940, reported that the Republican delegation was unpledged. In the Democratic primary, according to Davis, p. 293, unpledged slates were headed by Willis Allen, head of the California "Ham and Eggs" pension ticket which received 90,718 votes; and by Lt. Gov. Ellis E. Patterson, whose slate, backed by Labor's Non-Partisan League, received 48,337 votes.
7. Democratic delegates were pledged to Charles Sawyer (Ohio), according to Ohio Election Statistics, 1940, and Kravitz, op. cit., p. 10.

1944 Primaries

	Republican			Democratic	
	Votes	%		Votes	%
March 14 New Hampshire					
Unpledged delegates at large[1]	16,723	100.0	Unpledged delegates at large[1]	6,772	100.0
April 5 Wisconsin					
Douglas MacArthur (Wis.)	102,421	72.6	Franklin D. Roosevelt (N.Y.)	49,632	94.3
Thomas E. Dewey (N.Y.)	21,036	14.9	Others	3,014	5.7
Harold E. Stassen (Minn.)	7,928	5.6			
Wendell Willkie (N.Y.)	6,439	4.6			
Others	3,307	2.3			
April 11 Illinois					
MacArthur	550,354	92.0	Roosevelt	47,561	99.3
Dewey	9,192	1.5	Others	343	.7
Everett M. Dirksen (Ill.)	581	.1			
John W. Bricker (Ohio)	148	—			
Stassen	111	—			
Willkie	107	—			
Others	37,575	6.3			
April 11 Nebraska					
Stassen	51,800	65.7	Roosevelt	37,405	99.2
Dewey	18,418	23.3	Others	319	.8
Willkie	8,249	10.5			
Others	432	.5			
April 25 Massachusetts					
Unpledged delegates at large	53,511	100.0	Unpledged delegates at large	57,299	100.0
April 25 Pennsylvania					
Dewey[2]	146,706	83.8	Roosevelt	322,469	99.7
MacArthur[2]	9,032	5.2	Others	961	.3
Franklin D. Roosevelt (N.Y.)	8,815	5.0			
Willkie[2]	3,650	2.1			
Bricker[2]	2,936	1.7			
Edward Martin (Pa.)	2,406	1.4			
Stassen[2]	1,502	.9			
May 1 Maryland					
Unpledged delegates	17,600	78.9	[3]		
Willkie	4,701	21.1			
May 2 Alabama					
[3]			Unpledged delegates at large[4]	116,922	100.0
May 2 Florida					
[3]			Unpledged delegates at large[5]	118,518	100.0
May 2 South Dakota					
Charles A. Christopherson[6]	33,497	60.2	Fred Hildebrandt (S.D.)[6]	7,414	52.4
Others[6]	22,135	39.8	Others[6]	6,727	47.6

Republican	Votes	%	Democratic	Votes	%
May 9 Ohio					
Unpledged delegates at large [7]	360,139	*100.0*	Unpledged delegates at large [7]	164,915	*100.0*
May 9 West Virginia					
Unpledged delegates at large	91,602	*100.0*	Claude R. Linger (W.Va.)	59,282	*100.0*
May 16 California					
Earl Warren (Calif.)	594,439	*100.0*	Roosevelt	770,222	*100.0*
May 16 New Jersey					
Dewey	17,393	*86.2*	Roosevelt	16,884	*99.6*
Roosevelt [2]	1,720	*8.5*	Thomas E. Dewey (N.Y.)	60	*.4*
Willkie	618	*3.1*			
Bricker	203	*1.0*			
MacArthur	129	*.6*			
Stassen	106	*.5*			
May 19 Oregon					
Dewey [2]	50,001	*78.2*	Roosevelt	79,833	*98.7*
Stassen [2]	6,061	*9.5*	Others	1,057	*1.3*
Willkie [2]	3,333	*5.2*			
Bricker [2]	3,018	*4.7*			
MacArthur [2]	191	*.3*			
Others	1,340	*2.1*			
TOTALS					
MacArthur	662,127	*29.1*	Roosevelt	1,324,006	*70.9*
Warren	594,439	*26.2*	Unpledged delegates	464,426	*24.9*
Unpledged delegates	539,575	*23.8*	Linger	59,282	*3.2*
Dewey	262,746	*11.6*	Hildebrandt	7,414	*.4*
Stassen	67,508	*3.0*	Dewey	60	*—*
Christopherson	33,497	*1.5*	Others [9]	12,421	*.7*
Willkie	27,097	*1.2*			
Roosevelt	10,535	*.5*		1,867,609	
Bricker	6,305	*.3*			
Martin	2,406	*.1*			
Dirksen	581	*—*			
Others [8]	64,789	*2.9*			
	2,271,605				

1. Nine unpledged and two Dewey delegates won the Republican primary, and Roosevelt delegates won the Democratic primary, according to Kravitz, op. cit., p. 12.

2. Write-in.

3. No primary.

4. The Montgomery Advertiser of May 3, 1944, reported that these delegates were pro-Roosevelt but uninstructed.

5. The New York Times of May 3, 1944, reported that a contest for delegates took place between supporters of Roosevelt and supporters of Sen. Harry F. Byrd (D Va.). A vote breakdown showing Roosevelt and Byrd strength is unavailable.

6. The winning Republican slate was pledged to Stassen, the losing Republican slate to Dewey and the two Democratic slates to Roosevelt, according to the office of the South Dakota secretary of state and Kravitz, op. cit., p. 12.

7. Bricker delegates won the Republican primary and Joseph T. Ferguson delegates won the Democratic primary, according to Kravitz, op. cit., p. 13.

8. In addition to scattered votes, "others" includes Riley A. Bender who received 37,575 votes in the Illinois primary and Joe H. Bottum who received 22,135 in the South Dakota primary.

9. In addition to scattered votes, "others" includes Powell who received 6,727 votes in the South Dakota primary.

1948 Primaries

	Republican			Democratic		
	Votes	%		Votes	%
March 9 New Hampshire					
Unpledged delegates at large[1]	28,854	100.0	Unpledged delegates at large[1]	4,409	100.0
April 6 Wisconsin					
Harold E. Stassen (Minn.)	64,076	39.4	Harry S Truman (Mo.)	25,415	83.8
Douglas MacArthur (Wis.)	55,302	34.0	Others	4,906	16.2
Thomas E. Dewey (N.Y.)	40,943	25.2			
Others	2,429	1.5			
April 13 Illinois					
Riley A. Bender (Ill.)	324,029	96.9	Truman	16,299	81.7
MacArthur	6,672	2.0	Dwight D. Eisenhower (N.Y.)	1,709	8.6
Stassen	1,572	.5	Scott Lucas (Ill.)	427	2.1
Dewey	953	.3	Others[2]	1,513	7.6
Robert A. Taft (Ohio)	705	.2			
Others[2]	475	.1			
April 13 Nebraska					
Stassen	80,979	43.5	Truman	67,672	98.7
Dewey	64,242	34.5	Others	894	1.3
Taft	21,608	11.6			
Arthur Vandenberg (Mich.)	9,590	5.2			
MacArthur	6,893	3.7			
Earl Warren (Calif.)	1,761	.9			
Joseph W. Martin (Mass.)	910	.5			
Others	24	—			
April 20 New Jersey[3]					
Dewey	3,714	41.4	Truman	1,100	92.5
Stassen	3,123	34.8	Henry A. Wallace (Iowa)	87	7.3
MacArthur	718	8.0	Others	2	.2
Vandenberg	516	5.8			
Taft	495	5.5			
Dwight D. Eisenhower (N.Y.)	288	3.2			
Joseph W. Martin	64	.7			
Alfred E. Driscoll (N.J.)	44	—			
Warren	14	.2			
April 27 Massachusetts					
Unpledged delegates at large[4]	72,191	100.0	Unpledged delegates at large[4]	51,207	100.0
April 27 Pennsylvania					
Stassen[2]	81,242	31.5	Truman	328,891	96.0
Dewey[2]	76,988	29.8	Eisenhower	4,502	1.3
Edward Martin (Pa.)	45,072	17.5	Wallace	4,329	1.3
MacArthur[2]	18,254	7.1	Harold E. Stassen (Minn.)	1,301	.4
Taft[2]	15,166	5.9	Douglas MacArthur (Wis.)	1,220	.4
Vandenberg	8,818	3.4	Others	2,409	.7
Harry S Truman (Mo.)	4,907	1.9			
Eisenhower	4,726	1.8			
Henry A. Wallace (Iowa)	1,452	.6			
Others	1,537	.6			
May 4 Alabama					
[5]			Unpledged delegates at large[6]	161,629	100.0

Republican
Democratic

	Votes	%		Votes	%
May 4 Florida					
[5]			Others [7]	92,169	100.0
May 4 Ohio					
Unpledged delegates at large [8]	426,767	100.0	Unpledged delegates at large [8]	271,146	100.0
May 11 West Virginia					
Stassen	110,775	83.2	Unpledged delegates at large	157,102	100.0
Others	22,410	16.8			
May 21 Oregon					
Dewey	117,554	51.8	Truman	112,962	93.8
Stassen	107,946	47.6	Others	7,436	6.2
Others	1,474	.6			
June 1 California					
Warren	769,520	100.0	Truman	811,920	100.0
June 1 South Dakota					
Hitchcock [9]	45,463	100.0	Truman [9]	11,193	58.3
			Unpledged Delegates [9]	8,016	41.7

TOTALS					
Warren	771,295	29.1	Truman	1,375,452	63.9
Unpledged delegates	527,812	19.9	Unpledged delegates	653,509	30.4
Stassen	449,713	16.9	Eisenhower	6,211	.3
Bender	324,029	12.2	Wallace	4,416	.2
Dewey	304,394	11.5	Stassen	1,301	.1
MacArthur	87,839	3.3	MacArthur	1,220	.1
Hitchcock	45,463	1.7	Lucas	427	—
Edward Martin	45,072	1.7	Others	109,329	5.1
Taft	37,974	1.4			
Vandenberg	18,924	.7		2,151,865	
Eisenhower	5,014	.2			
Truman	4,907	.2			
Wallace	1,452	.1			
Joseph W. Martin	974	—			
Driscoll	44	—			
Others [10]	28,349	1.1			
	2,653,255				

1. Six unpledged and two Dewey delegates won in the Republican primary, and Truman delegates won in the Democratic primary, according to Kravitz, op. cit., p. 14.
2. Write-in.
3. Source: Kravitz, op. cit., p. 14.
4. The Boston Globe of April 28, 1948, reported that the Republican delegation was "generally unpledged" but was expected to support the "favorite son" candidacy of Sen. Leverett Saltonstall (R Mass.) on the first convention ballot. The Globe reported that Democratic delegates were presumed to favor Truman's nomination.
5. No primary.

6. Unpledged, anti-Truman slate, according to Kravitz, op. cit., p. 15.
7. Unpledged slate, according to Kravitz, ibid.
8. Taft won 44 delegates and Stassen nine in the Republican primary, and W.A. Julian won 55 delegates and Bixler one in the Democratic primary, according to Kravitz., ibid.
9. Republican delegates were unpledged, according to Kravitz, op. cit., p. 15. In the Democratic primary, according to Davis, p. 297, the slate led by South Dakota Democratic Party Chairman Lynn Fellows endorsed Truman and the slate headed by former Rep. Fred Hildebrandt (D S.D.) ran uninstructed.
10. In addition to scattered votes, "others" includes Byer who received 15,675 votes and Vander Pyl who received 6,735 votes in the West Virginia primary.

1952 Primaries

Republican	Votes	%	Democratic	Votes	%
March 11 New Hampshire					
Dwight D. Eisenhower (N.Y.)	46,661	50.4	Estes Kefauver (Tenn.)	19,800	55.0
Robert A. Taft (Ohio)	35,838	38.7	Harry S Truman (Mo.)	15,927	44.2
Harold E. Stassen (Minn.)	6,574	7.1	Douglas MacArthur (Wis.)	151	.4
Douglas MacArthur (Wis.)[1]	3,227	3.5	James A. Farley (N.Y.)	77.	.2
Others	230	.3	Adlai E. Stevenson (III.)	40	.1
March 18 Minnesota					
Stassen	129,706	44.4	Hubert H. Humphrey (Minn.)	102,527	80.0
Eisenhower[1]	108,692	37.2	Kefauver[1]	20,182	15.8
Taft[1]	24,093	8.2	Truman[1]	3,634	2.8
Earl Warren (Calif.)[1]	5,365	1.8	Dwight D. Eisenhower (N.Y.)	1,753	1.4
MacArthur[1]	1,369	.5			
Estes Kefauver (Tenn.)	386	.1			
Others	22,712	7.8			
April 1 Nebraska					
Taft[1]	79,357	36.2	Kefauver	64,531	60.3
Eisenhower[1]	66,078	30.1	Robert S. Kerr (Okla.)	42,467	39.7
Stassen	53,238	24.3			
MacArthur[1]	7,478	3.4			
Warren[1]	1,872	.9			
Others	11,178	5.1			
April 1 Wisconsin					
Taft	315,541	40.6	Kefauver	207,520	85.9
Warren	262,271	33.8	Others	34,005	14.1
Stassen	169,679	21.8			
Others	29,133	3.8			
April 8 Illinois					
Taft	935,867	73.6	Kefauver	526,301	87.7
Stassen	155,041	12.2	Stevenson	54,336	9.1
Eisenhower[1]	147,518	11.6	Truman	9,024	1.5
MacArthur[1]	7,504	.6	Eisenhower	6,655	1.1
Warren	2,841	.2	Others[1]	3,798	.6
Others	23,550	1.9			
April 15 New Jersey					
Eisenhower	390,591	60.7	Kefauver	154,964	100.0
Taft	228,916	35.6			
Stassen	23,559	3.7			
April 22 Pennsylvania					
Eisenhower	863,785	73.6	Kefauver[1]	93,160	53.3
Taft[1]	178,629	15.2	Eisenhower[1]	28,660	16.4
Stassen	120,305	10.3	Truman[1]	26,504	15.2
MacArthur[1]	6,028	.5	Robert A. Taft (Ohio)	8,311	4.8
Warren	3,158	.3	Averell Harriman (N.Y.)[1]	3,745	2.1
Harry S Truman (Mo.)	267	—	Stevenson[1]	3,678	2.1
Others	1,121	.1	Richard B. Russell (Ga.)[1]	1,691	1.0
			Others	9,026	5.2
April 29 Massachusetts					
Eisenhower[1]	254,898	69.8	Kefauver	29,287	55.7
Taft[1]	110,188	30.2	Eisenhower	16,007	30.5
			Truman	7,256	13.8

	Republican			Democratic		
		Votes	%		Votes	%
May 5 Maryland[2]						
[3]				Kefauver	137,885	74.8
				Unpledged delegates	46,361	25.2
May 6 Florida						
[3]				Russell	367,980	54.5
				Kefauver	285,358	42.3
				Others	21,296	3.2
May 6 Ohio						
Taft[4]		663,791	78.8	Kefauver[4]	305,992	62.3
Stassen[4]		178,739	21.2	Robert J. Bulkley (Ohio)[4]	184,880	37.7
May 13 West Virginia						
Taft		139,812	78.5	Unpledged delegates at large	191,471	100.0
Stassen		38,251	21.5			
May 16 Oregon						
Eisenhower		172,486	64.6	Kefauver	142,440	72.3
Warren		44,034	16.5	William O. Douglas (Wash.)	29,532	15.0
MacArthur		18,603	7.0	Stevenson	20,353	10.3
Taft[1]		18,009	6.7	Eisenhower[1]	4,690	2.4
Wayne L. Morse (Ore.)		7,105	2.7			
Stassen		6,610	2.5			
Others		350	.1			
June 3 California						
Warren		1,029,495	66.4	Kefauver	1,155,839	70.4
Thomas H. Werdel (Calif.)		521,110	33.6	Edmund G. Brown (Calif.)	485,578	29.6
June 3 South Dakota						
Taft		64,695	50.3	Kefauver	22,812	66.0
Eisenhower		63,879	49.7	Others[5]	11,741	34.0
June 17 District of Columbia[6]						
[3]				Harriman	14,075	74.9
				Kefauver	3,377	18.0
				Others[1]	1,329	7.1
TOTALS						
Taft		2,794,736	35.8	Kefauver	3,169,448	64.3
Eisenhower		2,114,588	27.1	Brown	485,578	9.9
Warren		1,349,036	17.3	Russell	369,671	7.5
Stassen		881,702	11.3	Unpledged delegates	237,832	4.8
Werdel		521,110	6.7	Bulkley	184,880	3.8
MacArthur		44,209	.6	Humphrey	102,527	2.1
Morse		7,105	.1	Stevenson	78,583	1.6
Kefauver		386	—	Truman	62,345	1.3
Truman		267	—	Eisenhower	57,765	1.2
Others		88,274	1.1	Kerr	42,467	.9
				Douglas	29,532	.6
		7,801,413		Harriman	17,820	.4
				Taft	8,311	.2
				MacArthur	151	—
				Farley	77	—
				Others[8]	81,019	1.6
					4,928,006	

1. Write-in.
2. Source: Kravitz, op. cit., p. 18, and the office of the Maryland secretary of state.
3. No primary.
4. Delegate-at-large vote.
5. These delegates ran on an uninstructed slate, according to Kravitz, op. cit., p. 19.
6. Source: David, Moos, and Goldman, Nominating Politics in 1952, Vol. 2, p. 331-332.
7. In addition to scattered votes, "others" includes Schneider who received 230

received 10,411 in the Nebraska primary; Ritter who received 26,208 and Stearns who received 2,925 in the Wisconsin primary; Slettendahl who received 22,712 in the Minnesota primary and Riley Bender who received 22,321 votes in the Illinois primary.

8. In addition to scattered votes, "others" includes Fox who received 18,322 votes and Charles Broughton who received 15,683 votes in the Wisconsin primary; Compton who received 11,331 and Shaw who received 9,965 in the Florida primary.

1956 Primaries

Republican			Democratic		
	Votes	%		Votes	%

March 13   New Hampshire

Dwight D. Eisenhower (Pa.)	56,464	98.9	Estes Kefauver (Tenn.)	21,701	84.6
Others	600	1.1	Others	3,945	15.4

March 20   Minnesota

Eisenhower	198,111	98.4	Kefauver	245,885	56.8
William F. Knowland (Calif.)	3,209	1.6	Adlai E. Stevenson (Ill.)	186,723	43.2
Others	51	—	Others	48	—

April 3   Wisconsin

Eisenhower	437,089	95.9	Kefauver	330,665[1]	100.0
Others	18,743	4.1			

April 10   Illinois

Eisenhower	781,710	94.9	Stevenson	717,742	95.3
Knowland	33,534	4.1	Kefauver[2]	34,092	4.5
Others	8,455	1.0	Others	1,640	.2

April 17   New Jersey

Eisenhower	357,066	100.0	Kefauver	117,056	95.7
Others	23	—	Others	5,230	4.3

April 24   Alaska (Territory)

Eisenhower	8,291	94.4	Stevenson	7,123	61.1
Knowland	488	5.6	Kefauver	4,536	38.9

April 24   Massachusetts

Eisenhower[2]	51,951	95.1	John W. McCormack (Mass.)[2]	26,128	47.9
Adlai E. Stevenson (Ill.)[2]	604	1.1	Stevenson[2]	19,024	34.9
Christian A. Herter (Mass.)[2]	550	1.0	Kefauver[2]	4,547	8.3
Richard M. Nixon (N.Y.)[2]	316	.6	Dwight D. Eisenhower (Pa.)[2]	1,850	3.4
John W. McCormack (Mass.)[2]	268	.5	John F. Kennedy (Mass.)[2]	949	1.7
Knowland[2]	250	.5	Averell Harriman (N.Y.)[2]	394	.7
Others[2]	700	1.3	Frank J. Lausche (Ohio)[2]	253	.5
			Others[2]	1,379	2.5

April 24   Pennsylvania

Eisenhower	951,932	95.5	Stevenson	642,172	93.6
Knowland	43,508	4.4	Kefauver[2]	36,552	5.3
Others	976	.1	Others	7,482	1.1

May 1   District of Columbia[3]

Eisenhower	18,101	100.0	Stevenson	17,306	66.2
			Kefauver	8,837	33.8

May 7   Maryland

Eisenhower	66,904	95.5	Kefauver	112,768	65.9
Unpledged delegates	3,131	4.5	Unpledged delegates	58,366	34.1

May 8   Indiana

Eisenhower	351,903	96.4	Kefauver	242,842[1]	100.0
Others	13,320	3.6			

Republican

	Votes	%

Democratic

	Votes	%

May 8 Ohio

John W. Bricker (Ohio)	478,453[1]	100.0	Lausche	276,670[1]	100.0

May 8 West Virginia

Unpledged delegates at large	111,883[1]	100.0	Unpledged delegates at large	112,832[1]	100.0

May 15 Nebraska

Eisenhower	102,576	99.8	Kefauver	55,265	94.0
Others	230	.2	Others	3,556	6.0

May 18 Oregon

Eisenhower	231,418[1]	100.0	Stevenson[2]	98,131	60.2
			Kefauver[2]	62,987	38.6
			Harriman[2]	1,887	1.2

May 29 Florida

Eisenhower	39,690	92.0	Stevenson	230,285	51.5
Knowland	3,457	8.0	Kefauver	216,549	48.5

June 5 California

Eisenhower	1,354,764[1]	100.0	Stevenson	1,139,964	62.6
			Kefauver	680,722	37.4

June 5 Montana

S.C. Arnold[4]	32,732	85.7	Kefauver	77,228[1]	100.0
Others	5,447	14.3			

June 5 South Dakota

Unpledged delegates[5]	59,374[1]	100.0	Kefauver	30,940[1]	100.0

TOTALS

	Votes	%		Votes	%
Eisenhower	5,007,970	85.9	Stevenson	3,051,347	52.3
Bricker	478,453	8.2	Kefauver	2,278,636	39.1
Unpledged delegates	174,388	3.0	Lausche	276,923	4.7
Knowland	84,446	1.4	Unpledged delegates	171,198	2.9
S.C. Arnold	32,732	.6	McCormack	26,128	.4
Stevenson	604	—	Harriman	2,281	—
Herter	550	—	Eisenhower	1,850	—
Nixon	316	—	Kennedy	949	—
McCormack	268	—	Others	23,280	.4
Others[6]	48,545	.8			
	5,828,272			5,832,592	

1. Figures obtained from Scammon's office. In America Votes, Scammon did not record vote totals if a candidate was unopposed or if the primary was strictly for delegate selection.
2. Write-in.
3. Source: Davis, op. cit., pp. 300-301.
4. Voters cast their ballots for S. C. Arnold, "stand-in" candidate for Eisenhower.
5. Slate unofficially pledged to Eisenhower but appeared on the ballot as "No preference."
6. In addition to scattered votes, "others" includes Lar Daly who received 8,364 votes in the Illinois primary, 13,320 votes in the Indiana primary and 5,447 votes in the Montana primary; and John Bowman Chapple who received 18,743 votes in the Wisconsin primary.

1960 Primaries

	Republican			Democratic		
	Votes	%		Votes	%

March 8   New Hampshire

Republican	Votes	%	Democratic	Votes	%
Richard M. Nixon (N.Y.)	65,204	89.3	John F. Kennedy (Mass.)	43,372	85.2
Nelson A. Rockefeller (N.Y.)[1]	2,745	3.8	Others	7,527	14.8
John F. Kennedy (Mass.)[1]	2,196	3.0			
Others	2,886	4.0			

April 5   Wisconsin

Republican	Votes	%	Democratic	Votes	%
Nixon	339,383[2]	100.0	Kennedy	476,024	56.5
			Hubert H. Humphrey (Minn.)	366,753	43.5

April 12   Illinois

Republican	Votes	%	Democratic	Votes	%
Nixon	782,849[2]	99.9	Kennedy[1]	34,332	64.6
Others[1]	442[2]	.1	Adlai E. Stevenson (Ill.)[1]	8,029	15.1
			Stuart Symington (Mo.)[1]	5,744	10.8
			Humphrey[1]	4,283	8.1
			Lyndon B. Johnson (Texas)[1]	442	.8
			Others[1]	337	.6

April 19   New Jersey

Republican	Votes	%	Democratic	Votes	%
Unpledged delegates at large	304,766[2]	100.0	Unpledged delegates at large	217,608[2]	100.0

April 26   Massachusetts

Republican	Votes	%	Democratic	Votes	%
Nixon[1]	53,164	86.0	Kennedy[1]	91,607	92.4
Rockefeller[1]	4,068	6.6	Stevenson[1]	4,684	4.7
Kennedy[1]	2,989	4.8	Humphrey[1]	794	.8
Henry Cabot Lodge (Mass.)[1]	373	.6	Richard M. Nixon (Calif.)[1]	646	.7
Adlai E. Stevenson (Ill.)[1]	266	.4	Symington[1]	443	.4
Barry Goldwater (Ariz.)[1]	221	.4	Johnson[1]	268	.3
Dwight D. Eisenhower (Pa.)[1]	172	.3	Others[1]	721	.7
Others[1]	592	1.0			

April 26   Pennsylvania

Republican	Votes	%	Democratic	Votes	%
Nixon	968,538	98.1	Kennedy[1]	183,073	71.3
Rockefeller[1]	12,491	1.3	Stevenson[1]	29,660	11.5
Kennedy[1]	3,886	.4	Nixon[1]	15,136	5.9
Stevenson[1]	428	—	Humphrey[1]	13,860	5.4
Goldwater[1]	286	—	Symington[1]	6,791	2.6
Others[1]	1,202	.1	Johnson[1]	2,918	1.1
			Rockefeller[1]	1,078	.4
			Others[1]	4,297	1.7

May 3   District of Columbia[3]

Republican	Votes	%	Democratic	Votes	%
Unpledged delegates	9,468	100.0	Humphrey	8,239	57.4
			Wayne L. Morse (Ore.)	6,127	42.6

May 3   Indiana

Republican	Votes	%	Democratic	Votes	%
Nixon	408,408	95.4	Kennedy	353,832	81.0
Others	19,677	4.6	Others	82,937	19.0

May 3   Ohio

Republican	Votes	%	Democratic	Votes	%
Nixon	504,072[2]	100.0	Michael V. DiSalle (Ohio)	315,312[2]	100.0

Republican

Democratic

	Votes	%		Votes	%
May 10 Nebraska					
Nixon	74,356	93.8	Kennedy	80,408	88.7
Rockefeller[1]	2,028	2.6	Symington[1]	4,083	4.5
Goldwater[1]	1,068	1.3	Humphrey[1]	3,202	3.5
Others[1]	1,805	2.3	Stevenson[1]	1,368	1.5
			Johnson[1]	962	1.1
			Others[1]	669	.7
May 10 West Virginia					
Unpledged delegates at large	123,756[2]	100.0	Kennedy	236,510	60.8
			Humphrey	152,187	39.2
May 17 Maryland					
[4]			Kennedy	201,769	70.3
			Morse	49,420	17.2
			Unpledged delegates	24,350	8.5
			Others	11,417	4.0
May 20 Oregon					
Nixon	211,276	93.1	Kennedy	146,332	51.0
Rockefeller[1]	9,307	4.1	Morse	91,715	31.9
Kennedy[1]	2,864	1.3	Humphrey	16,319	5.7
Goldwater[1]	1,571	.7	Symington	12,496	4.4
Others[1]	2,015	.9	Johnson	11,101	3.9
			Stevenson[1]	7,924	2.8
			Others[1]	1,210	.4
May 24 Florida					
Nixon	51,036[2]	100.0	George A. Smathers (Fla.)	322,235[2]	100.0
June 7 California					
Nixon	1,517,652[2]	100.0	Edmund G. Brown (Calif.)	1,354,031	67.7
			George H. McLain (Calif.)	646,387	32.3
June 7 South Dakota					
Unpledged delegates	48,461[2]	100.0	Humphrey	24,773[2]	100.0
TOTALS					
Nixon	4,975,938	89.9	Kennedy	1,847,259	32.5
Unpledged delegates	486,451	8.8	Brown	1,354,031	23.8
Rockefeller	30,639	.6	McLain	646,387	11.4
Kennedy	11,935	.2	Humphrey	590,410	10.4
Goldwater	3,146	.1	Smathers	322,235	5.7
Stevenson	694	—	DiSalle	315,312	5.5
Lodge	373	—	Unpledged delegates	241,958	4.3
Eisenhower	172	—	Morse	147,262	2.6
Others[5]	28,619	.5	Stevenson	51,665	.9
			Symington	29,557	.5
	5,537,967		Nixon	15,782	.3
			Johnson	15,691	.3
			Others[6]	110,192	1.9
				5,687,742	

1. Write-in.
2. Figures obtained from Scammon's office. In *America Votes,* Scammon did not record vote totals if a candidate was unopposed or if the primary was strictly for delegate selection.
3. Source: District of Columbia Board of Elections.
4. No primary.
5. In addition to scattered votes, "others" includes Paul C. Fisher who received

2,388 votes in the New Hampshire primary and Frank R. Beckwith who received 19,677 in the Indiana primary.
6. In addition to scattered votes, "others" includes Lar Daly who received 40,853 votes in the Indiana primary and 7,536 in the Maryland primary; Paul C. Fisher who received 6,853 votes in the New Hampshire primary; John H. Latham who received 42,084 in the Indiana primary and Andrew J. Easter who received 3,881 votes in the Maryland primary.

1964 Primaries

Republican	Votes	%	Democratic	Votes	%
March 10 New Hampshire					
Henry Cabot Lodge (Mass.)[1]	33,007	35.5	Lyndon B. Johnson (Texas)[1]	29,317	95.3
Barry M. Goldwater (Ariz.)	20,692	22.3	Robert F. Kennedy (N.Y.)[1]	487	1.6
Nelson A. Rockefeller (N.Y.)	19,504	21.0	Henry Cabot Lodge (Mass.)[*]	280	.9
Richard M. Nixon (Calif.)[1]	15,587	16.8	Richard M. Nixon (Calif.)[1]	232	.8
Margaret Chase Smith (Maine)	2,120	2.3	Barry M. Goldwater (Ariz.)[1]	193	.6
Harold E. Stassen (Pa.)	1,373	1.5	Nelson A. Rockefeller (N.Y.)[1]	109	.4
William W. Scranton (Pa.)[1]	105	.1	Others[1]	159	.5
Others	465	.5			
April 7 Wisconsin					
John W. Byrnes (Wis.)	299,612	99.7	John W. Reynolds (Wis.)	522,405	66.2
Unpledged delegate	816	.3	George C. Wallace (Ala.)	266,136	33.8
April 14 Illinois					
Goldwater	512,840	62.0	Johnson[1]	82,027	91.6
Smith	209,521	25.3	Wallace[1]	3,761	4.2
Henry Cabot Lodge[1]	68,122	8.2	Robert F. Kennedy[1]	2,894	3.2
Nixon[1]	30,313	3.7	Others[1]	841	.9
George C. Wallace (Ala.)[1]	2,203	.3			
Rockefeller[1]	2,048	.2			
Scranton[1]	1,842	.2			
George W. Romney (Mich.)[1]	465	.1			
Others[1]	437	.1			
April 21 New Jersey					
Henry Cabot Lodge[1]	7,896	41.7	Johnson[1]	4,863	82.3
Goldwater[1]	5,309	28.0	Wallace[1]	491	8.3
Nixon[1]	4,179	22.1	Robert F. Kennedy[1]	431	7.3
Scranton[1]	633	3.3	Others[1]	124	2.1
Rockefeller[1]	612	3.2			
Others[1]	304	1.6			
April 28 Massachusetts					
Henry Cabot Lodge[1]	70,809	76.9	Johnson[1]	61,035	73.4
Goldwater[1]	9,338	10.1	Robert F. Kennedy[1]	15,870	19.1
Nixon[1]	5,460	5.9	Lodge[1]	2,269	2.7
Rockefeller[1]	2,454	2.7	Edward M. Kennedy (Mass.)[1]	1,259	1.5
Scranton[1]	1,709	1.9	Wallace[1]	565	.7
Lyndon B. Johnson (Texas)[1]	600	.7	Adlai E. Stevenson (Ill.)[1]	452	.5
Smith[1]	426	.5	Hubert H. Humphrey (Minn.)[1]	323	.4
George C. Lodge (Mass.)[1]	365	.4	Others[1]	1,436	1.7
Romney[1]	262	.3			
Others[1]	711	.8			
April 28 Pennsylvania					
Scranton[1]	235,222	51.9	Johnson[1]	209,606	82.8
Henry Cabot Lodge[1]	92,712	20.5	Wallace[1]	12,104	4.8
Nixon[1]	44,396	9.8	Robert F. Kennedy[1]	12,029	4.8
Goldwater[1]	38,669	8.5	William W. Scranton (Pa.)[1]	8,156	3.2
Johnson[1]	22,372	4.9	Lodge[1]	4,895	1.9
Rockefeller[1]	9,123	2.0	Others[1]	6,438	2.5
Wallace[1]	5,105	1.1			
Others[1]	5,269	1.2			
May 2 Texas					
Goldwater	104,137	74.7	[2]		
Henry Cabot Lodge[1]	12,324	8.8			
Rockefeller	6,207	4.5			
Nixon[1]	5,390	3.9			
Stassen	5,273	3.8			
Smith	4,816	3.5			
Scranton[1]	803	.6			
Others[1]	373	.3			

Republican   ## Democratic

	Votes	%		Votes	%
May 5 District of Columbia[3]					
[3]			Unpledged delegates	41,095	100.0
May 5 Indiana					
Goldwater	267,935	67.0	Matthew E. Welsh (Ind.)	376,023	64.9
Stassen	107,157	26.8	Wallace	172,646	29.8
Others	24,588	6.2	Others	30,367	5.2
May 5 Ohio					
James A. Rhodes (Ohio)	615,754[4]	100.0	Albert S. Porter (Ohio)	493,619[4]	100.0
May 12 Nebraska					
Goldwater	68,050	49.1	Johnson[1]	54,713	89.3
Nixon[1]	43,613	31.5	Robert F. Kennedy[1]	2,099	3.4
Henry Cabot Lodge[1]	22,622	16.3	Wallace[1]	1,067	1.7
Rockefeller[1]	2,333	1.7	Lodge[1]	1,051	1.7
Scranton[1]	578	.4	Nixon[1]	833	1.4
Johnson[1]	316	.2	Goldwater[1]	603	1.0
Others[1]	1,010	.7	Others[1]	904	1.5
May 12 West Virginia					
Rockefeller	115,680[4]	100.0	Unpledged delegates at large	131,432[4]	100.0
May 15 Oregon					
Rockefeller	94,190	33.0	Johnson	272,099[4]	99.5
Henry Cabot Lodge	79,169	27.7	Wallace[1]	1,365[4]	.5
Goldwater	50,105	17.6			
Nixon	48,274	16.9			
Smith	8,087	2.8			
Scranton	4,509	1.6			
Others	1,152	.4			
May 19 Maryland					
Unpledged delegates	57,004	58.2	Daniel B. Brewster (Md.)	267,106	53.1
Others	40,994	41.8	Wallace	214,849	42.7
			Unpledged delegates	12,377	2.5
			Others	8,275	1.6
May 26 Florida					
Unpledged delegates	58,179	57.8	Johnson	393,339[4]	100.0
Goldwater	42,525	42.2			
June 2 California					
Goldwater	1,120,403	51.6	Unpledged delegates[5]	1,693,813	68.0
Rockefeller	1,052,053	48.4	Unpledged delegates[5]	798,431	32.0
June 2 South Dakota					
Unpledged delegates	57,653	68.0	Unpledged delegates	28,142[4]	100.0
Goldwater	27,076	32.0			

Republican

Democratic

TOTALS

Republican			Democratic		
Goldwater	2,267,079	38.2	Unpledged delegates	2,705,290	43.3
Rockefeller	1,304,204	22.0	Johnson	1,106,999	17.7
Rhodes	615,754	10.4	Wallace	672,984	10.8
Henry Cabot Lodge	386,661	6.5	Reynolds	522,405	8.4
Byrnes	299,612	5.0	Porter	493,619	7.9
Scranton	245,401	4.1	Welsh	376,023	6.0
Smith	224,970	3.8	Brewster	267,106	4.3
Nixon	197,212	3.3	Robert F. Kennedy	33,810	.5
Unpledged delegates	173,652	2.9	Henry Cabot Lodge	8,495	.1
Stassen	113,803	1.9	Scranton	8,156	.1
Johnson	23,288	.4	Edward M. Kennedy	1,259	—
Wallace	7,308	.1	Nixon	1,065	—
Romney	727	—	Goldwater	796	—
George C. Lodge	365	—	Stevenson	452	—
Others6	75,303	1.3	Humphrey	323	—
			Rockefeller	109	—
			Others7	48,544	.8
	5,935,339			6,247,435	

---

1. *Write-in.*
2. *No primary authorized.*
3. Source: *District of Columbia Board of Elections. No figures available for vote for delegates to Republican convention.*
4. *Figures obtained from Scammon's office. In* America Votes, *Scammon did not record vote totals if a candidate was unopposed or if the primary was strictly for delegate selection.*
5. *Gov. Edmund G. Brown (D Calif.) headed the winning slate of delegates and Mayor Sam Yorty of Los Angeles headed the losing slate.*

6. *In addition to scattered votes, "others" includes Norman LePage who received 82 votes in the New Hampshire primary; Frank R. Beckwith who received 17,884 votes and Joseph G. Ettl who received 6,704 votes in the Indiana primary; John W. Steffey who received 22,135 votes and Robert E. Ennis who received 18,859 votes in the Maryland primary.*
7. *In addition to scattered votes, "others" includes Lar Daly who received 15,160 votes, John H. Latham who received 8,067 votes and Fay T. Carpenter Swain who received 7,140 votes in the Indiana primary; and Andrew J. Easter who received 8,275 votes in the Maryland primary.*

1968 Primaries*

	Republican			Democratic	
	Votes	%		Votes	%

March 12   New Hampshire

Republican	Votes	%	Democratic	Votes	%
Richard M. Nixon (N.Y.)	80,666	77.6	Lyndon B. Johnson (Texas)[1]	27,520	49.6
Nelson A. Rockefeller (N.Y.)[1]	11,241	10.8	Eugene J. McCarthy (Minn.)	23,263	41.9
Eugene J. McCarthy (Minn.)[1]	5,511	5.3	Richard M. Nixon (N.Y.)[1]	2,532	4.6
Lyndon B. Johnson (Texas)[1]	1,778	1.7	Others	2,149	3.9
George W. Romney (Mich.)	1,743	1.7			
Harold E. Stassen (Pa.)	429	.4			
Others	2,570	2.5			

April 2   Wisconsin

Republican	Votes	%	Democratic	Votes	%
Nixon	390,368	79.7	McCarthy	412,160	56.2
Ronald Reagan (Calif.)	50,727	10.4	Johnson	253,696	34.6
Stassen	28,531	5.8	Robert F. Kennedy (N.Y.)[1]	46,507	6.3
Rockefeller[1]	7,995	1.6	Unpledged delegates	11,861	1.6
Unpledged delegates	6,763	1.4	George C. Wallace (Ala.)[1]	4,031	.5
Romney[1]	2,087	.4	Hubert H. Humphrey (Minn.)[1]	3,605	.5
Others	3,382	.7	Others	1,142	.2

April 23   Pennsylvania

Republican	Votes	%	Democratic	Votes	%
Nixon[1]	171,815	59.7	McCarthy	428,259	71.7
Rockefeller[1]	52,915	18.4	Robert F. Kennedy[1]	65,430	11.0
McCarthy[1]	18,800	6.5	Humphrey[1]	51,998	8.7
George C. Wallace (Ala.)[1]	13,290	4.6	Wallace[1]	24,147	4.0
Robert F. Kennedy (N.Y.)[1]	10,431	3.6	Johnson[1]	21,265	3.6
Reagan[1]	7,934	2.8	Nixon[1]	3,434	.6
Hubert H. Humphrey (Minn.)[1]	4,651	1.6	Others[1]	2,556	.4
Johnson[1]	3,027	1.1			
Raymond P. Shafer (Pa.)[1]	1,223	.4			
Others[1]	3,487	1.2			

April 30   Massachusetts

Republican	Votes	%	Democratic	Votes	%
Rockefeller[1]	31,964	30.0	McCarthy	122,697	49.3
John A. Volpe (Mass.)	31,465	29.5	Robert F. Kennedy[1]	68,604	27.6
Nixon[1]	27,447	25.8	Humphrey[1]	44,156	17.7
McCarthy[1]	9,758	9.2	Johnson[1]	6,890	2.8
Reagan[1]	1,770	1.7	Nelson A. Rockefeller (N.Y.)[1]	2,275	1.0
Kennedy[1]	1,184	1.1	Wallace[1]	1,688	.7
Others[1]	2,933	2.8	Others[1]	2,593	1.0

May 7   District of Columbia

Republican	Votes	%	Democratic	Votes	%
Nixon-Rockefeller[2]	12,102	90.1	Robert F. Kennedy[3]	57,555	62.5
Unpledged delegates[2]	1,328	9.9	Humphrey[3]	32,309	35.1
			Humphrey[3]	2,250	2.4

May 7   Indiana

Republican	Votes	%	Democratic	Votes	%
Nixon	508,362[4]	100.0	Robert F. Kennedy	328,118	42.3
			Roger D. Branigin (Ind.)	238,700	30.7
			McCarthy	209,695	27.0

May 7   Ohio

Republican	Votes	%	Democratic	Votes	%
James A. Rhodes (Ohio)	614,492[4]	100.0	Stephen M. Young (Ohio)	549,140[4]	100.0

Republican | Democratic

May 14 Nebraska[5]

Republican			Democratic		
Nixon	140,336	70.0	Robert F. Kennedy	84,102	51.7
Reagan	42,703	21.3	McCarthy	50,655	31.2
Rockefeller[1]	10,225	5.1	Humphrey[1]	12,087	7.4
Stassen	2,638	1.3	Johnson	9,187	5.6
McCarthy[1]	1,544	.8	Nixon[1]	2,731	1.7
Others	3,030	1.5	Ronald Reagan (Calif.)[1]	1,905	1.2
			Wallace[1]	1,298	.8
			Others	646	.4

May 14 West Virginia

Republican			Democratic		
Unpledged delegates at large	81,039[4]	100.0	Unpledged delegates at large	149,282[4]	100.0

May 28 Florida

Republican			Democratic		
Unpledged delegates	51,509[4]	100.0	George A. Smathers (Fla.)	236,242	46.1
			McCarthy	147,216	28.7
			Unpledged delegates	128,899	25.2

May 28 Oregon

Republican			Democratic		
Nixon	203,037	65.0	McCarthy	163,990	44.0
Reagan	63,707	20.4	Robert F. Kennedy	141,631	38.0
Rockefeller[1]	36,305	11.6	Johnson	45,174	12.1
McCarthy[1]	7,387	2.4	Humphrey[1]	12,421	3.3
Kennedy[1]	1,723	.6	Reagan[1]	3,082	.8
			Nixon[1]	2,974	.8
			Rockefeller[1]	2,841	.8
			Wallace[1]	957	.3

June 4 California

Republican			Democratic		
Reagan	1,525,091[4]	100.0	Robert F. Kennedy	1,472,166	46.3
			McCarthy	1,329,301	41.8
			Unpledged delegates	380,286	12.0

June 4 New Jersey

Republican			Democratic		
Nixon[1]	71,809	81.1	McCarthy[1]	9,906	36.1
Rockefeller[1]	11,530	13.0	Robert F. Kennedy[1]	8,603	31.3
Reagan[1]	2,737	3.1	Humphrey[1]	5,578	20.3
McCarthy[1]	1,358	1.5	Wallace[1]	1,399	5.1
Others[1]	1,158	1.3	Nixon[1]	1,364	5.0
			Others[1]	596	2.2

June 4 South Dakota

Republican			Democratic		
Nixon	68,113[4]	100.0	Robert F. Kennedy	31,826	49.5
			Johnson	19,316	30.0
			McCarthy	13,145	20.4

June 11 Illinois

Republican			Democratic		
Nixon[1]	17,490	78.1	McCarthy[1]	4,646	38.6
Rockefeller[1]	2,165	9.7	Edward M. Kennedy (Mass.)[1]	4,052	33.7
Reagan[1]	1,601	7.1	Humphrey[1]	2,059	17.1
Others[1]	1,147	5.1	Others[1]	1,281	10.6

Republican

	Votes	%
Reagan	1,696,270	37.9
Nixon	1,679,443	37.5
Rhodes	614,492	13.7
Rockefeller	164,340	3.7
Unpledged delegates	140,639	3.1
McCarthy	44,358	1.0
Stassen	31,598	.7
Volpe	31,465	.7
Robert F. Kennedy	13,338	.3
Wallace	13,290	.3
Nixon-Rockefeller[2]	12,102	.3
Johnson	4,805	.1
Humphrey	4,651	.1
Romney	3,830	.1
Shafer	1,223	—
Others[6]	17,707	.4
	4,473,551	

Democratic

	Votes	%
McCarthy	2,914,933	38.7
Robert F. Kennedy	2,304,542	30.6
Unpledged delegates	670,328	8.9
Young	549,140	7.3
Johnson	383,048	5.1
Branigin	238,700	3.2
Smathers	236,242	3.1
Humphrey	166,463	2.2
Wallace	33,520	.4
Nixon	13,035	.2
Rockefeller	5,116	.1
Reagan	4,987	.1
Edward M. Kennedy	4,052	.1
Others[7]	10,963	.1
	7,535,069	

* Delegate selection primaries were held in Alabama and New York. In America Votes, Scammon did not record vote totals if the primary was strictly for delegate selection and there was no presidential preference voting.

1. Write-in.

2. Prior to the primary, the District Republican organization agreed to divide the nine delegate votes, with six going to Nixon and three going to Rockefeller, according to the 1968 Congressional Quarterly Almanac, Vol. XXIV. Figures obtained from Scammon's office.

3. Figures obtained from Scammon's office. Two slates favored Humphrey; a member of an "independent" Humphrey slate received 2,250 votes.

4. Figures obtained from Scammon's office. In America Votes, Scammon did not record vote totals if a candidate was unopposed or if the primary was strictly for delegate selection.

5. In the American Party presidential primary, Wallace received 493 of the 504 votes cast, or 97.8% of the vote, according to the office of the Nebraska secretary of state.

6. In addition to scattered votes, "others" includes Willis E. Stone who received 527 votes, Herbert F. Hoover who received 247 votes, David Watumull who received 161 votes, William W. Evans who received 151 votes, Elmer W. Coy who received 73 votes and Don DuMont who received 39 votes in the New Hampshire primary; and Americus Liberator who received 1,302 votes in the Nebraska primary.

7. In addition to scattered votes, "others" includes John G. Crommelin who received 186 votes, Richard E. Lee who received 170 votes and Jacob J. Gordon who received 77 votes in the New Hampshire primary.

1972 Primaries*

	Republican			Democratic	
	Votes	%		Votes	%

March 7   New Hampshire

	Votes	%		Votes	%
Richard M. Nixon (Calif.)	79,239	67.6	Edmund S. Muskie (Maine)	41,235	46.4
Paul N. McCloskey (Calif.)	23,190	19.8	George S. McGovern (S.D.)	33,007	37.1
John M. Ashbrook (Ohio)	11,362	9.7	Sam Yorty (Calif.)	5,401	6.1
Others	3,417	2.9	Wilbur D. Mills (Ark.)[1]	3,563	4.0
			Vance Hartke (Ind.)	2,417	2.7
			Edward M. Kennedy (Mass.)[1]	954	1.1
			Hubert H. Humphrey (Minn.)[1]	348	.4
			Henry M. Jackson (Wash.)[1]	197	.2
			George C. Wallace (Ala.)[1]	175	.2
			Others	1,557	1.8

March 14   Florida

	Votes	%		Votes	%
Nixon	360,278	87.0	Wallace	526,651	41.6
Ashbrook	36,617	8.8	Humphrey	234,658	18.6
McCloskey	17,312	4.2	Jackson	170,156	13.5
			Muskie	112,523	8.9
			John V. Lindsay (N.Y.)	82,386	6.5
			McGovern	78,232	6.2
			Shirley Chisholm (N.Y.)	43,989	3.5
			Eugene J. McCarthy (Minn.)	5,847	.5
			Mills	4,539	.4
			Hartke	3,009	.2
			Yorty	2,564	.2

March 21   Illinois

	Votes	%		Votes	%
Nixon[1]	32,550	97.0	Muskie	766,914	62.6
Ashbrook[1]	170	.5	McCarthy	444,260	36.3
McCloskey[1]	47	.1	Wallace[1]	7,017	.6
Others[1]	802	2.4	McGovern[1]	3,687	.3
			Humphrey[1]	1,476	.1
			Chisholm[1]	777	.1
			Jackson[1]	442	—
			Kennedy[1]	242	—
			Lindsay[1]	118	—
			Others	211	—

April 4   Wisconsin

	Votes	%		Votes	%
Nixon	277,601	96.9	McGovern	333,528	29.6
McCloskey	3,651	1.3	Wallace	248,676	22.0
Ashbrook	2,604	.9	Humphrey	233,748	20.7
None of the names shown	2,315	.8	Muskie	115,811	10.3
Others	273	.1	Jackson	88,068	7.8
			Lindsay	75,579	6.7
			McCarthy	15,543	1.4
			Chisholm	9,198	.8
			None of the names shown	2,450	.2
			Yorty	2,349	.2
			Patsy T. Mink (Hawaii)	1,213	.1
			Mills	913	.1
			Hartke	766	.1
			Kennedy[1]	183	—
			Others	559	—

Republican

Democratic

	Votes	%		Votes	%
April 25 Massachusetts					
Nixon	99,150	81.2	McGovern	325,673	52.7
McCloskey	16,435	13.5	Muskie	131,709	21.3
Ashbrook	4,864	4.0	Humphrey	48,929	7.9
Others	1,690	1.4	Wallace	45,807	7.4
			Chisholm	22,398	3.6
			Mills	19,441	3.1
			McCarthy	8,736	1.4
			Jackson	8,499	1.4
			Kennedy[1]	2,348	.4
			Lindsay	2,107	.3
			Hartke	874	.1
			Yorty	646	.1
			Others	1,349	.2
April 25 Pennsylvania					
Nixon[1]	153,886	83.3	Humphrey	481,900	35.1
George C. Wallace (Ala.)[1]	20,472	11.1	Wallace	292,437	21.3
Others[1]	10,443	5.7	McGovern	280,861	20.4
			Muskie	279,983	20.4
			Jackson	38,767	2.8
			Chisholm[1]	306	—
			Others	585	—
May 2 District of Columbia					
[2]			Walter E. Fauntroy (D.C.)	21,217	71.8
			Unpledged delegates	8,343	28.2
May 2 Indiana					
Nixon	417,069	100.0	Humphrey	354,244	47.1
			Wallace	309,495	41.2
			Muskie	87,719	11.7
May 2 Ohio					
Nixon	692,828	100.0	Humphrey	499,680	41.2
			McGovern	480,320	39.6
			Muskie	107,806	8.9
			Jackson	98,498	8.1
			McCarthy	26,026	2.1
May 4 Tennessee					
Nixon	109,696	95.8	Wallace	335,858	68.2
Ashbrook	2,419	2.1	Humphrey	78,350	15.9
McCloskey	2,370	2.1	McGovern	35,551	7.2
Others	4	—	Chisholm	18,809	3.8
			Muskie	9,634	2.0
			Jackson	5,896	1.2
			Mills	2,543	.5
			McCarthy	2,267	.5
			Hartke	1,621	.3
			Lindsay	1,476	.3
			Yorty	692	.1
			Others	24	—

Primary Returns, 1972

Republican   ## Democratic

May 6   North Carolina

Nixon	159,167	94.8	Wallace	413,518	50.3
McCloskey	8,732	5.2	Terry Sanford (N.C.)	306,014	37.3
			Chisholm	61,723	7.5
			Muskie	30,739	3.7
			Jackson	9,416	1.1

May 9   Nebraska

Nixon	179,464	92.4	McGovern	79,309	41.3
McCloskey	9,011	4.6	Humphrey	65,968	34.3
Ashbrook	4,996	2.6	Wallace	23,912	12.4
Others	801	.4	Muskie	6,886	3.6
			Jackson	5,276	2.7
			Yorty	3,459	1.8
			McCarthy	3,194	1.7
			Chisholm	1,763	.9
			Lindsay	1,244	.6
			Mills	377	.2
			Kennedy[1]	293	.2
			Hartke	249	.1
			Others	207	.1

May 9   West Virginia

| Unpledged delegates at large | 95,813[3] | 100.0 | Humphrey | 246,596 | 66.9 |
| | | | Wallace | 121,888 | 33.1 |

May 16   Maryland

Nixon	99,308	86.2	Wallace	219,687	38.7
McCloskey	9,223	8.0	Humphrey	151,981	26.8
Ashbrook	6,718	5.8	McGovern	126,978	22.4
			Jackson	17,728	3.1
			Yorty	13,584	2.4
			Muskie	13,363	2.4
			Chisholm	12,602	2.2
			Mills	4,776	.8
			McCarthy	4,691	.8
			Lindsay	2,168	.4
			Mink	573	.1

May 16   Michigan

Nixon	321,652	95.5	Wallace	809,239	51.0
McCloskey	9,691	2.9	McGovern	425,694	26.8
Unpledged delegates	5,370	1.6	Humphrey	249,798	15.7
Others	30	—	Chisholm	44,090	2.8
			Muskie	38,701	2.4
			Unpledged delegates	10,700	.7
			Jackson	6,938	.4
			Hartke	2,862	.2
			Others	51	—

May 23   Oregon

Nixon	231,151	82.0	McGovern	205,328	50.2
McCloskey	29,365	10.4	Wallace	81,868	20.0
Ashbrook	16,696	5.9	Humphrey	51,163	12.5
Others	4,798	1.7	Jackson	22,042	5.4
			Kennedy	12,673	3.1
			Muskie	10,244	2.5
			McCarthy	8,943	2.2
			Mink	6,500	1.6
			Lindsay	5,082	1.2
			Chisholm	2,975	.7
			Mills	1,208	.3
			Others	618	.2

Republican   ## Democratic

May 23 Rhode Island	Votes	%		Votes	%
Nixon	4,953	88.3	McGovern	15,603	41.2
McCloskey	337	6.0	Muskie	7,838	20.7
Ashbrook	175	3.1	Humphrey	7,701	20.3
Unpledged delegates	146	2.6	Wallace	5,802	15.3
			Unpledged delegates	490	1.3
			McCarthy	245	.6
			Jackson	138	.4
			Mills	41	.1
			Yorty	6	—
June 6 California					
Nixon	2,058,825	90.1	McGovern	1,550,652	43.5
Ashbrook	224,922	9.8	Humphrey	1,375,064	38.6
Others	175	—	Wallace[1]	268,551	7.5
			Chisholm	157,435	4.4
			Muskie	72,701	2.0
			Yorty	50,745	1.4
			McCarthy	34,203	1.0
			Jackson	28,901	.8
			Lindsay	26,246	.7
			Others	20	—
June 6 New Jersey					
Unpledged delegates at large	215,719[3]	100.0	Chisholm	51,433	66.9
			Sanford	25,401	33.1
June 6 New Mexico					
Nixon	49,067	88.5	McGovern	51,011	33.3
McCloskey	3,367	6.1	Wallace	44,843	29.3
None of the names shown	3,035	5.5	Humphrey	39,768	25.9
			Muskie	6,411	4.2
			Jackson	4,236	2.8
			None of the names shown	3,819	2.5
			Chisholm	3,205	2.1
June 6 South Dakota					
Nixon	52,820	100.0	McGovern	28,017	100.0
TOTALS					
Nixon	5,378,704	86.9	Humphrey	4,121,372	25.8
Unpledged delegates	317,048	5.1	McGovern	4,053,451	25.3
Ashbrook	311,543	5.0	Wallace	3,755,424	23.5
McCloskey	132,731	2.1	Muskie	1,840,217	11.5
Wallace	20,472	.3	McCarthy	553,955	3.5
None of the names shown	5,350	.1	Jackson	505,198	3.2
Others[4]	22,433	.4	Chisholm	430,703	2.7
			Sanford	331,415	2.1
	6,188,281		Lindsay	196,406	1.2
			Yorty	79,446	.5
			Mills	37,401	.2
			Fauntroy	21,217	.1
			Unpledged delegates	19,533	.1
			Kennedy	16,693	.1
			Hartke	11,798	.1
			Mink	8,286	.1
			None of the names shown	6,269	—
			Others[5]	5,181	—
				15,993,965	

* Delegate selection primaries were held in Alabama and New York. In America Votes, Scammon did not record vote totals if the primary was strictly for delegate selection and there was no presidential preference voting.

1. Write-in.
2. No Republican primary in 1972.

3. Figures obtained from Scammon's office. In America Votes, Scammon did not record vote totals if the primary was strictly for delegate selection.
4. In addition to scattered votes, "others" includes Patrick Paulsen, who received 1,211 votes in the New Hampshire primary.
5. In addition to scattered votes, "others" includes Edward T. Coll, who received 280 votes in the New Hampshire primary and 589 votes in the Massachusetts primary.

1976 Primaries*

Republican	Votes	%	Democratic	Votes	%

February 24   New Hampshire

Republican	Votes	%	Democratic	Votes	%
Gerald R. Ford (Mich.)	55,156	49.4	Jimmy Carter (Ga.)	23,373	28.4
Ronald Reagan (Calif.)	53,569	48.0	Morris K. Udall (Ariz.)	18,710	22.7
Others[1]	2,949	2.6	Birch Bayh (Ind.)	12,510	15.2
			Fred R. Harris (Okla.)	8,863	10.8
			Sargent Shriver (Md.)	6,743	8.2
			Hubert H. Humphrey (Minn.)	4,596	5.6
			Henry M. Jackson (Wash.)	1,857	2.3
			George C. Wallace (Ala.)	1,061	1.3
			Ellen McCormack (N.Y.)	1,007	1.2
			Others	3,661	4.8

March 2   Massachusetts

Republican	Votes	%	Democratic	Votes	%
Ford	115,375	61.2	Jackson	164,393	22.3
Reagan	63,555	33.7	Udall	130,440	17.7
None of the names shown	6,000	3.2	Wallace	123,112	16.7
Others[1]	3,519	1.8	Carter	101,948	13.9
			Harris	55,701	7.6
			Shriver	53,252	7.2
			Bayh	34,963	4.8
			McCormack	25,772	3.5
			Milton J. Shapp (Pa.)	21,693	2.9
			None of the names shown	9,804	1.3
			Humphrey[1]	7,851	1.1
			Edward M. Kennedy (Mass.)[1]	1,623	0.2
			Lloyd Bentsen (Texas)	364	—
			Others	4,905	0.7

March 2   Vermont

Republican	Votes	%	Democratic	Votes	%
Ford	27,014	84.0	Carter	16,335	42.2
Reagan[1]	4,892	15.2	Shriver	10,699	27.6
Others[1]	251	—	Harris	4,893	12.6
			McCormack	3,324	8.6
			Others	3,463	9.0

March 9   Florida

Republican	Votes	%	Democratic	Votes	%
Ford	321,982	52.8	Carter	448,844	34.5
Reagan	287,837	47.2	Wallace	396,820	30.5
			Jackson	310,944	23.9
			None of the names shown	37,626	2.9
			Shapp	32,198	2.5
			Udall	27,235	2.1
			Bayh	8,750	.7
			McCormack	7,595	.6
			Shriver	7,084	.5
			Harris	5,397	.4
			Robert C. Byrd (W.Va.)	5,042	.4
			Frank Church (Idaho)	4,906	.4
			Others	7,889	.6

March 16   Illinois

Republican	Votes	%	Democratic	Votes	%
Ford	456,750	58.9	Carter	630,915	48.1
Reagan	311,295	40.1	Wallace	361,798	27.6
Lar Daly (Ill.)	7,582	1.0	Shriver	214,024	16.3
Others[1]	266	—	Harris	98,862	7.5
			Others[1]	6,315	.5

Republican

Democratic

	Votes	%		Votes	%
March 23 North Carolina					
Reagan	101,468	52.4	Carter	324,437	53.6
Ford	88,897	45.9	Wallace	210,166	34.7
None of the names shown	3,362	1.7	Jackson	25,749	4.3
			None of the names shown	22,850	3.8
			Udall	14,032	2.3
			Harris	5,923	1.0
			Bentsen	1,675	.3
April 6 Wisconsin					
Ford	326,869	55.2	Carter	271,220	36.6
Reagan	262,126	44.3	Udall	263,771	35.6
None of the names shown	2,234	.3	Wallace	92,460	12.5
Others[1]	583	—	Jackson	47,605	6.4
			McCormack	26,982	3.6
			Harris	8,185	1.1
			None of the names shown	7,154	1.0
			Shriver	5,097	.7
			Bentsen	1,730	.2
			Bayh	1,255	.2
			Shapp	596	.1
			Others[1]	14,473	2.0
April 27 Pennsylvania					
Ford	733,472	92.1	Carter	511,905	37.0
Reagan[1]	40,510	5.1	Jackson	340,340	24.6
Others[1]	22,678	2.8	Udall	259,166	18.7
			Wallace	155,902	11.3
			McCormack	38,800	2.8
			Shapp	32,947	2.4
			Bayh	15,320	1.1
			Harris	13,067	.9
			Humphrey[1]	12,563	.9
			Others	5,032	.3
May 4 District of Columbia					
[2]			Carter	10,521	31.6
			Walter E. Fauntroy (unpledged delegates)	10,149	30.5
			Udall	6,999	21.0
			Walter E. Washington (unpledged delegates)	5,161	15.5
			Harris	461	1.4
May 4 Georgia					
Reagan	128,671	68.3	Carter	419,272	83.4
Ford	59,801	31.7	Wallace	57,594	11.5
			Udall	9,755	1.9
			Byrd	3,628	.7
			Jackson	3,358	.7
			Church	2,477	.5
			Shriver	1,378	.3
			Bayh	824	.2
			Harris	699	.1
			McCormack	635	.1
			Bentsen	277	.1
			Shapp	181	—
			Others	2,393	.5

Republican   ## Democratic

May 4 Indiana	Votes	%		Votes	%
Reagan	323,779	51.3	Carter	417,480	68.0
Ford	307,513	48.7	Wallace	93,121	15.2
			Jackson	72,080	11.7
			McCormack	31,708	5.2

May 11 Nebraska	Votes	%		Votes	%
Reagan	113,493	54.5	Church	67,297	38.5
Ford	94,542	45.4	Carter	65,833	37.6
Others	379	.1	Humphrey	12,685	7.2
			Kennedy	7,199	4.1
			McCormack	6,033	3.4
			Wallace	5,567	3.2
			Udall	4,688	2.7
			Jackson	2,642	1.5
			Harris	811	.5
			Bayh	407	.2
			Shriver	384	.2
			Others[1]	1,467	.8

May 11 West Virginia	Votes	%		Votes	%
Ford	88,386	56.8	Byrd	331,639	89.0
Reagan	67,306	43.2	Wallace	40,938	11.0

May 18 Maryland	Votes	%		Votes	%
Ford	96,291	58.0	Edmund G. Brown Jr. (Calif.)	286,672	48.4
Reagan	69,680	42.0	Carter	219,404	37.1
			Udall	32,790	5.5
			Wallace	24,176	4.1
			Jackson	13,956	2.4
			McCormack	7,907	1.3
			Harris	6,841	1.2

May 18 Michigan	Votes	%		Votes	%
Ford	690,180	64.9	Carter	307,559	43.4
Reagan	364,052	34.3	Udall	305,134	43.1
Unpledged delegates	8,473	.8	Wallace	49,204	6.9
Others[1]	109	—	Unpledged delegates	15,853	2.2
			Jackson	10,332	1.5
			McCormack	7,623	1.1
			Shriver	5,738	.8
			Harris	4,081	.6
			Others[1]	3,142	.4

May 25 Arkansas	Votes	%		Votes	%
Reagan	20,628	63.4	Carter	314,306	62.6
Ford	11,430	35.1	Wallace	83,005	16.5
Unpledged delegates	483	1.5	Unpledged delegates	57,152	11.4
			Udall	37,783	7.5
			Jackson	9,554	1.9

May 25 Idaho	Votes	%		Votes	%
Reagan	66,743	74.3	Church	58,570	78.7
Ford	22,323	24.9	Carter	8,818	11.9
Unpledged delegates	727	.8	Humphrey	1,700	2.3
			Brown[1]	1,453	2.0
			Wallace	1,115	1.5
			Udall	981	1.3
			Unpledged delegates	964	1.3
			Jackson	485	.7
			Harris	319	.4

Republican

Democratic

	Votes	%		Votes	%
May 25 Kentucky					
Ford	67,976	50.9	Carter	181,690	59.4
Reagan	62,683	46.9	Wallace	51,540	16.8
Unpledged delegates	1,781	1.3	Udall	33,262	10.9
Others	1,088	.8	McCormack	17,061	5.6
			Unpledged delegates	11,962	3.9
			Jackson	8,186	2.7
			Others	2,305	.8
May 25 Nevada					
Reagan	31,637	66.3	Brown	39,671	52.7
Ford	13,747	28.8	Carter	17,567	23.3
None of the names shown	2,365	5.0	Church	6,778	9.0
			None of the names shown	4,603	6.1
			Wallace	2,490	3.3
			Udall	2,237	3.0
			Jackson	1,896	2.5
May 25 Oregon					
Ford	150,181	50.3	Church	145,394	33.6
Reagan	136,691	45.8	Carter	115,310	26.7
Others[1]	11,663	3.9	Brown[1]	106,812	24.7
			Humphrey	22,488	5.2
			Udall	11,747	2.7
			Kennedy	10,983	2.5
			Wallace	5,797	1.3
			Jackson	5,298	1.2
			McCormack	3,753	.9
			Harris	1,344	.3
			Bayh	743	.2
			Others[1]	2,963	.7
May 25 Tennessee					
Ford	120,685	49.8	Carter	259,243	77.6
Reagan	118,997	49.1	Wallace	36,495	10.9
Unpledged delegates	2,756	1.1	Udall	12,420	3.7
Others[1]	97	—	Church	8,026	2.4
			Unpledged delegates	6,148	1.8
			Jackson	5,672	1.7
			McCormack	1,782	.5
			Harris	1,628	.5
			Brown[1]	1,556	.5
			Shapp	507	.2
			Humphrey[1]	109	—
			Others[1]	492	.1
June 1 Montana					
Reagan	56,683	63.1	Church	63,448	59.4
Ford	31,100	34.6	Carter	26,329	24.6
None of the names shown	1,996	2.2	Udall	6,708	6.3
			None of the names shown	3,820	3.6
			Wallace	3,680	3.4
			Jackson	2,856	2.7
June 1 Rhode Island					
Ford	9,365	65.3	Unpledged delegates	19,035	31.5
Reagan	4,480	31.2	Carter	18,237	30.2
Unpledged delegates	507	3.5	Church	16,423	27.2
			Udall	2,543	4.2
			McCormack	2,468	4.1
			Jackson	756	1.3
			Wallace	507	.8
			Bayh	247	.4
			Shapp	132	.2

Republican

Democratic

	Votes	%		Votes	%
June 1 South Dakota					
Reagan	43,068	51.2	Carter	24,186	41.2
Ford	36,976	44.0	Udall	19,510	33.3
None of the names shown	4,033	4.8	None of the names shown	7,871	13.4
			McCormack	4,561	7.8
			Wallace	1,412	2.4
			Harris	573	1.0
			Jackson	558	1.0
June 8 California					
Reagan	1,604,836	65.5	Brown	2,013,210	59.0
Ford	845,655	34.5	Carter	697,092	20.4
Others[1]	20	—	Church	250,581	7.3
			Udall	171,501	5.0
			Wallace	102,292	3.0
			Unpledged delegates	78,595	2.3
			Jackson	38,634	1.1
			McCormack	29,242	.9
			Harris	16,920	.5
			Bayh	11,419	.3
			Others[1]	215	—
June 8 New Jersey					
Ford	242,122	100.00	Carter	210,655	58.4
			Church	49,034	13.6
			Jackson	31,820	8.8
			Wallace	31,183	8.6
			McCormack	21,774	6.0
			Others	16,373	4.5
June 8 Ohio					
Ford	516,111	55.2	Carter	593,130	52.3
Reagan	419,646	44.8	Udall	240,342	21.2
			Church	157,884	13.9
			Wallace	63,953	5.6
			Gertrude W. Donahey (unpledged delegates)	43,661	3.9
			Jackson	35,404	3.1

TOTALS

	Votes	%		Votes	%
Ford	5,529,899	53.3	Carter	6,235,609	38.8
Reagan	4,758,325	45.9	Brown	2,449,374	15.3
None of the names shown	19,990	0.2	Wallace	1,995,388	12.4
Unpledged delegates	14,727	0.1	Udall	1,611,754	10.0
Daly	7,582	0.1	Jackson	1,134,375	7.1
Others[3]	43,602	0.4	Church	830,818	5.2
			Byrd	340,309	2.1
	10,374,125		Shriver	304,399	1.9
			Unpledged delegates	248,680	1.5
			McCormack	238,027	1.5
			Harris	234,568	1.5
			None of the names shown	93,728	0.6
			Shapp	88,254	0.5
			Bayh	86,438	0.5
			Humphrey	61,992	0.4
			Kennedy	19,805	0.1
			Bentsen	4,046	—
			Others[4]	75,088	0.5
				16,052,652	

Delegate selection primaries were held in Alabama, New York and Texas. In America Votes, Scammon did not record vote totals if the primary was strictly for delegate selection and there was no presidential preference voting.

1. Write-in.

2. Ford unopposed. No primary held.

3. In addition to scattered write-in votes, "others" include Tommy Klein, who received 1,088 votes in Kentucky.

4. In addition to scattered write-in votes, "others" include Frank Ahern who received 1,487 votes in Georgia; Stanley Arnold, 371 votes in New Hampshire; Arthur O. Blessitt, 828 votes in New Hampshire and 7,889 in Georgia; Frank Bona, 135 votes in New Hampshire and 263 in Georgia; Billy Joe Clegg, 174 votes in New Hampshire; Abram Eisenman, 351 votes in Georgia; John S. Gonas, 2,288 votes in New Jersey; Jesse Gray, 3,574 votes in New Jersey; Robert L. Kelleher, 87 votes in New Hampshire, 1,603 in Massachusetts and 139 in Georgia; Rick Loewenherz, 49 votes in New Hampshire; Frank Lomento, 3,555 votes in New Jersey, Floyd L. Lunger, 3,935 votes in New Jersey; H. R. H. "Fifi" Rockefeller, 2,305 votes in Kentucky; George Roden, 153 votes in Georgia; Ray Rollinson, 3,021 votes in New Jersey; Terry Sanford, 53 votes in New Hampshire and 351 votes in Massachusetts; Bernard B. Schechter, 173 votes in New Hampshire.

1980 Primaries[1]

Republican	Votes	%	Democratic	Votes	%
February 17 Puerto Rico			**March 16**		
George Bush (Texas)[2]	111,940	60.1	Jimmy Carter (Ga.)	449,681	51.7
Howard H. Baker Jr. (Tenn.)[3]	68,934	37.0	Edward M. Kennedy (Mass.)	418,068	48.0
Benjamin Fernandez (Calif.)	2,097	1.1	Edmund G. Brown Jr. (Calif.)[5]	1,660	0.2
John B. Connally (Texas)[4]	1,964	1.1	Others	826	0.1
Harold Stassen (N.Y.)	672	0.4			
Robert Dole (Kan.)	483	0.3			
Others	281	0.1			
February 26 New Hampshire					
Ronald Reagan (Calif.)	72,983	49.6	Carter	52,692	47.1
Bush	33,443	22.7	Kennedy	41,745	37.3
Baker	18,943	12.1	Brown	10,743	9.6
John B. Anderson (Ill.)[6]	14,458	9.8	Lyndon LaRouche (N.Y.)	2,326	2.1
Philip M. Crane (Ill.)	2,618	1.8	Richard Kay (Ohio)	566	0.5
Connally	2,239	1.5	Others[7]	3,858	3.4
Dole	597	—			
Others[7]	1,876	1.3			
March 4 Massachusetts					
Bush	124,365	31.0	Kennedy	590,393	65.1
Anderson	122,987	30.7	Carter	260,401	28.7
Reagan	115,334	28.8	Brown	31,498	3.5
Baker	19,366	4.8	Others[7]	5,368	0.6
Connally	4,714	1.2	No preference	19,663	2.2
Crane	4,669	1.2			
Gerald R. Ford (Mich.)[7]	3,398	0.8			
Dole	577	—			
Fernandez	374	0.1			
Stassen	218	0.1			
Others[7]	2,581	0.6			
No preference	2,243	0.6			
March 4 Vermont					
Reagan	19,720	30.1	Carter	29,015	73.1
Anderson	19,030	29.0	Kennedy	10,135	25.5
Bush	14,226	21.7	Brown[7]	358	0.9
Baker	8,055	12.3	LaRouche[7]	6	—
Ford[7]	2,300	3.5	Others	189	0.5
Crane	1,238	1.9			
Connally	884	1.3			
Stassen	105	0.2			
Others[7]	53	—			
March 8 South Carolina					
Reagan	79,549	54.7			
Connally	43,113	29.6			
Bush	21,569	14.8			
Baker	773	0.5			
Fernandez	171	0.1			
Stassen	150	0.1			
Dole	117	0.1			
Nick Belluso	59	—			

Republican

Democratic

	Votes	%		Votes	%

March 11 Alabama

Reagan	147,352	69.7	Carter	193,734	81.6
Bush	54,730	25.9	Kennedy	31,382	13.2
Crane	5,099	2.4	Brown	9,529	4.0
Baker	1,963	0.9	William L. Nuckols	609	—
Connally	1,077	0.5	Bob Maddox	540	—
Stassen	544	0.3	Unpledged delegates	1,670	0.7
Dole	447	0.2			
Belluso	141	—			

March 11 Florida

Reagan	345,699	56.2	Carter	666,321	60.7
Bush	185,996	30.2	Kennedy	254,727	23.2
Anderson	56,636	9.2	Brown	53,474	4.9
Crane	12,000	2.0	Kay	19,160	1.7
Baker	6,345	1.0	No preference	104,321	9.5
Connally	4,958	0.8			
Stassen	1,377	0.2			
Dole	1,086	0.2			
Fernandez	898	0.1			

March 11 Georgia

Reagan	146,500	73.2	Carter	338,772	88.0
Bush	25,293	12.6	Kennedy	32,315	8.4
Anderson	16,853	8.4	Brown	7,255	1.9
Crane	6,308	3.2	Cliff Finch (Miss.)	1,378	0.4
Connally	2,388	1.2	Kay	840	0.2
Baker	1,571	0.8	LaRouche	513	0.1
Fernandez	809	0.4	Unpledged delegates	3,707	1.0
Dole	249	0.1			
Stassen	200	0.1			

March 18 Illinois

Reagan	547,355	48.4	Carter	780,787	65.0
Anderson	415,193	36.7	Kennedy	359,875	30.0
Bush	124,057	11.0	Brown	39,168	3.3
Crane	24,865	2.2	LaRouche	19,192	1.6
Baker	7,051	0.6	Anderson [7]	1,643	0.1
Connally	4,548	0.4	Others [7]	402	—
V. A. Kelley	3,757	0.3			
Dole	1,843	0.2			
Ford [7]	1,106	0.1			
Others	306	—			

March 25 Connecticut

Bush	70,367	38.6	Kennedy	98,662	46.9
Reagan	61,735	33.9	Carter	87,207	41.5
Anderson	40,354	22.1	LaRouche	5,617	2.7
Baker	2,446	1.3	Brown	5,386	2.6
Crane	1,887	1.0	Unpledged delegates	13,403	6.4
Connally	598	0.3			
Dole	333	0.2			
Fernandez	308	0.2			
Unpledged delegates	4,256	2.3			

Republican

	Votes	%

Democratic

	Votes	%

March 25 New York

Republican	Votes	%	Democratic	Votes	%
			Kennedy	582,757	58.9
			Carter	406,305	41.1

April 1 Kansas

Republican	Votes	%	Democratic	Votes	%
Reagan	179,739	63.0	Carter	109,807	56.6
Anderson	51,924	18.2	Kennedy	61,318	31.6
Bush	35,838	12.6	Brown	9,434	4.9
Baker	3,603	1.3	Finch	629	0.3
Connally	2,067	0.7	Maddox	632	0.3
Fernandez	1,650	0.6	Frank Ahern	571	0.2
Crane	1,367	0.5	Ray Rollinson	364	—
R. W. Yeager	1,063	0.4	None of the names shown	11,163	5.8
Alvin G. Carris	483	0.2			
Stassen	383	0.1			
William E. Carlson	311	—			
Donald Badgley	244	—			
None of the names shown	6,726	2.4			

April 1 Wisconsin

Republican	Votes	%	Democratic	Votes	%
Reagan	364,898	40.2	Carter	353,662	56.2
Bush	276,164	30.4	Kennedy	189,520	30.1
Anderson	248,623	27.4	Brown	74,496	11.8
Baker	3,298	0.4	LaRouche	6,896	1.1
Crane	2,951	0.3	Finch	1,842	0.3
Connally	2,312	0.3	Others [7]	509	0.1
Fernandez	1,051	0.1	None of the names shown	2,694	0.4
Stassen	1,010	0.1			
Others [7]	4,951	0.5			
None of the names shown	2,595	0.3			

April 5 Louisiana

Republican	Votes	%	Democratic	Votes	%
Reagan	31,212	74.9	Carter	199,956	55.7
Bush	7,818	18.8	Kennedy	80,797	22.5
Stassen	126	0.3	Brown	16,774	4.7
Belluso	155	0.3	Finch	11,153	3.1
Fernandez	84	0.2	Kay	3,362	0.9
C. Leon Pickett	67	—	Maddox	2,830	0.8
None of the names shown	2,221	5.3	Don Reaux	2,255	0.6
			Unpledged delegates	41,614	11.6

April 22 Pennsylvania

Republican	Votes	%	Democratic	Votes	%
Bush	626,759	50.5	Kennedy	736,854	45.7
Reagan	527,916	42.5	Carter	732,332	45.4
Baker	30,846	2.5	Brown	37,669	2.3
Anderson	26,890	2.1	Anderson [7]	9,182	0.6
Connally	10,656	0.9	Bush [7]	2,074	0.1
Stassen	6,767	0.5	Reagan [7]	1,097	0.1
Alvin J. Jacobson	4,357	0.4	Ford [7]	150	—
Fernandez	2,521	0.2	No preference	93,865	5.8
Others	4,699	0.4			

May 3 Texas

Republican	Votes	%	Democratic	Votes	%
Reagan	268,798	51.0	Carter	770,390	55.9
Bush	249,819	47.4	Kennedy	314,129	22.8
Unpledged delegates	8,152	1.5	Brown	35,585	2.6
			Unpledged delegates	257,250	18.7

Republican	Votes	%	Democratic	Votes	%

May 6 District of Columbia

Republican	Votes	%	Democratic	Votes	%
Bush	4,973	66.1	Kennedy	39,561	61.7
Anderson	2,025	26.9	Carter	23,697	36.9
Crane	270	3.6	LaRouche	892	1.4
Stassen	201	2.7			
Fernandez	60	0.8			

May 6 Indiana

Republican	Votes	%	Democratic	Votes	%
Reagan	419,016	73.7	Carter	398,949	67.7
Bush	92,955	16.4	Kennedy	190,492	32.3
Anderson	56,342	9.9			

May 6 North Carolina

Republican	Votes	%	Democratic	Votes	%
Reagan	113,854	67.6	Carter	516,778	70.1
Bush	36,631	21.8	Kennedy	130,684	17.7
Anderson	8,542	5.1	Brown	21,420	2.9
Baker	2,543	1.5	No preference	68,380	9.3
Connally	1,107	0.7			
Dole	629	0.4			
Crane	547	0.3			
No preference	4,538	2.7			

May 6 Tennessee

Republican	Votes	%	Democratic	Votes	%
Reagan	144,625	74.1	Carter	221,658	75.2
Bush	35,274	18.1	Kennedy	53,258	18.1
Anderson	8,722	4.5	Brown	5,612	1.9
Crane	1,574	0.8	Finch	1,663	0.6
Baker [7]	16	—	LaRouche	925	0.3
Ford [7]	14	—	Others [7]	49	—
Connally [7]	1	—	Unpledged delegates	11,515	3.9
Others [7]	8	—			
Unpledged delegates	4,976	2.5			

May 13 Maryland

Republican	Votes	%	Democratic	Votes	%
Reagan	80,557	48.2	Carter	226,528	47.5
Bush	68,389	40.9	Kennedy	181,091	38.0
Anderson	16,244	9.7	Brown	14,313	3.0
Crane	2,113	1.3	Finch	4,891	1.0
			LaRouche	4,388	0.9
			Unpledged delegates	45,879	9.6

May 13 Nebraska

Republican	Votes	%	Democratic	Votes	%
Reagan	155,995	76.0	Carter	72,120	46.9
Bush	31,380	15.3	Kennedy	57,826	37.6
Anderson	11,879	5.8	Brown	5,478	3.6
Dole	1,420	0.7	LaRouche	1,169	0.8
Crane	1,062	0.5	Others [7]	1,247	0.8
Stassen	799	0.4	Unpledged delegates	16,041	10.4
Fernandez	400	0.2			
Others [7]	2,268	1.1			

Republican	Votes	%	Democratic	Votes	%
May 20 Michigan					
Bush	341,998	57.5	Brown	23,043	29.4
Reagan	189,184	31.8	LaRouche	8,948	11.4
Anderson	48,947	8.2	Others [7]	10,048	12.8
Fernandez	2,248	0.4	Unpledged delegates	36,385	46.4
Stassen	1,938	0.3			
Others [7]	596	0.1			
Unpledged delegates	10,265	1.7			
May 20 Oregon					
Reagan	170,449	54.0	Carter	208,693	56.7
Bush	109,210	34.6	Kennedy	114,651	31.1
Anderson	32,118	10.2	Brown	34,409	9.3
Crane	2,324	0.7	Anderson [7]	5,407	1.5
Others [7]	1,265	0.4	Reagan [7]	2,206	0.6
			Bush [7]	1,838	0.5
May 27 Arkansas					
			Carter	269,375	60.1
			Kennedy	78,542	17.5
			Finch	19,469	4.3
			Unpledged delegates	80,904	18.0
May 27 Idaho					
Reagan	111,868	82.9	Carter	31,383	62.2
Anderson	13,130	9.7	Kennedy	11,087	22.0
Bush	5,416	4.0	Brown	2,078	4.1
Crane	1,024	0.8	Unpledged delegates	5,934	11.8
Unpledged delegates	3,441	2.6			
May 27 Kentucky					
Reagan	78,072	82.4	Carter	160,819	66.9
Bush	6,861	7.2	Kennedy	55,167	23.0
Anderson	4,791	5.1	Kay	2,609	1.1
Stassen	1,223	1.3	Finch	2,517	1.0
Fernandez	764	0.8	Unpledged delegates	19,219	8.0
Unpledged delegates	3,084	3.3			
May 27 Nevada					
Reagan	39,352	83.0	Carter	25,159	37.6
Bush	3,078	6.5	Kennedy	19,296	28.8
None of the names shown	4,965	10.5	None of the names shown	22,493	33.6
June 3 California					
Reagan	2,057,923	80.3	Kennedy slate	1,507,142	44.8
Anderson	349,315	13.6	Carter slate	1,266,276	37.6
Bush	125,113	4.9	Brown slate	135,962	4.0
Crane	21,465	0.8	LaRouche slate	71,779	2.1
Fernandez	10,242	0.4	Others [7]	51	—
Others [7]	14	—	Unpledged slate	382,759	11.4

Republican

Democratic

	Votes	%		Votes	%
June 3 New Mexico					
Reagan	37,982	63.8	Kennedy	73,721	46.3
Anderson	7,171	12.0	Carter	66,621	41.8
Bush	5,892	9.9	LaRouche	4,798	3.0
Crane	4,412	7.4	Finoh	4,490	2.8
Fernandez	1,795	3.0	Unpledged delegates	9,734	6.1
Stassen	947	1.6			
Unpledged delegates	1,347	2.3			
June 3 New Jersey					
Reagan	225,959	81.3	Kennedy	315,109	56.2
Bush	47,447	17.1	Carter	212,387	37.9
Stassen	4,571	1.6	LaRouche	13,913	2.5
			Unpledged delegates	19,499	3.5
June 3 Montana					
Reagan	68,744	86.6	Carter	66,922	51.5
Bush	7,665	9.7	Kennedy	47,671	36.7
No preference	3,014	3.8	No preference	15,466	11.9
June 3 Ohio					
Reagan	692,288	80.8	Carter	605,744	51.1
Bush	164,485	19.2	Kennedy	523,874	44.4
			LaRouche	35,268	3.0
			Kay	21,524	1.8
June 3 Rhode Island					
Reagan	3,839	72.0	Kennedy	26,179	68.3
Bush	993	18.6	Carter	9,907	25.8
Stassen	107	2.0	LaRouche	1,160	3.0
Fernandez	48	0.9	Brown	310	0.8
Unpledged delegates	348	6.5	Unpledged delegates	771	2.0
June 3 South Dakota					
Reagan slate	72,861	82.2	Kennedy slate	33,418	48.6
Bush	3,691	4.2	Carter slate	31,251	45.4
Stassen	987	1.1	Uncommitted slate	4,094	6.0
No preference	5,366	6.1			
June 3 West Virginia					
Reagan	115,407	83.6	Carter	197,687	62.2
Bush	19,509	14.1	Kennedy	120,247	37.8
Stassen	3,100	2.2			
June 3 Mississippi					
Reagan slate	23,028	89.4			
Bush slate	2,105	8.2			
Unslated	618	2.4			

Republican

Democratic

	Votes	%
TOTALS [8]		
Reagan	7,709,793	*60.8*
Bush	2,958,093	*23.3*
Anderson	1,572,174	*12.4*
Baker	112,219	*0.9*
Crane	97,793	*0.8*
Connally	80,661	*0.6*
Stassen	24,753	*0.2*
Fernandez	23,423	*0.2*
Dole	7,298	*0.1*
Jacobsen	4,357	—
Kelley	3,757	—
Yeager	1,063	—
Carris	483	—
Belluso	355	—
Carlson	311	—
Badgley	244	—
Pickett	67	—
Unpledged delegates	38,708	*0.3*
No preference	15,161	*0.1*
None of the names shown	14,286	*0.1*
Others	25,452	*0.2*
	12,690,451	

	Votes	%
Carter	9,593,335	*51.2*
Kennedy	6,963,625	*37.1*
Brown	573,636	*3.1*
LaRouche	177,784	*1.0*
Kay	48,061	*0.3*
Finch	48,032	*0.3*
Maddox	4,002	—
Reaux	2,255	—
Nuckols	609	—
Ahern	571	—
Rollinson	364	—
Unpledged delegates	950,378	*5.1*
No preference	301,695	*1.6*
None of the names shown	36,350	*0.1*
Others	47,128	*0.2*
	18,747,825	

1. In 1980, 35 states, the District of Columbia and Puerto Rico held presidential primaries. California Democrats and South Dakota Republicans and Democrats held state-type preference primaries. In New York, Democrats had a presidential preference, but Republicans held primaries for the selection of delegates only, without indication of presidential preference. In Mississippi, Republicans elected delegates by congressional districts pledged to candidates and the vote indicated is for the highest of each slate's candidates in each congressional district. In Arkansas, the Republicans did not hold a primary although Democrats did. In South Carolina, the Democrats did not hold a primary but Republicans did. The vote in Ohio is for at-large delegates pledged to specific candidates and elected as a group. The Republican and Democratic primaries in Puerto Rico were held on two different dates: February 17 and March 16, respectively.

2. Bush withdrew May 26.
3. Baker withdrew March 5.
4. Connally withdrew March 9.
5. Brown withdrew April 1.
6. Anderson withdrew April 24.
7. Write-in vote.
8. Totals exclude Puerto Rico, where citizens are unable to vote in the general election.

1984 Primaries

Republican			Democratic		
	Votes	%		Votes	%

February 28 New Hampshire

Ronald Reagan (Calif.)	65,033	86.1	Gary Hart (Colo.)	37,702	37.3
Harold E. Stassen (Pa.)	1,543	2.0	Walter F. Mondale (Minn.)	28,173	27.9
David Kelly (La.)	360	0.5	John Glenn (Ohio)	12,088	12.0
Gary Arnold (Minn.)	252	0.3	Jesse Jackson (Ill.)	5,311	5.3
Benjamin Fernandez (Calif.)	202	0.3	George McGovern (S.D.)	5,217	5.2
Others [1]	8,180	10.8	Ernest F. Hollings (S.C.)	3,583	3.5
			Alan Cranston (Calif.)	2,136	2.1
			Reubin Askew (Fla.)	1,025	1.0
			Stephen A. Koczak (D.C.)	155	0.2
			Gerald Willis (Ala.)	50	—
			Richard B. Kay (Fla.)	27	—
			Others [1]	5,664	5.6

March 6 Vermont [2]

Reagan	33,218	98.7	Hart	51,873	70.0
Others	425	1.3	Mondale	14,834	20.0
			Jackson	5,761	7.8
			Askew	444	0.6
			Others	1,147	1.5

March 13 Alabama

[3]			Mondale	148,165	34.6
			Glenn	89,286	20.8
			Hart	88,465	20.7
			Jackson	83,787	19.6
			Willis	6,153	1.4
			Hollings	4,759	1.1
			Unpledged delegates	4,464	1.0
			Askew	1,827	0.4
			Cranston	1,377	0.3

March 13 Florida

Reagan	344,150	100.0	Hart	463,799	39.2
			Mondale	394,350	33.4
			Jackson	144,263	12.2
			Glenn	128,209	10.8
			Askew	26,258	2.2
			McGovern	17,614	1.5
			Hollings	3,115	0.3
			Cranston	2,097	0.2
			Kay	1,328	0.1
			Koczak	1,157	0.1

Republican

	Votes	%

Democratic

	Votes	%

March 13 Georgia

Republican	Votes	%	Democratic	Votes	%
Reagan	50,793	100.0	Mondale	208,588	30.5
			Hart	186,903	27.3
			Jackson	143,730	21.0
			Glenn	122,744	17.9
			McGovern	11,321	1.7
			Hollings	3,800	0.6
			Unpledged delegates	3,068	0.4
			Willis	1,804	0.3
			Askew	1,660	0.2
			Cranston	923	0.1

March 13 Massachusetts

Republican	Votes	%	Democratic	Votes	%
Reagan	58,996	89.5	Hart	245,943	39.0
No preference	5,005	7.6	Mondale	160,893	25.5
Others	1,936	2.9	McGovern	134,341	21.3
			Glenn	45,456	7.2
			Jackson	31,824	5.0
			No preference	5,080	0.8
			Askew	1,394	0.2
			Hollings	1,203	0.2
			Cranston	853	0.1
			Others	3,975	0.6

March 13 Rhode Island

Republican	Votes	%	Democratic	Votes	%
Reagan	2,028	90.7	Hart	20,011	45.0
Unpledged delegates	207	9.3	Mondale	15,338	34.5
			Jackson	3,875	8.7
			Glenn	2,249	5.0
			McGovern	2,146	4.8
			Unpledged delegates	439	1.0
			Cranston	273	0.6
			Askew	96	0.2
			Hollings	84	0.2

March 18 Puerto Rico

[3]

Democratic	Votes	%
Mondale	141,698	99.1
Hart	874	0.6
Glenn	436	0.3
Sterling P. Davis (Miss.)	31	—

March 20 Illinois

Republican	Votes	%	Democratic	Votes	%
Reagan	594,742	99.9	Mondale	670,951	40.4
Others	336	0.1	Hart	584,579	35.2
			Jackson	348,843	21.0
			McGovern	25,336	1.5
			Glenn	19,800	1.2
			Betty Jean Williams (Ill.)	4,797	0.3
			Cranston	2,786	0.2
			Askew	2,182	0.1
			Others	151	—

	Republican			Democratic		
		Votes	%		Votes	%

March 27 Connecticut

[3]

				Hart	116,286	52.7
				Mondale	64,230	29.1
				Jackson	26,395	12.0
				Askew	6,098	2.8
				McGovern	2,426	1.1
				Hollings	2,283	1.0
				Unpledged delegates	1,973	0.9
				Glenn	955	0.4
				Cranston	196	0.1

April 3 New York

[3]

				Mondale	621,581	44.8
				Hart	380,564	27.4
				Jackson	355,541	25.6
				Glenn	15,941	1.1
				Cranston	6,815	0.5
				McGovern	4,547	0.3
				Askew	2,877	0.2
				Others	84	—

April 3 Wisconsin [4]

				Democratic		
"Ronald Reagan Yes"	280,608	95.2		Hart	282,435	44.4
"Ronald Reagan No"	14,047	4.7		Mondale	261,374	41.1
Others [1]	158	0.1		Jackson	62,524	9.8
				McGovern	10,166	1.6
				"None of the names shown"	7,036	1.1
				Glenn	6,398	1.0
				Cranston	2,984	0.5
				Hollings	1,650	0.3
				Askew	683	0.1
				Others	518	0.1

April 10 Pennsylvania

Reagan	616,916	99.3		Mondale	747,267	45.1
Others	4,290	0.7		Hart	551,335	33.3
				Jackson	264,463	16.0
				Cranston	22,829	1.4
				Glenn	22,605	1.4
				Lyndon H. LaRouche Jr. (Va.)	19,180	1.2
				McGovern	13,139	0.8
				Robert K. Griser (Pa.)	6,090	0.4
				Askew	5,071	0.3
				Hollings	2,972	0.2
				Others	1,343	0.1

May 1 District of Columbia

Reagan	5,692	100.0		Jackson	69,106	67.3
				Mondale	26,320	25.6
				Hart	7,305	7.1

Republican   # Democratic

	Votes	%			Votes	%

May 1 Tennessee

Reagan	75,367	90.9	Mondale		132,201	41.0
Unpledged delegates	7,546	9.1	Hart		93,710	29.1
Others	8	—	Jackson		81,418	25.3
			Unpledged delegates		6,682	2.1
			Glenn		4,198	1.3
			McGovern		3,824	1.2
			Others		30	—

May 5 Louisiana

Reagan	14,964	89.7	Jackson		136,707	42.9
Unpledged delegates	1,723	10.3	Hart		79,593	25.0
			Mondale		71,162	22.3
			Unpledged delegates		19,409	6.1
			LaRouche		4,970	1.6
			McGovern		3,158	1.0
			Griser		1,924	0.6
			Kay		1,344	0.4
			Koczak		543	0.2

May 5 Texas

Reagan	308,713	96.5	[3]			
Unpledged delegates	11,126	3.5				

May 8 Indiana

Reagan	428,559	100.0	Hart		299,491	41.8
			Mondale		293,413	40.9
			Jackson		98,190	13.7
			Glenn		16,046	2.2
			Bob Brewster (Fla.)		9,815	1.4

May 8 Maryland

Reagan	73,663	100.0	Mondale		215,222	42.5
			Jackson		129,387	25.5
			Hart		123,365	24.3
			Unpledged delegates		15,807	3.1
			LaRouche		7,836	1.5
			Glenn		6,238	1.2
			McGovern		5,796	1.1
			Cranston		1,768	0.3
			Hollings		1,467	0.3

May 8 North Carolina

[3]			Mondale		342,324	35.6
			Hart		289,877	30.2
			Jackson		243,945	25.4
			No preference		44,232	4.6
			Glenn		17,659	1.8
			McGovern		10,149	1.1
			Hollings		8,318	0.9
			Askew		3,144	0.3
			Cranston		1,209	0.1

Republican

Democratic

	Votes	%		Votes	%
May 8 Ohio					
Reagan	658,169	100.0	Hart	608,528	42.0
			Mondale	583,595	40.3
			Jackson	237,133	16.4
			McGovern	8,991	0.6
			Cranston	4,653	0.3
			LaRouche	4,336	0.3
May 15 Nebraska					
Reagan	145,245	99.9	Hart	86,582	58.2
Others	1,403	1.0	Mondale	39,635	26.6
			Jackson	13,495	9.1
			Unpledged delegates	4,631	3.1
			McGovern	1,561	1.0
			LaRouche	1,227	0.8
			Cranston	538	0.4
			Hollings	450	0.3
			Others	736	0.5
May 15 Oregon					
Reagan	238,594	98.0	Hart	233,638	58.5
Others [1]	4,752	2.0	Mondale	110,374	27.6
			Jackson	37,106	9.3
			Glenn	10,831	2.7
			LaRouche	5,943	1.5
			Others	1,787	0.5
May 15 Idaho					
Reagan	97,450	92.2	Hart	31,737	58.0
"None of the names shown"	8,237	7.8	Mondale	16,460	30.1
			Jackson	3,104	5.7
			"None of the names shown"	2,225	4.1
			LaRouche	1,196	2.2
June 5 California					
Reagan	1,874,897	100.0	Hart	1,155,499	38.9
Others [1]	78		Mondale	1,049,342	35.3
			Jackson	546,693	18.4
			Glenn	96,770	3.3
			McGovern	69,926	2.4
			LaRouche	52,647	1.8
			Others [1]	26	—
June 5 Montana					
Reagan	66,432	92.4	No preference	28,385	83.0
No preference	5,378	7.5	Hart [1]	3,080	9.0
Others	77	0.1	Mondale [1]	2,026	5.9
			Jackson [1]	388	1.1
			Others	335	1.0
June 5 New Jersey					
Reagan	240,054	100.0	Mondale	305,516	45.2
			Hart	200,948	29.7
			Jackson	159,788	23.6
			LaRouche	10,309	1.5

Republican   # Democratic

	Votes	%		Votes	%
June 5 New Mexico					
Reagan	40,805	94.9	Hart	87,610	46.7
Unpledged delegates	2,189	5.1	Mondale	67,675	36.1
			Jackson	22,168	11.8
			McGovern	5,143	2.7
			LaRouche	3,330	1.8
			Unpledged delegates	1,477	0.8
June 5 South Dakota					
[3]			Hart	26,641	50.7
			Mondale	20,495	39.0
			Jackson	2,738	5.2
			LaRouche	1,383	2.6
			Unpledged delegates	1,304	2.5
June 5 West Virginia					
Reagan	125,790	91.8	Mondale	198,776	53.8
Stassen	11,206	8.2	Hart	137,866	37.3
			Jackson	24,697	6.7
			LaRouche	7,274	2.0
			Alfred Timinski (N.J.)	632	0.2
June 12 North Dakota					
Reagan	44,109	100.0	Hart	28,603	85.1
			LaRouche	4,018	12.0
			Mondale [1]	934	2.8
TOTALS [5]					
Reagan	6,484,987	98.6	Mondale	6,811,214	37.8
"Ronald Reagan No"	14,047	0.2	Hart	6,503,968	36.1
Stassen	12,749	0.2	Jackson	3,282,431	18.2
Kelly	360	—	Glenn	617,380	3.4
Arnold	252	—	McGovern	334,801	1.9
Fernandez	202	—	LaRouche	123,649	0.7
Uncommitted	41,411	0.6	Askew	52,759	0.3
Others	21,643	0.3	Cranston	51,437	0.3
	6,575,651		Hollings	33,684	0.2
			Brewster	9,815	0.1
			Griser	8,014	—
			Willis	8,007	—
			Williams	4,797	—
			Kay	2,699	—
			Koczak	1,855	—
			Timinski	632	—
			Uncommitted	146,212	0.8
			Others	15,796	0.1
				18,009,217	

1. Write-in vote.
2. In Vermont's Liberty Union presidential primary, Dennis L. Serrette received 276 of the 309 votes cast, or 89.3 percent of the vote.
3. No primary.
4. Delegates could vote for or against Reagan within the Republican ticket.

5. Totals exclude Puerto Rico, where citizens are unable to vote in the general election.
6. The Uncommitted category includes votes cast on the following ballot lines: No preference, Unpledged delegates and "None of the names shown."

1988 Primaries

Republican			Democratic		
	Votes	%		Votes	%

February 16   New Hampshire

Republican	Votes	%	Democratic	Votes	%
George Bush (Maine)	59,290	37.6	Michael S. Dukakis (Mass.)	44,112	35.7
Robert Dole (Kan.)	44,797	28.4	Richard A. Gephardt (Mo.)	24,513	19.8
Jack F. Kemp (N.Y.)	20,114	12.8	Paul Simon (Ill.)	21,094	17.1
Pierre S. du Pont IV (Del.)	15,885	10.1	Jesse Jackson (Ill.)	9,615	7.8
Pat Robertson (Va.)	14,775	9.4	Albert Gore Jr. (Tenn.)	8,400	6.8
Alexander M. Haig Jr. (Pa.)	481	0.3	Bruce Babbitt (Ariz.)	5,644	4.6
Harold E. Stassen (Pa.)	130	—	Gary Hart (Colo.)	4,888	4.0
Paul B. Conley (N.Y.)	107	—	William J. du Pont IV (Ill.)	1,349	1.1
Mary Jane Rachner (Minn.)	107	—	David E. Duke (D.C.)	264	0.2
Others[1]	1,958	1.2	Lyndon H. LaRouche Jr. (Va.)	188	0.2
			William A. Marra (N.J.)	142	0.1
			Florenzo DiDonato	84	0.1
			Stephen A. Koczak (D.C.)	47	—
			Norbert G. Dennerll (Ohio)	18	—
			Others[1]	3,154	2.5

February 23   South Dakota

Republican	Votes	%	Democratic	Votes	%
Dole slate	51,599	55.2	Gephardt	31,184	43.6
Robertson slate	18,310	19.6	Dukakis	22,349	31.2
Bush slate	17,404	18.6	Gore	5,993	8.4
Kemp slate	4,290	4.6	Simon	3,992	5.6
Unpledged delegates slate	1,226	1.3	Hart	3,875	5.4
du Pont slate	576	0.6	Jackson	3,867	5.4
			Babbitt	346	0.5

March 1   Vermont[2]

Republican	Votes	%	Democratic	Votes	%
Bush	23,565	49.3	Dukakis	28,353	55.8
Dole	18,655	39.0	Jackson	13,044	25.7
Robertson	2,452	5.1	Gephardt	3,910	7.7
Kemp	1,877	3.9	Simon	2,620	5.2
du Pont	808	1.7	Hart	2,055	4.0
Haig	324	0.7	Others[1]	809	1.6
Others[1]	151	0.3			

March 5   South Carolina

Republican	Votes	%	Democratic	Votes	%
Bush	94,738	48.5	[3]		
Dole	40,265	20.6			
Robertson	37,261	19.1			
Kemp	22,431	11.5			
du Pont	316	0.2			
Haig	177	0.1			
Stassen	104	0.1			

March 8   Alabama

Republican	Votes	%	Democratic	Votes	%
Bush	137,807	64.5	Jackson	176,764	43.6
Dole	34,733	16.2	Gore	151,739	37.4
Robertson	29,772	13.9	Dukakis	31,306	7.7
Kemp	10,557	4.9	Gephardt	30,214	7.4
du Pont	392	0.2	Hart	7,530	1.9
Haig	300	0.1	Simon	3,063	0.8
			Babbitt	2,410	0.6
			Unpledged delegates	1,771	0.4
			LaRouche	845	0.2

Republican

Democratic

	Votes	%

				Votes	%

March 8   **Arkansas**

Republican	Votes	%	Democratic	Votes	%
Bush	32,114	47.0	Gore	185,758	37.3
Dole	17,667	25.9	Dukakis	94,103	18.9
Robertson	12,918	18.9	Jackson	85,003	17.1
Kemp	3,499	5.1	Gephardt	59,711	12.0
Unpledged delegates	1,402	2.1	Unpledged delegates	35,553	7.1
du Pont	359	0.5	Hart	18,630	3.7
Haig	346	0.5	Simon	9,020	1.8
			Duke	4,805	1.0
			Babbitt	2,614	0.5
			LaRouche	2,347	0.5

March 8   **Florida**

Republican	Votes	%	Democratic	Votes	%
Bush	559,820	62.1	Dukakis	521,041	40.9
Dole	191,197	21.2	Jackson	254,912	20.0
Robertson	95,826	10.6	Gephardt	182,861	14.4
Kemp	41,795	4.6	Gore	161,165	12.7
du Pont	6,726	0.7	Undecided	79,088	6.2
Haig	5,858	0.7	Hart	36,315	2.9
			Simon	27,620	2.2
			Babbitt	10,296	0.8

March 8   **Georgia**

Republican	Votes	%	Democratic	Votes	%
Bush	215,516	53.8	Jackson	247,831	39.8
Dole	94,749	23.6	Gore	201,490	32.6
Robertson	65,163	16.3	Dukakis	97,179	15.6
Kemp	23,409	5.8	Gephardt	41,489	6.7
du Pont	1,309	0.3	Hart	15,852	2.5
Haig	782	0.2	Simon	8,388	1.3
			Unpledged delegates	7,276	1.2
			Babbitt	3,247	0.5

March 8   **Kentucky**

Republican	Votes	%	Democratic	Votes	%
Bush	72,020	59.3	Gore	145,988	45.8
Dole	27,868	23.0	Dukakis	59,433	18.6
Robertson	13,526	11.1	Jackson	49,667	15.6
Kemp	4,020	3.3	Gephardt	28,982	9.1
Unpledged delegates	2,245	1.8	Hart	11,798	3.7
Stassen	844	0.7	Unpledged delegates	10,465	3.3
du Pont	457	0.4	Simon	9,393	2.9
Haig	422	0.3	Babbitt	1,290	0.4
			LaRouche	681	0.2
			Richard B. Kay (Fla.)	487	0.2
			Others	537	0.2

March 8   **Louisiana**

Republican	Votes	%	Democratic	Votes	%
Bush	83,687	57.8	Jackson	221,532	35.5
Robertson	26,295	18.2	Gore	174,974	28.0
Dole	25,626	17.7	Dukakis	95,667	15.3
Kemp	7,722	5.3	Gephardt	66,434	10.6
du Pont	853	0.6	Hart	26,442	4.2
Haig	598	0.4	Duke	23,390	3.7
			Simon	5,155	0.8
			Frank Ahern (La.)	3,701	0.6
			Babbitt	3,076	0.5
			LaRouche	1,681	0.3
			Dennerll	1,575	0.3
			Kay	823	0.1

Republican   # Democratic

	Votes	%		Votes	%
March 8 Maryland					
Bush	107,026	53.3	Dukakis	242,479	45.6
Dole	64,987	32.8	Jackson	152,642	28.7
Robertson	12,860	6.5	Gore	46,063	8.7
Kemp	11,909	5.9	Gephardt	42,059	8.0
du Pont	2,551	1.8	Simon	16,513	3.1
Haig	1,421	0.7	Unpledged delegates	14,948	2.8
			Hart	9,732	1.8
			Babbitt	4,750	0.9
			LaRouche	2,149	0.4
March 8 Massachusetts					
Bush	141,113	58.6	Dukakis	418,256	58.6
Dole	63,392	26.3	Jackson	133,141	18.7
Kemp	16,791	7.0	Gephardt	72,944	10.2
Robertson	10,891	4.5	Gore	31,631	4.4
du Pont	3,522	1.5	Simon	26,176	3.6
No preference	3,416	1.4	No preference	11,866	1.7
Haig	1,705	0.7	Hart	10,837	1.5
Others[1]	351	0.1	Babbitt	4,222	0.6
			DiDonato	1,971	0.3
			LaRouche	998	0.1
			Others[1]	1,405	0.2
March 8 Mississippi					
Bush	104,814	66.1	Jackson	160,651	44.7
Dole	26,855	16.9	Gore	120,364	33.5
Robertson	21,378	13.5	Dukakis	29,941	8.3
Kemp	5,479	3.5	Gephardt	19,693	5.5
			Hart	13,934	3.9
			Unpledged delegates	9,384	2.6
			Simon	2,118	0.6
			Babbitt	2,037	0.6
			LaRouche	1,295	0.4
March 8 Missouri					
Bush	168,812	42.2	Gephardt	305,287	57.8
Dole	164,394	41.1	Jackson	106,386	20.2
Robertson	44,705	11.2	Dukakis	61,303	11.7
Kemp	14,180	3.5	Simon	21,433	4.1
Unpledged delegates	5,563	1.4	Gore	14,549	2.8
du Pont	1,788	0.4	Hart	7,607	1.4
Haig	858	0.2	Unpledged delegates	6,635	1.3
			Duke	1,760	0.3
			Babbitt	1,377	0.3
			LaRouche	664	0.1
			Kay	372	—
			Koczak	241	—
			Dennerll	191	—
March 8 North Carolina					
Bush	124,260	45.4	Gore	235,669	34.7
Dole	107,032	39.1	Jackson	224,177	33.0
Robertson	26,861	9.8	Dukakis	137,993	20.3
Kemp	11,361	4.1	Gephardt	37,553	5.5
No preference	2,797	1.0	Hart	16,381	2.4
du Pont	944	0.3	No preference	16,337	2.4
Haig	546	0.2	Simon	8,032	1.2
			Babbitt	3,816	0.6

Republican

Democratic

	Votes	%		Votes	%

March 8   Oklahoma

Bush	78,224	37.4	Gore	162,584	41.4
Dole	73,016	34.9	Gephardt	82,596	21.0
Robertson	44,067	21.0	Dukakis	66,278	16.9
Kemp	11,439	5.5	Jackson	52,417	13.3
du Pont	938	0.4	Hart	14,336	3.7
Haig	715	0.3	Simon	6,901	1.8
Others	539	0.3	Duke	2,388	0.6
			Babbitt	1,601	0.4
			LaRouche	1,078	0.3
			Koczak	1,068	0.3
			Charles R. Doty (Okla.)	1,005	0.3
			Dennerll	475	0.1

March 8   Rhode Island

Bush	10,401	64.9	Dukakis	34,211	69.7
Dole	3,628	22.6	Jackson	7,445	15.2
Robertson	911	5.7	Gephardt	2,028	4.1
Kemp	792	4.9	Gore	1,939	4.0
Unpledged delegates	174	1.1	Simon	1,395	2.8
du Pont	80	0.5	Unpledged delegates	809	1.7
Haig	49	0.3	Hart	733	1.5
			Babbitt	469	1.0

March 8   Tennessee

Bush	152,515	60.0	Gore	416,861	72.3
Dole	55,027	21.6	Jackson	119,248	20.7
Robertson	32,015	12.6	Dukakis	19,348	3.3
Kemp	10,911	4.3	Gephardt	8,470	1.5
Unpledged delegates	2,340	0.9	Hart	4,706	0.8
Haig	777	0.3	Unpledged delegates	3,032	0.5
du Pont	646	0.3	Simon	2,647	0.5
Others[1]	21	—	Babbitt	1,946	0.3
			Others[1]	56	—

March 8   Texas

Bush	648,178	63.9	Dukakis	579,713	32.8
Robertson	155,449	15.3	Jackson	433,335	24.5
Dole	140,795	13.9	Gore	357,764	20.2
Kemp	50,586	5.0	Gephardt	240,158	13.6
Unpledged delegates	12,563	1.2	Hart	82,199	4.7
du Pont	4,245	0.4	Simon	34,499	1.9
Haig	3,140	0.3	Babbitt	11,618	0.7
			LaRouche	9,013	0.5
			Duke	8,808	0.5
			W. A. Williams	6,238	0.4
			Dennerll	3,700	0.2

March 8   Virginia

Bush	124,738	53.7	Jackson	164,709	45.1
Dole	60,921	26.0	Gore	81,419	22.3
Robertson	32,173	13.7	Dukakis	80,183	22.0
Kemp	10,809	4.6	Gephardt	15,935	4.4
Unpledged delegates	3,675	1.6	Simon	7,045	1.9
du Pont	1,229	0.5	Hart	6,266	1.7
Haig	597	0.3	Unpledged delegates	6,142	1.7
			Babbitt	2,454	0.7
			LaRouche	746	0.2

Republican | Democratic

	Votes	%		Votes	%

March 15   Illinois[4]

Republican			Democratic		
Bush	469,151	54.6	Simon	635,219	42.3
Dole	309,253	36.0	Jackson	484,233	32.3
Robertson	59,087	6.9	Dukakis	245,289	16.3
Kemp	12,687	1.5	Gore	77,265	5.1
du Pont	4,653	0.5	Gephardt	35,108	2.3
Haig	3,806	0.4	Hart	12,769	0.9
			LaRouche	6,094	0.4
			Babbitt	4,953	0.3

March 29   Connecticut

Republican			Democratic		
Bush	73,501	70.6	Dukakis	140,291	58.1
Dole	21,005	20.2	Jackson	68,372	28.3
Kemp	3,281	3.1	Gore	18,501	7.7
Unpledged delegates	3,193	3.1	Hart	5,761	2.4
Robertson	3,191	3.1	Simon	3,140	1.3
			Babbitt	2,370	1.0
			Unpledged delegates	1,951	0.8
			Gephardt	1,009	0.4

April 5   Wisconsin

Republican			Democratic		
Bush	295,295	82.2	Dukakis	483,172	47.6
Dole	28,460	7.9	Jackson	285,995	28.2
Robertson	24,798	6.9	Gore	176,712	17.4
Kemp	4,915	1.4	Simon	48,419	4.8
Uninstructed delegation	2,372	0.7	Gephardt	7,996	0.8
Haig	1,554	0.4	Hart	7,068	0.7
du Pont	1,504	0.4	Uninstructed delegation	2,554	0.3
Others[1]	396	0.1	Babbitt	2,353	0.2
			Others[1]	513	0.1

April 19   New York

[3]

Republican			Democratic		
			Dukakis	801,457	50.9
			Jackson	585,076	37.1
			Gore	157,559	10.0
			Simon	17,011	1.1
			Unpledged delegates	10,258	0.7
			Gephardt	2,672	0.2
			LaRouche	1,153	0.1

April 26   Pennsylvania

Republican			Democratic		
Bush	687,323	79.0	Dukakis	1,002,480	66.5
Dole	103,763	11.9	Jackson	411,260	27.3
Robertson	79,463	9.1	Gore	44,542	3.0
			Hart	20,473	1.4
			Simon	9,692	0.6
			Jennifer Alden Wesner (Pa.)	7,546	0.5
			Gephardt	7,254	0.5
			LaRouche	4,443	0.3

May 3   District of Columbia

Republican			Democratic		
Bush	5,890	87.6	Jackson	68,840	80.0
Dole	469	7.0	Dukakis	15,415	17.9
Robertson	268	4.0	Simon	769	0.9
Others[1]	93	1.4	Gore	648	0.8
			Gephardt	300	0.3
			Others	80	0.1

Republican

Democratic

	Votes	%		Votes	%
May 3 Indiana					
Bush	351,829	80.4	Dukakis	449,495	69.6
Dole	42,878	9.8	Jackson	145,021	22.5
Robertson	28,712	6.6	Gore	21,865	3.4
Kemp	14,236	3.6	Gephardt	16,777	2.6
			Simon	12,550	1.9
May 3 Ohio					
Bush slate	643,907	81.0	Dukakis slate	869,792	62.9
Dole slate	94,650	11.9	Jackson slate	378,866	27.4
Robertson slate	56,347	7.1	Gore slate	29,931	2.2
			James A. Traficant slate (Ohio)	29,912	2.2
			Hart slate	28,414	2.1
			Douglas Applegate slate (Ohio)	25,068	1.8
			Simon slate	15,524	1.1
			LaRouche slate	6,065	0.4
May 10 Nebraska[5]					
Bush	138,784	68.0	Dukakis	106,334	62.9
Dole	45,572	22.3	Jackson	43,380	25.7
Robertson	10,334	5.1	Gephardt	4,948	2.9
Kemp	8,423	4.1	Unpledged delegates	4,763	2.8
Others[1]	936	0.5	Hart	4,220	2.5
			Gore	2,519	1.5
			Simon	2,104	1.2
			LaRouche	416	0.2
			Others[1]	324	0.2
May 10 West Virginia					
Bush	110,705	77.3	Dukakis	254,289	74.8
Dole	15,600	10.9	Jackson	45,788	13.5
Robertson	10,417	7.3	Gore	11,573	3.4
Kemp	3,820	2.7	Hart	9,284	2.7
Stassen	1,604	1.1	Gephardt	6,130	1.8
Conley	994	0.7	Angus W. McDonald (W.Va.)	3,604	1.1
			Simon	2,280	0.7
			Babbitt	1,978	0.6
			LaRouche	1,482	0.4
			Duke	1,383	0.4
			Dennerll	1,339	0.4
			Traficant	967	0.3
May 17 Oregon					
Bush	199,938	72.8	Dukakis	221,048	56.8
Dole	49,128	17.9	Jackson	148,207	38.1
Robertson	21,212	7.7	Gephardt	6,772	1.7
Others[1]	4,208	1.5	Gore	5,445	1.4
			Simon	4,757	1.2
			LaRouche	1,562	0.4
			Others[1]	1,141	0.3

	Republican			Democratic		
		Votes	%		Votes	%

May 24   Idaho

	Votes	%		Votes	%
Bush	55,464	81.2	Dukakis	37,696	73.4
"None of the names shown"	6,935	10.2	Jackson	8,066	15.7
Robertson	5,876	8.6	"None of the names shown"	2,308	4.5
			Gore	1,891	3.7
			Simon	1,409	2.7

June 7   California[6]

	Votes	%		Votes	%
Bush	1,856,273	82.9	Dukakis	1,910,808	60.9
Dole	289,220	12.9	Jackson	1,102,093	35.1
Robertson	94,779	4.2	Gore	56,645	1.8
Others[1]	115	—	Simon	43,771	1.4
			LaRouche	25,417	0.8

June 7   Montana

	Votes	%		Votes	%
Bush	63,098	73.0	Dukakis	83,684	68.7
Dole	16,762	19.4	Jackson	26,908	22.1
No preference	6,520	7.5	No preference	4,083	3.4
			Gephardt	3,369	2.8
			Gore	2,261	1.9
			Simon	1,566	1.3

June 7   New Jersey

	Votes	%		Votes	%
Bush	241,033	100.0	Dukakis	414,829	63.4
			Jackson	213,705	32.7
			Gore	18,062	2.8
			LaRouche	2,621	0.4
			Marra	2,594	0.4
			Duke	2,491	0.4

June 7   New Mexico

	Votes	%		Votes	%
Bush	69,359	78.2	Dukakis	114,968	61.0
Dole	9,305	10.5	Jackson	52,988	28.1
Robertson	5,350	6.0	Hart	6,898	3.7
Unpledged delegates	2,569	2.9	Gore	4,747	2.6
Haig	2,161	2.4	Unpledged delegates	3,275	1.7
			Babbitt	2,913	1.5
			Simon	2,821	1.5

June 14   North Dakota

	Votes	%		
Bush	37,062	94.0	[7]	
Rachner	2,372	6.0		

Republican			Democratic		
	Votes	%		Votes	%

TOTALS   **TOTALS**

Republican			Democratic		
Bush	8,254,654	67.9	Dukakis	9,817,185	42.8
Dole	2,333,268	19.2	Jackson	6,685,699	29.1
Robertson	1,097,442	9.0	Gore	3,134,516	13.7
Kemp	331,333	2.7	Gephardt	1,388,356	6.0
du Pont	49,781	0.4	Simon	1,018,136	4.4
Haig	26,617	0.2	Hart	389,003	1.7
Stassen	2,682	—	Babbitt	77,780	0.3
Rachner	2,479	—	LaRouche	70,938	0.3
Conley	1,101	—	Duke	45,289	0.2
Uncommitted[8]	56,990	0.5	Traficant	30,879	0.1
Others[9]	8,768	0.1	Applegate	25,068	0.1
	12,165,115		Wesner	7,546	—
			Dennerll	7,298	—
			Williams	6,238	—
			Ahern	3,701	—
			McDonald	3,604	—
			Marra	2,736	—
			DiDonato	2,055	—
			Kay	1,682	—
			Koczak	1,356	—
			du Pont	1,349	—
			Doty	1,005	—
			Uncommitted[8]	232,498	1.0
			Others[10]	8,019	—
				22,961,936	

1. *Includes write-in votes.*

2. *In Vermont's Liberty Union presidential primary, Willa Kenoyer received 199 votes (68.9 percent), Herb Lewin received 65 votes (22.5 percent), and there were 25 scattered write-in votes (8.7 percent).*

3. *No primary.*

4. *In Illinois's Solidarity presidential primary, Lenora B. Fulani received 170 votes (100 percent).*

5. *In Nebraska's New Alliance presidential primary, Lenora B. Fulani received 10 votes (100 percent).*

6. *In California's American Independent presidential primary, James C. Griffin received 9,762 votes (64.4 percent), James Gritz received 5,401 votes (35.6 percent), and there were 3 scattered write-in votes (0.0 percent). In the Peace and Freedom presidential primary, Lenora B. Fulani received 2,117 votes (35.7 percent), Shirley Isaacson received 1,222 votes (20.6 percent), Larry Holmes received 1,042 votes (17.6 percent), Herb Lewin received 778 votes (13.1 percent), Willa Kenoyer received 411 votes (6.9 percent), Al Hamburg received 353 votes (6.0 percent), and there were 6 scattered write-in votes (0.1 percent).*

7. *No candidates' names appeared on the Democratic ballot. Tallied write-in votes were for Dukakis (2,890) and Jackson (515).*

8. *The Uncommitted category includes votes cast on the following ballot lines: Unpledged delegates, Undecided, No preference, Uninstructed delegation and "None of the names shown."*

9. *In addition to scattered write-in votes, "others" include Isabell Masters who received 539 votes in the Oklahoma primary; Robert F. Drucker who received 83 votes in the New Hampshire primary; William Horrigan who received 76 votes in the New Hampshire primary; Michael S. Levinson who received 43 votes in the New Hampshire primary.*

10. *In addition to scattered write-in votes, "others" include Anthony R. Martin-Trigona who received 598 votes — 537 votes in the Kentucky primary and 61 votes in the New Hampshire primary; Conrad W. Roy who received 122 votes in the New Hampshire primary; Osie Thorpe who received 96 votes — 80 votes in the District of Columbia primary and 16 votes in the New Hampshire primary; William King who received 36 votes in the New Hampshire primary; Edward T. O'Donnell who received 33 votes in the New Hampshire primary; Cyril E. Sagan who received 33 votes in the New Hampshire primary; Frank L. Thomas who received 28 votes in the New Hampshire primary; Claude R. Kirk who received 25 votes in the New Hampshire primary; Irwin Zucker who received 22 votes in the New Hampshire primary; A. A. Van Petten who received 10 votes in the New Hampshire primary; Stanley Lock who received 9 votes in the New Hampshire primary.*

1992 Primaries

Republican			Democratic		
	Votes	%		Votes	%

February 18   New Hampshire[1]

Republican			Democratic		
George Bush (Texas)	92,233	53.0	Paul E. Tsongas (Mass.)	55,638	33.2
Patrick J. Buchanan (Va.)	65,087	37.4	Bill Clinton (Ark.)	41,522	24.7
James P. Lennane (Fla.)	1,684	1.0	Bob Kerrey (Neb.)	18,575	11.1
Pat Paulsen (Calif.)	600	0.3	Tom Harkin (Iowa)	17,057	10.2
Harold E. Stassen (Minn.)	206	0.1	Edmund G. Brown (Calif.)	13,654	8.1
Jack Fellure (W.Va.)	36	—	Tom Laughlin (Calif.)	3,251	1.9
George Zimmermann (Texas)	31	—	Charles Woods (Nev.)	2,862	1.7
Tennie Rogers (Calif.)	20	—	Lawrence A. Agran (Calif.)	332	0.2
Others[2]	14,268	8.1	Eugene J. McCarthy (Va.)	211	0.1
			Lyndon H. LaRouche Jr. (Va.)	115	0.1
			Stephen Burke (N.Y.)	39	—
			Rufus T. Higginbotham (Texas)	31	—
			Tom Shiekman (Fla.)	23	—
			George W. Benns (N.Y.)	11	—
			Others[2]	14,498	8.7

February 25   South Dakota

Republican			Democratic		
Bush	30,964	69.3	Kerrey	23,892	40.2
Uncommitted	13,707	30.7	Harkin	15,023	25.2
			Clinton	11,375	19.1
			Tsongas	5,729	9.6
			Brown	2,300	3.9
			Agran	606	1.0
			LaRouche	441	0.7
			Others	137	0.2

March 3   Colorado

Republican			Democratic		
Bush	132,100	67.5	Brown	69,073	28.8
Buchanan	58,753	30.0	Clinton	64,470	26.9
Zimmermann	1,592	0.8	Tsongas	61,360	25.6
Paul S. Jensen (Colo.)	1,332	0.7	Kerrey	29,572	12.3
Rogers	535	0.3	Harkin	5,866	2.4
Others	1,378	0.7	Noncommitted	5,356	2.2
			Woods	1,051	0.4
			Agran	672	0.3
			Burke	532	0.2
			McCarthy	488	0.2
			LaRouche	328	0.1
			Tod H. Hawks	165	0.1
			Shiekman	76	—
			Jeffrey Marsh	59	—
			Louis McAlpine	48	—
			Ray Rollinson	46	—
			Others	481	0.2

March 3   Georgia

Republican			Democratic		
Bush	291,905	64.3	Clinton	259,907	57.2
Buchanan	162,085	35.7	Tsongas	109,148	24.0
			Brown	36,808	8.1
			Kerrey	22,033	4.8
			Uncommitted	17,256	3.8
			Harkin	9,479	2.1

March 3   Maryland

Republican			Democratic		
Bush	168,374	70.1	Tsongas	230,490	40.6
Buchanan	71,647	29.9	Clinton	189,905	33.5
			Brown	46,500	8.2
			Uncommitted	36,155	6.4
			Harkin	32,899	5.8
			Kerrey	27,035	4.8
			LaRouche	4,259	0.8

Republican
Democratic

	Votes	%		Votes	%
March 7 South Carolina					
Bush	99,558	66.9	Clinton	73,221	62.9
Buchanan	38,247	25.7	Tsongas	21,338	18.3
David Duke (La.)	10,553	7.1	Harkin	7,657	6.6
Others	482	0.3	Brown	6,961	6.0
			Uncommitted	3,640	3.1
			Bob Cunningham	1,369	1.2
			Woods	854	0.7
			Kerrey	566	0.5
			Angus W. McDonald	268	0.2
			LaRouche	204	0.2
			Others	336	0.3
March 10 Florida					
Bush	608,077	68.1	Clinton	570,566	50.8
Buchanan	285,386	31.9	Tsongas	388,124	34.5
			Brown	139,569	12.4
			Harkin	13,587	1.2
			Kerrey	12,011	1.1
March 10 Louisiana					
Bush	83,744	62.0	Clinton	267,002	69.5
Buchanan	36,525	27.0	Tsongas	42,508	11.1
Duke	11,955	8.8	Brown	25,480	6.6
Paulsen	1,186	0.9	McCarthy	15,129	3.9
Rogers	1,111	0.8	Woods	8,989	2.3
Zimmermann	474	0.4	Burke	4,294	1.1
Others	114	0.1	Harkin	4,033	1.0
			Agran	3,511	0.9
			LaRouche	3,082	0.8
			Kerrey	2,984	0.8
			Marsh	2,120	0.6
			Laughlin	1,857	0.5
			Hawks	1,469	0.4
			Rollinson	1,069	0.3
			McAlpine	870	0.2
March 10 Massachusetts[3]					
Bush	176,868	65.6	Tsongas	526,297	66.4
Buchanan	74,797	27.7	Brown	115,746	14.6
No preference	10,132	3.8	Clinton	86,817	10.9
Duke	5,557	2.1	Ralph Nader	32,881	4.1
Others[2]	2,347	0.9	No preference	12,198	1.5
			Kerrey	5,409	0.7
			Harkin	3,764	0.5
			McCarthy	3,127	0.4
			Agran	2,224	0.3
			LaRouche	2,167	0.3
			Others[2]	2,255	0.3
March 10 Mississippi					
Bush	111,794	72.3	Clinton	139,893	73.1
Buchanan	25,891	16.7	Brown	18,396	9.6
Duke	16,426	10.6	Tsongas	15,538	8.1
Rogers	189	0.1	Uncommitted	11,796	6.2
Others[2]	408	0.3	Harkin	2,509	1.3
			Kerrey	1,660	0.9
			LaRouche	1,394	0.7
			Others[2]	171	0.1

Republican
Democratic

	Votes	%		Votes	%
March 10 Oklahoma					
Bush	151,612	69.6	Clinton	293,266	70.5
Buchanan	57,933	26.6	Brown	69,624	16.7
Duke	5,672	2.6	Woods	16,828	4.0
Isabell Masters (Kan.)	1,830	0.8	Harkin	14,015	3.4
Rogers	674	0.3	Kerrey	13,252	3.2
			LaRouche	6,474	1.6
			McAlpine	2,670	0.6
March 10 Rhode Island					
Bush	9,853	63.0	Tsongas	26,825	52.9
Buchanan	4,967	31.8	Clinton	10,762	21.2
Uncommitted	444	2.8	Brown	9,541	18.8
Duke	326	2.1	Uncommitted	703	1.4
Others[2]	46	0.3	Kerrey	469	0.9
			Woods	408	0.8
			Harkin	319	0.6
			LaRouche	300	0.6
			McCarthy	235	0.5
			Laughlin	94	0.2
			Rollinson	91	0.2
			Agran	79	0.2
			Burke	48	0.1
			Others[2]	835	1.6
March 10 Tennessee					
Bush	178,219	72.5	Clinton	214,485	67.3
Buchanan	54,585	22.2	Tsongas	61,717	19.4
Duke	7,709	3.1	Brown	25,560	8.0
Uncommitted	5,022	2.0	Uncommitted	12,551	3.9
Others[2]	118	—	Harkin	2,099	0.7
			Kerrey	1,638	0.5
			Others[2]	432	0.1
March 10 Texas					
Bush	556,280	69.8	Clinton	972,151	65.6
Buchanan	190,572	23.9	Tsongas	285,191	19.2
Uncommitted	27,936	3.5	Brown	118,923	8.0
Duke	20,255	2.5	Woods	30,092	2.0
Zimmermann	1,349	0.2	Kerrey	20,298	1.4
Rogers	754	0.1	Harkin	19,617	1.3
			LaRouche	12,220	0.8
			Benns	7,876	0.5
			Higginbotham	7,674	0.5
			Hawks	4,924	0.3
			McAlpine	4,009	0.3
March 17 Illinois					
Bush	634,588	76.4	Clinton	776,829	51.6
Buchanan	186,915	22.5	Tsongas	387,891	25.8
Maurice Horton (Ill.)	9,637	1.2	Brown	220,346	14.6
			Uncommitted	67,612	4.5
			Harkin	30,710	2.0
			Kerrey	10,916	0.7
			LaRouche	6,599	0.4
			Agran	3,227	0.2

Republican			Democratic		
	Votes	%		Votes	%

March 17   Michigan

Republican			Democratic		
Bush	301,948	67.2	Clinton	297,280	50.7
Buchanan	112,122	25.0	Brown	151,400	25.8
Uncommitted	23,809	5.3	Tsongas	97,017	16.6
Duke	10,688	2.4	Uncommitted	27,836	4.8
Others[2]	566	0.1	Harkin	6,265	1.1
			Kerrey	3,219	0.5
			LaRouche	2,049	0.3
			Others[2]	906	0.2

March 24   Connecticut

Republican			Democratic		
Bush	66,356	66.7	Brown	64,472	37.2
Buchanan	21,815	21.9	Clinton	61,698	35.6
Uncommitted	9,008	9.1	Tsongas	33,811	19.5
Duke	2,294	2.3	Uncommitted	5,430	3.1
			Agran	2,688	1.6
			Harkin	1,919	1.1
			Kerrey	1,169	0.7
			McCarthy	1,036	0.6
			LaRouche	896	0.5

April 7   Kansas

Republican			Democratic		
Bush	132,131	62.0	Clinton	82,145	51.3
"None of the names shown"	35,450	16.6	Tsongas	24,413	15.2
Buchanan	31,494	14.8	"None of the names shown"	22,159	13.8
Paulsen	5,105	2.4	Brown	20,811	13.0
Duke	3,837	1.8	Kerrey	2,215	1.4
Masters	1,303	0.6	Gary Hauptli	1,303	0.8
Philip Skow	1,105	0.5	Woods	1,119	0.7
Zimmermann	766	0.4	Don Beamgard	1,009	0.6
Fellure	164	0.1	Harkin	940	0.6
Rogers	85	—	Hawks	765	0.5
Others	1,756	0.8	LaRouche	631	0.4
			Ralph Spelbring	537	0.3
			Marsh	160	0.1
			Agran	147	0.1
			McAlpine	131	0.1
			Others	1,766	1.1

April 7   Minnesota

Republican			Democratic		
Bush	84,841	63.9	Clinton	63,584	31.1
Buchanan	32,094	24.2	Brown	62,474	30.6
Uncommitted	4,098	3.1	Tsongas	43,588	21.3
Stassen	4,074	3.1	Uncommitted	11,366	5.6
Ross Perot[4] (Texas)	3,558	2.7	Ross Perot (Texas)[4]	4,250	2.1
Zimmermann	135	0.1	Harkin	4,077	2.0
Rogers	61	—	McCarthy	3,704	1.8
Others[2]	3,895	2.9	Kerrey	1,191	0.6
			Agran	1,042	0.5
			Woods	990	0.5
			LaRouche	532	0.3
			Burke	348	0.2
			McAlpine	183	0.1
			Hawks	111	0.1
			Marsh	106	0.1
			Others[2]	6,624	3.2

April 7   New York[5]

Republican			Democratic		
			Clinton	412,349	40.9
			Tsongas	288,330	28.6
			Brown	264,278	26.2
			Harkin	11,535	1.1
			Kerrey	11,147	1.1
			Agran	10,733	1.1
			McCarthy	9,354	0.9

Republican   # Democratic

	Votes	%		Votes	%

April 7   Wisconsin

Bush	364,507	75.6	Clinton	287,356	37.2
Buchanan	78,516	16.3	Brown	266,207	34.5
Duke	12,867	2.7	Tsongas	168,619	21.8
Uninstructed	8,725	1.8	Uninstructed	15,487	2.0
Stassen	3,819	0.8	McCarthy	6,525	0.8
Emmanuel L. Branch	1,013	0.2	Harkin	5,395	0.7
Others[2]	12,801	2.7	Agran	3,193	0.4
			LaRouche	3,120	0.4
			Kerrey	3,044	0.4
			Others[2]	13,650	1.8

April 28   Pennsylvania

Bush	774,865	76.8	Clinton	715,031	56.5
Buchanan	233,912	23.2	Brown	325,543	25.7
			Tsongas	161,572	12.8
			LaRouche	21,534	1.7
			Harkin	21,013	1.7
			Kerrey	20,802	1.6

May 5   District of Columbia

Bush	4,265	81.5	Clinton	45,716	73.8
Buchanan	970	18.5	Tsongas	6,452	10.4
			Uncommitted	5,292	8.5
			Brown	4,444	7.2

May 5   Indiana

Bush	374,666	80.1	Clinton	301,905	63.3
Buchanan	92,949	19.9	Brown	102,379	21.5
			Tsongas	58,215	12.2
			Kerrey	14,350	3.0

May 5   North Carolina

Bush	200,387	70.7	Clinton	443,498	64.1
Buchanan	55,420	19.5	No preference	106,697	15.4
No preference	27,764	9.8	Brown	71,984	10.4
			Tsongas	57,589	8.3
			Kerrey	6,216	0.9
			Harkin	5,891	0.9

May 12   Nebraska

Bush	156,346	81.4	Clinton	68,562	45.5
Buchanan	25,847	13.5	Brown	31,673	21.0
Duke	2,808	1.5	Uncommitted	24,714	16.4
Zimmermann	1,313	0.7	Tsongas	10,707	7.1
Rogers	751	0.4	Harkin	4,239	2.8
Others[2]	5,033	2.6	McCarthy	1,520	1.0
			LaRouche	1,148	0.8
			Woods	485	0.3
			Agran	280	0.2
			Others[2]	7,259	4.8

May 12   West Virginia

Bush	99,994	80.5	Clinton	227,815	74.2
Buchanan	18,067	14.6	Brown	36,505	11.9
Fellure	6,096	4.9	Tsongas	21,271	6.9
			McDonald	9,632	3.1
			Kerrey	3,152	1.0
			LaRouche	3,141	1.0
			Harkin	2,774	0.9
			Woods	1,487	0.5
			Spelbring	1,089	0.4

Republican			Democratic		
	Votes	%		Votes	%

May 19 Oregon

Republican	Votes	%	Democratic	Votes	%
Bush	203,957	67.1	Clinton	159,802	45.1
Buchanan	57,730	19.0	Brown	110,494	31.2
Duke	6,667	2.2	Tsongas	37,139	10.5
Others[2]	35,805	11.8	McCarthy	6,714	1.9
			LaRouche	3,096	0.9
			Woods	1,895	0.5
			Agran	1,652	0.5
			Others[2]	33,540	9.5

May 19 Washington

Republican	Votes	%	Democratic	Votes	%
Bush	86,839	67.0	Clinton	62,171	42.0
Perot[4]	25,423	19.6	Brown	34,111	23.1
Buchanan	13,273	10.2	Perot[4]	28,311	19.1
Stephen D. Michael	2,619	2.0	Tsongas	18,981	12.8
Duke	1,501	1.2	Harkin	1,858	1.3
			Kerrey	1,489	1.0
			LaRouche	1,060	0.7

May 26 Arkansas

Republican	Votes	%	Democratic	Votes	%
Bush	45,590	87.4	Clinton	342,017	68.0
Buchanan	6,551	12.6	Uncommitted	90,710	18.0
			Brown	55,234	11.0
			LaRouche	14,656	2.9

May 26 Idaho

Republican	Votes	%	Democratic	Votes	%
Bush	73,297	63.5	Clinton	27,004	49.0
"None of the names shown"	27,038	23.4	"None of the names shown"	16,029	29.1
Buchanan	15,167	13.1	Brown	9,212	16.7
			LaRouche	2,011	3.6
			Agran	868	1.6

May 26 Kentucky

Republican	Votes	%	Democratic	Votes	%
Bush	75,371	74.5	Clinton	207,804	56.1
Uncommitted	25,748	25.5	Uncommitted	103,590	28.0
			Brown	30,709	8.3
			Tsongas	18,097	4.9
			Harkin	7,136	1.9
			Kerrey	3,242	0.9

June 2 Alabama

Republican	Votes	%	Democratic	Votes	%
Bush	122,703	74.3	Clinton	307,621	68.2
Uncommitted	29,830	18.1	Uncommitted	90,863	20.2
Buchanan	12,588	7.6	Brown	30,626	6.8
			Woods	15,247	3.4
			LaRouche	6,542	1.4

June 2 California[6]

Republican	Votes	%	Democratic	Votes	%
Bush	1,587,369	73.6	Clinton	1,359,112	47.5
Buchanan	568,892	26.4	Brown	1,150,460	40.2
Others[2]	203	—	Tsongas	212,522	7.4
			McCarthy	60,635	2.1
			Kerrey	33,935	1.2
			Agran	24,784	0.9
			LaRouche	21,971	0.8
			Others[2]	190	—

June 2 Montana

Republican	Votes	%	Democratic	Votes	%
Bush	65,176	71.6	Clinton	54,989	46.8
No preference	15,098	16.6	No preference	28,164	24.0
Buchanan	10,701	11.8	Brown	21,704	18.5
			Tsongas	12,614	10.7

	Republican			Democratic		
		Votes	%		Votes	%
June 2	**New Jersey**					
Bush		240,535	77.5	Clinton	243,741	62.1
Buchanan		46,432	15.0	Brown	79,877	20.3
Perot[4]		23,303	7.5	Tsongas	45,191	11.5
				Perot[4]	12,478	3.2
				LaRouche	7,799	2.0
				George H. Ballard	2,067	0.5
				Robert F. Hanson	1,473	0.4
June 2	**New Mexico**					
Bush		55,522	63.8	Clinton	95,933	52.9
Uncommitted		23,574	27.1	Uncommitted	35,269	19.4
Buchanan		7,871	9.1	Brown	30,705	16.9
				Tsongas	11,315	6.2
				Harkin	3,233	1.8
				Agran	2,573	1.4
				LaRouche	2,415	1.3
June 2	**Ohio**					
Bush		716,766	83.3	Clinton	638,347	61.2
Buchanan		143,687	16.7	Brown	197,449	18.9
				Tsongas	110,773	10.6
				Louis Stokes (Ohio)	29,983	2.9
				Harkin	25,395	2.4
				Kerrey	22,976	2.2
				LaRouche	17,412	1.7
June 9	**North Dakota**					
Bush		39,863	83.4	Perot[4]	9,516	29.0
Paulsen		4,093	8.6	LaRouche	7,003	21.4
Perot[4]		3,852	8.1	Woods	6,641	20.3
				Shiekman	4,866	14.8
				Clinton[4]	4,760	14.5
TOTALS				**TOTALS**		
Bush		9,199,463	72.5	Clinton	10,482,411	51.8
Buchanan		2,899,488	22.8	Brown	4,071,232	20.1
Duke		119,115	0.9	Tsongas	3,656,010	18.1
Perot[4]		56,136	0.4	Kerry	318,457	1.6
Paulsen		10,984	0.1	Harkin	280,304	1.4
Horton		9,637	0.1	LaRouche	154,599	0.8
Stassen		8,099	0.1	McCarthy	108,678	0.5
Fellure		6,296	—	Woods	88,948	0.4
Zimmermann		5,660	—	Agran	58,611	0.3
Rogers		4,180	—	Perot[4]	54,755	0.3
Masters		3,133	—	Nader	32,881	0.2
Michael		2,619	—	Stokes	29,983	0.1
Lennane		1,684	—	McDonald	9,900	—
Jensen		1,332	—	McAlpine	7,911	—
Skow		1,105	—	Benns	7,887	—
Branch		1,013	—	Higginbotham	7,705	—
Uncommitted[7]		287,383	2.3	Hawks	7,434	—
Others[8]		79,220	0.6	Burke	5,261	—
		12,696,547		Laughlin	5,202	—
				Shiekman	4,965	—
				Marsh	2,445	—
				Ballard	2,067	—
				Spelbring	1,626	—
				Hanson	1,473	—
				Cunningham	1,369	—
				Hauptli	1,303	—
				Rollinson	1,206	—
				Beamgard	1,009	—
				Uncommitted[7]	750,873	3.7
				Others[9]	82,880	0.4
					20,239,385	

1. In New Hamphsire's Libertarian presidential primary, Andre V. Marrou received 3,219 votes (95.0 percent) and there were 168 scattered write-in votes (5.0 percent).

2. Includes write-in votes.

3. In Massachusetts' independent presidential primary, Howard Phillips received 352 votes (25.4 percent), "No preference" received 269 votes (19.4 percent), James Gritz received 177 votes (12.8 percent), Robert J. Smith received 54 votes (3.9 percent), Darcy G. Richardson received 36 votes (2.6 percent), Erik Thompson received 35 votes (2.5 percent), Earl F. Dodge received 26 votes (1.9 percent), J. Quinn Brisben received 24 votes (1.7 percent), Michael S. Levinson received 21 votes (1.5 percent), and there were 391 scattered write-in votes (28.2 percent).

4. Write-in votes.

5. No primary.

6. In California's American Independent presidential primary, Howard Phillips received 15,456 votes (99.9 percent) and there were 13 scattered write-in votes. In the Libertarian presidential primary, Andre V. Marrou received 15,002 votes (99.9 percent) and there were 12 scattered write-in votes. In the Peace & Freedom presidential primary, Lenora B. Fulani received 4,586 votes (51.6 percent), Ron Daniels received 2,868 votes (32.2 percent), R. Alison Star-Martinez received 1,434 votes (16.1 percent), and there were 6 scattered write-in votes.

7. The Uncommitted category includes votes cast on the following ballot lines: Uncommitted, Noncommitted, No preference, Uninstructed and "None of the names shown."

8. In addition to scattered write-in votes, "others" include Stephen A. Koczak who received 950 votes — 659 votes in the Colorado primary, 262 in the Kansas primary and 29 votes in the New Hampshire primary; Paul C. Daugherty who received 771 votes — 236 votes in the Kansas primary, 53 votes in the New Hampshire primary and 482 votes in the South Carolina primary; Jack J. H. Beemont who received 735 votes in the Kansas primary; Terrance R. Scott who received 719 votes in the Colorado primary; Billy Joe Clegg who received 518 votes — 408 votes in the Mississippi primary and 110 votes in the New Hampshire primary; Charles Doty who received 417 votes in the Kansas primary; Richard P. Bosa who received 349 votes in the New Hampshire primary; Sharon Anderson who received 300 votes in the Minnesota primary; John D. Merwin who received 223 votes in the New Hampshire primary; Beatrice Mooney who received 196 votes in the Minnesota primary; Thomas S. Fabish who received 183 votes — 44 votes in the Kansas primary, 114 votes in the Louisiana primary and 25 votes in the New Hampshire primary; Paul B. Conley who received 115 votes in the New Hampshire primary; Hubert D. Patty who received 93 votes — 62 votes in the Kansas primary and 31 votes in the New Hampshire primary; Georgiana Doer-schuck who received 57 votes in the New Hampshire primary; Michael Levinson who received 44 votes in the New Hampshire primary; Vincent Latchford who received 32 votes in the New Hampshire primary; F. Dean Johnson who received 24 votes in the New Hampshire primary; Norm Bertasavage who received 23 votes in the New Hampshire primary; Jack Trinsey who received 22 votes in the New Hampshire primary; Conrad A. Ryden who received 20 votes in the New Hampshire primary; Oscar A. Erickson who received 16 votes in the New Hampshire primary; Richard F. Reber who received 14 votes in the New Hampshire primary.

9. In addition to scattered write-in votes, "others" include John A. Barnes who received 892 votes in the Kansas primary; May Jane Rachner who received 620 votes in the Minnesota primary; Raymond Vanskiver who received 510 votes in the Kansas primary; Lenora B. Fulani who received 402 votes in the New Hampshire primary; William D. Pawley who received 364 votes in the Kansas primary; William P. Kreml who received 336 votes in the South Carolina primary; Susan C. Fey who received 308 votes in the Rhode Island primary; Patrick J. Mahoney who received 303 votes in the New Hampshire primary; Jim Hayes who received 279 votes in the Colorado primary; L. Douglas Wilder who received 240 votes — 103 votes in the New Hampshire primary and 137 votes in the South Dakota primary; Leonard Talbow who received 202 votes in the Colorado primary; John D. Rigazio who received 186 votes in the New Hampshire primary; Curly Thornton who received 177 votes — 125 votes in the New Hampshire primary and 52 votes in the Rhode Island primary; John J. Stardumsky who received 168 votes in the Rhode Island primary; Nathan Averick who received 112 votes — 105 votes in the Minnesota primary and 7 votes in the New Hampshire primary; Caroline P. Killeen who received 93 votes in the New Hampshire primary; John P. Cahill who received 83 votes in the New Hampshire primary; Paul Fisher who received 82 votes in the New Hampshire primary; Frank J. Bona who received 65 votes in the New Hampshire primary; Karl J. Hegger who received 61 votes in the New Hampshire primary; William Horrigan who received 53 votes in the New Hampshire primary; Dean A. Curtis who received 43 votes in the New Hampshire primary; Gilbert H. Holmes who received 39 votes in the New Hampshire primary; Ron Kovic who received 36 votes in the New Hampshire primary; Chris Norton who received 31 votes in the New Hampshire primary; Fanny R. Z. Monyek who received 29 votes in the New Hampshire primary; James B. Gay who received 28 votes in the New Hampshire primary; Barry J. Deutsch who received 26 votes in the New Hampshire primary; Cyril E. Sagan who received 26 votes in the New Hampshire primary; Edward T. O'Donnell who received 24 votes in the New Hampshire primary; Stephen H. Schwartz who received 17 votes in the New Hampshire primary.

1996 Primaries

Republican	Votes	%	Democratic	Votes	%
February 20 New Hampshire[1]					
Patrick J. Buchanan (Va.)	56,874	27.2	Bill Clinton (Ark.)	76,797	83.9
Bob Dole (Kan.)	54,738	26.2	Pat Paulsen (Calif.)	1,007	1.1
Lamar Alexander (Tenn.)	47,148	22.6	Lyndon H. LaRouche Jr. (Va.)	433	0.5
Malcolm S. "Steve" Forbes Jr. (N.J.)	25,505	12.2	Heather Anne Harder (Ind.)	369	0.4
Richard G. Lugar (Ind.)	10,838	5.2	Ted L. Gunderson (Nev.)	70	—
Alan Keyes (Md.)	5,572	2.7	Sal Casamassima (Texas)	45	—
Maurice "Morry" Taylor (Ill.)	2,944	1.4	Others[2]	12,841	14.1
Phil Gramm (Texas)	752	0.4			
Robert K. Dornan (Calif.)	529	0.3			
Susan Ducey (Pa.)	151	0.1			
Charles E. Collins (Fla.)	42	—			
Others[2]	3,845	1.8			
February 24 Delaware					
Forbes	10,709	32.7	Clinton	9,694	90.3
Dole	8,909	27.2	LaRouche	1,046	9.7
Buchanan	6,118	18.7			
Alexander	4,375	13.3			
Keyes	1,729	5.3			
Lugar	717	2.2			
Gramm	216	0.7			
February 27 Arizona[3]					
Forbes	115,962	33.4	Clinton	12,303	95.5
Dole	102,980	29.6	No preference	581	4.5
Buchanan	95,742	27.6			
Alexander	24,765	7.1			
Keyes	2,790	0.8			
Lugar	2,064	0.6			
Gramm	857	0.2			
Dornan	735	0.2			
Ducey	539	0.2			
Taylor	148	—			
Others	900	0.3			
February 27 North Dakota[4]					
Dole	26,832	42.1	Roland Riemers (N.D.)	651	41.1
Forbes	12,455	19.5	LaRouche	549	34.7
Buchanan	11,653	18.3	Vernon Clemenson (N.D.)	384	24.2
Gramm	5,997	9.4			
Alexander	4,008	6.3			
Keyes	2,030	3.2			
Lugar	559	0.9			
Taylor	200	0.3			
February 27 South Dakota[5]					
Dole	30,918	44.7	[6]		
Buchanan	19,780	28.6			
Forbes	8,831	12.8			
Alexander	6,037	8.7			
Keyes	2,378	3.4			
Uncommitted	677	1.0			
Gramm	387	0.6			
Taylor	162	0.2			
March 2 South Carolina					
Dole	124,904	45.1	[6]		
Buchanan	80,824	29.2			
Forbes	35,039	12.7			
Alexander	28,647	10.4			
Keyes	5,752	2.1			
Lugar	1,017	0.4			
Gramm	467	0.2			
Taylor	91	—			

	Republican			**Democratic**		
		Votes	%		Votes	%

March 3   Puerto Rico

	Votes	%			
Dole	233,742	97.9	6		
Gramm	1,454	0.6			
Alexander	1,273	0.5			
Forbes	1,078	0.5			
Buchanan	844	0.4			
Keyes	77	—			
Others	280	0.1			

March 5   Colorado

	Votes	%		Votes	%
Dole	108,123	43.6	Clinton	48,454	88.9
Buchanan	53,376	21.5	LaRouche	5,981	11.0
Forbes	51,592	20.8	Gunderson[7]	92	0.2
Alexander	24,184	9.8			
Keyes	9,052	3.7			
Lugar	1,603	0.6			

March 5   Connecticut

	Votes	%			
Dole	70,998	54.4	6		
Forbes	26,253	20.1			
Buchanan	19,664	15.1			
Alexander	6,985	5.4			
Keyes	2,209	1.7			
Uncommitted	1,699	1.3			
Lugar	1,495	1.1			
Taylor	430	0.3			
Dornan	401	0.3			
Gramm	284	0.2			

March 5   Georgia

	Votes	%		Votes	%
Dole	226,732	40.6	Clinton	95,103	100.0
Buchanan	162,627	29.1			
Alexander	75,855	13.6			
Forbes	71,276	12.7			
Keyes	17,538	3.1			
Lugar	1,971	0.4			
Gramm	1,095	0.2			
Dornan	1,005	0.2			
Collins	661	0.1			
Taylor	307	0.1			

March 5   Maine

	Votes	%		Votes	%
Dole	31,147	46.3	Clinton	23,879	88.4
Buchanan	16,478	24.5	Uncommitted	2,433	9.0
Forbes	9,991	14.8	LaRouche	715	2.6
Alexander	4,450	6.6			
Lugar	1,934	2.9			
Uncommitted	1,741	2.6			
Keyes	1,229	1.8			
Gramm	163	0.2			
Taylor	147	0.2			

March 5   Maryland

	Votes	%		Votes	%
Dole	135,522	53.3	Clinton	247,492	84.2
Buchanan	53,585	21.1	Uncommitted	33,417	11.4
Forbes	32,207	12.7	LaRouche	12,920	4.4
Alexander	14,061	5.5			
Keyes	13,718	5.4			
Lugar	2,872	1.1			
Gramm	1,174	0.5			
Dornan	757	0.3			
Taylor	350	0.1			

Republican

Democratic

	Votes	%		Votes	%
March 5 Massachusetts[8]					
Dole	135,946	47.7	Clinton	135,360	87.1
Buchanan	71,688	25.2	No preference	12,623	8.1
Forbes	39,605	13.9	LaRouche	5,212	3.4
Alexander	21,456	7.5	Others[2]	2,275	1.5
Keyes	5,224	1.8			
Lugar	4,743	1.7			
No preference	3,303	1.2			
Gramm	673	0.2			
Dornan	544	0.2			
Taylor	433	0.2			
Others[2]	1,218	0.4			
March 5 Rhode Island					
Dole	9,664	64.4	Clinton	7,825	89.1
Alexander	2,859	19.0	Uncommitted	535	6.1
Uncommitted	1,252	8.3	LaRouche	392	4.5
Lugar	487	3.2	Others[2]	28	0.3
Buchanan[7]	387	2.6			
Taylor	165	1.1			
Forbes[7]	128	0.9			
Keyes[7]	31	0.2			
Dornan[7]	1	—			
Gramm[7]	1	—			
Others[2]	34	0.2			
March 5 Vermont[9]					
Dole	23,419	40.3	Clinton	29,763	96.5
Buchanan	9,730	16.7	LaRouche	699	2.3
Forbes	9,066	15.6	Others[2]	376	1.2
Lugar	7,881	13.6			
Alexander	6,145	10.6			
Gramm	291	0.5			
Taylor	257	0.4			
Others[2]	1,324	2.3			
March 7 New York[10]					
Dole	599,748	55.1	[6]		
Forbes	325,211	29.9			
Buchanan	163,365	15.0			
March 12 Florida					
Dole	511,377	56.9	[6]		
Forbes	181,768	20.2			
Buchanan	162,770	18.1			
Keyes	16,631	1.9			
Alexander	14,142	1.6			
Dornan	4,465	0.5			
Lugar	3,236	0.4			
Gramm	2,994	0.3			
Taylor	1,133	0.1			
March 12 Louisiana					
Dole	37,170	47.8	Clinton	124,931	80.8
Buchanan	25,757	33.1	LaRouche	18,150	11.7
Forbes	10,265	13.2	Elvena E. Lloyd-Duffie (Ill.)	11,620	7.5
Keyes	2,464	3.2			
Alexander	1,642	2.1			
Taylor	491	0.6			

Republican

Democratic

	Votes	%		Votes	%
March 12 Mississippi					
Dole	91,639	60.3	Clinton	86,716	92.5
Buchanan	39,324	25.9	LaRouche	7,072	7.5
Forbes	12,119	8.0			
Keyes	2,907	1.9			
Alexander	2,781	1.8			
Dornan	2,123	1.4			
Gramm	475	0.3			
Lugar	141	0.1			
Taylor	84	0.1			
Others	332	0.2			
March 12 Oklahoma					
Dole	156,829	59.3	Clinton	279,454	76.2
Buchanan	56,949	21.5	LaRouche	46,392	12.7
Forbes	37,213	14.1	Lloyd-Duffie	40,758	11.1
Keyes	6,306	2.4			
Alexander	3,436	1.3			
Gramm	1,490	0.6			
Isabell Masters (Kan.)	1,052	0.4			
Lugar	538	0.2			
Collins	451	0.2			
Taylor	278	0.1			
March 12 Oregon					
Dole	206,938	50.8	Clinton	349,871	94.8
Buchanan	86,987	21.3	Others[2]	19,307	5.2
Forbes	54,121	13.3			
Alexander	28,332	7.0			
Keyes	14,340	3.5			
Lugar	4,971	1.2			
Gramm	2,117	0.5			
Dornan	1,872	0.5			
Taylor	1,344	0.3			
Others[2]	6,492	1.6			
March 12 Tennessee					
Dole	148,063	51.2	Clinton	122,538	88.9
Buchanan	72,928	25.2	Uncommitted	15,144	11.0
Alexander	32,742	11.3	Others[2]	115	0.1
Forbes	22,171	7.7			
Keyes	7,661	2.6			
Uncommitted	3,078	1.1			
Dornan	898	0.3			
Gramm	688	0.2			
Lugar	531	0.2			
Taylor	210	0.1			
Others[2]	416	0.1			
March 12 Texas					
Dole	567,164	55.6	Clinton	796,041	86.4
Buchanan	217,974	21.4	Fred Hudson (Texas)	32,232	3.5
Forbes	130,938	12.8	Harder	28,772	3.1
Keyes	41,746	4.1	LaRouche	28,137	3.1
Uncommitted	19,507	1.9	Gunderson	15,550	1.7
Alexander	18,745	1.8	Lloyd-Duffie	10,876	1.2
Gramm	18,629	1.8	Casamassima	9,648	1.0
Lugar	2,266	0.2			
Ducey	1,093	0.1			
Collins	633	0.1			
Taylor	458	—			
Others	650	0.1			

Republican   # Democratic

	Votes	%		Votes	%

March 19   Illinois[11]

Dole	532,467	65.1	Clinton	770,001	96.2
Buchanan	186,177	22.7	Lloyd-Duffie	16,045	2.0
Forbes	39,906	4.9	LaRouche	14,624	1.8
Keyes	30,052	3.7	Harder	6	—
Alexander	12,585	1.5			
Lugar	8,286	1.0			
Gramm	6,696	0.8			
Taylor	2,189	0.3			
Others[2]	6	—			

March 19   Michigan

Dole	265,425	50.6	Uncommitted	123,640	86.6
Buchanan	177,562	33.9	Others[2]	19,110	13.4
Forbes	26,610	5.1			
Uncommitted	23,109	4.4			
Keyes	15,995	3.1			
Alexander	7,631	1.5			
Lugar	2,175	0.4			
Gramm	1,755	0.3			
Dornan	1,723	0.3			
Taylor	1,018	0.2			
Others[2]	1,158	0.2			

March 19   Ohio

Dole	640,954	66.5	Clinton	713,153	91.8
Buchanan	208,012	21.6	LaRouche	63,377	8.2
Forbes	58,131	6.0			
Keyes	27,197	2.8			
Alexander	19,530	2.0			
Lugar	9,598	1.0			

March 19   Wisconsin

Dole	301,628	52.3	Clinton	347,629	97.6
Buchanan	194,733	33.8	Uninstructed	7,005	2.0
Forbes	32,205	5.6	Others[2]	1,534	0.4
Keyes	18,028	3.1			
Alexander	11,213	1.9			
Uninstructed	7,504	1.3			
Lugar	3,215	0.6			
Gramm	2,682	0.5			
Dornan	1,645	0.3			
Taylor	916	0.2			
Others[2]	2,806	0.5			

March 26   California[12]

Dole	1,619,931	66.1	Clinton	2,342,185	92.8
Buchanan	450,695	18.4	LaRouche	173,953	6.9
Forbes	183,367	7.5	Paulsen[7]	310	—
Keyes	93,577	3.8	Others[2]	6,924	0.3
Alexander	44,130	1.8			
Dornan	23,215	0.9			
Gramm	15,232	0.6			
Lugar	14,801	0.6			
Taylor	5,778	0.2			
Others[2]	1,586	0.1			

Republican

Democratic

	Votes	%		Votes	%

March 26   Nevada

			6		
Dole	72,932	*51.9*			
Forbes	27,063	*19.2*			
Buchanan	21,321	*15.2*			
"None of these candidates"	12,026	*8.6*			
Alexander	3,289	*2.3*			
Keyes	1,999	*1.4*			
Gramm	745	*0.5*			
Lugar	464	*0.3*			
Collins	305	*0.2*			
Taylor	94	*0.1*			
Others	399	*0.3*			

March 26   Washington

	Votes	%		Votes	%
Dole	76,155	*63.1*	Clinton	97,495	*98.5*
Buchanan	25,247	*20.9*	LaRouche	1,451	*1.5*
Forbes	10,339	*8.6*			
Keyes	5,610	*4.6*			
Alexander	1,600	*1.3*			
Gramm	630	*0.5*			
Lugar	587	*0.5*			
Dornan	516	*0.4*			

April 23   Pennsylvania

	Votes	%		Votes	%
Dole	435,031	*63.6*	Clinton	666,486	*92.0*
Buchanan	123,011	*18.0*	LaRouche	57,583	*8.0*
Forbes	55,018	*8.0*			
Keyes	40,025	*5.8*			
Lugar	31,119	*4.5*			

May 7   District of Columbia

	Votes	%		Votes	%
Dole	2,256	*75.5*	Clinton	20,568	*98.1*
Uncommitted	381	*12.8*	LaRouche	391	*1.9*
Buchanan	283	*9.4*			
Others[2]	67	*2.2*			

May 7   Indiana

	Votes	%		Votes	%
Dole	365,860	*70.8*	Clinton	329,536	*100.0*
Buchanan	100,245	*19.4*			
Forbes	50,802	*9.8*			

May 7   North Carolina

	Votes	%		Votes	%
Dole	202,863	*71.4*	Clinton	461,434	*80.6*
Buchanan	37,126	*13.1*	No preference	69,790	*12.2*
Keyes	11,759	*4.1*	LaRouche	40,936	*7.2*
Forbes	11,588	*4.1*			
No preference	10,918	*3.8*			
Alexander	7,400	*2.6*			
Lugar	2,558	*0.9*			

May 14   Nebraska[13]

	Votes	%		Votes	%
Dole	129,131	*75.7*	Clinton	81,854	*86.9*
Buchanan	17,741	*10.4*	LaRouche	10,228	*10.9*
Forbes	10,612	*6.2*	Others[2]	2,094	*2.2*
Keyes	5,132	*3.0*			
Alexander	4,423	*2.6*			
Lugar	1,127	*0.7*			
Dornan	847	*0.5*			
Taylor	460	*0.3*			
Others[2]	1,118	*0.7*			

Republican

Democratic

	Votes	%		Votes	%
May 14 West Virginia					
Dole	87,534	68.7	Clinton	257,087	86.5
Buchanan	20,928	16.4	LaRouche	40,034	13.5
Forbes	6,222	4.9			
Keyes	4,822	3.8			
Alexander	3,773	3.0			
Gramm	2,391	1.9			
Lugar	1,082	0.8			
Taylor	702	0.6			
May 21 Arkansas					
Dole	32,759	76.2	Clinton	239,287	75.8
Buchanan	10,067	23.4	Uncommitted	42,411	13.4
Uncommitted	150	0.3	LaRouche	20,669	6.6
			Lloyd-Duffie	13,136	4.2
May 28 Idaho					
Dole	74,011	62.3	Clinton	35,277	87.7
Buchanan	26,461	22.3	"None of the names shown"	4,951	12.3
"None of the names shown"	12,339	10.4			
Keyes	5,904	5.0			
May 28 Kentucky					
Dole	76,669	73.8	Clinton	211,667	76.7
Buchanan	8,526	8.2	Uncommitted	44,028	16.0
Uncommitted	4,793	4.6	LaRouche	20,324	7.4
Keyes	3,822	3.7			
Forbes	3,400	3.3			
Alexander	3,272	3.2			
Lugar	2,235	2.2			
Gramm	1,122	1.1			
June 4 Alabama					
Dole	160,097	75.5	Clinton	243,588	80.6
Buchanan	33,409	15.8	Uncommitted	45,764	15.2
Uncommitted	11,073	5.2	LaRouche	12,686	4.2
Keyes	7,354	3.5			
June 4 Montana					
Dole	72,176	61.3	Clinton	82,549	90.0
Buchanan	28,581	24.3	No preference	9,176	10.0
No preference	8,533	7.2			
Forbes	8,456	7.2			
June 4 New Jersey					
Dole	180,412	82.5	Clinton	254,004	95.2
Buchanan	23,789	10.9	LaRouche	12,736	4.8
Keyes	14,611	6.7			
June 4 New Mexico[14]					
Dole	53,300	75.6	Clinton	109,595	90.3
Buchanan	5,679	8.1	Uncommitted	11,767	9.7
Forbes	3,987	5.7			
Alexander	2,676	3.8			
Keyes	2,265	3.2			
Uncommitted	1,301	1.8			
Dornan	865	1.2			
Taylor	391	0.6			

Republican

	Votes	%
TOTALS		
Dole	8,427,601	59.2
Buchanan	3,021,935	21.2
Forbes	1,425,998	10.0
Alexander	495,590	3.5
Keyes	449,536	3.2
Lugar	127,111	0.9
Gramm	71,457	0.5
Dornan	42,141	0.3
Taylor	21,180	0.1
Collins	2,092	—
Ducey	1,783	—
Masters	1,052	—
Uncommitted[15]	123,765	0.9
Others[16]	22,698	0.2
	14,233,939	

Democratic

	Votes	%
TOTALS		
Clinton	9,730,184	88.5
LaRouche	597,081	5.4
Lloyd-Duffie	92,435	0.8
Hudson	32,232	0.3
Harder	29,147	0.3
Gunderson	15,712	0.1
Casamassima	9,693	0.1
Paulsen	1,317	—
Riemers	651	—
Clemenson	384	—
Uncommitted	423,265	3.8
Others[17]	64,294	0.6
	10,996,395	

1. In New Hampshire's Libertarian presidential primary, Harry Browne received 653 votes (40.5 percent), Irwin A. Schiff received 336 votes (20.8 percent) and there were 624 scattered write-in votes (38.6 percent).

2. Includes write-in votes.

3. The Arizona Democratic Party held its primary on March 9, 1996.

4. The North Dakota Democratic primary was nonbinding and did not elect delegates. In North Dakota's Libertarian presidential primary, Harry Browne received 147 votes (100.0 percent). In the Natural Law primary John Hagelin received 119 votes (100.0 percent).

5. In South Dakota's Libertarian presidential primary, Harry Browne received 325 votes (65.4 percent) and Irwin A. Schiff received 172 votes (34.6 percent).

6. No primary

7. Write-in votes.

8. In Massachusetts' Libertarian presidential primary, Harry Browne received 386 votes (44.4 percent), No preference received 237 votes (27.2 percent), Rick Tompkins received 111 votes (12.8 percent), Irwin A. Schiff received 66 votes (7.6 percent) and there were 70 scattered write-in votes (8.0 percent).

9. In Vermont's Liberty Union presidential primary, Mary Cal Hollis received 665 votes (80.1 percent) and there were 165 scattered write-in votes (19.9 percent).

10. Vote was for delegates only; there was no direct vote for candidates.

11. In Illinois' Libertarian presidential primary, Harry Browne received 1,278 votes (74.0 percent) and Irwin A. Schiff received 450 votes (26.0 percent).

12. In California's American Independent presidential primary, Howard Phillips received 19,204 votes (100.0 percent). In the Green presidential primary, Ralph Nader received 22,649 votes (100.0 percent). In the Libertarian presidential primary, Harry Browne received 7,258 votes (50.0 percent), Rick Tompkins received 3,400 votes (23.44 percent), Irwin A. Schiff received 2,215 votes (15.3 percent), Douglass J. Ohmen received 1,517 votes (10.5 percent) and there were 115 write-in votes (0.8 percent). In the Natural Law presidential primary, John Hagelin received 3,779 votes (100.0 percent). In the Peace and Freedom presidential primary, Monica Moorehead received 2,153 votes (33.9 percent), Jan Tucker received 1,512 votes (23.8 percent), Gerald Horne received 1,430 votes (22.5 percent), Mary Cal Hollis received 1,068 votes (16.8 percent), and there were 187 write-in votes (2.9 percent).

13. In Nebraska's Libertarian presidential primary, Harry Browne received 80 votes (89.9 percent) and there were 10 scattered write-in votes (11.1 percent). In the Libertarian Party of Iowa presidential primary, Harry Browne received 49 votes (77.8 percent) and there were 14 scattered write-in votes (22.2 percent).

14. In New Mexico's Green presidential primary, Ralph Nader received 976 votes (65.9 percent), Mary Cal Hollis received 395 votes (26.7 percent) and uncommitted delegates received 110 votes (7.4 percent).

15. The Uncommitted category includes votes cast on the following ballot lines: Uncommitted, No preference, Uninstructed, "None of these candidates" and "None of the names shown."

16. In addition to scattered write-in votes, "others" include Mary "France" Le Tulle who received 940 votes — 290 votes in the Nevada primary and 650 votes in the Texas primary; Billy Joe Clegg who received 415 votes — 297 votes in the Mississippi primary and 118 votes in the New Hampshire primary; Ann Jennings who received 304 votes in the Arizona primary; Richard P. Bosa who received 216 votes in the New Hampshire primary; Paul Jensen who received 172 votes — 99 votes in the Arizona primary and 73 votes in the Puerto Rico primary; Georgiana H. Doerschuck who received 154 votes in the New Hampshire primary; Joann V. Pharr who received 125 votes in the Arizona primary; Hilary Michael Milko who received 109 votes in the Nevada primary; Kenneth Hewitt who received 104 votes in the Arizona primary; Michael Stephen Levinson who received 94 votes — 59 votes in the Arizona primary and 35 votes in the New Hampshire primary; Richard D. Skillen who received 80 votes in the New Hampshire primary; Hubert David Patty who received 72 votes — 55 votes in the Arizona primary and 17 votes in the New Hampshire primary; Doug Fricke who received 64 votes in the Arizona primary; William James Flanagan who received 48 votes in the New Hampshire primary; Tennie Rogers who received 47 votes — 35 votes in the Mississippi primary and 12 in the New Hampshire primary; Charles Holden who received 38 votes in the Arizona primary; Russell J. Fornwalt who received 37 votes in the New Hampshire primary; Clyde Staggs who received 33 votes in the Arizona primary; John B. Hurd who received 26 votes in the New Hampshire primary; Gerald J. McManus who received 20 votes in the New Hampshire primary; C. A. Aldrich who received 19 votes in the Arizona primary.

17. In addition to scattered write-in votes, "others" include Carmen C. Chimento who received 656 votes in the New Hampshire primary; Caroline P. Killeen who received 391 votes in the New Hampshire primary; Bruce C. Daniels who received 312 votes in the New Hampshire primary; James D. Griffin who received 307 votes in the New Hampshire primary; Stephen Michael who received 94 votes in the New Hampshire primary; Willie Felix Carter who received 85 votes in the New Hampshire primary; Robert F. Drucker who received 81 votes in the New Hampshire primary; David Pauling who received 74 votes in the New Hampshire primary; Vincent S. Hamm who received 72 votes in the New Hampshire primary; Ronald W. Spangler who received 72 votes — 10 write-in votes in the California primary and 62 votes in the New Hampshire primary; Frank Legas who received 63 votes in the New Hampshire primary; Michael E. Dass who received 57 votes in the New Hampshire primary; Osie Thorpe who received 50 votes in the New Hampshire primary; Ben J. Tomeo who received 47 votes in the New Hampshire primary; John Safran who received 42 votes in the New Hampshire primary.

Presidential Nominating Campaigns, 1976-1996

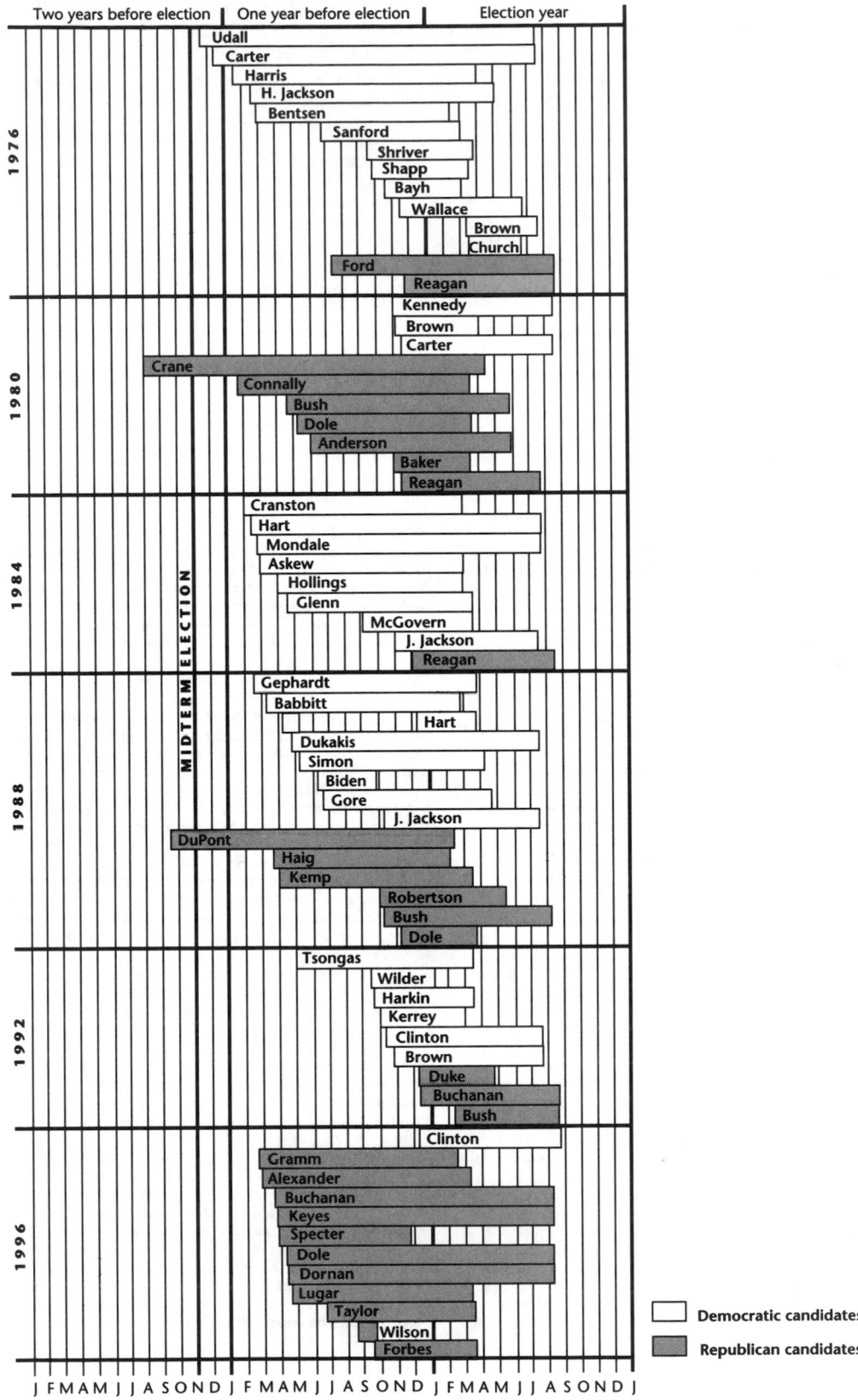

| Two years before election | One year before election | Election year |

1976
- Udall
- Carter
- Harris
- H. Jackson
- Bentsen
- Sanford
- Shriver
- Shapp
- Bayh
- Wallace
- Brown
- Church
- Ford
- Reagan

1980
- Kennedy
- Brown
- Carter
- Crane
- Connally
- Bush
- Dole
- Anderson
- Baker
- Reagan

1984
- Cranston
- Hart
- Mondale
- Askew
- Hollings
- Glenn
- McGovern
- J. Jackson
- Reagan

MIDTERM ELECTION

1988
- Gephardt
- Babbitt
- Hart
- Dukakis
- Simon
- Biden
- Gore
- J. Jackson
- DuPont
- Haig
- Kemp
- Robertson
- Bush
- Dole

1992
- Tsongas
- Wilder
- Harkin
- Kerrey
- Clinton
- Brown
- Duke
- Buchanan
- Bush

1996
- Clinton
- Gramm
- Alexander
- Buchanan
- Keyes
- Specter
- Dole
- Dornan
- Lugar
- Taylor
- Wilson
- Forbes

- □ Democratic candidates
- ■ Republican candidates

J F M A M J J A S O N D J F M A M J J A S O N D J F M A M J J A S O N D J

Source: *Selecting the President: From 1789 to 1996* (Washington, D.C.: Congressional Quarterly, 1997), 63.

Nominating Conventions

Although the presidential nominating convention has been a target of criticism throughout its existence, it has survived to become a traditional fixture of American politics. The convention owes its longevity and general acceptance in large part to the multiplicity of functions that the convention uniquely combines.

The convention is a nominating body that the Democrats, Republicans and most of the other major parties have used for 165 years to choose their candidates for president and vice president. The convention also produces a platform containing the party's positions on campaign issues. Convention delegates form the organization's supreme governing body and as such they make major decisions on party affairs. Between conventions such decisions are made by the national committee with the guidance of the party chair.

The convention provides a forum for compromise among the diverse elements within a party, allowing the discussion and often the satisfactory solution of differing points of view. As the ultimate campaign rally, the convention also gathers together thousands of party leaders and rank-and-file members from across the country in an atmosphere that varies widely, sometimes encouraging sober discussion but often resembling a carnival. But even though the process has drawn heavy criticism, the convention has endured because it successfully performs a variety of actions.

The convention is an outgrowth of the American political experience. Nowhere is it mentioned in the Constitution nor has the authority of the convention ever been a subject of congressional legislation. Rather, the convention has evolved along with the presidential selection process. The convention has been the accepted nominating method of the major political parties since the election of 1832, but internal changes within the convention system have been massive since the early, formative years.

Convention Sites

Before the Civil War, conventions frequently were held in small buildings, even churches, and attracted only several hundred delegates and a minimum of spectators. Transportation and communications were slow, so most conventions were held in the late spring in a city with a central geographical location. Baltimore, Md., was the most popular convention city in this period, playing host to the first six Democratic conventions (1832 through 1852), two Whig conventions, one National Republican convention, and the 1831 Anti-Masonic gathering — America's first national nominating convention. With the nation's westward expansion, the heartland city of Chicago, Ill., emerged as the most frequent convention center. Since its first one in 1860, Chicago has been the site of 25 major party conventions (14 Republican, 11 Democratic). The Democrats held their national convention in Chicago as recently as 1996. The Republicans chose that year to meet in San Diego — the first time that California city hosted a national party convention.

Locating and Financing Conventions

Since 1976, presidential elections have been publicly funded. Early on, the newly created Federal Election Commission (FEC) ruled that host-city contributions to conventions are allowable, enabling the parties to far exceed the technical limit on convention spending. In 1988, for example, the FEC allotted the two major parties $9.2 million each in public funds for their conventions. The money came from an optional checkoff for publicly financing presidential campaigns on federal income tax forms. (Congress raised the original $1 checkoff to $3 per taxpayer, beginning in 1993.) In 1988, the Republicans, however, spent a total of $18 million on their New Orleans convention, while the Democrats spent $22.5 million in Atlanta. To attract the Democratic convention, Atlanta levied a special tax on hotel guests, which enabled the host committee to offer a package of $5 million in borrowed money. For both conventions, General Motors (with FEC permission) provided fleets of cars at an estimated cost of $350,000.

In 1992, the Democrats spent a record $38.6 million on their New York City meeting, according to political scientist Herbert E. Alexander. For the 1996 conventions, the FEC allotted the two major parties $12.4 million each in public funds, but the total spending for each party, according to Alexander, was at least $30 million. No authoritative breakdown of 1996 convention costs was available, but major outlays typically go for construction, administration, office space, convention committees and police and fire protection. Besides adequate hotel and convention hall facilities, safety of the delegates and other attendees is increasingly a major consideration in selection of a national party convention site. The island location of Miami Beach, for example, made it easier to contain protest demonstrators and reportedly was a factor in its selection by the Republicans in 1968 and by both parties in 1972. For the party that controls the White House, often the overriding factor in site selection is the president's personal preference — as in the GOP's decision to meet in 1992 at President George Bush's adopted home

Sites of Major Party Conventions, 1832-1996

The following chart lists the 21 cities selected as the sites of major party conventions and the number of conventions they have hosted from the first national gathering for the Democrats (1832) and the Republicans (1856) through the 1996 conventions. The Democrats have hosted a total of 43 conventions; the Republicans 36.

	Total Conventions	Democratic Conventions		Republican Conventions	
		Number	Last Hosted	Number	Last Hosted
Chicago, Ill.	25	11	1996	14	1960
Baltimore, Md.	10	9	1912	1	1864
Philadelphia, Pa.	7	2	1948	5	1948
St. Louis, Mo.	5	4	1916	1	1896
New York, N.Y.	5	5	1992	0	—
San Francisco, Calif.	4	2	1984	2	1964
Cincinnati, Ohio	3	2	1880	1	1876
Kansas City, Mo.	3	1	1900	2	1976
Miami Beach, Fla.	3	1	1972	2	1972
Cleveland, Ohio	2	0	—	2	1936
Houston, Texas	2	1	1928	1	1992
Atlanta, Ga.	1	1	1988	0	—
Atlantic City, N.J.	1	1	1964	0	—
Charleston, S.C.	1	1	1860	0	—
Dallas, Texas	1	0	—	1	1984
Denver, Colo.	1	1	1908	0	—
Detroit, Mich.	1	0	—	1	1980
Los Angeles, Calif.	1	1	1960	0	—
Minneapolis, Minn.	1	0	—	1	1892
New Orleans, La.	1	0	—	1	1988
San Diego, Calif.	1	0	—	1	1996

city of Houston, or the Democrats' decision to meet in Atlantic City in 1964, because President Lyndon Johnson wanted a site within helicopter distance of Washington, and convenient to New York City.

The national committees of the two parties select the sites about one year before the conventions are to take place.

Call of the Convention

The second major step in the quadrennial convention process follows several months after the site selection with announcement of the convention call, the establishment of the three major convention committees — credentials, rules and platform (resolutions) — the appointment of convention officers and finally the holding of the convention itself. While these basic steps have undergone little change during the past 165 years, there have been major alterations within the nominating convention system.

The call to the convention sets the date and site of the meeting and is issued early in each election year, if not before. The call to the first Democratic convention, held in 1832, was issued by the New Hampshire legislature. Early Whig conventions were called by party members in Congress. With the establishment of national committees later in the 19th century, the function of issuing the convention call fell to these new party organizations. Each national committee currently has the responsibility for allocating delegates to each state.

Delegate Selection

Both parties have modified the method of allocating delegates to the individual states and territories. From the beginning of the convention system in the 19th century, both the Democrats and Republicans distributed votes to the states based on their Electoral College strength. The first major deviation from this procedure was made by the Republicans after their divisive 1912 convention, in which President William Howard Taft won renomination over former president Theodore Roosevelt. Taft's nomination was due largely to almost solid support from the South — a region vastly over-represented in relation to its number of Republican voters. Before their 1916 convention the Republicans reduced the allocation of votes to the Southern states. At their 1924 convention the Republicans applied the first bonus system, by which states were awarded extra votes for supporting the Republican presidential candidate in the previous election. The concept of bonus votes, applied as a reward to the states for supporting the party ticket, has been used and expanded by both parties since that time.

The Democrats first used a bonus system in 1944, completing a compromise arrangement with Southern states after abolishing the party's controversial two-thirds nominating rule in 1936. Since then both parties have used various delegate-allocation formulas. At their 1972 convention the Republicans revised the formula and added more than 900 new delegate slots. The Ripon Society, an organization of liberal Republicans, sued to have the new rules overturned. They argued that, because of the extra delegates awarded to states that voted Republican in the previous presidential election, small Southern and Western states were favored at the expense of the more populous but less Republican Eastern states. The challenge failed when the Supreme Court in February 1976 refused to hear the case and thus let stand a U.S. Court of Appeals decision upholding the rules.

Republican and Democratic Convention Delegates, 1932-1996

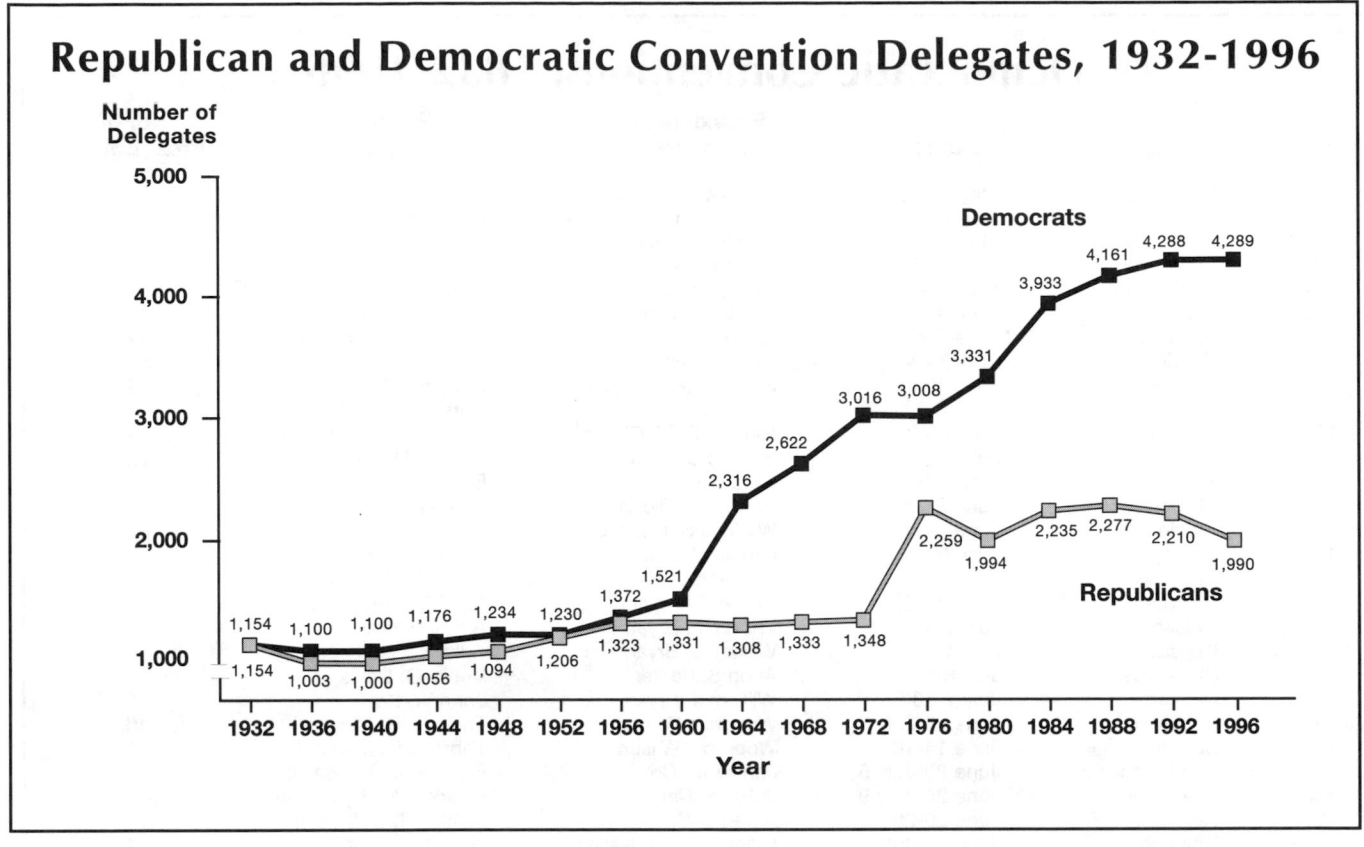

Only 116 delegates from 13 states attended the initial national nominating convention held by the Anti-Masons in 1831, but with the addition of more states and the adoption of increasingly complex voting-allocation formulas by the major parties, the size of conventions spiraled. The 1976 Republican convention had 2,259 delegates, while the Democrats in the same year had 3,075 delegates casting 3,008 votes. (The number of delegate votes was smaller than the number of delegates because Democratic Party rules provide for fractional voting.)

The expanded size of modern conventions in part reflected their democratization, with less command by a few party leaders and dramatic growth among youth, women and minority delegations. Increased representation by such groups was one of the major reasons given by the Republicans for the 60 percent increase in delegate strength authorized by the 1972 convention (and effective for the 1976 gathering). The Democrats adopted new rules in June 1978, expanding the number of delegates by 10 percent to provide extra representation for state and local officials. The new Democratic rules also required that women account for at least 50 percent of the delegates beginning with the 1980 convention. That party's national convention continued to grow throughout the next decade — from 3,933 delegates in 1984 to 4,289 in 1996. In 1996, 57 percent of the Democratic delegates were women; 33 percent were from minority groups.

In contrast, 1,990 delegates attended the 1996 Republican convention in San Diego. Unlike the Democrats, the Republican Party had no rules for the makeup of its convention delegates. Although 51 percent of the GOP registered voters in 1996 were women, only 39 percent of the convention delegates were women. However, while only 6 percent of registered Republican voters in 1996 were minorities, 8 percent of the Republican delegates were of minority groups.

With the increased size of conventions has come a formalization in the method of delegate selection, which at first was often haphazard and informal. At the Democratic convention in 1835, for example, Maryland had 188 delegates to cast the state's 10 votes. In contrast, Tennessee's 15 votes were cast by a traveling businessman who happened to be in the convention city at the time. While the number of delegates and the number of votes allocated tended to be equal or nearly so later in the 19th century, a few party bosses frequently exercised domination of national conventions.

Two basic methods of delegate selection were employed in the 19th century and continued to be used into the 20th: the caucus method, by which delegates were chosen by meetings at the local or state level, and the appointment method, by which delegates were appointed by the governor or a powerful state leader.

Presidential Primaries

A revolutionary new mechanism for delegate selection emerged during the early 1900s: the presidential primary election in which the voters directly elected convention delegates. Initiated in Florida in 1904, the presidential primary by 1912 was used by 13 states. In his first annual message to Congress the following year, President Woodrow Wilson advocated the establishment of a national primary to select presidential candidates: "I feel confident that I do not misinterpret the wishes or the expectations of the country when I urge the prompt enactment of legislation which will provide for primary elections throughout the country at which the voters of several parties may choose their nominees for the presidency without the intervention of nominating conventions." Wilson went on to suggest the retention of conven-

Democratic Conventions, 1832-1996

Year	City	Dates	Presidential Nominee	Vice Presidential Nominee	No. of Pres. Ballots
1832	Baltimore	May 21-23	Andrew Jackson	Martin Van Buren	1
1835	Baltimore	May 20-23	Martin Van Buren	Richard M. Johnson	1
1840	Baltimore	May 5-6	Martin Van Buren	—[1]	1
1844	Baltimore	May 27-29	James K. Polk	George M. Dallas	9
1848	Baltimore	May 22-25	Lewis Cass	William O. Butler	4
1852	Baltimore	June 1-5	Franklin Pierce	William R. King	49
1856	Cincinnati	June 2-6	James Buchanan	John C. Breckinridge	17
1860	Charleston	April 23-May 3	Deadlocked		57
	Baltimore	June 18-23	Stephen A. Douglas	Benjamin Fitzpatrick Herschel V. Johnson[2]	2
1864	Chicago	Aug. 29-31	George B. McClellan	George H. Pendleton	1
1868	New York	July 4-9	Horatio Seymour	Francis P. Blair	22
1872	Baltimore	July 9-10	Horace Greeley	Benjamin G. Brown	1
1876	St. Louis	June 27-29	Samuel J. Tilden	Thomas A. Hendricks	2
1880	Cincinnati	June 22-24	Winfield S. Hancock	William H. English	2
1884	Chicago	July 8-11	Grover Cleveland	Thomas A. Hendricks	2
1888	St. Louis	June 5-7	Grover Cleveland	Allen G. Thurman	1
1892	Chicago	June 21-23	Grover Cleveland	Adlai E. Stevenson	1
1896	Chicago	July 7-11	William J. Bryan	Arthur Sewall	5
1900	Kansas City	July 4-6	William J. Bryan	Adlai E. Stevenson	1
1904	St. Louis	July 6-9	Alton S. Parker	Henry G. Davis	1
1908	Denver	July 7-10	William J. Bryan	John W. Kern	1
1912	Baltimore	June 25-July 2	Woodrow Wilson	Thomas R. Marshall	46
1916	St. Louis	June 14-16	Woodrow Wilson	Thomas R. Marshall	1
1920	San Francisco	June 28-July 6	James M. Cox	Franklin D. Roosevelt	44
1924	New York	June 24-July 9	John W. Davis	Charles W. Bryan	103
1928	Houston	June 26-29	Alfred E. Smith	Joseph T. Robinson	1
1932	Chicago	June 27-July 2	Franklin D. Roosevelt	John N. Garner	4
1936	Philadelphia	June 23-27	Franklin D. Roosevelt	John N. Garner	Acclamation
1940	Chicago	July 15-18	Franklin D. Roosevelt	Henry A. Wallace	1
1944	Chicago	July 19-21	Franklin D. Roosevelt	Harry S. Truman	1
1948	Philadelphia	July 12-14	Harry S. Truman	Alben W. Barkley	1
1952	Chicago	July 21-26	Adlai E. Stevenson	John J. Sparkman	3
1956	Chicago	Aug. 13-17	Adlai E. Stevenson	Estes Kefauver	1
1960	Los Angeles	July 11-15	John F. Kennedy	Lyndon B. Johnson	1
1964	Atlantic City	Aug. 24-27	Lyndon B. Johnson	Hubert H. Humphrey	Acclamation
1968	Chicago	Aug. 26-29	Hubert H. Humphrey	Edmund S. Muskie	1
1972	Miami Beach	July 10-13	George McGovern	Thomas F. Eagleton R. Sargent Shriver[3]	1
1976	New York	July 12-15	Jimmy Carter	Walter F. Mondale	1
1980	New York	Aug. 11-14	Jimmy Carter	Walter F. Mondale	1
1984	San Francisco	July 16-19	Walter F. Mondale	Geraldine A. Ferraro	1
1988	Atlanta	July 18-21	Michael S. Dukakis	Lloyd Bentsen	1
1992	New York	July 13-16	Bill Clinton	Albert Gore Jr.	1
1996	Chicago	Aug. 26-29	Bill Clinton	Albert Gore Jr.	1

1. The 1840 Democratic convention did not nominate a candidate for vice president.

2. The 1860 Democratic convention nominated Benjamin Fitzpatrick, who declined the nomination shortly after the convention adjourned. On June 25 the Democratic National Committee selected Herschel V. Johnson as the party's candidate for vice president.

3. The 1972 Democratic convention nominated Thomas F. Eagleton, who withdrew from the ticket on July 31. On Aug. 8 the Democratic National Committee selected R. Sargent Shriver as the party's candidate for vice president.

tions for the purpose of declaring the results of the primaries and formulating the parties' platforms.

Before any action was taken on Wilson's proposal, the progressive spirit that spurred the growth of primaries died out. Not until after World War II, when widespread pressures for change touched both parties but especially the Democratic, was there a rapid growth in presidential primaries. In the mid-1980s some states reverted to the caucus method of delegate selection, but the revival trend soon abated. A record 44 primaries were held in 1996, including those in the District of Columbia and Puerto Rico.

In most states participation in the presidential primary is restricted to voters belonging to the party holding the primary. In some states, however, participation by voters outside the party is allowed by state-mandated open primaries, which override party rules to the contrary.

Democratic Rules in the 1980s and 1990s

In June 1982 the Democratic National Committee (DNC) adopted several changes in the presidential nominating process recommended by the party's Commission on Presidential Nominations, chaired by Gov. James B. Hunt Jr. of

Chief Officers and Keynote Speakers
At Democratic National Conventions, 1832-1996

Year	Chair National Committee	Temporary Chair	Permanent Chair	Keynote Speaker
1832		Robert Lucas, Ohio	Robert Lucas, Ohio	
1836		Andrew Stevenson, Va.	Andrew Stevenson, Va.	
1840		Isaac Hill, N.H.	William Carroll, Tenn.	
1844		Hendrick B. Wright, Pa.	Hendrick B. Wright, Pa.	
1848	Benjamin Hallet, Mass.	J.S. Bryce, La.	Andrew Stevenson, Va.	
1852	Robert M. McLane, Md.	Gen. Romulus M. Saunders, N.C.	John W. Davis, Ind.	
1856	David A. Smalley, Vt.	Samuel Medary, Ohio	John E. Ward, Ga.	
1860	August Belmont, N.Y.	Francis B. Flournoy, Ark.	Caleb Cushing, Mass.	
1864	August Belmont, N.Y.	William Bigler, Pa.	Horatio Seymour, N.Y.	
1868	August Belmont, N.Y.	Henry L. Palmer, Wis.	Horatio Seymour, N.Y.	
1872	Augustus Schell, N.Y.	Thomas Jefferson Randolph, Va.	James R. Doolittle, Wis.	
1876	Abram Stevens Hewitt, N.Y.	Henry M. Watterson, Ky.	John A. McClernand, Ill.	
1880	William H. Barnum, Conn.	George Hoadly, Ohio	John W. Stevenson, Ky.	
1884	William H. Barnum, Conn.	Richard B. Hubbard, Texas	William F. Vilas, Wis.	
1888	William H. Barnum, Conn.	Stephen M. White, Calif.	Patrick A. Collins, Mass.	
1892	William F. Harrity, Penn.	William C. Owens, Ky.	William L. Wilson, W.Va.	
1896	James K. Jones, Ark.	John W. Daniel, Va.	Stephen M. White, Calif.	
1900	James K. Jones, Ark.	Charles S. Thomas, Colo.	James D. Richardson, Tenn.	
1904	Thomas Taggart, Ind.	John Sharp Williams, Miss.	Champ Clark, Mo.	
1908	Norman E. Mack, N.Y.	Theodore A. Bell, Calif.	Henry D. Clayton, Ala.	
1912	William F. McCombs, N.Y.	Alton B. Parker, N.Y.	Ollie M. James, Ky.	
1916	Vance C. McCormick, Pa.	Martin H. Glynn, N.Y.	Ollie M. James, Ky.	
1920	George H. White, Ohio	Homer S. Cummings, Conn.	Joseph T. Robinson, Ark.	
1924	Clem Shaver, W.Va.	Pat Harrison, Miss.	Thomas J. Walsh, Mont.	
1928	John J. Raskob, Md.	Claude G. Bowers, Ind.	Joseph T. Robinson, Ark.	
1932	James A. Farley, N.Y.	Alben W. Barkley, Ky.	Thomas J. Walsh, Mont.	
1936	James A. Farley, N.Y.	Alben W. Barkley, Ky.	Joseph T. Robinson, Ark.	Alben W. Barkley, Ky.
1940	Edward J. Flynn, N.Y.	William B. Bankhead, Ala.	Alben W. Barkley, Ky.	William B. Bankhead, Ala.
1944	Robert E. Hannegan, Mo.	Robert S. Kerr, Okla.	Samuel D. Jackson, Ind.	Robert S. Kerr, Okla.
1948	J. Howard McGrath, R.I.	Alben W. Barkley, Ky.	Sam Rayburn, Texas	Alben W. Barkley, Ky.
1952	Stephen A. Mitchell, Ill.	Paul A. Dever, Mass.	Sam Rayburn, Texas	Paul A. Dever, Mass.
1956	Paul M. Butler, Ind.	Frank G. Clement, Tenn.	Sam Rayburn, Texas	Frank Clement, Tenn.
1960	Henry Jackson, Wash.	Frank Church, Idaho	LeRoy Collins, Fla.	Frank Church, Idaho
1964	John M. Bailey, Conn.	John O. Pastore, R.I.	John W. McCormack, Mass.	John O. Pastore, R.I.
1968	Lawrence F. O'Brien, Mass.	Daniel K. Inouye, Hawaii	Carl B. Albert, Okla.	Daniel K. Inouye, Hawaii
1972[1]	Lawrence F. O'Brien, Mass.		Lawrence F. O'Brien, Mass.	Reubin Askew, Fla.
1976	Robert S. Strauss, Texas		Lindy Boggs, La.	John Glenn, Ohio
				Barbara C. Jordan, Texas
1980	John C. White, Texas		Thomas P. O'Neill Jr., Mass.	Morris K. Udall, Ariz.
1984	Charles T. Manatt, Calif.		Martha Layne Collins, Ky.	Mario M. Cuomo, N.Y.
1988	Paul G. Kirk Jr., Mass.		Jim Wright, Texas	Ann W. Richards, Texas
1992	Ronald H. Brown, D.C.		Ann W. Richards, Texas	Bill Bradley, N.J.
				Zell Miller, Ga.
				Barbara C. Jordan, Texas
1996	Donald Fowler, S.C.		Thomas A. Daschle, S.D.	Evan Bayh, Ind.
			Richard A. Gephardt, Mo.	

1. A rule change eliminated the position of temporary chair.

North Carolina. The Hunt Commission, as it came to be known, suggested revisions to increase the power of party regulars and give the convention more freedom to act on its own. It was the fourth time in 12 years that the Democrats, struggling to repair their nominating process without repudiating earlier reforms, had rewritten their party rules. (*Changes in Democrats' Nominating Rules, box, p. 237*)

One major change in the Democrats' rules was the creation of a new group of "superdelegates," party and elected officials who would go to the 1984 convention uncommitted and would cast about 14 percent of the ballots. The DNC also adopted a Hunt Commission proposal to weaken the rule binding delegates to vote for their original presidential preference on the first convention ballot. But the new rule also allows a presidential candidate to replace any disloyal delegate with a more faithful one.

One of the most significant revisions was the Democrats' decision to relax proportional representation and end

Republican Conventions, 1856-1996

Year	City	Dates	Presidential Nominee	Vice Presidential Nominee	No. of Pres. Ballots
1856	Philadelphia	June 17-19	John C. Fremont	William L. Dayton	2
1860	Chicago	May 16-18	Abraham Lincoln	Hannibal Hamlin	3
1864	Baltimore	June 7-8	Abraham Lincoln	Andrew Johnson	1
1868	Chicago	May 20-21	Ulysses S. Grant	Schuyler Colfax	1
1872	Philadelphia	June 5-6	Ulysses S. Grant	Henry Wilson	1
1876	Cincinnati	June 14-16	Rutherford B. Hayes	William A. Wheeler	7
1880	Chicago	June 2-8	James A. Garfield	Chester A. Arthur	36
1884	Chicago	June 3-6	James G. Blaine	John A. Logan	4
1888	Chicago	June 19-25	Benjamin Harrison	Levi P. Morton	8
1892	Minneapolis	June 7-10	Benjamin Harrison	Whitelaw Reid	1
1896	St. Louis	June 16-18	William McKinley	Garret A. Hobart	1
1900	Philadelphia	June 19-21	William McKinley	Theodore Roosevelt	1
1904	Chicago	June 21-23	Theodore Roosevelt	Charles W. Fairbanks	1
1908	Chicago	June 16-19	William H. Taft	James S. Sherman	1
1912	Chicago	June 18-22	William H. Taft	James S. Sherman Nicholas Murray Butler[1]	1
1916	Chicago	June 7-10	Charles E. Hughes	Charles W. Fairbanks	3
1920	Chicago	June 8-12	Warren G. Harding	Calvin Coolidge	10
1924	Cleveland	June 10-12	Calvin Coolidge	Charles G. Dawes	1
1928	Kansas City	June 12-15	Herbert Hoover	Charles Curtis	1
1932	Chicago	June 14-16	Herbert Hoover	Charles Curtis	1
1936	Cleveland	June 9-12	Alfred M. Landon	Frank Knox	1
1940	Philadelphia	June 24-28	Wendell L. Willkie	Charles L. McNary	6
1944	Chicago	June 26-28	Thomas E. Dewey	John W. Bricker	1
1948	Philadelphia	June 21-25	Thomas E. Dewey	Earl Warren	3
1952	Chicago	July 7-11	Dwight D. Eisenhower	Richard M. Nixon	1
1956	San Francisco	Aug. 20-23	Dwight D. Eisenhower	Richard M. Nixon	1
1960	Chicago	July 25-28	Richard M. Nixon	Henry Cabot Lodge	1
1964	San Francisco	July 13-16	Barry Goldwater	William E. Miller	1
1968	Miami Beach	Aug. 5-8	Richard M. Nixon	Spiro T. Agnew	1
1972	Miami Beach	Aug. 21-23	Richard M. Nixon	Spiro T. Agnew	1
1976	Kansas City	Aug. 16-19	Gerald R. Ford	Robert Dole	1
1980	Detroit	July 14-17	Ronald Reagan	George Bush	1
1984	Dallas	Aug. 20-23	Ronald Reagan	George Bush	1
1988	New Orleans	Aug. 15-18	George Bush	Dan Quayle	1
1992	Houston	Aug. 17-20	George Bush	Dan Quayle	1
1996	San Diego	Aug. 12-15	Robert Dole	Jack Kemp	1

1. *The 1912 Republican convention nominated James S. Sherman, who died on Oct. 30. The Republican National Committee subsequently selected Nicholas Murray Butler to receive the Republican electoral votes for vice president.*

the ban on the "loophole" primary — winner take all by district. Proportional representation is the distribution of delegates among candidates to reflect their share of the primary or caucus vote. Mandated by party rules in 1980, it was blamed by some Democrats for the protracted primary fight between President Jimmy Carter and Sen. Edward M. Kennedy of Massachusetts. Because candidates needed only about 20 percent of the vote in most places to qualify for a share of the delegates, Kennedy was able to remain in contention. But while the system kept Kennedy going, it did nothing to help his chances of winning the nomination.

Although the Democrats' 1984 rules permitted states to retain proportional representation, they also allowed states to take advantage of two options that could help a front-running candidate build the momentum to wrap up the nomination early in the year.

One was a winner-take-more system. States could elect to keep proportional representation but adopt a winner bonus plan that would award the top vote-getter in each district one extra delegate.

The other option was a return to the loophole primary, which party rules outlawed in 1980 (with exemptions allowing Illinois and West Virginia to retain their loophole voting systems). In the loophole states, voters ballot directly for delegates, with each delegate candidate identified by presidential preference. Sometimes several presidential contenders win at least a fraction of the delegates in a given district, but the most common result is a sweep by the presidential front-runner, even if he has less than an absolute majority. Loophole primaries aid the building of a consensus behind the front-runner, while still giving other candidates a chance to inject themselves back into the race by winning a major loophole state decisively.

The DNC retained the delegate-selection season adopted in 1978, a three-month period stretching from the second Tuesday in March to the second Tuesday in June. But, in an effort to reduce the growing influence of early states in the nominating process, the Democrats required Iowa and New Hampshire to move their highly publicized elections to late winter. Party rules maintained the privileged status of Iowa

Chief Officers and Keynote Speakers
At Republican National Conventions, 1856-1996

Year	Chair National Committee	Temporary Chair	Permanent Chair	Keynote Speaker
1856	Edwin D. Morgan, N.Y.	Robert Emmet, N.Y.	Henry S. Lane, Ind.	
1860	Edwin D. Morgan, N.Y.	David Wilmot, Pa.	George Ashmun, Mass.	
1864	Edwin D. Morgan, N.Y.	Robert J. Breckinridge, Ky.	William Dennison, Ohio	
1868	Marcus L. Ward, N.J.	Carl Schurz, Mo.	Joseph R. Hawley, Conn.	
1872	William Claflin, Mass.	Morton McMichael, Pa.	Thomas Settle, N.C.	
1876	Edwin D. Morgan, N.Y.	Theodore M. Pomeroy, N.Y.	Edward McPherson, Pa.	
1880	J. Donald Cameron, Pa.	George F. Hoar, Mass.	George F. Hoar, Mass.	
1884	Dwight M. Sabin, Minn.	John R. Lynch, Miss.	John B. Henderson, Mo.	
1888	B.F. Jones, Pa.	John M. Thurston, Neb.	Morris M. Estee, Calif.	
1892	James S. Clarkson, Iowa	J. Sloat Fassett, N.Y.	William McKinley Jr., Ohio	
1896	Thomas H. Carter, Mont.	Charles W. Fairbanks, Ind.	John M. Thurston, Neb.	
1900	Marcus A. Hanna, Ohio	Edward O. Wolcott, Colo.	Henry Cabot Lodge, Mass.	
1904	Henry C. Payne, Wis.	Elihu Root, N.Y.	Joseph G. Cannon, Ill.	
1908	Harry S. New, Ind.	Julius C. Burrows, Mich.	Henry Cabot Lodge, Mass.	
1912	Victor Rosewater, Neb.	Elihu Root, N.Y.	Elihu Root, N.Y.	
1916	Charles D. Hilles, N.Y.	Warren G. Harding, Ohio	Warren G. Harding, Ohio	
1920	Will H. Hays, Ind.	Henry Cabot Lodge, Mass.	Henry Cabot Lodge, Mass.	Henry Cabot Lodge, Mass.
1924	John T. Adams, Iowa	Theodore E. Burton, Ohio	Frank W. Mortdell, Wyo.	
1928	William M. Butler, Mass.	Simeon D. Fess, Ohio	George H. Moses, N.H.	
1932	Simeon D. Fess, Ohio	L. J. Dickinson, Iowa	Bertrand H. Snell, N.Y.	
1936	Henry P. Fletcher, Pa.	Frederick Steiwer, Ore.	Bertrand H. Snell, N.Y.	Frederick Steiwer, Ore.
1940	John Hamilton, Kan.	Harold E. Stassen, Minn.	Joseph W. Martin Jr., Mass.	Harold E. Stassen, Minn.
1944	Harrison E. Spangler, Iowa	Earl Warren, Calif.	Joseph W. Martin Jr., Mass.	Earl Warren, Calif.
1948	Carroll Reece, Tenn.	Dwight H. Green, Ill.	Joseph W. Martin Jr., Mass.	Dwight H. Green, Ill.
1952	Guy George Gabrielson, N.J.	Walter S. Hallanan, W.Va.	Joseph W. Martin Jr., Mass.	Douglas MacArthur
1956	Leonard W. Hall, N.Y.	William F. Knowland, Calif.	Joseph W. Martin Jr., Mass.	Arthur B. Langlie, Wash.
1960	Thruston B. Morton. Ky.	Cecil H. Underwood, W.Va.	Charles A. Halleck, Ind.	Walter H. Judd, Minn.
1964	William E. Miller, N.Y.	Mark O. Hatfield, Ore.	Thruston B. Morton, Ky.	Mark O. Hatfield, Ore.
1968	Ray C. Bliss, Ohio	Edward W. Brooke, Mass.	Gerald R. Ford, Mich.	Daniel J. Evans, Wash.
1972	Robert Dole, Kan.	Ronald Reagan, Calif.	Gerald R. Ford, Mich.	Richard G. Lugar, Ind. Anne L. Armstrong, Texas
1976	Mary Louise Smith, Iowa	Robert Dole, Kan.	John J. Rhodes, Ariz.	Howard H. Baker Jr., Tenn.
1980	Bill Brock, Tenn.	Nancy Landon Kassebaum, Kan.	John J. Rhodes, Ariz.	Guy Vander Jagt, Mich.
1984	Frank J. Fahrenkopf Jr., Nev.	Howard H. Baker Jr., Tenn.	Robert H. Michel, Ill.	Katherine Ortega, N.M.
1988	Lee Atwater, S.C.	Elizabeth Hanford Dole, N.C.	Robert H. Michel, Ill.	Thomas H. Kean, N.J.
1992	Richard N. Bond, N.Y.	Kay Bailey Hutchison, Texas	Robert H. Michel, Ill.	Phil Gramm, Texas
1996	Haley Barbour, Miss.	Christine Todd Whitman, N.J. George W. Bush, Texas	Newt Gingrich, Ga.	Susan Molinari, N.Y.

and New Hampshire before other states but mandated that their initial nominating rounds be held only eight days apart in 1984. Five weeks had intervened between the Iowa caucuses and New Hampshire primary in 1980.

The DNC also retained rules requiring primary states to set candidate filing deadlines 30 to 90 days before the election and limiting participation in the delegate selection process to Democrats only. This last rule eliminated crossover primaries where voters could participate in the Democratic primary without designating their party affiliation. African Americans and Hispanics won continued endorsement of affirmative action in the new party rules. Women gained renewed support for the equal division rule, which required state delegations at the national convention to be divided equally between men and women.

The Democratic Party's 1988 presidential nominating process remained basically the same as that used in 1984. The rules adopted by the national committee included only minor modifications suggested by the party's rules review panel, the Fairness Commission.

The bloc of uncommitted party and elected officials (superdelegates) was expanded slightly to 16 percent and rearranged to reserve more convention seats for members of Congress, governors and the DNC; the rules restricting participation in Democratic primaries and caucuses to Democrats only was relaxed so the open primaries in Wisconsin and Montana could be conducted with the approval of the national party; and the share of the vote a candidate must win in a primary or caucus to qualify for delegates was lowered from the 20 percent level used in most places in 1984 to 15 percent.

Only the rule regarding the 15 percent "threshold" spawned much debate during the rules-writing process, and though the discussion of the issue seldom was acrimonious, it did reveal a yawning chasm in the party on what the proper role of the national convention should be.

Political Party Organization and Rules

Political parties in the United States are loosely organized. Anyone of voting age can become a party member simply by signing up. Millions of Americans do just that, while many others shun formal partisan affiliations but think of themselves as Democrats or Republicans nonetheless.

Cowboy humorist Will Rogers used to get laughs by saying, "I am not a member of any organized party. I am a Democrat." But the same line could also be applied to the Republicans, even if they sometimes seemed to be less disorganized than their major rivals.

Both parties have the same fluidity of membership, with the rolls open to independents as well as to supporters of the other party. Formally registering as a Democrat or Republican has the advantage of permitting participation in the party's nominating primaries and caucuses. Most states bar crossover voting in the other party's elections, largely for fear that Democrats would try to nominate the weakest Republican candidates, and vice versa.

There is little evidence, however, that most rank-and-file voters are as concerned about parties as such. While almost 33 million Americans voted in primaries in 1992, a far greater number waited for the general election that November — the first U.S. election in which more than 100 million people voted. (But the number of voters in primaries and in the general election declined in 1996 — the second time since 1988 that the absolute number of voters declined in the general election for president.) And in 1995, for the first time ever, a plurality of voters surveyed by the Gallup poll identified themselves as other" (36 percent) rather than as Republican or Democratic (32 percent each).

Party Structure

Loose though it is, each major party has an organizational structure — a necessity for continuity as an institution, fund raising and conducting election campaigns. Congress has officially recognized the role of the parties and public funding is provided for their presidential nominating conventions. Some states also provide funding for election campaigns.

Beginning at the precinct or neighborhood level, a series of progressively larger units make up the national organization. Next up the line are city, county, legislative district, congressional district and, just below the national committee, the state organizations.

There is no "chain of command." Each unit is more or less independent. The national chair exerts influence mainly through prestige and force of personality, rather than through any specified powers. The national committee elects the chair, but the president actually designates the chair of the party controlling the White House. *(National Party Chairs, box, p. 244)*

With its 426 members, the DNC is more than twice the size of the 162-member Republican National Committee. Fifty-four members make up the DNC executive committee — the 9 officers, 20 regional representatives, 10 "at-large" members elected by the DNC and 15 others representing Democratic affiliates.

Since 1984 the Democrats have occupied their own $6.4 million national headquarters at 430 South Capitol Street, S.E., in Washington. Previous locations in New York and Washington (including the Watergate offices burglarized by the Republicans in 1972) were rented.

Besides the chair, eight other DNC officers are elected: five vice chairs, treasurer, secretary and national finance chair. Party organizations in the states and territories elect their DNC members for four-year terms, ending with the next convention. They are the state chair and the next highest-ranking member of the opposite sex. Another 200 votes are distributed on a population basis, with each state or territory guaranteed at least two, equally divided among men and women.

Other DNC members are two U.S. senators, two House members, two members of the College Democrats and three representatives each from among Democratic governors, mayors, state legislators, county officials, municipal officials, Young Democrats and the National Federation of Democratic Women.

The RNC elects four officers — the chair, co-chair, secretary and treasurer for two-year terms. The party owns its national headquarters at 310 First Street, S.E., in Washington. The Republicans maintain a large field staff and generally have more money than the Democrats to dispense to campaigns.

Because of their large sizes, the full national committees seldom meet more than a few times during the four years between the national conventions, which are the parties' supreme governing bodies. In both parties, the day-to-day work of the national organization is done by the chair and the headquarters staff, under direction of the executive committee.

Operating Rules

The most important rules of both major parties deal largely with the selection of delegates to the quadrennial national nominating conventions. While the Democrats in recent years have experimented widely with these rules, mainly to give more representation to women, youth and minorities, Republicans have left their rules largely unchanged. *(GOP Primary Rules, box, p. 238)*

Beginning with reforms proposed by Sen. George S. McGovern of South Dakota, who won the nomination himself in 1972, the Democratic Party attempted to "democratize" the process. A succession of commissions headed by Barbara A. Mikulski of Maryland (1972), Morley Winograd of Michigan (1976), Gov. James B. Hunt Jr. of North Carolina (1980) and Donald L. Fowler of South Carolina (1988), succeeded in gaining equal representation for women, requiring proportional representation of delegates among primary vote-getters and giving convention votes to "superdelegate" party and elected officials.

For the 1992 convention, Democrats for the first time in two decades did not have a special commission intensively examining the nominating process. Nevertheless, the DNC again changed the rules somewhat. In 1996 the Democratic Party left its rules unchanged. *(Democratic Rules in the 1980s and 1990s, p. 232)*

Changes in Democrats' Nominating Rules

Between 1972 and 1992 Democrats tinkered with their nominating rules every four years, producing a system that, if not better than before, was always different. In 1996, the party left its rules unchanged for the first time in 20 years. The following chart shows the ebb and flow of the Democratic Party's rules changes, with a "✔" indicating the years these major rules were in effect.

	1972	1976	1980	1984	1988	1992	1996
Timing: Restrict delegate-selection events to a three-month period (the "window").			✔	✔	✔	✔	✔
Conditions of Participation: Restrict participation in delegate-selection events to Democrats.		✔	✔	✔	✔	✔	✔
Proportional Representation: Ban all types of winner-take-all contests.			✔			✔	✔
Ban all types of winner-reward contests (where winner receives extra delegates).						✔	✔
Delegate Loyalty: Give candidates the right to approve delegates identifying with their candidacy.		✔	✔	✔	✔	✔	✔
Bind delegates to vote for their original presidential preference at convention on first ballot.			✔				
Party and Elected Officials: Expand each delegation to include pledged party and elected officials.			✔	✔	✔	✔	✔
Further expand each delegation to include uncommitted party and elected officials ("superdelegates").				✔	✔	✔	✔
Demographic Representation: Encourage participation and representation of minorities and traditionally under-represented groups (affirmative action).				✔	✔	✔	✔
Require delegations to be equally divided between men and women.			✔	✔	✔	✔	✔

Most party leaders, including Democratic National Chairman Paul G. Kirk Jr., wanted a threshold of at least 15 percent because they thought it would help steadily shrink the field of presidential candidates during the primary and caucus season and ensure that the convention would be a "ratifying" body that confirmed the choice of the party's voters.

But civil rights leader and presidential candidate Jesse L. Jackson saw it differently, as did a cadre of liberal activists. They wanted a convention that was more "deliberative," and they complained that getting one was virtually impossible under the system as it existed because it discriminated against long-shot candidates and produced an artificial consensus behind one candidate.

Most Democratic leaders were satisfied with the way the nominating process operated in 1984, and they felt it would be a disaster for the party to go through a free-wheeling, multi-ballot convention. Not since 1952 — at the beginning of the television age — has a national party taken more than one ballot to nominate its candidate.

At the DNC meeting, some African American committee members joined with a few white liberal activists in proposing to eliminate the 15 percent threshold altogether. The proposal was rejected by voice vote. A second proposal to lower the threshold to 10 percent was defeated 92-178.

In 1990 the DNC made two basic changes that directly affected the delegate-selection process for the 1992 convention. One moved forward the officially sanctioned start of the presidential primary season by one week, from the second Tuesday in March to the first. This was an invitation to California to move its primary from June to March 3. (California declined in 1992, but in 1996 moved its primary from June to late March. This was part of a desire by both parties in 1992 to speed up the nomination contest and settle it by April or early May, so that united parties could organize their conventions with a focus on the November election.) The second

GOP Primary Rules

The Republican Party, wrote political scientist Nelson W. Polsby, "in many respects remains unreformed." Virtually anything has been permitted in the nominating process so long as it was not baldly discriminatory. And that has been the way GOP leaders have wanted it.

While the Democratic Party has a tightly crafted, nationalized set of rules that govern its nominating process, Republicans historically have shunned control by a central authority. The individual GOP state parties are given wide latitude to determine how their delegates are selected, with guidelines from the national party kept to a minimum.

The result has been a nominating procedure with a simplicity and continuity that the Democrats lack. A more homogeneous party than the Democrats, the Republicans have not felt the pressure for rules reform that had engulfed the Democrats. No major rules changes were made by the Republicans between 1974 and 1996.

Republicans, however, have not been able to operate totally in their own world. Campaign finance laws and the rising influence of mass media affected Republicans as well as Democrats. And in states where legislatures accommodated the Democrats and created a presidential primary, the Republicans were dragged along.

The Republican Party held 20 primaries in 1972, but over the next 24 years the number of primaries has steadily increased. In 1996 the party held a record 43 primaries, including those in the District of Columbia and Puerto Rico (the Democrats' record was 40 primaries in 1992). Primaries helped to select 85 percent of delegates to the GOP convention in 1996.

change banned winner-reward systems, which gave extra delegates to the winner of a primary or caucus. Fifteen states had used some form of winner-reward system in 1988.

The Democrats required all states in 1992 and thereafter to divide their publicly elected delegates proportionally among candidates who drew at least 15 percent of the primary or caucus vote.

The Democratic Party also continued to use superdelegates, expanding their number to 769 for the 1996 convention, or 18 percent of the 4,289 delegate votes.

During the 1972-1996 period the Republican Party followed an entirely different approach and made few changes in its nominating rules. While the Democratic rules were revised somewhat for each presidential cycle, the GOP rules remained stable. For the year 2000, however, the Republicans again changed their minds on the desirability of deciding the nomination contest by March or April; they provided a bonus for those states that choose their delegates to the 2000 GOP convention in May or June. (*GOP Primary Rules, box, above*)

Credentials Disputes

Before the opening of a convention the national committee compiles a temporary roll of delegates. The roll is referred to the convention's credentials committee, which holds hearings on the challenges and makes recommendations to the convention, the final arbiter of all disputes.

Some of the most bitter convention battles have concerned the seating of contested delegations. In the 20th century most of the heated credentials fights have concerned delegations from the South. In the Republican Party the challenges focused on the power of the Republican state organizations to dictate the selection of delegates. The issue was hottest in 1912 and 1952, when the party throughout most of the South was a skeletal structure whose power was restricted largely to selection of convention delegates. Within the Democratic Party the question of Southern credentials emerged after World War II on the volatile issues of civil rights and party loyalty. Important credentials challenges on these issues occurred at the 1948, 1952, 1964 and 1968 Democratic conventions.

There were numerous credentials challenges at the 1972 Democratic convention, but, unlike those at its immediate predecessors, the challenges involved delegations from across the nation and focused on violations of the party's newly adopted guidelines.

After their 1952 credentials battle, the Republicans established a contest committee within the national committee to review credentials challenges before the convention. After their divisive 1968 convention the Democrats also created a formal credentials procedure to review all challenges before the opening of the convention.

Equally important to the settlement of credentials challenges are the rules under which the convention operates. The Republican Party adopts a completely new set of rules at every convention. Although large portions of the existing rules are enacted each time, general revision is always possible.

After its 1968 convention the Democratic Party set out to reform itself and the convention system. The Commission on Rules and the Commission on Party Structure and Delegate Selection, both created by the 1968 convention, proposed many changes that were accepted by the national committee. As a result, a formal set of rules was adopted for the first time at the party's 1972 convention.

Controversial Rules

Although it did not have a formal set of rules before 1972, the Democratic Party operated with two controversial rules never used by the Republicans: the unit rule and the two-thirds nominating rule. The unit rule enabled the majority of a delegation, if authorized by its state party, to cast the entire vote of the delegation for one candidate or position. In use since the earliest Democratic conventions, the unit rule was abolished by the 1968 convention.

From their first convention in 1832 until the 1936 convention, the Democrats employed the two-thirds nominating rule, which required any candidate for president or vice president to win not just a simple majority but a two-thirds majority. Viewed as a boon to the South since it allowed that region a virtual veto power over any possible nominee, the rule was abolished with the stipulation that the South would receive an increased vote allocation at later conventions.

In its century of use the two-thirds rule frequently produced protracted, multi-ballot conventions, often giving the Democrats a degree of turbulence the Republicans, requiring only a simple majority, did not have. Between 1832 and 1932, seven Democratic conventions took more than 10 ballots to select a presidential candidate. In contrast, in their entire convention history, the Republicans have had just one convention that required more than 10 ballots to select a presidential candidate. *(Democrats' Two-Thirds Rule, box, right)*

One controversy that surfaced during the 1980 Democratic Party convention concerned a rule that bound delegates to vote on the first ballot for the candidates under whose banner they had been elected. Supporters of Sen. Kennedy had devoted their initial energies to prying the nomination from incumbent President Carter by defeating that rule. The final tally on the rule showed 1,936.42 delegates favoring the binding rule and 1,390.58 opposing it. Passage of the binding rule ensured Carter's renomination, and shortly after the vote Kennedy announced that his name would not be placed in nomination.

Convention Officers

Credentials, rules and platform are the three major convention committees, but each party has additional committees, including one in charge of convention arrangements.

Within the Republican Party the arrangements committee recommends a slate of convention officers to the national committee, which in turn refers the names to the committee on permanent organization for confirmation. The people the committee chooses are subject to the approval of the convention. In the Democratic Party, this function is performed by the rules committee.

In both the Democratic and Republican parties, the presiding officer during the bulk of the convention is the permanent chairman. Over the past quarter century the position usually has gone to the party's leader in the House of Representatives.

However, this loose precedent was broken in the Democratic Party by a rule adopted at the 1972 convention requiring that the presiding officer position alternate every four years between the sexes.

Party Platforms

The adoption of a party platform is one of the principal functions of a convention. The platform committee is charged with the responsibility of writing a party platform to be presented to the convention for its approval.

The main challenge before the platform committee is to write a platform all party candidates can use in their campaigns. For this reason, platforms often fit the description given them by Wendell L. Willkie, Republican presidential candidate in 1940: "fusions of ambiguity."

Despite the best efforts of platform-builders to resolve their differences in the comparative privacy of the committee room, they sometimes encounter so controversial a subject that it cannot be compromised. Under these conditions dissident committee members often submit a minority report to the convention floor. Open floor fights are not unusual and, like credentials battles, often reflect the strength of the various candidates.

When the party has an incumbent president, the platform often is drafted in the White House or at least has the approval of the president. Rarely does a party adopt a platform that is critical of an incumbent president of the same party. When Democratic delegates at their 1896 convention, inspired by William Jennings Bryan's "Cross of Gold" speech, repudiated President Grover Cleveland and his support for a gold standard for hard currency, and nominated Bryan for president on a "free silver" platform, they signaled a major sea change in American politics. A similar change took place

---

Democrats' Two-Thirds Rule

At their first convention in 1832, the Democrats adopted a rule requiring a two-thirds majority for nomination. Two presidential nominees— Martin Van Buren in 1844 and Champ Clark in 1912 — received majorities but failed to attain the two-thirds requirement.

On the first ballot in 1844 Van Buren received 146 of the 266 convention votes, 54.9 percent of the total. His total fell under a simple majority on succeeding roll calls and on the ninth ballot the nomination went to a dark-horse candidate, former governor James K. Polk of Tennessee.

In 1912 from the 10th through the 16th ballots Clark recorded a simple majority. He reached his peak on the 10th ballot, receiving 556 of the 1,094 convention votes, 50.8 percent of the total. The nomination, however, ultimately went to New Jersey governor Woodrow Wilson, who was selected on the 46th ballot.

At their 1936 convention, the Democrats voted to end the requirement for a two-thirds majority for nomination.

---

in 1948, when Democratic delegates led by Mayor Hubert Humphrey of Minneapolis overturned a recommendation by the platform committee and precipitated a walkout of Southern delegates by adopting a strong civil rights plank. Although overridden, President Harry S. Truman accepted the Humphrey plank—and won with it.

The first platform was adopted by the Democrats in 1840. It was a short document, fewer than 1,000 words. Since then the platforms with few exceptions have grown longer and longer, covering more issues and appealing to more and more interest groups. One of the exceptions to the growth trend was the 4,500-word Democratic platform of 1988 — about one-tenth the length of the 1984 platform. But by 1996 the Democrats' platform had grown again, to about 13,000 words, compared with about 28,000 words in its Republican counterpart.

The 1996 GOP platform was characterized by hard-line conservative stands on abortion and other social issues. Sen. Robert Dole, the party's nominee, sought to soften its stance and appeal to more middle-road non-party voters by giving prime time convention speaking slots to more moderate Republicans who publicly expressed disapproval with some of the platform, while affirming their support for a GOP victory in November.

Third Parties: Radical Ideas

Throughout American history, many daring and controversial political platforms adopted by third parties have been rejected as too radical by the major parties. Yet many of these proposals later have won popular acceptance and have made their way into the major party platforms — and into law. Ideas such as the abolition of slavery, prohibition, the graduated income tax, the popular election of senators, women's suffrage, minimum wages, Social Security and the 18-year-old vote were advocated by Populists, Progressives and other third parties long before they were finally accepted by the nation as a whole.

The radical third parties and their platforms have been anathema to the established wisdom of the day, denounced

Notable Credentials Fights

1848, Democratic. Two rival New York state factions, known as the Barnburners and the Hunkers, sent separate delegations. By a vote of 126 to 125, the convention decided to seat both delegations and split New York's vote between them. This compromise suited neither faction: the Barnburners bolted the convention; the Hunkers remained but refused to vote.

1860, Democratic. Dissatisfaction with the slavery plank in the party platform spurred a walkout by several dozen Southern delegates from the Charleston convention. When the tumultuous convention reconvened in Baltimore six weeks later, a credentials controversy developed on the status of the bolting delegates. The majority report of the credentials committee recommended that the delegates in question, except those from Alabama and Louisiana, be reseated. The minority report recommended that a larger majority of the withdrawing Charleston delegates be allowed to return. The minority report was defeated, 100-1/2 to 150, prompting a walkout by the majority of delegates from nine states.

1880, Republican. Factions for and against the candidacy of former president Ulysses S. Grant clashed on the credentials of the Illinois delegation. By a margin of 387 to 353, the convention rejected a minority report that proposed searing pro-Grant delegates elected at the state convention over other delegates elected at a congressional district caucus. Three other votes were taken on disputed credentials from different Illinois districts, but all were decided in favor of the anti-Grant forces by a similar margin. The votes indicated the weakness of the Grant candidacy. The nomination went to a dark-horse candidate, Rep. James A. Garfield of Ohio, on the 36th ballot.

1912, Republican. The furious struggle between President William Howard Taft and Theodore Roosevelt for the presidential nomination centered on credentials. The Roosevelt forces brought 72 delegate challenges to the floor of the convention, but the test of strength between the two candidates came on a procedural motion. By a vote of 567 to 507, the convention tabled a motion presented by the Roosevelt forces barring any of the delegates under challenge from voting on any of the credentials contests. This procedural vote clearly indicated Taft's control of the convention. All the credentials cases were settled in favor of the Taft delegates, and the presidential nomination ultimately went to the incumbent president.

1932, Democratic. Two delegations favorable to the front-runner for the presidential nomination, Franklin D. Roosevelt, came under challenge. However, in a show of strength, the Roosevelt forces won both contests: seating a Louisiana delegation headed by Sen. Huey P. Long by a vote of 638-3/4 to 514-1/4 and a Roosevelt delegation from Minnesota by an even wider margin, 658-1/4 to 492-3/4. Roosevelt won the nomination on the fourth ballot.

1952, Democratic. The refusal of three Southern states — Louisiana, South Carolina and Virginia — to agree to a party loyalty pledge brought their credentials into question. The Virginia delegation argued that the problem prompting the loyalty pledge was covered by state law. By a vote of 650-1/2 to 518, the convention approved the seating of the Virginia delegation. After Louisiana and South Carolina took positions similar to that of Virginia, they were seated by a voice vote.

1952, Republican. Sixty-eight delegates from three Southern states (Georgia, Louisiana and Texas) were the focal point of the fight for the presidential nomination between Gen. Dwight D. Eisenhower and Sen. Robert A. Taft of Ohio. The national committee, controlled by forces favorable to Taft, had voted to seat delegations friendly to the Ohio senator from these three states. But by a vote of 607 to 531 the convention seated the Georgia delegation favorable to Eisenhower. It seated the Eisenhower delegates from Louisiana and Texas without roll calls. The general went on to win the presidential nomination on the first ballot.

1968, Democratic. A struggle between the anti-Vietnam war forces, led by Sen. Eugene J. McCarthy of Minnesota, and the party regulars, headed by Vice President Hubert H. Humphrey, dominated the 17 cases considered by the credentials committee. Three of the cases, involving the Texas, Georgia and Alabama delegations, required roll calls on the convention floor. All were won by the Humphrey forces. By a vote of 1,368-1/4 to 956-3/4, the regular Texas delegation headed by Gov. John B. Connally was seated. A minority report to seat the entire Georgia delegation led by black leader Julian Bond was defeated, 1,043.55 to 1,415.45. And a minority report to seat a McCarthy-backed, largely black delegation from Alabama was also rejected, 880-3/4 to 1,607. Humphrey, having shown his strength during the credentials contests, went on to win an easy first ballot nomination.

1972, Democratic. The first test of strength at the convention between South Dakota senator George McGovern's delegates and party regulars came over credentials. Key challenges brought to the convention floor concerned the South Carolina, California and Illinois delegations. The South Carolina challenge was brought by the National Women's Political Caucus in response to alleged underrepresentation of women in the delegation. Although the caucus' position was supposedly supported by the McGovern camp, votes were withheld to avoid jeopardizing McGovern's chances of winning the important California contest. The caucus' challenge lost 1,429.05 to 1,555.75. The California challenge was of crucial importance to McGovern, since it involved 151 delegates initially won by the South Dakota senator in the state's winner-take-all primary, but stripped from him by the credentials committee. By a vote of 1,618.28 to 1,238.22, McGovern regained the contested delegates, thereby nailing down his nomination. With victory in hand, the dominant McGovern camp sought a compromise on the Illinois case, which pitted a delegation headed by Chicago's powerful mayor Richard Daley against an insurgent delegation composed of party reformers. Compromise was unattainable and with the bulk of McGovern delegates voting for the reformers, a minority report to seat the Daley delegates was rejected.

Major Platform Fights

1860, Democratic. A minority report on the slavery plank, stating that the decision on allowing slavery in the territories should be left to the Supreme Court, was approved, 165 to 138. The majority report (favored by the South) declared that no government — local, state or federal — could outlaw slavery in the territories. The acceptance of the minority report precipitated a walkout by several dozen Southern delegates and the eventual sectional split in the party.

1896, Democratic. The monetary plank of the platform committee, favoring free and unlimited coinage of silver at a ratio of 16 to 1 with gold, was accepted by the convention, which defeated a proposed gold plank, 626 to 303. During debate William Jennings Bryan made his famous "Cross of Gold" speech supporting the platform committee plank, bringing him to the attention of the convention and resulting in his nomination for president.

1908, Republican. A minority report, proposing a substitute platform, was presented by Sen. Robert M. La Follette of Wisconsin. Minority proposals included increased antitrust activities, enactment of a law requiring publication of campaign expenditures and popular election of senators. All the proposed planks were defeated by wide margins; the closest vote, on direct election of senators, was 114 for, 866 against.

1924, Democratic. A minority plank was presented that condemned the activities of the Ku Klux Klan, then enjoying a resurgence in the South and some states in the Midwest. The plank was defeated 542-7/20 to 543-3/20, the closest vote in Democratic convention history.

1932, Republican. A minority plank favoring repeal of the 18th Amendment (Prohibition) in favor of a state-option arrangement was defeated, 460-2/9 to 690-19/36.

1948, Democratic. An amendment to the platform, strengthening the civil rights plank by guaranteeing full and equal political participation, equal employment opportunity, personal security and equal treatment in the military service, was accepted, 651-1/2 to 582-1/2.

1964, Republican. An amendment offered by Sen. Hugh Scott of Pennsylvania to strengthen the civil rights plank by including voting guarantees in state as well as in federal elections and by eliminating job bias was defeated, 409 to 897.

1968, Democratic. A minority report on Vietnam called for cessation of the bombing of North Vietnam, halting of offensive and search-and-destroy missions by American combat units, a negotiated withdrawal of American troops and establishment of a coalition government in South Vietnam. It was defeated, 1,041-1/4 to 1,567-3/4.

1972, Democratic. By a vote of 1,852.86 to 999.34, the convention rejected a minority report proposing a government guaranteed annual income of $6,500 for a family of four. By a vote of 1,101.37 to 1,572.80, a women's rights plank supporting abortion rights was defeated.

1980, Democratic. The platform battle, one of the longest in party history, pitted President Jimmy Carter against his persistent rival, Sen. Edward M. Kennedy of Massachusetts. Stretching over 17 hours, the debate focused on Kennedy's economics plank, which finally was defeated by a voice vote. Yet Carter was forced to concede on so many specific points, including Kennedy's $12 billion anti-recession jobs programs, that the final document bore little resemblance to the draft initially drawn up by Carter's operatives.

1992, Democratic. A tax fairness plank offered by former senator Paul E. Tsongas of Massachusetts was defeated by a vote of 953 to 2,287. The plank called for a delay in any middle-class tax cut and tax credit for families with children until the deficit was under control.

---

as impractical, dangerous, destructive of moral virtues and even traitorous. They have been anti-establishment and more far-reaching in their proposed solutions to problems than the major parties have dared to be.

Major Parties: Broader Appeal

In contrast with the third parties, Democrats and Republicans traditionally have been much more chary of adopting radical platform planks. Trying to appeal to a broad range of voters, the two major parties have tended to compromise differences or to reject controversial platform planks.

The Democratic Party has been more ready than the Republicans to adopt once-radical ideas, but there is usually a considerable time lag between their origin in third parties and their eventual adoption in Democratic platforms. For example, while the Democrats by 1912 had adopted many of the Populist planks of the 1890s, the Bull Moose Progressives of that year already were way ahead of them in proposals for social legislation. Not until 1932 were many of the 1912 Progressive planks adopted by the Democrats.

Similarly, it was not until the 1960s that Democratic platforms incorporated many of the more far-reaching proposals originally put forward by the 1948 Progressive Party in that year.

Filling Vacancies

Starting with the Democratic convention of 1848, and the Republican Party's first national organizing meeting in 1856, both major parties have elected national committees to run the day-to-day business of the parties between conventions.

Since their beginning, one of the most important functions of national committees is to replace a candidate who dies or resigns after the convention adjourns, or after election day but before the electors cast their votes for president and vice president. This replacement power was assumed informally, but without controversy, at first; was granted by several national conventions during the Progressive Era (1900-1912); and was made part of both parties' permanent standing rules by the 1920s.

There have been four such vacancies.

In 1860, the Democratic designee for vice president, Sen. Benjamin Fitzpatrick of Alabama, declined the nomination after the ruinously chaotic Baltimore convention of that year finally adjourned. The national committee then nominated former Gov. Herschel V. Johnson of Georgia as Sen. Stephen A. Douglas' running mate.

Third Parties Usually Fade Rapidly

Most third party movements are like shooting stars, shining brightly in one election and then quickly disappearing. In the last century and a half, 11 third parties — plus independents John B. Anderson in 1980 and Ross Perot in 1992 — have drawn at least 5 percent of the popular vote in a presidential election. As of 1996 not one of the third parties was able to maintain its foothold in the electoral process. Four had disappeared by the next election, four others drew a smaller vote total and two merged with one of the major parties. It remained to be

seen how the Reform Party would fare in the 2000 election.

Each of these significant third parties, except the Socialists in 1912, made its best showing in its first election. (The Socialists, led by Eugene V. Debs, first ran in 1900, winning just 0.62 percent of the vote.) The following chart lists each party's presidential candidate and the percentage of the vote the party received in its most successful race and in the following election. A dash (—) indicates that the party had disappeared.

Party (Candidate)	Year	Percentage of Vote	Next Election
Anti-Mason (William Wirt)	1832	7.8%	endorsed Whig
Free Soil (Martin Van Buren)	1848	10.1	4.9%
Whig-American (Millard Fillmore)	1856	21.5	—
Southern Democrats (John C. Breckinridge)	1860	18.1	—
Constitutional Union (John Bell)	1860	12.6	—
Populist (James B. Weaver)	1892	8.5	endorsed Democrat
Progressive (Bull Moose) (Theodore Roosevelt)	1912	27.4	0.2
Socialist (Eugene V. Debs)	1912	6.0	3.2
Progressive (Robert M. La Follette)	1924	16.6	—
American Independent (George C. Wallace)	1968	13.5	1.4
John B. Anderson	1980	6.6	endorsed Democrat
Ross Perot	1992	18.9	created Reform Party
Reform Party (Ross Perot)	1996	8.5	1

1. *The Reform Party qualified for $30 million in federal matching funds for the 2000 election.*

In 1872, the Democratic nominee for president, Horace Greeley, founder of the *New York Tribune*, died shortly after election day. (Republican Ulysses S. Grant had won the election.) Greeley's dispirited party's national committee declined to select a replacement candidate, and the Democratic electors voted for four different candidates.

In 1912, Vice President James S. Sherman of New York died in office the week before election day. The Republican convention of that year had authorized the national committee to fill vacancies, and the committee quickly replaced Sherman. His name remained on state ballots as President William Howard Taft's running mate, but the eight Republican electors voted, as recommended by the committee, for the replacement candidate, Nicholas Murray Butler of New York, president of Columbia University.

Finally, in 1972, the Democratic nominee for vice president, Sen. Thomas Eagleton of Missouri, resigned his candidacy after the convention adjourned. The nominee for president, Sen. George McGovern, recommended R. Sargent Shriver of Illinois, former head of the Peace Corps, as his replacement running mate, and Shriver was selected by a

special meeting of an expanded national committee. *(Political Party Organization and Rules, box, p. 236)*

Communications and the Media

Major changes in the national nominating convention have resulted from the massive advances in transportation and communication technologies during the 20th century.

The revolution in transportation has affected the scheduling of conventions. In the 19th century, conventions were sometimes held a year or more before the election and at the latest were completed by late spring of the election year. With the ability of people to assemble quickly, conventions in recent years have been held later in the election year, usually in July or August. Advances in transportation also have affected site location. Geographic centrality is no longer a primary consideration in the selection of a convention city.

Radio coverage of conventions began in 1924; television coverage 16 years later. One of the first changes inspired by the media age was the termination of the custom that a presidential candidate not appear at the convention but accept

Chief Officers at Other National Party Conventions, 1831-1892

Year	Party	Temporary Chair	Chair
1831	Anti-Masonic		John C. Spencer, N.Y.
1831	National Republican	Abner Lacock, Pa.	James Barbour, Va.
1839	Whig	Isaac Bates, Mass.	James Barbour, Va.
1844	Whig	Andrew F. Hopkins, Ala.	Ambrose Spencer, N.Y.
1848	Whig	John A. Collier, N.Y.	John M. Morehead, N.C.
1852	Whig	George C. Evans, Maine	John G. Chapman, Md.
1843	Liberty		Leicester King
1848	Free Soiler		Charles Francis Adams, Mass.
1852	Free Soiler (Free Democrats)		Henry Wilson, Mass.
1856	American (Know-Nothing)		Ephraim Marsh
1860	Southern Democrat (Breckinridge Factor)		Caleb Cushing, Mass.
1860	Constitutional Union		Washington Hunt, N.Y.
1872	Liberal Republican	Stanley Matthews, Ohio	Carl Schurz, Mo.
1880	Greenback	Gilbert De La Matyr, Ind.	Richard Trevellick, Mich.
1888	Prohibition	H. A. Delano, Conn.	John P. St. John, Kans.
1892	Prohibition	John P. St. John, Kans.	Eli Ritter, Ind.
1892	People's (Populist)	C. H. Ellington, Ga.	H. L. Loricks, S.D.

his nomination in a ceremony several weeks later. Franklin D. Roosevelt was the first major party candidate to break this tradition when in 1932 he delivered his acceptance speech in person before the Democratic convention. Twelve years later Thomas E. Dewey became the first Republican nominee to give his acceptance speech to the convention. Since then the final activity of every Democratic and Republican convention has been the delivery of the acceptance speeches by the vice presidential and presidential nominees.

A second change was to cut back the frivolity and hoopla, and to emphasize the more important aspects of the convention process. Party leaders have also, in recent years, streamlined the schedule, with the assumption that the interest level of most of the viewing public for politics is limited. The result has been shorter speeches and generally fewer roll calls than at those conventions in the pre-television era.

Party leaders desire to put on a good show for the viewing public with the hope of winning votes for their party in November. The convention is a showcase, designed to present the party as both a model of democracy and an efficient, harmonious body. The schedule of convention activities is drawn up with an eye on the peak evening television viewing hours. There is an attempt to put the party's major selling points — the highly partisan keynote speech, the nominating ballots, and the candidates' acceptance speeches — on in prime time. (The effort to put acceptance speeches on in prime time has been especially strong since 1972, when

Democratic nominee George S. McGovern was forced to wait until 3 a.m. to make his speech.) Conversely, party leaders try to keep evidence of bitter party factionalism — such as explosive credentials and platform battles — out of the peak viewing period.

Both the Republicans and Democrats went to extraordinary lengths to turn their 1996 conventions into a tightly scripted, visually appealing television shows. But it seems that the harder the political parties try to win over American audiences, the less they have to show for their efforts. Many TV viewers voted with their remote controls — tuning out the 1996 conventions. Ratings for the three major networks' broadcasts of the conventions were off sharply from four years earlier.

In the media age the appearance of fairness is important, and in a sense this need to look fair and open has assisted the movement for party reform. Some influential party leaders, skeptical of reform of the convention, have found resistance difficult in the glare of television.

Before the revolution in the means of transportation and communication, conventions met in relative anonymity. Today conventions are held in all the privacy of a fishbowl, with every action and every rumor closely scrutinized. They have become media events and as such are targets for political demonstrations that can be not only an embarrassment to the party but a security problem as well.

In spite of its difficulties, the convention system has survived. As the nation has developed during the past century

National Party Chairs, 1848-1997

Name	State	Years of Service	Name	State	Years of Service
Democratic Party			**Republican Party (continued)**		
B. F. Hallett	Massachusetts	1848-52	Zachariah Chandler	Michigan	1876-79
Robert McLane	Maryland	1852-56	J. Donald Cameron	Pennsylvania	1879-80
David A. Smalley	Virginia	1856-60	Marshall Jewell	Connecticut	1880-83
August Belmont	New York	1860-72	D. M. Sabin	Minnesota	1883-84
Augustus Schell	New York	1872-76	B. F. Jones	Pennsylvania	1884-88
Abram S. Hewitt	New York	1876-77	Matthew S. Quay	Pennsylvania	1888-91
William H. Barnum	Connecticut	1877-89	James S. Clarkson	Iowa	1891-92
Calvin S. Brice	Ohio	1889-92	Thomas H. Carter	Montana	1892-96
William F. Harrity	Pennsylvania	1892-96	Mark A. Hanna	Ohio	1896-1904
James K. Jones	Arkansas	1896-1904	Henry C. Payne	Wisconsin	1904
Thomas Taggart	Indiana	1904-08	George B. Cortelyou	New York	1904-07
Norman E. Mack	New York	1908-12	Harry S. New	Indiana	1907-08
William F. McCombs	New York	1912-16	Frank H. Hitchcock	Massachusetts	1908-09
Vance C. McCormick	Pennsylvania	1916-19	John F. Hill	Maine	1909-12
Homer S. Cummings	Connecticut	1919-20	Victor Rosewater	Nebraska	1912
George White	Ohio	1920-21	Charles D. Hilles	New York	1912-16
Cordell Hull	Tennessee	1921-24	William R. Willcox	New York	1916-18
Clem Shaver	West Virginia	1924-28	Will Hays	Indiana	1918-21
John J. Raskob	Maryland	1928-32	John T. Adams	Iowa	1921-24
James A. Farley	New York	1932-40	William M. Butler	Massachusetts	1924-28
Edward J. Flynn	New York	1940-43	Hubert Work	Colorado	1928-29
Frank C. Walker	Pennsylvania	1943-44	Claudius H. Huston	Tennessee	1929-30
Robert E. Hannegan	Missouri	1944-47	Simeon D. Fess	Ohio	1930-32
J. Howard McGrath	Rhode Island	1947-49	Everett Sanders	Indiana	1932-34
William M. Boyle Jr.	Missouri	1949-51	Henry P. Fletcher	Pennsylvania	1934-36
Frank E. McKinney	Indiana	1951-52	John Hamilton	Kansas	1936-40
Stephen A. Mitchell	Illinois	1952-54	Joseph W. Martin Jr.	Massachusetts	1940-42
Paul M. Butler	Indiana	1955-60	Harrison E. Spangler	Iowa	1942-44
Henry M. Jackson	Washington	1960-61	Herbert Brownell Jr.	New York	1944-46
John M. Bailey	Connecticut	1961-68	B. Carroll Reece	Tennessee	1946-48
Lawrence F. O'Brien	Massachusetts	1968-69	Hugh D. Scott Jr.	Pennsylvania	1948-49
Fred Harris	Oklahoma	1969-70	Guy George Gabrielson	New Jersey	1949-52
Lawrence F. O'Brien	Massachusetts	1970-72	Arthur E. Summerfield	Michigan	1952-53
Jean Westwood	Utah	1972	C. Wesley Roberts	Kansas	1953
Robert Straus	Texas	1972-77	Leonard W. Hall	New York	1953-57
Kenneth Curtis	Maine	1977-78	H. Meade Alcorn Jr.	Connecticut	1957-59
John White	Texas	1978-81	Thruston B. Morton	Kentucky	1959-61
Charles Manatt	California	1981-85	William E. Miller	New York	1961-64
Paul Kirk	Massachusetts	1985-89	Dean Burch	Arizona	1964-65
Ronald H. Brown	Washington, D.C.	1989-93	Ray C. Bliss	Ohio	1965-69
David Wilhelm	Illinois	1993-94	Rogers C. B. Morton	Maryland	1969-71
Christopher Dodd (general chair)	Connecticut	1994-97	Robert Dole	Kansas	1971-73
			George Bush	Texas	1973-74
Donald Fowler	South Carolina	1994-97	Mary Louise Smith	Iowa	1974-77
Roy Romer (general chair)	Colorado	1997-	William Brock	Tennessee	1977-81
			Richard Richards	Utah	1981-83
Steven Grossman	Massachusetts	1997-	Paul Laxalt (general chair)	Nevada	1983-86
			Frank Fahrenkopf Jr.	Nevada	1983-89
Republican Party			Lee Atwater	South Carolina	1989-91
Edwin D. Morgan	New York	1856-64	Clayton Yeutter	Nebraska	1991-92
Henry J. Raymond	New York	1864-66	Rich Bond	New York	1992-93
Marcus L. Ward	New Jersey	1866-68	Haley Barbour	Mississippi	1993-97
William Claflin	Massachusetts	1868-72	Jim Nicholson	Colorado	1997-
Edwin D. Morgan	New York	1872-76			

Sources: Hugh A. Bone, *Party Committees and National Politics* (Seattle: University of Washington, 1958), 241-243; Congressional Quarterly, *The President, the Public, and the Parties,* 2nd ed. (Washington, D.C.: Congressional Quarterly, 1997), 42.

and a half, the convention has evolved as well, changing its form but retaining its variety of functions. Criticism has been leveled at the convention, but no substitute has yet been offered that would nominate a presidential ticket, adopt a party platform, act as the supreme governing body of the party, and serve as a massive campaign rally and propaganda forum. In addition to these functions, a convention is a place where compromise can take place — compromise often mandatory in a major political party that combines varying viewpoints.

Political Party Nominees, 1831-1996

Following is a comprehensive list of major and minor party nominees for president and vice president since 1831, when the first nominating convention was held by the Anti-Masonic Party. In many cases, minor parties made only token efforts at a presidential campaign. Often, third-party candidates declined to run after being nominated by the convention, or their names appeared on the ballots of only a few states. In some cases the names of minor candidates did not appear on any state ballots and they received only a scattering of write-in votes, if any.

The basic source for the 1832 to 1972 elections was Joseph Nathan Kane, *Facts About the Presidents*, 6th ed. (New York: H. W. Wilson Co., 1993). To verify the names appearing in Kane, Congressional Quarterly consulted the following additional sources: Richard M. Scammon, *America at the Polls* (Pittsburgh: University of Pittsburgh Press, 1965); Richard M. Scammon, *America Votes 8* (Washington, D.C.: Congressional

Quarterly, 1969); Richard M. Scammon, *America Votes 10* (Washington, D.C.: Congressional Quarterly, 1973); Richard B. Morris, ed. *Encyclopedia of American History*, (New York: Harper and Row, 1965); *Dictionary of American Biography*, (New York: Scribner's, 1928-1936); *Facts on File* (New York: Facts on File Inc., 1945-1975); Arthur M. Schlesinger, ed., *History of U.S. Political Parties*, Vols. I-IV, (New York: McGraw Hill, 1971); and *Who Was Who in America, 1607-1968*, Vols. I-V (Chicago: Marquis Co., 1943-1968). The source for the 1976 to 1996 elections was Congressional Quarterly's *America Votes* series, Vols. 12 (1977), 14 (1981), 16 (1985), 18 (1989), 20 (1993) and 22 (1997) published in Washington, D.C.

In cases where these sources contain information in conflict with Kane, the conflicting information is included in a footnote. Where a candidate appears in Kane *but could not be verified in another source*, an asterisk appears beside the candidate's name on the list.

1832 Election

Democratic Party
President: Andrew Jackson, Tennessee
Vice president: Martin Van Buren, New York
National Republican Party
President: Henry Clay, Kentucky
Vice president: John Sergeant, Pennsylvania
Independent Party
President: John Floyd, Virginia
Vice president: Henry Lee, Massachusetts
Anti-Masonic Party
President: William Wirt, Maryland
Vice president: Amos Ellmaker, Pennsylvania

1836 Election

Democratic Party
President: Martin Van Buren, New York
Vice president: Richard Mentor Johnson, Kentucky
Whig Party
President: William Henry Harrison, Hugh Lawson White, Daniel Webster
Vice president: Francis Granger, John Tyler
  The Whigs nominated regional candidates in 1836 hoping that each candidate would carry his region and deny Democrat Van Buren an electoral vote majority. Webster was the Whig candidate in Massachusetts; Harrison in the rest of New England, the Middle Atlantic states, and the West; and White in the South.
  Granger was the running mate of Harrison and Webster. Tyler was White's running mate.

1840 Election

Whig Party
President: William Henry Harrison, Ohio
Vice president: John Tyler, Virginia

Democratic Party
President: Martin Van Buren, New York
  The Democratic convention adopted a resolution that left the choice of vice-presidential candidates to the states. Democratic electors divided their vice-presidential votes among incumbent Richard M. Johnson (forty-eight votes), Littleton W. Tazewell (eleven votes), and James K. Polk (one vote).
Liberty Party
President: James Gillespie Birney, New York
Vice president: Thomas Earle, Pennsylvania

1844 Election

Democratic Party
President: James Knox Polk, Tennessee
Vice president: George Mifflin Dallas, Pennsylvania
Whig Party
President: Henry Clay, Kentucky
Vice president: Theodore Frelinghuysen, New Jersey
Liberty Party
President: James Gillespie Birney, New York
Vice president: Thomas Morris, Ohio
National Democratic Party
President: John Tyler, Virginia
Vice president: None
  Tyler withdrew in favor of the Democrat, Polk.

1848 Election

Whig Party
President: Zachary Taylor, Louisiana
Vice president: Millard Fillmore, New York
Democratic Party
President: Lewis Cass, Michigan
Vice president: William Orlando Butler, Kentucky
Free Soil Party
President: Martin Van Buren, New York
Vice president: Charles Francis Adams, Massachusetts

Political Party Nominees

Free Soil (Barnburners—Liberty Party)
President: John Parker Hale, New Hampshire
Vice president: Leicester King, Ohio
Later John Parker Hale relinquished the nomination.
National Liberty Party
President: Gerrit Smith, New York
Vice president: Charles C. Foote, Michigan

1852 Election

Democratic Party
President: Franklin Pierce, New Hampshire
Vice president: William Rufus De Vane King, Alabama
Whig Party
President: Winfield Scott, New Jersey
Vice president: William Alexander Graham, North Carolina
Free Soil
President: John Parker Hale, New Hampshire
Vice president: George Washington Julian, Indiana

1856 Election

Democratic Party
President: James Buchanan, Pennsylvania
Vice president: John Cabell Breckinridge, Kentucky
Republican Party
President: John Charles Fremont, California
Vice president: William Lewis Dayton, New Jersey
American (Know-Nothing) Party
President: Millard Fillmore, New York
Vice president: Andrew Jackson Donelson, Tennessee
Whig Party (the "Silver Grays")
President: Millard Fillmore, New York
Vice president: Andrew Jackson Donelson, Tennessee
North American Party
President: Nathaniel Prentice Banks, Massachusetts
Vice president: William Freame Johnson, Pennsylvania
Banks and Johnson declined the nominations and gave
their support to the Republicans.

1860 Election

Republican Party
President: Abraham Lincoln, Illinois
Vice president: Hannibal Hamlin, Maine
Democratic Party
President: Stephen Arnold Douglas, Illinois
Vice president: Herschel Vespasian Johnson, Georgia
Southern Democratic Party
President: John Cabell Breckinridge, Kentucky
Vice president: Joseph Lane, Oregon
Constitutional Union Party
President: John Bell, Tennessee
Vice president: Edward Everett, Massachusetts

1864 Election

Republican Party
President: Abraham Lincoln, Illinois
Vice president: Andrew Johnson, Tennessee
Democratic Party
President: George Brinton McClellan, New York
Vice president: George Hunt Pendleton, Ohio
Independent Republican Party
President: John Charles Fremont, California
Vice president: John Cochrane, New York
Fremont and Cochrane declined the nominations and gave
their support to the Republicans.

1868 Election

Republican Party
President: Ulysses Simpson Grant, Illinois
Vice president: Schuyler Colfax, Indiana
Democratic Party
President: Horatio Seymour, New York
Vice president: Francis Preston Blair Jr., Missouri

1872 Election

Republican Party
President: Ulysses Simpson Grant, Illinois
Vice president: Henry Wilson, Massachusetts
Liberal Republican Party
President: Horace Greeley, New York
Vice president: Benjamin Gratz Brown, Missouri
Independent Liberal Republican Party (Opposition Party)
President: William Slocum Groesbeck, Ohio
Vice president: Frederick Law Olmsted, New York
Democratic Party
President: Horace Greeley, New York
Vice president: Benjamin Gratz Brown, Missouri
Straight-Out Democratic Party
President: Charles O'Conor, New York
Vice president: John Quincy Adams, Massachusetts
Prohibition Party
President: James Black, Pennsylvania
Vice president: John Russell, Michigan
People's Party (Equal Rights Party)
President: Victoria Claflin Woodhull, New York
Vice president: Frederick Douglass
Labor Reform Party
President: David Davis, Illinois
Vice president: Joel Parker, New Jersey
Liberal Republican Party of Colored Men
President: Horace Greeley, New York
Vice president: Benjamin Gratz Brown, Missouri
National Working Men's Party
President: Ulysses Simpson Grant, Illinois
Vice president: Henry Wilson, Massachusetts

1876 Election

Republican Party
President: Rutherford Birchard Hayes, Ohio
Vice president: William Almon Wheeler, New York
Democratic Party
President: Samuel Jones Tilden, New York
Vice president: Thomas Andrews Hendricks, Indiana
Greenback Party
President: Peter Cooper, New York
Vice president: Samuel Fenton Cary, Ohio
Prohibition Party
President: Green Clay Smith, Kentucky
Vice president: Gideon Tabor Stewart, Ohio
American National Party
President: James B. Walker, Illinois
Vice president: Donald Kirkpatrick, New York

1880 Election

Republican Party
President: James Abram Garfield, Ohio
Vice president: Chester Alan Arthur, New York
Democratic Party
President: Winfield Scott Hancock, Pennsylvania
Vice president: William Hayden English, Indiana
Greenback Labor Party
President: James Baird Weaver, Iowa
Vice president: Benjamin J. Chambers, Texas

Prohibition Party
President: Neal Dow, Maine
Vice president: Henry Adams Thompson, Ohio
American Party
President: John Wolcott Phelps, Vermont
Vice president: Samuel Clarke Pomeroy, Kansas *

1884 Election

Democratic Party
President: Grover Cleveland, New York
Vice president: Thomas Andrews Hendricks, Indiana
Republican Party
President: James Gillespie Blaine, Maine
Vice president: John Alexander Logan, Illinois
Anti-Monopoly Party
President: Benjamin Franklin Butler, Massachusetts
Vice president: Absolom Madden West, Mississippi
Greenback Party
President: Benjamin Franklin Butler, Massachusetts
Vice president: Absolom Madden West, Mississippi
Prohibition Party
President: John Pierce St. John, Kansas
Vice president: William Daniel, Maryland
American Prohibition Party
President: Samuel Clark Pomeroy, Kansas
Vice president: John A. Conant, Connecticut
Equal Rights Party
President: Belva Ann Bennett Lockwood, District of Columbia
Vice president: Marietta Lizzie Bell Stow, California

1888 Election

Republican Party
President: Benjamin Harrison, Indiana
Vice president: Levi Parsons Morton, New York
Democratic Party
President: Grover Cleveland, New York
Vice president: Allen Granberry Thurman, Ohio
Prohibition Party
President: Clinton Bowen Fisk, New Jersey
Vice president: John Anderson Brooks, Missouri *
Union Labor Party
President: Alson Jenness Streeter, Illinois
Vice president: Charles E. Cunningham, Arkansas *
United Labor Party
President: Robert Hall Cowdrey, Illinois
Vice president: William H. T. Wakefield, Kansas *
American Party
President: James Langdon Curtis, New York
Vice president: Peter Dinwiddie Wigginton, California *
Equal Rights Party
President: Belva Ann Bennett Lockwood, District of Columbia
Vice president: Alfred Henry Love, Pennsylvania *
Industrial Reform Party
President: Albert E. Redstone, California *
Vice president: John Colvin, Kansas *

1892 Election

Democratic Party
President: Grover Cleveland, New York
Vice president: Adlai Ewing Stevenson, Illinois
Republican Party
President: Benjamin Harrison, Indiana
Vice president: Whitelaw Reid, New York
People's Party of America
President: James Baird Weaver, Iowa
Vice president: James Gaven Field, Virginia

Prohibition Party
President: John Bidwell, California
Vice president: James Britton Cranfill, Texas
Socialist Labor Party
President: Simon Wing, Massachusetts
Vice president: Charles Horatio Matchett, New York *

1896 Election

Republican Party
President: William McKinley, Ohio
Vice president: Garret Augustus Hobart, New Jersey
Democratic Party
President: William Jennings Bryan, Nebraska
Vice president: Arthur Sewall, Maine
People's Party (Populist)
President: William Jennings Bryan, Nebraska
Vice president: Thomas Edward Watson, Georgia
National Democratic Party
President: John McAuley Palmer, Illinois
Vice president: Simon Bolivar Buckner, Kentucky
Prohibition Party
President: Joshua Levering, Maryland
Vice president: Hale Johnson, Illinois *
Socialist Labor Party
President: Charles Horatio Matchett, New York
Vice president: Matthew Maguire, New Jersey
National Party
President: Charles Eugene Bentley, Nebraska
Vice president: James Haywood Southgate, North Carolina *
National Silver Party (Bi-Metallic League)
President: William Jennings Bryan, Nebraska
Vice president: Arthur Sewall, Maine

1900 Election

Republican Party
President: William McKinley, Ohio
Vice president: Theodore Roosevelt, New York
Democratic Party
President: William Jennings Bryan, Nebraska
Vice president: Adlai Ewing Stevenson, Illinois
Prohibition Party
President: John Granville Wooley, Illinois
Vice president: Henry Brewer Metcalf, Rhode Island
Social-Democratic Party
President: Eugene Victor Debs, Indiana
Vice president: Job Harriman, California
People's Party (Populist—Anti-Fusionist faction)
President: Wharton Barker, Pennsylvania
Vice president: Ignatius Donnelly, Minnesota
Socialist Labor Party
President: Joseph Francis Malloney, Massachusetts
Vice president: Valentine Remmel, Pennsylvania
Union Reform Party
President: Seth Hockett Ellis, Ohio
Vice president: Samuel T. Nicholson, Pennsylvania
United Christian Party
President: Jonah Fitz Randolph Leonard, Iowa
Vice president: David H. Martin, Pennsylvania
People's Party (Populist—Fusionist faction)
President: William Jennings Bryan, Nebraska
Vice president: Adlai Ewing Stevenson, Illinois
Silver Republican Party
President: William Jennings Bryan, Nebraska
Vice president: Adlai Ewing Stevenson, Illinois
National Party
President: Donelson Caffery, Louisiana
Vice president: Archibald Murray Howe, Massachusetts *

1904 Election

Republican Party
President: Theodore Roosevelt, New York
Vice president: Charles Warren Fairbanks, Indiana
Democratic Party
President: Alton Brooks Parker, New York
Vice president: Henry Gassaway Davis, West Virginia
Socialist Party
President: Eugene VIctor Debs, Indiana
Vice president: Benjamin Hanford, New York
Prohibition Party
President: Silas Comfort Swallow, Pennsylvania
Vice president: George W. Carroll, Texas
People's Party (Populist)
President: Thomas Edward Watson, Georgia
Vice president: Thomas Henry Tibbles, Nebraska
Socialist Labor Party
President: Charles Hunter Corregan, New York
Vice president: William Wesley Cox, Illinois
Continental Party
President: Austin Holcomb
Vice president: A. King, Missouri

1908 Election

Republican Party
President: William Howard Taft, Ohio
Vice president: James Schoolcraft Sherman, New York
Democratic Party
President: William Jennings Bryan, Nebraska
Vice president: John Worth Kern, Indiana
Socialist Party
President: Eugene Victor Debs
Vice president: Benjamin Hanford
Prohibition Party
President: Eugene WIlder Chafin, Illinois
Vice president: Aaron Sherman Watkins, Ohio
Independence Party
President: Thomas Louis Hisgen, Massachusetts
Vice president: John Temple Graves, Georgia
People's Party (Populist)
President: Thomas Edward Watson, Georgia
Vice president: Samuel Williams, Indiana
Socialist Labor Party
President: August Gillhaus, New York
Vice president: Donald L. Munro, Virginia
United Christian Party
President: Daniel Braxton Turney, Illinois
Vice president: Lorenzo S. Coffin, Iowa

1912 Election

Democratic Party
President: Woodrow Wilson, New Jersey
Vice president: Thomas Riley Marshall, Indiana
Progressive Party ("Bull Moose" Party)
President: Theodore Roosevelt, New York
Vice president: Hiram Warren Johnson, California
Republican Party
President: William Howard Taft, Ohio
Vice president: James Schoolcraft Sherman, New York
    Sherman died October 30; he was replaced by Nicholas
    Murray Butler, New York.
Socialist Party
President: Eugene Victor Debs, Indiana
Vice president: Emil Seidel, Wisconsin
Prohibition Party
President: Eugene Wilder Chafin, Illinois
Vice president: Aaron Sherman Watkins, Ohio

Socialist Labor Party
President: Arthur Elmer Reimer, Massachusetts
Vice president: August Gillhaus, New York[1]

1916 Election

Democratic Party
President: Woodrow Wilson, New Jersey
Vice president: Thomas Riley Marshall, Indiana
Republican Party
President: Charles Evans Hughes, New York
Vice president: Charles Warren Fairbanks, Indiana
Socialist Party
President: Allan Louis Benson, New York
Vice president: George Ross Kirkpatrick, New Jersey
Prohibition Party
President: James Franklin Hanly, Indiana
Vice president: Ira Landrith, Tennessee
Socialist Labor Party
President: Arthur Elmer Reimer, Massachusetts *
Vice president: Caleb Harrison, Illinois *
Progressive Party
President: Theodore Roosevelt, New York
Vice president: John Milliken Parker, Louisiana

1920 Election

Republican Party
President: Warren Gamaliel Harding, Ohio
Vice president: Calvin Coolidge, Massachusetts
Democratic Party
President: James Middleton Cox, Ohio
Vice president: Franklin Delano Roosevelt, New York
Socialist Party
President: Eugene Victor Debs, Indiana
Vice president: Seymour Stedman, Illinois
Farmer Labor Party
President: Parley Parker Christensen, Utah
Vice president: Maximilian Sebastian Hayes, Ohio
Prohibition Party
President: Aaron Sherman Watkins, Ohio
Vice president: David Leigh Colvin, New York
Socialist Labor Party
President: William Wesley Cox, Missouri
Vice president: August Gillhaus, New York
Single Tax Party
President: Robert Colvin Macauley, Pennsylvania
Vice president: R. G. Barnum, Ohio
American Party
President: James Edward Ferguson, Texas
Vice president: William J. Hough

1924 Election

Republican Party
President: Calvin Coolidge, Massachusetts
Vice president: Charles Gates Dawes, Illinois
Democratic Party
President: John William Davis, West Virginia
Vice president: Charles Wayland Bryan, Nebraska
Progressive Party
President: Robert La Follette, Wisconsin
Vice president: Burton Kendall Wheeler, Montana
Prohibition Party
President: Herman Preston Faris, Missouri
Vice president: Marie Caroline Brehm, California
Socialist Labor Party
President: Frank T. Johns, Oregon
Vice president: Verne L. Reynolds, New York

Socialist Party
President: Robert La Follette, New York
Vice president: Burton Kendall Wheeler, Montana
Workers Party (Communist Party)
President: William Zebulon Foster, Illinois
Vice president: Benjamin Gitlow, New York
American Party
President: Gilbert Owen Nations, District of Columbia
Vice president: Charles Hiram Randall, California[2]
Commonwealth Land Party
President: William J. Wallace, New Jersey
Vice president: John Cromwell Lincoln, Ohio
Farmer Labor Party
President: Duncan McDonald, Illinois *
Vice president: William Bouck, Washington *
Greenback Party
President: John Zahnd, Indiana *
Vice president: Roy M. Harrop, Nebraska *

1928 Election

Republican Party
President: Herbert Clark Hoover, California
Vice president: Charles Curtis, Kansas
Democratic Party
President: Alfred Emanuel Smith, New York
Vice president: Joseph Taylor Robinson, Arkansas
Socialist Party
President: Norman Mattoon Thomas, New York
Vice president: James Hudson Maurer, Pennsylvania
Workers Party (Communist Party)
President: William Zebulon Foster, Illinois
Vice president: Benjamin Gitlow, New York
Socialist Labor Party
President: Verne L. Reynolds, Michigan
Vice president: Jeremiah D. Crowley, New York
Prohibition Party
President: William Frederick Varney, New York
Vice president: James Arthur Edgerton, Virginia
Farmer Labor Party
President: Frank Elbridge Webb, California
Vice president: Will Vereen, Georgia[3]
Greenback Party
President: John Zahnd, Indiana *
Vice president: Wesley Henry Bennington, Ohio *

1932 Election

Democratic Party
President: Franklin Delano Roosevelt, New York
Vice president: John Nance Garner, Texas
Republican Party
President: Herbert Clark Hoover, California
Vice president: Charles Curtis, Kansas
Socialist Party
President: Norman Mattoon Thomas, New York
Vice president: James Hudson Maurer, Pennsylvania
Communist Party
President: William Zebulon Foster, Illinois
Vice president: James William Ford, New York
Prohibition Party
President: William David Upshaw, Georgia
Vice president: Frank Stewart Regan, Illinois
Liberty Party
President: William Hope Harvey, Arkansas
Vice president: Frank B. Hemenway, Washington
Socialist Labor Party
President: Verne L. Reynolds, New York
Vice president: John W. Aiken, Massachusetts
Farmer Labor Party
President: Jacob Sechler Coxey, Ohio
Vice president: Julius J. Reiter, Minnesota

Jobless Party
President: James Renshaw Cox, Pennsylvania
Vice president: V. C. Tisdal, Oklahoma
National Party
President: Seymour E. Allen, Massachusetts

1936 Election

Democratic Party
President: Franklin Delano Roosevelt, New York
Vice president: John Nance Garner, Texas
Republican Party
President: Alfred Mossman Landon, Kansas
Vice president: Frank Knox, Illinois
Union Party
President: William Lemke, North Dakota
Vice president: Thomas Charles O'Brien, Massachusetts
Socialist Party
President: Norman Mattoon Thomas, New York
Vice president: George A. Nelson, Wisconsin
Communist Party
President: Earl Russell Browder, Kansas
Vice president: James William Ford, New York
Prohibition Party
President: David Leigh Colvin, New York
Vice president: Alvin York, Tennessee
Socialist Labor Party
President: John W. Aikin, Massachusetts
Vice president: Emil F. Teichert, New York
National Greenback Party
President: John Zahnd, Indiana *
Vice president: Florence Garvin, Rhode Island *

1940 Election

Democratic Party
President: Franklin Delano Roosevelt, New York
Vice president: Henry Agard Wallace, Iowa
Republican Party
President: Wendell Lewis Willkie, New York
Vice president: Charles Linza McNary, Oregon
Socialist Party
President: Norman Mattoon Thomas, New York
Vice president: Maynard C. Krueger, Illinois
Prohibition Party
President: Roger Ward Babson, Massachusetts
Vice president: Edgar V. Moorman, Illinois
Communist Party (Workers Party)
President: Earl Russell Browder, Kansas
Vice president: James William Ford, New York
Socialist Labor Party
President: John W. Aiken, Massachusetts
Vice president: Aaron M. Orange, New York
Greenback Party
President: John Zahnd, Indiana *
Vice president: James Elmer Yates, Arizona *

1944 Election

Democratic Party
President: Franklin Delano Roosevelt, New York
Vice president: Harry S. Truman, Missouri
Republican Party
President: Thomas Edmund Dewey, New York
Vice president: John William Bricker, Ohio
Socialist Party
President: Norman Mattoon Thomas, New York
Vice president: Darlington Hoopes, Pennsylvania
Prohibition Party
President: Claude A. Watson, California
Vice president: Andrew Johnson, Kentucky

Socialist Labor Party
President: Edward A. Teichert, Pennsylvania
Vice president: Arla A. Albaugh, Ohio
America First Party
President: Gerald Lyman Kenneth Smith, Michigan
Vice president: Henry A. Romer, Ohio

1948 Election

Democratic Party
President: Harry S. Truman, Missouri
Vice president: Alben William Barkley, Kentucky
Republican Party
President: Thomas Edmund Dewey, New York
Vice president: Earl Warren, California
States' Rights Democratic Party
President: James Strom Thurmond, South Carolina
Vice president: Fielding Lewis Wright, Mississippi
Progressive Party
President: Henry Agard Wallace, Iowa
Vice president: Glen Hearst Taylor, Idaho
Socialist Party
President: Norman Mattoon Thomas, New York
Vice president: Tucker Powell Smith, Michigan
Prohibition Party
President: Claude A. Watson, California
Vice president: Dale Learn, Pennsylvania
Socialist Labor Party
President: Edward A. Teichert, Pennsylvania
Vice president: Stephen Emery, New York
Socialist Workers Party
President: Farrell Dobbs, New York
Vice president: Grace Carlson, Minnesota
Christian Nationalist Party
President: Gerald Lyman Kenneth Smith, Missouri
Vice president: Henry A. Romer, Ohio
Greenback Party
President: John G. Scott, New York
Vice president: Granville B. Leeke, Indiana *
Vegetarian Party
President: John Maxwell, Illinois
Vice president: Symon Gould, New York *

1952 Election

Republican Party
President: Dwight David Eisenhower, New York
Vice president: Richard Milhous Nixon, California
Democratic Party
President: Adlai Ewing Stevenson II, Illinois
Vice president: John Jackson Sparkman, Alabama
Progressive Party
President: Vincent William Hallinan, California
Vice president: Charlotta A. Bass, New York
Prohibition Party
President: Stuart Hamblen, California
Vice president: Enoch Arden Holtwick, Illinois
Socialist Labor Party
President: Eric Hass, New York
Vice president: Stephen Emery, New York
Socialist Party
President: Darlington Hoopes, Pennsylvania
Vice president: Samuel Herman Friedman, New York
Socialist Workers Party
President: Farrell Dobbs, New York
Vice president: Myra Tanner Weiss, New York
America First Party
President: Douglas MacArthur, Wisconsin
Vice president: Harry Flood Byrd, Virginia
American Labor Party
President: Vincent William Hallinan, California
Vice president: Charlotta A. Bass, New York

American Vegetarian Party
President: Daniel J. Murphy, California
Vice president: Symon Gould, New York *
Church of God Party
President: Homer Aubrey Tomlinson, New York
Vice president: Willie Isaac Bass, North Carolina *
Constitution Party
President: Douglas MacArthur, Wisconsin
Vice president: Harry Flood Byrd, Virginia
Greenback Party
President: Frederick C. Proehl, Washington
Vice president: Edward J. Bedell, Indiana
Poor Man's Party
President: Henry B. Krajewski, New Jersey
Vice president: Frank Jenkins, New Jersey

1956 Election

Republican Party
President: Dwight David Eisenhower, Pennsylvania
Vice president: Richard Milhous Nixon, California
Democratic Party
President: Adlai Ewing Stevenson II, Illinois
Vice president: Estes Kefauver, Tennessee
States' Rights Party
President: Thomas Coleman Andrews, Virginia
Vice president: Thomas Harold Werdel, California
Ticket also favored by Constitution Party.
Prohibition Party
President: Enoch Arden Holtwick, Illinois
Vice president: Edward M. Cooper, California
Socialist Labor Party
President: Eric Hass, New York
Vice president: Georgia Cozzini, Wisconsin
Texas Constitution Party
President: William Ezra Jenner, Indiana *
Vice president: Joseph Bracken Lee, Utah *
Socialist Workers Party
President: Farrell Dobbs, New York
Vice president: Myra Tanner Weiss, New York
American Third Party
President: Henry Krajewski, New Jersey
Vice president: Ann Marie Yezo, New Jersey
Socialist Party
President: Darlington Hoopes, Pennsylvania
Vice president: Samuel Herman Friedman, New York
Pioneer Party
President: William Langer, North Dakota *
Vice president: Burr McCloskey, Illinois *
American Vegetarian Party
President: Herbert M. Shelton, California *
Vice president: Symon Gould, New York *
Greenback Party
President: Frederick C. Proehl, Washington
Vice president: Edward Kirby Meador, Massachusetts *
States' Rights Party of Kentucky
President: Harry Flood Byrd, Virginia
Vice president: William Ezra Jenner, Indiana
South Carolinians for Independent Electors
President: Harry Flood Byrd, Virginia
Christian National Party
President: Gerald Lyman Kenneth Smith
Vice president: Charles I. Robertson

1960 Election

Democratic Party
President: John Fitzgerald Kennedy, Massachusetts
Vice president: Lyndon Baines Johnson, Texas
Republican Party
President: Richard Milhous Nixon, California
Vice president: Henry Cabot Lodge, Massachusetts

National States' Rights Party
President: Orval Eugene Faubus, Arkansas
Vice president: John Geraerdt Crommelin, Alabama
Socialist Labor Party
President: Eric Hass, New York
Vice president: Georgia Cozzini, Wisconsin
Prohibition Party
President: Rutherford Losey Decker, Missouri
Vice president: Earle Harold Munn, Michigan
Socialist Workers Party
President: Farrell Dobbs, New York
Vice president: Myra Tanner Weiss, New York
Conservative Party of New Jersey
President: Joseph Bracken Lee, Utah
Vice president: Kent H. Courtney, Louisiana
Conservative Party of Virginia
President: C. Benton Coiner, Virginia
Vice president: Edward M. Silverman, Virginia
Constitution Party (Texas)
President: Charles Loten Sullivan, Mississippi
Vice president: Merritt B. Curtis, District of Columbia
Constitution Party (Washington)
President: Merritt B. Curtis, District of Columbia
Vice president: B. N. Miller
Greenback Party
President: Whitney Hart Slocomb, California *
Vice president: Edward Kirby Meador, Massachusetts *
Independent Afro-American Party
President: Clennon King, Georgia
Vice president: Reginald Carter
Tax Cut Party (America First Party; American Party)
President: Lar Daly, Illinois
Vice president: Merritt Barton Curtis, District of Columbia
Theocratic Party
President: Homer Aubrey Tomlinson, New York
Vice president: Raymond L. Teague, Alaska *
Vegetarian Party
President: Symon Gould, New York
Vice president: Christopher Gian-Cursio, Florida

1964 Election

Democratic Party
President: Lyndon Baines Johnson, Texas
Vice president: Hubert Horatio Humphrey, Minnesota
Republican Party
President: Barry Morris Goldwater, Arizona
Vice president: William Edward Miller, New York
Socialist Labor Party
President: Eric Hass, New York
Vice president: Henning A. Blomen, Massachusetts
Prohibition Party
President: Earle Harold Munn, Michigan
Vice president: Mark Shaw, Massachusetts
Socialist Workers Party
President: Clifton DeBerry, New York
Vice president: Edward Shaw, New York
National States' Rights Party
President: John Kasper, Tennessee
Vice president: J. B. Stoner, Georgia
Constitution Party
President: Joseph B. Lightburn, West Virginia
Vice president: Theodore C. Billings, Colorado
Independent States' Rights Party
President: Thomas Coleman Andrews, Virginia
Vice president: Thomas H. Werdel, California *
Theocratic Party
President: Homer Aubrey Tomlinson, New York
Vice president: William R. Rogers, Missouri *
Universal Party
President: Kirby James Hensley, California
Vice president: John O. Hopkins, Iowa

1968 Election

Republican Party
President: Richard Milhous Nixon, New York
Vice president: Spiro Theodore Agnew, Maryland
Democratic Party
President: Hubert Horatio Humphrey, Minnesota
Vice president: Edmund Sixtus Muskie, Maine
American Independent Party
President: George Corley Wallace, Alabama
Vice president: Curtis Emerson LeMay, Ohio
LeMay replaced S. Marvin Griffin, who originally had been
selected.
Peace and Freedom Party
President: Eldridge Cleaver
Vice president: Judith Mage, New York
Socialist Labor Party
President: Henning A. Blomen, Massachusetts
Vice president: George Sam Taylor, Pennsylvania
Socialist Workers Party
President: Fred Halstead, New York
Vice president: Paul Boutelle, New Jersey
Prohibition Party
President: Earle Harold Munn Sr., Michigan
Vice president: Rolland E. Fisher, Kansas
Communist Party
President: Charlene Mitchell, California
Vice president: Michael Zagarell, New York
Constitution Party
President: Richard K. Troxell, Texas
Vice president: Merle Thayer, Iowa
Freedom and Peace Party
President: Richard Claxton (Dick) Gregory, Illinois
Vice president: Mark Lane, New York
Patriotic Party
President: George Corley Wallace, Alabama
Vice president: William Penn Patrick, California
Theocratic Party
President: William R. Rogers, Missouri
Universal Party
President: Kirby James Hensley, California
Vice president: Roscoe B. MacKenna

1972 Election

Republican Party
President: Richard Milhous Nixon, California
Vice president: Spiro Theodore Agnew, Maryland
Democratic Party
President: George Stanley McGovern, South Dakota
Vice president: Thomas Francis Eagleton, Missouri
Eagleton resigned and was replaced on August 8, 1972, by
Robert Sargent Shriver Jr., Maryland, selected by the Demo-
cratic National Committee.
American Independent Party
President: John George Schmitz, California
Vice president: Thomas Jefferson Anderson, Tennessee
Socialist Workers Party
President: Louis Fisher, Illinois
Vice president: Genevieve Gunderson, Minnesota
Socialist Labor Party
President: Linda Jenness, Georgia
Vice president: Andrew Pulley, Illinois
Communist Party
President: Gus Hall, New York
Vice president: Jarvis Tyner
Prohibition Party
President: Earle Harold Munn Sr., Michigan
Vice president: Marshall Uncapher
Libertarian Party
President: John Hospers, California
Vice president: Theodora Nathan, Oregon

People's Party
President: Benjamin McLane Spock
Vice president: Julius Hobson, District of Columbia
America First Party
President: John V. Mahalchik
Vice president: Irving Homer
Universal Party
President: Gabriel Green
Vice president: Daniel Fry

1976 Election

Democratic Party
President: James Earl (Jimmy) Carter Jr., Georgia
Vice president: Walter Frederick Mondale, Minnesota
Republican Party
President: Gerald Rudolph Ford, Michigan
Vice president: Robert Joseph Dole, Kansas
Independent candidate
President: Eugene Joseph McCarthy, Minnesota
Vice president: none[4]
Libertarian Party
President: Roger MacBride, Virginia
Vice president: David P. Bergland, California
American Independent Party
President: Lester Maddox, Georgia
Vice president: William Dyke, Wisconsin
American Party
President: Thomas J. Anderson, Tennessee
Vice president: Rufus Shackleford, Florida
Socialist Workers Party
President: Peter Camejo, California
Vice president: Willie Mae Reid, California
Communist Party
President: Gus Hall, New York
Vice president: Jarvis Tyner, New York
People's Party
President: Margaret Wright, California
Vice president: Benjamin Spock, New York
U.S. Labor Party
President: Lyndon H. LaRouche Jr., New York
Vice president: R. W. Evans, Michigan
Prohibition Party
President: Benjamin C. Bubar, Maine
Vice president: Earl F. Dodge, Colorado
Socialist Labor Party
President: Jules Levin, New Jersey
Vice president: Constance Blomen, Massachusetts
Socialist Party
President: Frank P. Zeidler, Wisconsin
Vice president: J. Quinn Brisben, Illinois
Restoration Party
President: Ernest L. Miller
Vice president: Roy N. Eddy
United American Party
President: Frank Taylor
Vice president: Henry Swan

1980 Election[5]

Republican Party
President: Ronald Wilson Reagan, California
Vice president: George Herbert Walker Bush, Texas
Democratic Party
President: James Earl (Jimmy) Carter Jr., Georgia
Vice president: Walter Frederick Mondale, Minnesota
National Unity Campaign
President: John B. Anderson, Illinois
Vice president: Patrick Joseph Lucey, Wisconsin
Libertarian Party
President: Edward E. Clark, California
Vice president: David Koch, New York

Citizens Party
President: Barry Commoner, New York
Vice president: LaDonna Harris, New Mexico
Communist Party
President: Gus Hall, New York
Vice president: Angela Davis, California
American Independent Party
President: John Richard Rarick, Louisiana
Vice president: Eileen M. Shearer, California
Socialist Workers Party
President: Andrew Pulley, Illinois
Vice president: Matilde Zimmermann
President: Clifton DeBerry, California
Vice president: Matilde Zimmermann
President: Richard Congress, Ohio
Vice president: Matilde Zimmermann
Right to Life Party
President: Ellen McCormack, New York
Vice president: Carroll Driscoll, New Jersey
Peace and Freedom Party
President: Maureen Smith, California
Vice president: Elizabeth Barron
Workers World Party
President: Deirdre Griswold, New Jersey
Vice president: Larry Holmes, New York
Statesman Party
President: Benjamin C. Bubar, Maine
Vice president: Earl F. Dodge, Colorado
Socialist Party
President: David McReynolds, New York
Vice president: Diane Drufenbrock, Wisconsin
American Party
President: Percy L. Greaves, New York
Vice president: Frank L. Varnum, California
President: Frank W. Shelton, Utah
Vice president: George E. Jackson
Middle Class Party
President: Kurt Lynen, New Jersey
Vice president: Harry Kieve, New Jersey
Down With Lawyers Party
President: Bill Gahres, New Jersey
Vice president: J. F. Loghlin, New Jersey
Independent Party
President: Martin E. Wendelken
Natural Peoples Party
President: Harley McLain, North Dakota
Vice president: Jewelie Goeller, North Dakota

1984 Election[6]

Republican Party
President: Ronald Wilson Reagan, California
Vice president: George Herbert Walker Bush, Texas
Democratic Party
President: Walter Fritz Mondale, Minnesota
Vice president: Geraldine Anne Ferraro, New York
Libertarian Party
President: David P. Bergland, California
Vice president: Jim Lewis, Connecticut
Independent Party
President: Lyndon H. LaRouche Jr., Virginia
Vice president: Billy Davis, Mississippi
Citizens Party
President: Sonia Johnson, Virginia
Vice president: Richard Walton, Rhode Island
Populist Party
President: Bob Richards, Texas
Vice president: Maureen Kennedy Salaman, California
Independent Alliance Party
President: Dennis L. Serrette, New Jersey
Vice president: Nancy Ross, New York

Communist Party
President: Gus Hall, New York
Vice president: Angela Davis, California
Socialist Workers Party
President: Mel Mason, California
Vice president: Andrea Gonzalez, New York
Workers World Party
President: Larry Holmes, New York
Vice president: Gloria La Riva, California
President: Gavrielle Holmes, New York
Vice president: Milton Vera
American Party
President: Delmar Dennis, Tennessee
Vice president: Traves Brownlee, Delaware
Workers League Party
President: Ed Winn, New York
Vice presidents: Jean T. Brust, Helen Halyard, Edward Bergonzi
Prohibition Party
President: Earl F. Dodge, Colorado
Vice president: Warren C. Martin, Kansas

1988 Election[7]

Republican Party
President: George Herbert Walker Bush, Texas
Vice president: James "Dan" Quayle, Indiana
Democratic Party
President: Michael Stanley Dukakis, Massachusetts
Vice president: Lloyd Millard Bentsen Jr., Texas
Libertarian Party
President: Ronald E. Paul, Texas
Vice president: Andre V. Marrou, Nevada
New Alliance Party
President: Lenora B. Fulani, New York
Vice president: Joyce Dattner
Populist Party
President: David E. Duke, Louisiana
Vice president: Floyd C. Parker
Consumer Party
President: Eugene Joseph McCarthy, Minnesota
Vice president: Florence Rice
American Independent Party
President: James C. Griffin, California
Vice president: Charles J. Morsa
National Economic Recovery Party
President: Lyndon H. LaRouche Jr., Virginia
Vice president: Debra H. Freeman
Right to Life Party
President: William A. Marra, New Jersey
Vice president: Joan Andrews
Workers League Party
President: Edward Winn, New York
Vice president: Barry Porster
Socialist Workers Party
President: James Warren, New Jersey
Vice president: Kathleen Mickells
Peace and Freedom Party
President: Herbert Lewin
Vice president: Vikki Murdock
Prohibition Party
President: Earl F. Dodge, Colorado
Vice president: George D. Ormsby
Workers World Party
President: Larry Holmes, New York
Vice president: Gloria La Riva, California
Socialist Party
President: Willa Kenoyer, Minnesota
Vice president: Ron Ehrenreich
American Party
President: Delmar Dennis, Tennessee
Vice president: Earl Jepson

Grassroots Party
President: Jack E. Herer, California
Vice president: Dana Beal
Independent Party
President: Louie Youngkeit, Utah
Third World Assembly
President: John G. Martin, District of Columbia
Vice president: Cleveland Sparrow

1992 Election[8]

Democratic Party
President: Bill Clinton, Arkansas
Vice president: Albert Gore Jr., Tennessee
Republican Party
President: George Herbert Walker Bush, Texas
Vice president: James "Dan" Quayle, Indiana
Independent
President: H. Ross Perot, Texas
Vice president: James Stockdale, California
Libertarian Party
President: Andre V. Marrou, Nevada
Vice president: Nancy Lord, Georgia
America First Party (Populist)
President: James "Bo" Gritz, Nevada
Vice president: Cyril Minett
New Alliance Party
President: Lenora B. Fulani, New York
Vice president: Maria E. Munoz, California
U.S. Taxpayers Party
President: Howard Phillips, Virginia
Vice president: Albion W. Knight, Maryland
Natural Law Party
President: John Hagelin, Iowa
Vice president: Mike Tompkins, Iowa
Peace and Freedom Party
President: Ron Daniels, California
Vice president: Asiba Tupahache
Independent
President: Lyndon H. LaRouche Jr., Virginia
Vice president: James L. Bevel
Socialist Workers Party
President: James Warren, New Jersey
Vice president: Willie Mae Reid
Independent
President: Drew Bradford
Grassroots Party
President: Jack E. Herer, California
Vice president: Derrick P. Grimmer
Socialist Party
President: J. Quinn Brisben, Illinois
Vice president: Barbara Garson
Workers League Party
President: Helen Halyard, Michigan
Vice president: Fred Mazelis, Michigan
Take Back America Party
President: John Yiamouyiannas
Vice president: Allen C. McCone
Independent
President: Delbert L. Ehlers
Vice president: Rick Wendt
Prohibition Party
President: Earl F. Dodge, Colorado
Vice president: George D. Ormsby
Apathy Party
President: Jim Boren
Vice president: Will Weidman
Third Party
President: Eugene A. Hem
Vice president: Joanne Roland
Looking Back Party
President: Isabell Masters, Kansas
Vice president: Walter Masters, Florida

American Party
    President: Robert J. Smith
    Vice president: Doris Feimer
Workers World Party
    President: Gloria La Riva, California
    Vice president: Larry Holmes, New York

1996 Election[9]

Democratic Party
    President: Bill Clinton, Arkansas
    Vice president: Albert Gore Jr., Tennessee
Republican Party
    President: Robert Dole, Kansas
    Vice President: Jack Kemp, New York
Reform Party
    President: H. Ross Perot, Texas
    Vice President: Pat Choate, District of Columbia
Green Party
    President: Ralph Nader, District of Columbia
    Vice President: Winona LaDuke, Minnesota
Libertarian Party
    President: Harry Browne, California
    Vice President: Jo Anne Jorgensen, South Carolina
U.S. Taxpayers Party
    President: Howard Phillips, Virginia
    Vice President: Herbert W. Titus, Virginia
Natural Law Party
    President: John Hagelin, Iowa
    Vice President: Mike Tompkins, North Carolina
Workers World Party
    President: Monica Moorehead, New York
    Vice President: Gloria La Riva, California

Peace and Freedom Party
    President: Marsha Feinland, California
    Vice President: Kate McClatchy, Massachusetts
Independent
    President: Charles E. Collins, Florida
    Vice President: Rosemary Giumarra
Socialist Workers Party
    President: James E. Harris, Georgia
    Vice President: Laura Garza, New York
Grassroots Party
    President: Dennis Peron, Minnesota
    Vice President: Arlin Troutt, Arizona
Socialist Party
    President: Mary Cal Hollis, Colorado
    Vice President: Eric Chester, Massachusetts
Socialist Equality Party
    President: Jerome White, Michigan
    Vice President: Fred Mazelis, Michigan
American Party
    President: Diane Beall Templin, California
    Vice President: Gary Van Horn, Utah
Prohibition Party
    President: Earl F. Dodge, Colorado
    Vice President: Rachel Bubar Kelly, Maine
Independent Party of Utah
    President: A. Peter Crane, Utah
    Vice President: Connie Chandler, Utah
America First Party
    President: Ralph Forbes, Arkansas
Independent Grassroots Party
    President: John Birrenbach, Minnesota
    Vice President: George McMahon, Iowa
Looking Back Party
    President: Isabell Masters, Kansas
    Vice President: Shirley Jean Masters, California
Independent
    President: Steve Michael, District of Columbia

*   *Candidates appeared in Joseph Nathan Kane,* Facts About the Presidents, *4th ed. (New York: H. W. Wilson, 1981), but could not be verified in another source.*

1. 1912: Arthur M. Schlesinger's History of American Presidential Elections (New York: McGraw-Hill, 1971) lists the Socialist Labor Party vice-presidential candidate as Francis. No first name is given.

2. 1924: Richard M. Scammon's America at the Polls (Pittsburgh: University of Pittsburgh Press, 1965) lists the American Party vice-presidential candidate as Leander L. Pickett.

3. 1928: America at the Polls lists the Farmer Labor Party vice-presidential candidate as L. R. Tillman.

4. 1976: McCarthy, who ran as an independent with no party designation, had no national running mate, favoring the elimination of the office. But as various state laws required a running mate, he had different ones in different states, amounting to nearly two dozen, all political unknowns.

5. 1980: In several cases vice-presidential nominees were different from those listed for most states, and the Socialist Workers and American Party nominees for president varied from state to state. For example, because Pulley, the major standard-bearer for the Socialist Workers Party was only twenty-nine years old, his name was not allowed on the ballot in some states (the Constitution requires presidential candidates to be at least thirty-five years old). Hence, the party ran other candidates in those states. In a number of states, candidates appeared on the ballot with variants of the party designations listed, without any party designation, or with entirely different party names.

6. 1984: Both Larry Holmes and Gavrielle Holmes were standard-bearers of the Workers World Party. Of the two, Larry Holmes was listed on more state ballots. Milton Vera was Gavrielle Holmes's vice-presidential running mate in Ohio and Rhode Island. The Workers League Party had three vice-presidential candidates: Jean T. Brust in Illinois; Helen Halyard in Michigan, New Jersey, and Pennsylvania; and Edward Bergonzi in Minnesota and Ohio.

7. 1988: The candidates listed include all those who appeared on the ballot in at least one state. In some cases, a party's vice-presidential candidate varied from state to state. Candidates' full names and states were not available from some parties.

8. 1992: The candidates listed include all those who appeared on the ballot in at least one state. In some cases a party's vice-presidential candidate varied from state to state. Candidates' states were not available from some parties.

9. 1996: The candidates listed include all those who appeared on the ballot in at least one state. In some cases a party's vice-presidential candidate varied from state to state. Candidates' states were not available from some parties.

Biographical Directory of Presidential And Vice Presidential Candidates

The names in the directory include all persons who have received electoral votes for president or vice president since 1789. Also included are prominent third party candidates who received popular votes but no electoral votes, and Nelson Aldrich Rockefeller, appointed vice president by Gerald Ford, who became president following the resignation of Richard M. Nixon.

The material is organized as follows: name, state of residence in the year(s) the individual received electoral votes, party or parties with which the individual identified when he or she received electoral votes, date of birth, date of death (where applicable), major offices held, and the year(s) of candidacy.

For the elections of 1789 through 1800, presidential electors did not vote separately for president or vice president. It was, therefore, difficult in many cases to determine if an individual receiving electoral votes in these elections was a candidate for the office of president or vice president. Where no determination could be made from the sources consulted by Congressional Quarterly, the year in which the individual received electoral votes is given with no specification as to whether the individual was a candidate for president or vice president.

The following sources were used: *American Leaders, 1789-1994: A Biographical Summary*, (Washington, D.C.: Congressional Quarterly, 1994); *Biographical Directory of the United States Congress, 1774-1989*, (Washington, D.C.: Government Printing Office, 1989); Rhodes Cook, *America Votes 22* (1997), (Washington, D.C.: Congressional Quarterly, 1997); *Dictionary of American Biography*, (New York: Scribner's, 1928-36); John A. Garraty, ed., *Encyclopedia of American Biography*, (New York: Harper and Row, 1974); Jaques Cattell Press, ed., *Who's Who in American Politics, 1977-78*, 6th ed. (New York: R. R. Bowker, 1977); Svend Petersen, *A Statistical History of the American Presidential Elections*, (Westport, Conn.: Greenwood Press, 1981); Richard M. Scammon, *America Votes 10* (1972), (Washington, D.C.: Congressional Quarterly, 1973); Richard M. Scammon and Alice V. McGillivray, *America Votes 12* (1976), (Washington, D.C.: Congressional Quarterly, 1977); *America Votes 14* (1980), (Washington, D.C.: Congressional Quarterly, 1981); *America Votes 18* (1988), (Washington, D.C.: Congressional Quarterly, 1989); *America Votes 20* (1992), (Washington, D.C.: Congressional Quarterly, 1993); *Who Was Who in America, 1607-1968*, (Chicago: Marquis, 1943-68).

Adams, Charles Francis - Mass. (Free Soil) Aug. 18, 1807 - Nov. 21, 1886; House, 1859-61; minister to Great Britain, 1861-68. Candidacy: VP - 1848.

Adams, John - Mass. (Federalist) Oct. 30, 1735 - July 4, 1826; Continental Congress, 1774; signer of Declaration of Independence, 1776; minister to Great Britain, 1785; U.S. vice president, 1789-97; U.S. president, 1797-1801. Candidacies: VP - 1789, 1792; P - 1796, 1800.

Adams, John Quincy - Mass. (Democratic-Republican, National Republican) July 11, 1767 - Feb. 23, 1848; Senate, 1803-08; minister to Russia, 1809-14; minister to Great Britain, 1815-17; secretary of state, 1817-25; U.S. president, 1825-29; House, 1831-48. Candidacies: P - 1820, 1824, 1828.

Adams, Samuel - Mass. (Federalist) Sept. 27, 1722 - Oct. 2, 1803; Continental Congress, 1774-81; signer of Declaration of Independence; governor, 1793-97. Candidacy: 1796.

Agnew, Spiro Theodore - Md. (Republican) Nov. 9, 1918 - Sept. 17, 1996; governor, 1967-69; U.S. vice president, 1969-73 (resigned Oct. 10, 1973). Candidacies: VP - 1968, 1972.

Anderson, John B. - Ill. (Republican, Independent) Feb. 15, 1922—; state's attorney, 1956-60; House, 1961-81. Candidacy: P - 1980.

Armstrong, James - Pa. (Federalist) Aug. 29, 1748 - May 6, 1828; House, 1793-95. Candidacy: 1789.

Arthur, Chester Alan - N.Y. (Republican) Oct. 5, 1830 - Nov. 18, 1886; collector, Port of N.Y., 1871-78; U.S. vice president, 1881; U.S. president, 1881-85. Candidacy: VP - 1880.

Banks, Nathaniel Prentice - Mass. (Liberal Republican) Jan. 30, 1816 - Sept. 1, 1894; House, 1853-57, 1865-73, 1875-79, 1889-91; governor, 1858-61. Candidacy: VP - 1872.

Barkley, Alben William - Ky. (Democratic) Nov. 24, 1877 - April 30, 1956; House, 1913-27; Senate, 1927-49, 1955-56; Senate majority leader, 1937-47; Senate minority leader, 1947-49; U.S. vice president, 1949-53. Candidacy: VP - 1948.

Bell, John - Tenn. (Constitutional Union) Feb. 15, 1797 - Sept. 10, 1869; House, 1827-41; Speaker of the House, 1834-35; secretary of war, 1841; Senate, 1847-59. Candidacy: P - 1860.

Benson, Allan Louis - N.Y. (Socialist) Nov. 6, 1871 - Aug. 19, 1940; writer, editor; founder of *Reconstruction Magazine,* 1918. Candidacy: P - 1916.

Bentsen, Lloyd Millard Jr. - Texas (Democratic) Feb. 11, 1921—; House 1948-55; Senate 1971-93; secretary of Treasury, 1993-94. Candidacy: VP - 1988.

Bidwell, John - Calif. (Prohibition) Aug. 5, 1819 - April 4, 1900; California pioneer; major in Mexican War; House, 1865-67. Candidacy: P - 1892.

Birney, James Gillespie - N.Y. (Liberty) Feb. 4, 1792 - Nov. 25, 1857; Kentucky Legislature, 1816-17; Alabama Legislature, 1819-20. Candidacies: P - 1840, 1844.

Blaine, James Gillespie - Maine (Republican) Jan. 31, 1830 - Jan. 27, 1893; House, 1863-76; Speaker of the House, 1869-75; Senate, 1876-81; secretary of state, 1881, 1889-92; president, first Pan American Congress, 1889. Candidacy: P - 1884.

Blair, Francis Preston Jr. - Mo. (Democratic) Feb. 19, 1821 - July 8, 1875; House, 1857-59, 1860, 1861-62, 1863-64; Senate, 1871-73. Candidacy: VP - 1868.

Bramlette, Thomas E. - Ky. (Democratic) Jan. 3, 1817 - Jan. 12, 1875; governor, 1863-67. Candidacy: VP - 1872.

Breckinridge, John Cabell - Ky. (Democratic, Southern Democratic) Jan. 21, 1821 - May 17, 1875; House, 1851-55; U.S. vice president, 1857-61; Senate, 1861; major general, Confederacy, 1861-65; secretary of war, Confederacy, 1865. Candidacies: VP - 1856; P - 1860.

Bricker, John William - Ohio (Republican) Sept. 6, 1893 - March 22, 1986; attorney general of Ohio, 1933-37; governor, 1939-45; Senate, 1947-59. Candidacy: VP - 1944.

Brown, Benjamin Gratz - Mo. (Democratic) May 28, 1826 - Dec. 13, 1885; Senate, 1863-67; governor, 1871-73. Candidacy: VP - 1872.

Bryan, Charles Wayland - Neb. (Democratic) Feb. 10, 1867 - March 4, 1945; governor, 1923-25, 1931-35; Candidacy: VP - 1924.

Bryan, William Jennings - Neb. (Democratic, Populist) March 19, 1860 - July 26, 1925; House, 1891-95; secretary of state, 1913-15. Candidacies: P - 1896, 1900, 1908.

Buchanan, James - Pa. (Democratic) April 23, 1791 - June 1, 1868; House, 1821-31; minister to Russia, 1832-34; Senate, 1834-45; secretary of state, 1845-49; minister to Great Britain, 1853-56; U.S. president, 1857-61. Candidacy: P - 1856.

Burr, Aaron - N.Y. (Democratic-Republican) Feb. 6, 1756 - Sept. 14, 1836; attorney general of N.Y., 1789-90; Senate, 1791-97; U.S. vice president, 1801-05. Candidacies: 1792, 1796, 1800.

Bush, George - Texas (Republican) June 12, 1924—; House, 1967-70; ambassador to the United Nations, 1971-73; chairman of the Republican National Committee, 1973-74; head of the U.S. liaison office in Peking, 1974-75; director of the Central Intelligence Agency, 1976-77; U.S. vice president, 1981-89; U.S. president, 1989-93. Candidacies: VP - 1980, 1984; P - 1988, 1992.

Butler, Benjamin Franklin - Mass. (Greenback, Anti-Monopoly) Nov. 5, 1818 - Jan. 11, 1893; House, 1867-75, 1877-79; governor, 1883-84. Candidacy: P - 1884.

Butler, Nicholas Murray - N.Y. (Republican) April 2, 1862 - Dec. 7, 1947; president, Columbia University, 1901-45; president, Carnegie Endowment for International Peace, 1925-45. Candidacy: VP - 1912. (Substituted as candidate after Oct. 30 death of nominee James S. Sherman.)

Butler, William Orlando - Ky. (Democratic) April 19, 1791 - Aug. 6, 1880; House, 1839-43. Candidacy: VP - 1848.

Byrd, Harry Flood - Va. (States' Rights Democratic, Independent Democratic) June 10, 1887 - Oct. 20, 1966; governor, 1926-30; Senate, 1933-65. Candidacies: P - 1956, 1960.

Calhoun, John Caldwell - S.C. (Democratic-Republican, Democratic) March 18, 1782 - March 31, 1850; House, 1811-17; secretary of war, 1817-25; U.S. vice president, 1825-32; Senate, 1832-43, 1845-50; secretary of state, 1844-45. Candidacies: VP - 1824, 1828.

Carter, James Earl Jr. - Ga. (Democratic) Oct. 1, 1924—; Georgia Legislature, 1963-67; governor, 1971-75; U.S. president, 1977-81. Candidacies: P - 1976, 1980.

Cass, Lewis - Mich. (Democratic) Oct. 9, 1782 - June 17, 1866; military and civil governor of Michigan Territory, 1813-31; secretary of war, 1831-36; minister to France, 1836-42; Senate, 1845-48, 1849-57; secretary of state, 1857-60. Candidacy: P - 1848.

Clay, Henry - Ky. (Democratic-Republican, National Republican, Whig) April 12, 1777 - June 29, 1852; Senate, 1806-07, 1810-11, 1831-42, 1849-52; House, 1811-14, 1815-21, 1823-25; Speaker of the House, 1811-14, 1815-20, 1823-25; secretary of state, 1825-29. Candidacies: P - 1824, 1832, 1844.

Cleveland, Stephen Grover - N.Y. (Democratic) March 18, 1837 - June 24, 1908; mayor of Buffalo, 1882; governor, 1883-85; U.S. president, 1885-89, 1893-97. Candidacies: P - 1884, 1888, 1892.

Clinton, Bill - Ark. (Democrat) Aug. 19, 1946—; attorney general of Arkansas, 1977-79; governor, 1979-81, 1983-92; U.S. president, 1993—. Candidacy: P - 1992, 1996.

Clinton, De Witt - N.Y. (Independent Democratic-Republican, Federalist) March 2, 1769 - Feb. 11, 1828; Senate, 1802-03; mayor of New York, 1803-07, 1810, 1811, 1813, 1814; governor, 1817-23, 1825-28. Candidacy: P - 1812.

Clinton, George - N.Y. (Democratic-Republican) July 26, 1739 - April 20, 1812; Continental Congress, 1775-76; governor, 1777-95, 1801-04; U.S. vice president, 1805-12. Candidacies: VP - 1789, 1792, 1796, 1804, 1808.

Colfax, Schuyler - Ind. (Republican) March 23, 1823 - Jan. 13, 1885; House, 1855-69; Speaker of the House, 1863-69; U.S. vice president, 1869-73. Candidacy: VP - 1868.

Colquitt, Alfred Holt - Ga. (Democratic) April 20, 1824 - March 26, 1894; House, 1853-55; governor, 1877-82; Senate, 1883-94. Candidacy: VP - 1872.

Coolidge, Calvin - Mass. (Republican) July 4, 1872 - Jan. 5, 1933; governor, 1919-21; U.S. vice president, 1921-23; U.S. president, 1923-29. Candidacies: VP - 1920; P - 1924.

Cox, James Middleton - Ohio (Democratic) March 31, 1870 - July 15, 1957; House, 1909-13; governor, 1913-15, 1917-21. Candidacy: P - 1920.

Crawford, William Harris - Ga. (Democratic-Republican) Feb. 24, 1772 - Sept. 15, 1834; Senate, 1807-13; president pro tempore of the Senate, 1812-13; secretary of war, 1815-16; secretary of the treasury, 1816-25. Candidacy: P - 1824.

Curtis, Charles - Kan. (Republican) Jan. 25, 1860 - Feb. 8, 1936; House, 1893-1907; Senate, 1907-13, 1915-29; president pro tempore of the Senate, 1911; Senate majority leader, 1925-29; U.S. vice president, 1929-33. Candidacies: VP - 1928, 1932.

Dallas, George Mifflin - Pa. (Democratic) July 10, 1792 - Dec. 31, 1864; Senate, 1831-33; minister to Russia, 1837-39; U.S. vice president, 1845-49; minister to Great Britain, 1856-61. Candidacy: VP - 1844.

Davis, David - Ill. (Democratic) March 9, 1815 - June 26, 1886; associate justice of U.S. Supreme Court, 1862-77; Senate, 1877-83; president pro tempore of the Senate, 1881. Candidacy: P - 1872.

Davis, Henry Gassaway - W.Va. (Democratic) Nov. 16, 1823 - March 11, 1916; Senate, 1871-83; chairman of Pan American Railway Committee, 1901-16. Candidacy: VP - 1904.

Davis, John William - W.Va., N.Y. (Democratic) April 13, 1873 - March 24, 1955; House, 1911-13; solicitor general, 1913-18; ambassador to Great Britain, 1918-21. Candidacy: P - 1924.

Dawes, Charles Gates - Ill. (Republican) Aug. 27, 1865 - April 3, 1951; U.S. comptroller of the currency, 1898-1901; first director of Bureau of the Budget, 1921-22; U.S. vice president, 1925-29; ambassador to Great Britain, 1929-32. Candidacy: VP - 1924.

Dayton, William Lewis - N.J. (Republican) Feb. 17, 1807 - Dec. 1, 1864; Senate, 1842-51; minister to France, 1861-64. Candidacy: VP - 1856.

Debs, Eugene Victor - Ind. (Socialist) Nov. 5, 1855 - Oct. 20, 1926; Indiana Legislature, 1885; president, American Railway Union, 1893-97. Candidacies: P - 1900, 1904, 1908, 1912, 1920.

Dewey, Thomas Edmund - N.Y. (Republican) March 24, 1902 - March 16, 1971; district attorney, New York County, 1937-41; governor, 1943-55. Candidacies: P - 1944, 1948.

Dole, Robert Joseph - Kan. (Republican) July 22, 1923—; House, 1961-69; Senate, 1969-96; Senate majority leader, 1985-87, 1995-96; Senate minority leader, 1987-95; chairman of the Republican National Committee, 1971-73. Candidacies: VP - 1976; P - 1996.

Donelson, Andrew Jackson - Tenn. (American "Know-Nothing") Aug. 25, 1799 - June 26, 1871; minister to Prussia, 1846-48; minister to Germany, 1848-49. Candidacy: VP - 1856.

Douglas, Stephen Arnold - Ill. (Democratic) April 23, 1813 - June 3, 1861; House, 1843-47; Senate, 1847-61. Candidacy: P - 1860.

Dukakis, Michael Stanley - Mass. (Democratic) Nov. 3, 1933—; governor, 1975-79, 1983-91. Candidacy: P - 1988.

Eagleton, Thomas Francis - Mo. (Democratic) Sept. 4, 1929—; attorney general of Missouri, 1961-65; lieutenant governor, 1965-68; Senate, 1968-87. Candidacy: VP - 1972. (Resigned from Democratic ticket July 31; replaced by R. Sargent Shriver Jr.)

Eisenhower, Dwight David - N.Y., Pa. (Republican) Oct. 14, 1890 - March 28, 1969; general of U.S. Army, 1943-48; Army chief of staff, 1945-48; president of Columbia University, 1948-51; commander of North Atlantic Treaty Organization, 1951-52; U.S. president, 1953-61. Candidacies: P - 1952, 1956.

Ellmaker, Amos - Pa. (Anti-Masonic) Feb. 2, 1787 - Nov. 28, 1851; elected to the House for the term beginning in 1815 but did not qualify; attorney general of Pennsylvania, 1816-19, 1828-29. Candidacy: VP - 1832.

Ellsworth, Oliver - Conn. (Federalist) April 29, 1745 - Nov. 26, 1807; Continental Congress, 1778-83; Senate, 1789-96; chief justice of United States, 1796-1800; minister to France, 1799. Candidacy: 1796.

English, William Hayden - Ind. (Democratic) Aug. 27, 1822 - Feb. 7, 1896; House, 1853-61. Candidacy: VP - 1880.

Everett, Edward - Mass. (Constitutional Union) April 11, 1794 - Jan. 15, 1865; House, 1825-35; governor, 1836-40; minister to Great Britain, 1841-45; president of Harvard University, 1846-49; secretary of state, 1852-53; Senate, 1853-54. Candidacy: VP - 1860.

Fairbanks, Charles Warren - Ind. (Republican) May 11, 1852 - June 4, 1918; Senate, 1897-1905; U.S. vice president, 1905-09. Candidacies: VP - 1904, 1916.

Ferraro, Geraldine Anne - N.Y. (Democratic) Aug. 26, 1935—; assistant district attorney, Queens County, 1974-78; House, 1979-85. Candidacy: VP - 1984.

Field, James Gaven - Va. (Populist) Feb. 24, 1826 - Oct. 12, 1901; major in the Confederate Army, 1861-65; attorney general of Virginia, 1877-82. Candidacy: VP - 1892.

Fillmore, Millard - N.Y. (Whig, American "Know-Nothing") Jan. 7, 1800 - March 8, 1874; House, 1833-35, 1837-43; N.Y. comptroller, 1847-49; U.S. vice president, 1849-50; U.S. president, 1850-53. Candidacies: VP - 1848; P - 1856.

Fisk, Clinton Bowen - N.J. (Prohibition) Dec. 8, 1828 - July 9, 1890; Civil War brevet major general; founder of Fisk University, 1866; member, Board of Indian Commissioners, 1874, president, 1881-90. Candidacy: P - 1888.

Floyd, John - Va. (Independent Democratic) April 24, 1783 - Aug. 17, 1837; House, 1817-29; governor, 1830-34. Candidacy: P - 1832.

Ford, Gerald Rudolph Jr. - Mich. (Republican) July 14, 1913—; House, 1949-73; House minority leader, 1965-73; U.S. vice president, 1973-74; U.S. president, 1974-77. Candidacy: P - 1976.

Frelinghuysen, Theodore - N.J. (Whig) March 28, 1787 - April 12, 1862; attorney general of New Jersey, 1817-29; Senate, 1829-35; president of Rutgers College, 1850-62. Candidacy: VP - 1844.

Fremont, John Charles - Calif. (Republican) Jan. 21, 1813 - July 13, 1890; explorer and Army officer in West before 1847; Senate, 1850-51; governor of Arizona Territory, 1878-81. Candidacy: P - 1856.

Garfield, James Abram - Ohio (Republican) Nov. 19, 1831 - Sept. 19, 1881; major general in Union Army during Civil War; House, 1863-80; U.S. president, 1881. Candidacy: P - 1880.

Garner, John Nance - Texas (Democratic) Nov. 22, 1868 - Nov. 7, 1967; House, 1903-33; House minority leader, 1929-31; Speaker of the House, 1931-33; U.S. vice president, 1933-41. Candidacies: VP - 1932, 1936.

Gerry, Elbridge - Mass. (Democratic-Republican) July 17, 1744 - Nov. 23, 1814; Continental Congress, 1776-80, 1783-85; signer of Declaration of Independence; Constitutional Convention, 1787; House, 1789-93; governor, 1810-12; U.S. vice president, 1813-14. Candidacy: VP - 1812.

Goldwater, Barry Morris - Ariz. (Republican) Jan. 1, 1909—; Senate, 1953-65, 1969-87. Candidacies: VP - 1960; P - 1964.

Gore, Albert Jr. - Tenn. (Democrat) March 31, 1948—; House, 1977-85; Senate, 1985-93; U.S. vice president, 1993—. Candidacy: VP - 1992, 1996.

Graham, William Alexander - N.C. (Whig) Sept. 5, 1804 - Aug. 11, 1875; Senate, 1840-43; governor, 1845-49; secretary of the Navy, 1850-52; Confederate Senate, 1864. Candidacy: VP - 1852.

Granger, Francis - N.Y. (Whig) Dec. 1, 1792 - Aug. 31, 1868; House, 1835-37, 1839-41, 1841-43; postmaster general, 1841. Candidacy: VP - 1836.

Grant, Ulysses Simpson - Ill. (Republican) April 27, 1822 - July 23, 1885; commander-in-chief, Union Army during Civil War; U.S. president, 1869-77. Candidacies: P - 1868, 1872.

Greeley, Horace - N.Y. (Liberal Republican, Democratic) Feb. 3, 1811 - Nov. 29, 1872; founder and editor, New York Tribune, 1841-72; House, 1848-49. Candidacy: P - 1872.

Griffin, S. Marvin - Ga. (American Independent) Sept. 4, 1907 - June 13, 1982; governor, 1955-59. Candidacy: VP - 1968. (Substituted as candidate until permanent candidate Curtis LeMay was chosen.)

Groesbeck, William Slocum - Ohio (Democratic) July 24, 1815 - July 7, 1897; House, 1857-59; delegate to International Monetary Conference in Paris, 1878. Candidacy: VP - 1872.

Hale, John Parker - N.H. (Free Soil) March 31, 1806 - Nov. 19, 1873; House, 1843-45; Senate, 1847-53, 1855-65; minister to Spain, 1865-69. Candidacy: P - 1852.

Hamlin, Hannibal - Maine (Republican) Aug. 27, 1809 - July 4, 1891; House, 1843-47; Senate, 1848-57, 1857-61, 1869-81; governor, 1857; U.S. vice president, 1861-65. Candidacy: VP - 1860.

Hancock, John - Mass. (Federalist) Jan. 23, 1737 - Oct. 8, 1793; Continental Congress, 1775-78, 1785-86; president of Continental Congress, 1775-77; governor, 1780-85, 1787-93. Candidacy: 1789.

Hancock, Winfield Scott - Pa. (Democratic) Feb. 14, 1824 - Feb. 9, 1886; brigadier general, commander of II Army Corps, Civil War. Candidacy: P - 1880.

Harding, Warren Gamaliel - Ohio (Republican) Nov. 2, 1865 - Aug. 2, 1923; lieutenant governor, 1904-05; Senate, 1915-21; U.S. president, 1921-23. Candidacy: P - 1920.

Harper, Robert Goodloe - Md. (Federalist) January 1765 - Jan. 14, 1825; House, 1795-1801; Senate, 1816. Candidacies: VP - 1816, 1820.

Harrison, Benjamin - Ind. (Republican) Aug. 20, 1833 - March 13, 1901; Union officer in Civil War; Senate, 1881-87; U.S. president, 1889-93. Candidacies: P - 1888, 1892.

Harrison, Robert H. - Md. 1745 - 1790; chief justice, General Court of Maryland, 1781. Candidacy: 1789.

Harrison, William Henry - Ohio (Whig) Feb. 9, 1773 - April 4, 1841; delegate to Congress from the Northwest Territory, 1799-1800; territorial governor of Indiana, 1801-13; House, 1816-19; Senate, 1825-28; U.S. president, 1841. Candidacies: P - 1836, 1840.

Hayes, Rutherford Birchard - Ohio (Republican) Oct. 4, 1822 - Jan. 17, 1893; major general in Union Army during Civil War; House, 1865-67; governor, 1868-72, 1876-77; U.S. president, 1877-81. Candidacy: P - 1876.

Hendricks, Thomas Andrews - Ind. (Democratic) Sept. 7, 1819 - Nov. 25, 1885; House, 1851-55; Senate, 1863-69; governor, 1873-77; U.S. vice president, 1885. Candidacies: P - 1872; VP - 1876, 1884.

Henry, John - Md. (Democratic-Republican) Nov. 1750 - Dec. 16, 1798; Continental Congress, 1778-80, 1785-86; Senate, 1789-97; governor, 1797-98. Candidacy - 1796.

Hobart, Garret Augustus - N.J. (Republican) June 3, 1844 - Nov. 21, 1899; New Jersey Senate, 1876-82; president of New Jersey Senate, 1881-82; Republican National Committee, 1884-96; U.S. vice president, 1897-99. Candidacy: VP - 1896.

Hoover, Herbert Clark - Calif. (Republican) Aug. 10, 1874 - Oct. 20, 1964; U.S. food administrator, 1917-19; secretary of commerce, 1921-28; U.S. president, 1929-33; chairman, Commission on Organization of the Executive Branch of Government, 1947-49, 1953-55. Candidacies: P - 1928, 1932.

Hospers, John - Calif. (Libertarian) June 9, 1918—; director of school of philosophy at University of Southern California. Candidacy: P - 1972.

Howard, John Eager - Md. (Federalist) June 4, 1752 - Oct. 12, 1827; Continental Congress, 1788; governor, 1788-91; Senate, 1796-1803. Candidacy: VP - 1816.

Hughes, Charles Evans - N.Y. (Republican) April 11, 1862 - Aug. 27, 1948; governor, 1907-10; associate justice of U.S. Supreme Court, 1910-16; secretary of state, 1921-25; chief justice of United States, 1930-41. Candidacy: P - 1916.

Humphrey, Hubert Horatio Jr. - Minn. (Democratic) May 27, 1911 - Jan. 13, 1978; mayor of Minneapolis, 1945-48; Senate, 1949-64, 1971-78; U.S. vice president, 1965-69. Candidacies: VP - 1964; P - 1968.

Huntington, Samuel - Conn., July 3, 1731 - Jan. 5, 1796; Continental Congress, 1776, 1778-81, 1783; president of the Continental Congress, 1779-81; governor, 1786-96. Candidacy: 1789.

Ingersoll, Jared - Pa. (Federalist) Oct. 24, 1749 - Oct. 31, 1822; Continental Congress, 1780-81; Constitutional Convention, 1787. Candidacy: VP - 1812.

Iredell, James - N.C. (Federalist) Oct. 5, 1751 - Oct. 20, 1799; associate justice of U.S. Supreme Court, 1790-99. Candidacy: 1796.

Jackson, Andrew - Tenn. (Democratic-Republican, Democratic) March 15, 1767 - June 8, 1845; House, 1796-97; Senate, 1797-98, 1823-25; territorial governor of Florida, 1821; U.S. president, 1829-37. Candidacies: P - 1824, 1828, 1832.

Jay, John - N.Y. (Federalist) Dec. 12, 1745 - May 17, 1829; Continental Congress, 1774-76, 1778-79; president of Continental Congress, 1778-79; minister to Spain, 1779; chief justice of United States, 1789-95; governor, 1795-1801. Candidacies: 1789, 1796, 1800.

Jefferson, Thomas - Va. (Democratic-Republican) April 13, 1743 - July 4, 1826; Continental Congress, 1775-76, 1783-84; author and signer of Declaration of Independence, 1776; governor, 1779-81; minister to France, 1784-89; secretary of state, 1790-93; U.S. vice president, 1797-1801; U.S. president, 1801-09. Candidacies: VP - 1792; P - 1796, 1800, 1804.

Jenkins, Charles Jones - Ga. (Democratic) Jan. 6, 1805 - June 14, 1883; governor, 1865-68. Candidacy: P - 1872.

Johnson, Andrew - Tenn. (Republican) Dec. 29, 1808 - July 31, 1875; House, 1843-53; governor, 1853-57; Senate, 1857-62, 1875; U.S. vice president, 1865; U.S. president, 1865-69. Candidacy: VP - 1864.

Johnson, Herschel Vespasian - Ga. (Democratic) Sept. 18, 1812 - Aug. 16, 1880; Senate, 1848-49; governor, 1853-57; senator, Confederate Congress, 1862-65. Candidacy: VP - 1860.

Johnson, Hiram Warren - Calif. (Progressive) Sept. 2, 1866 - Aug. 6, 1945; governor, 1911-17; Senate, 1917-45. Candidacy: VP - 1912.

Johnson, Lyndon Baines - Texas (Democratic) Aug. 27, 1908 - Jan. 22, 1973; House, 1937-49; Senate, 1949-61; Senate minority leader, 1953-55; Senate majority leader, 1955-61; U.S. vice president, 1961-63; U.S. president, 1963-69. Candidacies: VP - 1960; P - 1964.

Johnson, Richard Mentor - Ky. (Democratic) Oct. 17, 1780 - Nov. 19, 1850; House,

1807-19, 1829-37; Senate, 1819-29; U.S. vice president, 1837-41. Candidacies: VP - 1836, 1840.

Johnston, Samuel - N.C. (Federalist) Dec. 15, 1733 - Aug. 17, 1816; Continental Congress, 1780-81; governor, 1787-89; Senate, 1789-93. Candidacy: 1796.

Jones, Walter Burgwyn - Ala. (Independent Democratic) Oct. 16, 1888 - Aug. 1, 1963; Alabama Legislature, 1919-20; Alabama circuit court judge, 1920-35; presiding judge, 1935-63. Candidacy: P - 1956.

Julian, George Washington - Ind. (Free Soil, Liberal Republican) May 5, 1817 - July 7, 1899; House, 1849-51, 1861-71. Candidacies: VP - 1852, 1872.

Kefauver, Estes - Tenn. (Democratic) July 26, 1903 - Aug. 10, 1963; House, 1939-49; Senate, 1949-63. Candidacy: VP - 1956.

Kemp, Jack F. - N.Y. (Republican) July 13, 1935—; House, 1971-89; secretary of Housing and Urban Development, 1989-93. Candidacy: VP - 1996.

Kennedy, John Fitzgerald - Mass. (Democratic) May 29, 1917 - Nov. 22, 1963; House, 1947-53; Senate, 1953-60; U.S. president, 1961-63. Candidacy: P - 1960.

Kern, John Worth - Ind. (Democratic) Dec. 20, 1849 - Aug. 17, 1917; Senate, 1911-17; Senate majority leader, 1913-17. Candidacy: VP - 1908.

King, Rufus - N.Y. (Federalist) March 24, 1755 - April 29, 1827; Continental Congress, 1784-87; Constitutional Convention, 1787; Senate, 1789-96, 1813-25; minister to Great Britain, 1796-1803, 1825-26. Candidacies: VP - 1804, 1808; P - 1816.

King, William Rufus de Vane - Ala. (Democratic) April 7, 1786 - April 18, 1853; House, 1811-16; Senate, 1819-44, 1848-52; president pro tempore of the Senate, 1836, 1837, 1838, 1839, 1840, 1841, 1850; minister to France, 1844-46; U.S. vice president, 1853. Candidacy: VP - 1852.

Knox, Franklin - Ill. (Republican) Jan. 1, 1874 - April 28, 1944; secretary of the Navy, 1940-44. Candidacy: VP - 1936.

La Follette, Robert Marion - Wis. (Progressive) June 14, 1855 - June 18, 1925; House, 1885-91; governor, 1901-06; Senate, 1906-25. Candidacy: P - 1924.

Landon, Alfred Mossman - Kan. (Republican) Sept. 9, 1887 - Oct. 12, 1987; governor, 1933-37. Candidacy: P - 1936.

Lane, Joseph - Ore. (Southern Democratic) Dec. 14, 1801 - April 19, 1881; governor of Oregon Territory, 1849-50, 1853; House (territorial delegate), 1851-59; Senate, 1859-61. Candidacy: VP - 1860.

Langdon, John - N.H. (Democratic-Republican) June 26, 1741 - Sept. 18, 1819; Continental Congress, 1775-76, 1787; governor, 1805-09, 1810-12; Senate, 1789-1801; first president pro tempore of the Senate, 1789. Candidacy: VP - 1808.

Lee, Henry - Mass. (Independent Democratic) Feb. 4, 1782 - Feb. 6, 1867; merchant and publicist. Candidacy: VP - 1832.

LeMay, Curtis Emerson - Ohio (American Independent) Nov. 15, 1906 - Oct. 1, 1990; Air Force chief of staff, 1961-65. Candidacy: VP - 1968.

Lemke, William - N.D. (Union) Aug. 13, 1878 - May 30, 1950; House, 1933-41, 1943-50. Candidacy: P - 1936.

Lincoln, Abraham - Ill. (Republican) Feb. 12, 1809 - April 15, 1865; House, 1847-49. U.S. president, 1861-65 Candidacies: 1860, 1864.

Lincoln, Benjamin - Mass. (Federalist) Jan. 24, 1733 - May 9, 1810; major general in Continental Army, 1777-81. Candidacy: 1789.

Lodge, Henry Cabot Jr. - Mass. (Republican) July 5, 1902 - Feb. 27, 1985; Senate, 1937-44, 1947-53; ambassador to United Nations, 1953-60; ambassador to Republic of Vietnam, 1963-64, 1965-67. Candidacy: VP - 1960.

Logan, John Alexander - Ill. (Republican) Feb. 9, 1826 - Dec. 26, 1886; House, 1859-62, 1867-71; Senate, 1871-77, 1879-86. Candidacy: VP - 1884.

Machen, Willis Benson - Ky. (Democratic) April 10, 1810 - Sept. 29, 1893; Confederate Congress, 1861-65; Senate, 1872-73. Candidacy: VP - 1872.

Macon, Nathaniel - N.C. (Democratic-Republican) Dec. 17, 1757 - June 29, 1837; House, 1791-1815; Speaker of the House, 1801-07; Senate, 1815-28; president pro tempore of the Senate, 1826, 1827. Candidacy: VP - 1824.

Madison, James - Va. (Democratic-Republican) March 16, 1751 - June 28, 1836; Continental Congress, 1780-83, 1787-88; Constitutional Convention, 1787; House, 1789-97; secretary of state, 1801-09; U.S. president, 1809-17. Candidacies: P - 1808, 1812.

Mangum, Willie Person - N.C. (Independent Democrat) May 10, 1792 - Sept. 7, 1861; House, 1823-26; Senate, 1831-36, 1840-53. Candidacy: P - 1836.

Marshall, John - Va. (Federalist) Sept. 24, 1755 - July 6, 1835; House 1799-1800; secretary

of state, 1800-01; chief justice of United States, 1801-35. Candidacy: VP - 1816.

Marshall, Thomas Riley - Ind. (Democratic) March 14, 1854 - June 1, 1925; governor, 1909-13; U.S. vice president, 1913-21. Candidacies: VP - 1912, 1916.

McCarthy, Eugene Joseph - Minn. (Independent) March 29, 1916—; House, 1949-59; Senate, 1959-71. Candidacy: P - 1976.

McClellan, George Brinton - N.J. (Democratic) Dec. 3, 1826 - Oct. 29, 1885; general-in-chief of Army of the Potomac, 1861; governor, 1878-81. Candidacy: P - 1864.

McGovern, George Stanley - S.D. (Democratic) July 19, 1922—; House, 1957-61; Senate, 1963-81. Candidacy: P - 1972.

McKinley, William Jr. - Ohio (Republican) Jan. 29, 1843 - Sept. 14, 1901; House, 1877, 1885-91; governor, 1892-96; U.S. president, 1897-1901. Candidacies: P - 1896, 1900.

McNary, Charles Linza - Ore. (Republican) June 12, 1874 - Feb. 25, 1944; state Supreme Court judge, 1913-15; Senate, 1917-18, 1918-44; Senate minority leader, 1933-44. Candidacy: VP - 1940.

Miller, William Edward - N.Y. (Republican) March 22, 1914 - June 24, 1983; House, 1951-65; chairman of Republican National Committee, 1960-64. Candidacy: VP - 1964.

Milton, John - Ga. circa 1740 - circa 1804; secretary of state, Georgia, circa 1778, 1781, 1783. Candidacy: 1789.

Mondale, Walter Frederick - Minn. (Democratic) Jan. 5, 1928—; Senate, 1964-76; U.S. vice president, 1977-81; ambassador to Japan, 1993-96. Candidacies: VP - 1976, 1980; P - 1984.

Monroe, James - Va. (Democratic-Republican) April 28, 1758 - July 4, 1831; Continental Congress, 1783-86; Senate, 1790-94; minister to France, 1794-96, 1803; minister to England, 1803-07; governor, 1799-1802, 1811; secretary of state, 1811-14, 1815-17; U.S. president, 1817-25. Candidacies: VP - 1808; P - 1816, 1820.

Morton, Levi Parsons - N.Y. (Republican) May 16, 1824 - May 16, 1920; House, 1879-81; minister to France, 1881-85; U.S. vice president, 1889-93; governor, 1895-97. Candidacy: VP - 1888.

Muskie, Edmund Sixtus - Maine (Democratic) March 28, 1914 - March 26, 1996; governor, 1955-59; Senate, 1959-80; secretary of state, 1980-81. Candidacy: VP - 1968.

Nathan, Theodora Nathalia - Ore. (Libertarian) Feb. 9, 1923—; broadcast journalist;

National Judiciary Committee, Libertarian Party, 1972-75; vice chairperson, Oregon Libertarian Party, 1974-75. Candidacy: VP - 1972.

Nixon, Richard Milhous - Calif., N.Y. (Republican) Jan. 9, 1913 - April 22, 1994; House, 1947-50; Senate, 1950-53; U.S. vice president, 1953-61; U.S. president, 1969-74. Candidacies: VP - 1952, 1956; P - 1960, 1968, 1972.

Palmer, John McAuley - Ill. (Democratic, National Democratic) Sept. 13, 1817 - Sept. 25, 1900; governor, 1869-73; Senate, 1891-97. Candidacies: VP - 1872; P - 1896.

Parker, Alton Brooks - N.Y. (Democratic) May 14, 1852 - May 10, 1926; chief justice of N.Y. Court of Appeals, 1898-1904. Candidacy: P - 1904.

Pendleton, George Hunt - Ohio (Democratic) July 19, 1825 - Nov. 24, 1889; House, 1857-65; Senate, 1879-85; minister to Germany, 1885-89. Candidacy: VP - 1864.

Perot, H. Ross - Texas (Independent, Reform) June 27, 1930—; business executive and owner. Candidacy: P - 1992, 1996.

Pierce, Franklin - N.H. (Democratic) Nov. 23, 1804 - Oct. 8, 1869; House, 1833-37; Senate, 1837-42; U.S. president, 1853-57. Candidacy: P - 1852.

Pinckney, Charles Cotesworth - S.C. (Federalist) Feb. 25, 1746 - Aug. 16, 1825; president, state senate, 1779; minister to France, 1796. Candidacies: VP - 1800; P - 1804, 1808.

Pinckney, Thomas - S.C. (Federalist) Oct. 23, 1750 - Nov. 2, 1828; governor, 1787-89; minister to Great Britain, 1792-96; envoy to Spain, 1794-95; House, 1797-1801. Candidacy: 1796.

Polk, James Knox - Tenn. (Democratic) Nov. 2, 1795 - June 15, 1849; House, 1825-39; Speaker of the House, 1835-39; governor, 1839-41; U.S. president, 1845-49. Candidacies: VP - 1840; P - 1844.

Quayle, Dan - Ind. (Republican) Feb. 4, 1947—;House, 1977-81; Senate, 1981-89; U.S. vice president, 1989-93. Candidacies; VP - 1988, 1992.

Reagan, Ronald Wilson - Calif. (Republican) Feb. 6, 1911—; governor, 1967-75; U.S. president, 1981-89. Candidacies: P - 1980, 1984.

Reid, Whitelaw - N.Y. (Republican) Oct. 27, 1837 - Dec. 15, 1912; minister to France, 1889-92; editor-in-chief, *New York Tribune,* 1872-1905. Candidacy: VP - 1892.

Robinson, Joseph Taylor - Ark. (Democratic) Aug. 26, 1872 - July 14, 1937; House,

1903-13; governor, 1913; Senate, 1913-37; Senate minority leader, 1923-33; Senate majority leader, 1933-37. Candidacy: VP - 1928.

Rockefeller, Nelson Aldrich - N.Y. (Republican) July 8, 1908 - Jan. 26, 1979; governor, 1959-73; U.S. vice president, 1974-77 (nominated under the provisions of the 25th Amendment).

Rodney, Daniel - Del. (Federalist) Sept. 10, 1764 - Sept. 2, 1846; governor, 1814-17; House, 1822-23; Senate, 1826-27. Candidacy: VP - 1820.

Roosevelt, Franklin Delano - N.Y. (Democratic) Jan. 30, 1882 - April 12, 1945; assistant secretary of the Navy, 1913-20; governor, 1929-33; U.S. president, 1933-45. Candidacies: VP - 1920; P - 1932, 1936, 1940, 1944.

Roosevelt, Theodore - N.Y. (Republican, Progressive) Oct. 27, 1858 - Jan. 6, 1919; assistant secretary of the Navy, 1897-98; governor, 1899-1901; U.S. vice president, 1901; U.S. president, 1901-09. Candidacies: VP - 1900; P - 1904, 1912.

Ross, James - Pa. (Federalist) July 12, 1762 - Nov. 27, 1847; Senate, 1794-1803. Candidacy: VP - 1816.

Rush, Richard - Pa. (Democratic-Republican, National-Republican) Aug. 29, 1780 - July 30, 1859; attorney general, 1814-17; minister to Great Britain, 1817-24; secretary of the Treasury, 1825-29. Candidacies: VP - 1820, 1828.

Rutledge, John - S.C. (Federalist) Sept. 1739 - July 23, 1800; Continental Congress, 1774-75, 1782-83; governor, 1779-82; Constitutional Convention, 1787; associate justice of U.S. Supreme Court, 1789-91; chief justice of United States, 1795. Candidacy: 1789.

Sanford, Nathan - N.Y. (Democratic-Republican) Nov. 5, 1777 - Oct. 17, 1838; Senate, 1815-21, 1826-31. Candidacy: VP - 1824.

Schmitz, John George - Calif. (American Independent) Aug. 12, 1930—; House, 1970-73. Candidacy: P - 1972.

Scott, Winfield - N.J. (Whig) June 13, 1786 - May 29, 1866; general-in-chief of U.S. Army, 1841-61. Candidacy: P - 1852.

Sergeant, John - Pa. (National-Republican) Dec. 5, 1779 - Nov. 23, 1852; House, 1815-23, 1827-29, 1837-41. Candidacy: VP - 1832.

Sewall, Arthur - Maine (Democratic) Nov. 25, 1835 - Sept. 5, 1900; Democratic National Committee member, 1888-96. Candidacy: VP - 1896.

Seymour, Horatio - N.Y. (Democratic) May 31, 1810 - Feb. 12, 1886; governor, 1853-55, 1863-65. Candidacy: P - 1868.

Sherman, James Schoolcraft - N.Y. (Republican) Oct. 24, 1855 - Oct. 30, 1912; House, 1887-91, 1893-1909; U.S. vice president, 1909-12. Candidacies: VP - 1908, 1912. (Died during 1912 campaign; Nicholas Murray Butler replaced Sherman on the Republican ticket.)

Shriver, Robert Sargent Jr. - Md. (Democratic) Nov. 9, 1915—; director, Peace Corps, 1961-66; director, Office of Economic Opportunity, 1964-68; ambassador to France, 1968-70. Candidacy: VP - 1972. (Replaced Thomas F. Eagleton on Democratic ticket Aug. 8.)

Smith, Alfred Emanuel - N.Y. (Democratic) Dec. 30, 1873 - Oct. 4, 1944; governor, 1919-21, 1923-29. Candidacy: P - 1928.

Smith, William - S.C., Ala. (Independent Democratic-Republican) Sept. 6, 1762 - June 26, 1840; Senate, 1816-23, 1826-31. Candidacies: VP - 1828, 1836.

Sparkman, John Jackson - Ala. (Democratic) Dec. 20, 1899 - Nov. 16, 1985; House, 1937-46; Senate, 1946-79. Candidacy: VP - 1952.

Stevenson, Adlai Ewing - Ill. (Democratic) Oct. 23, 1835 - June 14, 1914; House, 1875-77, 1879-81; assistant postmaster general, 1885-89; U.S. vice president, 1893-97. Candidacies: VP - 1892, 1900.

Stevenson, Adlai Ewing II - Ill. (Democratic) Feb. 5, 1900 - July 14, 1965; assistant to the secretary of Navy, 1941-44; assistant to the secretary of state, 1945; governor, 1949-53; ambassador to United Nations, 1961-65. Candidacies: P - 1952, 1956.

Stockton, Richard - N.J. (Federalist) April 17, 1764 - March 7, 1828; Senate, 1796-99; House, 1813-15. Candidacy: VP - 1820.

Taft, William Howard - Ohio (Republican) Sept. 15, 1857 - March 8, 1930; secretary of war, 1904-08; U.S. president, 1909-13; chief justice of United States, 1921-30. Candidacies: P - 1908, 1912.

Talmadge, Herman Eugene - Ga. (Independent Democratic) Aug. 9, 1913—; governor, 1947, 1948-55; Senate, 1957-81. Candidacy: VP - 1956.

Taylor, Glen Hearst - Idaho (Progressive) April 12, 1904 - April 28, 1984; Senate, 1945-51. Candidacy: VP - 1948.

Taylor, Zachary - La. (Whig) Nov. 24, 1784 - July 9, 1850; major general, U.S. Army; U.S. president, 1849-50. Candidacy: P - 1848.

Tazewell, Littleton Waller - Va. (Democratic) Dec. 17, 1774 - May 6, 1860; House, 1800-01; Senate, 1824-32; president pro tempore of the Senate, 1832; governor, 1834-36. Candidacy: VP - 1840.

Telfair, Edward - Ga. (Democratic-Republican) 1735 - Sept. 17, 1807; Continental Congress, 1778, 1780-82; governor, 1789-93. Candidacy: 1789.

Thomas, Norman Mattoon - N.Y. (Socialist) Nov. 20, 1884 - Dec. 19, 1968; Presbyterian minister, 1911-31; author and editor. Candidacies: P - 1928, 1932, 1936, 1940, 1944, 1948.

Thurman, Allen Granberry - Ohio (Democratic) Nov. 13, 1813 - Dec. 12, 1895; House, 1845-47; Ohio Supreme Court, 1851-56; Senate, 1869-81; president pro tempore of the Senate, 1879, 1880. Candidacy: VP - 1888.

Thurmond, James Strom - S.C. (States' Rights Democrat) Dec. 5, 1902—; governor, 1947-51; Senate, 1954-56, 1956—; president pro tempore of the Senate, 1981-87; 1995—. Candidacies: P - 1948.

Tilden, Samuel Jones - N.Y. (Democratic) Feb. 9, 1814 - Aug. 4, 1886; governor, 1875-77. Candidacy: P - 1876.

Tompkins, Daniel D. - N.Y. (Democratic-Republican) June 21, 1774 - June 11, 1825; elected to the House for the term beginning in 1805 but resigned before taking seat; governor, 1807-17; U.S. vice president, 1817-25. Candidacies: VP - 1816, 1820.

Truman, Harry S. - Mo. (Democratic) May 8, 1884 - Dec. 26, 1972; Senate, 1935-45; U.S. vice president, 1945; U.S. president, 1945-53. Candidacies: VP - 1944; P - 1948.

Tyler, John - Va. (Whig) March 29, 1790 - Jan. 18, 1862; governor, 1825-27; Senate, 1827-36; U.S. vice president, 1841; U.S. president, 1841-45. Candidacies: VP - 1836, 1840.

Van Buren, Martin - N.Y. (Democratic, Free Soil) Dec. 5, 1782 - July 24, 1862; Senate, 1821-28; governor, 1829; secretary of state, 1829-31; U.S. vice president, 1833-37; U.S. president, 1837-41. Candidacies: VP - 1824, 1832; P - 1836, 1840, 1848.

Wallace, George Corley - Ala. (American Independent) Aug. 25, 1919—; governor, 1963-67, 1971-79, 1983-89. Candidacy: P - 1968.

Wallace, Henry Agard - Iowa (Democratic, Progressive) Oct. 7, 1888 - Nov. 18, 1965; secretary of agriculture, 1933-40; U.S. vice president, 1941-45; secretary of commerce, 1945-46. Candidacies: VP - 1940; P - 1948.

Warren, Earl - Calif. (Republican) March 19, 1891 - July 9, 1974; governor, 1943-53; chief justice of United States, 1953-69. Candidacy: VP - 1948.

Washington, George - Va. (Federalist) Feb. 22, 1732 - Dec. 14, 1799; First and Second Continental Congresses, 1774, 1775; commander-in-chief of armed forces, 1775-83; president of Constitutional Convention, 1787; U.S. president, 1789-97. Candidacies: P - 1789, 1792, 1796.

Watson, Thomas Edward - Ga. (Populist) Sept. 5, 1856 - Sept. 26, 1922; House, 1891-93; Senate, 1921-22. Candidacies: VP - 1896; P - 1904, 1908.

Weaver, James Baird - Iowa (Greenback, Populist) June 12, 1833 - Feb. 6, 1912; House, 1879-81, 1885-89; Candidacies: P - 1880, 1892.

Webster, Daniel - Mass. (Whig) Jan. 18, 1782 - Oct. 24, 1852; House, 1813-17, 1823-27; Senate, 1827-41, 1845-50; secretary of state, 1841-43, 1850-52. Candidacy: P - 1836.

Wheeler, Burton Kendall - Mont. (Progressive) Feb. 27, 1882 - Jan. 6, 1975; Senate, 1923-47. Candidacy: VP - 1924.

Wheeler, William Almon - N.Y. (Republican) June 30, 1819 - June 4, 1887; House, 1861-63, 1869-77; U.S. vice president, 1877-81. Candidacy: VP - 1876.

White, Hugh Lawson - Tenn. (Whig) Oct. 30, 1773 - April 10, 1840; Senate, 1825-35, 1835-40. Candidacy: P - 1836.

Wilkins, William - Pa. (Democratic) Dec. 20, 1779 - June 23, 1865; Senate, 1831-34; minister to Russia, 1834-35; House, 1843-44; secretary of war, 1844-45. Candidacy: VP - 1832.

Willkie, Wendell Lewis - N.Y. (Republican) Feb. 18, 1892 - Oct. 8, 1944; utility executive, 1933-40. Candidacy: P - 1940.

Wilson, Henry - Mass. (Republican) Feb. 16, 1812 - Nov. 22, 1875; Senate, 1855-73; U.S. vice president, 1873-75. Candidacy: VP - 1872.

Wilson, Woodrow - N.J. (Democratic) Dec. 28, 1856 - Feb. 3, 1924; governor, 1911-13; U.S. president, 1913-21. Candidacies: P - 1912, 1916.

Wirt, William - Md. (Anti-Masonic) Nov. 8, 1772 - Feb. 18, 1834; attorney general, 1817-29. Candidacy: P - 1832.

Wright, Fielding Lewis - Miss. (States' Rights Democratic) May 16, 1895 - May 4, 1956; governor, 1946-52. Candidacy: VP - 1948.

U.S. Constitution on Presidential Selection

Following are the constitutional provisions relating to selection of the president, including voting eligibility requirements. Also included is the 25th Amendment to the Constitution, ratified Feb. 10, 1967, providing for presidential succession because of disability, removal or resignation and for filling a vacancy in the vice presidency.

U.S. Constitution

Article II

Section 1. The executive Power shall be vested in a President of the United States of America. He shall hold his Office during the Term of four Years, and, together with the Vice President, chosen for the same term, be elected, as follows.

Each State shall appoint, in such Manner as the Legislature thereof may direct, a Number of Electors, equal to the whole Number of Senators and Representatives to which the State may be entitled in the Congress: but no Senator or Representative, or Person holding an Office of Trust or Profit under the United States, shall be appointed an Elector.

[The Electors shall meet in their respective States, and vote by Ballot for two Persons, of whom one at least shall not be an Inhabitant of the same State with themselves. And they shall make a List of all the Persons voted for, and of the Number of Votes for each; which List they shall sign and certify, and transmit sealed to the Seat of the Government of the United States, directed to the President of the Senate. The President of the Senate shall, in the Presence of the Senate and House of Representatives, open all the Certificates, and the Votes shall then be counted. The Person having the greatest Number of Votes shall be the President, if such Number be a Majority of the whole Number of Electors appointed; and if there be more than one who have such Majority, and have an equal Number of Votes, then the House of Representatives shall immediately chuse by Ballot one of them for President; and if no Person have a Majority, then from the five highest on the List the said House shall in like Manner chuse the President. But in chusing the President, the Votes shall be taken by States, the Representation from each State having one Vote; a quorum for this Purpose shall consist of a Member or Members from two thirds of the States, and a Majority of all the States shall be necessary to a Choice. In every Case, after the Choice of the President, the Person having the greatest Number of Votes of the Electors shall be the Vice President. But if there should remain two or more who have equal Votes, the Senate shall chuse from them by Ballot the Vice-President.][1]

The Congress may determine the Time of chusing the Electors, and the Day on which they shall give their Votes; which Day shall be the same throughout the United States.

No person except a natural born Citizen, or a Citizen of the United States, at the time of the Adoption of this Constitution, shall be eligible to the Office of President; neither shall any Person be eligible to that Office who shall not have attained to the Age of thirty five Years, and been fourteen Years a Resident within the United States.

Amendment XII *(Ratified July 27, 1804)*

The Electors shall meet in their respective states and vote by ballot for President and Vice-President, one of whom, at least, shall not be an inhabitant of the same state with themselves; they shall name in their ballots the person voted for as President, and in distinct ballots the person voted for as Vice-President, and they shall make distinct lists of all persons voted for as President, and of all persons voted for as Vice-President, and of the number of votes for each, which lists they shall sign and certify, and transmit sealed to the seat of the government of the United States, directed to the President of the Senate; . . .The person having the greatest number of votes for President, shall be the President, if such number be a majority of the whole number of Electors appointed; and if no person have such majority, then from the persons having the highest numbers not exceeding three on the list of those voted for as President, the House of Representatives shall choose immediately, by ballot, the President. But in choosing the President, the votes shall be taken by states, the representation from each state having one vote; a quorum for this purpose shall consist of a member or members from two-thirds of the states, and a majority of all the states shall be necessary to a choice. [And if the House of Representatives shall not choose a President whenever the right of choice shall devolve upon them, before the fourth day of March next following, then the Vice-President shall act as President, as in the case of the death or other constitutional disability of the President.—][2] The person having the greatest number of votes as Vice-President, shall be the Vice-President, if such number be a majority of the whole number of Electors appointed, and if no person have a majority, then from the two highest numbers on the list, the Senate shall choose the Vice President; a quorum for the purpose shall consist of two-thirds of the whole number of Senators, and a majority of the whole number shall be necessary to a choice. But no person constitutionally ineligible to the office of President shall be eligible to that of Vice-President of the United States.

Amendment XIV *(Ratified July 9, 1868)*

Section 1. All persons born or naturalized in the United States, and subject to the jurisdiction thereof, are citizens of the United States and of the State wherein they reside. No State shall make or enforce any law which shall abridge the privileges or immunities of citizens of the United States; nor shall any State deprive any person of life, liberty, or property, without due process of law; nor deny to any person within its jurisdiction the equal protection of the laws.

Section 2. Representatives shall be apportioned among the several States according to their respective numbers, counting the whole number of persons in each State, excluding Indians not taxed. But when the right to vote at any election for the choice of electors for President and Vice President of the United States, Representatives in Congress, the Executive and Judicial officers of a State, or the members of the Legislature thereof, is denied to any of the male inhabitants of such State, being twenty-one years of age,[3] and citizens of the United States, or in any way abridged, except for participation in rebellion, or other crime, the basis of representation therein shall be reduced in the proportion which the number of such male citizens shall bear to the whole number of male citizens twenty-one years of age in such State.

Section 3. No person shall be a Senator or Representative in Congress, or elector of President and Vice President, or hold any office, civil or military, under the United States, or under any State, who, having previously taken an oath, as a member of Congress, or as an officer of the United States, or as a member of any State legislature, or as an executive or judicial officer of any State, to support the Constitution of the United States, shall have engaged in insurrection or rebellion against the same, or given aid or comfort to the enemies thereof. But Congress may by a vote of two-thirds of each House, remove such disability.

Amendment XV *(Ratified February 3, 1870)*

Section 1. The right of citizens of the United States to vote shall not be denied or abridged by the United States or by any State on account of race, color, or previous condition of servitude.

Amendment XIX *(Ratified August 18, 1920)*

The right of citizens of the United States to vote shall not be denied or abridged by the United States or by any State on account of sex.

Amendment XX *(Ratified January 23, 1933)*

Section 1. The terms of the President and Vice President shall end at noon on the 20th day of January. . . .

Section 3. If, at the time fixed for the beginning of the term of the President, the President elect shall have died, the Vice President elect shall become President. If a President shall not have been chosen before the time fixed for the beginning of his term, or if the President elect shall have failed to qualify, then the Vice President elect shall act as President until a President shall have qualified; and the Congress may by law provide for the case wherein neither a President elect nor a Vice President elect shall have qualified, declaring who shall then act as President, or the manner in which one who is to act shall be selected, and such person shall act accordingly until a President or Vice President shall have qualified.

Section 4. The Congress may by law provide for the case of the death of any of the persons from whom the House of Representatives may choose a President whenever the right of choice shall have devolved upon them, and for the case of the death of any of the persons from whom the Senate may choose a Vice President whenever the right of choice shall have devolved upon them.

Amendment XXIII *(Ratified March 29, 1961)*

Section 1. The District constituting the seat of Government of the United States shall appoint in such manner as the Congress may direct:

A number of electors of President and Vice President equal to the whole number of Senators and Representatives in Congress to which the District would be entitled if it were a State, but in no event more than the least populous State; they shall be in addition to those appointed by the States, but they shall be considered, for the purposes of the election of President and Vice President, to be electors appointed by a State; and they shall meet in the District and perform such duties as provided by the twelfth article of amendment.

Amendment XXIV *(Ratified January 23, 1964)*

Section 1. The right of citizens of the United States to vote in any primary or other election for President or Vice President, for electors for President or Vice President, or for Senator or Representative in Congress, shall not be denied or abridged by the United States or any State by reason of failure to pay any poll tax or other tax.

Amendment XXV *(Ratified Feb. 10, 1967)*

Section 1. In case of the removal of the President from office or of his death or resignation, the Vice President shall become President.

Section 2. Whenever there is a vacancy in the office of the Vice President, the President shall nominate a Vice President who shall take office upon confirmation by a majority vote of both Houses of Congress.

Section 3. Whenever the President transmits to the President pro tempore of the Senate and the Speaker of the House of Representatives his written declaration that he is unable to discharge the powers and duties of his office, and until he transmits to them a written declaration to the contrary, such powers and duties shall be discharged by the Vice President as Acting President.

Section 4. Whenever the Vice President and a majority of either the principal officers of the executive departments or of such other body as Congress may by law provide, transmit to the President pro tempore of the Senate and the Speaker of the House of Representatives their written declaration that the President is unable to discharge the powers and duties of his office, the Vice President shall immediately assume the powers and duties of the office as Acting President.

Thereafter, when the President transmits to the President pro tempore of the Senate and the Speaker of the House of Representatives his written declaration that no inability exists, he shall resume the powers and duties of his office unless the Vice President and a majority of either the principal officers of the executive departments or of such other body as Congress may by law provide, transmit within four days to the President pro tempore of the Senate and the Speaker of the House of Representatives their written declaration that the President is unable to discharge the powers and duties of his office. Thereupon Congress shall decide the issue, assembling within forty-eight hours for that purpose if not in session. If the Congress, within twenty-one days after receipt of the latter written declaration, or, if Congress is not in session, within twenty-one days after Congress is required to assemble, determines by two-thirds vote of both Houses that the President is unable to discharge the powers and duties of his office, the Vice President shall continue to discharge the same as Acting President; otherwise, the President shall resume the powers and duties of his office.

Amendment XXVI *(Ratified July 1, 1971)*

Section 1. The right of citizens of the United States, who are eighteen years of age or older, to vote shall not be denied or abridged by the United States or by any State on account of age.

1. *Superseded by the 12th Amendment.*
2. *Changed to Jan. 20 by the 20th Amendment, ratified in 1933.*
3. *Superseded by the 19th and 26th Amendments.*

Bibliography

Books

Abramson, Paul R., John H. Aldrich and David W. Rohde. *Change and Continuity in the 1992 Elections.* Rev. ed. Washington, D.C.: Congressional Quarterly, 1995.

Asher, Herbert. *Presidential Elections and American Politics: Votes, Candidates, and Campaigns since 1952.* 5th ed. Pacific Grove, Calif.: Brooks-Cole, 1992.

Bagby, Wesley. *The Road to Normalcy: The Presidential Campaign and Election of 1920.* New York: AMS Press, 1962.

Barber, James D. *The Presidential Character: Predicting Performance in the White House.* 4th ed. Englewood Cliffs, N.J.: Prentice-Hall, 1992.

Bartels, Larry M. *Presidential Primaries and the Dynamics of Public Choice.* Princeton, N.J.: Princeton University Press, 1988.

Best, Judith. *The Case Against Direct Election of the President: A Defense of the Electoral College.* Ithaca, N.Y.: Cornell University Press, 1975.

Black, Earl, and Merle Black. *The Vital South: How Presidential Elections Are Won.* Cambridge, Mass.: Harvard University Press, 1992.

Brams, Steven J. *The Presidential Election Game.* New Haven, Conn.: Yale University Press, 1978.

Burnham, Walter D. *Critical Elections and the Mainsprings of American Politics.* New York: Norton, 1971.

Ceaser, James, and Andrew Busch. *Upside Down and Inside Out: The 1992 Elections and American Politics.* Lanham, Md.: Rowman and Littlefield, 1993.

Congressional Quarterly. *National Party Conventions 1831-1996.* Washington, D.C.: Congressional Quarterly, 1997.

Congressional Quarterly. *Selecting the President: From 1789-1996.* Washington, D.C.: Congressional Quarterly, 1997.

Cook, Rhodes, and Alice V. McGillivray. *U.S. Primary Elections: President, Congress, Governors: 1995-1996.* Washington, D.C.: Congressional Quarterly, 1997.

Crotty, William, ed. *America's Choice: The Election of 1992.* Guilford, Conn.: Dushkin, 1993.

David, Paul T., and James W. Ceasar. *Proportional Representation in Presidential Nominating Politics.* Charlottesville: University Press of Virginia, 1980.

Davis, James W. *The Presidential Primaries: Road to the White House.* 1967. Reprint. Westport, Conn.: Greenwood Press, 1980.

Di Clerico, Robert E., and Eric M. Uslaner. *Few Are Chosen: Problems in Presidential Selection.* New York: McGraw-Hill, 1984.

Drew, Elizabeth. *Portrait of an Election: The 1980 Presidential Campaign.* New York: Simon and Schuster, 1981.

Durbin, Thomas, ed. *Nomination and Election of the President and Vice President of the United States, 1992, Including the Manner of Selecting Delegates to National Party Conventions.* Washington, D.C.: U.S. Government Printing Office, 1992.

Ewing, Cortez A. M. *Presidential Elections from Abraham Lincoln to Franklin Roosevelt.* 1940. Reprint. Westport, Conn.: Greenwood Press, 1972.

Flanigan, William H., and Nancy H. Zingale. *Political Behavior of the American Electorate.* 8th ed. Washington, D.C.: CQ Press, 1994.

Gammon, Samuel R., Jr. *The Presidential Campaign of 1832.* 1922. Reprint. Saint Clair Shores, Mich.: Scholarly Press, 1972.

Germond, Jack W., and Jules Witcover. *Blue Smoke and Mirrors: How Reagan Won and Why Carter Lost the Election of 1980.* New York: Viking, 1981.

Gray, Lee L. *How We Choose a President: The Election Year.* 5th ed. New York: St. Martin's Press, 1980.

Gunderson, Robert G. *The Log-Cabin Campaign.* 1957. Reprint. Westport, Conn.: Greenwood Press, 1977.

Haworth, Paul L. *The Hayes-Tilden Disputed Presidential Election of 1876.* 1906 Reprint. New York: AMS Press, 1979.

Hess, Stephen. *The Presidential Campaign: An Essay.* 3rd ed. Washington, D.C.: Brookings, 1988.

Hirschfield, Robert S., ed. *Selection Election: A Forum on the American Presidency.* Hawthorne, N.Y.: Hawthorne, 1982.

Hoyt, Edwin P. *Jumbos and Jackasses: A Popular History of the Political Wars.* Garden City, N.Y.: Doubleday, 1960.

Jamieson, Kathleen Hall. *Packaging the Presidency: A History and Criticism of Presidential Campaign Advertising.* 3rd ed. New York: Oxford University Press, 1996.

Jensen, Merrill, ed. *The Documentary History of the First Federal Elections, 1788-1790.* Madison, Wis.: Madison House, 1991.

Joint Center for Political Studies. *Picking a President: A Guide to Delegate Selection in the United States.* Washington, D.C.: Joint Center for Political Studies, 1980.

Keech, William R., ed. *Winner Take All: Report of the Twentieth Century Task Force on Reform of the Presidential Election Process.* New York: Holmes and Meier, 1978.

Kessel, John H. *Presidential Campaign Politics.* 4th ed. Pacific Grove, Calif.: Brook-Cole, 1992.

Key, V. O., Jr. *The Responsible Electorate: Rationality in Presidential Voting, 1936-1960.* Cambridge, Mass.: Harvard University Press, 1966.

Kirkpatrick, Samuel A., ed. *American Electoral Behavior: Change and Stability.* Beverly Hills, Calif.: Sage, 1976.

Kleppner, Paul. *Who Voted?: The Dynamics of Electoral Turnout, 1870-1980.* New York: Praeger, 1982.

——, and Walter D. Burnham. *The Evolution of American Electoral System.* Westport, Conn.: Greenwood Press, 1982.

Longley, Lawrence D. *The Politics of Electoral College Reform.* New Haven, Conn.: Yale University Press, 1972.

Maisel, L. Sandy. *Parties and Elections in America: The Electoral Process.* 2nd ed. New York: McGraw-Hill, 1993.

Mayhew, David R. *Divided We Govern: Party Control, Lawmaking & Investigations.* New Haven, Conn.: Yale University Press, 1991.

Mazmanian, Daniel A. *Third Parties in Presidential Elections.* Washington, D.C.: Brookings, 1974.

McGillivray, Alice V. *Presidential Primaries and Caucuses: 1992. A Handbook of Election Statistics.* Washington, D.C.: Congressional Quarterly, 1992.

Michener, James A. *Presidential Lottery: Political System.* 2nd ed. Washington, D.C.: CQ Press, 1988.

Moore, John. *Speaking of Washington: Facts, Firsts, and Folklore.* Washington, D.C.: Congressional Quarterly, 1993.

Nelson, Michael, ed. *The Presidency and the Political System.* 4th ed. Washington, D.C.: CQ Press, 1994.

——, ed. *The Elections of 1992.* Washington, D.C.: CQ Press, 1993.

——, ed. *The Elections of 1996.* Washington, D.C.: CQ Press, 1997.

Newman, Bruce I. *The Marketing of the President: Political Marketing as a Campaign Strategy.* Thousand Oaks, Calif.: Sage, 1994.

Norrander, Barbara. *Super Tuesday: Regional Politics and Presidential Primaries.* Lexington: University Press of Kentucky, 1992.

Overacker, Louise. *The Presidential Primary.* 1926. Reprint. New York: Arno, 1974.

Page, Benjamin I. *Choices and Echoes in Presidential Elections: Rational Man and Electoral Democracy.* Chicago: University of Chicago Press, 1978.

Peel, Roy V. *The 1928 Campaign: An Analysis.* 1931. Reprint. Salem, N.H.: Ayer, 1974.

——. *The 1932 Campaign: An Analysis.* 1935. Reprint. New York: Da Capo Press, 1973.

Peirce, Neal, and Lawrence D. Longley. *The People's President: The Electoral College and the Emerging Consensus for a Direct Vote Alternative.* Rev. ed. New Haven, Conn.: Yale University Press, 1981.

Petersen, Svend. *A Statistical History of the American Presidential Elections.* Westport, Conn.: Greenwood Press, 1981.

Polsby, Nelson W., and Aaron Wildavsky. *Presidential Elections: Contemporary Strategies of American Electoral Politics.* 8th ed. New York: Free Press, 1991.

Ranney, Austin. *Federalization of Presidential Primaries.* Washington, D.C.: American Enterprise Institute, 1978.

Robinson, Edgar E. *The Presidential Vote, 1896-1932.* New York: Octagon Books, 1970.

——. *They Voted for Roosevelt: The Presidential Vote, 1932-1944.* 1947. Reprint. New York: Octagon Books, 1970.

Roseboom, Eugene H. *A History of Presidential Elections: From George Washington to Jimmy Carter.* 4th ed. New York: Macmillan, 1979.

Rosenstone, Steven J., Roy L. Behr and Edward Lazarus. *Third Parties in America: Citizen Response to Major Party Failure.* Princeton, N.J.: Princeton University Press, 1984.

Runyon, John H. *Source Book of American Presidential Campaign and Election Statistics, 1948-1968.* New York: Ungar, 1971.

Sayre, Wallace S. *Voting for President: The Electoral College and the American Political System.* Washington, D.C.: Brookings, 1970.

Scammon, Richard M. *America Votes: A Handbook of Contemporary Election Statistics.* Vols. 1-2. New York: Macmillan, 1956-58. *America Votes.* Vols. 3-5. Pittsburgh: University of Pittsburgh, 1959-64. *America Votes.* Vols. 6-11. Washington, D.C.: Congressional Quarterly, 1966-75.

——. and Alice V. McGillivray. *America Votes.* Vols. 12-21. Washington, D.C.: Congressional Quarterly, 1977-95.

Schlesinger, Arthur M., Jr., ed. *History of American Presidential Elections.* 4 vols. New York: McGraw Hill, 1971.

——. *The Coming to Power: Critical Presidential Elections in American History.* New York: Chelsea House, 1981.

Singer, Aaron, ed. *Campaign Speeches of American Presidential Candidates, 1928-1972.* New York: Ungar, 1976.

——. *Campaign Speeches of American Presidential Candidates, 1948-1984.* New York: Ungar, 1985.

Smith, Jeffrey A. *American Presidential Elections: Trust and the Rational Voter.* New York: Praeger, 1980.

Stanwood, Edward. *History of the Presidency.* 2 vols. 1928. Reprint. New York: Kelley, 1975.

Stavis, Ben. *We Were the Campaign: New Hampshire to Chicago for McCarthy.* Boston: Beacon Press, 1969.

Tate, Katherine. *From Protest to Politics: The New Black Voters in American Elections.* Cambridge: Harvard University Press, 1993.

Wattenberg, Martin P. *The Rise of Candidate-Centered Politics: Presidential Elections of the 1980s.* Cambridge: Harvard University Press, 1991.

Wayne, Stephen J. *The Road to the White House, 1992: The Politics of Presidential Elections.* New York: St. Martin's Press, 1992.

Weinbaum, M. G., and L. H. Gold. *Presidential Election, A Simulation with Readings.* 2nd ed. Hillsdale, Ill.: Dryden, 1974.

White, Theodore H. *America in Search of Itself: The Making of the President, 1956-1980.* New York: Harper and Row, 1982.

Articles

Aldrich, John H. "Rational Choice and Turnout." *American Journal of Political Science* 37 (February 1993): 246-278.

Axelrod, Robert. "Where the Votes Come from: An Analysis of Electoral Coalitions, 1952-1968. *American Political Science Review* 66 (March 1972): 11-20.

Bayh, Birch. "Electing a President: The Case for Direct Popular Election." *Harvard Journal on Legislation* (January 1969): 1-12.

Brody, Richard, and Lee Sigelman. "Presidential Popularity and Presidential Elections: An Update and Extension." *Public Opinion Quarterly* 47 (Fall 1983): 325-329.

Cohen, Jeffrey Elliot, and David C. Nice. "Party Unity and Presidential Election Performance: 1936-1980." *Presidential Studies Quarterly* 12 (Summer 1982): 317-329.

Eshelman, Edwin D. "Congress and Electoral Reform: An Analysis of Proposals for Changing Our Method of Selecting a President." *Christian Century,* Feb. 5, 1969, 178-181.

Feerick, John D. "The Electoral College: Why It Ought to Be Abolished." *Fordham Law Review* (October 1968): 43.

Felson, Marcus, and Seymour Sudman. "The Accuracy of Presidential Preference Primary Polls." *Public Opinion Quarterly* 39 (Summer 1975): 232-236.

Freund, Paul A. "Direct Election of the President: Issues and Answers." *American Bar Association Journal* (August 1970): 733.

Gossett, William T. "Direct Popular Election of the President." *American Bar Association Journal* (March 1970): 230.

Kessel, John H. "The Seasons of Presidential Politics." *Social Science Quarterly* 58 (December 1977): 418-435.

Kirkpatrick, Samuel A., William Lyons and Michael R. Fitzgerald. "Candidates, Parties, and Issues in the American Electorate: Two Decades of Change." *American Politics Quarterly* 3 (July 1975): 247-283.

Leighley, Jan E., and Jonathan Nagler. "Socioeconomic Class Bias in Turnout: 1964-1988: The Voters Remain the Same." *American Political Science Review* 86 (September 1992): 725-736.

Lengle, James I. "Divisive Presidential Primaries and Party Electoral Prospects, 1932-1976." *American Politics Quarterly* 8 (July 1980): 261-277.

Lipset, Seymour Martin. "The Significance of the 1992 Election." *PS: Political Science and Politics* 26 (March 1993): 7-16.

Livingston, James. "The Presidency and the People." *Democracy* 3 (Summer 1983): 41-49.

Moran, Jack, and Mark Fenster. "Voter Turnout in Presidential Primaries: A Diachronic Analysis." *American Politics Quarterly* 10 (October 1982): 453-476.

Powell, G. Bingham, Jr. "American Voter Turnout in Comparative Perspective." *American Political Science Review* 80 (March 1986): 17-43.

"Presidential Primaries: Proposals for a New System." *Congressional Quarterly Weekly Report,* July 8, 1972, 1650-1655.

Roettger, Walter B., and Hugh Winebrenner. "The Voting Behavior of American Political Scientists: The 1980 Presidential Election." *Western Political Quarterly* 36 (March 1983): 134-148.

Sievers, H. J. "Reform of the Electoral College." *America,* Nov. 16, 1968, 465.

Index